Parallel Scientific Computing in C++ and MPI

This book provides a seamless approach to numerical algorithms, modern programming techniques, and parallel computing. Oftentimes such concepts and tools are taught serially across different courses and different textbooks, and hence the interconnections among them are not immediately apparent. The necessity of integrating concepts and tools usually comes after such courses are concluded (e.g., during a first job or a thesis project), thus forcing the student to synthesize what is perceived to be three independent subfields into one in order to produce a solution. Although this process is undoubtedly valuable, it is time consuming and in many cases it may not lead to an effective combination of concepts and tools. Moreover, from the pedagogical point of view, the integrated seamless approach can stimulate the student simultaneously through the eyes of multiple disciplines, thus leading to enhanced understanding of subjects in scientific computing.

The book includes both basic as well as advanced topics and places equal emphasis on the discretization of partial differential equations and on solvers. Some of the advanced topics include wavelets, high-order methods, nonsymmetric systems, and parallelization of sparse systems. The material of the book has been used in many courses at the undergraduate and graduate levels at Princeton University, Brown University, and MIT for students from engineering, computer science, physics, and mathematics.

George Em Karniadakis is Professor of Applied Mathematics at Brown University. In addition to pioneering spectral methods for unstructured grids, microfluidic simulations, and fast methods in uncertainty modeling, he has published more than 200 papers covering topics such as numerical methods, parallel computing, and various applications in fluid mechanics. He has also co-authored two popular books.

Robert M. Kirby II is Assistant Professor of Computer Science at the University of Utah. He specializes in large-scale scientific computing and visualization, with particular focus on software design, parallel computing, and direct numerical simulation of flow–structure interactions.

Parallel Scientific Computing in C++ and MPI

A Seamless Approach to Parallel Algorithms and Their Implementation

GEORGE EM KARNIADAKIS   **ROBERT M. KIRBY II**

CAMBRIDGE
UNIVERSITY PRESS

PUBLISHED BY THE PRESS SYNDICATE OF THE UNIVERSITY OF CAMBRIDGE
The Pitt Building, Trumpington Street, Cambridge, United Kingdom

CAMBRIDGE UNIVERSITY PRESS
The Edinburgh Building, Cambridge CB2 2RU, UK
40 West 20th Street, New York, NY 10011-4211, USA
477 Williamstown Road, Port Melbourne, VIC 3207, Australia
Ruiz de Alarcón 13, 28014 Madrid, Spain
Dock House, The Waterfront, Cape Town 8001, South Africa

http://www.cambridge.org

First published 2003

Printed in the United States of America

Typefaces Stone Serif 9/12 pt., Franklin Gothic Cond, and Futura Cond. Obl.   *System* LATEX 2_ε [TB]

A catalog record for this book is available from the British Library.

Library of Congress Cataloging in Publication Data
Karniadakis, George.
  Parallel scientific computing in C++ and MPI : a seamless approach to parallel
  algorithms and their implementation / George Em Karniadakis and Robert M. Kirby II.
    p. cm.
  Includes bibliographical references and index.
  ISBN 0-521-81754-4 – ISBN 0-521-52080-0 (pb.)
  1. Parallel processing (Electronic computer) 2. C++ (Computer program language)
  3. Data transmission systems. I. Kirby, Robert M., 1975– II. Title.
  QA76.58 .K37   2003
  004'.35 – dc21   2002034805

ISBN 0 521 81754 4 hardback
ISBN 0 521 52080 0 paperback

Contents

Preface and Acknowledgments

Scientific computing is by its very nature a practical subject – it requires tools and a lot of practice. To solve realistic problems we need not only fast algorithms but also a combination of good tools and fast computers. This is the subject of the current book, which emphasizes equally all three: algorithms, tools, and computers. Oftentimes such concepts and tools are taught *serially* across different courses and different textbooks, and hence the interconnections among them are not immediately apparent. We believe that such a close integration is important from the outset.

The book starts with a heavy dosage of C++ and basic mathematical and computational concepts, and it ends emphasizing advanced parallel algorithms that are used in modern simulations. We have tried to make this book fun to read, to somewhat demystify the subject, and thus the style is sometimes informal and personal. It may seem that this happens at the expense of rigor, and indeed we have tried to limit notation and the proving of theorems. Instead, we emphasize concepts and useful "tricks of the trade" with many code segments, remarks, reminders, and warnings throughout the book.

The material of this book has been taught at different times to students in engineering, physics, computer science, and applied mathematics at Princeton University, Brown University, and MIT over the past fifteen years. Different segments have been taught to undergraduates and graduates, and to novices as well as to experts. To this end, on all three subjects covered, we start with simple introductory concepts and proceed to more advanced topics; such bandwidth, we believe, is one strength of this book.

We have been involved in large-scale parallel computing for many years from benchmarking new systems to solving complex engineering problems in computational mechanics. We represent two different generations of computational science and supercomputing, and our fields of expertise are both overlapping and complementary. The material we selected to include in this book is based on our experiences and needs as computational scientists for high-order accuracy, modular code, and domain decomposition. These are necessary ingredients for pushing the envelope in simulation science and allow one to test new theories and concepts or solve very large specific engineering problems accurately.

In addition to integrating C++ and MPI concepts and programs into the text, we also provide with this book a *software suite* containing all the functions and programs discussed. It is our belief, as stated earlier, that mastery of this subject requires both a knowledge of the tools and substantial practice using the tools. Part of the integration that we are attempting to achieve is attained when the reader is able to go immediately from the textbook to the computer to experiment with the concepts that have been presented. We envision the software suite allowing the reader to do the following: to verify the concepts presented in the book by using the programs that are provided, to extend the programs in the book to implement concepts that may have been discussed but not programmed, and to tackle problems different from those presented using the software provided.

HOW TO USE THIS BOOK

The current book is appropriate for use by students in engineering and physics, computer science, and applied mathematics. It is designed to be more like a textbook and less of a research monograph. The material can be used to fill two semesters with the following breakdown: The first semester will cover Chapters 1 to 5 at the senior undergraduate or first-year graduate level. The second semester will cover the remainder of the book in a first- or second-year graduate course. Chapters 1 to 5 cover all the basic concepts in algorithms, C++, and MPI. Chapters 6 to 10 cover discretization of differential equations and corresponding solvers and present more advanced C++ and MPI tools. The material in Chapter 3 on approximation of functions and discrete data is fundamental and precedes other topics. In the basic material on discretization, we separated *explicit* from *implicit* approaches because the parallel computational complexity of the two is fundamentally different.

A lighter course, for example, a quarter course or a lower level undergraduate course, could be based on Chapters 1 to 5 by leaving out the MPI material and possibly other advanced topics such as wavelets, advanced quadrature rules, and systems of nonlinear equations. There are other possibilities as well. A graduate-level course on numerical linear algebra can be based on Sections 4.1.6 and 4.1.7 and Chapters 7 to 10. Assuming that the student has a C++ background or even another high-performance language, then the addition of MPI material in Sections 2.3, 3.4, 4.3, and 5.13 will constitute one full-semester course on parallel numerical linear algebra. Another possibility for a quarter course is to simply teach the algorithms in Chapters 5 to 8 covering traditional numerical analysis. Supplementary notes from the instructor, for example, theorem proofs and more case studies, can make this a full-semester course.

The book is designed so that it can be used with or without the C++ and MPI tools and associated concepts, but we strongly encourage the instructor to teach the course as a seamless integration of both algorithms and tools.

ACKNOWLEDGMENTS

We are grateful to Dr. Ma Xia and Dr. C. Evangelinos for their help and advice regarding the material of this topic and for some of the figures they provided. We would also like to thank Ms. Madeline Brewster for her help in formatting the book and for typing a major portion of it. The first author is grateful for the many years of funding by the Office of Naval Research, the Air Force Office of Scientific Research, and the Department of Energy.

Finally, we would like to thank our families for their continuous love, patience, and understanding, especially during this long project.

George Em Karniadakis
Robert M. Kirby II

1

Scientific Computing and Simulation Science

1.1 WHAT IS SIMULATION?

Science and engineering have undergone a major transformation at the research level as well as at the development and technology level. The modern scientist and engineer spend more and more time in front of a laptop, a workstation, or a parallel supercomputer and less and less time in the physical laboratory or in the workshop. The virtual wind tunnel and the virtual biology laboratory are not a thing of the future; they are here! The old approach of "cut and try" has been replaced by "simulate and analyze" in several key technological areas such as aerospace applications, synthesis of new materials, design of new drugs, and chip processing and microfabrication. The new discipline of nanotechnology will be based primarily on large-scale computations and numerical experiments. The methods of scientific analysis and engineering design are changing continuously, affecting both our approach to the phenomena that we study as well as the range of applications that we address. Whereas there is an abundance of software available to be used as almost a "black box," working in new application areas requires good knowledge of fundamentals and mastering of effective new tools.

In the classical scientific approach, the physical system is first simplified and set in a form that suggests what type of phenomena and processes may be important and, correspondingly, what experiments are to be conducted. In the absence of any known type of governing equations, dimensional inter dependence between physical parameters can guide laboratory experiments in identifying key parametric studies. The database produced in the laboratory is then used to construct a simplified "engineering" model that, after field-test validation, will be used in other areas of research, product development, and design and possibly lead to new technological applications. This approach has been used almost invariably in every scientific discipline, from engineering and physics to chemistry and biology.

The simulation approach follows a parallel path but with some significant differences. First, the phase of the physical model analysis is more elaborate: The physical system is cast in a form governed by a set of partial differential equations, which represent continuum approximations to microscopic models. Such approximations are not possible for all systems, and sometimes the microscopic model should be used directly. Second, the laboratory experiment is replaced by simulation, that is, by a numerical experiment based on a discrete model. Such a model may represent a discrete approximation of the continuum partial differential equations, or it may simply represent a statistical representation of the microscopic model. Finite difference approximations on a grid are examples of the first case, and Monte Carlo methods are examples of the second case. In either case, these algorithms have to be converted to software using an appropriate computer language, debugged, and run on a workstation or a parallel supercomputer. The output is usually a large number of files of a few megabytes to hundreds of gigabytes, being especially large for simulations of time-dependent phenomena. To be useful, this numerical database needs to be put into graphical form using various visualization tools, which may not always be suited for the particular application considered. Visualization can be especially useful during simulations where interactivity is required as the grid may be changing or the number of molecules may be increasing.

The simulation approach has already been followed by the majority of researchers across disciplines in the past few decades. The question is whether this is a new science and how one could formally obtain such skills. Moreover, does this constitute fundamental new knowledge or is it a "mechanical procedure," an ordinary skill that a chemist, a biologist, or an engineer will acquire easily as part of "training on the job" without specific formal education? It seems that the time has arrived where we need to reconsider boundaries between disciplines and reformulate the education of the future *simulation scientist*, an interdisciplinary scientist.

Let us reexamine some of the requirements following the various steps in the simulation approach. The first task is to select the right representation of the physical system by making consistent assumptions to derive the governing equations and the associated boundary conditions. The conservation laws should be satisfied; the entropy condition should not be violated; the uncertainty principle should be honored. The second task is to develop the right algorithmic procedure to discretize the continuum model or represent the dynamics of the atomistic model. The choices are many, but which algorithm is the most accurate one, or the simplest one, or the most efficient one? These algorithms do not belong to a discipline! Finite elements, first developed by the famous mathematician Richard Courant and rediscovered by civil engineers, have found their way into every engineering discipline as well as into physics, geology, and other fields. Molecular dynamics simulations are practiced by chemists, biologists, material scientists, and others. The third task is to compute efficiently in the ever-changing world of supercomputing. How efficient the computation is translates to how realistic of a problem is solved and therefore how useful the results can be to applications. The fourth task is to assess the accuracy of the results in cases where no direct confirmation from physical experiments is possible, such as in nanotechnology or in biosystems or in astrophysics. Reliability of the predicted numerical answer is an important issue in the simulation approach because some of the answers may lead to new physics or false physics contained in the discrete model or induced by the algorithm but not derived from the physical problem. Finally, visualizing the simulated phenomenon, in most cases in three-dimensional space and in time, by employing proper computer graphics (a separate specialty on its own) completes the full simulation cycle. The rest of the steps followed are similar to those of the classical scientific approach.

In classical science we are dealing with matter and therefore *atoms*, but in simulation we are dealing with information and therefore *bits*; so it is atoms versus bits. We should, therefore, recognize the simulation scientist as a separate scientist, the same way we recognized just a few decades ago the computer scientist as different than the electrical engineer or the applied mathematician. The new scientist is certainly not a computer scientist, although he or she should be computer literate in both software and hardware. The simulation scientist, is not a physicist, although a sound physics background is needed. Nor is he or she an applied mathematician, although expertise in mathematical analysis and approximation theory is needed.

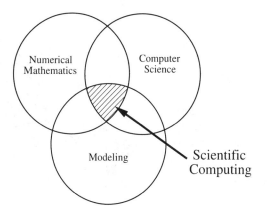

With the rapid and simultaneous advances in software and computer technology, especially commodity computing and the so-called soupercomputing, every scientist and engineer will have on his or her desk an advanced simulation kit of tools consisting of a software library and multiprocessor computers that will make analysis, product development, and design more optimal and cost effective. But what the future scientists and engineers will need, first and foremost, is a solid interdisciplinary education.

Figure 1.1: Definition of scientific computing as the intersection of numerical mathematics, computer science, and modeling.

Scientific computing is the heart of simulation science, and this is the subject of this book. The emphasis is on a balance between classical and modern elements of numerical mathematics and of computer science, but we have selected the topics based on broad modeling concepts encountered in physico-chemical and biological sciences, or even economics (see Figure 1.1).

1.2 A SEAMLESS APPROACH PATH

Our aim in writing this book has been to provide the student, the future simulation scientist, with a seamless approach to numerical algorithms, modern programming techniques, and parallel computing. Often times such concepts and tools are taught serially across different courses and different textbooks, and hence the interconnection between them is not immediately apparent. The necessity of integrating concepts and tools usually comes after such courses are concluded, for example, during a first job or a thesis project, thus forcing the student to synthesize what is perceived to be three independent subfields into one to produce a solution. Although this process is undoubtly valuable, it is time consuming and in many cases it may not lead to an effective combination of concepts and tools. Moreover, from the pedagogical point of view, the integrated seamless approach can stimulate the student simultaneously through the eyes of multiple disciplines, thus leading to enhanced understanding of subjects in scientific computing.

As discussed in the previous section, in the scientific simulation approach there are several successive stages that lead from

1. the real-world problem to its mathematical formulation,
2. the mathematical description to the computer implementation and solution, and
3. the numerical solution to visualization and analysis.

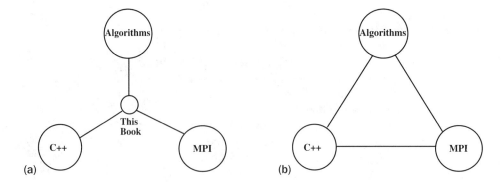

Figure 1.2: (a) Simultaneous integration of concepts in contrast with (b) the classical serial integration.

In this book, we concentrate on stage 2, which includes not only the mathematics of numerical linear algebra and discretization but also the implementation of these concepts in C++ and MPI.

There are currently several excellent textbooks and monographs on these topics, but these lack the type of integration that we propose. For example, the book by Golub and Ortega [45] introduces pedagogically all the basic parallel concepts, but a gap remains between the parallel formulation and its implementation. Similarly, the books by Trefethen and Bau [88] and Demmel [26] provide rigor and great insight into numerical linear algebra algorithms, but they do not provide sufficient material on discretization and implementation. Popular books in C++ (e.g., by Stroustrup [86]) and MPI (e.g., by Pacheco [73]) are references that teach programming using disconnected algorithmic examples, which is useful for acquiring general programming skills but not for parallel scientific computing. Our book treats numerics, parallelism, and programming equally and simultaneously by placing the reader at a vantage point between the three areas, as shown in the schematic of Figure 1.2a, and in contrast with the classical approach of connecting the three subjects serially, as illustrated in Figure 1.2b.

1.3 THE CONCEPT OF PROGRAMMING LANGUAGE

In studying computer languages, we want to study a new way of interacting with the computer. Most people are familiar with the use of software purchased online or from your local computer store; such software ranges from word processors and spreadsheets to interactive games. But have you ever wondered how these things are created? How do you actually "write" software? Throughout this book we will be teaching through both lecture and example how to create computer software that solves scientific problems. Our purpose is not to teach you how to write computer games and the like, but the knowledge gained here can be used to devise your own software endeavors.

It has been stated by some that the computer is a pretty dumb device, in that it only understands two things – *on* and *off*. Like sending Morse code over a telegraph wire with signals of dots and dashes, the computer uses sequences of zeros and ones as its language. The zeros and ones may seem inefficient, but it is not just the data used, but the rules applied to the data that make the computer powerful. This concept, in theory, is no different than human language. If we were to set before you a collection of symbols, say a, b, c, d,...z, and indicate to you that you can use these to express even the most complex thoughts and emotions of the human mind and heart, you would think we were crazy. Just twenty-six little symbols? How can this be? We know, however, that it is not merely the symbols that are important but the rules used to combine the symbols. If you adhere to the rules defined by the English language, then books like this can be written using merely combinations of the twenty-six characters! How is this similar to the computer? The computer is a complex device for executing instructions. These instructions are articulated by using our *two-base* characters, 0 and 1, along with a collection of rules for combining them together. This brings us to our first axiom:

AXIOM I: *Computers are machines that execute instructions. If someone is not telling the computer what to do, it does nothing.*

Most people have had some experience with computers, and immediately they will read this statement and say: "Hey, I have had my computer do all kinds of things that I didn't want!" Ah, but read the axiom carefully. The key to this axiom is the use of the term *someone*. The one thing to keep in mind is that some human, or collection of humans, developed software to tell the computer what to do. At a relatively low level, this would be the people who wrote the operating system used by the computer. At a higher level, this would be the people who developed the word processor or game that you were using. In both cases, however, someone determined how the computer would act and react to your input. We want you, after reading this book and understanding the concepts herein, to be able to be in the driver's seat. This leads us to our second axiom:

AXIOM II: *Computer programming languages allow humans a simplified means of giving the computer instructions.*

We tell you that we want you to be in the driver's seat, and you tell us "I don't want to learn how to communicate in zeros and ones. Learning English was hard enough!" You can imagine how slowly the computer age would have progressed if every programming class consisted of the following lecture scheme. Imagine the first day of class. On the first day, the instructor tells you that you will be learning the two basic components of the computer language today: 0 and 1. The instructor may force you to say zero and one a few times and then to write zero and one many times on a piece of paper for practice, but then, what else would there be to learn concerning your character set? Class dismissed. Then, for the rest of the semester, you would spend your time learning how to combine zeros and ones to get the computer to do what you want. Your first assignment might be to add two numbers a and b and to store the result in c (i.e., c = a + b). You end up with something that looks like the following:

```
01011001010001000111010101000100
01011001011100100010100101000011
00111010101000100111010100100101
01011101010101010101010000111101
```

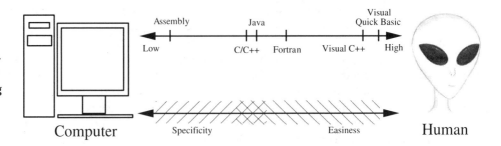

Figure 1.3: Programming languages provide us a means of bridging the gap between the computer and the human.

This seems like a longwinded way of saying

$$c = a + b,$$

but this is what the computer understands, so this is how we must communicate with it. However, humans do not communicate in this fashion. Human language and thought use a higher abstraction than this. How can we make a bridge for this gap? We bridge this gap via programming languages (see Figure 1.3).

The first programming language we will mention is *assembly*. The unique property of assembly is that for each instruction, there is a one-to-one correspondence between a command in assembly and a computer-understandable command (in zeros and ones). For instance, instead of writing

0101100101000100011101010101000100

as a command, you could write "load a $1." This tells the computer to load the contents of the memory location denoted by "a" into register $1 in the computer's CPU (central processing unit). This is much better than before. Obviously, this sequence of commands is much easier for the human to understand. This was a good start, but assembly is still considered a "low-level language." By low level we mean that one instruction in assembly is equal to one computer instruction. But as we said earlier, we want to be able to think on a higher level. Hence, "higher level" languages were introduced. Higher level languages are those in which one instruction in the higher level language equals one or more computer-level instructions. We want a computer language where we can say "c = a + b"; this would be equivalent to saying

```
load a $1
load b $2
add $1 $2 $3
save $3 c
```

One high-level instruction was equivalent to four lower level instructions (here written in pseudo-assembly so that you can follow what is going on). This is preferable for many reasons. First, we as humans would like to spend our time thinking about how to solve the problem, not just trying to remember (and write) all the assembly code! Second, by writing in a higher level language, we can write code that can work on multiple computers, because the translation of the higher level code can be done by a compiler into the assembly code of the processor on which we are running.

As you read through this book and do the exercises found herein, always be mindful that our goal is to utilize the computer for accomplishing scientific tasks encountered in simulation science. At a high level, there is a science or engineering problem to solve, and we want to use the computer as a tool for solving the problem. The means by which we will use the computer is through the writing and execution of programs written using the computing language C++ and the parallel message passing libraries of MPI.

1.4 WHY USE C++ AND WHAT IS MPI?

The algorithms we present in the book can certainly be implemented in other languages (e.g., FORTRAN or Java) as well as using other communication libraries, such as PVM (parallel virtual machine). However, we commit to a specific language and parallel library to provide the student with the immediate ability to experiment with the concepts presented. To this end, we have chosen C++ as our programming language for a multitude of reasons. First, it provides an object-oriented infrastructure that accommodates a natural breakdown of the problem into a collection of data structures and operations on those structures. Second, the use of C++ transcends many disciplines beyond engineering, where traditionally FORTRAN has been the prevailing language. Third, C++ is a language naturally compatible with the basic algorithmic concepts of

- partitioning,
- recursive function calling,
- dynamic memory allocation, and
- encapsulation.

Similarly, we commit to MPI (message passing interface) as a message passing library because it accommodates a natural and simple partitioning of the problem, it provides portability and efficiency, and it has received wide acceptance by academia and industry.

The simultaneous integration we propose in this book will be accomplished by carefully presenting related concepts from all three subareas. Moving from one chapter to the next requires different dosages of new material in algorithms and tools. This is explained graphically in Figure 1.4, which shows that although new algorithms are introduced at an approximately constant rate, the introduction of new C++ and MPI material vary inversely. We begin with an emphasis on the basics of the language, which allows the student to immediately work on the simple algorithms introduced initially; as the book progresses and the computational complexity of algorithms increases the use of parallel constructs and libraries is emphasized.

More specifically, to help facilitate the student's immersion into object-oriented thinking, we provide a library of *classes* and *functions* for use throughout the book. The classes contained in this library are used from

Figure 1.4: Progression of new material throughout the book in the three areas shown in Figure 1.2.

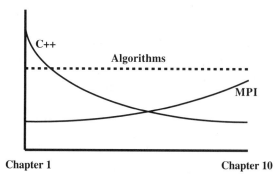

Chapter 1   Chapter 10

the very beginning of the book as a natural, user-defined extension of C++. As the book progresses, the underlying logic and programming implementation of these classes are explained, bringing the student to a deeper understanding of the development of C++ classes. We will denote all classes used within the book and not inherent to C++ with the letters SC, such as the classes *SCVector* and *SCMatrix*.

The SC notation is used to clearly distinguish between C++ defined and user-defined data types and also to accentuate the utility of user-defined types within the C++ programming language. As students become more familiar and confident in their ability to devise and use data types, we encourage them to use these facilities provided by the language for more effective programming and problem solving. All the codes of this book and many more examples are included in the *software suite*, which is distributed with this book.

Software

Suite

1.5 WHAT ABOUT OpenMP?

Because of the recent proliferation of distributed shared-memory (DSM) machines in the scientific computing community, there is much interest in how best to appropriately utilize both the distributed and the shared-memory partitioning of these systems. MPI provides an efficient means of parallel communication among a *distributed* collection of machines; however, not all MPI implementations take advantage of *shared memory* when it is available between processors (the basic premise being that two processors, which share common memory, can communicate with each other faster through the use of the shared medium than through other communication means).

OpenMP (open multi processing) was introduced to provide a means of implementing shared-memory parallelism in FORTRAN and C/C++ programs. Specifically, OpenMP specifies a set of environment variables, compiler directives, and library routines to be used for shared-memory parallelization. OpenMP was specifically designed to exploit certain characteristics of shared-memory architectures such as the ability to directly access memory throughout the system with low latency and very fast shared-memory locks. To learn more about OpenMP, visit **www.openmp.org**.

A new parallel programming paradigm is emerging in which both the MPI and OpenMP are used for parallelization. In a distributed shared-memory architecture, OpenMP would be used for intranode communication (i.e., between a collection of processors that share the same memory subsystem) and MPI would be used for internode communication (i.e., between distinct distributed collections of processors). The combination of these two parallelization methodologies may provide the most effective means of fully exploiting modern DSM systems.

1.6 ALGORITHMS AND TOP TEN LIST

The Greeks and Romans invented many scientific and engineering algorithms, but it is believed that the term "algorithm" stems from the name of the ninth-century Arab mathematician *al-Khwarizmi*, who wrote the book *al-jabr wa'l muqabalach*, which eventually evolved into today's high school algebra textbooks. He was perhaps the first to stress systematic procedures for solving mathematical problems. Since then, some truly ingenious algorithms have been invented, but the algorithms that have formed the foundations of scientific computing as a separate discipline were developed in the second part of the twentieth century. Dongarra and Sullivan put together a list of the *top ten algorithms* of the twentieth century [33]. According to these authors, the following algorithms (listed in chronological order) had the greatest influence on science and engineering in the past:

1. **1946:** The Monte Carlo method for modeling probabilistic phenomena.
2. **1947:** The Simplex method for linear optimization problems.
3. **1950:** The Krylov subspace iteration method for fast linear solvers and eigen-solvers.
4. **1951:** The Householder matrix decomposition to express a matrix as a product of simpler matrices.
5. **1957:** The FORTRAN compiler that liberated scientists and engineers from programming in assembly.
6. **1959–1961:** The QR algorithm to compute many eigenvalues.
7. **1962:** The Quicksort algorithm to put things in numerical or alphabetical order fast.
8. **1965:** The fast Fourier transform to reduce operation count in Fourier series representation.
9. **1977:** The integer relation detection algorithm, which is useful for bifurcations and in quantum field theory.
10. **1987:** The fast multipole algorithm for N-body problems.

Although there is some debate as to the relative importance of these algorithms or the absence of other important methods in the list (e.g., finite differences and finite elements), this selection by Dongarra and Sullivan reflects some of the thrusts in scientific computing in the past. The appearance of the FORTRAN compiler, for example, represents the historic transition from assembly language to higher level languages, as discussed earlier. In fact, the first FORTRAN compiler was written in 23,500 assembly language instructions! FORTRAN has been used extensively in the past, especially in the engineering community, but most of the recent scientific computing software has been rewritten in C++ (e.g., the Numerical Recipes [75]).

In this book we will cover in detail the algorithms 3, 4, 6, and 8 from the aforementioned mentioned list, including many more recent versions, which provide more robustness with respect to round-off errors and efficiency in the context of parallel computing. We will also present discretizations of ordinary and partial differential equations using several finite difference formulations.

Many new algorithms will probably be invented in the twenty-first century – hopefully some of them from the readers of this book! As Dongarra and Sullivan noted, "This century will not be very restful for us, but is not going to be dull either!"

2

Basic Concepts and Tools

In this chapter we introduce the main themes that we will cover in this book and provide an introduction for each of them. We begin with a brief overview of C++ and define the two basic concepts of *functions* and *classes* as well as other syntactic elements of the language. We then introduce basic mathematical concepts that include elements of linear algebra, vector orthogonalization, and corresponding codes and software. Finally, we introduce parallel programming and review some generic parallel architectures as well as standard parallel algorithms for basic operations (e.g., the *fan-in* algorithm for recursive doubling). We also provide a brief overview of the main MPI commands.

2.1 INTRODUCTION TO C++

An ancient proverb states that the beginning of a thousand-mile journey begins with a single step. For us, this single step will be a brief overview of the C++ programming language. This introduction is not designed to be all-inclusive, but rather it should provide the scaffolding from which we will build concepts throughout this book. Admittedly, what you will read now may seem daunting in its scope, but as you become more familiar with the concepts found herein, you will be able to use the C++ language as a tool for furthering your understanding of deeper mathematical and algorithmic concepts presented later in the book. With this in mind, let us begin our thousand-mile journey with this first step.

Any programming language can be broken down into two high-level concepts:

- data and
- operations on data.

Though this may seem like a trivial statement, quite often in science and engineering problems the real work that needs to be done is identifying what are the relevant data and what operations need to be executed on these data to obtain the desired results. From the programming point of view, we will assume that you already have a clear concept of what data are needed to solve the problem and what algorithms will be acting on the data; we will focus on translating these needs into the programming language.

We have chosen to present this material in a top-down manner; that is, we will start from the high level of the program and work our way down toward lower and lower levels of detail. At the end of this section, we will recapitulate what we have learned and show how all the pieces do indeed fit together though an example. We start with the idea of a program, or "code" as it is sometimes referred to within the scientific computing community. A program is a sequence of instructions acting on a collection of data. Just as this chapter had a starting point, every program must have a starting point, and in C++, the starting point of execution is the "main" function, which is called **main**. This tells the computer where to start execution of your program. The simplest C++ code that can be written is the following:

```
int main(int argc, char ** argv){
}
```

This piece of code will compile and execute, but it will do absolutely nothing. Though it may contain data inputted through the arguments *argc* and *argv*, it contains no operations on these data. It merely provides the computer with a starting point of execution and then immediately terminates because all executable commands have been executed (which in this case is none!).

This is your first C++ program. In keeping with programming tradition, your first nontrivial C++ program should be the following:

```
#include<iostream.h>

int main(int argc, char ** argv){
    cout << "Hello World" << endl;
}
```

Software

Suite

At this stage, you should type in this program, compile it using your native C++ compiler, and execute it. The result of this program should be that the statement "Hello World" is printed to your screen. If you have problems with this exercise, see Appendix A.

In theory, you now have your first C++ program. You have written the code, compiled and linked the code, and are able to execute the code on your native machine. Now that this first step is behind us, let us jump into discussing some of the basic concepts, one of which we have just gained some experience: the concept of a function.

2.1.1 Two Basic Concepts in C++

There are two basic concepts used throughout the C++ programming language: the concepts of

- *function* and of
- *class*.

The C programming language, upon its inception, had at least one self-defining feature: *modularity*. The C language was designed to be modular, and this modularity was accomplished through the employment of functions. Almost everything in C is a function, and some have said that "...all C really is a big function calling a bunch of other functions." Well, this is almost right. The C language basically consists of two components, a core language specification that contains basic data types and constructs (such as **if** statements, **for** statements, etc., some of which we discuss later on in this chapter) and a collection of libraries, each of which contains many predefined functions. C++ built on this philosophy and introduced the "class" as a second fundamental building block of the language. Within C++, functions and classes are intertwined to create the desired program.

We begin by defining what we mean by a *function* and a *class*. Functions and classes can be distinguished by their fundamental premises. The primary premise of a function revolves around what the function does, whereas the fundamental premise of a class revolves around the data that the class contain. Functions are designed to be abstractions of algorithms; classes (at least as presented in this book) are an abstraction of data and operations on these data. We will clarify this distinction by examining the two concepts in more detail.

Functions

Functions are abstractions that encapsulate a concept or algorithm. The concept of a function is probably not new to you. In mathematics, we see functions all the time. We define functions so that we can abstract a particular operation or collection of operations into one statement. In mathematics, we note functions in a manner like

$$f(x) = x^3 - x^2 + 2.$$

We understand that if we evaluate the function at the point $x = 2$, denoted $f(2)$, this is equivalent to substituting the number 2 into the expression $x^3 - x^2 + 2$, yielding $2^3 - 2^2 + 2 = 6$. We hence would say that $f(2) = 6$. In mathematical parlance, we would add rigor to all that we have done so far and state this collection of operations as follows:

> *Given x as a real number, define $f(x)$ as a function returning a real number, where the definition of $f(x)$ is given by the expression $f(x) = x^3 - x^2 + 2$.*

This example demonstrates the three major components of a function:

Figure 2.1: A schematic of a function in C++.

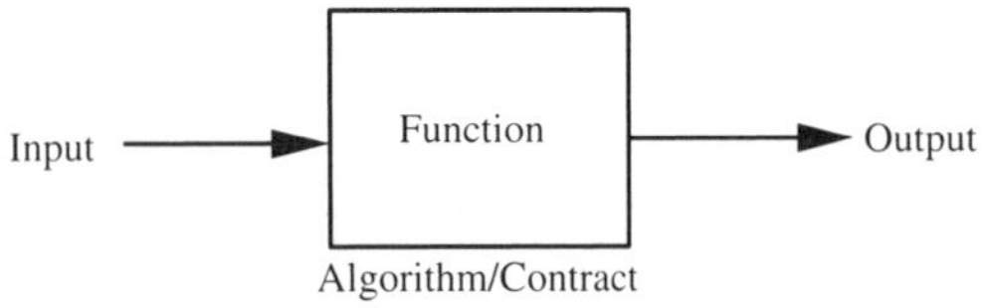

• *input, output,* and *contract (or algorithm)*.

We specified the valid range of parameters that can be inputted into this function (mathematically referred to as the domain of the function); we specified the range in which the output would lie (mathematically referred to as the range of the function); and finally we specified what, given a particular input, the function will do. The same holds true for C++. For a function, we need to specify the input, output, and contract.

Input ⟶ [Function] ⟶ Output

Algorithm/Contract

In C++, the process of specifying the input, output, and contract is done in two stages (see Figure 2.1).[1] These two stages are specifying the following for each function:

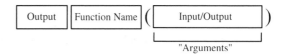

Figure 2.2: Schematic of the syntax of a C++ function.

- function declaration and
- function definition.

A function's declaration accomplishes several things in one step. It declares the name of the function and the data types of the input and output of the function. The function definition specifies what the function will accomplish given particular input data. Hence, the definition of a function is the algorithmic explanation of the contract of the function.

A schematic for the syntax used for the declaration of a C++ function is given in Figure 2.2. Using this as our guide, let us attempt to formulate our mathematical function into a C++ function. For the purposes of this demonstration, let us assume that we have a data type called *float*, which is the floating point representation of a real number. The function declaration of our function "f" is given by

```
float f(float x);
```

Examining our schematic given in Figure 2.2, we can dissect this code to understand what is going on. Let us see if we have met the three components of a function declaration. First, we specified the name of the function, "f." Next, we specified that the valid input to our function is a floating point value. Finally, we specified that our function returns a floating point value. Hence, we now have declared our function! What does declaration really mean though? Declaration of a function allows us to use this function throughout our code with the assumption that this function will act upon the contract of the function (later specified by the definition of the function). A key thing to realize is that

- *a function must be declared before it can be used.*

Because of this fact, many programmers place all their function declarations at the beginning of their C++ program so that all functions are accessible everywhere. You will notice throughout this book that either we place our function declarations within a *header file* (the files with a *.h* extension) that is included at the beginning of a program or we directly insert the function declarations after the *include* files and prior to the *main* function definition. An example template of this type of file setup is shown at the end of this section.

Another important fact is that within the *argument list* (the list of inputs and outputs given as arguments to the function) the names specified are irrelevant. The compiler is only concerned about the data type. Hence, it would be perfectly valid to write

```
float f(float);
```

---

[1] According to the language standard, it is possible to combine both of these items into one statement satisfying the requirement for both simultaneously. For pedagogical clarity, we will always keep the two stages separate.

Why do we have a variable name there, if it is just to be ignored? The most practical reason we put variable names in function declarations is that we normally "cut and paste" the function declaration from the function definition. The function definition *does* require variable names to be used. We will now give the function definition so that this becomes more apparent:

```
float f(float x){
    float y;

    y = x*x*x - x*x + 2;

    return y;
}
```

Notice that the function definition has a very similar beginning to that of the function declaration. As before, you specify the function name and the input and output data types. The difference, however, is that the function definition is the implementation of our contract. For the function definition, including specific variable names within the argument list is essential because we will use these variable names throughout the definition to refer to the data that were inputted. In C++, when data are inputted into a function, the information is *passed by value*. This means that when the function is called, a copy of the information is created for the function to use, and so the function does not use the original data. This is an important and yet subtle point about C++. We will discuss this in more detail later (see Section 3.1.2). For now, the thing to remember is that the function takes from its argument list the information passed to it, and it stores a copy of the information in a variable specified by the name given in the argument list.

In this example, we declare a variable y in which we temporarily store the value of our function, given by the expression **x*x*x - x*x + 2**, and then we return the value of the variable y. The *return* statement designates the variable from which a value is to be returned from the function back to the caller. If we were to examine a code snippet, we could use our function just as we did mathematically by writing

```
float w;

w = f(2);
```

If were to print the value of w, we would see that the returned value is the floating point value 6.000. Some of this process will become more clear after we have discussed basic data types. The key items to remember from this discussion are the following:

- Every function must have a function declaration and definition.
- Function declarations specify the name of the function and the data types of the inputs and outputs.

- Function definitions specify the implementation of the algorithm used to carry out the contract of the function.
- Variable names in function declarations *do not* matter.
- Variable names in function definitions *do* matter because they specify how the data are to be referred to in the implementation of the function.
- Variables passed to C++ functions are passed by *value* unless otherwise specified.

PUTTING IT INTO PRACTICE

Software
Suite

Recall our little main function we wrote, compiled, and ran at the beginning of this section. Let us now combine that code with our new function.

```
#include <iostream.h> // inclusion of library header file
                      // for use of cout

float f(float x);     // function declaration

int main(int argc, char ** argv){
   float w;
   w = f(2);
   cout << "The value of w is: " << w << endl;
}

float f(float x){     // function definition
   float y;
   y = x*x*x - x*x + 2;
   return y;
}
```

If you were to compile and run this code, you would obtain a statement on your screen that says: The value of w is: 6.00.

In this program, we use an object named *cout*, the declaration of which is found in the system header file *iostream.h*. The object *cout* is used for printing to standard output, which in many cases is the screen. For now, it is sufficient to know that the << symbols delineate expressions to be printed. In the code shown here, the first statement to be printed is the string "The value of w is:"; then the program prints the value associated with the variable *w* and then the end-of-line character denoted by the term *endl*. We will speak more about *cout* later in this chapter.

Classes

Classes are abstractions that encapsulate data and operations on these data. In C++, the concept of classes is used to simplify through encapsulation very complex data structures. A class consists of two parts: *data* and *methods operating on the data* (see Figure 2.3). What you will find is that methods are merely functions that are "attached" to classes. The concept of a method is analogous to that of a function, with the primary

C++ Class

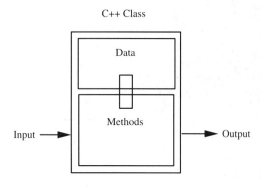

Figure 2.3: A C++ class encapsulates data and methods acting on these data.

focus of a method being to act on the data of the class, and not on arbitrary inputted data.

For example, in the Gram–Schmidt routines in Section 2.2.9, we utilize several user-defined classes; among those classes is the class SCVector. Vector does not exist as a basic data type in C++; however, the language allows us to define a new type, called SCVector, that consists of a collection of basic data types and operations on these data. The declaration for the class SCVector is given at the end of this paragraph. We will not go over every detail now but will defer explicit explanation until later in this book (see Section 3.1.8). However, we call your attention to the two basic concepts of classes in C++:

1. encapsulated data and
2. methods acting on these data.

In this class, the variables *dimension* and *data* are encapsulated by the class, and all the remaining methods (in the section marked "public") act on these basic data.

We now present the class declaration of the SCVector class:

```
class SCVector{
private:
  int    dimension;   // dimension of the vector
  double *data; // pointer to array containing
      vector components

public:
  SCVector(int dim); // default constructor
  SCVector(const SCVector& v); // copy constructor
  SCVector(int col, const SCMatrix &A); //secondary constructor
  ~SCVector(); //destructor

  int    Dimension() const; //dimension of the vector
  double Length();       // Euclidean norm of the vector
  void   Normalize();   // normalize vector

  double Norm_l1();
  double Norm_l2();
  double Norm_linf();

  //***********************
  // User-Defined Operators
  //***********************
  int operator==(const SCVector& v) const;
```

```
    int operator!=(const SCVector& v) const;
    SCVector & operator=(const SCVector& v);

    double  operator()(const int i) const;
    double& operator()(const int i);

    void Print() const;

};
```

We will explain classes more thoroughly later (Section 3.1.8), but let us take this opportunity to point out a few features of classes:

- In the class described here, there are several "constructors." A **constructor** is the first method that is called when an object is instantiated. These methods can be used to initialize data, set up information within the class, etc.
- A **destructor** is the method called prior to an object being deleted. The operating system will call this method (if it is available) to allow the object to "clean up for itself" prior to the operating system (OS) finishing the job by freeing the memory to which the class was allocated.
- Notice that some methods of this class modify the data contained within the object, whereas others merely compute things based upon the data within the object. For instance, the function *Normalize* does exactly that – it normalizes the vector data contained with the object to have norm one. The function *Norm_l2*, however, does not modify the data contained with the object it merely computes the Euclidean norm of the vector based upon the information within the object.
- Classes allow us to define what are referred to as **overloaded operators**. In the declaration on the SCVector class, we have listed these as "user-defined operators." In addition to defining new data types, we can also define (or redefine) how common unary and binary operators act on those objects (such as defining what "+" means when two newly defined objects are involved).

2.1.2 Learning the Syntax and Other Basic Commands

Getting Past ";" and "{ }"

As you may have already noticed from the small amount of code that we have presented to you, the symbols ";" and "{ } " are integral to C++. We will briefly describe the purpose of these symbols here.

In general, the ";" is used to terminate an executable statement; hence this is why you see it at the conclusion of the commands listed in the previous section. Having such a symbol denote the end of an executable statement allows the compiler to easily delineate between statements.

The { } brackets (called curly brackets) are used to denote *scope*. We will not go into all the nuances of scope right now other than to tell you that the scope of a variable or a function is the area of code in which that variable or function can be used.

Table 2.1: Integer data types.

Type	Description
short	Short integer
int	Integer
long	Long integer

Table 2.2: Floating point data types.

Type	Description
float	Single precision
double	Double precision

Table 2.3: Character data type.

Type	Description
char	Character

Basic Data Types

In C++, variables are used to store information. In this section we go over some of the basic data types available in C++ (see Appendix A for more information). Just like in mathematics, a variable is a symbol used to denote a particular value, either numerical or character. One way of thinking of a variable is that it is a box in which information can be stored. In C++, all variables must have a *type*. The *type* tells the computer what kind of box to create, the dimension of the box, the shape, etc. The syntax for creating a variable is

<type> <variable list>

Some basic data types are listed in Tables 2.1–2.3. Given these conventions, we see that to declare a variable called x of type *int*, we would write

int x;

This allocates a block of memory of the size of an integer, and it would assign the symbol x to refer to that location in memory. Hence, from now on, if we act on the variable x, we are acting on the content of the memory assigned to x. This may sound odd at first, but this is one of the subtle differences between computer programming and mathematics. One thing that most people do not realize is that the computer does not have integer memory, floating point memory, or character memory.[2] As far as the computer is concerned, memory is memory. The data type that is used tells the computer *how to interpret memory*. A particular set of four bytes can be used in one program to represent an integer, and in another program to represent a float. The computer does not care. What is important is that the computer needs to know how to interpret the *bit pattern* of the four bytes. Does it interpret the collection of bits as an integer or a float or as some other variable type? Coming to grips with this notion will be very important when we start discussing the idea of addresses, the subject of pointers, etc. For now, just remember two key things about data types: The data type you specify tells the computer

- the number of bytes to use to hold the data and
- how to interpret the bit pattern specified in those bytes.

Now that you know that variables exist, and you know some of the basic types, here are some rules to remember when using variables:

- Variables must be declared before they are used.
- Variable names can be of arbitrary length.
- Variable names *are* case sensitive.
- Variables are to be assumed to be uninitialized. *Do not* rely on the operating system to initialize or zero values for you.

---

[2] Computers do in fact have specialized memory within the processor, called *registers*, that are either integer or float/double.

- Variable lists may be used. If we wish to allocate three integer variables *a*, *b*, and *c*, we may do so as follows: `int a,b,c;`. All three variables will be declared as integers. It is also perfectly valid to declare each one with a separate statement.
- Variables may be initialized by either constants or expressions within the declaration statement. Hence, if we wanted to initialize the integer variable *a* to zero, we could do the following: `int a=0;`. You can also do this in the context of variable lists. Suppose you want to initialize the integer variable *b* to one, but not the other variables. You can do this as follows: `int a,b=1,c;`.

Table 2.4: Binary arithmetic operations.

Symbol	Interpretation
+	Addition
−	Subtraction
*	Multiplication
/	Division

Basic Operations

Now that we have some concept of variables, the natural question to ask is: "What can we do with them ?" C++ provides a collection of basic operations, some of which are listed in Table 2.4.

The operations presented look very much like the operations you would expect in mathematics. We must make two special notes, however. The first note concerns the assignment operator, and the second note concerns order of precedence and associativity. In C++, the symbol "=," which we, in English, pronounce "equals," should be interpreted as "is assigned the value of"; for example $x = 2$ is to be read x "is assigned the value of" 2. Take the following C++ code example:

```
int x,y,z;

x = 2;
y = 4;

z = x + y;
```

The C++ interpretation of this code is as follows: First, declare three variables, x, y, and z as integers. Next, assign x the value 2, then assign y the value 4. We then add the values of x and y and assign to z the newly computed value. The ordering is important. In mathematics, we may say $p = q$ or $q = p$, and both statements mean that p is equal to q. However, in C++, $p = q$ says that the variable p is assigned the same value as the variable q, whereas $q = p$ says that the variable q is assigned the value of p. As you can see, these two statements are not equivalent.

The second item to note is that operators have both precedence and associativity. The C++ operator precedence and associativity are provided in Table 2.5. What does operator precedence and associativity really mean to the programmer? Examine the following example: Assume that we want to add six numbers: 1, 2, 3, 4, 5, and 6. Mathematically, we write this operation as $1 + 2 + 3 + 4 + 5 + 6$. However, if we implement this expression, keeping in mind that we are dealing with a

Table 2.5: Unitary +, −, and * have higher precedence than the binary forms.

Operations	Associativity
( ) [ ] −> .	Left to right
! ~ ++ -- + − * & (type) sizeof	Right to left
* / %	Left to right
+ −	Left to right
<< >>	Left to right
< <= > >=	Left to right
== !=	Left to right

binary operator "+," then we would write the following for summing: $1 + 2 = 3$, $3 + 3 = 6$, $6 + 4 = 10$, $10 + 5 = 15$, and $15 + 6 = 21$. We begin by adding the first two numbers together, and then we accumulate as we come to each new value. The same is true for the computer. When the computer is faced with the expression

```
int x,y,z,w;

x = 2.0;
y = 3.0;
z = 4.0;

w = x + y + z;
```

it interprets this as being equivalent to

```
int x,y,z,w;

x = 2.0;
y = 3.0;
z = 4.0;

w = x + y;
w = w + z;
```

Notice that in the second expression, each evaluation involves only one binary expression. Hence associativity is left to right in this case. Now suppose we had the following expression:

```
int x,y,z,w;

x = 2.0;
y = 3.0;
z = 4.0;

w = x + y * z;
```

The computer interprets this to be the following:

```
int x,y,z,w;

x = 2.0;
y = 3.0;
z = 4.0;

w = y * z;
w = w + x;
```

Why do we perform multiplication prior to addition? The multiplication operator has precedence over the addition operator, and hence all multiplications are done first. This is a very important concept to realize.

Order of operations is important. Precedence can make all the difference!	**Key Concept**

One thing we should mention is the use of () in expressions. Notice in the precedence table that () are at the top of the list. This is for a reason. The use of () gives the programmer the right to specify the order of precedence by explicitly placing () within the expression. For instance, in the following piece of code:

```
int x,y,z,w;

x = 2.0;
y = 3.0;
z = 4.0;

w = (x + y) * z;
```

the computer interprets this to be the following:

```
int x,y,z,w;

x = 2.0;
y = 3.0;
z = 4.0;

w = x + y;
w = w * z;
```

We have in effect told the computer the precedence order that we, the programmer, want by explicitly specifying that the addition is to be done first and then the multiplication. This brings us to a good, sound coding rule:

Use () to explicitly denote the order or precedence that is desired. () cost you nothing in terms of computational time, yet they can save you hours of debugging time trying to find an order-of-precedence error.	**Key Concept**

The Boolean Expression

One of the most fundamental concepts used in computer science is the concept of a Boolean expression. A Boolean expression returns a value of either *true* or *false*. In C++, *true* and *false* are valid values of the enumerated (variable) type *bool*. For now, we will merely concern ourselves with the fact that *true* may be converted to the integer value "1" and *false* may be converted to the integer value "0". As you will see in the three fundamental structures presented next, Boolean expressions are used to determine the flow of control. Flow of control tells us, simply which C++ statements should be

executed in a particular situation. Both the unary and binary Boolean operators are presented in Tables 2.6 and 2.7.

There are several key facts to know about these operators. First, they are binary operators just like + and − (addition and subtraction, respectively). Thus, you can assign a variable the value obtained by using them. For example, the following code is perfectly legitimate:

```
#include <iostream.h>

int main(int argc, char ** argv){
    int a,b,c;

    a = 3;
    b = 5;

    c = a < b;

    cout << "The value of c = " << c << endl;
}
```

Table 2.6: Unitary Boolean operations.

Symbol	Interpretation
!	NOT

Table 2.7: Binary Boolean operations.

Symbol	Interpretation
&&	AND
||	OR
>	Greater than
>=	Greater than or equal to
<	Less than
<=	Less than or equal to
==	Equal to

If we were to print the value of *c* immediately following the assignment statement (as we have in this code through the use of the *cout* statement), we would find that the value of *c* is 1, because it is true that the 3 < 5. The ability to assign a variable the value of a Boolean expression holds true for all Boolean binary operators.

Two other operators that may not be as familiar to most readers are the Boolean AND (&&) and Boolean OR (\|\|). These two operators are commonly used to simplify logical expressions so that several cases can be considered in one statement. The Boolean values of these two expressions are:

```
OR (||)        AND (&&)
   0 1            0 1
 0 0 1          0 0 0
 1 1 1          1 0 1
```

These two tables should be interpreted in the following manner. Suppose we have two variables *a* and *b*. The Boolean value of variable *a* is denoted by the values on the left of the table, and the Boolean value of the variable *b* is denoted by the values on the top of the table. If we were to execute the operation *a* <operator> *b* (where <operator> is either OR or AND), then the result of this operation is given by the value in the square given by the respective row and column given by the values of *a* and *b*. Hence, if $a = 1$ and $b = 0$, **a\|\|b** yields the value 1 (true) whereas **a&&b** yields the value 0 (false). These logical relationships are very important and hence should be memorized.

You may be wondering what happens if you use these Boolean operations on regular values. Let us suppose that you had the following piece of code. What happens to the variable *c*?

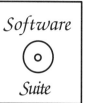

```
#include <iostream.h>

int main(int argc, char ** argv){
    int a,b,c;
```

```
    a = 3;
    b = 5;

    c = a && b;

    cout << "The value of c = " << c << endl;
}
```

Under such circumstances, *a* and *b* are implicitly cast to Boolean expressions before the AND operation is performed. Implicit casting does not affect the actual value of *a* or *b* but merely internally converts these values so that the computer can do the appropriate Boolean operation that you have requested. In such cases the following implicit casting rule is applied:

Any number not equal to zero (either positive or negative) denotes true (the logical value 1), and zero denotes false (the logical value 0).

If we now try to answer the question of what will the computer do, we see that the computer will first implicitly cast *a* and *b* to their appropriate values, which in this case are both logical true since both are nonzero, and then the AND operation will be carried out. Looking at the table, we see that (true && true) equals true, and hence the value of *c* is true (cast to the value 1).

An Example: The Collatz Problem

We will now proceed to explain three fundamental flow of control structures in C++: the **if** statement, the **while** statement, and the **for** statement. We will motivate our discussion of these three constructs with the following problem, known as the *Collatz Problem*. The problem itself is given by a very simple algorithm:

Start with any integer greater than zero; if the number is even, divide it by two; otherwise multiply it by three and add one to it. Iterate this process until the number you reach is the number one.

Hence, if you start with the value 10, the sequence of numbers what you will obtain from this algorithm is the sequence 10, 5, 16, 8, 4, 2, 1. In Figure 2.4 we plot the iterate value versus iteration for two different initial guesses, 100 and 1,000. The description of the algorithm is quite simple, and the patterns given by plotting the iterated solution versus iteration number are intriguing; however, the problem that has stumped mathematicians for decades is the following proposition attributed to Collatz:

Given any integer greater than one, the algorithm just described will terminate (i.e., the value will reach one) in a finite number of iterations.

Since the algorithm is fairly simple to implement, many explicit numerical tests have been done that demonstrate that for extremely large numbers this proposition holds true. However, at the time of this writing no theoretical proof exists for Collatz's proposition.

We will present two pieces of code that implement the algorithm just described. The first algorithm, denoted Collatz-A, makes the assumption that Collatz is right; the other, Collatz-B, is a little less confident that the proposition holds true!

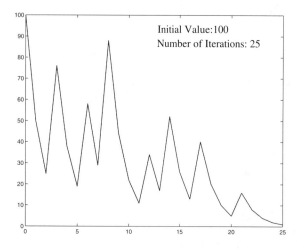

Initial Value:100
Number of Iterations: 25

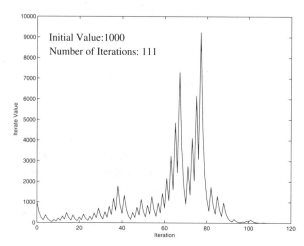

Initial Value:1000
Number of Iterations: 111

Figure 2.4: Iteration history of the Collatz algorithm for two different initial guesses, $n = 100$ and $n = 1,000$.

ALGORITHM COLLATZ-A

```
#include<iostream.h>

int main(int argc, char ** argv){
  int i,xn;
  int initial_guess = 100; // **declaration and initialization
                           //   by a constant within the same
                           //   statement

  xn = initial_guess;
  i = 0;

  while(xn != 1){

    cout << i << " " << xn << endl;

    if(xn%2==0) // use of integer modulus operator
      xn = xn/2;
    else
      xn = 3*xn+1;

    i=i+1;
  }
}
```

ALGORITHM COLLATZ-B

```
#include <iostream.h>

int main(int argc, char ** argv){
  int i,xn;
  int max_iterations = 1000;  // declaration and initialization
```

```
    int initial_guess = 100;     // declaration and initialization

    xn = initial_guess;

    for(i=0;i<max_iterations;i=i+1){

      cout << i << " " << xn << endl;

      if(xn == 1)
        break;        // use of break statement to exit for loop
                      // when the condition xn==1 is true

      if(xn%2==0)
        xn = xn/2;
      else
        xn = 3*xn+1;
    }
}
```

The fundamental difference between these two implementations is the choice of whether to use the *while* statement or the *for* statement. In the Collatz-A code, the *while* statement will terminate only if our iterate value reaches one; if it never reaches one, our program will run forever (or until the system administrator kills your process thinking you accidently left some mindless process running). Collatz-B, however, places a limit on the maximum number of iterations that you will allow before giving up on Collatz. Because both algorithms utilize the *if* statement, we will focus there first. We then move on to descriptions of the *for* and *while* statements.

The IF Statement

The *if* statement is truly at the core of any programming language. Almost all computer architectures implement a form of the *if* statement as part of their fundamental set of computer instructions. This is done because when someone sets up a computer problem, the programmer is quite often confronted with algorithmic decisions in which if something is true, then a particular piece of code should be executed, and if it is not true, then another piece of code should be executed. Such logical decisions are not unique to programming; they are fundamental to the way in which we, as humans, think. For this particular algorithm, the "if" decision is based on whether the iterate value is odd or even. The way in which we implemented this was as follows:

```
if(xn%2==0)
  xn = xn/2;
else
  xn = 3*xn+1;
```

Here, we check if the *xn* modulus 2 is 0 (i.e., if the remainder from dividing *xn* by 2 is 0); if it is, this implies that *xn* is even, and thus we should divide *xn* by 2. Otherwise, *xn* is odd, and thus we should multiply it by 3 and add 1. From this you can see the basic structure of the *if* statement. The basic structure is expressed in the following two logical examples: 1. if A then B and 2. if A then B else C.

Several examples are now provided so that you can see the syntactic structure of these statements. There are a few things to point out. First, notice that if no {} brackets are used, only the next statement immediately following the *if* statement is executed as part of the *if*. This is a common programming mistake – people think that their *if* statement encompasses many statements, but because they forgot to use {} brackets, only the first statement is executed as part of the *if*. The other thing to notice is that you are not limited to only one statement in the conditional. You can have logical statements such as if A then B, C, D, E, ... Just remember, you need to use the {} brackets to denote this collection of commands!

EXAMPLES.

```
if( boolean statement )
    statement 1;

if( boolean statement )
    statement 1;
else
    statement 2;

if( boolean statement ){
    statement 1;
    statement 2;
    ...
}

if( boolean statement ){
    statement 1;
    statement 2;
}
else{
    statement 3;
    statement 4;
}

if( boolean statement ){
    statement 1;
    statement 2;
}else if{
    statement 3;
    statement 4;
}
```

The WHILE Statement

The *while* statement is commonly used for executing a set of instructions while something is true. For Collatz-A, in which we presume that Collatz was right, we continue to iterate until our iterate xn reaches the value of one.

Two example *while* statements are presented here. Note that the rules concerning {} discussed for *if* statements hold true here also. Multiple statements can be executed as part of the *while* if {} are used to denote the extent of the statements.

EXAMPLES.

```
while( boolean expression )
    statement 1;

while( boolean expression ){
    statement 1;
    statement 2;
    ...
}
```

The FOR Statement

For scientific programming in general, one of the most common statements used is the *for* statement, which initiates a *for loop*. *For* loops are used to denote a finite number of times a particular set of instructions is to be executed. In Collatz-B, we only allow a finite number of iterations to occur, in this case 1,000. If the iterate value has not reached the value one after 1,000 iterations, the loop terminates. The *for* statement used for Collatz-B is as follows:

```
for(i=0;i<max_iterations;i=i+1){

    // ... statements ...

}
```

We begin by initializing a variable *i* to the value zero. The second part of the statement means that as long as *i* is less than *max_iterations*, the statements contained within the {} should be executed. The third component of the statement says to increment the value of *i* by one (i.e., i = i + 1) at the conclusion of each iteration. Hence, in block form, the expression becomes

```
Initialize i = 0

head: if i <  max_iterations, terminate
      Execute statements
      Increment the value of i by one
      Return (go to) to the statement 'head'
```

Hence if *max_iterations* is equal to zero, the loop will never execute. For any integer value of *max_iterations* greater than zero, the statements inside the *for* statement will execute *max_iteration* times.

There are many variations of the *for* statement, all of which follow the concept illustrated in the example here.

EXAMPLES.

```
for( statement 1; boolean expression; statement 2)
   statement 3;

for( statement 1; boolean expression; statement 2){
   statement 3;
   statement 4;
}
```

In the place of statement 1, we normally have the initialization of the looping variable. Then, we have a Boolean expression that tells us when the loop is to end. Then, finally, we have an increment statement, which updates the looping variable. Although in this case we have used solely integers, the *for* statement does not require it. If we were marching across an evenly spaced grid on [0, 1] with grid spacing h, we could equally have used the following *for* loop:

```
int N = 10; // Number of points with which discretize
double x, h = 1.0/(N-1); // ** Grid spacing; initialization
                     //    by an expression.

for(x=0.0; x<=1.0; x = x+h){ //** notice that we can use
                              // float/double within the for

 // ... appropriate statements here .....

}
```

2.1.3 Learning to Print

The printing routines to standard output (i.e., the screen) are handled by the class *cout*. The declaration of *cout* can be found in the *iostream.h* header file. You will notice that we included it in every program we have written so far that has used output to the screen. This file must be included in any program using the *cout* statement.

Recall our Collatz example previously described. In that example, we wanted to print the value of i at each iteration and the value of xn for that iteration, so we used the following statement:

```
cout << i << " " << xn << endl;
```

The printing to standard output is initiated by *cout*. Following the *cout* class, the symbols "<<" are used to delineate between items to print. In this case, we want to print the value of i, followed by a space (here denoted by the string " "), followed by the value of xn. The symbol "endl" denotes printing the end-of-line character. If we wanted to print the final iteration count only, we could execute the following statement after the *while* or *for* statement:

```
cout << "The final iteration number is: " << i << endl;
```

The general rule for the *cout* statement is that strings (denoted by quotation marks) are printed literally; that is, exactly what is placed between quotes is printed. When variables are placed in the *cout* statement, it is tacitly assumed that the contents of the variable are to be printed, and not the variable name itself.

We now present some general remarks concerning the *cout* statement:

- The $<<$ used with *cout* is actually an *overloaded* operator. The class *cout* encapsulates into an object the information necessary to accomplish printing to standard output. The $<<$ operator is defined for all predefined variable types (int, float, double, etc.) and allows us to "feed" *cout* with the data that we wish to have printed to the screen.
- Instead of using **endl**, you can also use the end-of-line character **\n** called *newline*. For example, instead of

  ```
  cout << "The final answer is yes" << endl;
  ```

  you could equally use the following:

  ```
  cout << "The final answer is yes\n";
  ```

  The **\n** character is considered one character, and hence it can be stored in a single variable of type *char*.

2.1.4 Learning to Read

Printing to the screen is important, but what about inputting information into the computer? To read from standard input (i.e., the keyboard) we use the object *cin*. The declaration of *cin* can be found in the *iostream.h* header file. This file must be included in any program using the *cin* statement.

The *cin* statement allows us to read data from the keyboard. In the Collatz programs that we presented earlier, every time the user wanted to produce the pattern for a different number, the user would have to change the value of the initial guess variable and then recompile the program. Suppose in our Collatz problem that we wanted the user to input the initial value from the keyboard so that the program could be compiled just once and use the inputted information each time it ran. To accomplish this, we can use the *cin* statement as follows:

```
#include <iostream.h>

int main(int argc, char ** argv){
  int i,xn;
  int max_iterations = 1000;  // declaration and initialization
  int initial_guess = 100;    // declaration and initialization

  cout << "Input a new value: ";

  cin >> initial_guess;

  xn = initial_guess;
```

```
for(i=0;i<max_iterations;i=i+1)}

// .... remainder of the program given previously
```

In this code, we query the user for a new value (using *cout* to print a message to the screen), and then we use *cin* to retrieve the user's keyboard input and place it into the variable *initial_guess*. Using the *cin* statement as shown here, we can now compile this program once and rerun it, allowing the user to input new values for which to obtain a Collatz sequence.

We now present some general remarks concerning the *cin* statement:

- Just as << was on overloaded operator for *cout*, >> is an overloaded operator for *cin*. The operator >> is used to delineate between inputted items.
- *cin* ignores white space when reading from standard input. Suppose that we want to input two integers into our program; we write the following:

```
int A,B;

cout << "Input two integers:";
cin >> A >> B;
```

The user could then type two integers separated by any number of white spaces (which *cin* would ignore), and *cin* would put the two integers into the variables *A* and *B*.

- *cin* reads successively through the inputted stream of information. For example, suppose that you wanted to input an integer and a floating point number into your program. We write the following:

```
int A;
float B;

cout << "Input two integers:";
cin >> A >> B;
```

If the user inputs an integer and a float separated by white space, all will work as expected. If the user, however, accidentally enters the floating point number first, the program will read up to the decimal point to obtain the integer (e.g., if 10.3 is entered, *cin* will read the value 10 into the variable *A*) and then will continue from that point to read the floating point value (which for this case will be the value 0.3) into the variable *B*.

For a more comprehensive description of the *cin* operator, we suggest that the reader consult [86].

2.1.5 How to Program in Style

Though C++ is quite tolerant of programming styles, humans are not. Someone can write a perfectly legitimate C++ code (syntactically and semantically), and yet it would be virtually incomprehensible to anyone else but the programmer (and in some cases, it may even baffle the programmer if he or she has not looked at it for a while). In general, it is good practice to follow a few basic stylistic rules when programming:

- Write comments for the nonobvious. Here, nonobvious refers both to algorithmic tricks used *and* to programming tricks used.
- Space lines of code appropriately. White space and blank lines are ignored by the compiler, hence you should use them to your advantage. A properly spaced code is much easier to read than a compacted, mangled piece of code.
- Use indentation to denote scope. When programming *for, if, while*, etc., you should use indentation to denote scope. For example, examine the differences between the following two codes:

```
for(i=0;i<N;i=i+1){
y[i] = 0.0;
for(j=0;j<N;j=j+1){
y[i] = y[i] + A[i][j]*x[j];
}
}
```

versus

```
for(i=0;i<N;i=i+1){
    y[i] = 0.0;
    for(j=0;j<N;j=j+1){
        y[i] = y[i] + A[i][j]*x[j];
    }
}
```

As you can see, the indentation of the statements leads to immediate recognition of the nesting of the statements. This type of "spot-check" ability is very important when searching for either algorithmic or syntactic bugs.

How to Comment Code

C++ provides two means of commenting code: the single line comment and the block comment. The single line comment is denoted by //. When the compiler reaches the // statement, it ignores all characters that follow up to the line return. Thus, we can use this comment symbol to comment our previous coding example as follows:

```
//This code computes the matrix-vector product A*x,
//and puts the result in y

for(i=0;i<N;i=i+1){       //loop over the rows
    y[i] = 0.0;           //initialize to zero
    for(j=0;j<N;j=j+1){  //loop over the columns
        y[i] = y[i] + A[i][j]*x[j];
    }//end for j
}//end for i
```

The second means of commenting is by using the /* */ syntax. The C++ compiler will ignore everything between /* and */, even if this spans across several lines. Hence, if we wanted to comment out the loops in the previous code, we could do the following:

```
/*
for(i=0;i<N;i=i+1){
   y[i] = 0.0;
   for(j=0;j<N;j=j+1){
       y[i] = y[i] + A[i][j]*x[j];
   }
} */
```

By placing these symbols before and after this block of code, we have commented out the entire block of code. Obviously, this is not the only (nor the primary) use of comment blocks. The purpose of this form of commenting is to allow the user to place more detailed (multiline) descriptions of algorithmic components of the code.

PUTTING IT INTO PRACTICE

We now introduce a full C++ program using the previously discussed coding examples. This program contains all the essential items necessary to compile and execute our Collatz algorithm (in this particular case, we are looking at *Collatz-A*).

```
#include <iostream.h>
#include <iomanip.h>

int main(int argc, char ** argv){
  int i,xn;
  int initial_guess = 100;

  xn = initial_guess;
  i = 0;
  while(xn != 1){
    cout << i << " " << xn << endl;
    if(xn == 1)
      break;
    if(xn%2==0)
      xn = xn/2;
    else
      xn = 3*xn+1;
    i=i+1;
  }
}
```

The general format of our code is as follows: At the top of the file we place our "include" statements. These statements are called "precompiled directives." This means that they are instructions to be carried out before the compilation is done. In this case, the "#include" statement tells the compiler to insert the variable and function declarations found in the header file "iostream.h" and "iomanip.h." Since we have no other functions than our *main* function, we have no other functions to declare. Our program begins with a *main* function, which tells the computer where to start executing. Inside this function we place the C++ description of the algorithm we want executed.

To recapitulate, the general format of our C++ codes will be as follows:

```
/********************************;
/*      Include Statements        */
/********************************/

#include <iostream.h>       //Input/Output Header File
#include <iomanip.h>        //Input/Output Manipulation
                                 Header File
#include <fstream.h>        //File Input/Output Header File
#include <string.h>         //String Manipulation Header File
#include <math.h>           //Math Library Header File

//  ..... etc .....

/****************************************/
/* User-Defined Variable Declarations    */
/****************************************/

// Items such as Class declarations, etc.

/********************************/
/*      Function Declarations      */
/********************************/

// User-defined function declarations.

/********************************/
/*        Main Program          */
/********************************/
int main(int argc, char ** argv){

   // ... Algorithm ...

}

/********************************/
/*      Function Definitions      */
/********************************/
```

Quite often throughout this book we will omit repeating this basic structure; we will focus merely on providing algorithm and function definitions. Algorithms described throughout this book can be inserted into the C++ programming shell outlined here, compiled, and executed. When deviations from this style are needed, they will be explicitly mentioned in the text.

2.2 MATHEMATICAL AND COMPUTATIONAL CONCEPTS

2.2.1 Notation

We will denote a vector by a bold letter, so the transpose of a vector $\mathbf{x}$ of length n is $\mathbf{x}^T = (x_1, x_2, x_3, \ldots, x_n)$. We will denote a matrix of size $m \times n$ by a capital bold letter, say matrix $\mathbf{A}$, which has entries $(a_{ij}; i = 1, \ldots, m; j = 1, \ldots, n)$. We will often write the matrix $\mathbf{A}$ in terms of its columns $\mathbf{a}_j$, each one having m entries. We will also use the symbol $\mathcal{O}(n^p)$ (read as "order of" n^p) to denote either asymptotic computational complexity or convergence rate.

2.2.2 Binary Numbers and Round-off

Appreciation of the finite arithmetic in scientific computing is very important, and sloppy handling of arithmetic precision often leads to erroneous results or even disasters in large scientific computations. It has been reported, for example, that the Patriot missile failure in Dharan, Saudi Arabia, on February 25, 1991, which resulted in twenty-eight deaths, is ultimately attributable to poor handling of rounding errors. Similarly, the explosion of an *Ariane 5* rocket just after lift-off on its maiden voyage off French Guinea, on June 4, 1996, was ultimately the consequence of simple overflow (the conversion from a 64-bit floating point value to a 16-bit signed integer value).

While we are familiar and more comfortable with the base-10 arithmetic system, a computer is restricted to a binary numbering system. The number 126, for example, has the representation

$$126 = 1 \times 10^2 + 2 \times 10^1 + 6 \times 10^0$$

in the base-10 system, or equivalently

$$01111110_2 = 0 \times 2^7 + 1 \times 2^6 + 1 \times 2^5 + 1 \times 2^4 + 1 \times 2^3 + 1 \times 2^2 + 1 \times 2^1 + 0 \times 2^0$$

in the base-2 system. This is the **floating point** representation.

In computing we call each place in a binary number a digit or a **bit**, and we call a group of 8 bits a **byte**. Similarly, we call 1,024 bytes a kilobyte (1 kB) and 1,048,576 bytes a megabyte (1 MB), and so on. An equivalent way to write the number 126 in scientific notation is

$$\underbrace{+}_{sign} \quad \underbrace{.126}_{fraction} \quad \underbrace{\times 10^3}_{exponent}$$

Therefore, in the computer we need to store the sign, the fraction, and the exponent separately. To this end, there is a standard notation adopted by the IEEE (Institute of Electrical and Electronic Engineers) for binary arithmetic, which is used in most computers (the old Cray computers did not follow this convention). There are two types of floating point numbers, depending on the number of binary digits (bits) we store: Specifically, in the **single precision** (*float* type in C++) we have 8 bits for the exponent and 23 bits in the fraction whereas in the **double precision** (*double* type in C++) we have 11 bits for the exponent and 52 bits for the fraction. In both cases we need to also reserve 1 bit for the sign. What this means simply is that there is a lower and an upper bound on the size of numbers we can deal with in the computer. In the single precision type this range extends from 2^{-126} to 2^{128} and in the double precision from 2^{-1022} to 2^{1024}, so clearly the latter allows great flexibility in dealing with very small or very large numbers. The lower limit in this range determines an *underflow* whereas the upper limit determines an *overflow*. What value a variable takes on when it overflows or underflows depends on both the variable type and the computing architecture on which you are running. Even this large range, however, may not be sufficient in certain applications, and one may need to extend it by using **double extended precision** (*long double* in C++), which can store up to a total of 128 bits. In practice, it is more efficient to use *adaptive* arithmetic only when it is needed, for example in refining the mesh down to very small length scales to resolve small vortices in a flow simulation.

The finite arithmetic in computing implies that the *effective zero* in the computer is about 6×10^{-8} for single precision and 10^{-16} for double precision. We can determine the value of *machine epsilon* by finding the value of $1/2^p$ such that to the computer

$$1.0 + \frac{1}{2^p} = 1.0.$$

This is accomplished by increasing the value of p incrementally and monitoring the point at which the computer cannot distinguish between the value 1 and the value $1 + 1/2^p$. This procedure is implemented for both floating point and double precision variables in the following two functions:

```
float FloatMachineEps(){
  float   fmachine_e, ftest;
  fmachine_e = 1.0;

  ftest = 1.0 + fmachine_e;
  while(1.0 != ftest){
    fmachine_e = fmachine_e/2.0;
    ftest = 1.0 + fmachine_e;
  }

  return fmachine_e;
}

double DoubleMachineEps(){
  double dmachine_e, dtest;
  dmachine_e = 1.0;

  dtest = 1.0 + dmachine_e;
  while(1.0 != dtest){
```

Software

⊙

Suite

Table 2.8: Machine
zero for *float* and
double precision for a
Pentium 4 processor.

```
        dmachine_e = dmachine_e/2.0;
        dtest = 1.0 + dmachine_e;
    }

    return dmachine_e;

}
```

Variable type	Machine zero
float	5.96046e-08
double	1.11022e-16

Now, a natural question is: "How do I use these functions?" For starters, we would write the following program, which uses both functions:

```
#include <iostream.h>

float FloatMachineEps();
double DoubleMachineEps();

int main(int * argc, char ** argv[]){
    float fep;
    double dep;

    fep = FloatMachineEps();
    dep = DoubleMachineEps();

    cout << "Machine epsilon for single precision is:";
    cout << fep << endl;

    cout << "Machine epsilon for double precision is:";
    cout << dep << endl;

}
```

The machine-zero values obtained by running this program on a Pentium 4 processor are given in Table 2.8.

Key Concept

Notice the structure of this code:

1. function Declarations,
2. "main" Function, and
3. function definitions.

This code example demonstrates two important concepts. First, it demonstrates that in computing, it is important to understand how arithmetic works on your machine. Second, this example demonstrates that with very little programming, a user can investigate the machine upon which the code is running. We must be mindful that no computer can accomplish infinite precision arithmetic; it is limited to finite precision. Finite precision arithmetic is explained as follows: When the exact value of a basic operation (e.g., addition of two numbers) is not represented with a sufficient number of digits, it is then approximated with the closest floating point number. The approximation error incurred is referred to as the *round-off* error. It is for this reason that such a fundamental property of addition as the associative property is not always satisfied in the computer. For example,

$$-1.0 + (1.0 + \epsilon) \neq (-1.0 + 1.0) + \epsilon$$

because on the left-hand side a very small number is added to a large number and that change may not be represented exactly (due to round-off error) in the computer.

2.2.3 Condition Number

The condition number is a very useful measure of the sensitivity of the numerical solution to a slight change in the input. This number is proportional to the magnitude of the first derivative of the solution. This can be formally shown by considering a solution $\phi(x)$ and recomputing it for a slightly perturbed input, that is, $x + \delta x$, where δx is the perturbation. Using the Taylor series expansion and keeping the first term only, we obtain

$$\phi(x + \delta x) \approx \phi(x) + \phi'(x)\delta x.$$

Thus, the change in the function value is

$$\frac{|\phi(x + \delta x) - \phi(x)|}{|\phi(x)|} \approx \frac{|\phi'(x)||x|}{|\phi(x)|} \times \frac{|\delta x|}{|x|}$$

Using this equation we define as *condition number* the first term in the product of the right-hand side. It represents the relative error in the solution (response) given a small change in the input expressed by the independent variable x.

2.2.4 Vector and Matrix Norms

We define the most important norms that we will use to measure errors in this book. We need norms both for vectors as well as for matrices. The norm of a vector $\mathbf{x}^T = (x_1, x_2, x_3, \ldots, x_n)$ of length n is a scalar that obeys the following rules:

- $\| \mathbf{x} \| \geq 0$.
- $\| \mathbf{x} \| = 0 \Leftrightarrow \mathbf{x} = 0$.
- $\| \alpha\mathbf{x} \| = |\alpha| \| \mathbf{x} \|$, where α is a scalar.
- $\| \mathbf{x} + \mathbf{y} \| \leq \| \mathbf{x} \| + \| \mathbf{y} \|$.

Some of the most commonly used norms are

- the discrete L_∞ norm defined as $\quad \| \mathbf{x} \|_\infty = \max_i |x_i|$,
- the discrete L_2 norm defined as $\quad \| \mathbf{x} \|_2 = \left(\sum_{i=1}^n x_i^2\right)^{\frac{1}{2}}$,
- the discrete L_1 norm defined as $\quad \| \mathbf{x} \|_1 = \sum_{i=1}^n |x_i|$, and
- the L_p norm defined as $\quad \| \mathbf{x} \|_p = \left(\sum_{i=1}^n |x_i|^p\right)^{1/p}$.

There is a theorem of equivalence of vector norms; by this we mean that

$\| \mathbf{x} \|_p$ *is equivalent to* $\| \mathbf{x} \|_q$ *if there exist numbers A(p,q,n) and B(p,q,n) so that*

$$\| \mathbf{x} \|_p \leq A \| \mathbf{x} \|_q,$$

$$\| \mathbf{x} \|_q \leq B \| \mathbf{x} \|_p.$$

THEOREM: *All L_p norms are equivalent for $p \geq 1$ and the size of the vector is n finite.*

REMARK: For $p > q > 1$, then $\| \mathbf{x} \|_p \leq \| \mathbf{x} \|_q \leq n \| \mathbf{x} \|_p$, where n is the vector length.

This theorem is the reason why we sometimes omit the subindex in the norm notation. As an example, the L_1 norm and the L_2 norm are equivalent but not equal. In practice, this means that either one can be used to measure errors and the convergence result we obtain in our analysis would not depend on the particular norm.

THE CAUCHY-SCHWARZ INEQUALITY is very useful in numerical analysis. For any two vectors $\mathbf{x}$ and $\mathbf{y}$ we have

$$|(\mathbf{x}, \mathbf{y})| \leq \| \mathbf{x} \|_2 \| \mathbf{y} \|_2,$$

where $(\mathbf{x}, \mathbf{y})$ is the inner product of the two vectors (see Section 2.2.7) defined as $(x, y) = \sum_{i=1}^{n} x_i y_i$.

MATRIX NORMS: The matrix norm generated by the vector norm $\| \mathbf{x} \|_p$ is defined by

$$\| \mathbf{A} \|_p = \max_{x \neq \mathbf{0}} \frac{\| \mathbf{A}\mathbf{x} \|_p}{\| \mathbf{x} \|_p}.$$

Similarly, we have the following:

- The L_∞ norm generates $\| \mathbf{A} \|_\infty = \max_i \sum_{j=1}^{n} |a_{ij}|$, which is the maximum row sum.
- The L_1 norm generates $\| \mathbf{A} \|_1 = \max_j \sum_{i=1}^{n} |a_{ij}|$, which is the maximum column sum.
- The L_2 norm generates the average matrix norm, that is, $\| \mathbf{A} \|_2 = \sqrt{\max \lambda(\mathbf{A}^*\mathbf{A})}$, where $\mathbf{A}^*\mathbf{A}$ is a positive symmetric matrix with positive real eigenvalues. Here $\mathbf{A}^*$ denotes the complex conjugate matrix of $\mathbf{A}$, which in the case of real matrix entries is the transpose of $\mathbf{A}$, that is, $\mathbf{A}^* = \mathbf{A}^T$.

There are also two useful inequalities involving matrix norms:

$$\| \mathbf{A} + \mathbf{B} \| \leq \| \mathbf{A} \| + \| \mathbf{B} \|,$$

$$\| \mathbf{A}\mathbf{x} \| \leq \| \mathbf{A} \| \| \mathbf{x} \|.$$

In these inequalities we assume that a specific norm, as defined in this section, is chosen.

2.2.5 Eigenvalues and Eigenvectors

The eigenvalues and corresponding eigenvectors of a matrix $\mathbf{A}$ are determined by solving

$$\mathbf{A}\mathbf{x} = \lambda\mathbf{x} \Rightarrow (\mathbf{A} - \lambda\mathbf{I})\mathbf{x} = 0,$$

where

$$\mathbf{I} = \begin{bmatrix} 1 & & & & & \\ & 1 & & & O & \\ & & 1 & & & \\ & & & \ddots & & \\ O & & & & 1 \end{bmatrix}$$

is the identity matrix. The eigenvectors $\mathbf{x}$ are nonzero if the determinant is zero, that is, if

$$\det(\mathbf{A} - \lambda\mathbf{I}) = 0,$$

and this equation determines the eigenvalues λ. It can be rewritten as

$$\det(\mathbf{A} - \lambda\mathbf{I}) = \Pi_{i=1}^{n}(a_{ii} - \lambda_i) + p_{n-1}(\lambda) = 0,$$

where a_{ii} are the diagonal elements of $\mathbf{A}$ and $p_{n-1}(\lambda)$ is a $(n-1)$th-order polynomial. Therefore, an $n \times n$ matrix has exactly n eigenvalues, that is, the roots of this nth-order polynomial, which may be real or complex and simple or multiple. However, this approach is rarely used in practice to compute the eigenvalues because it is computationally very expensive and also unstable. This is illustrated with the *Wilkinson matrix*

$$\mathbf{W} = \begin{bmatrix} 1 & & & & & \mathcal{O}(\epsilon) \\ & 2 & & & & \\ & & 3 & & & \\ & & & \ddots & & \\ & & & & 19 & \\ \mathcal{O}(\epsilon) & & & & & 20 \end{bmatrix},$$

where by $\mathcal{O}(\epsilon)$ we denote possible round-off error. In the absence of round-off error, the eigenvalues are determined by

$$(1 - \lambda)(2 - \lambda)(3 - \lambda) \cdots (19 - \lambda)(20 - \lambda) = 0,$$

and thus $\lambda_i = i$. However, for $\epsilon \neq 0$ the *characteristic* polynomial is

$$\lambda^{20} - 210\lambda^{19} + \cdots + 20! + \epsilon\lambda^{19}.$$

Let us assume that $\epsilon = 10^{-11}$; then we obtain

$$\lambda_i = 1, 2, \ldots, 8, 9, 10.01, 11.3, 12.5 \pm 0.5i, 14.5 \pm 0.5i, \ldots, 20.$$

Therefore, the presence of even slight noise in the data results in several eigenvalues being wrong, even complex in this case!

Similarity Transformation

Next, we provide some basic background on linear algebra. First, we define the *similarity transformation*. Specifically, we say that the matrix $\mathbf{A}$ is *similar* to matrix $\mathbf{B}$ if

A and **B** have the same eigenvalues (i.e., the same eigenspectrum) but not necessarily the same eigenvectors. Therefore, the transformation

$$\mathbf{A} \longrightarrow \mathbf{PAP}^{-1},$$

where **P** is a nonsingular matrix, leads to a matrix $\mathbf{B} = \mathbf{PAP}^{-1}$, which is similar to **A**. This can be proved based on the definitions. Let us assume

$$\mathbf{Ax} = \lambda \mathbf{x}$$

and

$$\mathbf{PAP}^{-1}\mathbf{y} = \mu \mathbf{y}.$$

Then

$$\mathbf{AP}^{-1}\mathbf{y} = \mathbf{P}^{-1}\mu \mathbf{y} = \mu \mathbf{P}^{-1}\mathbf{y}$$

and by defining $\mathbf{x} = \mathbf{P}^{-1}\mathbf{y}$, we have $\mu = \lambda$, so all n eigenvalues are the same for both **A** and $\mathbf{PAP}^{-1}$. We also note that if **P** is an orthogonal matrix then $\mathbf{P}^{-1} = \mathbf{P}^{T}$ and then $\mathbf{PAP}^{T}$ is similar to **A**. In theory, any nonsingular matrix **P** can be used in the similarity transformation, but the best choice in practice is to use an orthonormal matrix. The reason is that with finite arithmetic ill-conditioned matrices, unlike orthonormal matrices, amplify the round-off error and may lead to erroneous results.

REMARK 1: The transpose matrix $\mathbf{A}^{T}$ is similar to matrix **A** since they have the same characteristic polynomial. However, they do not have the same eigenvectors. In contrast, the inverse matrix $\mathbf{A}^{-1}$ has the same eigenvectors with **A** but inverse eigenvalues, λ_i^{-1}. This is true because

$$\mathbf{Ax} = \lambda \mathbf{x} \Rightarrow \mathbf{x} = \mathbf{A}^{-1}\lambda \mathbf{x} \Rightarrow \lambda^{-1}\mathbf{x} = \mathbf{A}^{-1}\mathbf{x}.$$

REMARK 2: The matrix $\mathbf{A}^{k}$, where k is a positive integer, has eigenvalues λ^{k}, where λ are the eigenvalues of **A**. However, $\mathbf{A}^{k}$ and **A** have the same eigenvectors. This can be extended further and it is easy to show that if we construct the *polynomial matrix*

$$p(\mathbf{A}) \equiv \alpha_0 \mathbf{A}^0 + \alpha_1 \mathbf{A} + \alpha_2 A^2 + \cdots + \alpha_k \mathbf{A}^k,$$

then

$$p(\lambda_1), \ p(\lambda_2), \ p(\lambda_3) \ldots p(\lambda_n)$$

are the eigenvalues of $p(\mathbf{A})$. Correspondingly, the eigenvectors of **A** are also eigenvectors of $p(\mathbf{A})$. As an example, the eigenvalues of $p_1(\mathbf{A}) = \mathbf{A} + \sigma\mathbf{I}$ are $(\lambda_i + \sigma)$.

We have already seen that computing the eigenvalues accurately from the determinant may not always be possible, although the Newton–Raphson method of Chapter 4 is an accurate method of computing the roots of polynomials, but it may be inefficient. In Chapter 10 we present several methods to compute iteratively and selectively the maximum and minimum eigenvalues and corresponding eigenvectors.

2.2.6 Memory Management

Before we present **BLAS** (Basic Linear Algebra Subroutines) in the next section, we will give you some preliminary information concerning memory management that will help to make the next discussion more relevant.

In this section, we will discuss two issues:

- memory layout for matrices and
- cache blocking.

Our discussion will be directed toward understanding how memory layout in main memory and cache (see Figure 2.11) affect performance.

integer a
array of floats x

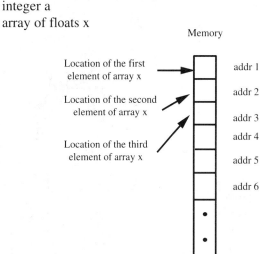

Figure 2.5: Schematic showing the memory layout for an integer variable and an array of floating point values. The partitioned strip denotes the memory of the computer, and the labels *addr* to the right denote the address of the parcel of memory.

Memory Layout for Matrices

Computer memory consists of a linearly addressable space, as illustrated in Figure 2.5. In this illustration, we denote memory as a one-dimensional partitioned strip. To the right of the strip, the labels *addr* denote the address of the parcel of memory. By linearly addressable we mean that $addr\ 2 = addr\ 1 + addrset$, where *addrset* is the memory offset between two contiguous blocks of addressable memory.[3] Single variables and one-dimensional arrays fit quite nicely into this concept since a single integer variable needs only one parcel of memory, and the array needs only one parcel of memory per element of the array.

How are two-dimensional arrays stored in memory? Because memory is linearly addressable, to store a two-dimensional array we must decide how to decompose the matrix into one-dimensional units. There are two obvious means of doing this: decomposing the matrix into a collection of rows or decomposing the matrix into a collection of columns. The first is referred to as "row-major order"; the latter is referred to as "column-major order." This concept is illustrated in Figure 2.6.

After examining Figure 2.6, we draw your attention to the following statements:

- The amount of memory used by both ordering is the same. Nine units of memory are used in both cases.
- The linear ordering is different. Although both orderings start with the same entry (S_{00}), the next addressable block in memory contains a different entry of **S** (S_{01} for row-major order versus S_{10} for column-major order). This important observation will be discussed further in just a moment.

---

[3] We have remained general because different architectures allow different addressable sets. Some architectures are bit addressable, some byte addressable, and some only word addressable. We will not delve further into this matter, but the interested reader should consult a computer architecture book for more details.

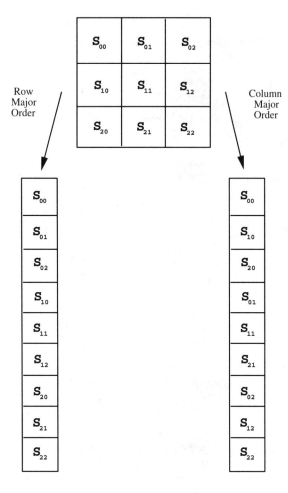

Row
Major
Order

Column
Major
Order

Figure 2.6: The 3 × 3 matrix S is decomposed by row-major ordering on the left and by column-major ordering on the right.

- If **S** is a symmetric matrix (meaning $S_{ij} = S_{ji}$), then row-major ordering and column-major ordering appear identical.
- C++ uses row-major ordering whereas FORTRAN uses column-major ordering. In Section 5.1.4 we discuss how multidimensional arrays are allocated in C++ and how row-major ordering comes into play.

One other item needs to be mentioned before we can conclude this discussion. As shown in Figure 2.11, most modern computing architectures have several layers of memory between what we have referred to as "main memory" and the central processing unit. Main memory is normally much slower than the CPU, and hence engineers decided to insert smaller but faster memory between main memory and the CPU (in this discussion, we will lump register memory in with the CPU and will refer to level 1 (L_1) and level 2 (L_2) cache simply as "cache"). If all the items necessary to accomplish a computation could fit into cache, then the total time to execute the instructions would be reduced because the time cost of *loads* and *stores* to memory would be accelerated.

In general, even for programs in which not all the data can fit into cache, the use of cache decreases the total time cost by using cached data as much as possible. This is referred to as **cache reuse**. The goal is that once some piece of information has been loaded into cache, it should be reused as much as possible (since access to it is much faster than accessing the same data from main memory). Whenever a piece of needed information is found in cache, we have what is referred to as a **cache hit**. Whenever a piece of information cannot be found in cache, and hence it must be obtained from main memory (by loading it into cache), we have what is referred to as a **cache miss**.

Items from main memory are loaded in blocks of size equal to the size of a **cache line**, a term that comes from the size of the lines going from main memory modules to the cache memory modules. Hence, if you want to access one element of an array, and it is not in cache (a miss), an entire cache line's worth of information will be loaded into cache, which may include many contiguous elements of the array. We draw your attention to Figure 2.7. In this illustration, we are examining the memory layout during a matrix–vector multiplication. The 3 × 3 matrix **A** is stored in row-major order followed by a 3 × 1 vector **x**. In this simplified example, our cache consists of nine units that are loaded/stored in blocks of three units (our cache line is of size three units).

At macro time t_0, the first element of **A** is needed, so an entire cache line's worth of information is loaded, which in this case consists of three units. Hence, the entire first row of **A** is loaded into cache. The first element of the vector **x** is needed, and hence an entire cache line's worth of information is loaded, which is equal to all of **x**. To accomplish the dot product of the first row of **A** with the vector **x**, the other entries already in cache are needed. Thus, we have several cache hits as other computations are accomplished to obtain the end result of the dot product, b_1. At macro time t_1, the first item in the second row of **A** is needed, and hence there is a cache miss. An entire cache line of information is loaded, which in this case is the entire second row. Again, many computations can be accomplished until another cache miss happens, in which case new information must be loaded into cache.

Although this is a very simplied example, it demonstrates how memory layout can be very important to *cache reuse*. What would have happened if we had stored the matrix **A**

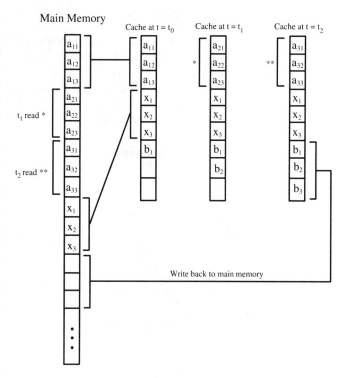

Figure 2.7: Main memory and cache layout for a matrix–vector multiplication.

in column-major order but had implemented the algorithm described? Because of the particular cache size and cache line size, we would have had a cache miss almost every time we needed an entry of **A**, and hence the total time cost would have been greatly increased because of the excessive direct use of main memory instead of the fast cache.

Cache Blocking

The concept of *cache blocking* involves structuring the data and operations on these data so that maximum cache reuse can be achieved (i.e., to maximize cache hits). In our example, we have achieved this by choosing to store the matrix **A** in row-major order for the particular algorithm that we implemented.

Keep this concept in mind during the discussion of BLAS in the next section. In several cases, different implementations are given for the same mathematical operation, some depending on whether your matrix is stored in column-major order or in row-major order. In the end, the computational time used to run your program can be significantly altered by paying attention to which algorithm is most efficient with which memory layout. Taking into account cache characteristics when determining the data partition used is very important and can greatly enhance or deteriorate the performance of your program.

2.2.7 Basic Linear Algebra – BLAS

Basic operations with vectors and matrices dominate scientific computing programs, and thus to achieve high efficiency and clean computer programs an effort has been made in the past few decades to standardize and optimize such operations. Two of the most basic operations with vectors that appear in a code repeatedly are **inner (dot) product** and **outer product**. The inner or dot product returns a scalar; however, the outer product returns a matrix. For example:

INNER PRODUCT

$$[a_1 \, a_2 \, a_3 \ldots] \begin{bmatrix} b_1 \\ b_2 \\ b_3 \\ \vdots \end{bmatrix} = c,$$

where c is the scalar value of the inner product, and $c = 0$ implies that the two vectors are orthogonal, a terminology similar to vector calculus.

OUTER PRODUCT

$$\begin{bmatrix} a_1 \\ a_2 \\ a_3 \\ \vdots \end{bmatrix} [b_1 \, b_2 \, b_3 \ldots] = \begin{bmatrix} a_1 b_1 & a_1 b_2 & a_1 b_3 \cdots \\ a_2 b_1 & a_2 b_2 & a_2 b_3 \cdots \\ a_3 b_1 & a_3 b_2 & a_3 b_3 \cdots \\ \vdots \end{bmatrix}.$$

In addition to the inner and outer products, there are several other standard matrix and vector operations that are used repeatedly in scientific computing. A convenient taxonomy is based on their computational complexity (i.e., the number of floating point operations required to complete an operation). In the previous example with the inner product of vectors with length n, we require n multiplications and $(n-1)$ additions or a total of approximately $2n$ operations. We denote the computational complexity of the *inner product* as $\mathcal{O}(n)$ (read as "order n"). Similarly, we can estimate the computational complexity of the *outer product* to be $\mathcal{O}(n^2)$. We can then define levels of operations as

$$\mathcal{O}(n), \quad \mathcal{O}(n^2), \quad \text{and} \quad \mathcal{O}(n^3),$$

and this is exactly what has been done with the **BLAS** (basic linear algebra subprograms), a collection of routines that perform specific vector and matrix operations. BLAS were first proposed by Lawson et al. [67] and further developed in [27, 29]. BLAS serve as building blocks in many computer codes, and their performance on a certain computer usually reflects the performance of that code on the same computer. This is why most of the computer vendors optimize BLAS for specific architectures. BLAS provide both efficiency and modularity. The most recent trend has been to develop a new generation of "self-tuning" BLAS libraries targeting the rich but complex memory systems of modern processors.

The adaptive BLAS software is called **ATLAS**, which stands for automatically tuned linear algebra software [93]. ATLAS is an implementation of empirical optimization procedures that allow for many different ways of performing a kernel operation with corresponding timers to determine which approach is best for a particular platform. More specifically, ATLAS uses two techniques: *multiple implementation* and *code generation*. In the latter, a highly parameterized code is written that generates many different kernel implementations. In the former, different handwritten versions of the same kernel are explicitly provided. The ATLAS framework also allows the user to supply machine-specific implementations for other operations, for example *prefetch* instructions and even different timers to affect optimization.

LEVEL "1"

The first level, **BLAS1**, includes $\mathcal{O}(n)$ operations; these include scalar–vector multiplication, vector addition, inner (dot) product, vector multiplication, and the "*saxpy*" operation. The latter simply means "scalar alpha x plus y" and serves as a mnemonic rule for adding a vector to another vector multiplied with a scalar:

$$c = dot(\mathbf{x}, \mathbf{y}),$$

$$c = c + x(i)y(i); \quad i = 1, n$$

and also

$$\mathbf{z} = saxpy(\alpha, \mathbf{x}, \mathbf{y}),$$

$$z(i) = \alpha x(i) + y(i); \quad i = 1, n.$$

In these expressions the equal sign implies "assignment" rather than equality as is common in computer programming.

A typical performance of the double precision (*ddot*) inner product on the Intel Pentium 4 (1.7 GHz) (see Figure 2.12) is shown in Figure 2.8. Specifically, the ATLAS version of BLAS is employed with two different options of handling the data: "Hot" implies that the vector is in cache and "cold" implies that is out of cache. This processor has two levels of cache, which are both on the chip (see Figure 2.12). The primary (L_1) cache is 16 kB whereas the secondary (L_2) cache is 256 kB.[4] We see that the "hot/hot" combination results in the best performance, which, however, is less than half of the maximum possible speed of 1.7 Gflops for a single operation per cycle. However, when the vector sizes exceed the cache size, at an array size of approximately 10,000, the performance asymptotes to approximately 250 Mflops, which is only a fraction of the maximum speed.

---

[4] This is a relatively small cache. The new processors have cache of several megabytes.

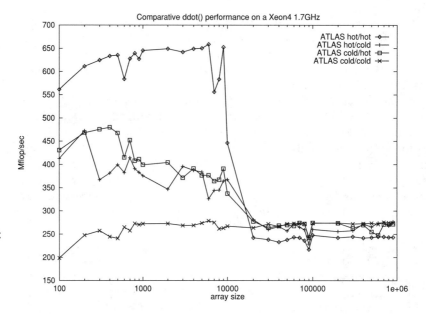

Figure 2.8:
Performance of the dot
product on the Intel
Pentium 4 with speed
1.7 GHz. (Courtesy of
C. Evangelinos.)

LEVEL "2"

The second level, **BLAS2**, includes $\mathcal{O}(n^2)$ operations, specifically the most important operation in scientific computing: *matrix–vector* multiplication.[5] There are two ways of performing this operation depending on how we access the matrix **A**, either by row or by column:

- $\mathbf{z} = \text{MatVec}.ij(\mathbf{A}, \mathbf{x})$. This is the row version.

    Initialize $z(i) = 0.0$ for $i = 1, n$
    Begin Loop $i = 1, n$
         Begin Loop $j = 1, n$
                           $z(i) = z(i) + A(i, j)x(j)$
         End Loop
    End Loop

- $\mathbf{z} = \text{MatVec}.ji(\mathbf{A}, \mathbf{x})$. This is the *saxpy* version. We give an example of this version as it may be less familiar to the reader compared to the inner product version:

$$\begin{bmatrix} 1 & 2 \\ 3 & 4 \end{bmatrix}\begin{bmatrix} 5 \\ 6 \end{bmatrix} = 5\begin{bmatrix} 1 \\ 3 \end{bmatrix} + 6\begin{bmatrix} 2 \\ 4 \end{bmatrix}.$$

The *saxpy* version is basically a linear combination of the columns of the matrix **A** with weights given by the entries of the vector. We will also refer to this version as the FORTRAN programming version since the matrix **A** is accessed by columns,

---

[5] The matrix–vector BLAS routine has the name *dgemv* (double precision) but also the name *mxv* is used.

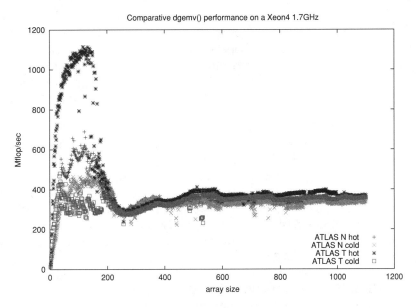

Figure 2.9: Performance of the matrix–vector multiplication on the Intel Pentium 4 with speed of 1.7 GHz. (Courtesy of C. Evangelinos.)

which is the way that matrices are stored in FORTRAN language. The loop that implements the column version is as follows:

Initialize $z(i) = 0.0$ for $i = 1, n$
Begin Loop $j = 1, n$
     Begin Loop $i = 1, n$
                      $z(i) = z(i) + A(i, j)x(j)$
     End Loop
End Loop

It is different from the row version only in the order of the loops (i then j instead of the j then i presented here).

• *Gaxpy* (General **A** **x** plus **y**). This is an operation that involves matrix–vector products, which is the generalization of *saxpy*:

$$\mathbf{z} = \mathbf{y} + \mathbf{Ax}; \quad \mathbf{z} = gaxpy \;\; (\mathbf{A}, \;\; \mathbf{x}, \;\; \mathbf{y})$$
$$\downarrow \quad\quad \downarrow \quad \downarrow$$
$$m \times n \quad n \quad m$$

To compute a *gaxpy* we use the *saxpy* operation in the following loop:

     $\mathbf{z} = \mathbf{y}$
Begin Loop $j = 1, n$
               $z = z + x(j) \underbrace{A(., j)}_{\text{column}}$

End Loop

A typical performance of the double precision (*dgemv*) matrix–vector operation on the Intel Pentium 4 (1.7 GHz) is shown in Figure 2.9. Specifically, the ATLAS version of the BLAS2 routine is employed with different ways of handling the matrix, accessing it either with unit stride ("T" stands for transpose) or with larger stride ("N" stands for normal). Similarly to the *dot* operation in Figure 2.8, *hot* and *cold* refer to *in-cache* or *out-of-cache* operations, respectively. Here we see that the maximum achievable speed is larger than the BLAS1 level operation of Figure 2.8, but again in these matrices with a rank of 200 the out-of-cache operations result in inferior performance.

LEVEL "3"

In this level we have the *matrix–matrix* multiplication, which is an $\mathcal{O}(n^3)$ operation. It can be accomplished in six different ways, based on the basic operations of lower computational complexity of levels 1 and 2.[6] These six different loop arrangements were first proposed by Dongarra, et al. [31]. The corresponding BLAS are **BLAS3**. We present here the inner (dot) product version, the middle product or *saxpy* version, and the outer product version. The other three ways are similar to the three versions that we present here and form the "dual" algorithms. In all cases the basic loop is

$$c_{ij} = c_{ij} + a_{ik}b_{kj}$$

for the matrix multiplication $\mathbf{C} = \mathbf{A}\,\mathbf{B}$, so it is the order of indexing that is different. To make ideas more clear we present a specific example with a 2×2 matrix–matrix multiplication.

- Inner (dot) product version:

$$\begin{bmatrix} 1 & 2 \\ 3 & 4 \end{bmatrix}\begin{bmatrix} 5 & 6 \\ 7 & 8 \end{bmatrix} = \begin{bmatrix} 1\cdot5+2\cdot7 & 1\cdot6+2\cdot8 \\ 3\cdot5+4\cdot7 & 3\cdot6+4\cdot8 \end{bmatrix}.$$

- Middle (*saxpy*) product version:

$$\begin{bmatrix} 1 & 2 \\ 3 & 4 \end{bmatrix}\begin{bmatrix} 5 & 6 \\ 7 & 8 \end{bmatrix} = \begin{bmatrix} 5\begin{bmatrix} 1 \\ 3 \end{bmatrix} + 7\begin{bmatrix} 2 \\ 4 \end{bmatrix} & 6\begin{bmatrix} 1 \\ 3 \end{bmatrix} + 8\begin{bmatrix} 2 \\ 4 \end{bmatrix} \end{bmatrix}.$$

- Outer product version:

$$\begin{bmatrix} 1 & 2 \\ 3 & 4 \end{bmatrix}\begin{bmatrix} 5 & 6 \\ 7 & 8 \end{bmatrix} = \begin{bmatrix} 1 \\ 3 \end{bmatrix}\begin{bmatrix} 5 & 6 \end{bmatrix} + \begin{bmatrix} 2 \\ 4 \end{bmatrix}\begin{bmatrix} 7 & 8 \end{bmatrix}.$$

Although mathematically equivalent, the different versions can have very different levels of computer performance because of the different ways that they access memory.

Next we write the general loops for the three versions presented here for matrices $\mathbf{A}(m \times r)$, $\mathbf{B}(r \times n)$, and $\mathbf{C} = \mathbf{A}\mathbf{B}$. The asymptotic operation count for this operation is $\mathcal{O}(2mnr)$ flops.

- Inner (dot) product version or **MatMat.ijk** algorithm. Matrix $\mathbf{A}$ is accessed by rows and matrix $\mathbf{B}$ by columns, whereas the matrix $\mathbf{C}$ is constructed row by

---

[6] The matrix–matrix BLAS routine has the name *dgemm* (double precision) but also the name *mxm* is used.

row:

Initialize	$C(i, j) = 0.0$ for $i = 1, m; j = 1, n$
Begin Loop	$i = 1, m$
Begin Loop	$j = 1, n$
Begin Loop	$k = 1, r$
	$C(i, j) = C(i, j) + A(i, k)B(k, j)$
End Loop	
End Loop	
End Loop	

- Dual inner (dot) product version or **MatMat.jik** algorithm. Matrix **A** is accessed by rows and matrix **B** by columns, whereas the matrix **C** is constructed column by column (note that the ordering of the i and j loops has changed):

Initialize	$C(i, j) = 0.0$ for $i = 1, m; j = 1, n$
Begin Loop	$j = 1, n$
Begin Loop	$i = 1, m$
Begin Loop	$k = 1, r$
	$C(i, j) = C(i, j) + A(i, k)B(k, j)$
End Loop	
End Loop	
End Loop	

- Middle (*Gaxpy*) product version or **MatMat.jki** algorithm. Matrix **A** and matrix **B** are both stored by columns, so we have repeated matrix–vector multiplications of matrix **A** with columns of **B**, and this is done using the *linear combination* version of BLAS2:

Initialize	$C(i, j) = 0.0$ for $i = 1, m; j = 1, n$
Begin Loop	$j = 1, n$
Begin Loop	$k = 1, r$
Begin Loop	$i = 1, m$
	$C(i, j) = C(i, j) + A(i, k)B(k, j)$
End Loop	
End Loop	
End Loop	

Notice that this operation can be accomplished by using the *gaxpy* operation as follows:

$$C(., j) = gaxpy(A, B(., j), C(., j))$$

The dual operation of the outer product is MatMat.ikj, and it is implemented with a loop similar to that shown, where we need to exchange i and j.

- Outer product version or **MatMat.kji** algorithm. Here matrix **A** is accessed by columns and matrix **B** is accessed by rows in order to form outer products:

Begin Loop $\qquad k = 1, r$
$\qquad$ Begin Loop $\qquad j = 1, n$
$\qquad\qquad$ Begin Loop $\qquad i = 1, m$
$$C(i, j) = \underbrace{C(i, j) + A(i, k)B(k, j)}_{saxpy}$$
$\qquad\qquad$ End Loop
$\qquad$ End Loop
End Loop

The dual operation for the outer product version is MatMat.kij, and it is implemented with a loop similar to that shown, where we need to exchange i for j.

A typical performance of the double precision (*dgemm*) matrix–matrix operation on the Intel Pentium 4 (1.7 GHz) is shown in Figure 2.10. Specifically, the ATLAS version of the BLAS3 routine is employed with different ways of handling the matrix, accessing it either T or N, hot or cold, as before. Here ATLAS employs *cache blocking* by carefully partitioning the matrices into blocks and making effective reuse of the data. This results in a performance that is approximately the same for all different ways of accessing the data. If no such fine tuning were performed, the asymptotic performance would drop dramatically for matrices of rank above 100. It is interesting to note here that the asymptotic performance is well above 1.7 Gflops, which corresponds to a single operation per cycle. This is because one of the two available floating point units of Pentium 4 (the SSE2) is capable of executing any pairwise operation of eight available registers every cycle for a maximum performance of *four* single or *two* double precision flops per cycle at IEEE 754 precision.

Figure 2.10: Performance of the matrix–matrix multiplication on the Intel Pentium 4 with a speed of 1.7 GHz. (Courtesy of C. Evangelinos.)

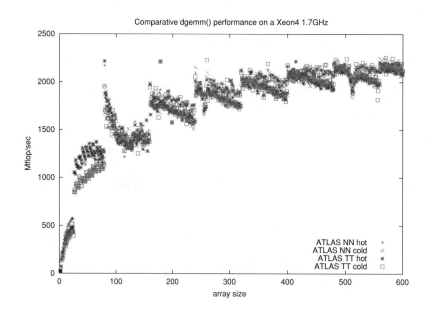

BLAS and Memory Access

The practical difference in the various ways of implementing matrix–vector and matrix–matrix operations lies in the way we access memory and the type of memory, that is, main memory or cache memory, as the latter is typically ten times faster than the former. To appreciate this difference we sketch in Figure 2.11 a pyramid of hierarchies (see [30] for more details) in today's typical computer that shows the relative distance between the CPU and the various levels of memory. The larger the size of memory, the longer it takes to access it. A layout of the Intel Pentium 4 is shown in Figure 2.12.

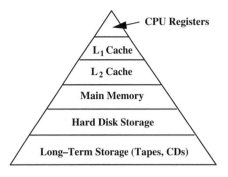

The cost associated with the BLAS programs can be computed by taking into account the total number of floating operations while also including the cost associated with *memory access* to load the operands. The following time estimate (T) is a conservative one, as it assumes that there is no overlap between computation and loading of data:

Figure 2.11: Memory hierarchies in a typical computer.

$$T = n_f \times \delta t + n_m \times \tau = n_f \times \delta t \left(1 + \frac{n_m}{n_f} \times \frac{\tau}{\delta t}\right),$$

Figure 2.12: Block diagram of the Intel Pentium 4.

where n_f is the number of floating point operations, n_m is the number of memory references, and δt and τ are the times to execute a floating point operation and the time to load an operand, respectively, and both are fixed for a given computer model.

From this equation, we can see that the ratio n_m/n_f plays an important role in minimizing the total time. For each BLAS routine we can estimate this ratio for the three levels of operation. For example:

- For BLAS1 such as the *saxpy* operation, we have that $n_f = 2n$, $n_m = 3n + 1$, and thus $n_m/n_f \to 3/2$ for large n.
- For BLAS2 (matrix–vector multiplication) we have that $n_f = 2n^2$, $n_m = n^2 + 3n$, and thus $n_m/n_f \to 1/2$ for large n.
- Finally, for BLAS3 (matrix–matrix multiplication) we have that $n_f = 2n^4$, $n_m = 4n^3$, and thus $n_m/n_f \to 2/n$ for large n.

From the three levels of operations, it is clear that the matrix–matrix multiplication is the most *efficient* one because the number of memory references per flop decreases for larger size matrices. This is the reason that the asymptotic performance measured in Figures 2.8–2.10 is maximum for the matrix–matrix operation. It is, therefore, a good practice in writing code to involve more matrix–matrix multiplications and use BLAS2 or BLAS1 less often, if possible.

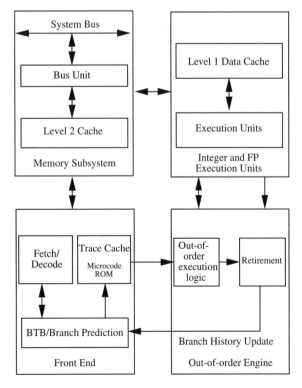

REMARK 1: There are also several other routines in all levels of BLAS for different operations, for example, generation of plane rotations in BLAS1, solvers of triangular equations in BLAS2, and multiplications of a general matrix by a triangular matrix in BLAS3. The reader can find all this information on the Web using the URL for the *netlib* freeware libraries **(http://www.netlib.org/blas and also http://www.netlib.org/atlas)**.

REMARK 2: BLAS accommodate both single and double precision, corresponding to prefixes *s* and *d*, respectively, in the names of subroutines. For a subset of routines (*dot* products and *matrix–vector* products) extended precision is also available for very high accuracy computations (prefix *e*). BLAS also accommodate complex arithmetic.

2.2.8 Exploiting the Structure of Sparse Matrices

The asymptotic limit of computational complexity in obtaining

$$\mathbf{C}(m \times n) = \mathbf{A}(m \times r)\mathbf{B}(r \times n)$$

is $\mathcal{O}(2nmr)$, but this limit overpredicts the count of operations for small size matrices. In practice, we often encounter sparse matrices, and thus we have to be able to obtain a better estimate for the operation count taking into account that sparsity. One such example is the multiplication of two upper triangular square matrices $\mathbf{A}$ and $\mathbf{B}$ ($n \times n$), which contain a_{ij} and b_{ij} as entries. The resulting matrix $\mathbf{C}$ (shown for the case of $n = 3$),

$$\mathbf{C} = \begin{bmatrix} a_{11}b_{11} & a_{11}b_{12} + a_{12}b_{22} & a_{11}b_{13} + a_{12}b_{23} + a_{13}b_{33} \\ 0 & a_{22}b_{22} & a_{22}b_{23} + a_{23}b_{33} \\ 0 & 0 & a_{33}b_{33} \end{bmatrix}$$

is also upper triangular.

To implement the general case of multiplication of upper triangular matrices, we write the following loop:

Initialize $\qquad$ $C(i, j) = 0.0$ for $i = 1, n; j = 1, n$
Begin Loop $\qquad$ $i = 1, n$
$\qquad$ Begin Loop $\qquad\qquad$ $j = i, n$
$\qquad\qquad$ Begin Loop $\qquad\qquad\qquad$ $k = i, j$
$\qquad\qquad\qquad\qquad$ $\underbrace{C(i, j) = C(i, j) + A(i, k)B(k, j)}_{2(j-i+1) \text{ flops}}$
$\qquad\qquad$ End Loop
$\qquad$ End Loop
End Loop

Notice that this is the inner product version MatMat.ijk but with the lower limits in the index j and k modified so that only entries in the upper triangular matrix are involved in the computation. Clearly, we want to avoid multiplying zero entries! To evaluate the flop count, we sum the amount of arithmetic associated with the most deeply nested statements in the algorithm. To this end, we obtain

$$\sum_{i=1}^{n}\sum_{j=i}^{n} 2(j-i+1) = \sum_{i=1}^{n}\sum_{j=1}^{n-i+1} 2j \approx \sum_{i=1}^{n} 2\frac{(n-i+1)^2}{2} = \sum_{i=1}^{n} i^2 \approx \frac{n^3}{3}. \qquad (2.1)$$

Note that we used the following sums in the above derivation:

$$\sum_{p=1}^{n} p = \frac{n(n+1)}{2} \approx \frac{n^2}{2}$$

and also

$$\sum_{p=1}^{n} p^2 = \frac{n^3}{3} + \frac{n^2}{2} + \frac{n}{6} \approx \frac{n^3}{3}.$$

The corresponding cost for computing these matrices as full matrices is $2n^3$, and thus the savings with this algorithm is sixfold.

In the same spirit, we could exploit the structure of other sparse matrices both in computing and in storing them. A particular structure that is often encountered in solving numerical partial differential equations is that of **banded matrices**, where we have a tridiagonal matrix $[a(i), b(i), c(i)]$ with $b(i)$ on the diagonal:

$$\mathbf{A} = \begin{pmatrix} b_1 & a_1 & & & \mathbf{0} \\ c_1 & b_2 & a_2 & & \\ & \ddots & \ddots & \ddots & a_{n-1} \\ \mathbf{0} & & c_{n-1} & b_n & \end{pmatrix}.$$

First, it is advantageous to store such matrices in terms of their diagonals $[a, b, c]$. Next, we can easily verify that

$$\mathbf{Ax} = \mathbf{bx} \oplus^u \mathbf{ax}_1 \oplus^l \mathbf{cx}_2,$$

where $\mathbf{x}^T = (x_1, \ldots, x_n)$ is a vector of length n but $x_1^T = (x_2, x_3, \ldots, x_n)$ and $x_2^T = (x_1, x_2, \ldots, x_{n-1})$ are vectors of length $(n-1)$. Because of this mismatching in vector length, the summation $\oplus$ in this equation should be interpreted appropriately; that is, we should add ($\oplus^u$) the diagonal $\mathbf{a}$ above the main diagonal $\mathbf{b}$ (here the second term in the sum) to the first component of $\mathbf{bx}$ and also add ($\oplus^l$) the diagonal $\mathbf{c}$ below the main diagonal to the last component of $\mathbf{bx}$. Also, the multiplications between all vectors should be performed in an elementwise fashion.

2.2.9 Gram–Schmidt Vector Orthogonalization

Important operations in scientific computing are vector orthogonalization and normalization. The Gram–Schmidt process starts with n linearly independent vectors $\mathbf{x}_i$ and ends with n orthonormal vectors $\mathbf{q}_i$, that is, vectors that are orthogonal to each other and that also have L_2 norms of unity. Let us consider the vectors $\mathbf{x}_i$, $i = 0, \ldots, n-1$

each of length m. We want to produce vectors $\mathbf{q}_i$, $i = 0, \ldots, n - 1$, where the first vector $\mathbf{q}_0$ is the normalized $\mathbf{x}_0$, the vector $\mathbf{q}_1$ is orthogonal to $\mathbf{q}_0$ and normalized, the vector $\mathbf{q}_2$ is orthogonal to $\mathbf{q}_0$ and $\mathbf{q}_1$, and so on. The idea is to produce a vector

$$\mathbf{y}_i = \mathbf{x}_i - (\mathbf{q}_{i-1}^T \mathbf{x}_i) \mathbf{q}_{i-1} - \cdots - (\mathbf{q}_0^T \mathbf{x}_i) \mathbf{q}_0 \, ,$$

which subtracts the projection of $\mathbf{x}_i$ onto each vector $\mathbf{q}_j$ for $j = 0, \ldots, i - 1$. Having obtained $\mathbf{y}_i$ we can then normalize it to obtain the corresponding orthonormal vector, that is,

$$\mathbf{q}_i = \frac{\mathbf{y}_i}{\| \mathbf{y}_i \|_2} \, .$$

We can summarize this algorithm as follows:

Initialize: Compute $r_{00} = \| \mathbf{x}_0 \|_2$. If $r_{00} = 0$ STOP; else $\mathbf{q}_0 = \mathbf{x}_0 / r_{00}$.
Begin Loop: For $j = 0, \ldots, n - 1$ Do:

    1. Compute $r_{ij} = \mathbf{q}_i^T \mathbf{x}_j$, $i = 0, \ldots, j - 1$
    2. $\mathbf{y}_j = \mathbf{x}_j - \sum_{i=0}^{j-1} r_{ij} \mathbf{q}_i$
    3. $r_{jj} = \| \mathbf{y}_j \|_2$
    4. If $r_{jj} = 0$ STOP
      else $\mathbf{q}_j = \mathbf{y}_j / r_{jj}$

End Loop.

EXAMPLE. Let us assume that we want to orthonormalize the vectors

$$\mathbf{x}_0 = \begin{bmatrix} 1 \\ 0 \\ 2 \end{bmatrix} \text{ and } \mathbf{x}_1 = \begin{bmatrix} 2 \\ 3 \\ 0 \end{bmatrix} .$$

Thus, following the algorithm just listed, we obtain

- $r_{00} = (1^2 + 0^2 + 2^2)^{1/2} = 2.2367$ and $\mathbf{q}_0 = \dfrac{1}{2.2367}(1\ 0\ 2)^T$,
  so

  $$\mathbf{q}_0 = \begin{bmatrix} 0.4472 \\ 0 \\ 0.8942 \end{bmatrix} ;$$

- $r_{01} = q_0^T \mathbf{x}_1 = 0.8942$
  and

  $$\mathbf{y}_1 = \mathbf{x}_1 - r_{01} \mathbf{q}_0 = \begin{bmatrix} 2 \\ 3 \\ 0 \end{bmatrix} - 0.8942 \begin{bmatrix} 0.4472 \\ 0 \\ 0.8942 \end{bmatrix} = \begin{bmatrix} 1.6001 \\ 3 \\ -0.7996 \end{bmatrix} ,$$

  so

  $$r_{11} = \| y_1 \|_2 = \left[(1.6001)^2 + 3^2 + (-0.7996)^2 \right]^{1/2} = 3.4928$$

and

$$\mathbf{q}_1 = \frac{\mathbf{y}_1}{r_{11}} = \begin{bmatrix} 0.45811 \\ 0.85890 \\ 0.22890 \end{bmatrix}.$$

Notice that we can write

$$\begin{bmatrix} 1 & 2 \\ 0 & 3 \\ 2 & 0 \end{bmatrix} = \begin{bmatrix} 0.4472 & 0.45811 \\ 0 & 0.85890 \\ 0.8942 & 0.22890 \end{bmatrix} \begin{bmatrix} 2.2367 & 0.8942 \\ 0 & 3.4928 \end{bmatrix}.$$

This algorithm is presented using common mathematical abstractions, such as vectors and matrices. The beauty of C++ is that these mathematical abstractions can be implemented in C++ as "user-defined" data types, in particular for this case, as *classes*. We now present the implementation of this algorithm in C++, utilizing some predefined user-defined classes that we have created. Explanation of the class syntax of this function will be given later in Section 3.1.8, along with details as to how to create your own user-defined data types.

GRAM–SCHMIDT CODE

Software

Suite

In the coding example that follows, we are using the *SCVector class* that we previously defined (Section 2.1.1). Because we have defined the SCVector class to have mathematical properties just like what we would expect, we see that we can translate the algorithm given previously directly into the code. Admittedly, some of the C++ syntax in the function that follows goes beyond what you have been taught thus far; the details of the class implementation of this code will be given later on in this book (see Section 3.1.8). What you should notice, however, is that classes, such as SCVector, allow you to more closely model the mathematical definitions used in the algorithmic description of the solution of the problem.

```
SCstatus GramSchmidt(SCVector * x, SCVector * q){
  int i,j;
  int dim = x[0].Dimension();
  SCVector y(dim);
  SCMatrix r(dim);

  r(0,0) = x[0].Norm_l2();

  if(r(0,0)==0.0)
    return(FAIL);
  else
    q[0] = x[0]/r(0,0);

  for(j=1;j<dim;j++){            // corresponds to Begin Loop
    for(i=0;i<=j-1;i++)
      r(i,j) = dot(q[i],x[j]); // corresponds to step 1
```

```
    y = x[j];
    for(i=0;i<=j-1;i++)
      y = y - r(i,j)*q[i];        // corresponds to 2

    r(j,j) = y.Norm_l2();         // corresponds to 3

    if(r(j,j) == 0.0)
      return(FAIL);
    else
      q[j] = y/r(j,j);            // corresponds to 4
  }

  return(SUCCESS);
}
```

Observe in this code that we allocate within this function an SCMatrix *r*, which we use throughout the function, and which is discarded when the function returns to its calling function. We may want to retain *r*, however. In this case, we can create a function that has an identical name as the previous function but contains an additional variable within the argument list. The name and the argument list are used to distinguish which function we are referring to when we call the function. (This concept will be discussed further in Section 4.1.4.)

In the function that follows, we pass into the function *GramSchmidt* a SCMatrix *r* that it populates over the course of the computation.

```
SCstatus GramSchmidt(SCVector * x, SCVector * q, SCMatrix &r){
  int i,j;
  int dim = x[0].Dimension();
  SCVector y(dim);

  r(0,0) = x[0].Norm_l2();

  if(r(0,0)==0.0)
    return(FAIL);
  else
    q[0] = x[0]/r(0,0);

  for(j=1;j<dim;j++){                 // corresponds to Begin Loop
    for(i=0;i<=j-1;i++)
      r(i,j) = dot(q[i],x[j]);  // corresponds to step 1

    y = x[j];
    for(i=0;i<=j-1;i++)
      y = y - r(i,j)*q[i];        // corresponds to step 2

    r(j,j) = y.Norm_l2();         // corresponds to step 3

    if(r(j,j) == 0.0)
      return(FAIL);
```

Software

Suite

```
      else
         q[j] = y/r(j,j);            // corresponds to 4
   }

   return(SUCCESS);
}
```

> Classes can help you more closely mimic the natural data structures of the problem. We are not confined to working with only the low-level concepts of integers, floats, and characters.

Key Concept

QR Factorization and Code

Another important point we will often use in this book is a special **matrix factorization**. In particular, if the vectors x_i, $i = 0, \ldots, n-1$ form the columns of a matrix X of size $m \times n$, q_i, $i = 0, \ldots, n-1$ form the columns of matrix Q, and r_{ij} are the entries of a square $n \times n$ matrix R (which turns out to be upper triangular) the following equation is valid:

$$X = QR.$$

This is known as *QR decomposition (or factorization) of the matrix* X, and it has important implications in obtaining eigenvalues and solutions of linear systems.

We now present a C++ function that accomplishes the QR decomposition of a matrix.

Just as was stated, we input a matrix X to be decomposed into the matrices Q and R. We begin by creating two arrays of vectors q and v, which will serve as input to our original Gram–Schmidt routine. As you will see, this routine contains only two basic components:

Software ⊙ *Suite*

1. a data management component, which allows us to go from matrices to a collection of vectors and back, and
2. a call to the Gram–Schmidt routine that we wrote previously (and now you understand why we may have wanted to be able to retrieve the value of the SCMatrix r).

This routine demonstrates one important issue in scientific computing: the compromise between computational time and programmer's time. In this case, one may argue that if we were to write a routine specifically for QR decomposition, then we could reduce some of the cost of the data management section and thus have a "more optimal code." However, this consideration must be balanced by considering how much computational time is used for data manipulation versus the time to properly write and debug an entirely new function. In this particular case, in theory, we have already written and tested our **GramSchmidt(v,q,R)** function, and hence we are confident that if we give the Gram–Schmidt function proper inputs, it will return the correct solution. Hence, we can focus our programming and debugging on the extension of the concept, rather than on the details of optimization. Optimization is certainly important if we were to be calling this routine many times in a particular simulation; however, optimization-savy individuals, as the old saying goes, often miss the forest for the trees!

```
SCstatus QRDecomposition(SCMatrix X, SCMatrix &Q, SCMatrix &R){
  int i,j;
  int num_vecs = X.Rows();
  int dim = X.Columns();
  SCstatus scflag;

  Vector *q = new SCVector[num_vecs](),
         *v = new Vector[num_vecs]();

  for(i=0;i<num_vecs;i++){
    q(i).Initialize(dim);
    v(i).Initialize(dim);
  }

  for(i=0;i<num_vecs;i++){
    for(j=0;j<dim;j++)
      v[i](j) = X(j,i);
  }

  scflag = GramSchmidt(v,q,R);

  for(i=0;i<num_vecs;i++)
    for(j=0;j<dim;j++)
      Q(j,i) = q[i](j);

  return scflag;
}
```

Modified Gram–Schmidt Algorithm and Code

Notice that the Gram–Schmidt method breaks down at the kth stage if $\mathbf{x}_k$ is linearly dependent on the previous vectors $\mathbf{x}_j$, $j = 0, \ldots, k-2$ because $\| \mathbf{x}_k \|_2 = 0$. It has also been observed that, in practice, even if there are no actual linear dependencies, orthogonality may be lost because of finite arithmetic and round-off problems, as discussed earlier. To this end, a **modified Gram–Schmidt** process has been proposed and this code is almost always used in computations. Specifically, an intermediate result is obtained,

$$\mathbf{y}_j^0 = \mathbf{q}_j - (\mathbf{q}_0^T \mathbf{x}_j)\mathbf{q}_0,$$

which we project onto $\mathbf{q}_0$ (instead of the original $\mathbf{x}_j$), as follows:

$$\mathbf{y}_j^1 = \mathbf{y}_j^0 - (\mathbf{q}_1^T \mathbf{y}_j^0)\mathbf{q}_1 \,,$$

and so on. This process then involves successive one-dimensional projections. In the following, we present a row-oriented version of the modified Gram–Schmidt algorithm.

Initialize: Set $\mathbf{q}_i = \mathbf{x}_i, \quad i = 0, \ldots, n-1.$
Begin Loop: For $i = 0, \ldots, n-1$ *Do:*

$$r_{ii} = ||\mathbf{q}_i||_2$$

$$\mathbf{q}_i = \mathbf{q}_i / r_{ii}$$

For $j = i+1, \ldots, n-1$ *Do:*

$$r_{ij} = \mathbf{q}_i^T \mathbf{q}_j$$

$$\mathbf{q}_j = \mathbf{q}_j - r_{ij}\mathbf{q}_i$$

End Loop

End Loop.

We now present a C++ implementation of the modified Gram–Schmidt algorithm. With the exception of the commented block of code, the remaining code is identical to the original code already provided.

Software

Suite

```
SCstatus ModifiedGramSchmidt(SCVector * x, SCVector * q,
    SCMatrix &r){
  int i,j;
  int dim = x[0].Dimension();
  SCVector(dim);

  r(0,0) = x[0].Norm_l2();

  if(r(0,0)==0)
    return(FAIL);
  else
    q[0] = x[0]/r(0,0);

  for(j=1;j<dim;j++){

    /********************************************************/
    /* We replace the following block of lines from the    */
    /* original Gram-Schmidt algorithm already presented,   */
    /* for(i=0;i<=j-1;i++)                                   */
    /*     r(i,j) = dot(q[i],x[j]);                          */
    /*                                                        */
    /*     y = x[j];                                          */
    /*     for(i=0;i<=j-1;i++)                                */
```

```
/*              y = y - r(i,j)*q[i];                        */
/*                                                          */
/* with the modification described here. The               */
/* following lines implement that modification.            */
/************************************************************/

        y = x[j];

        for(i=0;i<=j-1;i++){
          r(i,j) = dot(q[i],y);
          y = y - r(i,j)*q[i];
        }

        /************************************************************/
        /*                   End of Modification                    */
        /************************************************************/

        r(j,j) = y.Norm_12();

        if(r(j,j) == 0)
          return(FAIL);
        else
          q[j] = y/r(j,j);
      }

    return(SUCCESS);

  }
```

REMARK 1: The computational complexity of the Gram–Schmidt process is $\mathcal{O}(mn^2)$ irrespective of which version is used. This is evident by comparing the comment block inserted into the modified Gram–Schmidt code. If you carefully examine the deleted code versus the newly inserted code, you will see that the number of operations performed are identical. It is often the case in scientific computing that although two algorithms may be identical mathematically (i.e., in infinite precision), one algorithm is inherently better than the other when implemented numerically. Furthermore, in this case, we see that we achieve an additional benefit from the modified algorithm at no additional cost.

REMARK 2: The loss of orthogonality of $\mathbf{Q}$ in the modified Gram–Schmidt method depends on the condition number $\kappa(\mathbf{A})$ of the matrix $\mathbf{A}$ obtained by using the specified vectors as columns [8]. In general, the orthogonality of $\mathbf{Q}$ can be completely lost with the classical Gram–Schmidt method whereas the orthogonality property may not be lost with the *modified* Gram–Schmidt method but it may not be acceptable when the matrix $\mathbf{A}$ is ill-conditioned. A better approach is to employ the Householder method (discussed in Section 9.3), which is more accurate and also computationally less expensive. For example, the cost for Gram–Schmidt is $\mathcal{O}(mn^2)$ whereas for the Householder method it is $\mathcal{O}(mn^2 - n^3/3)$.

2.3 PARALLEL COMPUTING

Imagine a large hall like a theater, except that the circles and galleries go right round through the space usually occupied by the stage. The walls of this chamber are painted to form a map of the globe... A myriad of computers are at work upon the weather of the part of the map where each sits, but each computer attends only to one equation or part of an equation. The work of each region is coordinated by an official of higher rank... From the floor of the pit a tall pillar rises to half the height of the hall. It carries a large pulpit on its top. In this sits the man in charge of the whole theater; he is surrounded by several assistants and messengers. One of his duties is to maintain a uniform speed of progress in all parts of the globe. In this respect he is like the conductor of an orchestra in which the instruments are slide rules and calculating machines. But instead of waving a baton he turns a beam of blue light upon those who are behindhand.

Lewis F. Richardson, "Weather Prediction by Numerical Process" (1922)

This prophetic quote describes quite accurately the many hardware and software ingredients of a modern parallel computer. It refers to a *multiple instruction–multiple data type* and involves *domain decomposition* as the mode of partitioning the work load. The concepts of *master node* that synchronizes the processes as well as of *load balancing* are also included in the statement.

In the following, we briefly review some parallel computer architectures and introduce parallel concepts and tools.

2.3.1 From Supercomputing to Soupercomputing

A *supercomputer* is the fastest computer of its time; today's supercomputer is tomorrow's desktop or laptop computer. One of the first supercomputers of historical significance was the Cray-1. It was used quite successfully in many applications involving large-scale simulation in the early 1980s. The Cray-1 was not a parallel computer, however, but it employed a powerful (at the time) vector processor with many vector registers attached to the main memory (see Figure 2.13). Today, all supercomputers are parallel computers. Some are based on specialized processors and networks, but the majority are based on commodity hardware and open-source operating system and applications software. In this section, we will review briefly some of the history and the recent trends.

Types of Parallel Computers

A popular taxonomy for parallel computers is the description introduced by Michael Flynn in the mid-1960s [36] of the programming model as single instruction–multiple data stream (SIMD) or multiple instruction–multiple data stream (MIMD). On a SIMD computer, such as the Thinking Machines CM-2 or the NCUBE Inc. computers of the 1980s, each processor performs the same arithmetic operation (or stays idle) during each computer clock, as controlled by a central control unit (see Figure 2.14). In this model (also referred to as a data parallel program) high-level languages (e.g., CM FORTRAN, C^*, and Lisp) are used, and computation and communication among processors are synchronized implicitly at every clock period.

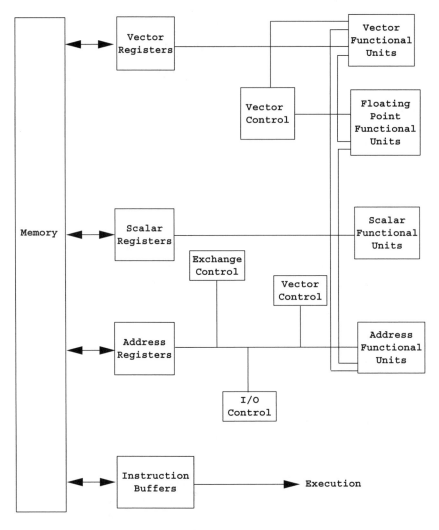

CRAY-1

**Figure 2.13:
Schematic of the first
Cray computer, the
Cray-1.**

On a MIMD computer (see Figure 2.15) each of the parallel processing units executes operations independently of the others, subject to synchronization through appropriate message passing at specified time intervals. Both parallel data distribution as well as the message passing and synchronization are under user control. Examples of MIMD systems include the Intel Gamma and Delta Touchstone computers and, with fewer but more powerful processors, the Cray C-90 and the first generation of IBM SP2 (all made in the 1990s).

Although it is often easier to design compilers and programs for SIMD multiprocessors because of the uniformity among processors, such systems may be subject to great computational inefficiencies. This is due to their inflexibility when stages of a

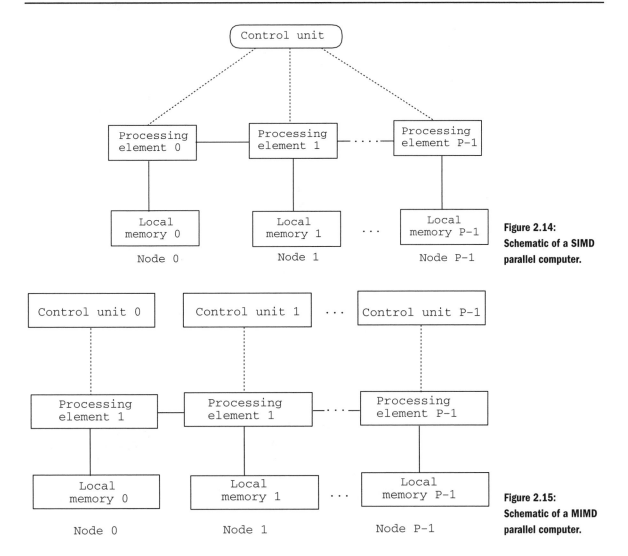

Figure 2.14:
Schematic of a SIMD
parallel computer.

Figure 2.15:
Schematic of a MIMD
parallel computer.

computation are encountered in which large number of identical operations are not involved. There has been a natural evolution of multiprocessor systems toward the more flexible MIMD model, especially the merged programming model in which there is a single program (perhaps executing distinct instructions) on each node. This merged programming model is a hybrid between the data parallel model and the message passing model and was successfully exemplified in the Connection Machine CM-5. In this SPMD (single program–multiple data) model, data parallel programs can enable or disable the message passing mode, and thus one can take advantage of the best features of both models.

MIMD computers can have either shared memory as the SGI Origin 2000 or distributed memories as in the IBM SP system. The issue of shared memory requires further

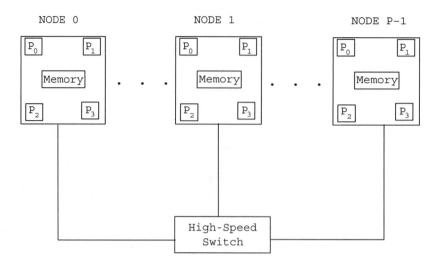

Figure 2.16:
Schematic of generic
parallel computer.

clarification as it is different from the centralized memory. Shared memory means that a single address space can be accessed by every processor through a synchronized procedure. In nonshared memory systems explicit communication procedures are required. The prevailing paradigm in parallel computing today is one where the physical memory is distributed, but the address space is shared as this is more flexible and makes an easier programming environment.

PC Clusters

The most popular and cost-effective approach to parallel computing is cluster computing, based, for example, on PCs running the Linux operating system (hereafter referred to merely as Linux). The effectiveness of this approach depends on the communication network connecting the PCs together, which may vary from fast Ethernet to Myrinet that can broadcast messages at a rate of several gigabits per second (Gbs).

Issues of computer design, balancing memory, network speed, and processing speed can be addressed by examining the generic parallel computer (GPC) depicted in Figure 2.16. The key components of the GPC are an interconnecting set of P processing elements (PE) with distributed local memories, a shared global memory, and a fast disk system (DS). The GPC serves as a prototype of most PC-based clusters that have dominated supercomputing in the past decade both on the scientific and commercial fronts.

The first PC cluster was designed in 1994 at NASA Goddard Space Flight Center to achieve one gigaflop. Specifically, sixteen PCs were connected together using a standard Ethernet network. Each PC had an Intel 486 microprocessor with sustained performance of about 70 Mflops. This first PC cluster was built for only $40,000. This compares to $1 million, which was the cost for a commercial equivalent supercomputer at that time. It was named *Beowulf* after the lean hero of medieval times who defeated the giant Grendel. In 1997 researchers at the Oak Ridge National Laboratory built a

Beowulf cluster from many obsolete PCs of various types; for example, in one version it included seventy-five PCs with Intel 486 microprocessors, fifty-three Intel Pentium PCs, and five fast Alpha workstations. Dubbed the *stone soupercomputer* because it was built at almost no cost, this PC heterogeneous cluster was able to perform important simulations producing detailed national maps of ecoregions based on almost 100 million degrees of freedom [54]. A picture of this first soupercomputer is shown in Figure 2.17.

Building upon the success of the first such system, the BEOWULF project [7, 81], several high-performance systems have been built that utilize commodity microprocessors with

Figure 2.17: Soupercomputer of the Oak Ridge National Laboratory. (Courtesy of F. Hoffman.)

fast interconnects exceeding 1 Gbs in bandwidth. *Moore's law* (an empirical statement made in 1965 by the Intel co-founder Gordon Moore) suggests that the performance of a commodity microprocessor doubles every eighteen months, which implies that, even without fundamental changes in the fabrication technology, processors with a speed of several tens of gigaflops can become available. Nanotechnology can help in prolonging the validity of this statement, which has held true for at least four decades. New developments include the terahertz transistor, and the packaging of more than one billion transistors on a single chip will hopefully keep Moore's law alive. Intel's Pentium 4 (see Figure 2.12) has about forty-two million transistors.

In addition to enhancements in the speed of individual processors, there have been several key developments that have enabled commodity supercomputing:

- the development and maturization of the free operating system Linux, which is now available for all computer platforms; the freely distributable system and the open-source software movement has established Linux as the operating system of choice, so almost all PC clusters are Linux based;
- the MPI standard that has made parallel coding portable and easy; there are several implementations such as MPICH, SCore, etc., but they all share the same core commands we present in this book; and
- the rapid advances in interconnect and fast switches with small latencies, which are now widely available unlike the early days of proprietary and expensive systems available only by a few big vendors.

Grid Supercomputing

The computational grid is a new distributed computing paradigm, similar in spirit to the electric power grid. It provides scalable high-performance mechanisms for discovering and negotiating access to geographically remote resources. It came about via

Internet and World Wide Web advances and through increases in network speed that *double* about every nine months. This is twice the rate of Moore's law, and it implies that the performance of a wide area network (WAN) increases by two orders of magnitude every five years!

Computing on remote platforms involves several steps: to first identify the available sites, to negotiate fast access to them, and to configure the local hardware and software to access them. The Grid provides the hardware and software infrastructure that allows us to do this. The community-based open-source Globus toolkit is the most popular software infrastructure [38]; see also **http://www.globus.org**. It implements protocols for secure identification, allocation, and release of resources from a globally federated pool of supercomputers (i.e., the Grid).

The Grid also allows the implementation of network-enabled solvers for scientific computing, such as the package NetSolve [14]. NetSolve searches for available computational resources within the Grid and chooses the best available resource based upon some sort of matchmaking procedure. It consists of three parts: a client, an agent, and a server. The client is the user issuing a request that is received by the agent. The latter allocates the best server or servers, which perform the computation and return the results to the client. The server is a daemon[7] process, which is on the alert awaiting requests from the client.

Performance Measurements and Top 500

Unfortunately, there is no universal yardstick to measure the performance of parallel computers. In fact the use of a single number to characterize performance, such as the peak performance quoted by the manufacturer, is often misleading. It is common to evaluate performance in terms of benchmark runs consisting of kernels, algorithms, and applications so that different aspects of the computer system are measured. This approach, however, is still dependent on the quality of software rather than just hardware characteristics. The controversy over performance evaluation methods has been recognized by the computer science community and there have been several recent attempts to provide more objective performance metrics for parallel computers [57]. A discussion of some of the most popular benchmarks, the BLAS routines, was presented in Section 2.2.7, and more information can be found on the Web at **http://www.netlib.org/benchmark**.

A good basis for performance evaluation of supercomputers is also provided in the Top500 list; see **http://www.top500.org/**. This list was created by Dongarra in the early 1990s and it is updated twice a year. It reports the sites around the world with the 500 most powerful supercomputers. Performance on a LINPACK benchmark [28] is the measure used to rank the computers. This is a code that solves a system of linear equations (see Chapter 9) using the best software for each platform. Based on the data collected so far and the current teraflop sustained speeds achieved, it is predicted that

---

[7] A daemon is a program that runs continuously, and whose purpose is to handle periodic service requests that the operating system expects to receive.

the first petaflop/s (10^{15} floating point operations per second) supercomputer would be available around 2010 or perhaps sooner.

2.3.2 Mathematical Parallelism and Recursive-Doubling

We now review briefly the mathematics of parallelism. There are many basic mathematical operations that have a high degree of parallelism, and by this we mean that they can be performed simultaneously and independently of each other. Consider, for example, the elementwise multiplication of two vectors $\mathbf{x}$, $\mathbf{y}$ to produce another vector $\mathbf{c}$, that is,

$$c_i = x_i y_i, \quad i = 1, \ldots, N.$$

Clearly, in this case all N products can be obtained simultaneously, and thus we can imagine each term in this product being evaluated by a different computer. In this particular example there is of course no need to engage N different processors to do such a simple operation, but the point we want to make is that for this operation there are no dependencies among the different pairs of data. This is an example of *perfect mathematical parallelism*. This form of parallelism also applies to the task of finding the maximum in each pair of a set of N pairs of numbers, that is, $\max(x_i, y_i)$, $i = 1, \ldots, N$. This operation is also perfectly parallel, and we will refer to such problems as EP (embarrassingly parallel).

Notice, however, that if we attempt to find the absolute maximum number in these pairs we introduce interdependencies among the data, and such an operation is not perfectly parallel anymore. The same is true for simple BLAS operations, for example the evaluation of an inner (dot) product, that is,

$$c = \sum_{i=1}^{N} x_i y_i,$$

where c is a scalar. This requires the summation of all N product pairs $(x_i y_i)$, which is clearly a *serial* operation as it involves accumulation of the sum of a next pair to the previous accumulation, and so on. Another such example is the evaluation of a polynomial $p(x)$, for instance

$$p(x) = a_0 + a_1 x + a_2 x^2 + a_3 x^3 + \cdots + a_N x^N,$$

at a specific point x_0, which is also an accumulation operation. For this example, a straightforward computation would require recomputing the powers of x or else we would require extra storage. This last issue can be avoided by resorting to *Horner's rule* and alternating multiplications and additions appropriately. For example, the polynomial

$$p(x) = 2 + 3x + 7x^2 + 4x^3 + x^4$$

can be computed from the equivalent equation

$$p(x) = 2 + (3 + (7 + (4 + x)x)x)x,$$

which can be computed recursively with $(N - 1)$ multiplication and N additions. This is an important point: Observe that the mathematical result of the two forms is the same; however the number of operations that must be accomplished to obtain the result is different. This type of operation rearrangement for optimization is common (and powerful) in scientific computing. This particular operation, however, is still *serial* because to proceed with the next iteration we need the results from the previous one.

Let us now revisit the computation of the inner product already mentioned. To be able to perform the addition of the terms $(x_i y_i)$ faster than in the straightforward serial fashion from left to right, we can break the sum into two smaller sums (assuming for convenience that N is an even number). For example, we have that the two sets are

$$\sum_{i=1}^{N/2} x_i y_i \quad \text{and} \quad \sum_{i=N/2+1}^{N} x_i y_i .$$

We can compute the two sums separately and then collect the two results and perform another sum to obtain the final result. The total number of additions is, of course, the same [i.e., $(N - 1)$], but assuming that we can execute the two big sums simultaneously the *wall clock* time is almost half of what it was before. We can estimate more precisely the wall clock time by assuming that it takes the computer a time δt to perform an addition. This time δt is related to the processor speed, and it is in the range of several *nanoseconds* for a relatively fast computer. The total time required for the straightforward approach is $T_1 = (N - 1)\delta t$. Then, the total time required after we break up the problem into two subproblems is $T_2 = (N/2 - 1)\delta t + \delta t + C$, where C represents the time required to collect the two results from the subsums. We can measuse the *speedup* of this *data partionining* method from the ratio

$$S_2 = \frac{T_1}{T_2} = \frac{N - 1}{N/2 + C/\delta t} .$$

For efficiency we want S_2 to be larger than one, which will be true if the relative communication-to-computation time $C/\delta t$ is small. If this cost is negligible then for N very large we obtain $S_2 \approx 2$, which is the theoretical maximum speedup.

This simple exercise illustrates how we can extract parallelism from an operation that is seemingly serial at a first glance. Moreover, this data partitioning approach can be continued *recursively* so that the subsums are smaller and smaller, until we reach a single pair of numbers in this particular approach. This **divide-and-conquer** approach is fundamental to parallel processing. It is also known by other names, such as the *fan-in* algorithm or the *recursive-doubling* algorithm. Another advantage of recursive-doubling is that it leads to enhanced numerical stability because when we sum a large set of numbers in a serial fashion significant accumulation of errors can occur. However, the recursive-doubling algorithm and corresponding pairwise summation is assured to be more stable.

We can now generalize the aforementioned example by assuming that we have P computer processors available and that $P = N$, with $N = 2^q$, so that we can reduce the evaluation of a *dot product* into a summation of two numbers on each processor. The total number of stages or branches in this tree, which is illustrated in Figure 2.18 for the case of $N = 8$, is q; here $q = 3$. Using the afore-mentioned recursive thinking, we can estimate the *speedup factor* to be

$$S_P = \frac{T_1}{T_P} = \frac{(N-1)\delta t}{q\delta t + qC},$$

where we include a total communication cost of qC assuming that in each stage the communication time penalty to collect terms and send them to other processors is C; let us denote the relative time by $\alpha = C/\delta t$. We can rewrite the speedup factor in terms of the problem size N or the number of processors P as

$$S_P = \frac{N-1}{(1+\alpha)\log_2 N} = \frac{P-1}{(1+\alpha)\log_2 P}.$$

We see from the last equation that even for zero communications ($\alpha = 0$), the theoretical maximum speedup factor is

$$S_P = \frac{P-1}{\log_2 P} < P \quad \text{and} \quad \eta_P = \frac{P-1}{P\log_2 P},$$

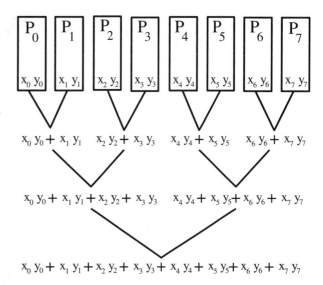

Figure 2.18: Inner (dot) product operation following the fan-in algorithm for $N = P = 8$.

where the last equation defines the *parallel efficiency* η_P. For an EP (embarrassingly parallel) problem we have that $\eta_P = 1$ or 100%. It is clear that in this recursive algorithm the parallel efficiency is less than perfect even if we ignore communications among the processors. At successive stages of the computations fewer and fewer processors are involved in the computation, and in fact in the last stage only two processors are involved while $(P - 2)$ are staying idle. The parallel efficiency, therefore, should reflect this load imbalance among the P processors.

If communication is taken into account in this simple model, which assumes that $C = \alpha\delta t$, then we have that

$$S_P(\alpha = 1) = \frac{1}{2}S_P(\alpha = 0).$$

Therefore, we are computing at only 50% parallel efficiency. In practice, there are other factors that may limit the parallel efficiency even more. For example, the number of processors may not match exactly with the size of the problem, the total problem or subproblems may not fit in the memory, or a startup time penalty known as *latency* may slow down the transferring of data. In this latter case, a better model for the communication cost is

$$C = L + \beta l,$$

where L is the latency, l is the message length, and β^{-1} is the *bandwidth*, which reflects the maximum rate at which messages can be exchanged. Latency is significant when we transfer small parcels of data often, but for longer messages it is a subdominant time

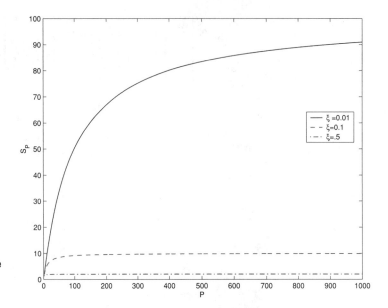

Figure 2.19: Speedup factor versus number of processors for three different degrees of parallelizable code.

cost. Typical ranges for L are from a few nanoseconds to a few microseconds, and it is usually inversely proportional to the cost of the computer multiprocessor.

2.3.3 Amdahl's Law

A more general model for the speedup factor was proposed by Gene Amdahl (1967) and is thus often referred to as *Amdahl's law* [2]. In its simplest form it assumes that some percentage, say ξ, of the program or code cannot be parallelized, and that the remaining $(1 - \xi)$ is perfectly parallel. Neglecting any other communication, delays such as memory contention, latencies, etc. Amdahl's model for speedup states that

$$S_P = \frac{T_1}{[\xi + (1 - \xi)/P]T_1} = \frac{1}{\xi + \frac{1-\xi}{P}},$$ (2.2)

and thus an upper bound in the limit of $P \to \infty$ is $S_P \leq 1/\xi$. This implies that even if $\xi = 1\%$ (meaning only 1% of the program is not parallelizable) for $P = 100$ we have that $S_{100} = 50$, so we operate at half the maximum efficiency; see also Figure 2.19.

Although useful, this performance measure S_P can sometimes be misleading because it may favor inefficient but highly parallelizable algorithms instead of more efficient algorithms that may be more difficult to map onto a parallel multiprocessor computer. Also, the derivation of Amdahl's law relies on the assumption that the serial work ξ is independent of the size of the problem size N. In practice, it has been observed that ξ decreases as a function of problem size. Therefore, the upper bound on the speedup factor S_P usually increases as a function of problem size. Another anomaly is the *superlinear speedup*, which means that the speedup factor has been measured to be more than P. This may happen because of memory access and cache mismanagement or because the serial implementation on a single processor is suboptimal.

There are several industry standard benchmark programs such as Whetstone, ScaLAPACK, and LINPACK. These benchmarks have been used extensively in all advanced computer system evaluations, but specific benchmarks have also been developed to evaluate shared, distributed, and hybrid memory parallel computers. These vary from simple parallel loops to measure the ability of parallelizing compilers to the PER-FECT benchmark, which consists of thirteen programs including several fluid dynamics programs, to the MIMD benchmarks (e.g., Genesis) consisting of fast Fourier transforms (FFTs); partial differential equations, molecular dynamics, and linear algebra. A particularly popular set of benchmarks, the NAS parallel benchmarks, was developed at NASA Ames. They comprise a suite of eight programs with three versions for serial, machine-dependent, and MPI-based implementations **(see http://www.nas.nasa.gov/ Software/NPB)**.

Measures of performance based on Amdahl's law are particularly effective for small programs that do not require extensive and intensive use of computer memory. Most computer benchmarks are of this sort, but they do not in fact fulfill many of the requirements for the solution of large-scale simulations.

2.3.4 MPI – <u>M</u>essage <u>P</u>assing <u>I</u>nterface

Parallel computing, in its conceptual form, appears to be a very reasonable concept. Many of the concepts found in parallel computing have analogous concepts in social areas such as business management. The idea of many people working together toward one goal is similar to many processes working together toward one solution. The idea of wanting to partition the work so that all processors are busy and none remain idle is similar to wanting to keep your team busy, with none having to sit around waiting on someone else for information. From this perspective, we see that parallel computing is a natural extension of the concept of *divide and conquer*; that is, we first begin with a problem we want to solve, we then access the available resources we can use toward solving the problem (which in the case of computing will be the number of processors that can be used), and we then attempt to partition the problem into manageable pieces that can be done concurrently by each person on the team.

Parallel computing is a divide-and-conquer strategy.	**Key Concept**

The most common difficulty that people have with this concept is not the divide-and-conquer component; most often, we are quite comfortable with the *concept of*

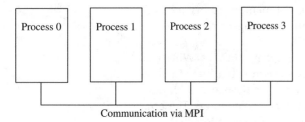

Communication via MPI

Figure 2.20: Schematic of MPI *processes* working together.

partitioning a problem into workable subproblems. However, it may be difficult (1) to see how a specific problem can be partitioned efficiently to be solved in parallel and (2) to understand how you can get computers to work in parallel. Both of these issues, at varying levels, will be addressed in this book.

Throughout this book, we will be discussing how to take specific numerical algorithms and partition them among multiple processors. Hence, at this stage of your reading, we will focus on the second of the two major difficulties:

- understanding and implementing parallel programming on a computer.

The first issue that we will draw your attention to is that the goal of this book is not to give detailed descriptions of the hardware and software mechanisms used for implementing parallel computers. Our goal in this book, and the goal of most simulation scientists, is to *use* the parallel computing tools already designed and created for them. Hence, we focus on the problem we are trying to solve, and not on the intricate details of getting computers to communicate with each other. To this end, we have chosen to employ MPI, a message-passing interface, for handling our parallel computing communication needs.

There are many good books on MPI itself, for example, [51] and [73], both of which give some of the history and the developmental rationale behind a message-passing interface. We will not cover this information other than to mention that the basic premise behind MPI is that multiple parallel processes work concurrently toward a common goal using "messages" as their means of communicating with each other. This idea is illustrated in Figure 2.20. Multiple MPI processes may run on different processors, and these processes communicate through the infrastructure provided by MPI. As users, we need not know the implementation of this infrastructure; we need only to know how to take advantage of it! To this end, almost everything in MPI can be summed up in the single idea of "Message Sent – Message Received."

Key Concept

Almost everything in MPI can be summed up in the single idea of "Message Sent – Message Received."

We will be discussing the mechanics of this process, that is, the MPI routines to use to accomplish this, throughout this book. Let us begin our parallel computing experience by understanding from a high level the differences between our previous "serial" codes (those programs that we have been addressing so far) and our new "parallel" codes. Up to now, every program that we have discussed has had one single thread of execution. A simplistic breakdown is the following: The program started, data were allocated, work was done on these data, and an answer was produced. All the steps were presented in a serial fashion: A, then B, then C, etc. Think of this model as the "you working alone" model. You, as a single person, have a goal to accomplish, and you set out with a specific collection of tasks that need to be done to get the job done. You decide an order in which these need to be accomplished, and then you plow through them one by one. Now, imagine that you are working with someone else toward a common goal. You must now ask yourself the following question:

- How can I partition the problem so that we can utilize our resources and accomplish the goal in the least amount of time (or with the least effort)?
     This is a parallelization question!

This parallelization question can be broken down into the following two questions:

- What work can be accomplished concurrently?
- When is communication between concurrent processes necessary?

Take the following example: Suppose that you are taking a class in which this book is being used as the text. The goal (hopefully) is for everyone to read the text. If there is only one copy of the text, then one possible strategy is for the instructor to prepare an ordered list of all those in the class, and for each person to read the text when it is his or her turn. This is thus a serial process; you as a student must wait until your turn to read the book and must remain idle (with respect to the reading the book) until you have obtained a copy. However, if the goal is for everyone to read the book, then a more optimal solution with respect to time is for everyone to have a copy of the book simultaneously! Then each person can be reading the book concurrently. This is an example of an **Embarrassingly Parallel Algorithm**.

Now, how would such an algorithm be implemented in parallel using MPI? We will begin with a modification of our "Hello World" program. We must first specify our goal: We want each process to print to the screen "Hello World!" Because this does not require any communication, doing this concurrently by all the processes involved should be possible.

Our first MPI program to accomplish this is the following program:

Software

Suite

```
#include <iostream.h>
#include <mpi.h>

int main(int argc, char ** argv){

  MPI_Init(&argc,&argv);

  cout << "Hello World!" << endl;

  MPI_Finalize();
}
```

Compilation and execution details for MPI programs is provided in Appendix B.1. What is the first thing that you should notice about MPI? The programming interface to MPI is a collection of functions! MPI is a library of functions designed to handle all the nitty-gritty details of message passing on the architecture on which you want to run. We notice several things immediately about this program:

- We included *mpi.h*. This provides us with the function declarations for all MPI functions.
- We must have a beginning and an ending. The beginning is in the form of an *MPI_Init()* call, which indicates to the operating system that this is an MPI program and allows the OS to do any necessary initialization. The ending is in the form of an *MPI_Finalize()* call, which indicates to the OS that "cleanup" with respect to MPI can commence.
- If the program is embarrassingly parallel, then the operations done between the MPI initialization and finalization involve no communication.

When you compile and run this program, you obtain a collection of "Hello World!" messages printed to your screen. The number of messages is equal to the number of processes on which you ran the program.[8] This is your first parallel program!

The two MPI functions that you used in the previous program have the following form:

- **MPI_Init**

```
int MPI_Init(
        int*      argc_ptr       /*  in/out  */,
        char**    argv_ptr[ ]    /*  in/out  */)
```

- **MPI_Finalize**

```
int MPI_Finalize(void)
```

In this book, we will take for granted the information that is passed to MPI_Init. Just as in Figure 2.20, our MPI program started up a number of processes, each of which printed its message. The most natural question to ask is:

- *How does a process know which number it is?*

There are two important commands very commonly used in MPI:

- **MPI_Comm_rank**

```
int MPI_Comm_rank(
        MPI_Comm      comm     /*  in   */,
        int*          result   /*  out  */)
```

---

[8] Though the printing by the program is done concurrently, the computer must serialize the output to write it to the screen. We still consider this to be an embarrassingly parallel process.

• **MPI_Comm_size**

```
int MPI_Comm_size(
        MPI_Comm    comm   /*  in   */,
        int*        size   /*  out  */)
```

The first of these two functions, *MPI_Comm_rank*, provides you with your process identification or **rank** (which is an integer ranging from 0 to $P - 1$, where P is the number of processes on which you are running). *MPI_Comm_size* provides you with the total number of processes that have been allocated. The argument *com* is called the **communicator**, and it essentially is a designation for a collection of processes that can communicate with each other. MPI has functionality to allow you to specify various communicators (differing collections of processes); however, in this book, whenever a communicator must be specified, we will always use *MPI_COMM_WORLD*, which is predefined within MPI and consists of all the processes initiated when we run our parallel program.

If you were running a $P = 8$ process job, *MPI_Comm_size* would pass back the number 8 as the total number of processes running, and *MPI_Comm_rank* would return to you a number 0, 1, ..., 7 denoting within which process you currently were executing. How do you use this information?

Let us modify our previous code to not only have each MPI process print out "Hello World!" but also to tell us which process the message is coming from and how many total processes with which it is joined.

```
#include <iostream.h>
#include <mpi.h>

int main(int argc, char ** argv){
  int mynode, totalnodes;

  MPI_Init(&argc,&argv);
  MPI_Comm_size(MPI_COMM_WORLD, &totalnodes);
  MPI_Comm_rank(MPI_COMM_WORLD, &mynode);

  cout << "Hello world from process " << mynode;
  cout << " of " << totalnodes << endl;

  MPI_Finalize();
}
```

When run with four processes, the screen output may look like:

```
Hello world from process 0 of 4
Hello world from process 3 of 4
Hello world from process 2 of 4
Hello world from process 1 of 4
```

Software
Suite

Note, as we pointed out, that the output to the screen may not be ordered correctly since all processes are trying to write to the screen at the same time, and the operating system has to decide on an ordering. However, the thing to notice is that each process called out with its process identification number and the total number of MPI processes of which it was a part.

It is at this point that we want to make a critical observation: When running with MPI, all processes use the same compiled binary, and hence all processes are running the exact same code. What in an MPI distinguishes a parallel program running on P processors from the serial version of the code running on P processors? Two things distinguish the parallel program:

1. Each process uses its *process rank* to determine what part of the algorithm instructions are meant for it.
2. Processes communicate with each other to accomplish the final task.

Even though each process receives an identical copy of the instructions to be executed, this does not imply that all processes will execute the same instructions. Because each process is able to obtain its process rank (using *MPI_Comm_rank*), it can determine which part of the code it is supposed to run. This is accomplished through the use of **if** statements. Code that is meant to be run by one particular process should be enclosed within an **if** statement, which verifies the process identification number of the process. If the code is not placed with **if** statements specific to a particular *id*, then the code will be executed by all processes (as in the case of the code listed here). Shortly we will show you a parallel program in which this fact is illustrated.

We, as of yet, have not actually accomplished the second point, communicating between processes (from the programmers point of view); we have merely relied on the operating system and other software system layers to handle the initiation and termination of our MPI processes across multiple processors. Recall that we said that MPI can be summed up in the concept of sending and receiving messages. Sending and receiving is done with the following two functions: *MPI_Send* and *MPI_Recv*. Below we present the function syntax, argument list description, a usage example, and some remarks for the *MPI_Send* and *MPI_Recv* commands.

| MPI |

FUNCTION CALL SYNTAX

```
int MPI_Send(
        void*         message    /*  in  */,
        int           count      /*  in  */,
        MPI_Datatype  datatype   /*  in  */,
        int           dest       /*  in  */,
        int           tag        /*  in  */,
        MPI_Comm      comm       /*  in  */,
```

```
int MPI_Recv(
        void*           message    /*  out  */,
        int             count      /*  in   */,
        MPI_Datatype    datatype   /*  in   */,
        int             source     /*  in   */,
        int             tag        /*  in   */,
        MPI_Comm        comm       /*  in   */,
        MPI_Status*     status     /*  out  */)
```

UNDERSTANDING THE ARGUMENT LISTS

MPI

- *message* – starting address of the send/recv buffer.
- *count* – number of elements in the send/recv buffer.
- *datatype* – data type of the elements in the send buffer.
- *source* – process rank to send the data.
- *dest* – process rank to receive the data.
- *tag* – message tag.
- *comm* – communicator.
- *status* – status object.

EXAMPLE OF USAGE

MPI

```
int mynode, totalnodes;
int datasize;   // number of data units to be sent/recv
int sender;     // process number of the sending process
int receiver;   // process number of the receiving process
int tag;        // integer message tag

MPI_Status status;   // variable to contain status
                            information

MPI_Init(&argc,&argv);
MPI_Comm_size(MPI_COMM_WORLD, &totalnodes);
MPI_Comm_rank(MPI_COMM_WORLD, &mynode);

// Determine datasize

double * databuffer = new double[datasize];

// Fill in sender, receiver, tag on sender/receiver
        processes,
// and fill in databuffer on the sender process.

if(mynode==sender)
  MPI_Send(databuffer,datasize,MPI_DOUBLE,receiver,
           tag,MPI_COMM_WORLD);

if(mynode==receiver)
```

```
MPI_Recv(databuffer,datasize,MPI_DOUBLE,sender,tag,
        MPI_COMM_WORLD,&status);

// Send/Recv complete
```

MPI

REMARKS

- In general, the *message* array for both the sender and receiver should be of the same type and both of size at least *datasize*.
- In most cases the *sendtype* and *recvtype* are identical.
- The tag can be any integer between 0 and 32767.
- *MPI_Recv* may use for the tag the wildcard *MPI_ANY_TAG*. This allows an MPI_Recv to receive from a send using any tag.
- *MPI_Send* cannot use the wildcard *MPI_ANY_TAG*. A specific tag must be specified.
- *MPI_Recv* may use for the source the wildcard *MPI_ANY_SOURCE*. This allows an *MPI_Recv* to receive from a send from any source.
- *MPI_Send* must specify the process rank of the destination. No wildcard exists.

Software

Suite

To get you started, we will begin with a small numerical example. Imagine that we want to sum up all the numbers from 1 to 1,000. We could implement this as the following *serial code*:

```
#include<iostream.h>

int main(int argc, char ** argv){
  int sum;

  sum = 0;

  for(int i=1;i<=1000;i=i+1)
     sum = sum + i;

  cout << "The sum from 1 to 1000 is: " << sum << endl;
}
```

Instead, let us use multiple processes to do the job. Now admittedly, multiple processes are not needed for this job, but the point of this exercise is for you to see how we partition the problem. The first thing we realize is that to effectively sum all the numbers from 1 to 1,000 using multiple processes, we want to partition the sums across the processes. Suppose that we use only two processes; then we want process 0 to sum from 1 to 500, and process 1 to sum from 501 to 1,000, and then at the end, the two values are added together to obtain the total sum of all numbers from 1 to 1,000. A schematic of this is provided in Figure 2.21. Given P processes, the problem of summing is partitioned into P subproblems, and then at the end all processes send their information to process 0 for the final accumulation of the results.

The first question we must ask ourselves is "How do we partition the processing?" Recall from our prior discussion that every
process can find out how many total processes are being used and
which process it is (by using *MPI_Comm_size* and *MPI_Comm_rank*, respectively). Let *mynode* be the variable storing the result of the call
to *MPI_Comm_rank*, and let *totalnodes* be the variable storing the result of the call to *MPI_Comm_size*. Then, the formula for partitioning
the sums across the processes is given by the following code:

Figure 2.21: Gather-
ing of all information
to one process using
sends and receives.

```
startval = 1000*mynode/totalnodes+1;
endval =   1000*(mynode+1)/totalnodes;
```

If you use only one process, then *totalnodes* = 1 and *mynode* = 0, and hence
startval = 1 and *endval* = 1,000. If you are using two processes, then *totalnodes* = 2,
and *mynode* is either 0 or 1. For *mynode* = 0, *startval* = 1 and *endval* = 500, and for
mynode = 1, *startval* = 501 and *endval* = 1,000. You can continue this procedure until
you are using 1,000 processes, at which point each process is only summing one value
(i.e., not summing at all!), and all the values are sent to process 0 for accumulation.

Once we have the starting value and ending value of our sum, each process can
execute a *for* loop to sum up the values between its *startval* and its *endval*. Then, once
the local accumulation is done, each process (other than process 0) sends its sum to
process 0.

The code that follows is a C++/MPI program that accomplishes this

```
#include<iostream.h>
#include<mpi.h>

int main(int argc, char ** argv){
  int mynode, totalnodes;
  int sum,startval,endval,accum;
  MPI_Status status;

  MPI_Init(argc,argv);
  MPI_Comm_size(MPI_COMM_WORLD, &totalnodes); // get totalnodes
  MPI_Comm_rank(MPI_COMM_WORLD, &mynode);     // get mynode

  sum = 0; // zero sum for accumulation
  startval = 1000*mynode/totalnodes+1;
  endval =   1000*(mynode+1)/totalnodes;

  for(int i=startval;i<=endval;i=i+1)
    sum = sum + i;

  if(mynode!=0)
    MPI_Send(&sum,1,MPI_INT,0,1,MPI_COMM_WORLD);
  else
    for(int j=1;j<totalnodes;j=j+1){
```

Software
○
Suite

```
            MPI_Recv(&accum,1,MPI_INT,j,1,MPI_COMM_WORLD, &status);
            sum = sum + accum;
        }

    if(mynode == 0)
        cout << "The sum from 1 to 1000 is: " << sum << endl;

    MPI_Finalize();

}
```

We will present more detailed information about the *MPI_Send* and *MPI_Recv* commands later in this book (see Section 3.4). Note, however, the general structure of the message passing. First, observe that there is an *if* statement, which distinguishes between whether you are process 0 or any other process. Why? Recall that all processes other than process 0 are **sending**, whereas process 0 is **receiving**. We should design our programs so that for each message sent using the command *MPI_Send*, there is some receiving process.

Hence, whereas each process other than 0 has one *MPI_Send* call, process 0 has $(P-1)$ *MPI_Recv* calls (where P is the total number of processes used). This is an important concept to understand. Oftentimes an MPI program has been sitting idle because one process was sending, and there were no process waiting to receive!

This portion of the text was not meant to be all inclusive, nor are you expected to be able to go out and write MPI codes using *sends* and *receives* with blinding efficiency (especially since we have not yet explained the argument lists for *MPI_Send* and *MPI_Recv*). However, as you go through this book, you will slowly but surely accumulate MPI knowledge and experience, and at the end, you will *hopefully* be writing C++/MPI code with confidence!

2.4 HOMEWORK PROBLEMS

1. Prove that the condition number in the L_2 norm of an othogonal matrix is 1 and that the condition number (in any norm) of a matrix is greater than or equal to 1.

2. Use the classical Gram–Schmidt and the modified Gram–Schmidt algorithms to orthonormalize the vectors

$$\mathbf{x}_0 = \begin{pmatrix} 1 \\ 10^{-4} \\ 0 \end{pmatrix} \text{ and } \mathbf{x}_1 = \begin{pmatrix} 1 \\ 0 \\ 10^{-4} \end{pmatrix}.$$

Compare the two results. What do you observe?

3. Find the eigenvalues of an $n \times n$ matrix with all entries equal to 1.

4. Modify Collatz-B so that instead of using the expression $x_{n+1} = 3x_n + 1$ you use $x_{n+1} = 5x_n + 1$. Use the number 100 as an initial guess and set the maximum number of iterations to 10,000. What do you observe? Postulate as to why this happens.
   (*Hint*: Have you ever played an arcade game in which you eventually were scoring a negative number?)

5. The Fibonacci sequence is a sequence of integers created by the following inductive process: Given $f_0 = 0$ and $f_1 = 1$, the next number in the sequence is equal to the sum of the previous two numbers, that is,

$$f_n = f_{n-1} + f_{n-2}.$$

This process can be continued indefinitely and produces the Fibonacci sequence: $0, 1, 1, 2, 3, 5, 8, 13, \ldots$.

   (a) Write a program that allows the user to input a desired number of terms N of the Fibonacci sequence and outputs the sequence $f_0, f_1, \ldots, f_N$ to the screen.

   (b) Modify your program so that you keep track of the ratio f_n/f_{n-1}. How many terms do you need so that the difference between f_n/f_{n-1} and f_{n-1}/f_{n-2} is less than 1.0×10^{-5}?

   (c) What is the value of this ratio? The number you have converged to is called the *Golden Mean*.

6. The harmonic series $\sum_{k=1}^{\infty} 1/k$ diverges, that is, it grows without bound as we include more terms. Consider the truncation that includes the first n terms, which we call partial sum S_n. This can be computed recursively from $S_n = S_{n-1} + 1/n$ with $S_1 = 1$. What is the largest S_n that can be obtained in your computer in single precision?

7. The Pythagorean theorem states that the sum of the squares of the sides of a right triangle is equal to the square of the hypotenuse. Thus, if x and y are the lengths of the two sides of a right triangle, and z is the length of the hypotenuse, then $x^2 + y^2 = z^2$. Fermat, a lawyer and amateur mathematician during the 1600s, postulated that there exists no other integer m (other than $m = 2$) such that $x^m + y^m = z^m$ for the sides of a right triangle.

   (a) Write a function *power* that takes as input a double precision number x and an integer m and returns as output a double precision number that is equal to the value of x raised to the power m (i.e., x^m).

   (b) Write a function *pythagoreus* that takes as input two double precision numbers x and y and an integer m and returns as output a double precision number that is equal to the value of $x^m + y^m$. Use the function *power* written from (a).

   (c) Write a program that queries the user for three values: two double precision numbers that equal the length of two of the sides of a right triangle and an integer N. Your program should first use the function *pythagoreus* to determine the value of the square of the hypotenuse. Then you should write a loop that checks to see if there exists any integer $2 < m \leq N$ such that $z^m = x^m + y^m$. If you find such a value of m, print the result and break out of the loop. If you do not find a value m such that this expression is true, print a message that states that no value can be found for the value N provided by the user.

8. Change the stride of the summing example given in Section 2.3 (by making the stride of the additions equal to the number of processors). This will require devising new formulas for the variables *startval* and *endval* and changing the $i = i + 1$ used within the summing loop to some other increment.

9. Modify the summing example as follows:

   (a) At the beginning of the main function, add an integer variable *master*, and initialize this value to some number between zero and the number of processors minus one.

   (b) Modify the *MPI_Send/MPI_Recv* sequence such that all processes except *master* send and process *master* receives.
   (*Hint*: From the example, in the *MPI_Send*, the "0," denotes that you are sending to process zero; in the *MPI_Recv*, the j denotes the process from which a message is being received. These will need to be modified.)

   (c) Output the sum from *master*.

   (d) Add *cout* statements so that each sending process prints a message stating to whom it is sending, and add *cout* statements so that the receiving process acknowledges from whom it has received.

10. Modify the summing example as follows:

   (a) Instead of summing integers, change the appropriate variables so that you will now sum doubles. You will need to use *MPI_DOUBLE* instead of *MPI_INT* within the MPI calls. Verify that you obtain the same answer as the integer case.

   (b) Change the sum so that you are summing $1/i$ instead of i.

   (c) At the top of the program, immediately following the **#include<iostream.h>** statement, add **#include<iomanip.h>**. Then prior to calling the cout statement, add the following line:
   ```
   cout << setprecision(20);
   ```
   After making these changes and recompiling, run your program on two, four, and eight processes. What differences in the sum of $1/i$ do you see? Postulate as to why this is so.

11. Modify the parallel MPI code to do the following:

    (a) Have process 0 query the user for the number of elements over which to sum.

    (b) From process 0, distribute to all processes the number of elements to sum (using sends and receives) and appropriately calculate the interval over which each process is to sum.

    (c) Accomplish the summing as is already done in the program.

    (d) After creating the final answer on process 0, print the result.

3

Approximation

Two of the most common tasks in scientific computing are interpolation of discrete data and approximation by known functions of the numerical solution, the source terms, and the boundary or initial conditions. Therefore, we need to perform these tasks both accurately and efficiently. The data are not always nicely distributed on a uniform lattice or grid, and thus we must learn how to manage these situations as well. We often use polynomials to represent discrete data because they are easy to "manipulate," that is, differentiate and integrate. However, *sines* and *cosines* as well as special functions called *wavelets* are very effective means to perform interpolation and approximation, and they have very interesting properties.

In this section, we will study various such representations and their corresponding C++ implementations. We consider cases where the data are just sufficient to determine exactly the representation (deterministic case) as well as cases where the data are more than the information needed (overdetermined case).

Finally, we will present a more detailed discussion of *MPI_Send* and *MPI_Recv*, the two fundamental building blocks of MPI.

3.1 POLYNOMIAL REPRESENTATION

In this section we will study different ways of interpolating data on equidistant and more general grids using polynomials. We will discuss both accuracy and efficiency and will introduce C++ arrays and other concepts to effectively implement the algorithms.

3.1.1 Vandermonde and Newton Interpolation

Assuming that we have the data available on the discrete set of points $\{x_0, x_1, \ldots, x_N\}$ with corresponding values $\{f(x_0), f(x_1), \ldots f(x_N)\}$, then we can construct a function $f(x)$ that passes through the pairs $(x_i, f(x_i))$ by the approximation

$$f(x) \approx p_N(x) = \sum_{k=0}^{N} a_k \phi_k(x),$$

where $p_N(x)$ is referred to as the interpolating polynomial, $\phi_k(x)$ are *a priori* known polynomials, and a_k are the *unknown* coefficients. We call $\phi_k(x)$ the *basis*, and its choice is very important in obtaining an *efficient* approximation. For example, assuming that

$\phi_k(x) = x^k$, $k = 0, \ldots, N$, then we have the following representation at the known pair $(x_i, f(x_i))$:

$$f(x_i) = a_0 + a_1 x_i + a_2 x_i^2 + \cdots + a_N x_i^N, \quad i = 0, \ldots N.$$

All together we have $(N + 1)$ such equations for the $(N + 1)$ unknowns a_i, $i = 0, \ldots, N$. This system of equations can be recast in matrix form with the vector of unknowns $\mathbf{a}^T = (a_0, a_1, a_2, \ldots, a_N)$ as

$$\begin{bmatrix} 1 & x_0 & x_0^2 & \ldots & x_0^N \\ 1 & x_1 & x_1^2 & \ldots & x_1^N \\ \vdots & \vdots & \vdots & & \vdots \\ 1 & x_N & x_N^2 & \ldots & x_N^N \end{bmatrix} \begin{bmatrix} a_0 \\ a_1 \\ \vdots \\ a_N \end{bmatrix} = \begin{bmatrix} f(x_0) \\ f(x_1) \\ \vdots \\ f(x_N) \end{bmatrix},$$

or in compact form as

$$\mathbf{V}\mathbf{a} = \mathbf{f},$$

where the matrix $\mathbf{V}$ is known as the *Vandermonde matrix*. This matrix is nonsingular because we assume that all $\{x_0, x_1, \ldots x_N\}$ are distinct points, and therefore there exists a unique polynomial of order N that represents this data set. We could obtain the vector of coefficients $\mathbf{a}$ from

$$\mathbf{a} = \mathbf{V}^{-1}\mathbf{f},$$

by inverting the Vandermonde matrix $\mathbf{V}$ and subsequently performing matrix–vector multiplications with $f(x_i)$. This, however, is an expensive operation with a cost of $\mathcal{O}(N^3)$ to invert the matrix $\mathbf{V}$ (see Chapter 9), and it is rarely used in practice.

One approach to reducing the computational complexity is to simply change the basis to

$$\phi_k(x) = \Pi_{i=0}^{k-1}(x - x_i),$$

so $f(x)$ is now approximated by

$$f(x) \approx a_0 + a_1(x - x_0) + a_2(x - x_0)(x - x_1) + \cdots + a_N(x - x_0)(x - x_1)\ldots(x - x_{N-1}). \quad (3.1)$$

Notice that we still use a polynomial basis, but we have simply shifted it with respect to the coordinates of the data points. This simple shift turns out to have a dramatic effect since now the *new* unknown coefficients can be computed by inverting the system

$$\begin{bmatrix} 1 & 0 & & \ldots & & 0 \\ 1 & (x_1 - x_0) & \ldots & & & 0 \\ \vdots & \vdots & & & & \vdots \\ 1 & (x_N - x_0) & \ldots & (x_N - x_0)(x_N - x_1)\ldots(x_N - x_{N-1}) \end{bmatrix} \begin{bmatrix} a_0 \\ a_1 \\ \vdots \\ a_N \end{bmatrix} = \begin{bmatrix} f(x_0) \\ f(x_1) \\ \vdots \\ f(x_N) \end{bmatrix},$$

which is a lower triangular matrix and requires only $\mathcal{O}(N^2)$ operations to obtain the vector of unknown coefficients. This is done by simple forward substitution and can be implemented readily using BLAS2.

REMARK: It is instructive to compare this method, which is called *Newton interpolation*, with the Vandermonde interpolation. Assuming that we use Gauss elimination to obtain the vector of unknown coefficients (see Chapter 9), we see that the change of basis in the Newton approach takes us directly to the second stage of Gauss elimination, which is the *forward substitution*, whereas in the Vandermonde approach we have to essentially perform an *LU* decomposition of the matrix **V** (see Section 9.1), which is an $\mathcal{O}(N^3)$ operation. However, the Vandermonde matrix is a special one, and its inversion can also be done in $\mathcal{O}(N^2)$ operations (e.g., using FFTs; see Section 3.2). Thus, the two approaches discussed here are computationally equivalent.

Newton Interpolation: Recursive Algorithm

There is a nice recursive property that we can deduce from Newton's interpolation method. This property can be used for writing compact C++ code as we shall see in the next section.

Solving for the first few coefficients, we obtain

$$a_0 = f(x_0)$$

$$a_1 = \frac{f(x_1) - f(x_0)}{x_1 - x_0}$$

$$a_2 = \frac{\frac{f(x_2) - f(x_0)}{x_2 - x_0} - \frac{f(x_1) - f(x_0)}{x_1 - x_0}}{x_2 - x_1}$$

$$\vdots$$

and so we see that the coefficient

$$a_k = \mathcal{F}(x_0, x_1, \ldots, x_k),$$

that is, the kth coefficient, is a function of the first k function values $f(x_k)$. $\mathcal{F}$ is a function of both the x_k variables and the $f(x_k)$ data (and hence, in the end, since $f(x)$ is a function of x, then really $\mathcal{F}$ is just a function of the x_k's as given here).

To obtain a recursive relation for the coefficient a_k we need to write the approximation in the grid

$$G_0^k \equiv \{x_i\}, \quad i = 0, \ldots k,$$

where the subscript denotes the starting index and the superscript denotes the ending index. To this end, we consider the two subsets

$$G_0^{k-1} \equiv \{x_0, x_1, \ldots, x_{k-1}\}$$

and

$$G_1^k \equiv \{x_1, x_2, \ldots, x_k\}$$

of k grid points each. We also denote the corresponding polynomial approximations by $p_0^k(x)$, $p_0^{k-1}(x)$, and p_1^k formed by using the grids G_0^k, G_0^{k-1}, and G_1^k, respectively. We then observe that

$$(x_0 - x_k)p_0^k(x) = (x - x_k)p_0^{k-1}(x) - (x - x_0)p_1^k(x), \qquad (3.2)$$

as the polynomial $p_0^k(x)$ passes through all the pairs

$$(x_i, f(x_i)), \quad i = 0, \ldots, k.$$

Next, upon substitution of $p_0^k(x)$, $p_0^{k-1}(x)$, and $p_1^k(x)$ in Equation (3.2) by their full expansions, which are

$$p_0^k(x) = a_0 + a_1(x - x_0) + \cdots + a_k(x - x_0) \ldots (x - x_{k-1})$$

$$p_0^{k-1}(x) = a_0 + a_1(x - x_0) + \cdots + a_{k-1}(x - x_0) \ldots (x - x_{k-2})$$

$$p_1^k(x) = b_1 + b_2(x - x_1) + \cdots + b_k(x - x_1) \ldots (x - x_{k-1}),$$

and comparing the coefficients of highest polynomial power, x^k, we obtain

$$(x_0 - x_k)a_k = a_{k-1} - b_k$$

or

$$(x_0 - x_k)\mathcal{F}(x_0, x_1, \ldots, x_k) = \mathcal{F}(x_0, x_1, \ldots, x_{k-1}) - \mathcal{F}(x_1, x_2, \ldots, x_k),$$

and therefore

$$\mathcal{F}(x_0, x_1, \ldots, x_k) = \frac{\mathcal{F}(x_0, \ldots, x_{k-1}) - \mathcal{F}(x_1, \ldots, x_k)}{x_0 - x_k}. \qquad (3.3)$$

We thus obtain the higher *divided differences* (i.e., coefficients) from the lower ones from Equation (3.3).

We illustrate this procedure on a grid G_0^2 containing three grid points (x_0, x_1, x_2), so that

$$\mathcal{F}(x_0) = f(x_0), \quad \mathcal{F}(x_1) = f(x_1), \quad \mathcal{F}(x_2) = f(x_2),$$

then at the next level

$$\mathcal{F}(x_0, x_1) = \frac{\mathcal{F}(x_0) - \mathcal{F}(x_1)}{x_0 - x_1},$$

$$\mathcal{F}(x_1, x_2) = \frac{\mathcal{F}(x_1) - \mathcal{F}(x_2)}{x_1 - x_2},$$

and

$$\mathcal{F}(x_0, x_1, x_2) = \frac{\mathcal{F}(x_0, x_1) - \mathcal{F}(x_1, x_2)}{x_0 - x_2},$$

and so on, for grids with more points.

3.1.2 Arrays in C++

So far, when we have discussed variables in C++, we have referred to single variables, such as the variables *mynode* and *totalnode* presented in Section 2.3.4. Now, mathematically, we just introduced a collection of variables in the form of a sequence: $x_0, x_1, x_2, \ldots, x_N$. If you were to write a program that involved such a sequence of numbers, how would you declare these variables? Of course, to start with, you may use the knowledge you gained from Section 2.1.2 to decide how to declare the variables. The variable declaration would look like the following (for $N = 5$):

```
double x0,x1,x2,x3,x4,x5;
```

This does not seem too difficult. However, imagine that you want to use 100 points! Do you want to type x0, x1,..., x99? And even more annoying, suppose that you want to compare the results of running a program using 50 points compared to those using 1,000 points! Do not be dismayed; C++ has a solution to your problem! The C++ solution to this problem is the concept of *arrays*. In C++, you can allocate a block of memory locations using arrays. There are two means of accomplishing this: *static allocation* and *dynamic allocation*. We will discuss both briefly.

Static Allocation of Arrays

The first means by which you can allocate an array is to *statically* allocate the array. For our purposes, we will take this to mean that prior to both compilation and execution, the size of the array is known. In the previous section, we discussed the idea of using a discrete set of points $\{x_0, x_1, \ldots, x_N\}$ for interpolation. For a specific example, let us take $N = 99$ (so that the total number of points is 100), and let us assume that we want our grid points to be evenly spaced in the interval $[0, 1]$.

The following piece of code would statically allocate an array of 100 doubles and would fill in those variables with their appropriate positions in the interval $[0, 1]$:

Software

Suite

```
#include <iostream.h>

int main(int argc, char * argv[]){
  int i;
  double x[100];
  double dx = 1.0/99.0;

  for(i=0;i<100;i++)
    x[i] = i*dx;

  for(i=0;i<100;i++)
    cout << "x[" << i << "] = " << x[i] << endl;
}
```

Let us now examine in detail the statements in this program. First, notice the syntax used for allocating static arrays:

```
<type> <variable name>[ size ]
```

Here, *size* is the number of memory positions that you want allocated. In our example, we wanted 100 doubles to be allocated. Once the allocation is done, how do we access these variables? C++ uses [ ] for accessing variables in an array. In our allocation, x[0] is the first element, x[1] is the second element, etc. There are several key points for you to realize:

- C++ array indexing always begins at 0. Hence, the first position in an array is always the position denoted by [0].
- C++ does not verify that you do not overrun an array. To overrun an array is to attempt to access a memory location that has not been allocated to the array. In our example, trying to access x[100] would be illegal because we only allocated an array containing 100 elements (indexed 0, ..., 99). C++ will not complain when compiling, but such overrunning may cause a segmentation fault (or even far worse, the program may run normally but give the wrong results!). You should be very careful not to overrun arrays!
- When *statically* allocating arrays, you cannot use a variable for the size parameter. Hence the following C++ code is *invalid*:

```
int npts = 100;
double x[npts];
```

Your C++ compiler will complain that this is illegal! This is because it is not until the program is actually executed that the value of *npts* is known to the program (recall that upon execution *npts* is both allocated in memory and then intialized to the value 100). This type of operation *can* be done with dynamic memory allocation, which will also be discussed momentarily.

- We can, however, index the array using variables. In our example, we are able to iterate through all the values of the array using a *for* loop.

PROGRAMMER BEWARE!

- C++ arrays always begin their indexing at 0
- Array allocations are done by *size*, not by the final index value! Hence if you allocate an array with 100 elements, you would index them from 0, ..., 99!

Warning

Implicit and Explicit Casting

At this stage, let us interject a brief note concerning a common mistake made by programmers first learning C++. Notice in the preceding example that we have allocated a variable *dx*, and we have initialized it to 1.0/99.0. What would happen if we were to write 1/99? The answer is that the variable would be set to 0.0 instead of 0.01010101 as we would have expected. Why you might ask? All binary operations in C++ are type-specific. Although we use the "+" symbol to add two integers together, and we also use the "+" to add two floats together, the operations that the computer accomplishes to execute these two operations are different. What happens when you want to mix and match variable types? Suppose that you want to add $10.0 + 1$, where 10.0 is a floating point value and 1 is an integer. C++ will implicitly cast the value 1 to 1.0 (i.e., from an integer value to a floating point value), and then it will carry out the binary operation of "+" between two floating point values. Casting is the conversion

Implicit Casting Order

Example

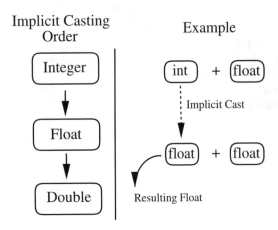

Figure 3.1: Implicit casting precedence.

of information stored by a variable from one type to another. Implicit casting implies that the casting operation is done automatically for you (C++ also allows explicit casting, which we also mention in the following). The order of casting is presented in Figure 3.1. In the figure, there is a pictorial example of implicit casting.

Why will 1/99 yield the value 0? Since the value 1 is an integer, and the value 99 is an integer, then the division operator used will be the integer division operator /. As an integer operation, 99 divides 1 zero times, and hence the solution is zero! However, if we were to write 1.0/99, we now have a floating point value divided by an integer, and hence the computer must first cast the integer value to a float. Operationally, the computer would first cast the value 99 to the value 99.0, and then it would use the floating point division operator "/" to divide 1.0 by 99.0, yielding 0.01010101.

Warning

PROGRAMMER BEWARE!

• Incorrect assumptions concerning implicit casting can lead to erroneous answers!

C++ also allows *explicit casting*; that is, it allows you, the programmer, to specify that you want a value cast to a different type. The syntax used for explicit casting is the following:

```
(type to cast to) <variable name>
```

For example, suppose that we want to explicity cast the value of an integer variable to a floating point variable. We could write the following:

```
int x = 1;
float y;

y = (float) x;
```

In this example, the value of x is explicitly cast to a floating point value, and then the floating point variable is assigned that value. In the preceding example, if you were not using the explicit casting operator (float), the variable would have to be implicitly cast. Explicit casting is useful in identifying to both you – the programmer – and to the computer the places that you expect a casting call to occur.

Dynamic Allocation of Arrays

Recall from our static allocation example, we stated that for an array to be allocated statically, the size of the array must be known prior to compilation and execution.

Suppose that we want to specify the size of an array "on the fly"; that is, suppose that we want the user to be able to input the size of an array and the program, while executing, to allocate the properly sized array. How can this be done? This can be accomplished in C++ using dynamic allocation. Dynamic allocation occurs using the **new** operator.

Let us reexamine our earlier example. Suppose that we want the user to be able to input the number of points into which he or she would like to partition the interval [0, 1]. This can be accomplished with the following code:

```
#include <iostream.h>

int main(int argc, char * argv[]){
  int i,npts;
  double *x;   //declaration of pointer variable 'x'
  double dx;

  cout << "Enter the number of points in [0,1]: ";
  cin >> npts;

  x = new double[npts]; // dynamic allocation of npts doubles
  dx = 1.0/(npts-1);

  for(i=0;i<npts;i++)
    x[i] = i*dx;

  for(i=0;i<npts;i++)
    cout << "x[" << i << "] = " << x[i] << endl;

  delete[] x;  // deallocation of dynamically allocated
               // memory

}
```

We will now analyze the differences between this code and the one presented previously: First, you will notice that we allow the user to input the number of points into the program. This is accomplished through the use of *cin*. This class, like *cout*, is declared in the system header file *iostream.h*. By using *cin*, we can obtain data from standard input, which in this case is from the keyboard. Recall from the previous chapter the following facts:

- *cin* reads from standard input (which for us is the keyboard).
- Observe that the direction of the >> is opposite to that of *cout*. This is for a reason. For *cout*, you are taking information from the variables that you provide to the expression and are providing that information to the operating system to be written to the screen. In the case of *cin*, you obtain data from the operating system and place it into the variables provided in the calling statement.
- The program must read one data item for each variable in the *cin* input list. Hence if we have the statement **cin >> a >> b;** where both *a* and *b* are declared as integers, then *cin* will expect that there are two distinct integers for it to read from standard input.

- You may place one or more blank (space) characters to delineate numerical values.
- Any blank space prior to the value to be read is ignored.

Immediately following the computer's execution of the *cin* statement, the variable *npts* has a value equal to the number of points that the programmer wants for this discretization. Next, we allocate an array *dynamically* using the **new** operator. This is but one step in a three-step process (to be described further in just a moment). We then do the operations just as we had done before, and we conclude by "freeing" the memory that we allocated by using the **delete/delete[]** operator. To recapitulate, the three steps that occur in dynamic memory allocation are:

1. declaration of a *pointer* variable,
2. allocation of memory using the **new** operator, and
3. deallocation of memory using the **delete/delete[]** operator.

We will now discuss each of these three steps individually. We begin with the first step: declaration of a *pointer* variable. Pointers are variables that hold *addresses*. They may hold addresses to integer variables; they may hold addresses to floating point or double precision variables. Pointer variables are type-specific.

Key Concept   Pointer variables are in general type-specific.

In the previous example, we have obtained from the *cin* statement the number of points that the user wants to use. This is stored in the integer variable *npts*. We now want to allocate an array of size *npts*. First, notice that we have declared a variable *x* of type double*. The use of the "*" prior to the variable name designates this as a pointer variable (i.e., a variable that holds the address in memory of a double) instead of declaring a double. To recapitulate:

```
double x;
```

declares a variable named "x" of type double (that is, *x* is a variable valid for containing a double precision number), whereas

```
double *x;
```

declares a variable named "x" of type "double *,"[1] which is a variable valid to contain the address in memory of a double precision variable. For now, you should take this mechanism for granted; this distinction will become more apparant as we use pointers more and more.

One common mistake when declaring multiple pointers is to misplace the *. Take for example the following two declarations:

```
double *x1,y1;
double *x2,*y2;
```

---

[1] Programmers quite often actually say "double star" when pronouncing this variable type.

The first of these two statements declares a variable named $x1$ of type double* and then declares a variable named $y1$ *of type double* (not double*). However, in the second declaration, both $x2$ and $y2$ are declared of type double star.

Once a pointer variable has been declared, we can ask the operating system to allocate for us a block of memory to contain our collection of doubles. This process is accomplished through the use of **new**. The **new** command asks the operating system (OS) for a block of memory of the type and size for which we ask, and it returns to us the *address* of that block of memory. If no memory is available (or for whatever other reason the OS may decide not to be cooperative), the **new** command will return *NULL*, which is called the "Null pointer" or "Null address." This implies that we have not successfully obtained our request. In the preceding code, we ask the OS for *npts* doubles in the following syntactic form:

```
<address> new <type>[ size ]
```

If the OS is successful in giving us the memory we request, we will have a block of memory that we can access just as we did in the static memory allocation case. To access the first double in the array, we access $x[0]$, and so forth.

At the conclusion of our program, or at some stage of the program where the array is no longer needed, we should release the memory used for this array back to the operating system for reuse. This process is called *deallocating* memory. To accomplish this deallocation, we use the **delete**[] command. In our case

```
delete[] x;
```

informs the OS that the memory that was allocated to the pointer variable x is no longer needed and can therefore be released. There are actually two delete operators, **delete** and **delete**[], that are used for informing the OS that dynamically allocated memory can be reclaimed. The distinction between the aforementioned operators is the following:

- **delete** (with no [] following it) is used when only a single object has been allocated. Suppose we were to allocate space to hold an integer as follows:

  ```
  int * a = new int;
  ```

  Space for only one integer was allocated (i.e., one integer object was allocated); hence to deallocate we would merely use **delete** as follows:

  ```
  delete a;
  ```

- **delete**[] is used when an array of objects has been allocated. Suppose we were to allocate space to hold 20 integers as follows:

  ```
  int * a = new int[20];
  ```

  Space for 20 integers was allocated (i.e., an array of 20 integer objects was allocated); hence to deallocate we would use the **delete**[] as follows:

  ```
  delete[] a;
  ```

REMARK: Both **delete** and **delete**[ ] take only one argument. A comma-separated list is not valid, and although it will compile, it will not give the desired result.

ALLOCATION/DEALLOCATION RULE OF THUMB. If your allocation statement **new** requires the use of [ ], then so does the deallocation statement **delete**.

Warning

PROGRAMMER BEWARE!

• Once memory is deallocated, you should not use it!

Passing Arrays to Functions

Finally, we want to draw your attention to passing arrays in C++. Passing arrays in C++ comes down to passing the pointer variable. Whether you declared the array dynamically or statically, you still end up passing a pointer. This is one subtle point that is not apparent when you declare arrays statically: Statically declared arrays are really just pointers in disguise. Whether you are dealing with statically declared or dynamically declared arrays, you will pass them to functions in the same fashion.

In the program that follows, we have encapsulated the generation of the grid into a function called "CreateGrid_EvenlySpaced." This function takes as arguments the size of the array *npts* and the pointer variable *x*. With these two pieces of information, the function can successfully fill in the array, as had been done before.

Software
○
Suite

```cpp
#include <iostream.h>
#include "SCchapter3.h" //contains declaration of
                        //CreateGrid_EvenlySpaced

int main(int argc, char * argv[]){
  int i,npts;
  double *x;
  double dx;

  cout << "Enter the number of points in [0,1]: ";
  cin >> npts;

  x = new double[npts];

  CreateGrid_EvenlySpaced(npts, x, 0.0, 1.0);

  for(i=0;i<npts;i++)
    cout << "x[" << i << "] = " << x[i] << endl;

  delete[] x;

}

// Definition of CreateGrid_EvenlySpaced is in SCchapter3.cpp
```

```
void  CreateGrid_EvenlySpaced(int npts, double *x,
                              double a, double b){
  double dx = (b-a)/(npts-1.0);

  for(int i=0;i<npts;i++)
    x[i] = a + i*dx;

  return;
}
```

There are three things that we want to draw your attention to in this example:

1. Note that in both the declaration and definition of the function *CreateGrid_EvenlySpaced* we declare *x* as a variable of type double*; this is important. The compiler needs to know (and recognize) that it is passing an address.

2. Note also that we have to pass *npts* into the function *CreateGrid_EvenlySpaced*. What if we did not? Recall that variables within functions are local to the function. Hence, if we do not explicitly *tell* the function that the size of the array is *npts*, it has no way of knowing it!

3. Observe that for including the standard header file *iostream.h* we use **#include<iostream.h>**, whereas to include our user-defined header file *SCchapter3.h* we use **#include "SCchapter3.h"**. The angled bracket notation <...> is to be used when including standard library headers obtained from the standard include directory (files such as *iostream.h, iomanip.h, math.h*, etc.). To include user-defined header files from the current directory, quotation marks "..." are used.

Passing by Value versus Passing by Reference

Recall in the previous chapter that we mentioned that unless otherwise stated all variables passed to a function are, by default, *passed by value*. We now want to clarify the difference among the ideas of *passing by value, passing by reference*, and *passing the address*.

- *Passing by value* – When a variable is passed to a function by *value*, a new memory location is allocated, and a copy of the contents of the variable is placed in the new memory location. The function may then locally modify the contents of the new location. When the function returns, the new memory location is released and its contents are lost. Consider the following program:

```
#include <iostream.h>

void func(int a);

int main(int argc, char * argv[]){
  int b;

  b = 4;
  func(b);
  cout << "value of b = " << b << endl;
}
```

```
void func(int a){
  cout << "value of a = " << a << endl;
  a = 64;
}
```

In this program, the variable *b* is passed to the function *func* by value. When the function is executed, a new memory location (distinct from the memory location of the variable *b*) is allocated on the function stack and is assigned to the variable name *a* locally within the function. The contents of *b* are copied into the location associated with the variable *a*. The first *cout* statement prints that the value of *a* is 4. The local function variable *a* is then assigned the value 64, and the function returns. Upon returning, the local memory is returned to the system. The second *cout* statement prints that the value of *b* is still 4; it was unaffected by the function.

- *Passing by reference* – When a variable is passed to a function by *reference*, no new memory location is allocated; instead, the local variable within the function is assigned to refer to the *same* memory location as the variable being passed. Consider the following program:

```
#include <iostream.h>

void func(int &a);

int main(int argc, char * argv[]){
  int b;

  b = 4;
  func(b);
  cout << "value of b = " << b << endl;
}

void func(int &a){
  cout << "value of a = " << a << endl;
  a = 64;
}
```

In this program, the variable *b* is passed to the function *func* by reference. Notice the placement of the & in both function declaration and definition; this syntax informs the compiler that we want the variable passed by reference. When the function is executed, the local variable *a* is assigned to the same memory location as *b*. The first *cout* statement will print that the value of *a* is 4. The local function variable *a* is then assigned the value 64, and the function returns. Since the local variable *a* referred to the same memory location as *b*, the second *cout* statement prints that the value of *b* is 64.

- *Passing the address* – Instead of passing by value or by reference, we have the third option of passing (explicitly) the address of the variable. When an address is passed, the address value is stored in a pointer variable of the appropriate type.

Consider the following program:

```cpp
#include <iostream.h>

void func(int *a);

int main(int argc, char * argv[]){
  int b;

  b = 4;
  func(&b);
  cout << "value of b = " << b << endl;
}

void func(int *a){
  cout << "value of a = " << *a << endl;
  *a = 64;
}
```

In the function *func* in this program, we declare the input argument to be a pointer to an integer. When the function *func* is called from within *main*, we use the *operator* &, which stands for "take the address of." Inside of the function *func*, an integer pointer variable is created, and the address of *b* is stored there. The contents of the memory location to which *a* points can be accessed using the *operator* ∗, which stands for "the memory location that is pointed to by." The first *cout* statement will print that the value of ∗*a* is 4. The memory to which *a* points is then assigned the value 64, and the function returns. Since the local variable *a* pointed to the same memory location as *b*, the second *cout* statement prints that the value of *b* is 64.

Code for Recursive Newton's Algorithm

Let us now try to use the C++ concepts we have just introduced to implement Newton's recursive algorithm. To accomplish this, we first need to look at how to partition the problem. The first thing we observe from the mathematical description of Section 3.1.1 is that we will need to generate an array of doubles, which will contain the differencing coefficients a_k from the formulation given previously. First, we need to have:

1. the number of interpolation points,
2. a grid of points at which the interpolation is to be exact,
3. an array containing the function we wish to interpolate evaluated at the interpolating grid, and
4. an array to store the Newton differencing coefficients a_k.

Let us take the top-down approach. First, assume that we have the four items just enumerated. The following function encapsulates the calculation of the differencing

Software
Suite

coefficients:

```
void NewtonDiffTable(int npts, double *xpts, double *funcvals,
 double * newton_coeffs){
   int i,j;
   for(i=0;i<npts;i++)
     newton_coeffs[i] = NewtonDiffFunction(0,i, xpts, funcvals);
}
```

In this function, *npts* is the number of interpolating points, *xpts* is an array containing the interpolating grid, and *funcvals* is an array containing the function we wish to interpolate evaluated at the interpolating grid. For each coefficient a_i (contained within the array element *newton_coeffs[i]*), we call the following *NewtonDiffFunction*:

```
double NewtonDiffFunction(int start_index, int ending_index,
   double * xpts, double * funcvals){
   double val;

   int diff = ending_index-start_index;

   if(diff == 0){
     val = funcvals[start_index];
   }
   else{
     val = (NewtonDiffFunction(start_index,ending_index-1,
                               xpts,funcvals) -
     NewtonDiffFunction(start_index+1,ending_index,
                               xpts,funcvals))/
          (xpts[start_index]-xpts[ending_index]);
   }

   return val;
}
```

As input, this function takes a starting index and an ending index (both of which are assumed to be in between 0 and (*npts*−1)), the interpolating grid, and the function to be interpolated evaluated on that grid. What is different about this function? It calls itself! This is a powerful concept, called *recursive function calling*, that can be used in C++. In the function here, notice that we are able to replicate in C++ code the mathematical recursive relation given in Equation (3.3).

For the recursion to be effective, we must have two things:

1. a recursive relationship and
2. a stopping condition.

> **Key Concept**
>
> Recursive functions require two things: a recursive definition and a stopping condition.

The first item seems quite obvious; recursion requires a recursive definition. The second item, although it sounds trivial, is often the stumbling block – often we do not know when the recursive relationship ends. In the example code given here, the recursive definition is given in Equation (3.3) and the stopping condition is determined by the condition that the starting index be the same as the ending index. From our previous mathematical definitions, we know that when the starting index and ending index are the same, then the Newton formula gives back the value of the function evaluated at that index value.

Once we have successfully calculated the Newton divided differences, we can now implement our Newton interpolating polynomial as follows:

```
double NewtonInterpolant(double x, int npts, double * xpts,
  double * newton_coeffs){
  int i,j;
  double sum = 0.0, xval;

  for(i=0;i<npts;i++){
    xval = 1.0;
    for(j=0;j<i;j++)
      xval = xval*(x-xpts[j]);
    sum = sum + newton_coeffs[i]*xval;
  }

  return sum;
}
```

As *input*, this function takes a value x (which is the value at which we want to know the value of the interpolating polynomial), the number of interpolating points *npts*, an array of interpolating points *xpts*, and the array of previously calculated Newton divided differences. As *output*, this function gives the value of the interpolating polynomial evaluated at the point x. Observe that this code replicates the mathematical definition given in Equation (3.1).

We will now use the previously defined functions in a program. Here we have provided a program that interpolates the *Runge function*

$$f(x) = \frac{1}{1 + 25x^2}, \quad x \in [-1, 1]. \tag{3.4}$$

This code queries the user for the degree of the interpolating polynomial and prints on the screen the values of the interpolating polynomial evaluated at 1,000 evenly spaced points on the interval $[-1, 1]$. This example demonstrates the use of

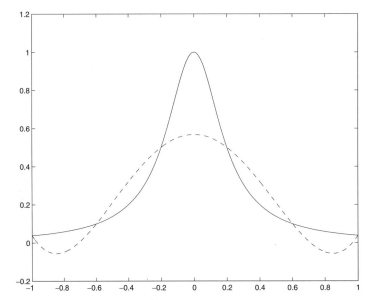

Figure 3.2:
Comparison of the
solution (solid curve)
and fifth-order interpo-
lation polynomial
(dashed curve)
obtained using the
Newton differencing
program.

output/input with *cout/cin* respectively, dynamic memory allocation, and recursive functions (through the calling of the *NewtonDiffTable* function). In Figure 3.2, we plot the results of running the program when the degree of the interpolating polynomial is set to five.

```
#include <iostream.h>
#include "SCchapter3.h"

double func(double x);

int main(int argc, char * argv[]){
  int i;
  int degree, polypnts;
  int npts = 1000;        //number of points used for plotting
  double xpt, soln, approx;

  cout << "Enter the degree of the interpolating polynomial: ";
  cin >> degree;

  polypnts = degree+1; //number of points is
                       //   equal to 1 + degree

  double * poly_xpts = new double[polypnts];
  double * func_vals = new double[polypnts];
  double * newton_coeffs = new double[polypnts];

  CreateGrid_EvenlySpaced(polypnts, poly_xpts, -1.0, 1.0);
```

```
   for(i=0;i<polypnts;i++){
     func_vals[i] = func(poly_xpts[i]);
   }

   NewtonDiffTable(polypnts, poly_xpts, func_vals,
                   newton_coeffs);

   for(i=0;i<npts;i++){
     xpt = -1.0 + 2.0*i/(npts-1);
     soln = func(xpt);
     approx = NewtonInterpolant(xpt, polypnts,
                                poly_xpts, newton_coeffs);
     cout << xpt << " " << soln << " " << approx << endl;
   }

   delete[] poly_xpts;
   delete[] func_vals;
   delete[] newton_coeffs;
}

double func(double x){
   double y;

   y = 1.0 + 25.0*x*x;
   y = 1.0/y;

   return y;
}
```

We will conclude this section by making some observations concerning this code.

- Notice that we have variable declarations after executable statements. This is one major difference between the programming language C (and many other programming languages) and C++. In many languages, all declarations must be made prior to executable statements. This is *not true* in C++. In C++, variables may be declared at any point within the program. Observe that we declare three pointer variables (double * variables) following the input sequence. Our primary reason for often placing all the variable declarations at the beginning of a function is clarity.
- In Chapter 2 we mentioned that in C++ it is possible to initialize a variable with an executable statement and not just a constant. This is exactly what we have done in this program. Observe that we initialize each new double* variable with the results of the *new* operator.
- For each item we want to delete, we must execute an individual delete[] statement. You *cannot* combine them like variable declaration in the following manner:

```
   delete[] poly_xpts, func_vals, newton_coeffs;
```

Though the compiler will not complain about such a statement, only the last variable will have the valid operation done to it. Both **delete** and **delete**[] take only one argument.

3.1.3 Lagrangian Interpolation

Another basis that is often used in practice to interpolate data primarily on nonequidistant grids is Lagrangian interpolation. Here, the basis $\phi_k(x)$ is equal to the Lagrangian polynomial, which is defined by

$$h_k(x) = \Pi \left(\frac{(x - x_i)}{(x_k - x_i)} \right), \quad i = 0, 1, \dots N; \quad i \neq k. \tag{3.5}$$

This is a polynomial of degree N and satisfies the equation

$$h_i(x_j) = \delta_{ij},$$

where δ_{ij} is the Kronecker delta

$$\delta_{ij} = \begin{cases} 1, i = j, \\ 0, i \neq j. \end{cases}$$

Software

Suite

PUTTING IT INTO PRACTICE

The following code implements this definition and returns values of the Lagrange polynomial.

```
double LagrangePoly(double x, int pt, int npts, double * xpts){
  int i;
  double h=1.0;

  for(i=0;i<pt;i++)
    h = h * (x - xpts[i])/(xpts[pt]-xpts[i]);

  for(i=pt+1;i<npts;i++)
    h = h * (x - xpts[i])/(xpts[pt]-xpts[i]);

  return h;
}
```

This code is relatively simple, yet there is one point to which we would like to draw your attention. Notice in the mathematical definition of Lagrange polynomials that there is the condition $i \neq j$, which in the code here translates into i != pt. This can be implemented in one of two ways:

1. As was done here, by breaking the sum into two parts, and having separate *for* loops for each part.
2. Having one *for* loop ranging from $0 \leq i < npts$, in which inside the *for* loop there is an *if* statement that checks if the value of the looping variable is the same as the value of pt.

Thus, the alternative function definition is the following:

```
double LagrangePoly(double x, int pt, int npts, double * xpts){
  int i;
  double h=1.0;

  for(i=0;i<npts;i++)
     if(i!=pt)
        h = h * (x - xpts[i])/(xpts[pt]-xpts[i]);

  return h;
}
```

These two definitions accomplish the same objective; however, their efficiency may be different. The reason for the efficiency difference comes from the repeated use of the *if* statement. The *if* statement is, in general, a very difficult computer instruction to optimize because the value of the Boolean expression is not known ahead of time, and hence which branch of the *if* the computer will have to execute is uncertain until the Boolean expression is evaluated. Hence, avoiding unnecessary *if* statements is, in general, a good policy because it allows the compiler to accomplish more code optimization.[2]

Avoid *if* statements within *for* loops.

Key Concept

Returning to the mathematics, by definition, then, we have that

$$f(x) = \sum_k a_k \phi_k(x)$$

or

$$f(x) = \sum_k f(x_k) h_k(x),$$

which in C++ is implemented as follows:

```
double LagrangeInterpolant(double x, int npts, double *xpts,
   double * funcvals){
  int i;
  double sum = 0.0;
```

---

[2] In recent years, there has been considerable work in processor design to incorporate what is referred to as "branch prediction." During runtime, the processor monitors the behavior of branches and attempts to predict which branch of the *if* will be taken. By doing so (i.e., if it predicts correctly) it can pipeline instructions with no additional cost resulting from the branching statement. If it is wrong, it will incur the normal branching penalty (in terms of pipelining).

```
for(i=0;i<npts;i++){
  sum = sum + funcvals[i]*LagrangePoly(x,i,npts,xpts);
}
return sum;
}
```

We can reuse the program presented for the Newton divided differences (previous section) to now perform Lagrange interpolation. First, we can remove the declaration of the Newton differencing coefficients, and we can also remove the call to the function *NewtonDiffTable*. Now, instead of calling *NewtonInterpolant(...)*, we will call *LagrangeInterpolant(...)* with its appropriate arguments. We have extracted the relevant code from the program presented earlier and now present a modified version of the code. The key thing to observe is that by writing modular code, we have increased code reuseability.

```
double * poly_xpts = new double[polypnts];
double * func_vals = new double[polypnts];

CreateGrid_EvenlySpaced(polypnts, poly_xpts, -1.0, 1.0);

for(i=0;i<polypnts;i++){
  func_vals[i] = func(poly_xpts[i]);
}

for(i=0;i<npts;i++){
  xpt = -1.0 + 2.0*i/(npts-1);
  soln = func(xpt);
  approx =  LagrangeInterpolant(xpt, polypnts,
                                poly_xpts, func_vals);
  cout << xpt << " " << soln << " " << approx << endl;
}

delete[] poly_xpts;
delete[] func_vals;
```

**Key
Concept**

Modular code is *reuseable* code

The coefficients in this polynomial representation are the function values at the grid points. Therefore, this approach is very efficient, especially for a "static" grid, because the Lagrangian polynomials can be constructed once, stored, and used repeatedly. However, in a dynamic grid where the grid points $\{x_i\}$ change, we need to recompute *all* Lagrangian polynomials, and this may be costly.

3.1.4 The Runge Phenomenon

Up to this point, we have assumed that all polynomial interpolation formulas converge irrespective of the distribution of points x_i (i.e., uniform with equidistant spacing

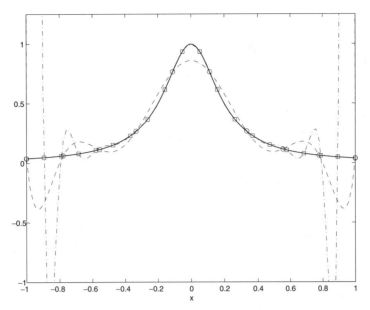

Figure 3.3: Plot of the Runge function (Equation (3.4); solid curve) and approximations using ten equidistant points (dashed curve) and twenty equidistant points (dashed-dot curve).

or nonuniform with arbitrary spacing). We have to wonder, however, if the type of function we try to approximate matters. Usually, polynomial approximation in the neighborhood of a point is safe, but as we try to extend this interpolation *in the large*, that is, away from the given data, proper conditions have to be satisfied, as we will illustrate in this section. First, we state a fundamental theorem that justifies polynomial approximation.

WEIERSTRASS THEOREM (1885): *Any continuous function defined in a finite range can be approximated to any degree of accuracy by polynomial powers.*

Although this theorem is reassuring it does not suggest what is the appropriate type of polynomial approximation. Specifically, the question still remains whether equidistant data always produce stable and convergent polynomial approximations. Experience shows that the answer to this question is negative, and in fact it was O. Runge in 1901 who first discovered this troubling fact by considering the function

$$f(x) = \frac{1}{1 + 25x^2}, \quad x \in [-1, 1]. \tag{3.6}$$

In Figure 3.3 we plot this function along with a polynomial approximation on ten and twenty equidistant points. We observe that the approximation is accurate around the origin but at $x \geq \pm 0.72$ the interpolating polynomial does not converge; taking more than ten points makes the oscillations worse. However, by interpolating the Runge function at special nonequidistant points, obtained from

$$x_k = \cos(k\pi/N), \ i = 0, \ldots, N,$$

we obtain a stable polynomial approximation, which converges fast to the exact solution as the number of grid points increases; this is shown in Figure 3.4. These special

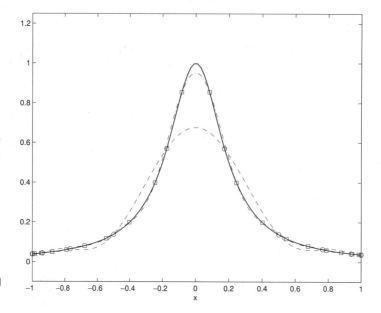

Figure 3.4: Plot of the Runge function (Equation (3.4); solid curve) and approximations using ten points (dashed line) and twenty points (dashed-dot curve) following the *cosine-law* distribution of grid points.

points are the *roots of the derivatives* of Chebyshev polynomials, which we will study in the next section. Other type of approximations, such as trigonometric interpolation, may also be stable (see Section 3.2.4).

For equidistant polynomial interpolation, how can we know in advance which functions have stable polynomial approximations? We know that for Taylor-type expansions this question relates to the analyticity of a function in the complex plane, and we are perhaps familiar with the Taylor circle inside which there are no singularities. The same picture emerges here also except that the circle is replaced by an oval-shape region, which is shown in Figure 3.5. The proof is rather elaborate and the interested reader is referred to the book by Lanczos [66].

THEOREM: *The necessary and sufficient condition for convergence of equidistant polynomial interpolation is that a function not have any singularities in the oval region Ω corresponding to the definition interval of $f(x)$ with $x \in [-1, 1]$.*

The Runge function of Equation (3.4) has singularities at $z = \pm i/5$, and this is the reason for the unstable behavior close to the end points. The more general Runge function

$$f(x) = \frac{\epsilon^2}{\epsilon^2 + x^2}, \quad x \in [-1, 1],$$

has a singularity at $x = \pm i\epsilon$. This is a very tough function to approximate, as at $x = 0$ we have $f(0) = 1$ but at distance only ϵ away we have $f(\epsilon) = \frac{1}{2}$, independent of the value of ϵ. You can appreciate what happens when $\epsilon = 10^{-6}$!

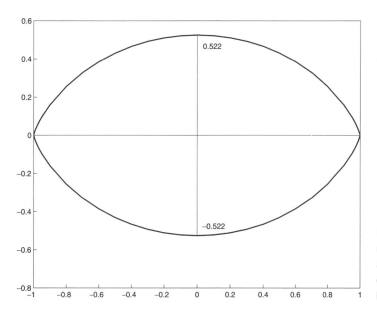

Figure 3.5: Region of required analyticity for a function for stable equidistant polynomial interpolation.

3.1.5 Chebyshev Polynomials

Spectral approximations and more specifically polynomial approximations using Chebyshev polynomials are a very effective means of representing relatively smooth data and also numerical solutions of partial differential equations. Just as before, we can write our polynomial approximation $p_N(x)$ as truncated series of the form

$$f(x) \approx p_N(x) = \sum_{k=0}^{N} a_k T_k(x),$$

where $T_k(x)$ is the kth Chebyshev polynomial. The Chebyshev polynomial series converges very fast; the polynomials are determined from recursion relations such as

$$T_0(x) = 1; \quad T_1(x) = x; \quad T_{n+1}(x) = 2xT_n(x) - T_{n-1}(x), \quad n \geq 1. \tag{3.7}$$

The following code implements this recursive formula; plots of $T_k(x)$, $k = 0, 1, 2, 3, 4$ are shown in Figure 3.6.

```
double ChebyshevPoly(int degree, double x){
  double value;

  switch(degree){
  case 0:
    value = 1.0;
    break;
  case 1:
    value = x;
    break;
```

Software

Suite

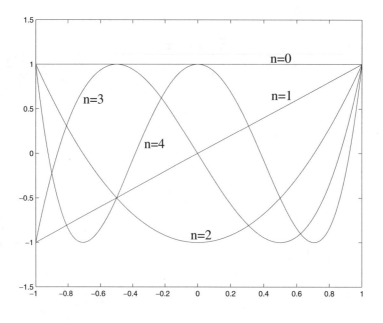

Figure 3.6: Chebyshev polynomials of order 0 through 4 in the interval $[-1, 1]$.

```
default:
    value = 2.0*x*ChebyshevPoly(degree-1,x) -
            ChebyshevPoly(degree-2,x);
}

return value;
}
```

In this example, there are two things that we want to point out. First, notice that for this particular example, we have *two* explicit stopping conditions: when $k = 0$ and when $k = 1$. This is because our recurrence relation contains references to $(k-1)$ and $(k-2)$, and hence we need both to be valid to get the kth term. The second thing to observe in this example is the use of a not previously mentioned C++ statement, the **switch** statement.

The SWITCH Statement

The switch statement is a convenient way of replacing a collection of *if–else* statements. In the example here, we have the following logic: If the value of degree is 0, then return the number 1.0, else if the value of degree is 1, return the value of x, or else the value is what is given by the recurrence relation. We could implement this using *if–else* statements as follows:

```
if(degree == 0)
    value = 1.0;
else{
    if(degree == 1)
        value = x;
    else
```

```
      value = 2.0*x*ChebyshevPoly(degree-1,x) -
              ChebyshevPoly(degree-2,x);
}
```

However, C++ has a statement named **switch** that accomplishes this type of logic for you. The syntax of a switch statement is as follows:

```
switch( variable ){

  case a:
     statement 1;
     break;

  case b:
     statement 2;
     statement 3;
     break;

  default:
     statement 4;
}
```

Here, "variable" is the variable that you want to test; "a," "b," etc. are the *constant* values that you want to test against. (These cannot be variables; they must be constants.) When the *switch* is executed, the first *case* in which the variable is equivalent to the case is where execution begins. All statements below that *case* statement are executed. Hence, when all the statements that you want done for a particular case have been executed, you must use a **break** statement to exit the switch. The *default* case is the case that is executed if no other cases have matched the variable.

PROGRAMMER BEWARE!

• Do not forget to put break statements between independent cases!

Warning

Because of the "flow-through" nature of the switch statement, one can group cases together. Suppose, for example, that we wanted to implement a *statement* that executes statement 1 if cases 0 and 1 are true and executes statement 2 otherwise. The following pseudo-code example demonstrates the implementation of this logic:

```
switch(degree){
   case 0:
   case 1:
      statement 1;
      break;
   default:
      statement 2;
}
```

In this example, if either case 0 or case 1 is true, then statement 1 (and only statement 1, because of the *break* statement) will be executed. For all other values of the variable degree, statement 2 will be executed.

Key Concept	**Switch** is a nice organizational tool for implementing *if–else* relationships.

Properties of Chebyshev Polynomials

Next, we summarize some important properties of the Chebyshev polynomials:

- **Symmetry**: $T_n(-x) = (-1)^n T_n(x)$.
- The **leading coefficient** is 2^{n-1}, $n \geq 1$.
- **Zeros**: The roots of $T_n(x)$ are $x_k = \cos\left(\frac{2k+1}{n} \cdot \frac{\pi}{2}\right)$, $k = 0, 1, \ldots, n-1$. These are called *Gauss points* and we will use them later in numerical integration. The roots of its derivative $T_k'(x)$, which are the locations of extrema for $T_k(x)$, are the *Gauss–Lobatto points* and are given by $x_k' = \cos\frac{k\pi}{n}$. We also have that

$$T_n(x_k') = (-1)^k, \quad k = 0, 1, 2, \ldots.$$

- **Orthogonality** in the continuous inner product is

$$\int_{-1}^{1} T_i T_j \frac{dx}{\sqrt{(1-x^2)}} = (T_i, T_j) = \begin{cases} 0, & i \neq j, \\ \pi/2, & i = j \neq 0, \\ \pi, & i = j = 0. \end{cases}$$

We often use orthogonality in the discrete inner product:

$$\sum_{k=0}^{m} T_i(x_k) T_j(x_k) = \begin{cases} 0, & i \neq j, \\ \frac{m+1}{2}, & i = j \neq 0, \\ m+1, & i = j. \end{cases}$$

- **Lagrangian Interpolant**: The Chebyshev Lagrangian interpolant through N Gauss points has a simple form:

$$h_k(x) = \frac{T_N(x)}{T_N'(x_k)(x - x_k)}, \quad x \neq x_k.$$

- **Grid Transformation**: The following grid transformation maps the Gauss–Lobatto points $x_k = \cos(k\pi/N)$, $k = 0, \ldots, N$ to a new set of grid points ξ_k obtained from

$$\xi_k = \frac{\sin^{-1}(\alpha x_k)}{\sin^{-1}(\alpha)}, \tag{3.8}$$

where $\alpha \in (0, 1]$ defines the exact distribution. For $\alpha \to 0$ the new points are equidistant and the Chebyshev approximation resembles the Fourier method.

However, for stability of the approximation the new points cannot be exactly equidistant, and thus $\alpha > 0$.

- **Minimax Property**: Of all the nth-degree polynomials with leading coefficient 1, the polynomial $2^{1-n}T_n(x)$ has the smallest maximum norm in the interval $[-1, 1]$. The value of its maximum norm is 2^{1-n}.

Approximation Error and Convergence Rate

Let us assume that we are given the values of a function $f(x)$ on a grid of $(m+1)$ points, and we use a polynomial $p(x)$ to represent the data on this grid. The error [or remainder $r(x)$] in the approximation of a function $f(x)$ is then

$$|f(x) - p(x)| = \frac{(x - x_0)(x - x_1)\ldots(x - x_m)|f^{(m+1)}(\xi)|}{(m+1)!},$$

where $\xi \in [x_0, x_m]$. This error behaves like the polynomial curve

$$r(x) \sim (x - x_0)(x - x_1)(x - x_2)\ldots(x - x_m),$$

which oscillates, similar in fact to the least-squares approximation (Section 3.1.7), and unlike the Taylor expansion approximation where the error increases exponentially as $\sim (x - x_0)^{m+1}$.

Now, we can attempt to find the optimum distribution of the grid points, which means that we seek to minimize the maximum magnitude of

$$q(x) \equiv (m+1)!\, p(x) = (x - x_0)(x - x_1)\ldots(x - x_m).$$

To this end, we can use the minimax property to obtain

$$q(x) = 2^{-m}T_{m+1}(x);$$

thus $\{x_k\}$ are the zeros of the Chebyshev polynomial $T_{m+1}(x)$, and thus the grid points x_k are the roots of $T_{m+1}(x)$, that is,

$$x_k = \cos\left(\frac{2k+1}{m+1}\frac{\pi}{L}\right), k = 0, 1, \ldots m.$$

We now state Rivlin's *minimax error* theorem:

MINIMAX ERROR THEOREM: *The maximum pointwise error of a Chebyshev series expansion that represents an arbitrary function $f(x)$ is only a small constant away from the minimax error, that is, the smallest possible pointwise error of any Nth-degree polynomial. The following inequality applies:*

$$\| f(x) - \sum_{k=0}^{N} a_k T_k(x) \|_\infty \leq 4\left(1 + \frac{\ln N}{\pi^2}\right) \cdot \| f(x) - mm(x) \|_\infty,$$

where mm(x) is the best possible polynomial.

Note that for $N = 128$ the prefactor is less than 5 and for $N = 2{,}688{,}000$ the prefactor is $4\left(1 + \frac{\ln N}{\pi^2}\right) \approx 10$. Therefore, the Chebyshev expansion series is within a decimal point of the *minimax approximation*.

The convergence of Chebyshev polynomial expansions is similar to Fourier cosine series, as the following transformation applies:

$$x = \cos\theta \quad \text{and} \quad T_n(\cos\theta) = \cos(n\theta).$$

Assuming an infinite expansion of the form

$$f(x) = \sum_{k=0}^{\infty} a_k T_x(x)$$

then

$$a_k = \frac{1}{\pi c_k} \int_0^{\pi} f(\cos\theta) \cos k\theta \, d\theta = \frac{2}{\pi c_k} \int_{-1}^{1} f(x) T_k(x) \frac{dx}{\sqrt{1-x^2}} \, ,$$

where we have defined

$$c_k = \begin{cases} 2, k = 0, \\ 1, k > 0. \end{cases}$$

The convergence rate of the expansion series is defined by the decaying rate of the coefficients a_k. To this end, if

- $f^{(p)}(x)$ is continuous $\forall \, |x| \leq 1, \quad p = 0, 1, 2, \ldots, n-1$, and
- $f^{(n)}(x)$ is integrable

then

$$a_k \ll \frac{1}{k^n} \, .$$

This implies that for infinitely differentiable functions the convergence rate is extremely fast. This convergence is called *exponential*, and it simply means that if we double the number of grid points the approximation error will decrease by two orders of magnitude (i.e., a factor of 100), instead of a factor of 4, which would correspond to interpolation with quadratic polynomials and second-order convergence rate. This estimate also shows that in the Chebyshev approximation we can exploit the regularity, that is, the *smoothness*, of the function to accelerate the convergence rate of the expansion. Also, notice that unlike the Fourier series (see Section 3.2), the convergence of a Chebyshev series does not depend on the values of $f(x)$ at the end points, because the boundary terms vanish automatically.

Finally, an important consequence of the rapid convergence of Chebyshev polynomial expansions of smooth functions is that they can be differentiated normally termwise, that is,

$$\frac{d^p f(x)}{dx^p} = \sum_{k=0}^{\infty} a_k \frac{d^p T_k(x)}{dx^p} \, .$$

In computing Chebyshev derivatives higher than the first, inaccurate results may be obtained because of round-off error. In particular, it has been observed that round-off error may be significant for the *second derivative* for $N > 128$, for the *third derivative* for $N > 64$, and for the *fourth derivative* for $N > 32$. These errors can be reduced if the grid transformation given by Equation (3.8) is employed.

EXAMPLE. The following example, first presented in Gottlieb and Orszag [49], shows the fast convergence of Chebyshev discretization. The exact representation for the *sine* function corresponding to wave number M is

$$\sin M\pi(x+\alpha) = 2\sum_{n=0}^{\infty} \frac{1}{c_n} J_n(M\pi) \sin(M\pi\alpha + \frac{1}{2}n\pi) T_n(x),$$

where $J_n(x)$ is the Bessel function of order n. We can argue that $J_n(M\pi) \to 0$ exponentially fast for $n > M\pi$, given that the Bessel function can be approximated by

$$J_n(M\pi) \approx \frac{1}{\sqrt{2\pi n}} \left(e \underbrace{\frac{M\pi}{2n}}_{\leq 1} \right)^n \quad \text{if} \quad \frac{n}{M} > \pi.$$

This result leads to the following heuristic rule for Chebyshev series approximation, proposed by Gottlieb and Orszag:

QUASI-SINUSOIDAL RULE OF THUMB *To resolve M complete waves it is required that Mπ modes be retained, or in other words π polynomials should be retained per wavelength.*

Although very good, such a resolution capability is less than that of a Fourier method that requires approximately two points per wave! In fact, this rule is an asymptotic result, and a more practical rule for the total number of points N is

$$N = 6 + 4(M-1),$$

which has been verified in many numerical experiments.

3.1.6 Hermite Interpolation and Splines

We now turn to piecewise polynomial interpolation using relatively low order polynomials, unlike the single domain global interpolation. As we know from our previous discussion, the more (distinct) grid points that we introduce into the polynomial approximation, the higher the order of the interpolating polynomial. As the degree of the polynomial increases, the interpolating polynomial becomes more oscillatory. One solution to this problem is to use multiple piecewise polynomials of low order instead of one high-order polynomial. This has the advantage that the interpolation error is proportional to a lower order derivative, resulting in better accuracy and more flexibility. The method of splines, first used in naval architecture, is a very effective approach and facilitates smooth transition between subdomains.

To proceed, let us first consider cubic *Hermite interpolation* where both function and derivatives are interpolated. The interpolation problem can be stated as follows:

- *Given data for the function values y and slopes s, $(x_L; y_L; s_L)$ and $(x_R; y_R; s_L)$ at the left (x_L) and right (x_R) boundaries of one-dimensional domain, find a cubic polynomial*

$$p(x) = a_0 + a_1(x - x_L) + a_2(x - x_L)^2 + a_3(x - x_L)^2(x - x_R)$$

with the four unknown coefficients obtained from

$$p(x_L) = y_L, \quad p(x_R) = y_R,$$

$$p'(x_L) = s_L, \quad p'(x_R) = s_R.$$

The first derivative is

$$p'(x) = a_1 + 2a_2(x - x_L) + a_3[2(x - x_L)(x - x_R) + (x - x_L)^2]$$

and by substituting the known data at the boundaries, we have

$$p(x_L) = y_L = a_0, \quad a_0 + a_1 \Delta x + a_2(\Delta x)^2 = y_R,$$

$$p'(x_L) = s_L = a_1, \quad a_1 + 2a_2 \Delta x + a_3(\Delta x)^2 = s_R,$$

where $\Delta x \equiv x_R - x_L$ is the domain size. We recast these in matrix–vector form as follows:

$$\begin{bmatrix} 1 & & & \mathbf{O} \\ 0 & 1 & & \\ 1 & \Delta x & \Delta x^2 & \\ 0 & 1 & 2\Delta x & \Delta x^2 \end{bmatrix} \begin{bmatrix} a_0 \\ a_1 \\ a_2 \\ a_3 \end{bmatrix} = \begin{bmatrix} y_L \\ s_L \\ y_R \\ s_R \end{bmatrix},$$

and we see that the coefficient matrix is lower triangular.

The solution is obtained by forward substitution:

$$a_0 = y_L, \quad a_2 = y_L'',$$

$$a_1 = s_L, \quad a_3 = y_L''',$$

where we have defined the *forward differences* at the left boundary as

$$y_L' \equiv \frac{y_R - y_L}{\Delta x}, \quad y_L'' \equiv \frac{y_L' - s_L}{\Delta x}, \quad y_L''' \equiv \frac{s_L - 2y_L' + s_R}{\Delta x^2}.$$

THEOREM ON ACCURACY OF HERMITE INTERPOLATION: *For a function $f(x)$ interpolated by a cubic Hermite polynomial $p(x)$ in a domain of size Δx, the error is bounded from above by*

$$\| f(x) - p(x) \|_\infty \leq \frac{\| f^{(4)}(x) \|_\infty}{384} (\Delta x)^4.$$

This theorem guarantees that if the domain is divided into 100 subintervals then the error will be reduced by a factor of 10^8! The proof is based on evaluating the *maximum* contribution of the remainder at the midpoint of the domain.

Figure 3.7:
Interpolation in the
interval $x \in [x_I, x_{I+1}]$.

CONSTRUCTING CUBIC SPLINES. Having obtained simple formulas for Hermite cubic polynomial interpolation, we now proceed to construct formulas for different types of cubic splines. Here we replace the extra information given for first derivatives (s_L, s_R) at the end points of the domain by imposing continuity at the interior points. We assume, therefore, that the entire domain is subdivided into subdomains or cells and that the function and its derivatives are continuous at the breakup points, which we call the interior points. We can state the problem of constructing splines as follows:

Figure 3.8:
Interpolation in the
interval $x \in$
$[x_{I+1}, x_{I+2}]$.

- *Given the data points* $(x_1, y_1), \ldots, (x_n, y_n)$, *find a piecewise cubic interpolant* $S(x)$ *so that* $S(x)$, $S'(x)$, *and* $S''(x)$ *are continuous at all interior points* x_i, $i = 2, \ldots, (n-1)$.

To achieve this we have to choose the slopes $(s_i, i = 1, \ldots, n)$ at all points appropriately. To maintain continuity of the slopes we simply assign a single value at each point. However, we have to enforce continuity of the second derivative explicitly. To this end, we consider the subdomain $x \in [x_i, x_{i+1}]$ and apply Hermite interpolation as before where the point x_i is the left boundary and the point x_{i+1} is the right boundary, as shown in Figure 3.7.

We then construct the cubic polynomial

$$p_i(x) = y_i + s_i(x - x_i) + y_i''(x - x_i)^2 + y_i'''(x - x_i)^2(x - x_{i+1}),$$

where

$$y_i' = \frac{y_{i+1} - y_i}{\Delta x_i}, \quad y_i'' = \frac{y_i' - s_i}{\Delta x_i}, \quad y_i''' = \frac{s_i - 2y_i' + s_{i+1}}{(\Delta x_i)^2},$$

with $\Delta x_i \equiv x_{i+1} - x_i$. We also obtain the second derivative

$$p_i''(x) = 2y_i'' + y_i'''[4(x - x_i) + 2(x - x_{i+1})].$$

Next, we move to the adjacent cell $x \in [x_{i+1}, x_{i+2}]$ and apply Hermite interpolation on this interval (see Figure 3.8).

We construct the polynomial

$$p_{i+1}(x) = y_{i+1} + s_{i+1}(x - x_{i+1}) + y_{i+1}''(x - x_{i+1})^2 + y_{i+1}'''(x - x_{i+1})^2(x - x_{i+2})$$

and its second derivative

$$p_{i+1}''(x) = 2y_{i+1}'' + y_{i+1}'''[4(x - x_{i+1}) + 2(x - x_{i+2})].$$

Next, we enforce continuity of second derivative at x_{i+1} and obtain equations for the *unknown slopes*:

$$\frac{2}{\Delta x_i}(2s_{i+1} + s_i - 3y_i') = \frac{2}{\Delta x_{i+1}}(3y_{i+1}' - 2s_{i+1} - s_{i+2}),$$

which can be rewritten as

$$\Delta x_{i+1}s_i + 2(\Delta x_i + \Delta x_{i+1})s_{i+1} + \Delta x_i s_{i+2} = 3(\Delta x_{i+1}y_i' + \Delta x_i y_{i+1}'), \qquad (3.9)$$

$$i = 1, \ldots, n - 2.$$

These equations can be recast in a matrix–vector form with a tridiagonal coefficient matrix. However, we have no information for the slopes s_1, s_n (the end slopes), and thus we cannot solve for the slopes yet; we need additional information, the type of which specifies different classes of splines:

- **I. The Complete Spline**: Here the additional information is given at the end points where the end slopes are explicitly specified, that is, $s_1 = S_L$ and $s_n = S_R$.
- **II. The Natural Spline**: In this case the *curvature* [i.e., $p''(x)$] at the end points is set to *zero*, that is,

$$p_1''(x_L) = 0 \Rightarrow s_1 = \frac{1}{2}(3y_1' - s_2) \quad \text{and} \quad s_n = \frac{1}{2}(3y_{n-1}' - s_{n-1}).$$

- **III. The Not-a-Knot Spline**: In this case, no explicit information on the end points is provided, but instead we use continuity of the *third derivative* $p'''(x)$ at the points x_2 and x_{n-1}. Using

$$p_i'''(x) = 6\frac{s_i + s_{i+1} - 2y_i'}{(\Delta x_i)^2},$$

and enforcing the continuity condition, we obtain

$$s_1 = -s_2 + 2y_1' + \left(\frac{\Delta x_1}{\Delta x_2}\right)^2 (s_2 + s_3 - 2y_2').$$

This forms the first row in the triagonal matrix–vector system, which now has a bandwidth of *two* instead of *one*. A similar equation is valid for the other end (last row in the matrix–vector system).

- **IV. The B-Spline**: An example of a very popular cubic spline derived from this Hermite interpolation is the *basic* or *B-spline*. It corresponds to zero slopes at the end points (i.e., $s_L = s_R = 0$), and it is symmetric. Its support is five points, that is, it is nonzero within four equidistant intervals Δx. It is defined by the five points

$$(x_i, y_i) = [(0, 0), (1, 1), (2, 4), (3, 1), (4, 0)].$$

Solving the matrix–vector system constructed from Equation (3.9),

$$\begin{bmatrix} 2 & 1 & & & \\ 1 & 4 & 1 & & \\ & 1 & 4 & 1 & \\ & & 1 & 4 & 1 \\ & & & 1 & 2 \end{bmatrix} \begin{bmatrix} s_1 \\ s_2 \\ s_3 \\ s_4 \\ s_5 \end{bmatrix} = 3 \begin{bmatrix} 1 \\ 4 \\ 0 \\ -4 \\ -1 \end{bmatrix},$$

we obtain

$$B(x) \equiv S(x) = \begin{cases} x^3, & 0 \le x \le 1, \\ 4 - 6(2 - x)^2 + 3(2 - x)^3, & 1 \le x \le 2, \\ 4 - 6(2 - x)^2 - 3(2 - x)^3, & 2 \le x \le 3, \\ (4 - x)^3, & 3 \le x \le 4, \end{cases}$$

and it is zero everywhere else, as shown in Figure 3.9. Note that the B-spline, which has its origin in applications of beam vibrations, satisfies a *minimum*

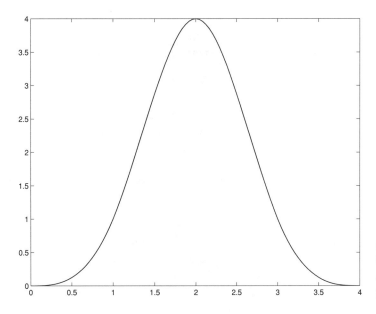

Figure 3.9: Plot of the B-spline. Its support extends over four intervals.

principle. Specifically, the B-spline has the smallest bending energy

$$E(B(x)) = \int_0^N \left(\frac{d^2 B}{dx^2}\right)^2 dx,$$

among all functions or other splines that go through the same data points.

Next, we state a theorem that gives upper bounds for the error of spline interpolation up to the third derivative. This depends on the end points, so the theorem is for the *complete spline:*

THEOREM ON ACCURACY OF COMPLETE SPLINES: *Let $S(x)$ be the cubic spline that interpolates $f(x)$, $x \in [a, b]$, at points $x_i = i \Delta x$, where $\Delta x = \frac{(b-a)}{n}$, $i = 0, \ldots, n$, and also $s_L = f'(a)$ and $s_R = f'(b)$; then*

$$\| S^{(r)}(x) - f^{(r)}(x) \|_2 \leq \epsilon_r \| f^{(4)} \|_2 (\Delta x)^{4-r}, \quad r = 0, 1, 2, 3,$$

where $\epsilon_0 = \frac{1}{384}$, $\epsilon_1 = \frac{1}{24}$, $\epsilon_2 = \frac{3}{8}$, and $\epsilon_3 = 1$.

3.1.7 Least-Squares Approximation

What we have dealt with so far are interpolations for which the number of unknowns matches the number of constraints in the function values or slopes. The cubic splines are perhaps a slight exception, as extra information is needed to determine them, but they too could be cast in a form of a linear system

$$\mathbf{C}\mathbf{a} = \mathbf{y},$$

where $\mathbf{a}$ is the vector of unknowns and $\mathbf{y}$ is the vector of prescribed values.

In practical scientific computing, however, the opposite situation may occur: We may have much *more information* than we actually require. For example, consider the case of data analysis in an experiment with many measurements and with the dependent variable following a quadratic trend. It is clear that, unless we are really lucky, not all measurements will lie on a parabola! It is also clear that not all measurements have the same confidence associated with them, and this should be reflected in the polynomial interpolant. The question then is, "What type of parabola best fits the data and has built in the measurement accuracy reported?"

A similar situation arises in the problem of smoothing the data, a familiar task in engineering, and Gauss was the first to provide a general treatment of this subject. He introduced the *bracket notation* that we will use here; that is, for a set of m grid points we define

$$[y] \equiv y_1 + \ldots + y_m$$

and the moments

$$[wx^k] \equiv w_1 x_1^k + w_2 x_2^k + \cdots + w_m x_m^k.$$

To obtain the least-squares polynomial, we assume that we have m points and the pairs (x_i, y_i), $i = 1, \ldots, m$, and we try to represent them with a polynomial $p(x)$ of degree n:

$$p(x) = a_0 + a_1 x + a_2 x^2 + \cdots + a_n x^n,$$

where $m \geq n + 1$. The strict inequality corresponds to an overdetermined system that we discuss in this section. In matrix–vector form, if we follow the straightforward path, as in the Vandermonde approach (Section 3.1.1), we have that

$$\mathbf{C}(m \times (n+1)) \times \mathbf{a}(n+1) = \mathbf{y}(m),$$

so the matrix $\mathbf{C}$ is *rectangular*, and for $m > (n+1)$ this system does not always have a solution.

However, there is a *minimum principle* associated with this problem. That is, instead of solving the system $\mathbf{Ca} = \mathbf{y}$ we attempt to find the vector $\mathbf{a}$ such that we minimize the residual

$$r(\mathbf{a}) = \| \mathbf{Ca} - \mathbf{y} \|_2.$$

This results in solving a system of the form

$$\mathbf{C}^T \mathbf{C} \, \mathbf{a} = \mathbf{C}^T \mathbf{y}, \tag{3.10}$$

where $\mathbf{C}^T \mathbf{C}$ is a symmetric, positive definite matrix if $\mathbf{C}$ has linearly independent columns.

This may not be obvious at first but following Gauss, we can derive the *normal equations* that result in the matrix–vector form of Equation (3.10). To this end, we compute the residual

$$r_i = a_0 + a_1 x_i + \cdots + a_n x_i^n - y_i$$

at each measurement point x_i, $i = 1, \ldots, m$. We now form the sum of the square of all the m residuals,

$$R(a_0, a_1, \ldots, a_n) = \sum_{i=1}^{m} w_i r_i^2,$$

where w_i is a weight that reflects *confidence* in the accuracy of measurement at point x_i. The next step is to minimize the residual R by taking its derivatives with respect to all a_i and setting them to zero, that is,

$$\frac{\partial R}{\partial a_i} = 0 \quad \text{for} \quad i = 1, \ldots, n.$$

Using the Gauss notation, this yields

$$a_0[wx^0] + a_1[wx^1] + \ldots + a_n[wx^n] = [wy],$$

$$a_0[wx^1] + a_1[wx^2] + \ldots + a_n[wx^{n+1}] = [wxy],$$

$$\vdots$$

$$a_0[wx^n] + a_1[wx^{n+1}] + \ldots + a_n[wx^{2n}] = [wx^n y].$$

We also note that the unknowns are $(a_0, a_1, \ldots, a_n)$ and that the coefficient matrix $\mathbf{H}$ is

$$\mathbf{H} = \begin{bmatrix} [wx^0] & [wx^1] & \ldots & [wx^n] \\ [wx^1] & [wx^2] & \ldots & [wx^{n+1}] \\ \vdots & \vdots & & \\ [wx^n] & [wx^{n+1}] & \ldots & [wx^{2n}] \end{bmatrix},$$

which is an $(n+1) \times (n+1)$ matrix, the *Hankel matrix*, with its cross-diagonals constant. Also, if we form

$$\mathbf{W} = \begin{bmatrix} w_1 & & & \\ & w_2 & \mathbf{0} & \\ \mathbf{0} & & \ddots & \\ & & & w_m \end{bmatrix}$$

the matrix of weights, then we can write the Hankel matrix as

$$\mathbf{H} = \mathbf{V}^T \mathbf{W} \mathbf{V},$$

where

$$\mathbf{V} = \begin{bmatrix} 1 & x_1 & \ldots & x_1^n \\ 1 & x_2 & \ldots & x_2^n \\ \vdots & \vdots & & \\ 1 & x_m & \ldots & x_m^n \end{bmatrix}$$

is the *rectangular* Vandermonde matrix; it is nonsingular if at least $(n+1)$ points (out of the total m points) are distinct. The normal equations can be recast in matrix–vector form as

$$(\mathbf{V}^T\mathbf{W}\mathbf{V})\mathbf{a} = \mathbf{V}^T\mathbf{W}\mathbf{y},$$

where

$$\mathbf{y}^T = (y_1, y_2, \ldots, y_m)$$

are the measurements.

The normal equations are, in some sense, a generalization of the Vandermonde approach where the set

$$(1, x, x^2, \ldots, x^n)$$

is used as basis $\phi_k(x)$ in the expansion

$$f(x) \approx \sum_{k=0}^{n} a_k \phi_k(x).$$

We can *change the basis*, as we did in the case of deterministic interpolation, to arrive at a better algorithm to compute the coefficients $(a_0, a_1, \ldots, a_n)$ via *recursion*. To this end, minimization of

$$R(a_0, a_1, \ldots a_n) = \sum_{i=1}^{m} w_i [f(x_i) - y_i]^2$$

results in a coefficient matrix $\mathbf{G}((n+1) \times (n+1))$ with elements

$$g_{ij} = \sum_{k=1}^{m} w_k \phi_i(x_k) \phi_j(x_k)$$

for the system $\mathbf{Ga} = \mathbf{b}$ or

$$g_{ij}a_j = b_i \quad \text{with} \quad b_i = \sum_{k=1}^{m} w_k \phi_i(x_k) y_k.$$

If this basis is *orthonormal*, that is, if

$$\sum_{k=1}^{m} w_k \phi_i(x_k) \phi_j(x_k) = \begin{cases} 0, & i \neq j, \\ 1, & i = j, \end{cases}$$

then the matrix $\mathbf{G}$ is a *diagonal matrix* and the computation of the unknown vector $\mathbf{a}$ becomes a trivial matter. We have seen that the Chebyshev polynomials are orthonormal but their construction requires special Gauss–Lobbato points (see Section 3.1.5). Here the key is to discover a similar *three-term recurrence formula* for a given *arbitrary* distribution of points $\{x_i\}$. We expect that such a three-term recurrence formula is possible given that the Gram–Schmidt orthogonality procedure of this form for vectors leads to that form (see Section 2.2.9); similar results should be expected for polynomials.

Let us call the basis $\phi_k(x) = q_k(x)$, where $q_k(x)$ is the orthonormal polynomial that, by assumption, satisfies the recursion

$$q_{j+1}(x) = xq_j(x) - \alpha_{j+1}q_j(x) - \beta_j q_{j-1}(x), \quad j = 1, \ldots, (n-1). \tag{3.11}$$

We need to find recurrence relations for the constants α_{i+1} and β_j as well as initial conditions. From the orthonormality constraint we have that

$$q_0(x) = 1$$

and by assuming that

$$q_1(x) = x - \alpha_1,$$

we require orthonormality, that is

$$\sum_{i=1}^{m} w_i q_0(x_i) q_1(x_i) = 0$$

or

$$\sum_{i=1}^{m} w_i (x_i - \alpha_1) = 0$$

or

$$\sum_{i=1}^{m} w_i \alpha_1 = \sum_{i=1}^{m} w_i x_i \Rightarrow \alpha_1 = \frac{1}{\gamma_0} \sum_{i=1}^{m} w_i x_i,$$

where

$$\gamma_0 \equiv \sum_{i=1}^{m} w_i$$

and, in general, we define

$$\gamma_k \equiv \sum_{i=1}^{m} w_i q_k^2(x_i).$$

Similarly, we can obtain the coefficients α_2 and β_2 by insisting that $q_2(x)$ be orthogonal to $q_1(x)$ and $q_0(x)$, which are the two previous polynomials. By induction we obtain the general result from the following two orthogonality constraints:

$$\sum_{i=1}^{m} w_i q_{j+1}(x_i) q_j(x_i) = 0, \quad q_{j+1} \perp q_j, \tag{3.12}$$

$$\sum_{i=1}^{m} w_i q_{j+1}(x_i) q_{j-1}(x_i) = 0, \quad q_{j+1} \perp q_{j-1}. \tag{3.13}$$

These conditions are sufficient to prove that $q_{j+1} \perp q_k$, $k = 0, \ldots, j - 2$.

By substituting the recurrence formula [Equation (3.11)] for q_{j+1} in Equations (3.12) and (3.13), we obtain

$$\alpha_{j+1} = \frac{1}{\gamma_j} \sum_{i=1}^{m} w_i x_i q_j^2(x_i)$$

and

$$\beta_j = \frac{1}{\gamma_{j-1}} \sum_{i=1}^{m} w_i \underbrace{[x_i q_{j-1}(x_i)]}_{Eq.\ 3.11} q_j(x_i)$$

$$= \frac{1}{\gamma_{j-1}} \sum w_i [q_j(x_i) + \alpha_j q_{j-1}(x_i) + \beta_{j-1} q_{j-2}(x_i)] \cdot q_j(x_i)$$

$$= \frac{1}{\gamma_{j-1}} \sum w_i q_j^2(x_i) = \frac{\gamma_j}{\gamma_{j-1}}$$

$$\Rightarrow \beta_j = \frac{\gamma_j}{\gamma_{j-1}}.$$

We can now write the following recursive algorithm for computing the orthogonal polynomials $q_k(x)$:

Initialize:

$$\gamma_0 = \sum_{i=1}^{m} w_i; \quad q_0(x) = 1; \quad q_1(x) = x - \frac{1}{\gamma_0} \sum_{i=1}^{m} w_i x_i$$

Begin Loop: $j = 1, n-1$

$$\gamma_j = \sum_{i=1}^{m} w_i q_j^2(x_i)$$

$$\beta_j = \frac{\gamma_j}{\gamma_{j-1}}$$

$$\alpha_{j+1} = \frac{1}{\gamma_j} \sum_{i=1}^{m} w_i x_i q_j^2(x_i)$$

$$q_{j+1}(x) = x q_j(x) - \alpha_{j+1} q_j(x) - \beta_j q_{j-1}(x)$$

End Loop

Having constructed all the orthogonal polynomials $q_k(x)$, we can compute the unknown coefficients from

$$a_k = \frac{1}{\gamma_k} \sum_{i=1}^{m} w_i q_k(x_i) y_i, \quad k = 0, 1, \ldots, n,$$

and finally

$$f(x) \approx \sum_{k=0}^{n} a_k q_k(x)$$

is the *least-squares polynomial*.

REMARK: There is a similarity between the procedure we just described and the **QR decomposition** presented in Section 2.2.9. Recall that the problem of finding a least-square polynomial is equivalent to solving the system

$$\mathbf{C}^T \mathbf{C} \mathbf{a} = \mathbf{C}^T \mathbf{y}.$$

We can apply QR decomposition to matrix $\mathbf{C}$ to obtain

$$\mathbf{C} = \mathbf{QR},$$

and the first equation becomes

$$\mathbf{R}^T \mathbf{R}\, \mathbf{a} = \mathbf{R}^T \mathbf{Q}^T \mathbf{y}$$

or

$$\mathbf{R}\, \mathbf{a} = \mathbf{Q}^T \mathbf{y}$$

with $\mathbf{R}$ being upper triangular. The vector of unknown coefficients $\mathbf{a}$ is then obtained by back substitution. In practice, another version of QR factorization the *Householder triangulaziation*, is preferable. We will study this in Chapter 9.

PUTTING IT INTO PRACTICE

From the preceding discussion, we see that given a set of data, we need to calculate and store three quantities: α_i, β_i, and the set of least-squares coefficients. We will accomplish this with the function presented in the following. This function takes as input the number of points over which the least-squares approximation is to be calculated (*npts*), an array of positions x, data values (or function values) at the previously mentioned spatial points stored in the array *funcvals*, and the degree of the least-squares approximation *ndeg*. Then as output arrays this routine will fill in the arrays *alpha*, *beta*, and *lscoeffs*. Note that this function assumes that all the arrays have been allocated.

```
void LS_ComputeCoeffs(int npts, double *xpts, double *funcvals,
        int ndeg, double *alpha, double *beta, double *lscoeffs){
  int i,j;
  double xi,tmpd;
  double * gamma = new double[ndeg+1];

  /////////////////////////////
  // Compute average first
  xi = 0.0;
  for(i=0;i<npts;i++){
    xi += xpts[i];
  }
  xi /= (double) npts;
  /////////////////////////////

  gamma[0] = npts;
  alpha[0] = beta[0] = 0.0;
  alpha[1] = xi;
```

Software ⊙ *Suite*

```
for(j=1;j<=ndeg-1;j++){
  gamma[j]    = 0.0;
  alpha[j+1] = 0.0;
  for(i=0;i<npts;i++){
    tmpd = LS_OrthoPoly(j,xpts[i],alpha,beta);
    gamma[j] += tmpd*tmpd;
    alpha[j+1] += xpts[i]*tmpd*tmpd;
  }
  alpha[j+1] /= gamma[j];
  beta[j] = gamma[j]/gamma[j-1];
}

gamma[ndeg] = 0.0;

for(i=0;i<npts;i++){
  tmpd = LS_OrthoPoly(ndeg,xpts[i],alpha,beta);
  gamma[ndeg] += tmpd*tmpd;
}

beta[ndeg] = gamma[ndeg]/gamma[ndeg-1];

for(j=0;j<=ndeg;j++){
  lscoeffs[j] = 0.0;
  for(i=0;i<npts;i++)
    lscoeffs[j] = lscoeffs[j] + funcvals[i]*
                  LS_OrthoPoly(j,xpts[i],alpha,beta);
  lscoeffs[j] /= gamma[j];
}

delete[] gamma;

return;
}
```

There are two issues that we would like to point your attention to as you examine this function:

REMARK 1: If you examine the mathematical formulation carefully, you notice that the function relies on the orthogonal polynomial function being defined. The definition for the orthogonal polynomial requires the α and β to be defined. At first glance, there appears to be a circular dependency! However, such is not the case. Observe that whenever the orthogonal polynomial needs to know α and β, they have already been properly calculated. This is a highly inductive process. The ordering of calculation is very important in this routine. You should take the time to chart out the dependencies; observe how timing is everything!

REMARK 2: Dynamic memory allocation within functions is quite natural, and most programmers have no problem allocating arrays within functions. However, many programmers become negligent and do not deallocate the temporary memory that they needed. In the function presented here, the array *gamma* is allocated for temporary usage within this function. Note that this temporary array is deallocated (using the **delete[]** command) just prior to the function returning. Recall that the local variables within a function are local to the function and go away when the function concludes. Hence, if memory is allocated to *gamma* and is not returned to the system prior to the function returning, that memory is "lost" for the remainder of the runtime of your program! This is what is referred to as a *memory leak*. If you view memory as a conserved quantity (that is, that for every allocation there is a deallocation), then if you forget to deallocate a piece of memory prior to it being inaccessible by the user (in this case owing to the pointer variable going away when the function returns), then memory has "leaked," and hence the total amount of memory available for dynamic memory allocation is reduced.

PROGRAMMER BEWARE!

- Beware of memory leaks! For every allocate (**new**) there should be a deallocate (**delete[]**).

Warning

Using the Switch

Once again, we use the concept of recursion for quickly implementing the mathematical definition of the orthogonal polynomial. Again, we have two base cases, when the index of the polynomial is 0 or 1; for all other positive values of the index, the value of the polynomial is calculated using the recursion relation.

Software
Suite

```
double LS_OrthoPoly(int j, double x, double *alpha,
  double*beta){
int i;
double value;

switch(j){
case 0:
  value = 1.0;
  break;
case 1:
  value = x - alpha[j];
  break;
default:
  value = (x-alpha[j])*LS_OrthoPoly(j-1,x,alpha,beta) -
    beta[j-1]*LS_OrthoPoly(j-2,x,alpha,beta);
  break;
 }

 return value;
}
```

Once the coefficients have been calculated, then the least-squares approximating polynomial can be evaluated at any point. Next we present the implementation of this function.

```
double LSApproximatingPoly(int ndeg, double x, double *alpha,
   double *beta, double *lscoeffs){
   double value = 0.0;

   for(int i=0;i<=ndeg;i++)
     value += lscoeffs[i]*LS_OrthoPoly(i, x, alpha, beta);

   return value;

}
```

C++ Compound Assignment

Look carefully at the previous function. You will notice something new: the "+=" operator. This is a convenient C++ shorthand used for accumulation. The C++ statement

```
a += b;
```

is equivalent to the statement

```
a = a + b;
```

which is to be interpreted as taking the value of b and accumulating it to a. Table 3.1 gives a collection of these "shorthand" programming notations used in C++.

Pre- and postincrementing/decrementing may be somewhat confusing at first, but consider the following code:

```
j = i++;
k = ++p;
```

in which we use the postincrementor in the first line and the preincrementor in the second line. If we expand this shorthand notation into its traditional C++ code, we obtain the following:

```
j = i;
i = i + 1;

p = p + 1;
k = p;
```

Notice that in the first example, the postincrementor is used, so the assignment is accomplished first and then the increment. The exact opposite happens when the preincrementor is used. When used as an individual statement (such as we have used it in **for** statements), the two give identical results.

Table 3.1: C++ compound assignment operations.

Shorthand	Description
i++	Preincrement, i = i + 1
++i	Postincrement, i = i + 1
i−−	Predecrement, i = i − 1
−−i	Postdecrement, i = i − 1
i += j	i = i + j
i −= j	i = i − j
i *= j	i = i * j
i /= j	i = i / j

PROGRAMMER BEWARE!

- C++ shorthand can be convenient but deadly! A slip of the finger and += can be =+, which is a valid C++ statement, setting one value as the positive value of another value! But that was not what was intended!

Warning

We next present a program that uses the functions just described. Notice the general structure of this program:

1. Query the user to obtain information.
2. Allocate necessary memory (dynamically).
3. Produce a grid, and evaluate the function to be approximated.
4. Compute least-squares coefficients by calling LS_ComputeCoeffs.
5. Evaluate approximating polynomial on a fine grid for plotting.
6. Deallocate dynamic memory used within the program.

Software

Suite

```cpp
#include <iostream.h>
#include "SCchapter3.h"

double func(double x);

int main(int argc, char * argv[]){
  int i;
  int degree, polypnts;
  int npts = 1000;       //number of points used for plotting
  double xpt, soln, approx;

  cout << "Enter the degree of the least-squares polynomial: ";
  cin >> degree;

  cout << "Enter the number of points to use for evaluation: ";
  cin >> polypnts;

  double * poly_xpts = new double[polypnts];
  double * func_vals = new double[polypnts];
  double * alpha      = new double[degree+1];
  double * beta       = new double[degree+1];
  double * lscoeffs   = new double[degree+1];

  CreateGrid_EvenlySpaced(polypnts, poly_xpts, -1.0, 1.0);

  for(i=0;i<polypnts;i++){
    func_vals[i] = func(poly_xpts[i]);
  }

  LS_ComputeCoeffs(polypnts, poly_xpts, func_vals, degree,
                   alpha, beta, lscoeffs);
```

```
for(i=0;i<npts;i++){
  xpt = -1.0 + 2.0*i/(npts-1);
  soln = func(xpt);
  approx = LSApproximatingPoly(degree, xpt, alpha,
                                       beta, lscoeffs);
  cout << xpt << " " << soln << " " << approx << endl;
}

delete[] alpha;
delete[] beta;
delete[] lscoeffs;
delete[] poly_xpts;
delete[] func_vals;
}

double func(double x){
  double y;

  y = 1.0 + 25.0*x*x;
  y = 1.0/y;

  return y;
}
```

Key Concept

As a programmer, you should have a game plan! Always take a few moments to formulate the general structure of your program; this will save you much time in the end.

3.1.8 Introduction to Classes

In the previous chapter, we discussed the two fundamental concepts within C++: the idea of *functions* and the idea of *classes*. In this section, we will present a brief overview of how to declare, define, and use classes. We will use as an example the class *SCVector* found in the *software suite*. We will then illustrate the rationale of classes by defining a new class to be used in a least-squares example.

This section is meant only to be a brief overview of classes for the cases where classes are used in this book. To discover the full power of classes (through inheritance, etc.), we refer the reader to [86].

Software
Suite

Class Declaration

Classes are *user-defined* data types. We first present the declaration of our user-defined class *SCVector*, and then we will comment on the specifics of the declaration.

```
class SCVector{
  private:
```

```
  int    dimension;
  double *data;

 public:
  SCVector(int dim);
  SCVector(const SCVector& v);
  SCVector(int col, const SCMatrix &A);
  ~SCVector();

  int    Dimension() const;
  double Length();      /* Euclidean Norm of the Vector */
  void   Normalize();

  double Norm_l1();
  double Norm_l2();
  double Norm_linf();
  double MaxMod();
  double ElementofMaxMod();
  int MaxModindex();

  //***********************
  // User-Defined Operators
  //***********************
  int operator==(const SCVector& v) const;
  int operator!=(const SCVector& v) const;
  SCVector & operator=(const SCVector& v);

  double  operator()(const int i) const;
  double& operator()(const int i);

  void Print() const;
  void Initialize(double a);
  void Initialize(double *v);
};
```

We now present some remarks concerning this code.

- Observe the structure of a class declaration. First, there is the use of the key word *class*, followed by the user-defined variable name, which will be used later when creating instantiations of this class. Within the {}, there are three key words used to denote accessibility:
    1. *Private* refers to those variables and functions that cannot be accessed from outside of the object, and for which access is noninheritable.
    2. *Protected* refers to those variables and functions that cannot be accessed from outside of the object, and for which access is inheritable.
    3. *Public* refers to those variables and functions that can be accessed from outside of the object.

  Those variables and methods within the private section are only accessible from within the object, whereas variables and methods in the public section are accessible outside the object.

- The declaration of a class must be concluded by a ";".
- You may have noticed that we used the term *object* in these definitions, and you may have assumed that we really meant class. We did not. In C++ nomenclature, a *class* refers to the declaration of the user-defined variable, whereas an *object* is an instance of a variable of that type. Take for example the predefined variable type *int*. In C++ parlance, we would refer to our declaration of *int* as the class and to every variable that we create as "an object of type *int*."
- Within the private section of this class, we have declared two variables, *dimension* and *data*, that can be used within the object.
- In the public section, we have declared a collection of methods that access or modify the data contained within the object.

Method Definitions

We now discuss some of the method definitions for this class found within the *software suite*.

Each method has the following structure:

```
<return type> ClassName::MethodName(<argument list>)
```

The return type, method name, and argument list are similar to what we have seen with functions. In the case of a class method, we also designate the class to which the method is assigned (using the "ClassName::" syntax).

CONSTRUCTOR. A constructor is the first function that is called when the object is instantiated. In this case, the constructor requires the input of the dimension of the vector. The constructor then uses this information to initialize the local variable *dimension* and to allocate memory that is assigned to the local variable *data*.

```
SCVector::SCVector(int dim){
  dimension = dim;
  data = new double[dimension];

  for(int i=0;i<dimension;i++)
    data[i] = 0.0;
}
```

COPY CONSTRUCTOR. A copy constructor is used whenever a copy is required (either by the programmer or the program). The object to be copied is passed as an argument to this method. Notice that the argument is passed as a *const* (meaning that within the method we cannot change the value of the object *v*) and that it is passed by reference (denoted by the "&") so that no new memory allocation is required to store the contents of *v* (as opposed to if we had passed by value). The current object is initialized so that it is a copy of *v*.

```
SCVector::SCVector(const SCVector &v){
  dimension = v.Dimension();
  data = new double[dimension];
```

Software Suite

```
   for(int i=0;i<dimension;i++)
     data[i] = v.data[i];
}
```

DESTRUCTOR. This method is called automatically when the object is released back to the operating system. Its purpose is to clean up the storage contained within the object.

```
SCVector::~SCVector(){
  dimension = 0;
  delete[] data;
  data = NULL;
}
```

GENERAL METHODS. From the class declaration previously presented, we present two method definitions, one that merely accesses the data with the object to provide a result and the second that acts upon the data contained within the object. Consider the following two method definitions:

```
double SCVector::Norm_l2(){
  double sum = 0.0;
  for(int i=0;i<dimension;i++)
    sum += data[i]*data[i];
  return(sqrt(sum));
}

void SCVector::Normalize(){
  double tmp = 1.0/Norm_l2();
  for(int i=0;i<dimension;i++)
    data[i] = data[i]*tmp;
}
```

In the first method, we use the information stored within the class (contained within *data*) to compute the L_2 norm of the vector, and we return this information at the conclusion of the function. In the second method, we act upon the data contained within the object by normalizing the value of the vector to one. Notice that within the *Normalize* method we call local class method *Norm_l2* to obtain the discrete L_2 norm of the vector.

Overloaded Operators

In addition to class methods, we can also *overload* operators so that they are appropriately defined for our new user-defined data type. Consider the following operator declaration:

```
SCVector operator+(const SCVector& v1, const SCVector& v2);
```

and corresponding operator definition

```
SCVector operator+(const SCVector& v1, const SCVector& v2){
  int min_dim = min_dimension(v1,v2);
  SCVector x(min_dim);
  for(int i=0;i<min_dim;i++)
    x(i) = v1(i) + v2(i);
  return x;
}
```

The basic syntax is as follows:

```
<return type> operator<symbol>(<argument 1>,<argument 2>)
```

where the return type, symbol, and arguments are to be supplied by the programmer. Using this syntax we appropriately define what it means to add (using the binary operator "+") two SCVector objects. We will illustrate how this is used in the following.

Object Allocation and Usage

To understand how all the information presented here is used, consider the following code:

```
SCVector a(3),b(3),c(3);  //allocate SCVectors a,b,c
                          //Constructor is called automatically to
                          //allocate memory and provide default
                          //initialization

a(0) = 1.0;  //Initialize the values of 'a' using () operator
a(1) = 2.0;  //defined for the class SCVector
a(2) = 3.0;

b(0) = -2.0; //Initialize the values of 'b'using () operator
b(1) = 1.0;  //defined for the class SCVector
b(2) = 3.0;

c = a+b;     //Use overloaded operator '+' to compute
             //the sum of a and b, and use the
             //overloaded operator '=' to assign
             //the value to 'c'

c.Print();   //Use print method to print the value of c
```

Execution of this code within a program would yield the result [-1.0; 3.0; 6.0] printed to standard output.

PUTTING IT INTO PRACTICE

The least-squares example presented earlier provides a good motivation for using *classes*. Observe that associated with each least-squares approximating polynomial we form, we need to keep track of three arrays – *alpha*, *beta*, and *lscoeffs* – for each approximating polynomial! Is this doable? Certainly. But from an organizational standpoint, we would like to be able to automatically associate the appropriate arrays with the right polynomials. Imagine that we were asked to handle 20–100 least-squares approximations simultaneously! This is doable but extremely messy. However, recall that classes can provide us a means of organizing our data.

First, we begin by giving the class *declaration*:

```
class LSPoly{
 private:
  int ndeg;
  double *alpha, *beta, *lscoeffs;

  double LSPolyOrtho(int j, double x);

 public:
  LSPoly();
  ~LSPoly();

  void PrintCoeffs();
  int Initialize(int npts, int in_ndeg, double * xpts,
                 double * funcvals);
  double Evaluate(double x);
};
```

In addition to the four variables *ndeg*, *alpha*, *beta*, and *lscoeffs* declared within the class, five methods associated with this class have declared. We present the definitions of these five methods and provide a brief explanation of each.

DEFAULT CONSTRUCTOR. This method is called automatically when the object is instantiated if no other constructor is called. Observe that in this case we initialize variables to either zero or NULL (whichever is appropriate for the variable type).

```
LSPoly::LSPoly(){
  ndeg = 0;
  alpha = NULL;
  beta = NULL;
  lscoeffs = NULL;
}
```

DESTRUCTOR. This method is called automatically when the object is destroyed.

```
LSPoly::~LSPoly(){
  delete[] alpha;
```

```
  delete[] beta;
  delete[] lscoeffs;

  ndeg = 0;
  alpha = NULL;
  beta = NULL;
  lscoeffs = NULL;
}
```

PRIVATE METHOD. The next method is a "private" method; that is, it can only be called from within the object. This means that the only valid places that this function can be called are within other methods defined within the object.

```
double LSPoly::LSPolyOrtho(int j,double x){
  int i;
  double value;

  switch(j){
  case 0:
    value = 1.0;
    break;
  case 1:
    value = x - alpha[j];
    break;
  default:
    value = (x-alpha[j])*LSPolyOrtho(j-1,x) -
      beta[j-1]*LSPolyOrtho(j-2,x);
    break;
  }

  return value;
}
```

PUBLIC METHOD. The next three methods are "public" methods; that is, they can be accessed from outside the object. The first method accomplishes the initialization of the class that consists of computing the values stored in *alpha*, *beta*, and *gamma*. The second method allows us to print the contents of the object, and the third method allows us to evaluate the least-squares approximation using the information stored within the object.

```
int LSPoly::Initialize(int npts, int in_ndeg, double * xpts,
                       double * funcvals){
  int i,j;
  double xi,tmpd;

  if(alpha!=NULL){
    cerr << "Error:: LSPoly has already been initialized\n";
```

```
      return 0;
  }

  ndeg = in_ndeg;

  /* Storage for this object */
  lscoeffs = new double[ndeg+1];
  alpha = new double[ndeg+1];
  beta = new double[ndeg+1];

  /* Storage for just this method */
  double * gamma = new double[ndeg+1];

  /////////////////////////
  // Compute average first
  xi = 0.0;
  for(i=0;i<npts;i++){
    xi += xpts[i];
  }
  xi /= (double) npts;
  /////////////////////////

  gamma[0] = npts;
  alpha[0] = beta[0] = 0.0;
  alpha[1] = xi;

  for(j=1;j<=ndeg-1;j++){
    gamma[j]   = 0.0;
    alpha[j+1] = 0.0;
    for(i=0;i<npts;i++){
      tmpd = LS_OrthoPoly(j,xpts[i],alpha,beta);
      gamma[j] += tmpd*tmpd;
      alpha[j+1] += xpts[i]*tmpd*tmpd;
    }
    alpha[j+1] /= gamma[j];
    beta[j] = gamma[j]/gamma[j-1];
  }

  gamma[ndeg] = 0.0;

  for(i=0;i<npts;i++){
    tmpd = LSPolyOrtho(ndeg,xpts[i]);
    gamma[ndeg] += tmpd*tmpd;
  }

  beta[ndeg] = gamma[ndeg]/gamma[ndeg-1];

  for(j=0;j<=ndeg;j++){
    lscoeffs[j] = 0.0;
```

```
      for(i=0;i<npts;i++)
        lscoeffs[j] = lscoeffs[j] + funcvals[i]*
                           LSPolyOrtho(j,xpts[i]);
      lscoeffs[j] /= gamma[j];
    }

    delete[] gamma;

    return 1;
}
void LSPoly::PrintCoeffs(){
   cout << endl;
   cout << "********************************" << endl;
   cout << "i\talpha\tbeta\tlscoeffs" << endl;

   for(int j=0;j<=ndeg;j++){
     cout << j << "\t" << alpha[j] << "\t";
     cout << beta[j] << "\t" << lscoeffs[j] << endl;
   }

   cout << "********************************" << endl << endl;

   return;
}
double LSPoly::Evaluate(double x){
   double value = 0.0;

   for(int i=0;i<=ndeg;i++)
     value += lscoeffs[i]*LSPolyOrtho(i,x);

   return value;
}
```

Now, we want to put it all together into one piece of code. Using the preceding information, we have now declared a class named LSPoly, and we have provided definitions to all its methods. We now use this new user-defined variable in the program that follows.

```
#include <iostream.h>
#include "SCchapter3.h"

double func(double x);

int main(int argc, char * argv[]){
  int i;
  int degree, polypnts;
  int npts = 1000;       //number of points used for plotting
  double xpt, soln, approx;

  LSPoly poly;  // Our user-defined class!
```

```
      cout << "Enter the degree of the least-squares polynomial: ";
      cin >> degree;

      cout << "Enter the number of points to use for evaluation: ";
      cin >> polypnts;

      double * poly_xpts = new double[polypnts];
      double * func_vals = new double[polypnts];

      CreateGrid_EvenlySpaced(polypnts, poly_xpts, -1.0, 1.0);

      for(i=0;i<polypnts;i++){
        func_vals[i] = func(poly_xpts[i]);
      }

      poly.Initialize(polypnts,degree,poly_xpts,func_vals);

      for(i=0;i<npts;i++){
        xpt = -1.0 + 2.0*i/(npts-1);
        soln = func(xpt);
        approx = poly.Evaluate(xpt);
        cout << xpt << " " << soln << " " << approx << endl;
      }

      delete[] poly_xpts;
      delete[] func_vals;
    }

    double func(double x){
      double y;

      y = 1.0 + 25.0*x*x;
      y = 1.0/y;

      return y;
    }
```

We want to draw your attention to certain key items within this program:

- We begin by instantiating a variable of type LSPoly, just like creating a "regular" (predefined) variable. As previously stated, when the variable is initiated, the constructor is called.

- To access both variables and methods that are public, we use the "." notation.

  ```
  <variable name>.<object variable>
  ```

  or

  ```
  <variable name>.<method>( ... <method argument list> ... )
  ```

  In our example, we access the *Initialize* method as follows:

  ```
  poly.Initialize(polypnts,degree,poly_xpts,func_vals);
  ```

where *poly* is the name of the object and *Initialize* is the name of the public method that we want to access.

If, instead of the object, we were using a pointer to the object, we use the "−>" notation as follows:

```
<pointer variable name>-><object variable>
```

or

```
<pointer variable name>-><method>( ... <method argument list>
                                     ... )
```

- All the information necessary for the least-squares approximation is stored within the object, and hence the call for evaluating the least-squares polynomial is merely the call

```
approx = poly.Evaluate(xpt);
```

3.1.9 Multidimensional Interpolations

We can extend the interpolation methods we have presented so far in two or three dimensions by constructing appropriate two- or three-dimensional polynomials. In two dimensions, for example, we have

$$f(x, y) = \sum_k \alpha_k \phi_k(x, y),$$

Figure 3.10: Standard domains for the quadrilateral (left) and triangular (right) expansion in terms of the Cartesian coordinates ξ_1, ξ_2.

where α_k are the unknown coefficients, and the exact form of the polynomial basis $\phi_k(x, y)$ depends on the shape of the computational domain. To simplify the presentation, we first consider canonical domains, and subsequently we present mapping techniques to deal with more general domains. The approach presented here is typically followed in finite element methods (see [63]), where polynomial approximations in subdomains (the "elements") are required; however, this polynomial approximation is general and easy to implement.

3.1.10 Simple Domains

The canonical domains we consider are the square and the triangular domains with the coordinates $\xi_1 \in [-1, 1]$ and $\xi_2 \in [-1, 1]$ being the normalized coordinates as shown in Figure 3.10. Similar extensions can be constructed in three dimensions for a standard hexahedron and a tetrahedron. In Figure 3.11 we construct *Pascal's diagram* to demonstrate graphically the polynomial space for each region.

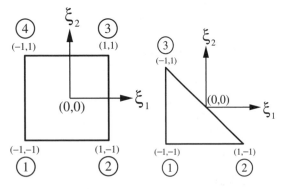

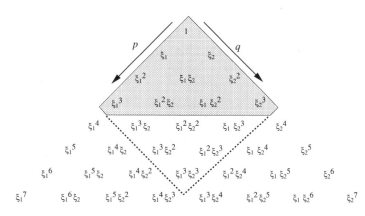

Figure 3.11: Pascal's diagram showing the polynomial space for the triangular expansion (shaded region) and square region (shaded region plus values within dotted line). The example here is for a cubic polynomial approximation.

We first consider the square domain, for which it is computationally efficient to split directions by constructing tensor products of the form

$$f(\xi_1, \xi_2) \approx \sum_p \sum_q \alpha_{pq} \phi_p(\xi_1) \phi_q(\xi_2).$$

Let us rewrite this equation using one-dimensional Lagrangian interpolants $h_i(\xi)$, that is,

$$f(\xi_1, \xi_2) \approx \sum_p \sum_q f_{pq} h_p(\xi_1) h_q(\xi_2),$$

where f_{pq} are the function values at the node (p, q).

In the standard square, *bilinear interpolation* is achieved by employing the one-dimensional linear interpolants

$$h_i(\xi) = \frac{1}{2}(1 \pm \xi), \quad i = 1, 2$$

and thus

$$f(\xi_1, \xi_2) \approx \frac{1}{4}[f_1(1 - \xi_1)(1 - \xi_2)] + \frac{1}{4}[f_2(1 + \xi_1)(1 - \xi_2)]$$

$$+ \frac{1}{4}[f_3(1 + \xi_1)(1 + \xi_2)] + \frac{1}{4}[f_4(1 - \xi_1)(1 + \xi_2)],$$

where we have used a counterclockwise convention to number the corners of the domain, and f_i denotes the function values at each vertex starting from the lower left corner (see Figure 3.10).

PUTTING IT INTO PRACTICE

We can implement this formula as follows:

```
double Square_2dInterpolant(SCPoint x, int npts,
   double *funcvals){
  double value = 0.;
  double h[4];
```

Software

Suite

```
if(npts != 4){
  cerr << "Error in Square_2dInterpolant -- ";
  cerr << "Invalid npts given" << endl;
  return value;
}

h[0] = 0.5*(1.0-x(0));
h[1] = 0.5*(1.0+x(0));
h[2] = 0.5*(1.0-x(1));
h[3] = 0.5*(1.0+x(1));

value = funcvals[0]*h[0]*h[2] + funcvals[1]*h[1]*h[2] +
        funcvals[2]*h[1]*h[3] + funcvals[3]*h[0]*h[3];

return value;
}
```

In this routine, we rely on the use of the data type SCPoint, which is a user-defined *class* included in the *software suite*. What is important for you to know concerning SCPoint is that if P is a variable of type SCPoint, then the coordinate (x, y) is stored as $(P(0), P(1))$. Hence, in this two-dimensional example, we are providing an SCPoint that has two accessible values, $x(0)$ and $x(1)$: $x(0) = \xi_0$ and $x(1) = \xi_1$.

Let us observe a few items within this code:

- Notice that because we know how many interpolants we will need, we can use static allocation of an array for holding the temporary values of the interpolants. If instead of four points we knew that we would use nine points, then we could allocate h[9] instead of h[4]. Obviously this is much easier than typing h0, h1, ... h8! It would also be perfectly valid to use dynamic memory allocation here; we have chosen not to for optimization reasons. For such a small number of variables, the cost of dynamic memory allocation outweighs the convenience.

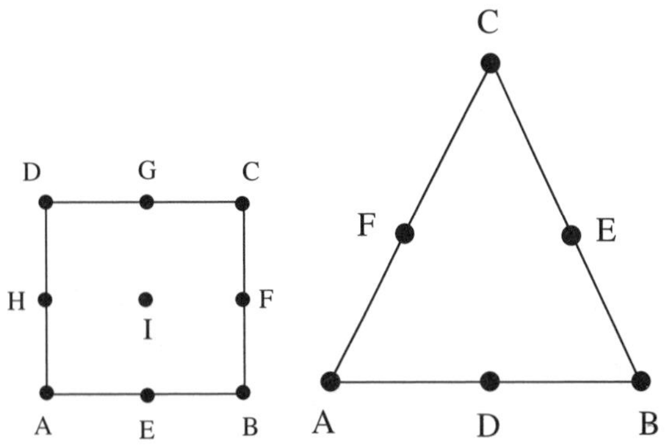

Figure 3.12: Domain and points where the data are specified for a square (left) and a triangle (right).

- In this function, we introduce the concept of *argument checking*. We have written the preceding function with the intention of providing the two-dimensional bilinear interpolation. From the theory, we see that this requires that four function values be given. What would happen if we are only given three function values (that is, what if the user had only allocated and assigned values for funcvals[0], funcvals[1], and funcvals[2])? Using this function would be invalid, and in all likelihood our program would crash! Quite often programmers introduce *checks* into their code to help minimize such mistakes. In this case, we check to make sure that we have received *npts* = 4; if not, we issue a warning that we received an invalid *npts* value, and we return 0.0.

- Notice that we used *cerr* instead of *cout*. The object *cerr* is an output object like *cout* and is also declared in *iostream.h*. The difference between *cout* and *cerr* is that *cerr* writes to **standard error** instead of standard output (which may or may not be the same actual output device).

Carefully designed argument checking can save you hours of debugging time. Plan ahead for your own possible mistakes – and prevent them from occurring.

Key Concept

High-Order Interpolation

Higher order approximations can be constructed if more information about the function $f(x)$ is given. Typically, that information may be available at the midpoints of the edges of the domain or even at the center of the domain. In this case, we need to first construct higher order one-dimensional Lagrangian interpolants. Let us consider the cases of having one or two extra interior points distributed equidistantly along the edge. From their definition we have that

$$h_3(\xi) = 1 - \xi^2 \quad \text{and} \quad h_4(\xi) = 1 - 27\xi^3 - 9\xi^2 + 27\xi + 9.$$

With these four one-dimensional Lagrangian interpolants we can construct up to third-order polynomial approximations in a square domain if information is given at all the points A, B, ..., I, as shown in Figure 3.12. As an example, let us assume that we have available $f(A)$, $f(B)$, $f(C)$, $f(D)$, and $f(E)$. Then the interpolants (also called *shape functions*) are as follows:

$$h_A = \frac{1}{4}(1 - \xi_1)(1 - \xi_2) - \frac{1}{2}h_E, \quad h_B = \frac{1}{4}(1 + \xi_1)(1 - \xi_2) - \frac{1}{2}h_E,$$

$$h_C = \frac{1}{4}(1 - \xi_1)(1 + \xi_2), \quad h_D = \frac{1}{4}(1 + \xi_1)(1 + \xi_2),$$

$$h_E = \frac{1}{2}(1 - \xi_1^2).$$

Let us now assume that in addition we also have function values at the points I and F. Then the above interpolants can be easily modified to handle this case as well by adding extra terms that reflect this interaction:

$$h_A = \frac{1}{4}(1 - \xi_1)(1 - \xi_2) - \frac{1}{2}h_E - \frac{1}{4}h_I, \quad h_B = \frac{1}{4}(1 + \xi_1)(1 - \xi_2) - \frac{1}{2}h_E - \frac{1}{2}h_F - \frac{1}{4}h_I,$$

$$h_C = \frac{1}{4}(1 - \xi_1)(1 + \xi_2) - \frac{1}{2}h_F - \frac{1}{4}h_I, \quad h_D = \frac{1}{4}(1 + \xi_1)(1 + \xi_2) - \frac{1}{4}h_I,$$

$$h_E = \frac{1}{2}(1 - \xi_1^2)(1 - \xi_2) - \frac{1}{2}h_I, \quad h_F = \frac{1}{2}(1 + \xi_1)(1 - \xi_2^2) - \frac{1}{2}h_I,$$

$$h_I = (1 - \xi_1^2)(1 - \xi_2^2).$$

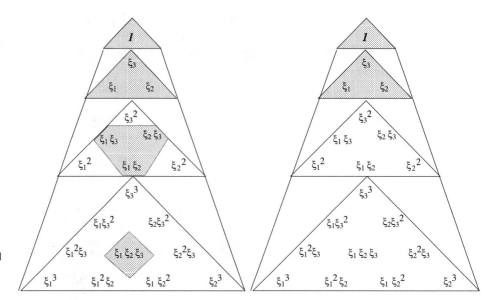

Figure 3.13: Pascal's diagram for hexahedral (left) and tetrahedal (right) domains.

These approximations can be extended to *hexahedral domains* using the tensor-product form. For example, in the case of *trilinear interpolation* with the function values specified at the eight vertices the shape functions are

$$h_i(\xi_1, \xi_2, \xi_3) = \frac{1}{8}(1 \pm \xi_1)(1 \pm \xi_2)(1 \pm \xi_3).$$

For higher order interpolations similar constructions can be obtained with the approximating polynomials defined by the hierarchy shown in Figure 3.13a, which is Pascal's diagram for hexahedral domains. For more details see [63, Chapter 3].

Nontensor Products

For a *triangular region*, however, tensor products are not so easily constructed unless special coordinate systems and transformations are introduced (see[63]). For linear interpolation, the shape functions are constructed, for example, by collapsing the corners D and C of the square to obtain

$$h_i^{\mathrm{tr}} = h_i^{\mathrm{sq}} = \frac{1}{4}(1 + (-1)^i r)(1 - s), \quad i = A, B,$$

and

$$h_C^{\mathrm{tr}} = h_C^{\mathrm{sq}} + h_D^{\mathrm{sq}} = \frac{1}{2}(1 + \xi_2).$$

These can be recomputed after we renormalize the coordinates so that $\xi_1 \in [0, 1]$ and $\xi_2 \in [0, 1]$ to obtain

$$h_A = 1 - \xi_1 - \xi_2, \quad h_B = \xi_1, \quad h_C = \xi_2.$$

Furthermore, if we have data at the midpoints of the edges of the triangle (see Figure 3.12b) we can construct complete *quadratic interpolation* using the shape functions

$$h_A = 1 - \xi_1 - \xi_2 - \frac{1}{2}h_D - \frac{1}{2}h_F,$$

$$h_B = \xi_1 - \frac{1}{2}h_D - \frac{1}{2}h_E,$$

$$h_C = \xi_2 - \frac{1}{2}h_E - \frac{1}{2}h_F, \quad h_D = 4\xi_1(1 - \xi_1 - \xi_2),$$

$$h_E = 4\xi_1\xi_2, \quad h_F = 4\xi_2(1 - \xi_1 - \xi_2).$$

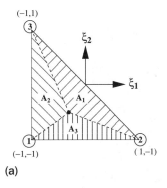
(a)

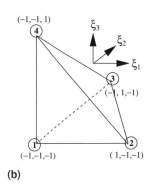
(b)

Figure 3.14: (a) The area coordinate system in the standard triangular region. Each coordinate l_1, l_2, and l_3 can be interpreted as the ratio of areas A_1, A_2, and A_3 over the total area. (b) The standard tetrahedral region for the definition of volume coordinates.

Another popular way of constructing linear interpolations in a triangular region is by using the area (and volume in three dimensions) coordinates, otherwise known as *barycentric* or *triangular/tetrahedral* coordinates.

The area coordinate system is illustrated in Figure 3.14a for the standard triangle. Any point in the triangle is described by the three coordinates l_1, l_2, and l_3, which can be interpreted as the ratio of the areas A_1, A_2, and A_3 over the total area $A = A_1 + A_2 + A_3$, that is,

$$l_1 = \frac{A_1}{A}, \qquad l_2 = \frac{A_2}{A}, \qquad l_3 = \frac{A_3}{A}.$$

Therefore l_1, l_2, and l_3 have a unit value at the vertices marked 1, 2, and 3 in Figure 3.14a, respectively. By definition these coordinates satisfy the relationship

$$l_1 + l_2 + l_3 = 1,$$

and they can be expressed in terms of ξ_1, ξ_2 as

$$l_1 = \frac{1}{2}(1 - \xi_1) - \frac{1}{2}(1 + \xi_2),$$

$$l_2 = \frac{1}{2}(1 + \xi_1),$$

$$l_3 = \frac{1}{2}(1 + \xi_2).$$

A similar construction follows for volume coordinates l_1, l_2, l_3, l_4, which are defined as having a unit value at the vertices marked 1, 2, 3, 4 in Figure 3.14b. In terms of the local Cartesian coordinates the volume coordinate system is defined as

$$l_1 = \frac{-(1 + \xi_1 + \xi_2 + \xi_3)}{2}, \qquad l_2 = \frac{(1 + \xi_1)}{2},$$

$$l_3 = \frac{(1 + \xi_2)}{2}, \qquad l_4 = \frac{(1 + \xi_3)}{2}.$$

3.1.11 Curvilinear Domains

In many practical simulation problems we need to perform polynomial interpolation in regions that may be of an arbitrary shape and orientation, as illustrated in Figure 3.15.

Figure 3.15: To construct a C^0 expansion from multiple elements of specified shapes (for example, triangles or rectangles), each elemental region Ω^e is mapped to a standard region Ω_{st} in which all local operations are evaluated [63].

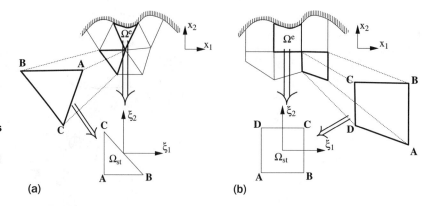

(a)   (b)

Such general domains can be broken into subdomains that are triangular or quadrilateral regions. These can then be transformed to standard regions, as shown in Figure 3.10. To treat these more general domains we follow the method presented in [63]; we introduce a one-to-one mapping denoted by

$$x_1 = \chi_1^e(\xi_1, \xi_2), \qquad x_2 = \chi_2^e(\xi_1, \xi_2)$$

in two dimensions, and similarly

$$x_1 = \chi_1^e(\xi_1, \xi_2, \xi_3), \qquad x_2 = \chi_2^e(\xi_1, \xi_2, \xi_3), \qquad x_3 = \chi_3^e(\xi_1, \xi_2, \xi_3)$$

in three dimensions.

For elemental shapes with straight sides a simple mapping may be constructed using linear interpolation. For example, to map a triangular region (as in Figure 3.15a) assuming that the coordinates of the triangle $\{(x_1^A, x_2^A), (x_1^B, x_2^B), (x_1^C, x_2^C)\}$ are known we can use

$$x_1 = \chi(\xi_1, \xi_2) = \frac{1}{2}x_1^A(-\xi_2 - \xi_1) + \frac{1}{2}x_1^B(1 + \xi_1) + \frac{1}{2}x_1^C(1 + \xi_2). \tag{3.14}$$

A similar approach leads to the bilinear mapping for an arbitrary shaped straight-sided quadrilateral where only the vertices need to be prescribed. For the straight-sided quadrilateral with vertices labeled as shown in Figure 3.15b the mapping is

$$x_1 = \chi_1(\xi_1, \xi_2) = x_1^A \frac{(1 - \xi_1)}{2} \frac{(1 - \xi_2)}{2} + x_1^B \frac{(1 + \xi_1)}{2} \frac{(1 - \xi_2)}{2}$$
$$+ x_1^D \frac{(1 - \xi_1)}{2} \frac{(1 + \xi_2)}{2} + x_1^C \frac{(1 + \xi_1)}{2} \frac{(1 + \xi_2)}{2}. \tag{3.15}$$

When developing a mapping it is important to ensure that the *Jacobian* of the mapping to the standard region is *nonzero* and of the same sign. To satisfy this condition when using the mappings given here, we require all elemental regions to have internal corners with angles that are less than $180°$ and so are convex.

To describe a straight-sided region we only need to know the values of the vertex locations. However, to describe a curved region we need more information. Specifically, as illustrated in Figure 3.16, we need a description of the shape of each edge in terms

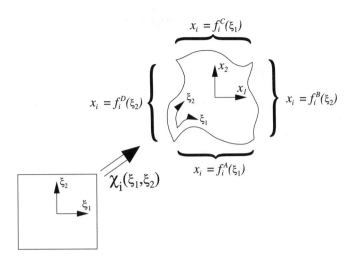

Figure 3.16: A general curved element can be described in terms of a series of parametric functions $f^A(\xi_1)$, $f^B(\xi_2)$, $f^C(\xi_1)$, and $f^D(\xi_2)$. By representing these functions as a discrete expansion we can construct a mapping $\chi_I(\xi_1, \xi_2)$ relating the standard region (ξ_1, ξ_2) to the deformed region (x_1, x_2) [63].

of a series of parametric functions, which we define as $f_i^A(\xi_1)$, $f_i^B(\xi_2)$, $f_i^C(\xi_1)$ and $f_i^D(\xi_2)$. Since our mapping $\chi_i(\xi_1, \xi_2)$ maps the whole of the standard region to the curvilinear quadrilateral domain, the parameter can be taken as the local coordinate ξ_1 or ξ_2.

A practical algorithm for doing this is the method of *blending function* as originally proposed by Gordon and Hall [48]. For the quadrilateral region shown in Figure 3.16 the *linear blending* function is given by

$$
\begin{aligned}
\chi_i(\xi_1, \xi_2) = {} & f^A(\xi_1)\frac{(1-\xi_2)}{2} + f^C(\xi_1)\frac{(1+\xi_2)}{2} \\
& + f^D(\xi_2)\frac{(1-\xi_1)}{2} + f^B(\xi_2)\frac{(1+\xi_1)}{2} \\
& - \frac{(1-\xi_1)}{2}\frac{(1-\xi_2)}{2} f^A(-1) - \frac{(1+\xi_1)}{2}\frac{(1-\xi_2)}{2} f^A(1) \\
& - \frac{(1-\xi_1)}{2}\frac{(1+\xi_2)}{2} f^C(-1) - \frac{(1+\xi_1)}{2}\frac{(1+\xi_2)}{2} f^C(1),
\end{aligned}
\tag{3.16}
$$

where the vertex points are continuous [for example, $f^A(-1) = f^D(-1)$] and hence the last four may also be expressed in terms of f^B and f^D. The mapping function of a curve-sided element is constructed by approximating the edge function in terms of the Lagrange polynomial, that is,

$$
f_i^A(\xi_1) \approx \sum_{p=0} f_i^A(\xi_{1,p}) h_p(\xi_1),
$$

and then using the linear blending function equation (3.16).

3.2 FOURIER SERIES REPRESENTATION

In this section, we will consider interpolations based on bases $\phi_k(x) = e^{ikx}$, $\cos kx$, and $\sin kx$. These are the Fourier representations in terms of complex exponentials, or cosines and sines, respectively; that is, we represent an arbitrary function in terms of pure *harmonic functions*. The Fourier method works in the *frequency domain* (or wavenumber domain) to provide information in the *physical domain*. This ability to relate frequency and space or time domains has made the Fourier transform one of the most useful tools of numerical and mathematical analysis. With the discovery of a fast algorithm in 1965, which reduces its computational complexity from $\mathcal{O}(N^2)$ to $\mathcal{O}(N \log_2 N)$, the FFT (fast Fourier transform) is also an extremely effective tool in scientific computing.

3.2.1 Convergence

The main idea of Fourier series is to represent a function $y = f(x)$ with a *basis* consisting of *sines* and *cosines* or *complex exponentials*. However, unlike the polynomial approximation, the convergence of Fourier series is not always guaranteed in the pointwise sense for an arbitrary function. Here, we will follow the exposition of Lanczos to present the basic material (see [66]).

In general, if the function $f(x)$ satisfies the *Dirichlet* conditions, it converges, but such conditions are too restrictive. Specifically, a function satisfies the Dirichlet conditions if the following are true:

- $f(x)$ is defined at every point in the interval $x \in [-\pi, \pi]$.
- $f(x)$ is single valued, piecewise continuous, and finite; for example, the function $f(x) = \log x$ is excluded.
- $f(x)$ is of bounded variation; that is, $f(x)$ cannot have an infinite number of maxima and minima.

A function that satisfies the Dirichlet conditions can be expanded into the following *convergent* infinite series:

$$f(x) = \frac{1}{2}a_0 + a_1 \cos x + a_2 \cos 2x + \cdots + b_1 \sin x + b_2 \sin 2x + \cdots, \qquad (3.17)$$

where the *Fourier coefficients* are computed from

$$a_k = \frac{1}{\pi} \int_{-\pi}^{\pi} f(x) \cos kx \, dx$$

and

$$b_k = \frac{1}{\pi} \int_{-\pi}^{\pi} f(x) \sin kx \, dx.$$

Equivalently, we can use complex exponentials as the basis to write

$$f(x) = \sum_{k=-\infty}^{\infty} c_k e^{ikx} \quad \text{with} \quad c_k = \frac{1}{2\pi} \int_{-\pi}^{\pi} f(x) e^{-ikx} dx. \qquad (3.18)$$

Also, the two sets of coefficients are related:

$$a_k = c_k + c_{-k}, \tag{3.19}$$

$$b_k = \frac{1}{i}(c_k - c_{-k}). \tag{3.20}$$

The truncated version of this series is called a *discrete Fourier series* and has the form

$$f_N(x) = \sum_{k=-(N-1)}^{N-1} c_k e^{ikx}.$$

As we will see momentarily, it can be constructed by sampling the function at N equidistant points

$$x_k = \frac{2\pi k}{N}, \quad k = 0, \ldots N - 1.$$

EXAMPLE. The Fourier coefficients of the Dirac function $\delta(x)$ are

$$a_k = \frac{1}{\pi} \int \delta(x) \cos kx \, dx = \frac{1}{\pi},$$

$$b_k = \frac{1}{\pi} \int \delta(x) \sin kx \, dx = 0,$$

$$c_k = \frac{1}{2\pi} \int \delta(x) e^{ikx} dx = \frac{1}{2\pi}.$$

The Fourier series of $\delta(x)$ for $N = 16$ and $N = 32$ are shown in Figure 3.17. The peak is sharper at higher values of N. The Dirac function does not satisfy the Dirichlet conditions.

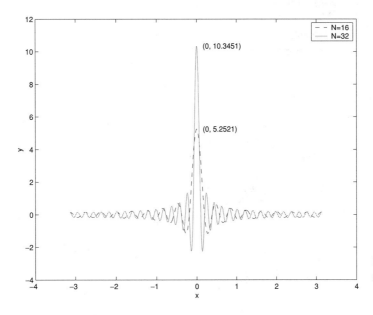

Figure 3.17: Fourier series of $\delta(x)$ for $N = 16$ and $N = 32$.

Dirichlet Kernel

We now return to the question of convergence and specifically the validity of Equations (3.17) and (3.18). What Dirichlet did was to substitute back into Equation (3.17) or (3.18) the expressions for the Fourier coefficients a_k, b_k, and c_k and truncate after N terms; then he let $N \to \infty$ to obtain

$$f_N(x) = \int_{-\pi}^{\pi} f(z) D_N(x - z) dz,$$

where

$$D_N(t) = \frac{\sin(N + 1/2)t}{2\pi \sin\left(\frac{t}{2}\right)}$$

is the **Dirichlet kernel**.

The Dirichlet kernel contains the partial sum

$$\sum_{-N}^{N} e^{ikt} = e^{-iNt}\left[1 + e^{it} + e^{2it} + \cdots + e^{2Nit}\right] = \frac{e^{i(N+1/2)t} - e^{-i(N+1/2)t}}{e^{i(1/2)t} - e^{-i(1/2)t}} = \frac{\sin\left(N + \frac{1}{2}\right)t}{\sin\frac{1}{2}t}.$$

This Dirichlet kernel can be thought as a "lens" that focuses the action at the point $z = x$. To ensure that $\lim_{N \to \infty} f_N(x) = f(x)$, it requires a very strong focusing power around the point $t = 0$ of the kernel $D_N(t)$. Mathematically, this can be expressed by the following two conditions (see [66]):

$$\text{(A)} \quad \lim_{N \to \infty} \int_{\epsilon}^{\pi} |D_N(t)| dt = 0,$$

$$\text{(B)} \quad \lim_{N \to \infty} \int_{-\epsilon}^{\epsilon} D_N(t) dt = 1$$

Condition (A) is not satisfied by the Dirichlet kernel because its secondary maxima are comparable to the primary maximum at $t = 0$.

Fejer's Construction

A different path to convergence was suggested by Fejer, who proposed an alternative summation procedure. He only imposed the constraint

$$\int_{-\pi}^{+\pi} |f(x)| dx < \infty,$$

which states that $f(x)$ is an *absolutely integrable* function. For example, the function $y = \log x$ is absolutely integrable but the function $y = 1/x$ is not. He then considered the partial sums

$$S_0 = \frac{1}{2}a_0,$$

$$S_1 = \frac{1}{2}a_0 + a_1 \cos x + b_1 \sin x,$$

$$\vdots$$

$$S_N = \frac{1}{2}a_0 + a_1 \cos x + \cdots + a_N \cos Nx + b_1 \sin x + \cdots + b_N \sin Nx$$

and constructed the sequence

$$f_1 = S_0, \quad f_2 = \frac{S_0 + S_1}{2}, \ldots, S_N = \frac{S_0 + S_1 + \cdots + S_{N-1}}{N}.$$

This sequence leads to the kernel

$$F_N(t) = \frac{\sin^2(Nt/2)}{2\pi N \sin^2(t/2)},$$

which is very focused and satisfies conditions (A) and (B). Unlike the previous case, the Fejer sequence converges at all points including points of discontinuity, where it converges at the *arithmetic mean* of the values at either side of the discontinuity.

3.2.2 Periodic Extension of Functions

Consider now that $f(x)$ is defined in the interval $x \in [0, \pi]$. We can still represent the function as a Fourier series by appropriately extending it. That is, we define it in the interval $x \in [-\pi, x]$ as well by representing it by either an even or an odd function. The Fourier series will then involve *cosines* or *sines*, respectively. If $f(x)$ is not zero at the boundary points the reflection as an odd function will cause a discontinuity at $x = 0, \pi$, which will lead to the so-called Gibbs phenomenon. This is manifested by wiggles around the discontinuity that affect the solution everywhere. This is avoided for an even function.

An example of a periodic extension for the function $y = x/\pi$, where $x \in [0, \pi]$, is shown in Figure 3.18. Both odd and even constructions are shown, with the latter resulting in a C^0 continuous extended function.

Let us now assume that $f(0) = 0$ and also $f(\pi) = 0$. Then we should expand $f(x)$ using a *sine series* because both the (extended) function and first derivative are continuous. We can compare the convergence rates of the two representations by performing integration by parts. For the *cosine series*

$$\int f(x) \cos kx \, dx = \frac{f(x) \sin kx}{k} - \frac{1}{k} \int f'(x) \sin kx \, dx,$$

and the second term gives

$$\int f'(x) \sin kx \, dx = -\frac{f'(x) \cos kx}{k} + \frac{1}{k} \int f''(x) \cos kx \, dx.$$

Thus, the convergence of

$$\int_0^\pi f(x) \cos kx \, dx$$

is dictated by the boundary term

$$\frac{(-1)^k f'(\pi) - f'(0)}{k^2} \sim \frac{1}{k^2}.$$

In contrast, the *sine series* representation leads to

$$\int_0^\pi f(x) \sin kx \, dx \to \frac{f(0) - (-1)^k f(\pi)}{k} \sim \frac{1}{k}.$$

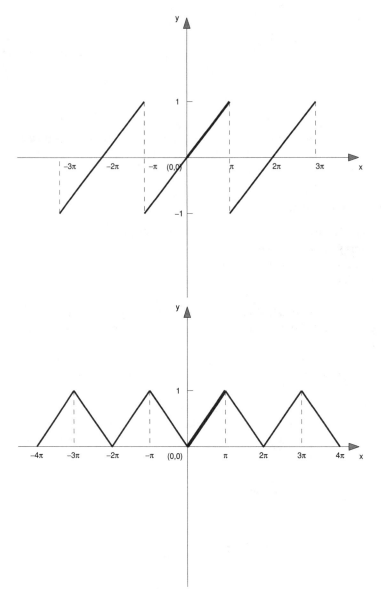

Figure 3.18: Periodic extensions of the function $y = x/\pi$, where $x \in [0, \pi]$ using an odd function extension (upper) and an even function extension (lower).

Now if

$$f(0) = f(\pi) = 0$$

this implies

$$\int_0^\pi f(x) \sin kx \, dx \to \frac{f''(x) \cos kx}{k^3} \to \frac{(-1)^k f''(\pi) - f''(0)}{k^3} \sim \frac{1}{k^3}.$$

Therefore, we conclude that in this case the sine series converges like $1/k^3$ (versus $1/k^2$ for the cosine series) and therefore the former is a better approach.

Some Properties of the Fourier Series

Fourier series have many interesting properties; see for example [62]. Two of the most important ones that are useful in theoretical work are

- **Bessel's inequality**, which states that projections are smaller than the projected function and thus

$$\int_{-\pi}^{\pi} \left[\frac{1}{2}a_0 + a_1 \cos x + \cdots + b_N \sin Nx \right]^2 dx \le \int_{-\pi}^{\pi} [f(x)]^2 \, dx, \text{ and}$$

- **Parseval's formula**, which is a direct consequence of the above, and states that

$$\pi[a_0^2 + a_1^2 + b_1^2 + a_2^2 + b_2^2 + \cdots] = \int_{-\pi}^{\pi} [f(x)]^2 dx.$$

This is obtained from Bessel's inequality, which in the limit of $N \to \infty$ becomes an equality; it is simply the definition of the Fourier series. Integrating both sides and using orthogonality we obtain Passeval's formula. This equation is very useful as it connects a vector of coefficients to a function in a unique way.

3.2.3 Differentiation and the Lanczos Filter

Taking derivatives of Fourier series of functions that are discontinuous is not a straightforward matter. Lanczos has devised a clever method in dealing with this, which we explain next.

Let us consider the truncated Fourier series

$$f_N(x) = \sum_{k=-(N-1)}^{N-1} c_k e^{ikx}$$

and from that the truncation error, which we also call the *residual*:

$$\eta_N(x) = \sum_{k=N}^{\infty} (c_k e^{ikx} + c_{-k} e^{-ikx}) = e^{iNx} \underbrace{\sum_{k=0}^{\infty} c_{N+k} e^{ikx}}_{\rho_N(x)} + e^{-iNx} \underbrace{\sum_{k=0}^{\infty} c_{-N-k} e^{ikx}}_{\rho_{-N}(x)}.$$

Examining the residual more carefully we observe that it consists of two contributions, $\rho_N(x)$, which is slowly varying, and e^{iNx}, which is rapidly varying. Thus, the error in the Fourier series has the structure of a *modulated wave*. This will have consequences when we attempt to take the derivative, the error of which is

$$\eta_N'(x) = iNe^{iNx}\rho_N(x) + e^{iNx}\rho_N'(x) - iNe^{-iNx}\rho_{-N}(x) + e^{-iNx}\rho_{-N}'(x).$$

We see that the differentiation of the high-frequency wave produces divergent terms proportional to N as $N \to \infty$.

To overcome this difficulty, Lanczos introduced a new differentiation operator $\mathcal{D}_N$ so that

$$\mathcal{D}_N \to \frac{d}{dx}, \quad N \to \infty.$$

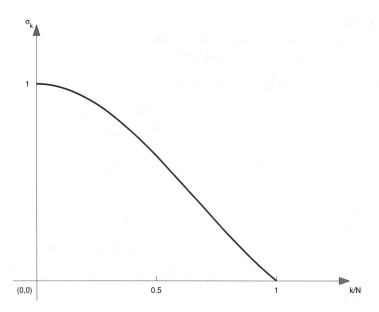

Figure 3.19: Plot of the Lanczos filter of Equation (3.21).

It is defined by

$$\mathcal{D}_N f = -\frac{f(x + \pi/N) - f(x - \pi/N)}{2\pi/N}.$$

If we apply, for example, this operator to the function $f(x) = e^{ikx}$ we obtain

$$\mathcal{D}_N e^{ikx} = i\frac{\sin k/N\,\pi}{\pi/N}e^{ikx} = \left(\frac{\sin \frac{\pi k}{N}}{k\frac{\pi}{N}}\right)(ik)e^{ikx},$$

where we recognize the term in parenthesis *(ik)* as being the d/dx derivative of e^{ikx}. We can then write

$$\mathcal{D}_N = \sigma_k \frac{d}{dx},$$

where

$$\sigma_k = \frac{\sin \pi k/N}{k\pi/N} \tag{3.21}$$

is the **Lanczos filter.** A plot of the Lanczos filter is shown in Figure 3.19. It has the value $\sigma_k = 1$ around the origin and it tends to zero for $k \to N$. Therefore, the action of this filter is to attenuate the contribution of the high frequencies.

We now apply the new differentiation operator to the residual previously obtained to get

$$\mathcal{D}_N \eta_N(x) = -e^{iNx}\mathcal{D}_N \rho_N(x) - e^{iNx}\mathcal{D}_N \rho_{-N}(x).$$

Both $\rho_N(x)$ and $\rho_{-N}(x)$ are smooth functions and their differentiation produces bounded terms. In addition, we observe that there are now no divergent terms (e.g., terms

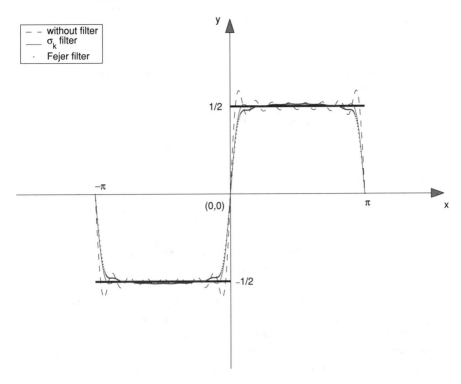

Figure 3.20: Step function and approximations using the Fourier series, the Lanczos-filtered series, and the Fejer construction; $N = 8$.

proportional to N) and thus the residual error for the new differentiation tends to zero, and in fact in the limit as $N \to \infty$ the derivative of $f(x)$ is obtained correctly at all points.

EXAMPLE 1. We first examine the action of the Lanczos filter in the approximation of $f(x)$ by a Fourier series. We choose the function shown in Figure 3.20, which has a discontinuity at $x = 0$ and is constant at values $\pm 1/2$ in the rest of the interval $x \in [-\pi, \pi]$.

Its Fourier representation is a sine series of the form

$$y(x) = \frac{2}{\pi}\left(\sin x + \frac{\sin 3x}{3} + \frac{\sin 5x}{5} + \cdots\right),$$

which we also plot in Figure 3.20 for $N = 8$. We observe the Gibbs phenomenon around the origin and also around $x = \pm\pi$ (i.e., the loss of convergence), which is not improved for higher values of N. We also plot the filtered Fourier series, that is, the modified series where each of the coefficients has been multiplied by σ_k; in this case a smooth representation is obtained. Finally, for comparison we also include the Fejer construction: the arithmetic mean of the partial sums. We see that this representation is also smooth but not as accurate as the Lanczos-filtered function.

We now turn to the question of differentiation of this function. Clearly

$$y'(x) = 0,$$

except at $x = 0$ where the derivative does not exist. The termwise standard differentiation of $y = f(x)$ gives

$$y'_N(x) = \frac{2}{\pi}(\cos x + \cos 3x + \cos 5x + \cdots),$$

which does not converge at any point x, except at $x = \pm\pi/2$. Thus, the singularity at $x = 0$ propagates its effect globally!

We then apply the Lanczos recipe, that is,

$$y'_N(x) = \frac{2}{\pi}\left[\frac{\sin\frac{\pi}{2N}}{\pi/2N}\cos x + \frac{\sin\frac{3\pi}{2N}}{\frac{3\pi}{2N}}\cos 3x + \cdots\right].$$

Now $y'(x)$ converges at all points, except at $x = 0$, where it grows to ∞, so that $\int_{-\epsilon/2}^{\epsilon/2} y'_N(x)dx \Rightarrow 1$, which is the $\delta(x)$ function!

EXAMPLE 2. We can also use the Lanczos recipe to construct Fourier series expansions for functions that are not absolutely square integrable, such as the function $y = 1/x$. To this end, we consider the function $y = \log x$, where $x \in [0, \pi]$, which is absolutely square integrable, and thus its Fourier series converges (recall Fejer). We then use the Lanczos recipe to take its derivative and observe that

$$x^{-1} = \frac{d}{dx}\log x;$$

thus we have the Fourier series

$$x^{-1} = \sum_k \sigma_k \frac{d}{dx}[\text{Fourier series of } \log x].$$

3.2.4 Trigonometric Interpolation

Trigonometric interpolation is a powerful tool in representing data and does not suffer from some of the problems we encountered with polynomial interpolation for certain functions (e.g. the Runge function). In fact, we can argue that generally trigonometric interpolation is superior to polynomial interpolation for data on equidistant grids.

We now consider the approximation problem, where we have a number m of basis functions involved that is less than the number of available data equidistant points n. Let us denote the function values by

$$y_\alpha = f(x_\alpha)$$

and the representation by

$$\bar{y} = \sum_{k=1}^{m} c_k\varphi_k(x), \ m \leq n.$$

As we have already seen in Section 3.1.7, in general $y_\alpha \neq \bar{y}(\alpha)$, and thus we try to minimize the square of this error. This is the method of least squares, which we apply here first for the case of

$$\varphi_k(x) = e^{ikx}.$$

The coefficients c_k are then computed using the minimization procedure outlined in Section 3.1.7 to get

$$c_k = \frac{1}{\gamma_k} \sum_{\alpha=1}^{N} y_\alpha \varphi_k^*(x_\alpha),$$

where $\varphi_k^*(x) = e^{-ikx}$ denotes the complex conjugate of $\varphi_k(x)$. Also, γ_k are normalization factors given by

$$\gamma_k = \sum_{\alpha=1}^{N} \varphi_k(x_\alpha) \varphi_k^*(x_\alpha).$$

The orthonormality condition implies that

$$\sum_{\alpha=1}^{N} \bar{y}_\alpha^2 = c_1^2 + c_2^2 + \cdots + c_m^2,$$

and thus the error in the approximation is

$$\eta^2 = \sum_{\alpha=1}^{N} (y_\alpha - \bar{y}_\alpha)^2 = \sum_{\alpha=1}^{N} y_\alpha^2 - (c_1^2 + c_2^2 + \cdots + c_m^2).$$

In summary, assuming that the positions of the data points x_α are chosen so that

$$x_\alpha = \alpha \frac{\pi}{N}, \quad a = -N, -(N-1), \ldots, (N-1), N$$

then the trigonometric interpolation problem using the complex exponentials as a basis is given by

$$\begin{cases} \bar{y}(x) = \sum_{k=-m}^{m} c_k e^{ikx}, \, m \leq N, \\ c_k = \frac{1}{2N} \sum_{\alpha=-N}^{N} y_\alpha e^{-ikx\alpha}, \end{cases}$$

where in the second sum the end values should be multiplied by 1/2.

We can also employ a real basis, either sines or cosines, to perform the approximation depending on whether the function $f(x)$ is odd or even, respectively.

For example, if the function is odd we employ the *sine series*

$$f(x) \approx b_1 \sin x + b_2 \sin 2x + \cdots + b_m \sin mx,$$

where

$$b_k = \frac{2}{N} \sum_{\alpha=1}^{N-1} y_\alpha \sin k\alpha \frac{\pi}{N}.$$

For $m = N$ we do not have an overdetermined problem anymore, and thus we can fit the data exactly to produce a sine *interpolation* instead of *approximation*. We note here, however, that b_N is undetermined in this case as we effectively have only $(N-1)$ data points. This is because $f(\pi) = 0$ in the previous approximation since $\sin kx = 0$ at $x = \pi$. Although the condition $f(0) = 0$ is satisfied automatically because of the odd property, the condition $f(\pi) = 0$ may not necessarily be true. This means that a Gibbs phenomenon may develop, which will limit convergence of the approximation to $1/k$. To enhance the convergence rate we can construct the following function:

$$g(x) = f(x) - (\alpha + \beta x),$$

which satisfies the conditions $g(0) = g(\pi) = 0$ if

$$\alpha = f(0) \quad \text{and} \quad \beta = \frac{f(\pi) - f(0)}{\pi}.$$

The sine representation of $g(x)$ now leads to a convergence rate dictated by $1/k^3$.

We can also employ the *cosine series* to approximate an even function. The expansion now has the form

$$f(x) \approx \frac{1}{2}a_0 + a_1 \cos x + \cdots + a_m \cos mx,$$

where

$$a_k = \frac{2}{N} \sum_{\alpha=0}^{N} y_\alpha \cos k\alpha \frac{\pi}{N}.$$

Here again in this summation the end values are multiplied by $1/2$. Notice also that to obtain an *interpolation* instead of an *approximation* the last term is replaced by $(1/2)a_N \cos Nx$.

REMARK: All the summations discussed here can be executed efficiently using the fast Fourier transforms covered in the next section.

3.2.5 Noisy Data

We can also use the properties of trigonometric interpolation to process noisy data, that is, to remove the major part of the noise that is superimposed on our data. Using wavelets is a great way of doing that (see Section 3.3) but we can also use Fourier analysis.

We have seen in the previous section that we can construct a sine Fourier series to approximate a function, which converges as $\sim 1/n^3$. However, any amount of noise, which can be thought of as a pulse of short duration, would lower the convergence of the series significantly, most probably to $\sim 1/n$.

- *The key idea is then to differentiate between good data and noise by looking at the decay of coefficients, for example $1/n^3$ versus $1/n$.*

Let us assume that we sample the function $f(x_k)$ over an interval L at the points

$$x_k = 0, h, 2h, \ldots, Nh.$$

Then, as before, we construct a new function $g(x)$ based on

$$\begin{cases} g(x) = f(x) - (\alpha + \beta x), \\ g(-x) = -g(x), \end{cases}$$

which leads to

$$g(x) = f(x) - f(0) - \frac{f(L) - f(0)}{L} x.$$

We then expand

$$g(x) = b_1 \sin \frac{\pi}{L} x + b_2 \sin \frac{2\pi}{L} x + \cdots,$$

where

$$b_k = \frac{2}{N} \sum_{\alpha=1}^{N-1} g(\alpha h) \sin k\alpha \frac{\pi}{N}.$$

From the physical point of view, we may not want any *overtones* contained in the harmonic analysis of $f(x)$ beyond a "cutoff" frequency v_0 so we set

$$b_k = 0, \quad k \leq m,$$

so that

$$\frac{m\pi}{L} x = 2\pi v_0 x$$

$$\Rightarrow \frac{m}{N} = 2v_0 h.$$

Therefore, we can represent the actual data by

$$g(x) \approx \sum_{k=1}^{m} b_k \sin k \frac{\pi}{L} x,$$

up to wavenumber (or frequency) m determined from the equation for $\frac{m}{N}$. In practice, the lower wavenumbers are also contaminated; that is, the coefficients $b_k \leq m$ are also influenced by noise but not as much as the upper part of the spectrum, which is produced entirely by noise.

3.2.6 Matrix Representation

Let us assume again that the function $f(x)$ is sampled at N equidistant points with spacing $\frac{2\pi}{N}$ between successive neighbors, with the first point at $x = 0$. The values of the function represented by the truncated Fourier series are given by

$$f_n = \sum_{k=0}^{N-1} c_k e^{ikn\frac{2\pi}{N}}, \quad n = 0, 1, \ldots, N - 1.$$

Let

$$w \equiv e^{\frac{2\pi i}{N}},$$

where $w^N = e^{2\pi i} = 1$, so w is the Nth root of unity. Then

$$f_n = \sum_{k=0}^{N-1} c_k w^{kn}.$$

We can then determine the Fourier coefficients c_k by solving the following linear system:

$$c_0 + c_1 + c_2 + \cdots + c_{N-1} = f_0,$$

$$c_0 + c_1 w + c_2 w^2 + \cdots + c_{N-1} w^{N-1} = f_1,$$

$$c_0 + c_1 w^{N-1} + c_2^{2(N-1)} + \cdots + c_{N-1} w^{(N-1)^2} = f_{N-1},$$

which we rewrite in matrix form as

$$\begin{bmatrix} 1 & 1 & \ldots & 1 \\ 1 & w & & w^{N-1} \\ \vdots & \vdots & & \vdots \\ 1 & w^{N-1} & & w^{(N-1)^2} \end{bmatrix} \begin{bmatrix} c_0 \\ c_1 \\ \vdots \\ c_{N-1} \end{bmatrix} = \begin{bmatrix} f_0 \\ f_1 \\ \vdots \\ f_{N-1} \end{bmatrix}.$$

The coefficients matrix, which we denote by $\mathbf{W}$, has a special structure similar to the Vandermonde matrix defined in Section 3.1.1 of polynomial interpolation. It can be readily inverted, since

$$\mathbf{W}\mathbf{W}^* = N\mathbf{I} \Rightarrow \mathbf{W}^{-1} = \frac{1}{N}\mathbf{W}^*,$$

where $\mathbf{W}^*$ is the complex conjugate of matrix $\mathbf{W}$. This can be easily verified by considering any entry of a matrix resulting from multiplying $\mathbf{W}$ with $\mathbf{W}^*$ and using orthogonality of vectors for the row-column combination.

Note that we can normalize the matrix $\mathbf{W}$ to produce a *unitary matrix* $\mathbf{U}$ by a simple rescaling, that is,

$$\mathbf{U} = \frac{\mathbf{W}}{\sqrt{N}}.$$

Circulant Matrices

We first give the definition:

- A *circulant* matrix is a periodic matrix with constant diagonals of the form

$$\mathbf{C} = \begin{bmatrix} c_0 & c_{N-1} & c_{N-2} & \ldots & c_1 \\ c_1 & c_0 & c_{N-1} & \ldots & c_2 \\ \vdots & \vdots & \vdots & & \vdots \\ c_{N-1} & c_{N-2} & c_{N-3} & \ldots & c_0 \end{bmatrix}.$$

There is a special relationship between the circular matrix and the Fourier matrix **W**. In general, the matrix **C** can be factored as

$$\mathbf{C} = \mathbf{Q}\mathbf{\Lambda}\mathbf{Q}^{-1},$$

where **Q** contains the eigenvectors of **C** as columns and $\mathbf{\Lambda}$ is a diagonal matrix containing the eigenvalues. For a circulant matrix

$$\mathbf{Q} = \mathbf{W};$$

that is, the eigenvectors of the circulant matrix **C** are the columns of the Fourier matrix **W**. This can be shown directly by substituting the columns of **W** into the eigenproblem

$$\mathbf{C}\mathbf{x} = \lambda\mathbf{x}.$$

3.2.7 The Fast Fourier Transform (FFT)

The fast Fourier transform (FFT) leads to a very smart factorization of the Fourier matrix **W** of size N. It produces a product of about $\mathcal{O}(\log_2 N)$ matrices with only about $\mathcal{O}(N \log_2 N)$ nonzero entries (total). Therefore, the cost to compute the discrete Fourier transform or its inverse is $\mathcal{O}(N \log_2 N)$ instead of $\mathcal{O}(N^2)$. The term $\log_2 N$ suggests a *fan-in* type algorithm (see Section 2.3.2) – this is what we will explain in this section.

We start by considering the system

$$\mathbf{C} = \mathbf{W}\mathbf{f},$$

where **W** is the Fourier matrix of order $N \times N$, **f** is the vector containing the function values at N points, and **C** is the vector of the Fourier coefficients. We recall the Vandermonde structure of the Fourier matrix, for example for $N = 4$ we have

$$\mathbf{W}_4 = \begin{bmatrix} 1 & 1 & 1 & 1 \\ 1 & w_4 & w_4^2 & w_4^3 \\ 1 & w_4^2 & w_4^4 & w_4^6 \\ 1 & w_4^3 & w_4^6 & w_4^9 \end{bmatrix} = \begin{bmatrix} 1 & 1 & 1 & 1 \\ 1 & i & -1 & -i \\ 1 & -1 & 1 & -1 \\ 1 & -i & -1 & i \end{bmatrix},$$

where $w_4 = e^{\frac{2\pi i}{4}} = \cos\frac{2\pi}{4} + i\sin\frac{2\pi}{4} = i$.

The special structure of $\mathbf{W}_4$ as well as the properties of the principal roots of unity suggest that the matrix $\mathbf{W}_8$ relates to $\mathbf{W}_4$. This is because $w_8^2 = w_4$, and in general

$$w_N^2 = w_M,$$

where $M = N/2$.

For example, the second row of $\mathbf{W}_8$ is

$$[1 \ \ w_8 \ \ w_8^2 \ \ w_8^3 \ \ w_8^4 \ \ w_8^5 \ \ w_8^6 \ \ w_8^7],$$

which we rewrite as

$$[1 \; w_8 \; w_4 \; w_8 w_4 \; w_4^2 \; w_8 w_4^2 \; w_4^3 \; w_8 w_4^3].$$

This can be further split into two subvectors of half size. The first one involves only w_4, that is,

$$[1 \; w_4 \; w_4^4 \; w_4^3],$$

formed by taking every other entry, starting with the first one. The second subvector is then

$$w_8[1 \; w_4 \; w_4^2 \; w_4^3],$$

and it is the same as the first subvector with a prefactor w_8.

We thus see that the rows of $\mathbf{W}_8$ are closely related to $\mathbf{W}_4$, and we can derive similar relations for $\mathbf{W}_{10}$, $\mathbf{W}_{32}$, and so on. This is the key observation that led Cooley and Tukey in the formulation of the FFT in 1965 [17]. It is based on the old idea of **divide and conquer**. Assuming that we have a Fourier matrix $\mathbf{W}_N$, where $N = 2^m$, then we can split the matrix in successive steps to smaller and smaller matrices. This is only part of the job as we still need to perform matrix–vector multiplications, and finally to compute the Fourier coefficients.

More formally, the nth function value is

$$f_n = \sum_{k=0}^{N-1} w_N^{nk} c_k = \sum_{k=0}^{M-1} w_N^{2nk} c_{2k} + \sum_{k=0}^{M-1} w_N^{(2k+1)n} c_{2k+1},$$

where $M = N/2$ or

$$f_n = \sum_{k=0}^{M-1} w_M^{nk} c_k^{\mathrm{e}} + w_N^n \sum_{k=0}^{M-1} w_M^{nk} c_k^{\mathrm{o}} \tag{3.22}$$

since $w_N^2 = w_M$; also, we have denoted by c^{e} and c^{o} the even and odd parts of the vector $\mathbf{c}$, respectively. Notice that this formula gives us only the *first half* of the Fourier coefficients from $n = 0, \ldots, (M-1)$. To obtain the other half we substitute $(n+M)$ instead of n and use the fact that

$$w_M^{k(n+M)} = w_M^{nk} \cdot w_M^{kM} = w_M^{nk}$$

and also

$$w_N^{n+M} = w_N^n \cdot w_N^M = w_N^n \cdot e^{\frac{2\pi i M}{N}} = w_N^n \cdot e^{\pi i} = -w_N^n.$$

Therefore:

$$f_{n+M} = \sum_{k=0}^{M-1} w_M^{nk} c_k^{\mathrm{e}} - w_N^n \sum_{k=0}^{M-1} w_M^{nk} c_k^{\mathrm{o}}. \tag{3.23}$$

The matrix–vector product $\mathbf{Wc}$ is then computed from Equations (3.22) and (3.23).

This is the *first level* of splitting into even and odd parts. However, assuming $N = 2^m$, we can repeat this process m more times in a *recursive fashion*. The cost at each level includes the two matrix–vector multiplications of length $M = N/2$ plus the multiplication by the prefactor w_N^k in Equations (3.22) and (3.23). The basic cost model for this recursion is

$$C(N) = \alpha C \left(\frac{N}{2} \right) + \beta \left(\frac{N}{2} \right),$$

which leads to the estimate

$$C(N) \sim \mathcal{O}(5N \log_2 N)$$

versus $\mathcal{O}(8N^2)$ operations for the direct computation.

REMARK 1: Although the FFT is a recursive algorithm, traditional implementations are based on simple nested loops, which have been proved to be more efficient. However, on more modern architectures where cache utilization is important, the recursive procedure is better (see FFTW in Section 3.2.8).

REMARK 2: In addition to its computational simplicity, the FFT has less round-off error than the direct summation approach.

REMARK 3: For N that has the general form

$$N = 2^\alpha 3^\beta 4^\gamma 5^\delta 6^\epsilon,$$

it is still possible to perform FFTs by splitting the function into several parts, not only its odd and even components (see [87]). The corresponding cost is

$$\mathcal{O} \left(N \left(5\alpha + 9\frac{1}{3}\beta + 8\frac{1}{2}\gamma + 13\frac{3}{5}\delta + 13\frac{1}{3}\epsilon - 6 \right) \right).$$

REMARK 4: The real-to-real transform can be computed in half the number of operations, for example, in $\mathcal{O}\left(\frac{5}{2}N \log_2 N\right)$. This is done by defining

$$g_k = f_{2k} + i f_{2k+1}, \quad k = 0, 1, \ldots M,$$

where $M = N/2$. Then we take an M-length transform of g_k and set $c_m = c_0$. We extract all the coefficients from

$$c_k = \frac{1}{2}(a\tilde{g}_k + \tilde{g}^*_{M-k}) - \frac{i}{2}e^{\frac{2\pi i k}{N}}[\tilde{g}_k - \tilde{g}^*_{M-k}], \quad k = 0, 1, \ldots, M - 1,$$

where we have denoted the Fourier coefficients of g with $\tilde{g}$, and the star denotes complex conjugate.

3.2.8 The Fastest Fourier Transform in the West – FFTW

The Fastest Fourier Transform in the West (FFTW) is a C subroutine that contains *adaptive software* for real and complex one-dimensional and multidimensional FFTs. Unlike conventional implementations that use loops instead of recursion, in the FFTW explicitly *recursive* implementation is followed because of theoretical evidence that *divide-and-conquer algorithms improve locality.*

FFTW is not a new FFT algorithm, but it is simply a smart implementation that attempts to exploit a given processor architecture by interacting with its pipeline and its memory hierarchy. It derives its name from the fact that in benchmark tests it has proven to be faster than any other publicly available FFT software. FFTW was developed by Frigo and Johnson at MIT in the late 1990s [40]. It is similar in spirit to the ATLAS software described in Chapter 2. The key idea is that the standard Cooley–Tukey algorithm is adapted to the specific hardware employed in the computation.

To adapt to any hardware, FFTW runs several diagnostic tests in a preprocessing stage. More specifically, the code is divided into two parts:

- the executor and
- the codelet generator.

The *executor* computes the transform by first building a *plan*. This plan consists of a sequence of instructions that specifies the operation of the executor. The codelets are highly optimized fragments of C code that the executor uses. The exact combination of codelets that will be used depends on the plan, which contains diagnostics and measurements for the particular computer employed. The plan itself is also activated at runtime, but it is determined before the actual computation starts. It employs dynamic programming and a cost-minimization algorithm, which targets the execution time and not the number of floating point operations.

Therefore, the plan is created first as follows:

Figure 3.21: Comparisons of FFTW with other FFT implementations on the 1.7 GHz Pentium 4 processor. The other FFT implementations are in C and FORTRAN.

```
fftw_plan fftw_create_plan(int n, fft_direction dir, int flags)
```

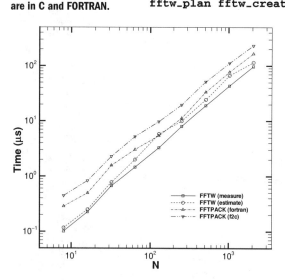

This function creates a plan for computing a one-dimensional Fourier transform. Here *n* is the size of the transform, which can be an arbitrary integer, $dir = -1$ or 1 are flags that denote direction and can be substituted by the aliases *FFTW_FORWARD* and *FFTW_BACKWARD*, respectively. Also, *flags* is a Boolean, which provides different options. For example, the *FFTW_MEASURE* finds the optimal plan by computing several FFTs and measuring their execution time. Clearly, this takes time so the first time around when you run the FFTW it is expensive. However, the computed plan can be used for subsequent runs, which are really fast! An alternative is to use the flag *FFTW_ESTIMATE* to provide a "best guess" of an optimal plan without actually running any diagnostic FFTs.

A typical code that uses the complex one-dimensional FFTW looks like the following:

```
#include<fftw.h>
...
{
fftw_complex in[N], out[N];
fftw_plan p;
...
p=fftw_create_plan(N,FFTW_FORWARD,FFTW_MEASURE);
...
fftw_one(p,in,out);
...
fftw_destroy_plan(p);
}
```

An example of typical performance of the one-dimensional FFTW is provided in Figure 3.21, which shows the superior performance of the FFTW on the Pentium 4 processor. We also compare the *FFTW_MEASURE* versus the *FFTW_ESTIMATE* options and show that even for this relatively small size N of the transform tested, the optimal plan that the former uses makes a substantial difference.

The FFTW has also been implemented for parallel environments for both shared memory and distributed memory platforms. In particular, the MPI FFTW routines use distributed data, with the array divided according to the rows; that is, each processor gets a subset of the rows of data. The FFTW supplies a routine that reports how much data resides on each processor. A typical name of the MPI FFTW routines is

```
#include<fftw_mpi.h>
...
fftwnd_mpi(p, 1, data, NULL, FFTW_NORMAL_ORDER);
...
```

This code uses a complex two-dimensional MPI FFTW.

For details on how to use the FFTW, including the MPI FFTW, the reader should consult **www.fftw.org**, which is the official internet site maintained by the developers of this adaptive software.

3.3 WAVELET SERIES REPRESENTATION

Wavelets are an alternative, relatively recent family of basis functions to represent a function in the form

$$f(x) = \sum d_{jk} \psi(2^j x - k),$$

where d_{jk} are the unknown coefficients. They can be orthonormal or not, smooth or

Figure 3.22: Multistep function.

not, and compact or not. They allow a decomposition of a function in such a way that its wavenumbers depend on the position x. They can also represent segmented functions (e.g., the multistep function shown in Figure 3.22).

It is almost impossible to represent such a function with a Fourier series. However, using wavelets we can construct a special basis, called the *Walsh basis* functions (see Figure 3.23), that can approximate the multistep function very accurately. Specifically, the function shown in Figure 3.22 is represented by the first six basis functions of the Walsh family using the following coefficients (from first to sixth):

$$0.3200, \quad 0.9601, \quad 0.7266, \quad 0.4120, \quad 0.7446, \quad 0.2679.$$

We note here that the Walsh basis functions are defined in the same interval as the original function (i.e., the basis is global not local, similar to the Fourier representation). In contrast, some of the best wavelets, as we will see in the following, have a compact support; that is, they are *local*.

3.3.1 Basic Relations

There are two basic concepts that are used in this field: the *scaling function* $\phi(x)$ and the *wavelet* $\psi(x)$. More specifically, we use the integer *translations*,

$$\phi(x - k) \quad \text{and} \quad \psi(x - k), \quad k \in \mathcal{Z},$$

and also their *dilations*,

$$\phi(2^j x) \quad \text{and} \quad \psi(2^j x), \quad j \in \mathcal{Z}.$$

Almost always we need both translations and dilations, which we obtain by combining these above concepts to give

$$\phi(2^j x - k) \quad \text{and} \quad \psi(2^j x - k).$$

Here, we will refer to 2^{-j} as the scale of level j.

Using one of the oldest scaling functions and wavelets, from the *Haar family*, we can construct the entire Walsh family. The basic Haar scaling function is a (positive) constant pulse, whereas the Haar basic wavelet is a combined positive–negative pulse (sometimes we will refer to it as the *mother Haar wavelet*). In Figure 3.24 we show how to construct the first two Walsh basis functions from the Haar basic units.

In fact, we can generate the entire Walsh family by using the mother wavelet; we only need the scaling function for the very first Walsh basis. This decomposition of a function into hierarchical components is known as *multiresolution analysis*; we will generalize it to arbitrary functions later. Actually, the functions cannot quite be arbitrary – they need to be in L_2, that is, in the space of absolutely square integrable, similar to the condition that Fejer considered in his Fourier construction (see Section 3.2.1).

In addition to L_2, the two spaces

$$V_j = \left\{ \sum_{k=-\infty}^{\infty} c_{jk} \phi(2^j x - k) : \sum_{k=-\infty}^{\infty} |c_{jk}|^2 < \infty \right\}$$

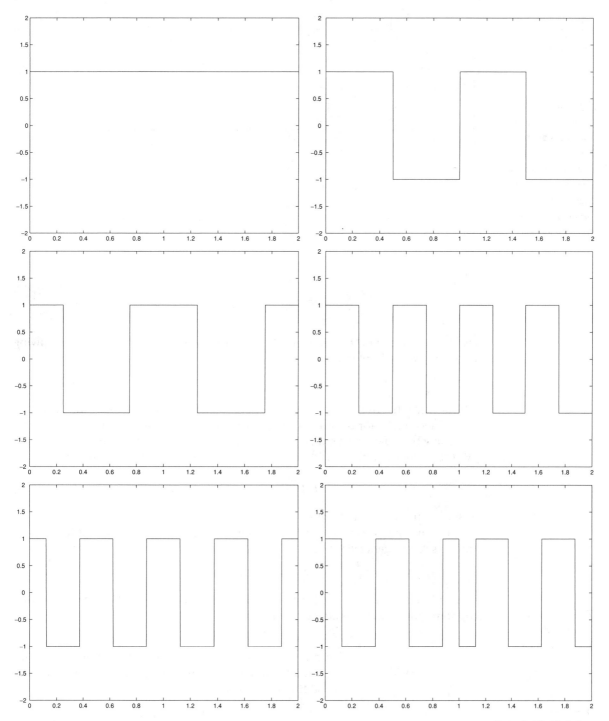

Figure 3.23: First six basis functions of the Walsh family.

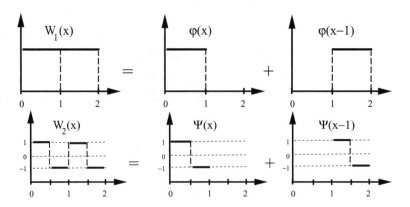

Figure 3.24: The first Walsh basis function (upper) is expressed in terms of the Haar scaling function. The second Walsh basis function (lower) is expressed in terms of the Haar wavelet.

and

$$W_j = \left\{ \sum_{k=-\infty}^{\infty} d_{jk} \psi(2^j x - k) : \sum_{k=-\infty}^{\infty} |d_{jk}|^2 < \infty \right\}$$

are also very useful in the following. Based on these definitions, we have the following important *hierarchy* of spaces:

$$\ldots \subset V_{-1} \subset V_0 \subset V_1 \ldots \subset L_2.$$

We conclude that the subspaces for the scaling functions are nested. Schematically, we have, for example, for the Haar scaling function the picture shown in Figure 3.25.

Using the Haar wavelet we can also infer a relationship between the spaces V_j and W_j. Let us, for example, consider the scaling function $\phi(2x - 1)$; then we can write

$$\phi(2x - 1) = \frac{1}{2}\phi(x) - \frac{1}{2}\psi(x), \tag{3.24}$$

as shown in the sketch of Figure 3.26.

In terms of spaces Equation (3.24) can be written as $V_1 = V_0 + W_0$, but it turns out that this can be generalized to

$$V_{j+1} = V_j + W_j, \quad \forall j \in \mathcal{Z}.$$

In addition, the Haar scaling function and wavelet are orthogonal, which means that the corresponding spaces are orthogonal, that is,

$$V_j \perp W_j.$$

Figure 3.25: Schematic illustration of the spaces V_0 and V_1.

In general, however, this orthogonality condition may not be valid for all types of wavelets, and instead the following condition is satisfied:

$$V_j \cap W_j = \emptyset \quad \forall j \in \mathcal{Z};$$

that is, the intersection of the scaling function and wavelet spaces is the empty set.

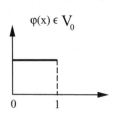

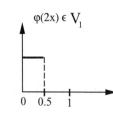

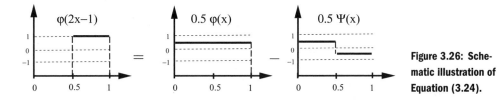

Figure 3.26: Schematic illustration of Equation (3.24).

The fact that there is hierarchy in spaces $V_j \subset V_{j+1}$ and also that $W_j \subset V_{j+1}$ leads to the following two fundamental equations, also known as *two-scale relations*:

$$\phi(x) = \sum_k p_k \phi(2x - k) \tag{3.25}$$

and

$$\psi(x) = \sum_k q_k \phi(2x - k). \tag{3.26}$$

Thus, the wavelet can be obtained from the scaling function. For special cases (e.g., *orthonormal wavelets*), we have

$$\psi(x) = \sum_k (-1)^k p_{1-k} \phi(2x - k), \tag{3.27}$$

which will be discussed in detail later.

EXAMPLES.

- For the Haar wavelet $\psi(x) = \phi(2x) - \phi(2x - 1)$, where $\phi(x)$ is the Haar scaling (box) function, we have $p_0 = 1$ and $p_1 = 1$.
- For the hat wavelet, corresponding to the hat function $N_2(x)$: $\psi(x) = \phi(2x) - \frac{1}{2}\phi(2x - 1) - \frac{1}{2}\phi(2x + 1)$, the coefficients are $p_0 = 1/2$, $p_1 = 1$, and $p_2 = 1/2$ from Equation (3.27).

3.3.2 Dilation Equation

The nested property of the spaces V_j leads to the two-scale *dilation* equation of the form

$$\phi(x) = \sum_k p_k \phi(2x - k).$$

For example, for the Haar scaling function, we have that

$$\phi(x) = \phi(2x) + \phi(2x - 1)$$

since

$$p_0 = p_1 = 1,$$

$$p_k = 0, \ |k| > 1.$$

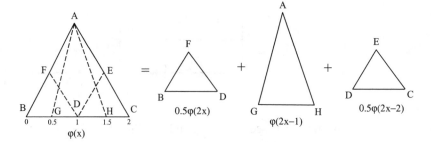

Figure 3.27: Solution
of the dilation
equation for the hat
wavelet $N_2(x)$.

Let us also consider the new scaling function we introduced previously,

$$\phi(x) = N_2(x) = \int_0^1 N_1(x - t)\,dt,$$

where $N_1(x)$ is the box Haar function. Then, the dilation equation is

$$\phi(x) = \frac{1}{2}\phi(2x) + \phi(2x - 1) + \frac{1}{2}\phi(2x - 2)$$

since

$$p_0 = \frac{1}{2}, \ p_1 = 1, \ p_2 = \frac{1}{2},$$

as we have already seen for the wavelet $\psi(x)$, and

$$p_k = 0, \quad |k| > 2.$$

Schematically, this can be justified as shown in Figure 3.27.

So far we have shown that the coefficients p_k form a finite set, typically very small and consisting of the first few nonzero values. This shows *compact support*, but there are cases for which the p_k are all nonzero. Obtaining them is not always easy. Dilation equations are interesting on their own right, and here we review three different approaches to solving them (see [85]).

Iteration for Dilation Equation

Here we iterate on the two-scale dilation equation

$$\phi_n(x) = \sum_k p_k \phi_{n-1}(2x - k),$$

where $\sum_k p_k = 2$. This condition is based on the normalization $\int \phi(x)\,dx = 1$ and can be derived by multiplying the dilation equation by 2 and integrating, that is,

$$2\int \phi\,dx = \sum_k p_k \int \phi(2x - k)\,d(2x - k) \Rightarrow \sum_k p_k = 2.$$

To initialize we need to set the value of ϕ_0 for $n = 1$. For Daubechies wavelets (see Section 3.3.4) we set ϕ_0 equal to the Haar scaling function $N_1(x)$. An appropriate initial choice is made for other families of wavelets.

- If $p_0 = 2$ then $p_k = 0$, $|k| > 1$, and the iteration converges to a delta function.
- If $p_0 = p_1 = 1$ the iteration converges to the Haar scaling function; that is, we have invariance, since $\phi_n = \phi_0$.
- If $p_0 = \frac{1}{2}$, $p_1 = 1$, $p_2 = \frac{1}{2}$ we recover the hat function $N_2(x)$, as demonstrated in Figure 3.27.
- If $p_0 = \frac{1}{8}$, $p_1 = \frac{4}{2}$, $p_2 = \frac{2}{3}$, $p_3 = \frac{1}{2}$, $p_4 = \frac{1}{8}$ the iteration converges to the cubic B-spline $N_4(x)$. This can be written as

$$N_4(x) = \int_0^1 N_3(x - t)dt,$$

where $N_3(x)$ is the quadratic B-spline, which in turn is

$$N_3(x) = \int_0^1 N_2(x - t)dt,$$

and $N_2(x)$ is the hat function of Figure 3.27.

Fourier Transform for Dilation Equation

We can also obtain the scaling function by Fourier transforming the two-scale difference equation, that is,

$$\hat{\phi}(z) = \sum_k p_k \int \phi(2x - k)e^{izx}dx$$

$$= \sum_k p_k e^{ikz/2} \int \phi(2x - k)e^{i\frac{2x-k}{2}z}\frac{1}{2}d(2x - k)$$

$$= \left(\frac{1}{2}\sum_k p_k e^{i\frac{kz}{2}}\right) \cdot \int \phi(t)e^{itz/2}dt$$

$$\equiv P\left(\frac{z}{2}\right) \cdot \hat{\phi}\left(\frac{z}{2}\right),$$

where

$$P(z) = \frac{1}{2}\sum_k p_k e^{ikz} \tag{3.28}$$

is the *transfer function* and $P(0) = 1$. We have thus obtained

$$\hat{\phi}(z) = P\left(\frac{z}{2}\right) \cdot \hat{\phi}\left(\frac{z}{2}\right),$$

where also $\hat{\phi}(0) = 1 = \int \phi(x)dx$ by the normalization condition.

Using this equation for $\hat{\phi}$ we have that

$$\hat{\phi}\left(\frac{z}{2}\right) = P\left(\frac{z}{4}\right) \cdot \hat{\phi}\left(\frac{z}{4}\right),$$

and so on for $\hat{\phi}\left(\frac{z}{4}\right)$, $\hat{\phi}\left(\frac{z}{8}\right)$, etc. Thus,

$$\hat{\phi}(z) = \Pi_{n=1}^N P\left(\frac{z}{2^n}\right) \cdot \hat{\phi}\left(\frac{z}{2^N}\right),$$

and for

$$N \to \infty, \quad \frac{z}{2^N} \to 0 \Rightarrow \hat{\phi}\left(\frac{2}{2^N}\right) \to 1.$$

Thus

$$\hat{\phi}(z) \to \Pi_{n=1}^{\infty} P\left(\frac{z}{2^n}\right),$$

and the inverse transform of $\hat{\phi}(z)$ gives the scaling function $\phi(x)$.

For example:

- Let $p_0 = 2$, then $P(z) = 1 \Rightarrow \hat{\phi}(z) = 1 \Rightarrow \phi(x) = \delta(x)$, the Dirac function.
- Let $p_0 = p_1 = 1$, so $P(z) = \frac{1}{2}\left[1 + e^{iz}\right]$. Then

$$P\left(\frac{z}{2}\right) P\left(\frac{z}{4}\right) P\left(\frac{z}{8}\right) \dots P\left(\frac{z}{2^N}\right) = \frac{1}{2}(1 + e^{iz/2})$$

$$\cdot \frac{1}{2}(1 + e^{iz/4}) \cdot \frac{1}{2}(1 + e^{iz/8}) \dots \frac{1}{2}(1 + e^{\frac{iz}{2^N}})$$

$$\Rightarrow \frac{1 - e^{iz}}{(-iz)} = \int_0^1 e^{izx} dx.$$

The inverse transform then gives $\phi(x) = N_1(x)$, which is the Haar scaling function.

Recursion for Dilation Equation

The idea here is that we can construct $\phi(x)$ numerically, *point by point*. That is, assuming that we know $\phi(k)$ (at the integer points), then we can use the dilation equation to obtain ϕ at $k/2$, then at $k/4$, and ultimately at $k/2^N$. The question then becomes: How do we obtain the values $\phi(k)$? These are obtained as solutions of the eigenvalue problem constructed from the algebraic equations at points

$$x = 0, \pm 1, \pm 2, \dots$$

within the range of support. Specifically, we set up an eigensystem

$$\phi = -\mathbf{P}\phi,$$

where

$$\phi = [\dots \phi(1), \phi(2), \phi(3) \dots]^T$$

and $\mathbf{P}$ is a relatively sparse matrix containing the coefficients p_k.

We will demonstrate this approach later for the Daubechies wavelets.

3.3.3 Discrete Wavelet Transform: Mallat's Algorithm

Let $f(x) \in L_2$, and we want to approximate it by

$$f_n(x) \approx f(x), \quad f_n(x) \in V_n.$$

Then, given the hierarchy of spaces and the fact that

$$V_{j+1} = V_j + W_j,$$

a unique decomposition of $f_n(x)$ in terms of its components $g_j(x) \in W_j$ exists. In particular, we can write

$$f_n(x) = \underbrace{f_{n-m}(x)}_{\in V_{n-m}} + \left\{ \underbrace{g_{n-m}(x) + \cdots + g_{n-1}(x)}_{\in W_{n-m} \ldots W_{n-1}} \right\}, \qquad (3.29)$$

where m is a positive integer that depends on the filter size.

That is, the function is decomposed into one component (the "blur" or "DC") that can be represented in the space V_{n-m} of scaling functions *plus* contributions at various scales that can be represented by wavelets. This decomposition makes sense as the "blur" represents the "mean" whereas the wavelets represent the "fluctuations," since they have zero mean by construction. The wavelet contributions correspond to the following wavelet series:

$$g_j(x) = \sum_k d_{jk} \psi_{jk}(x).$$

Most but not all wavelets are orthogonal, so here we extend the concept of orthogonality to *biorthogonality*. To this end, we introduce the *dual wavelet* $\tilde{\psi}(x) \in L_2$, where the following inner product expresses the *biorthogonality* condition:

$$\langle \psi_{jk}(x), \tilde{\psi}_{jk}(x) \rangle = \int_{-\infty}^{\infty} \psi_{jk}(x) \tilde{\psi}_{\ell m}^*(x) dx = \delta_{j\ell} \delta_{km},$$

where the star * denotes complex conjugate (some wavelets are complex functions). Also, the normalization condition

$$\psi_{jk} = 2^{j/2} \psi(2^j x - k)$$

is usually employed to relate the wavelet basis functions to the mother wavelet.

With these definitions, we can now obtain the discrete wavelet transform in the general case. To this end, we rewrite Equation (3.29) as

$$g_j(x) = f_n(x) - [f_j(x) + g_{n-1}(x) + \cdots + g_{j+1}(x)],$$

and taking the inner product, we get

$$\langle g_j(x), \tilde{\psi}(2^j x - k) \rangle = \langle f_n(x), \tilde{\psi}(2^j x - k) \rangle,$$

as the rest of the terms drop out because of biorthogonality. Thus,

$$d_{jk} = \langle g_j(x), \tilde{\psi}_{jk}(x) \rangle = \langle f_n(x), \tilde{\psi}_{jk}(x) \rangle \qquad (3.30)$$

$$= 2^{j/2} \int_{-\infty}^{\infty} f_n(x) [\tilde{\psi}(2^j x - k)]^* dx,$$

which is the *discrete wavelet transform* of $f_n(x)$.

We now turn to searching for algorithms that enable us to decompose or reconstruct the approximation $f_n(x)$ quickly. Using the scaling function as basis, we can write

$$f_n(x) = \sum_k c_{nk}\phi(2^n x - k).$$

Also, from the relation $V_1 = V_0 + W_0$, we have that

$$\phi(2x - m) = \sum_k [a_{m-2k}\phi(x - k) + b_{m-2k}\psi(x - k)], \quad \forall m \in \mathbb{Z}. \qquad (3.31)$$

Similarly, from $V_n = V_{n-1} + W_{n-1}$, we conclude that

$$\underbrace{f_n(x)}_{\in V_n} = \underbrace{f_{n-1}(x)}_{\in V_{n-1}} + \underbrace{g_{n-1}(x)}_{\in W_{n-1}},$$

where

$$f_{n-1}(x) = \sum_k c_{n-1,k}\phi(2^{n-1}x - k), \qquad (3.32)$$

$$g_{n-1}(x) = \sum_k d_{n-1,k}\psi(2^{n-1}x - k). \qquad (3.33)$$

These relations are useful in helping us obtain the set of coefficients

$$\{c_{nk}\} \text{ and } \{d_{nk}\} \text{ from } \{c_{n-1,k}\} \text{ and } \{d_{n-1,k}\}.$$

Comparing, for example, Equations (3.31) with (3.32) and (3.33), we obtain

$$\begin{cases} c_{n-1,k} = \sum_m a_{m-2k}c_{n,m}, \\[2mm] d_{n-1,k} = \sum_m b_{m-2k}c_{n,m}. \end{cases}$$

These operations represent *discrete convolution* and can be performed fast. More precisely, there should be a change in sign, between, for example, $a_{m-2k} \to a_{2k-m}$; also, only the double-indexed entries should be sampled. This procedure is known as the *Mallat algorithm* [69]. It can compute all coefficients in $\mathcal{O}(N)$ arithmetic operations, that is, even faster than the FFT, which has $\mathcal{O}(N \log_2 N)$ arithmetic operations.

This analysis gives the decomposition of $f_n(x)$. In terms of *reconstruction*, that is, to obtain $f_n(x)$ from $\{f_{n-1}(x) \text{ and } g_{n-1}(x)\}$, we start with the two-scale difference equations

$$\phi(x) = \sum_k p_k\phi(2x - k),$$

$$\psi(x) = \sum_k q_k\phi(2x - k)$$

and thus

$$c_{n,k} = \sum_m [p_{k-2m}c_{n-1,m} + q_{k-2,m}d_{n-1,m}],$$

where again the aforementioned corrections are needed to make this an exact convolution, which can be computed fast. This is the *inverse Mallat's algorithm*.

3.3.4 Some Orthonormal Wavelets

Orthonormal wavelets form a very special class of basis functions. They satisfy the following condition among spaces at different scales:

$$W_i \perp W_j, \quad i \neq j.$$

Also, the space of finite-energy function L_2 can be represented by an orthogonal sum of the subspaces W_j, which we express as

$$L_2 = \oplus_{-\infty}^{\infty} W_j.$$

It is read as "the direct sum of W_j" and we refer to it as the *wavelet decomposition* of L_2.

The condition of *orthonormality* is expressed best by the Fourier transform. That is, if

$$\sum_{k=-\infty}^{\infty} |\hat{\phi}(\omega + 2\pi k)|^2 = 1$$

then the function $\phi(x) \in L_2$ is orthonormal (see [16]). One can show that the orthogonality condition between W_j and V_j, and correspondingly between $\psi(x)$ and $\phi(x)$, gives

$$q_k = (-1)^k p_{1-k};$$

that is, the wavelet coefficients are determined solely by the scaling function coefficients, so

$$\psi(x) = \sum_k (-1)^k p_{1-k} \phi(2x - k). \tag{3.34}$$

Based on that, the orthogonal decomposition $V_1 = V_0 \oplus W_0$ leads to

$$\phi(2x - m) = \sum_k \frac{1}{2} [p_{m-2k} \phi(x - k) + (-1)^m p_{2k-m+1} \psi(x - k)],$$

which is a *decomposition relation* of functions $\phi(x)$ and $\psi(x)$.

Next, we provide some examples of orthonormal wavelets.

Haar Wavelet

The oldest of all is the Haar wavelet, which we have already studied. It corresponds to the box scaling function with $p_0 = p_1 = 1$ and $p_k = 0$ for all the other coefficients ($k > 1$). Using Equation (3.34), we can write

$$\psi(x) = \phi(2x) - \phi(2x - 1)$$
$$= N_1(2x) - N_1(2x - 1).$$

Shannon Wavelet

The Shannon wavelet uses the scaling function

$$\phi(x) = \frac{\sin \pi x}{\pi x},$$

which is identical to the Lanczos filter (see Section 3.2.3). The coefficients of the Shannon scaling function are

$$p_k = \begin{cases} 1, & k = 0, \\[2mm] (-1)^{\frac{k-1}{2}} \dfrac{2}{\pi k}, & k = 2m - 1, \\[2mm] 0, & k = 2m. \end{cases}$$

Based on Equation (3.34), we then obtain

$$\psi(x) = \sum_k (-1)^k p_{1-k} \phi(2x - k),$$

which leads to

$$\psi(x) = \frac{\sin 2\pi x - \cos \pi x}{\pi \left(x - \frac{1}{2} \right)}. \tag{3.35}$$

A plot of the Shannon wavelet is shown in Figure 3.28.

Orthonormal Spline Wavelets

We have discussed splines in Section 3.1.6 and here we examine how we can use them as orthonormal wavelets. In general, the translates of B-splines are not orthogonal,

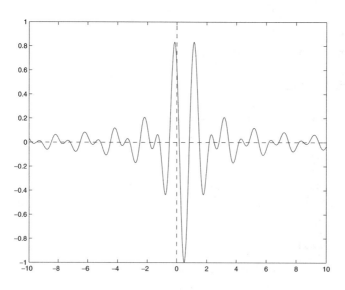

Figure 3.28: Shannon wavelet.

and thus a special orthonormalization procedure needs to be employed. The result is that
the orthonormalized splines will no longer be
polynomials.

Following Chui [16], we first define the B-
splines recursively from

$$N_m(x) = \int_{-\infty}^{\infty} N_{m-1}(x-t)N_1(t)dt$$

$$= \int_0^1 N_{m-1}(x-t)dt,$$

where $N_1(t)$ is the box function. The two-scale
equation for the B-splines is

$$N_m(x) = \sum_{k=0}^{m} 2^{-m+1} \binom{m}{k} N_m(2x-k),$$

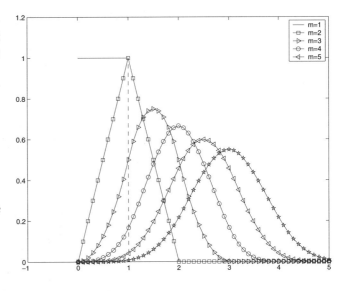

Figure 3.29: B-splines
(cardinal) from first to
fifth order.

and $N_m(x)$ is an $(m-1)$-order polynomial with continuity (smoothness)

$$N_m(x) \in C^{m-2}.$$

Plots are shown in Figure 3.29 for various orders; they are smooth but not orthonormal.

To orthonormalize $N_m(x)$ to produce $N_m^{\perp}(x)$, Chui has introduced the complex conjugate of the reflection of $N_m(x)$, that is, $N_m^*(-x)$, as the *dual function*. To this end, we
have

$$N_{2m}(m+x) = \int_{-\infty}^{\infty} N_m(t)N_m^*(t-x)dt = \frac{1}{2\pi} \int_0^{2\pi} \left\{ \sum_{k=-\infty}^{\infty} |\hat{N}_m(\omega + 2\pi k)|^2 \right\} e^{i\omega x} d\omega,$$

where the last term refers to the Fourier transform of $N_m(x)$.

If we define

$$E_m(z) \equiv \sum_{k=-m+1}^{m-1} N_{2m}(m+k)z^k$$

the orthonormalization procedure leads to

$$N_m^{\perp}(\omega) = \frac{\hat{N}_m(\omega)}{[E_m(z^2)]^{1/2}}, \quad z = e^{-i\frac{\omega}{2}}.$$

Also, the transfer function can be expressed via $E_m(z)$ (see [16]):

$$P(z) \equiv \frac{1}{2} \sum_k p_k z^k = \left(\frac{1+z}{2} \right)^m \left[\frac{E_m(z)}{E_m(z^2)} \right]^{1/2}.$$

Finally, the mth-order orthonormal wavelet, also known as the **Battle–Lemarié**

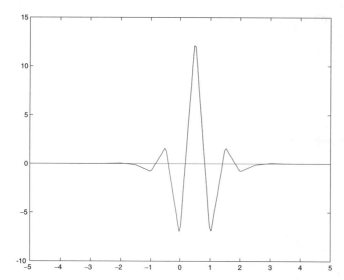

Figure 3.30: Battle–Lemarié wavelet of order $m = 2$ (linear).

wavelet, is given by

$$\psi_m(x) = \sum_k (-1)^k p_{1-k} N_m^{\perp}(2x - k). \qquad (3.36)$$

In practice, it is more convenient to define the Battle–Lemarié wavelet in terms of its Fourier transform:

$$\hat{\psi}_m(\omega)$$

$$= -\left(\frac{4}{i\omega}\right)^m \left[\sin^{2m}\left(\frac{\omega}{4}\right)\right] z \left[\frac{E_m(-z)}{E_m(z)E_m(z^2)}\right]^{1/2},$$

where $z = e^{-i\omega/2}$.

A plot of the Battle–Lemarié wavelet is shown in Figure 3.30 for $m = 2$.

The Daubechies Wavelets

The Daubechies wavelets are very special because they are very compact but also orthonormal; therefore, no special procedure is needed to orthonormalize them. They can be defined by means of the transfer function

$$P(z) = \frac{1}{2} \sum_{n=0}^{N} p_n z^n = \left(\frac{1+z}{2}\right)^m S_{N-m}(z),$$

where $S_{N-m}(z)$ is a polynomial of degree $(N - m)$ and $S_{N-m}(1) = 1$; the latter implies that $P(1) = 1$. Computing S_{N-m} is not trivial and the interested reader is referred to [22].

The inverse Fourier transform of the product

$$\hat{\phi}_m(\omega) = \Pi_{j=1}^{\infty} P\left(e^{-i\omega/2^j}\right)$$

gives the Daubechies scaling function.

An alternative way is to use iteration, as discussed earlier, for example,

$$\phi_{m;j+1}(x) = \sum_{k=0}^{N} p_k \phi_{m;j}(2x - k),$$

starting with $\phi_{m;0} = N_2(x)$, the linear B-spline, and iterate to a converged solution to obtain $\phi_m(x)$.

Having obtained the scaling function, we can then obtain the Daubechies wavelets from

$$\psi_m(x) = \sum_{k=-N+1}^{1} (-1)^k p_{1-k} \phi_m(2x - k).$$

The Daubechies scaling function and wavelet of orders $m = 4$ and 7 are shown in Figures 3.31 and Figure 3.32, respectively.

As we see from the plots, the Daubechies wavelets are compact but not very smooth; in fact, here polynomial smoothness has been sacrificed for compactness! The

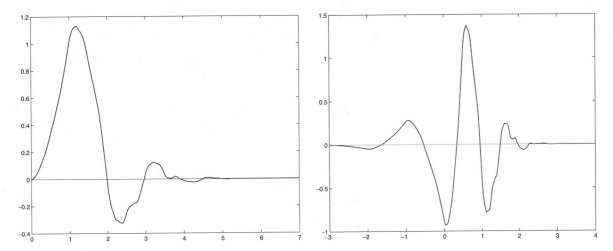

smoothness of the Daubechies wavelets increases with the order but only by about half a derivative each time; for example, ψ_4 is $C^{0.55}$, which is fractionally continuous. In contrast, we recall that the B-splines with $m = 4$ are C^2 continuous.

More specifically, the Daubechies wavelet of fourth order ($m = 4$) is defined by the coefficients

$$p_0 = \frac{1 + \sqrt{3}}{4}, \quad p_1 = \frac{3 + \sqrt{3}}{4},$$

$$p_2 = \frac{3 - \sqrt{3}}{4}, \quad p_3 = \frac{1 - \sqrt{3}}{4}.$$

We can now use these coefficients to construct $\phi_4(x)$, the scaling function, by recursion,

Figure 3.31: Scaling function (left) and wavelet (right) of the Daubechies family; $m = 4$.

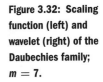

Figure 3.32: Scaling function (left) and wavelet (right) of the Daubechies family; $m = 7$.

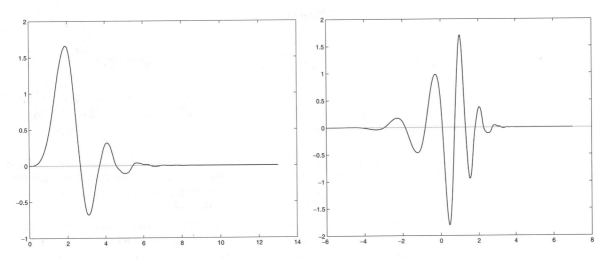

as discussed earlier. First, we set up an eigenvalue problem by applying the dilation equation at the integer points $x = 1$ and $x = 2$ in the open interval $x \in (0, 3)$:

$$\phi_4(1) = \frac{1 + \sqrt{3}}{4}\phi_4(2) + \frac{3 + \sqrt{3}}{4}\phi(1),$$

$$\phi_4(2) = \frac{3 - \sqrt{3}}{4}\phi_4(2) + \frac{1 - \sqrt{3}}{4}\phi_4(1).$$

The eigenvalues of the 2×2 eigensystem are 1 and 1/2; the former leads to

$$\phi_4(1) = \frac{1 + \sqrt{3}}{2} \quad \text{and} \quad \phi_4(2) = \frac{1 - \sqrt{3}}{2}.$$

Having obtained these values, we now set $x = 1/2, 1/2^2, 1/2^3$ and so on at all dyadic points to compute values of $\phi_4(x)$ at many other points.

The accuracy of the approximation depends on the order p of zeros of the transfer function

$$P(z) = \frac{1}{2}\sum_k p_k e^{ikz}.$$

This turns out to be equivalent to the following condition for the coefficients p_k:

$$\sum (-1)^k k^m p_k = 0, \quad m = 0, 1, \ldots, p - 1.$$

Correspondingly, the first p *moments* of the wavelet $\psi(x)$ are zero; that is,

$$\int x^m \psi(x)dx = 0, \quad \forall m = 0, \ldots, p - 1.$$

The fourth-order Daubechies scaling function $\phi_4(x)$ has $p = 2$ in contrast with the cubic spline, which has $p = 4$. The corresponding error bound is

$$\| f(x) - \sum p_k \phi(2^j x - k) \| \leq C \cdot 2^{-jp} \| f^{(p)}(x) \|;$$

that is, the error is $\mathcal{O}(h^p)$, where $h = 2^{-j}$.

3.4 BACK TO PARALLEL COMPUTING: SEND AND RECEIVE

The information that we provided in Chapter 2 was accurate but incomplete. In this section we want to supply more information about sending and receiving in MPI. After this section, throughout the book, we will begin to directly integrate MPI concepts into the lessons.

Recall from our previous discussion that for each call to *MPI_Send*, there should be a call to *MPI_Recv*. Here we give the declarations (which can be found in **mpi.h** on your parallel computer) for both *MPI_Send* and *MPI_Recv*. Let us investigate each one separately. Throughout the book, we will use the formats here for presenting MPI functions. The return value and name will be provided followed by the argument list (both variable type and variable name) and comments denoting whether the variable is intended to act as input (in) to or output (out) of the function.

• MPI_Send

```
int MPI_Send(
        void*           message     /* in  */,
        int             count       /* in  */,
        MPI_Datatype    datatype    /* in  */,
        int             dest        /* in  */,
        int             tag         /* in  */,
        MPI_Comm        comm        /* in  */)
```

The first item in the argument list is the starting *address* from which the data item is to be retrieved. You can translate this as "the *pointer* variable." The second piece of information is the count, which is the number of items to send. The third item is the data type, which can be among the following:

- MPI_INT,
- MPI_FLOAT,
- MPI_DOUBLE, or
- MPI_CHAR.

See Appendix B for a full listing of all the allowable variable types. Here we only provide the four basic types that we have introduced thus far. The fourth argument is the processor identification number to which the message is to be sent. This processor **id** is the integer that is obtained locally on the processor by calling *MPI_Comm_rank*() (recall that, in the previous example, we stored the local process number in the variable *mynode*). The fifth argument is a tag, which is an integer used to delineate between successive messages. Suppose that you were going to send messages one right after the other to and from one processor to the next. Then you would assign two different tag numbers so that you can guarantee the ordering that the processor will receive the information. The final argument provides information concerning which processes are within the current communication group. For our purposes, this argument will always be set to *MPI_COMM_WORLD*.

Now, on the receiving side, we have the following:

• MPI_Recv

```
int MPI_Recv(
        void*           message     /* out */,
        int             count       /* in  */,
        MPI_Datatype    datatype    /* in  */,
        int             source      /* in  */,
        int             tag         /* in  */,
        MPI_Comm        comm        /* in  */,
        MPI_Status*     status      /* out */)
```

Again, the first item in the argument list is the starting *address* into which the data are to be placed, the second argument is the count, and the third argument identifies the type of information to be sent. Instead of specifying the destination, the fourth argument is the source of the information, which is the process identifier of the source of the message to be received. The fifth and sixth arguments were just discussed in the preceding paragraph. The final argument is a special type of variable that supplies status information. Examining *status.MPI_ERROR* can provide the programmer with error information when something goes wrong. For more information concerning the content and use of *MPI_Status*, we refer the reader to [73].

For the purposes of illustration, let us examine the following MPI code. We want to create an array on each process, but to only initialize it on process 0. Once the array has been initialized on process 0, then it is sent out to each process.

Software

Suite

```cpp
#include<iostream.h>
#include<mpi.h>

int main(int argc, char * argv[]){
  int i;
  int nitems = 10;
  int mynode, totalnodes;
  MPI_Status status;

  double * array;

  MPI_Init(&argc,&argv);
  MPI_Comm_size(MPI_COMM_WORLD, &totalnodes);
  MPI_Comm_rank(MPI_COMM_WORLD, &mynode);

  array = new double[nitems];

  if(mynode == 0){
    for(i=0;i<nitems;i++)
      array[i] = (double) i;
  }

  if(mynode==0)
    for(i=1;i<totalnodes;i++)
      MPI_Send(array,nitems,MPI_DOUBLE,i,1,MPI_COMM_WORLD);
  else
    MPI_Recv(array,nitems,MPI_DOUBLE,0,1,MPI_COMM_WORLD,
        &status);

  for(i=0;i<nitems;i++){
    cout << "Processor " << mynode;
    cout << ": array[" << i << "] = " << array[i] << endl;
  }

  delete[] array;

  MPI_Finalize();

}
```

We draw your attention to the following:

• We first do the MPI initialization and information gathering calls described in the previous chapter (*MPI_Init*, *MPI_Comm_size*, and *MPI_Comm_rank*).
• We then create, on each process, an array using dynamic memory allocation.
• On process 0 only (i.e., `mynode == 0`), we initialize the array to contain the ascending index values. Observe that we *explicitly cast* the integer index value i to a double precision number to be stored in `array[i]`.
• On process 0, we proceed with (`totalnodes-1`) calls to *MPI_Send*.
• On all other processes other than 0, we call *MPI_Recv* to receive the sent message.
• On each individual process, we print the results of the sending/receiving pair.
• On each individual process, we deallocate the dynamic memory that we had allocated.

Though this program is simple, it contains most of the necessary components for getting up and running with MPI.

Let us conclude this section by making some remarks that will be useful both in understanding the program presented here and in understanding MPI programs to follow.

• Whenever you send and receive data, MPI assumes that you have provided nonoverlapping positions in memory. This remark will be extremely relevant when we study collective routines in the chapters to follow. We will point this fact out again.
• As we pointed out in the previous chapter, *MPI_COMM_WORLD* is referred to as a **communicator**. In general, a communicator is a collection of processes that can send messages to each other. *MPI_COMM_WORLD* is predefined in all implementations of MPI, and it consists of all MPI processes running after the initial execution of the program.
• In the send/receive discussions here, we were required to use a *tag*. The tag variable is used to distinguish upon receipt between two messages sent by the same process. The order of sending does not necessarily guarantee the order of receiving. Tags are used to distinguish between messages. MPI allows the tag *MPI_ANY_TAG*, which can be used by *MPI_Recv* to accept any valid tag from a sender. You *cannot* use *MPI_ANY_TAG* in the *MPI_Send* command, however.
• Similar to the *MPI_ANY_TAG* wildcard for tags, there is also an *MPI_ANY_SOURCE* wildcard that can also be used by *MPI_Recv*. By using it in an *MPI_Recv*, a process is ready to receive from any sending process. Again, you *cannot* use *MPI_ANY_SOURCE* in the *MPI_Send* command. There is no wildcard for sender destinations.
• When you pass an array to *MPI_Send/MPI_Recv*, it need not have exactly the number of items to be sent – *it must have greater than or equal to the number of items to be sent*. Suppose, for example, that you had an array of 100 items, but you only wanted to send the first 10 items. You can do so by passing the array to *MPI_Send* and only stating that 10 items are to be sent.

Throughout the remainder of this book we will building upon the basic foundation introduced here to accomplish more serious tasks of parallel scientific computing.

3.5 HOMEWORK PROBLEMS

3.5.1 Homework Problems for Section 3.1

1. In the previous chapter's exercises, a recursive relationship was given for generating the Fibonacci sequence. Write a recursively called function that takes as input at least the maximum number of terms to generate (your function may have more inputs) and prints the Fibonacci sequence to the screen.

2. The Vandermonde matrix of rank n is defined by

$$V_n \equiv \begin{bmatrix} 1 & x_0 & x_0^2 & \dots & x_0^n \\ 1 & x_1 & x_1^2 & \dots & x_1^n \\ \vdots & \vdots & \vdots & \vdots & \vdots \\ 1 & x_n & x_n^2 & \dots & x_n^n \end{bmatrix}.$$

Prove the following result for its determinant:

$$\det V_n = d_0 \, d_1 \dots d_{n-1},$$

where

$$d_k \equiv (x_{k+1} - x_k)(x_{k+1} - x_{k-1}) \dots (x_{k+1} - x_0).$$

3. Compute (by hand) the second-order polynomial $p_2(x)$ so that

$$p_2(0) = 3, \quad p_2(1) = 2, \quad p_2(3) = 5,$$

using the Vandermonde, Newton, and Lagrange approaches.

4. Construct the third-order Lagrange polynomials for the following functions in the interval $[x_0, x_n]$:

    (a) $f(x) = \ln x$, $x_0 = 1$, $x_1 = 1.1$, $x_2 = 1.3$, $x_3 = 1.4$;
    (b) $f(x) = 5\cos x + 3\sin x$, $x_0 = 0$, $x_1 = 0.25$, $x_2 = 0.5$, $x_3 = 1.0$.

5. Consider the Runge function with $\epsilon = 10^{-n}$, where $n = 1$ (case A) and $n = 5$ (case B). How many Chebyshev modes are required to approximate it with 10% (engineering) or 1% (scientific) accuracy for both cases A and B?

6. Consider the function $f(x) = \sin 2\pi x$, where $x \in [-1, 1]$.

    (a) Write a program for computing the interpolating polynomial $p_n(x)$ at the points $x_i^n = -1 + \frac{2i}{n}$ with $i = 0, 1, \dots, n$ for $n = 6, 12, 18, 24$ using the Lagrange approach. Plot the maximum pointwise error versus n.

(b) Do the same as in (a) but use a Chebyshev distribution of points to represent $f(x)$.

(c) Repeat (a) and (b) using the Newton approach.

(d) Write a program that asks the user which approach to use and which distribution to use. Integers may be used to delineate between approaches and between point distributions (i.e., Lagrange = 0, Newton = 1, etc.)

7. Estimate the number of multiplications required to compute $f(x) = \sum_{k=0}^{n} a_k q_k(x)$, where $q_k(x)$ is a general orthogonal polynomial. Show that if $q_k(x)$ is a Chebyshev polynomial then the number of required multiplications can be reduced to half the number required in the general case.

8. Modify the class defined for least squares to be an interpolation class. Encapsulate all the inner workings of interpolation into one object.

9. Represent the data in the table

x	0	0.1	0.2	0.3	0.4	0.5	0.6	0.7	0.8	0.9	1.0
$g(x)$	5	3.8	3.5	3.4	3.3	3.35	3.7	4.0	4.5	5.1	5.5

by a function of the form

$$g(x) = \alpha x^{-1} + \beta x^2,$$

using a procedure similar to least squares. Determine the values of α, β that minimize the least-squares error.

(**Note**: The resulting system of nonlinear equations may be solved iteratively; for help visit www.netlib.org.)

10. **Multivariate polynomial interpolation:** In most problems in simulation science the dependent variable is a function of more than one independent variable; for example, $y = f(x_1, x_2)$ is a bivariate function. We want to develop a least-squares multivariate approximation using the quadratic polynomial

$$y = c_0 + \alpha_1 x + \beta_1 y + \alpha_2 x^2 + \beta_2 y^2 + c_1 xy.$$

Obtain the equation for c_i, α_i, β_i that minimizes the least-squares error and formulate the problem in matrix form.

11. Determine a B-spline that goes through the end points for the following control points:

x	0	0	1	2	2	4	4
$f(x)$	0	1	1/2	1/2	2	2	0

12. Construct a fourth-order polynomial that approximates the function $f(x) = \sqrt{x}$ and goes through the points 0, 1, 2, 3, 4. Also, approximate this function with a cubic B-spline and compare the average and maximum approximation errors of the two approaches.

13. Using the *MPI_Send* and *MPI_Recv* functions, write an MPI program that accomplishes piecewise Lagrange interpolation. As in the preceding problem, consider the function $f(x) = \sin 2\pi x$, where $x \in [-1, 1]$. Write a program that accomplishes the following:

    (a) Partition the interval $[-1, 1]$ based upon the number of processors used.
    (b) For each process, use only four interpolation points (third-order polynomial) in which two of the points are the end points of the subdomain used for that process.
    (c) For each process, evaluate your interpolant at 30 points on its subdomain.
    (d) For each process, send all 30 points to process 0 for collection.
    (e) Have only process 0 print out the resulting interpolant evaluated at 30*P points (where P is the number of processes used).

14. **Mappings in polynomial approximations:** As we have seen in Section 3.1.4, regions of rapid variation in a function may lead to global spurius oscillations. An effective remedy is to introduce a new coordinate system $x = q(s, \alpha)$, where x is the physical coordinate and the transformed coordinate satisfies $-1 \le s \le 1$. The parameter α is associated with the steepness and its location.

    Two such mappings have been introduced by [6] that work effectively with Chebyshev approximations.

    The first mapping $x \mapsto s$ employs

    $$x = \alpha_2 + \tan[(s - s_0)\lambda]/\alpha_1,$$

    where

    $$s_0 = \frac{k-1}{k+1}, \quad k = \tan^{-1}[\alpha_1(1 + \alpha_2)]/\tan[\alpha_1(1 - \alpha_2)]$$

    and

    $$\lambda = \tan^{-1}[\alpha_1(1 - \alpha_2)]/(1 - s_0).$$

    Here α_1 expresses the degree of steepness and α_2 the location of rapid variation.

    The second mapping has the form

    $$x = \sin^{-1}(\alpha_1 s)/\sin^{-1}(\alpha_1), \quad 0 \le \alpha_1 \le 1.$$

    This mapping expands the boundary regions and compresses the interior regions. As $\alpha_1 \to 1$ the Gauss–Lobatto points become more uniformly spaced.

    Consider the Runge function $f(x) = 1/(1 + 25x^2)$ with $x \in [-1, 1]$, and use both mappings to approximate $f(x)$. Systematically vary the values of α_1 and α_2 to find optimum values for $N = 4, 8, 12, 24$, and 32 grid points. Make a log-linear plot of the L_2 and L_∞ errors versus N and compare your answers to the unmapped case, as in Figures 3.3 and 3.4.

15. Construct shape functions for a square domain $[-1, 1] \times [-1, 1]$ and a cubic domain $[-1, 1] \times [-1, 1] \times [-1, 1]$ for which there are only three nodes per edge (i.e., two vertices and a middle node) but not an interior node. Repeat for the case where there are four equidistant nodes per edge but no interior node.

16. Construct shape functions for a triangular domain and a tetrahedron domain each with edges of unit length and with a middle node per edge as well as one interior node.

17. Modify the code for multidimensional interpolation presented in Section 3.1.10 handle more than just bilinear interpolation. Given nine points, you should be able to go up to bicubic interpolation. Modify the code presented earlier to handle at least four points and up to nine points. This implies that your function has to be intelligent concerning the number of points that it passes. Let us first examine the things that will and will not change:

(a) Observe that the argument list itself need not change. Only the information passed into the function will change.

b) The user will now specify *npts* to be some value other than (or possibly including) four. The first thing to change is the static memory allocation of the array. No longer is an array of four elements sufficient. Should we move to dynamic memory allocation based on *npts*? No. Even though it would be perfectly legitimate to use dynamic memory allocation in this case, it is just as easy to allocate a static array for the maximum number of elements, which in this case is nine. In this case, it is "cheaper" to allocate a few extra doubles (in the case that *npts* is less than nine) than to both allocate and deallocate memory dynamically.

(a) You must now, of course, change the *argument checking*. No longer should you check to see if *npts* is exactly equal to four; rather you must check if *npts* lies between four and nine (inclusive).

(c) Now you must introduce the interpolation formulas for the various interpolants. We have already provided the first four formulas.

(d) The final issue is to check into which *npts* category you fall. Did the user want *npts* = 4, *npts* = 5, ..., or *npts* = 9? Since there are a small number of possibilities, try using a switch statement. Recall that the layout will look like the following:

```
switch(npts)
   case 4:
     // formulas for npts = 4
   break;

   case 5:
     // formulas for npts = 5
   break;

   case 6:
     // formulas for npts = 6
   break;

   case 7:
     // formulas for npts = 7
   break;
```

```
case 8:
  // formulas for npts = 8
break;

case 9:
  // formulas for npts = 9
break;
default:
  //add error statement here for when an
  //invalid npts is given
}
```

One thing that we would like to point out in this example is that we have made a programming decision to sacrifice optimality for generality. Experienced programmers would be quick to point out that the structure given here is not optimal and that if you were going to be doing thousands or millions of interpolations, it would be better for you to write a function for each case separately (hence eliminating the switch statement, and even the argument checking). The tradeoff in this case is that we have only one function to maintain. This balance between generality and optimality is one which you will constantly be confronted with as a programmer. The balance you reach is almost always application and situation dependent.

3.5.2 Homework Problems for Section 3.2

1. Let $f = \sum a_k e^{ikx}$ and $g = \sum b_k e^{ikx}$, and we construct the product $fg = \sum c_k e^{ikx}$. What is the relationship between c_k and b_k, a_k?

2. Construct the cosine and sine series of the function $f(x) = x^3$. Do the two series converge at the same rate? Plot the partial sums for each representation retaining $N = 2, 4, 8, 16, 32$ terms. What do you observe?

3. Compute the square of the Fourier matrix $\mathbf{W}$ of order $N = 1,024$ using matrix–matrix multiplication (e.g., *dgemm* from BLAS3) and also using the discrete fast Fourier transforms using the fact that this is a product of two circulant matrices. What do you observe?

4. Consider the function $f(x) = 1$, $x \in [0, 1]$, and $f(x) = -1$, $x \in [1, 2]$. Obtain its Fourier coefficients and use the Lanczos filter to improve the approximation. What is the asymptotic rate of convergence before and after the filtering in the L_1 and L_2 norms? You can obtain the answers either analytically or numerically.

5. Use a double Fourier series representation to expand in real double Fourier series the function

$$f(x, y) = x + y \quad x, y \in [-\pi, \pi].$$

6. **Chebyshev transforms**: Derive an algorithm for a fast Chebyshev transform based on the fast Fourier transform. Write a C++ code for it and obtain timings on your

computer for various sizes N. How does your algorithm compare to the matrix–vector multiplication? Specifically, at what value of N do we have the break-even point?

3.5.3 Homework Problems for Section 3.3

1. Use the Fourier transform approach to plot the Battle–Lemarié wavelet of order $m = 4$.

2. Use the iteration approach to plot the Daubechies scaling functions and wavelets of orders $m = 5$ and 9.

3. Obtain the discrete wavelet transform of the function f using the Daubechies wavelets of fourth order.

4. Derive Equation 3.35 for the Shannon wavelet.

4

Roots and Integrals

In this chapter we apply the approximation theory we presented in Chapter 3 to find solutions of linear and nonlinear equations and to perform integration of general functions. Both subjects are classical, but they serve as basic tools in scientific computing operations and in solving systems of ordinary and partial differential equations. With regard to root finding, we consider both scalar as well as systems of nonlinear equations. We present different versions of the Newton–Raphson method, the steepest descent method, and the conjugate gradient method (CGM); we will revisit the latter in Chapter 9. With regard to numerical integration we present some basic quadrature approaches, but we also consider advanced quadrature rules with singular integrands or in unbounded domains.

On the programming side, we first introduce the concept of passing a function to a function; in the previous chapter we were passing variables. This allows an easy implementation of recursion, which is so often encountered in scientific computing. We offer several C++ examples from root finding and numerical integration applications that make use of *recursion*, and we show an effective use of *classes* and *overloaded operators*. We also address parallel programming with emphasis on domain decomposition, specifically the concept of *reduction operations*. We introduce the MPI commands *MPI_Reduce* and *MPI_Allreduce* for accomplishing reduction operations among a collection of processes.

4.1 ROOT-FINDING METHODS

There are many problems in scientific computing where we need to find the root of a nonlinear equation or systems of algebraic equations. For example, a polynomial equation arises in computing the eigenvalues from the characteristic polynomial, or general transcendental equations need to be solved to obtain the dispersion relation in wave dynamics problems. Another example is the computation of a square root of a number. For example, the computation of $\sqrt{3}$ can be turned into finding the root of the equation $f(x) = x^2 - 3 = 0$, and this can be solved *iteratively* very fast, starting from an educated guess! For an initial guess of $x_0 = 1.5$ we substitute in the formula

$$x_{n+1} = \frac{1}{2}(x_n + \frac{3}{x_n}), \quad n = 1, 2, \ldots,$$

Table 4.1: Numerical approximation of $\sqrt{3}$.

Iteration	Root approximation	Error
0	1.50000000	2.32050808e-01
1	1.75000000	1.79491924e-02
2	1.73214286	9.20495740e-05
3	1.73205081	2.44585041e-09
$\vdots$		

and obtain $x_1 = 1.75$ in one iteration versus the exact value 1.7320508. More iterations will result in predicting accurately more and more digits; in fact, we double the number of correct digits in each iteration! This formula comes from the Newton–Raphson algorithm, and it is often used in mathematical libraries of computers for the square-root function.

In the following we provide our own implementation of this function and construct Table 4.1 showing the iteration count and associated error when computing $\sqrt{3}$ using this function.

```
double SquareRoot(double value, double guess, int iterations){
  int i;
  double xn = guess;

  for(i=0; i<iterations;i++)
    xn = 0.5*(xn + value/xn);

  return xn;
}
```

In this function, observe that upon calculation of the next value x_{n+1}, we immediately place it in the variable **xn**. This is because in this iterative scheme, once the new value is computed, the previous value is not needed. An alternative version of the function is the following:

```
double SquareRoot(double value, double guess, double tol){
  int i;
  int maxit = 100;
  double xn2, xn = guess;

  for(i=0; i<maxit;i++){
    xn2 = 0.5*(xn + value/xn);
    if(fabs(xn2-xn)<tol)
       return xn2;
    xn = xn2;
  }
```

Software ◉ *Suite*

```
    cerr << "Maximum number of iterations reached ";
    cerr << "without convergence" << endl;
    return xn2;
}
```

In this function, instead of inputting the number of iterations, we input a tolerance. As we calculate updated values, we check to see if the absolute value of the difference between successive iterates is less than the tolerance. Note the following remarks:

- We *do* need to separately store the new value (**xn2**) so that it can be compared with the old value.
- We have chosen to set a maximum number of iterations instead of using a *while* loop.
- We use the function **fabs**, which is a function whose declaration is contained within *math.h*, and which takes as input a double precision number and gives back the double precision absolute value of that number. (**Note:** A function **abs** exists also, but it takes as input integers and returns the integer absolute value. Because of implicit casting, oftentimes people make the mistake of using **abs** when they should be using **fabs**, and they obtain the wrong result.)
- We return directly from the *for* loop once the tolerance condition has been met. By using return, we terminate the loop tacitly by exiting the function.

We are familiar with root-finding methods for the first- and second-order polynomial equations for which we can derive closed-form solutions, and these solutions have been known to Egyptians for centuries and also to Babylonians for more than forty centuries! Clearly, we do not need to use a computer to obtain solutions for these equations, but things become much harder as the order of the polynomial increases, and in fact fifth- or higher order polynomials *cannot* be solved in closed form, as Lagrange first discovered in the late eighteenth century. For third- and fourth-order polynomial equations, analytical formulas are available. They were first obtained by the Italian mathematician Ferrari; however, they are very complex and thus not very useful.

In this section, we will study methods and corresponding code fragments to obtain solutions of *general nonlinear equations* as well as *systems* of general nonlinear equations, but it instructive to start with polynomial equations. The methods that we will develop are *iterative* and are easy to program, but they require good knowledge of the basic theory. We need

- to know how fast the algorithms converge,
- to know when to terminate the iterative process, and
- to make an initial guess to start the iteration, sometimes an educated guess!

In the following, we show how we can use the approximation theory of the previous chapter to achieve these goals.

4.1.1 Polynomial Equations

CUBIC POLYNOMIALS. Let us first consider a cubic polynomial equation of the form

$$f(\xi) = \xi^3 + a\xi^2 + b\xi - c = 0,$$

where a, b, and c are real numbers so that we have at least one real root. Here we will follow the analysis of Lanczos [66]. The first step is to *rescale* this equation in a more convenient form by introducing the transformation

$$x = \alpha\xi, \ a_1 = \alpha a, \ b_1 = \alpha^2 b, \ c_1 = \alpha^3 c,$$

and by substitution we obtain

$$f(x) = x^3 + a_1 x^2 + b_1 x - c_1 = 0.$$

By taking $\alpha = 1/\sqrt[3]{c}$ we obtain $c_1 = 1$, and therefore

$$f(0) = -1 < 0 \quad \text{and} \quad f(\infty) > 0.$$

We also have that the three roots satisfy

$$x_1 \, x_2 \, x_3 = 1.$$

Next, we examine the sign of $f(x)$ at $x = 1$; if $f(1) > 0$ there exists one *real* root in the interval $[0, 1]$, but if $f(1) < 0$ there must be one real root in the interval $[1, \infty]$. In this case, we simply introduce another transformation, that is,

$$\bar{x} = \frac{1}{x},$$

mapping $[1, \infty] \to [0, 1]$. It is then sufficient to find the real root of a cubic equation in the interval $[0, 1]$.

TELESCOPING OF A POWER SERIES BY SUCCESSIVE REDUCTIONS is an elegant way of reducing a high-order polynomial to a lower order by taking advantage of the properties of the Chebyshev polynomials discussed in Section 3.1.5. In particular, we will use the *shifted* Chebyshev polynomials defined by

$$T_k^*(x) = T_k(2x - 1), \quad x \in [0, 1], \tag{4.1}$$

which we tabulate in Table 4.2. We will make use of the following facts:

- The shifted Chebyshev polynomials have the largest coefficient of the highest power of x among all polynomials defined in the same interval.
- They are bounded by ± 1, just like the standard Chebyshev polynomials.
- They are defined in the interval of interest; here $x \in [0, 1]$.

Let us consider, for example, the third-order shifted Chebyshev polynomial $T_3^*(x) = 32 x^3 - 48 x^2 + 18 x - 1$; then

$$x^3 = \frac{48x^2 - 18x + 1}{32} + \frac{T_3^*(x)}{32},$$

Table 4.2: Coefficients of the first six shifted Chebyshev polynomials $T_n^*(x)$. The underlined numbers correspond to negative coefficients, and the sequence is from the lowest to highest power; for example, $T_3^*(x) = -1 + 18x - 48x^2 + 32x^3$, $T_0^*(x) = 1$.

$n = 1$:	1, 2
$n = 2$:	1, 8, 8
$n = 3$:	1, 18, 48, 32
$n = 4$:	1, 32, 160, 256, 128
$n = 5$:	1, 50, 400, 1120, 1280, 512
$n = 6$:	1, 72, 840, 3584, 6912, 6144, 2048

and because of the boundness of $T_3^*(x)$, we can approximate

$$x^3 \approx 1.5x^2 - 0.5625x + 0.03125 \quad (\pm 0.03125),$$

where the term in the parenthesis is the error $\pm 1/32$, which in this case is about 3%.

EXAMPLE. The following example illustrates the main points discussed so far. Let us consider the cubic polynomial equation

$$\xi^3 + \xi^2 - 1.5\xi - 50 = 0.$$

We first perform the transformation

$$\alpha = 1/\sqrt[3]{50} \approx 0.2714 \Rightarrow f(x)$$
$$= x^3 + 0.2714x^2 - 0.1105x - 1 = 0,$$

and subsequently, we examine the sign of $f(x)$ at $x = 1$:

$$f(1) = 0.1609 > 0 \Rightarrow x_1 \in [0, 1].$$

The next step is to reduce the cubic equation to a quadratic equation and apply the formula of the Babylonians! To this end, we use the shifted Chebyshev polynomial $T_3^*(x)$ and Equation (4.1) to obtain

$$1.7714x^2 - 0.673x - 0.9687 = 0,$$

which has a positive root $x_1 = 0.9534$ and a negative root, which we disregard. We now transform back to obtain

$$\xi_1 = \frac{x_1}{\alpha} = \frac{0.9534}{0.2714} = 3.513.$$

The residual is $f(3.513) = 0.42$, and although this value is not 0, it is relatively small compared to the constant $c = 50$; it corresponds to an error of 0.4%! The more accurate value obtained with the Newton–Raphson method is 3.5030. If, however, this is not an acceptable accuracy, then this "educated" guess can serve as an initial value in one of the algorithms that we will present in this section.

FOURTH-ORDER POLYNOMIALS. We can proceed similarly with fourth-order polynomial equations of the form

$$x^4 + c_1x^3 + c_2x^2 + c_3x + c_4 = 0,$$

which can be turned into the form

$$(x^2 + \alpha x + \beta)^2 = (ax + b)^2,$$

and by taking the square root we reduce this to two quadratic equations. The question is how to obtain α, β, a, and b in terms of c_i, $i = 1, 2, 3, 4$. This is accomplished via a series of simple transformations:

$$\alpha = c_1/2, \ A = c_2 - \alpha^2, \ B = c_3 - \alpha A.$$

We then form the cubic equation

$$f(\xi) \equiv \xi^3 + (2A - \alpha^2)\xi^2 + (A^2 + 2B\alpha - 4c_4)\xi - B^2 = 0,$$

which has a positive real root since $f(0) = -B^2 < 0$. We now use the previous method for cubic polynomials to determine the real root, which we call ξ_1. Having obtained ξ_1, we determine all the coefficients of the two quadratic equations from

$$\alpha = \frac{1}{2}c_1, \ \beta = \frac{1}{2}(A + \xi_1), \ a = \sqrt{\xi_1}, \ b = \frac{a}{2}(\alpha - B/\xi_1).$$

Again, this real root can be used as an initial guess to obtain more accurate answers from the algorithms presented later in this section.

HIGH-ORDER POLYNOMIALS. Obtaining good approximations for the roots of high-order polynomials is a much more difficult job and may require many function evaluations to locate approximately real roots. However, high-order polynomials have typically complex roots, so here we review a method first proposed by Bernoulli that provides an approximation to the *absolutely largest* root. Let us consider the polynomial

$$f(x) = x^n + a_1 x^{n-1} + \cdots + a_n = (x - x_1)(x - x_2)\dots(x - x_n),$$

were x_i, $i = 1, 2, \ldots, n$ denote the roots of the polynomial $f(x)$. We can then compute the ratio

$$-\frac{f'(x)}{f(x)} = \frac{1}{x_1 - x} + \frac{1}{x_2 - x} + \cdots + \frac{1}{x_n - x}.$$

If x_0 is an initial guess that happens to be close to one of the roots, say x_1, then by comparing terms in this expansion we can see that one term dominates, that is,

$$\frac{1}{x_0 - x_1} \sim -\frac{f'(x_0)}{f(x_0)}.$$

Thus, we have managed to isolate one root, and, in fact, we can make this estimate sharper by taking the derivative $(m - 1)$ times to obtain

$$-\frac{1}{(m-1)!}\left[\frac{f'(x)}{f(x)}\right]^{(m-1)} = \frac{1}{(x_1 - x)^m} + \cdots + \frac{1}{(x_n - x)^m}$$

$$\Rightarrow \frac{1}{(x_1 - x_0)^m} \sim -\frac{1}{(m-1)!}\left[\frac{f'(x_0)}{f(x_0)}\right]^{(m-1)}.$$

By choosing m sufficiently high we can put the "spotlight" on the root x_1 with increasing accuracy. This method, however, requires a lot of work as it involves the computation of derivatives, although approximate ways have been suggested by Lanczos to do this efficiently, for example, the so-called *method of moments*. The interested reader should consult Lanczos's book [66] for more details.

4.1.2 Fixed Point Iteration

One approach to solving nonlinear equations is by iteration, where the equation $f(x) = 0$ is rearranged as

$$x = g(x), \tag{4.2}$$

with $f(x) = x - g(x)$. We can set up a *fixed point iteration* of the form

$$x_{n+1} = g(x_n),$$

which upon convergence ("steady state") leads to $x_{n+1} \to s$, and thus Equation (4.2) is satisfied. It turns out that the key to convergence, as we will see in the theorem to follow, is the first derivative of $g(x)$. We demonstrate this by a simple example of a quadratic polynomial, which is used often to model *chaos*.

Let us consider

$$g(x) = \alpha x(1 - x) = \alpha x - \alpha x^2,$$

with α being the bifurcation parameter, the meaning of which will become clear momentarily. We want to solve

$$x_{n+1} = \alpha x_n - \alpha x_n^2. \tag{4.3}$$

We note that the maximum value of $g(x)$ is $g(1/2) = \alpha/4$, and therefore for $\alpha < 4$, $x_n \in [0, 1]$; that is, the sequence of numbers produced by the iteration process remains bounded within the range $[0, 1]$. Let us consider a specific example, and take $\alpha = 2$. Then

$$x_{n+1} = 2x_n - 2x_n^2$$

and in steady state, that is, upon convergence, we have that $x_n \to s$ and also $x_{n+1} \to s$, so the fixed or *stationary points* are given by the equation

$$s = 2s - 2s^2,$$

which has two roots, the stationary points, at $s = 0$ and $1/2$.

We then evaluate the first derivative at the stationary points, and

- if $|g'(s)| < 1$, the stationary point s is *attractive*;
- otherwise, it is *repulsive*.

This can be seen by constructing the graph of $g(x)$ and following the sequence generated by the iterative equation. In this case, we have that $g'(0) = 2$, which is a repulsive point, and $g'(1/2) = 0$, which is an attractive point, and in fact very attractive!

This process can be easily generalized for the simple iteration equation we have considered to obtain the stationary points $s_1 = 0$ and $s_2 = (\alpha - 1)/\alpha$. At the second point, we have

$$g'(s_2) = 2 - \alpha \quad \text{and} \quad |2 - \alpha| < 1 \Rightarrow -1 < 2 - \alpha < 1 \Rightarrow 1 < \alpha < 3.$$

Therefore, we have found the range within which the bifurcation parameter α results in an attractive point and thus a convergent iteration process. Similarly, it is easy to show that $g'(s_1) = \alpha$, so as long as $\alpha < 1$ we have a convergent iteration process.

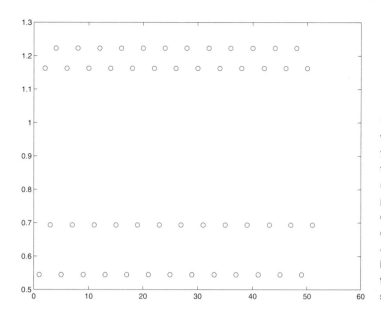

Figure 4.1: Plot of the values (vertical axis) of the time series versus the iteration number (horizontal axis) produced from the quadratic chaos equation (4.3); $\alpha = 0.249$. The iteration converges to four different values at steady state.

We can of course substitute back into Equation (4.2) to obtain

$$g_1(x) = g(g(x)) = \alpha(\alpha x - \alpha x^2) - \alpha(\alpha x - \alpha x^2)^2,$$

which has four stationary points. By proceeding as before and examining the derivative $g_1'(s)$, we find that we have an instability and thus divergence for $\alpha > 3.45$. In fact, for higher values of α the system bifurcates even further to a *period-doubling cascade*. The ratio between the length of one stability window and the next approaches a universal constant $\delta = 4.69920166\ldots$, which is known as the *Feigenbaum's constant* in chaos theory.

EXAMPLE. Next, we present an example of the iteration process for the quadratic chaos equation, which converges for some small value of the bifurcation parameter; for larger values it oscillates between different values even at steady state; and for even larger values it is unstable and diverges. Consider the iteration

$$x_{n+1} = (1 + 10\alpha)x_n - 10\alpha x_n^2, \quad x_0 = 0.1. \qquad (4.4)$$

We find that for $\alpha = 0.18$ this iteration converges to 1, but for $\alpha = 0.23$ it jumps between 1.18 and 0.69. For $\alpha = 0.25$ it jumps among 1.23, 0.54, 1.16, and 0.70. For the value $\alpha = 0.3$ no discernible pattern is displayed; note also a window of *order* just above $\alpha = 0.28$ and then a return to chaos again! The plots in Figures 4.1 and 4.2 show schematically this strange but interesting behavior.

After this introductory example, we are now ready to state the theorem on convergence of fixed point iteration.

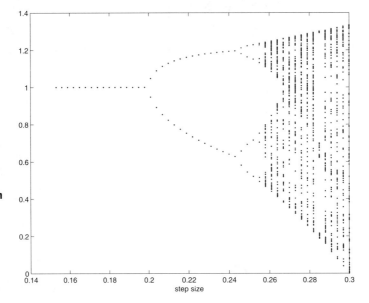

Figure 4.2: Bifurcation diagram. Plotted are the converged values of the iteration in Equation (4.4) versus the bifurcation parameter (step size) α.

THEOREM OF CONVERGENCE OF FIXED POINT ITERATION: *Let s be a solution of $x = g(x)$ and g have a continuous derivative in some interval I containing s. Then if $|g'(s)| \leq K < 1$ in I, the iteration process $x_{n+1} = g(x_n)$ converges for any initial value x_0 in I.*

PROOF. From the mean value theorem we have that there exists a point $t_1 \in [x, s]$: $g(x) - g(s) = g'(t_1)(x - s)$. Then

$$|x_n - s| = |g(x_{n-1}) - g(s)| = |g'(t_1)|\,|x_{n-1} - s|$$

$$\leq K|x_{n-1} - s|$$

$$= K|g(x_{n-2}) - g(s)|$$

$$\leq K|g'(t_2)|\,|x_{n-2} - s|$$

$$\leq K^2|x_{n-2} - s|$$

$$\vdots$$

$$\leq K^n|x_0 - s| \to 0.$$

Here $t_i, i = 1, 2, \ldots \in I$, as well. Note that $g(x)$ is called a *contraction*, and in general a *contraction mapping* is defined as

$$|g(u) - g(v)| \leq K|u - v|, \quad K < 1.$$

ROUND-OFF ERROR. Associated with such an iteration process are round-off errors, which, however, can be quantified. To this end, consider the iteration

$$x_n = g(x_{n-1}) + \delta_n,$$

where $|\delta_n| \leq \delta$ and $\delta \ll 1$ denotes the known machine accuracy. We then have

$$
\begin{aligned}
|x_n - s| &= |g(x_{n-1}) - g(s) + \delta_n| \\
&\leq K|x_{n-1} - s| + \delta \\
&\leq K(K|x_{n-2} - s| + \delta) + \delta \\
&\vdots \\
&\leq K^n|x_0 - s| + \delta(1 + K + K^2 + \cdots + K^{n-1}) \\
&\leq K^n|x_0 - s| + \frac{\delta}{1 - K},
\end{aligned}
$$

where in the last line we used the limit of a geometric series since $K < 1$.

ERROR ESTIMATE. Similarly, we can obtain an error estimate by comparing two successive approximations:

$$
\begin{aligned}
|x_{n+1} - x_n| &= |g(x_n) - g(x_{n-1})| \\
&\leq K|x_n - x_{n-1}| \\
&\vdots \\
&\leq K^n|x_1 - x_0|.
\end{aligned}
$$

For fixed n and $m > n$ we have

$$
\begin{aligned}
|x_m - x_n| &\leq |x_m - x_{m-1}| + |x_{m-1} - x_{m-2}| + \cdots + |x_{n+1} - x_n| \\
&\leq (K^{m-1} + K^{m-2} + \cdots + K^n)|x_1 - x_0| \\
&= \frac{K^n}{1 - K}|x_1 - x_0|.
\end{aligned}
$$

Since $x_m \to s$ as $m \to \infty$ for convergence, then

$$|x_n - s| \leq \frac{K^n}{1 - K}|x_1 - x_0|.$$

We can now define the **convergence rate** as the ratio of two successive error estimates. Let $e_n \equiv x_n - s$ and $s = g(s)$; then

$$e_{n+1} = x_{n+1} - s = g(s + e_n) - g(s) = g'(t)e_n,$$

from the mean value theorem, $t \in [x_n, s]$, and thus

$$\lim_{n \to \infty} \frac{e_{n+1}}{e_n} = g'(s).$$

If $g'(s) = 0$ and $g'(x)$ is continuous (as in the case of the very attractive point at $s = 0$ that we encountered in the example earlier), then

$$e_{n+1} = g(s + e_n) - g(s) = g'(s)e_n + g''(s)\frac{e_n^2}{2} + \cdots$$

and therefore

$$\lim_{n \to \infty} \frac{e_{n+1}}{e_n^2} = \frac{1}{2}g''(s),$$

which shows **quadratic convergence**; that is, at every iteration the number of correct digits is doubled!

4.1.3 Newton–Raphson Method

We now present the most popular method in root finding, which was proposed independently by Newton and Raphson. It combines the ideas of the iterative process already discussed and of approximation presented in Section 3.1. Let us consider again the equation

$$f(x) \equiv x - g(x) \quad \text{and} \quad f(s) = 0,$$

and denote by h the distance between the exact solution s and an initial guess x_0. Then, we use Taylor expansion around x_0 to obtain

$$f(s) = 0 = f(h + x_0) = f(x_0) + hf'(x_0) + \frac{h^2}{2}f''(x_0) + \cdots.$$

By neglecting terms higher than second order in h, we obtain

$$h_0 \equiv h = -\frac{f(x_0)}{f'(x_0)}.$$

We can now propose an improved guess $x_1 = x_0 + h_0$, which leads to a hopefully shorter distance

$$h_1 = -\frac{f(x_1)}{f'(x_1)},$$

and so on.

We summarize this iterative process as follows:

$$x_{n+1} = x_0 + h_0 + \cdots + h_n,$$

$$h_n = -\frac{f(x_n)}{f'(x_n)}, \quad n = 1, 2, \ldots,$$

where x_0 is the initial guess that starts the iteration. Alternatively, we can write these two equations as a single equation,

$$x_{n+1} = x_n \underbrace{- \frac{f(x_n)}{f'(x_n)}}_{g(x_n)}, \tag{4.5}$$

assuming that $f'(s) \neq 0$. The convergence rate can then be obtained by examining the first derivative $g'(s)$:

$$g'(x) = 1 - \frac{f'^2 - ff''}{(f')^2} = f\frac{f''}{(f')^2} \to 0 \text{ as } x \to s.$$

We also have that

$$g''(x) = \frac{(ff'')'(f')^2 - 2f'f''ff''}{(f')^4} = \frac{ff'''f' + f'^2f'' - 2ff''^2}{(f')^3} \neq 0 \text{ as } x \to s.$$

In general, $g''(s) \neq 0$, and therefore the convergence rate of the Newton–Raphson method is second order (**quadratic convergence**).

EXAMPLE. Let us revisit the example of finding the square root of a positive number that we discussed in the introduction of this section. We assume that

$$f(x) = x^2 - C$$

and therefore

$$s = \sqrt{C}$$

is the exact answer. We now use the preceding Newton–Raphson formula

$$f'(x_n)(x_{n+1} - x_n) = -f(x_n),$$

and thus

$$2x_n(x_{n+1} - x_n) = C - (x_n)^2 \Rightarrow x_{n+1} = \frac{1}{2}\left(x_n + \frac{C}{x_n}\right).$$

Therefore, we compute the square root $\sqrt{C}$ by averaging x and C/x. The convergence is quadratic, that is,

$$x_{n+1} - \sqrt{C} = \frac{1}{2x_n}(x_n - \sqrt{C})^2.$$

At every iteration step the difference $(x_n - \sqrt{C})$, which is the error, is squared!

Improved Convergence

We can improve the convergence rate of the Newton–Raphson method by retaining the second-order term in the Taylor expansion, that is,

$$f(x_0) + h[f'(x_0) + \frac{h}{2}f''(x_0)] = 0$$

$$\Rightarrow h = -\frac{f(x_0)}{f'(x_0) + \frac{h}{2}f''(x_0)}.$$

In this equation, we can compute a provisional value for h in the denominator, say h_n^*, from the linear Taylor expansion at the previous iteration as

$$h_n^* = -\frac{f(x_n)}{f'(x_n)} \Rightarrow \frac{1}{h_n} = -\frac{f'(x_n)}{f(x_n)} + \frac{1}{2}\frac{f''(x_n)}{f'(x_n)}.$$

This two-step approach is a general procedure called the *predictor–corrector* method and is used often in scientific computing. The idea is to first predict with a lower order but explicit method and subsequently to correct the answer with a higher order method.

Multiple Roots

So far we have only treated the case of a single root, but we also need to have fast methods to compute multiple roots. In such cases, both the function and some of its derivatives vanish at the root location, depending on the multiplicity.

Let us first examine the case of a **double root** and consider an initial guess x_0; if it is close to the exact root s then $f(x_0) \to 0$ and also $f'(x_0) \to 0$. Therefore, the standard Newton–Raphson method will converge slowly because the term

$$g'(x_0) = f(x_0) \frac{f''(x_0)}{[f'(x_0)]^2}$$

will be finite or slowly decaying to zero, and

$$\lim_{n \to \infty} \frac{e_{n+1}}{e_n} = g'(s) \neq 0,$$

which indicates only first-order convergence for a double root. We can improve convergence by solving the quadratic equation with respect to h

$$\frac{1}{2} f''(x_0)h^2 + f'(x_0)h + f(x_0) = 0,$$

derived from Taylor's expansion, to obtain two roots $h_\pm$ and then setting

$$x_1 = x_0 \pm h_\pm$$

and proceeding with the iteration.

In the case of a **triple root**

$$f(x_0) \to 0, \quad f'(x_0) \to 0, \quad f''(x_0) \to 0,$$

and we need to solve a cubic equation to obtain the proper distance to update the guess, that is,

$$\frac{1}{6} f'''(x_0)h^3 + \frac{1}{2} f''(x_0)h^2 + f_0'(x_0)h + f(x_0) = 0.$$

By solving this equation we obtain three values h_1, h_2, h_3, and thus we can update $x_1 = x_0 + h_i$, $i = 1, 2, 3$, and so on for the next iteration.

A *better approach* in dealing with multiple roots is presented in the following. We assume that the function $f(x)$ has a **root of multiplicity** p, so we can write

$$f(x) = (x - s)^p h(x), \quad p > 1, \quad h(s) \neq 0,$$

and

$$g(x) \equiv x - \frac{f(x)}{f'(x)},$$

whose derivative as $x \to s$ determines the convergence rate. We obtain

$$g'(x) = 1 - \frac{ph^2(x) + (x - s)^2(h'(x))^2 - (x - s)^2 h(x) h''(x)}{p^2 h^2(x) \left[1 + (x - s)\frac{h'(x)}{ph(x)}\right]^2}.$$

Upon convergence we have that $x \to s$, and thus

$$g'(s) \to 1 - \frac{1}{p} \neq 0 \quad \text{for} \quad p > 1.$$

Clearly, $|g'(s)| < 1$, and the method converges, but it is only first order. However, we note that if we redefine $g(s)$ so that

$$g(x) \equiv x - p\frac{f(x)}{f'(x)},$$

we obtain quadratic convergence, as $g'(x \to s) \to 0$, and we use the theorem of convergence of the previous section. The iterative process is then

$$x_{n+1} = x_n - p\frac{f(x_n)}{f'(x_n)}, \quad n = 0, 1, \ldots.$$

Yet another way to obtain second-order convergence for a multiple root is to define the function

$$\phi(x) = \frac{f(x)}{f'(x)},$$

which upon convergence ($x \to s$) has the simple form

$$\phi(x \to s) \to \frac{x - s}{p},$$

with a *single* root at $x = s$, and thus Newton–Raphson will converge quadratically fast. However, this method requires three function evaluations [$f(x)$, $f'(x)$, and $f''(x)$], and thus it is more expensive than the previous one.

- In general, it is impossible to achieve second-order convergence with only one function evaluation.

The initial guess is very important in starting the iterative process in the Newton–Raphson algorithm. The following theorem states the proper conditions for convergence:

THEOREM OF CONVERGENCE OF NEWTON–RAPHSON METHOD : *Suppose that $f'(x) \neq 0$, that $f''(x)$ does not change sign in the interval $[a, b]$, and that $f(a) f(b) < 0$. If*

$$|\frac{f(a)}{f'(a)}| < (b - a) \, and \, |\frac{f(b)}{f'(b)}| < (b - a)$$

then the Newton–Raphson method converges from an arbitrary initial approximation $x_0 \in [a, b]$.

4.1.4 Passing Functions to Functions in C++

One thing that we will find useful throughout this chapter is the concept of passing functions to functions, just as you pass variables to functions. Why is this useful? When writing modular code, quite often you write essential library routines once, and compile them once, and then merely link them to your current program when you compile. Take for example our Newton–Raphson algorithm. Notice that the algorithm is described independently of the particular function with which you are working; it merely relies on the fact that you have a function $f(x)$ and its derivative $f'(x)$. We want to write code in such a way that we can change our function and its derivative, and never have to change our core Newton–Raphson implementation. This can be accomplished by passing functions to functions.

Just as in the case of a variable, within the argument of the function to which you are passing the function, you must provide information as to what is being passed. In the case of passing a function, the information that is needed is as follows:

- the name that the function to be called within the routine,
- the argument types of the function that you are passing, and
- the return value of the function that you are passing.

This procedure will be made more clear in the examples that follow.

Software Suite

PUTTING IT INTO PRACTICE
In the following examples, there are two main concepts that we would like to draw your attention to:

- passing functions to functions and
- using different functions with the same name.

We begin with passing functions to functions. The next example is our implementation of the Newton–Raphson method. Recall that, for this algorithm, we require both the function and its derivative. We thus require two functions, here called "func" and "func_der" within our code to be passed to the NewtonRaphson routine.

```
double NewtonRaphson(double x0, double (*func)(double),
                     double (*func_der)(double),
    int max_iter, int multiplicity){
  double x,p = (double) multiplicity;
  const double tolerance = 1.0e-14;

  for(int i=0;i<max_iter;i++){
    x = x0 - p*func(x0)/func_der(x0);
    if(fabs(func(x))<tolerance) break;
    x0 = x;
  }

  return x;
}
```

We make the following remarks:

- Observe how this function is notified that a function is being passed to it. In the second argument of the argument list, we specify as the argument

    ```
    double (*func)(double)
    ```

    notifying the function of the return type (in this case *double*), name of the passed function to be used within the function (in this case *func*), and the argument types of the passed function (in this case *double*). In the third argument we pass another function with the same return type and argument list types, but with a different name (*func_der*).
- We wrote the *if* statement on one line – this is perfectly valid in C++. Since by definition an *if* statement executes the next executable statement given that the check is evaluated to be true, then we can condense an *if* statement having only one executable statement to one line. We suggest that if the executable statement that follows the *if* is complicated, you do not condense both the *if* and the next executable statement to one line.
- We can sacrifice memory for optimization. Notice that within the *if* statement, we evaluate *func(x)*. If the tolerance criterion is not met, we set $x0 = x$ and begin the iteration again, which requires that we evaluate *func(x0)*. If the function *func* is expensive to compute, it is advantageous to save the function evaluation to a variable that we use both in the *if* statement and in the case that the tolerance is not met.

Look at the following function. What is the difference between this function and the preceding one?

```
double NewtonRaphson(double x0, double (*func)(double),
                     double (*func_der)(double), int max_iter){
  double x, p = 1; // here, p stands for the multiplicity;
                   // we assume default p=1
  const double tolerance = 1.0e-14;

  for(int i=0;i<max_iter;i++){
    x = x0 - p*func(x0)/func_der(x0);
    if(fabs(func(x))<tolerance) break;
    x0 = x;
  }

  return x;
}
```

The answer is that the second function does not require you to pass the variable "multiplicity." The second implementation of the *NewtonRaphson* function assumes the multiplicity is one. Why do we point this out? Notice that we used the same function name for both functions. C++ allows you to have multiple functions with the same name *as long as* the argument lists are different. By different, we mean either in number of arguments or in the type of variable.

Key Concept	C++ allows multiple functions with the same name *as long as* the argument lists are different.

In the preceding example, the argument list of one function has fewer variables than the argument list of the other function, and hence the compiler can distinguish them as two different functions. This concept is useful in writing general software libraries, in that you can handle many different function cases by having functions with the same name but different argument lists.

Warning	**PROGRAMMER BEWARE!** • Having different return types does not imply having different functions

The compiler cannot tell the difference between two functions that have identical names and arguments; it can only distinguish different return types!

Also, observe that in the preceding function we use the keyword **const**. This identifier should be used in conjunction with a variable declaration and initialization as follows:

```
const <type> <variable name> = <constant value>;
```

where `<type>` is the variable type, `<variable name>` is the variable name we have chosen to use, and `<constant value>` is a value of the appropriate type that we would like to remain constant. Once a variable has been declared constant within a function, it cannot be changed within the function. Using **const** reinforces that something is meant to be a constant and guarantees that the programmer does not accidentally reset the value to something else (which would imply that the value was not constant!).

We provide another example of the *NewtonRaphson* routine, now with three functions being passed to this routine. In this case, we pass a functional implementation of the second derivative of the function to this routine so that the convergence rate for multiple roots can be computed.

```
double NewtonRaphson(double x0, double (*func)(double),
      double (*func_der)(double),
              double (*func_secondder)(double), int max_iter,
      int multiplicity){
  double x,p = (double) multiplicity;
  const double tolerance = 1.0e-14;

  cout << "-----------------------------------" << endl;
  cout << "x \t f(x) \t g'(x)" << endl;

  for(int i=0;i<max_iter;i++){
```

```
        cout << x0 << "\t" << func(x0) << "\t" <<  (1-p) +
          p*func(x0)*func_secondder(x0)/pow(func_der(x0),2) <<
              endl;;
        x = x0 - p*func(x0)/func_der(x0);
        if(fabs(func(x))<tolerance) break;
        x0 = x;
      }

      return x;
    }
```

We can now put into practice what we have learned. The following program uses the last *NewtonRaphson* function to compute the roots of

$$(x - 2)^3(x + 2) = 0.$$

```
#include <iostream.h>
#include "SCchapter4.h"

const double alpha = 2.0; // global constant

double func(double x);
double func_der(double x);
double func_secondder(double x);

int main(int argc, char * argv[]){
  int max_iter = 100;
  int multiplicity = 1;
  double x0 = 1;

  double x =  NewtonRaphson(x0,func,func_der,func_secondder,
    max_iter,multiplicity);

  cout << x << " " << fabs(func(x)) <<endl;;
}

double func(double x){
  double value = (x-alpha)*(x-alpha)*(x-alpha)*(x+alpha);
  return(value);
}

double func_der(double x){
  double value = 3*(x-alpha)*(x-alpha)*(x+alpha)+
    (x-alpha)*(x-alpha)*(x-alpha);

  return(value);
}

double func_secondder(double x){
  double value = 6*(x-alpha)*(x+alpha)+6*(x-alpha)*(x-alpha);
  return(value);
}
```

Observe that we declare and define our implementations of the function, derivative function, and second derivative function just as we have always done previously. Now, when it is time to call the *NewtonRaphson* routine we place into the argument list the function names in the appropriate places within the argument list, just as if we were passing these functions as variables.

4.1.5 Secant Method

The Newton–Raphson method requires that we know the function analytically, so that we can differentiate it analytically. However, there are instances where we only know the function values and therefore we need to construct the derivative using finite differences. General finite difference methods will be covered in detail in Sections 5.1 and 6.1, but here we use the simple backward-difference formula to approximate the first derivative, that is,

$$f'(x_n) \approx (\Delta f)_1 \equiv \frac{f(x_n) - f(x_{n-1})}{x_n - x_{n-1}}.$$

The secant method extrapolates along the chord that connects the points x_n and x_{n-1} instead of extrapolating along the tangent at x_{n-1} as is done by the Newton–Raphson method. This is a first-order, $\mathcal{O}(h)$, approximation to the derivative; however, the overall convergence rate of the secant method is about 1.6 compared with 2 for the Newton–Raphson method.

In comparing the secant method with the Newton–Raphson method in situations where both approaches can be applied, we have a *break-even point* determined approximately by the equation of cost in computing

$$f'(x) = \theta \times (\text{cost of } f(x)).$$

Then if $\theta > 0.4$, it is more efficient to use the secant method. Note that $(0.4 = 2 - 1.6)$ reflects the difference in convergence rate of the two methods.

Error Analysis of the Secant Method

In the following, we provide a brief proof on the convergence rate of the secant method, following the derivation in [72].

We use Newton's interpolating formula presented in Chapter 3 and the mean value theorem:

$$f(x) = f(x_n) + (x - x_n)(\Delta f)_1 + (x - x_{n-1})(x - x_n)\frac{1}{2}f''(\xi),$$

where we defined earlier

$$(\Delta f)_1 = \frac{f_n - f_{n-1}}{x_n - x_{n-1}}.$$

Now x_{n+1} satisfies the secant method equation: $0 = f_n + (x_{n+1} - x_n)(\Delta f)_1$.
We also have for the exact solution

$$0 = f_n + (s - x_n)(\Delta f)_1 + \frac{1}{2}(s - x_{n-1})(s - x_n)f''(\xi),$$

and by subtracting, we obtain

$$(s - x_{n+1})(\Delta f)_1 + \frac{1}{2}(s - x_{n-1})(s - x_n) f''(\xi) = 0.$$

From the mean value theorem we have that for a special point ξ^*, $(\Delta f)_1 = f'(\xi^*)$, and therefore the error

$$e_{n+1} = \underbrace{\frac{f''(\xi)}{2 f'(\xi^*)}}_{C} e_n e_{n-1}.$$

We have assumed that $f''(x)$ is continuous, and thus it is bounded, so we can always find the constant C. Let us now assume that

$$|\epsilon_{n+1}| = K|\epsilon_n|^m,$$

and substitute into the previous equation to arrive at

$$K|e_n|^m \approx C|e_n| \, (K^{-1/m}|e_n|^{1/m}) \Rightarrow m = 1 + 1/m \rightarrow m = \frac{1}{2}(1 \pm \sqrt{5}).$$

We can only accept the (+) sign and thus we obtain that the convergence rate is $m \approx$ 1.618 (recall that this value is the *golden ratio*, which we computed from the Fibonacci sequence in the exercises in Chapter 2).

4.1.6 Systems of Nonlinear Equations

The Newton–Raphson method can be generalized in a straightforward manner to systems of nonlinear equations by introducing the Jacobian operator. Let us consider the $n \times n$ system

$$f_1(x_1, \ldots, x_n) = 0,$$

$$f_2(x_1, \ldots, x_n) = 0,$$

$$\vdots$$

$$f_n(x_1, \ldots, x_n) = 0,$$

which we rewrite in compact form as

$$\mathbf{f}(\mathbf{x}) = \mathbf{0}.$$

Then, the iterative Newton–Raphson method for this system is

$$\mathbf{J}_n(\mathbf{x}_{n+1} - \mathbf{x}_n) = -\mathbf{f}(\mathbf{x}_n),$$

where we define the Jacobian operator as

$$\mathbf{J} = \frac{\partial f_i}{\partial x_j}.$$

We also note that here the subscripts $n, (n+1), \ldots$ denote iteration number but also components of the vector $\mathbf{x}$.

CONVERGENCE. Next, we examine the conditions that guarantee that the Newton–Raphson method for a system converges at a rate similar to the scalar equations, that is, at quadratic rate. This is done by examining the partial derivatives of

$$\mathbf{g}(\mathbf{x}) \equiv \mathbf{x} - \mathbf{J}^{-1}\mathbf{f}(\mathbf{x}),$$

and by differentiation

$$\frac{\partial \mathbf{g}(\mathbf{x})}{\partial x_j} = \frac{\partial \mathbf{x}}{\partial x_j} - \frac{\partial}{\partial x_j}\left[\mathbf{J}^{-1}(\mathbf{x})\mathbf{f}(\mathbf{x})\right]$$

$$= \frac{\partial \mathbf{x}}{\partial x_j} - \mathbf{J}^{-1}(\mathbf{x})\frac{\partial \mathbf{f}}{\partial x_j} - \mathbf{f}(\mathbf{x})\frac{\partial \mathbf{J}^{-1}(\mathbf{x})}{\partial x_j}.$$

At the solution $\mathbf{x} = \mathbf{s}$, this expression becomes

$$\frac{\partial \mathbf{g}(\mathbf{s})}{\partial x_j} = \mathbf{I} - \mathbf{J}^{-1}(\mathbf{s})\mathbf{J}(\mathbf{s}) - \mathbf{f}(\mathbf{s})\frac{\partial \mathbf{J}^{-1}(\mathbf{s})}{\partial x_j} \to 0,$$

where $\mathbf{I}$ is the identity operator. Furthermore, to determine the last term, $\frac{\partial}{\partial x_j}[\mathbf{J}^{-1}(\mathbf{x})]$, we note that

$$\frac{\partial}{\partial x_j}[\mathbf{J}^{-1}\mathbf{J}] = \frac{\partial \mathbf{I}}{\partial \mathbf{x}} = \mathbf{0} = \mathbf{J}^{-1}\frac{\partial \mathbf{J}}{\partial \mathbf{x}} + \mathbf{J}\frac{\partial \mathbf{J}^{-1}}{\partial \mathbf{x}},$$

and therefore

$$\frac{\partial \mathbf{J}^{-1}}{\partial x_j} = -\mathbf{J}^{-1}\frac{\partial \mathbf{J}}{\partial x_j}\mathbf{J}^{-1}.$$

From this analysis, we see that we need only require that

- $\mathbf{f}(\mathbf{x})$ have two derivatives and
- $\mathbf{J}(\mathbf{x})$ be nonsingular at the solution or root.

Then, the convergence of Newton–Raphson's method is *quadratic*, similar to the scalar case. The theorem below gives the precise conditions for convergence.

CONVERGENCE THEOREM: *Let us assume that*

$$\| \mathbf{J}^{-1}(\mathbf{x}_0) \| \le a \quad and \quad \| \mathbf{x}_0 - \mathbf{x}_1 \| \le b$$

and also that

$$\sum_{k=1}^{n}\left|\frac{\partial^2 f_i(\mathbf{x})}{\partial x_j \partial x_k}\right| \le \frac{c}{n}, \quad \forall\, \mathbf{x} : \| \mathbf{x} - \mathbf{x}_0 \| \le 2b, \quad i, j = 1, 2, \ldots, n.$$

If in addition $a\,b\,c \le 1/2$, then the Newton–Raphson iterates are uniquely defined and lie in the 2b-sphere, that is,

$$\| \mathbf{x}_k - \mathbf{x}_0 \| \le 2b,$$

$$\lim_{k \to \infty} \mathbf{x}_k = \mathbf{s}, \quad \| \mathbf{x}_k - \mathbf{s} \| \le \frac{2b}{2^k}.$$

The problem with the Newton–Raphson method for systems is that it is computationally expensive as it requires the solution of a linear system in each iteration to invert the Jacobian matrix $\mathbf{J}$. It also requires the construction of the n^2 entries in the Jacobian matrix, which are partial derivatives of $\mathbf{f}(\mathbf{x})$. To this end, several modifications have been proposed and many different versions are used in practice, depending on the particular application. Next, we present two simple popular versions.

MODIFIED NEWTON. Here the Jacobian is computed only initially and used for all subsequent iterations, that is,

$$\mathbf{J}_0(\mathbf{x}_{n+1} - \mathbf{x}_n) = -\mathbf{f}(\mathbf{x}_n) \,.$$

This, however, lowers the convergence to first order, as can be seen for the scalar example presented earlier for the square root (here $\mathbf{J}_0 = 2x_0.$):

$$(x_{n+1} - \sqrt{C}) = \left[1 - \frac{x_n + \sqrt{C}}{2x_0} \right] (x_n - \sqrt{C}),$$

which clearly indicates linear convergence.

QUASI-NEWTON. Here we use the values from the *first two iterations* $\mathbf{x}_1, \mathbf{x}_0$ and we define $\Delta\mathbf{x} \equiv \mathbf{x}_1 - \mathbf{x}_0$ and $\Delta\mathbf{f} \equiv \mathbf{f}_1 - \mathbf{f}_0$. The idea is to adjust $\mathbf{J}_1$ to satisfy $\mathbf{J}_1\Delta\mathbf{x} = \Delta\mathbf{f}$, and thus

$$\mathbf{J}_1 = \mathbf{J}_0 + \frac{(\Delta\mathbf{f} - \mathbf{J}_0\Delta\mathbf{x})(\Delta\mathbf{x})^T}{(\Delta\mathbf{x})^T(\Delta\mathbf{x})} \,,$$

and then $\mathbf{x}_2 = \mathbf{x}_1 - \mathbf{J}^{-1}\mathbf{f}$. Convergence is faster than linear but not quite quadratic. An extension of this approach with modifications to preserve symmetry of $\mathbf{J}$ is used in finite element methods [84].

Continuation Method

We have seen so far through the theorems and through examples how crucial the initial condition (guess) is for the Newton–Raphson method to converge, and this is especially true for systems of nonlinear equations. In problems where we have to solve nonlinear equations many times (e.g., in time-dependent simulations), we can use the solution of the previous time step. Similarly, assuming that we study the instability of a system that depends on a bifurcation parameter α, we need to solve

$$\mathbf{f}(\mathbf{x}, \alpha) = \mathbf{0}$$

for several values of α. One approach that is often used in practice is to linearize the equations for the critical value of the bifurcation parameter, say at α_c, for example right at the onset of the bifurcation (instability), and compute the solution to the linear system of equations. We can then use that solution as a initial guess to obtain a solution for a value of $\alpha > \alpha_c$ but with the difference $(\alpha - \alpha_c)$ not too large. This process can continue for a larger value of α, and so on. This is the *continuation method*, as we assume that the systems of equations define dependent variables that are continuously differentiable in α.

If there is no bifurcation parameter explicitly included in the equations, we can still use the continuation method by introducing a *fictitious* parameter α and rewriting the system of equations as

$$\mathbf{h}(\mathbf{x}, \alpha) = (1 - \alpha)\mathbf{f}(\mathbf{x}_0) - \mathbf{f}(\mathbf{x}), \quad \alpha \in [0, 1],$$

where $\mathbf{x}_0$ is a first solution guess, which may or may not satisfy the original system $\mathbf{f}(\mathbf{x}) = \mathbf{0}$. We see that for $\alpha = 0$ the guess solution is a root for $\mathbf{h}(\mathbf{x})$, and for $\alpha = 1$ we recover the system we want to solve. This suggests that we can start with the guess solution $\mathbf{x}_0$ and $\alpha = 0$ and continue in small increments of α up to $\alpha = 1$.

4.1.7 Solution via Minimization: Steepest Descent and Conjugate Gradients

In this section we present ways of solving systems of linear and nonlinear algebraic equations by attempting to obtain the minimum of an appropriately defined functional. We will focus on two useful methods: steepest descent and conjugate gradients.

Method of Steepest Descent

We have already mentioned the computational complexity associated with the computation of the Jacobian $\mathbf{J}$, but even worse, sometimes we may not be able to compute it at all. In this case, we can still use an approach similar to the secant method in which we replace the inverse Jacobian with a scalar constant α, as follows:

$$\mathbf{x}_{n+1} - \mathbf{x}_n = -\alpha \mathbf{f}(\mathbf{x}_n). \tag{4.6}$$

The step size α is important, but it is the direction of the path that we follow namely, along the tangent direction $-\mathbf{f}(\mathbf{x}_n)$–that gives this method the name of the *steepest descent*.

To appreciate this, let us introduce the antiderivative of the system of equations we try to solve, which is a scalar function

$$P(x_1, \ldots, x_n) \quad \text{and} \quad f_i = \frac{\partial P}{\partial x_i} = 0.$$

We can then interpret $\mathbf{f}(\mathbf{x})$ as the gradient of the parent function $P(\mathbf{x})$. Obtaining the solution is equivalent to minimizing the parent function, as we set all its partial derivatives equal to zero. For example, for a system of *linear equations* $\mathbf{Ax} = \mathbf{b}$, the parent function that we minimize has the simple quadratic form

$$P(\mathbf{x}) = \frac{1}{2}\mathbf{x}^T \mathbf{A}\mathbf{x} - \mathbf{x}^T \mathbf{b}$$

because the location of the minimum coincides with the solution $\mathbf{x} = \mathbf{A}^{-1}\mathbf{b}$. For nonlinear equations, however, the parent function is more difficult to obtain.

Since $\mathbf{f} = \nabla P$ and the gradient operator points toward increasing values of the scalar P, that is, along paths of *steepest ascent*, it is clear that $-\mathbf{f}(\mathbf{x}_n)$ points along paths of *steepest descent* [see Equation (4.6)], and it is perpendicular to iso-contours of $P(\mathbf{x})$. The iso-surfaces of a *positive-definite* quadratic $P(\mathbf{x})$ is an ellipsoid centered about the global minimum; the semiaxes of the ellipsoid are related to the eigenvalues of the corresponding matrix $\mathbf{A}$. If the eigenvalues of $\mathbf{A}$ are all equal, then the iso-surfaces of P would be spheres, and thus the steepest descent direction would point toward the sphere center. However, the eigenvalues are typically very different in magnitude; in extreme cases the sphere may be a *thin ellipsoid,* in which case convergence to the minimum may be very slow or may even fail. This is expressed in the following theorem, which is valid for the *linear* case:

FIRST THEOREM OF CONVERGENCE FOR QUADRATIC P: *The eigenspectrum of the matrix* $\mathbf{A}$ *defines the convergence of the steepest descent method as follows:*

$$P(x_k) + \frac{1}{2}\mathbf{b}^T\mathbf{A}^{-1}\mathbf{b} \leq \left(1 - \frac{1}{\kappa_2(\mathbf{A})}\right)\left(P(x_{k-1}) + \frac{1}{2}\mathbf{b}^T\mathbf{A}^{-1}\mathbf{b}\right).$$

Here

$$\kappa_2(A) = \frac{\lambda_{\max}}{\lambda_{\min}}$$

is the condition number of the *positive-definite* symmetric matrix $\mathbf{A}$, and if it is large the convergence is very slow. The condition number expresses the aspect ratio of the ellipsoid, that is, the ratio of its two semiaxes.

The step size α can be chosen properly so that a monotonic convergence is guaranteed. The following theorem presents the appropriate choice for α.

SECOND THEOREM OF CONVERGENCE FOR QUADRATIC P: *Consider the vector* $\mathbf{f} \equiv \nabla P = \mathbf{A}\mathbf{x} - \mathbf{b}$. *By computing the step size in the steepest descent method from*

$$\alpha = \frac{\mathbf{f}^T\mathbf{f}}{\mathbf{f}^T\mathbf{A}\mathbf{f}} \tag{4.7}$$

then

$$P(\mathbf{x}) = P(\mathbf{x} - 2\alpha\mathbf{f}) \quad and \quad P(\mathbf{x} - \alpha\mathbf{f}) - P(\mathbf{x}) \leq 0$$

for an arbitrary vector $\mathbf{x}$.

This theorem simply states that if we move by an amount 2α along the steepest descent, we will end up on the other side of the ellipsoid formed by the iso-contours of $P(\mathbf{x})$. If we move only by an amount α, then we guarantee that we get closer to the global minimum. This is proven by considering

$$P(\mathbf{x} - 2\alpha\mathbf{f}) = \frac{1}{2}(\mathbf{x} - 2\alpha\mathbf{f})^T\mathbf{A}(\mathbf{x} - 2\alpha\mathbf{f}) - (\mathbf{x} - 2\alpha\mathbf{f})^T\mathbf{b},$$

which is rearranged to

$$P(\mathbf{x} - 2\alpha\mathbf{f}) = P(\mathbf{x}) - 2\alpha\mathbf{f}^T\mathbf{f} + 2\alpha^2\mathbf{f}^T\mathbf{A}\mathbf{f},$$

so by choosing α as suggested by the theorem we prove the first statement. The second statement is straightforward to prove with this choice of α, and upon substitution we obtain

$$P(\mathbf{x} - \alpha\mathbf{f}) = P(\mathbf{x}) - \frac{1}{2}\frac{(\mathbf{f}^T\mathbf{f})^2}{\mathbf{f}^T\mathbf{A}\mathbf{f}} \leq P(\mathbf{x}).$$

The steepest descent algorithm with *adaptive step* size α for the linear system $f \equiv \mathbf{Ax} - \mathbf{b} = 0$ can then be summarized as follows:

STEEPEST DESCENT ALGORITHM

Initialize: Choose $\mathbf{x}_0 \Rightarrow \mathbf{f}_0 = \mathbf{Ax}_0 - \mathbf{b}$.
Begin Loop: for $n = 1, 2, \ldots$

$$\alpha_n = \frac{\mathbf{f}_n^T\mathbf{f}_n}{\mathbf{f}_n^T\mathbf{A}\mathbf{f}_n}$$

$$\mathbf{x}_{n+1} = \mathbf{x}_n - \alpha_n\mathbf{f}_n$$

$$\mathbf{f}_{n+1} = \mathbf{Ax}_n - \mathbf{b}$$

endfor

End Loop

For *nonlinear* systems this algorithm can also be used but the step size α_n may not be optimum and convergence could be slow.

Conjugate Gradient Method – CGM

A more effective method than the steepest descent is one that not only takes adaptive steps but also *turns adaptively* in the pursuit of the minimum of the parent function. To this end, we can improve the search direction so that instead of $\mathbf{f}(\mathbf{x}_n)$, we follow the direction of the steepest descent $\mathbf{p}$, which is conjugate to the previous search directions

$$\mathbf{p}_n = -\mathbf{f}_n + \beta_{n-1}\mathbf{p}_{n-1}, \tag{4.8}$$

where β_{n-1} changes in each iteration *adaptively* and can be computed from the projection

$$\beta_{n-1} = \frac{\mathbf{f}_n^T(\mathbf{f}_n - \mathbf{f}_{n-1})}{\mathbf{f}_{n-1}^T\mathbf{f}_{n-1}}, \tag{4.9}$$

as we will show later. The conjugate gradient formula is then

$$\mathbf{x}_{n+1} - \mathbf{x}_n = \alpha_n\mathbf{p}_n, \tag{4.10}$$

where $\mathbf{p}_n$ is computed from Equation (4.8) and the step size α_n could also be computed adaptively. For nonlinear problems there are no known formulas that can do that but for linear problems there is a nice theory that we will present next. We note that for $\beta_{n-1} = 0$ we recover the steepest descent method.

CGM for Linear Systems

We will present several different solution algorithms for linear systems in Chapter 9, but CGM is one of the very best. The success of the conjugate gradient method in obtaining solutions of systems of nonlinear equations quickly is based upon the theory of conjugate gradients for *linear systems of equations* and the remarkable properties that are inherent in this method. In the following, we develop this theory for the linear system

$$\mathbf{Ax} = \mathbf{b} \Rightarrow \mathbf{r} \equiv \mathbf{b} - \mathbf{Ax},$$

where $\mathbf{r}$ is defined as the residual. It is zero exactly when we reach the minimum of the the quadratic parent function

$$P(\mathbf{x}) = \frac{1}{2}\mathbf{x}^T\mathbf{Ax} - \mathbf{x}^T\mathbf{b},$$

where we assume that $\mathbf{A}$ is *positive-definite* and *symmetric*.

First, we need to define conjugate directions. In general, the vectors $\mathbf{p}$ and $\mathbf{q}$ are said to be conjugate or A-orthogonal if

$$\mathbf{p}^T\mathbf{Aq} = 0.$$

The idea of the CGM is to perform searches in a set of conjugate directions $\mathbf{p}_i$ satisfying the A-orthogonality condition, that is,

$$\mathbf{p}_i^T\mathbf{Ap}_j = 0.$$

As an example, the eigenvectors of the matrix $\mathbf{A}$ satisfy this property since

$$\mathbf{v}_i^T\mathbf{Av}_j = \mathbf{v}_i^T\lambda\mathbf{v}_j = \lambda\mathbf{v}_i^T\mathbf{v}_j = 0, \quad i \neq j.$$

Let us now assume that we have a symmetric positive-definite matrix $\mathbf{A}$ that has size $n \times n$. Then at each iteration $(k + 1)$ we obtain the conjugate direction, that is, the solution, from

$$\mathbf{x}_{k+1} = \mathbf{x}_k + \alpha\mathbf{p}_k,$$

where α will be chosen to minimize the quadratic functional, and $\mathbf{p}_k$ will be computed adaptively, as we will see in the following. First, we can show that

$$P(\mathbf{x}_{k+1}) = P(\mathbf{x}_k) + \frac{1}{2}\alpha^2\mathbf{p}_k^T\mathbf{Ap}_k - \alpha\mathbf{p}_k^T\mathbf{r}_k,$$

where we have used $\mathbf{r}_k = \mathbf{b} - \mathbf{A}\mathbf{x}_k$. Next, we minimize the quadratic P with respect to α by setting

$$\frac{\partial P}{\partial \alpha} = 0,$$

which leads to

$$\alpha_k \equiv \alpha = \frac{(\mathbf{p}_k, \mathbf{r}_k)}{(\mathbf{p}_k, \mathbf{A}\mathbf{p}_k)}.$$

Here we have defined the inner (dot) product

$$(\mathbf{a}, \mathbf{b}) \equiv \mathbf{a}^T \mathbf{b}$$

to simplify the notation, and we will use that in the following.

THEOREM ON CONJUGATE DIRECTIONS: *Let* $\mathbf{A}$ *be a symmetric positive-definite matrix of size* $n \times n$. *Then after n conjugate direction searches in the n-dimensional space, we obtain* $\mathbf{r}_n = \mathbf{0}$, *and thus we reach a minimum of the parent function* $P(\mathbf{x})$.

    PROOF. We will make use of the A-orthogonality property defining the conjugate directions. First, from the repeated action of the iteration $\mathbf{x}_k = \mathbf{x}_{k-1} + \alpha_{k-1}\mathbf{p}_{k-1}$ we obtain

$$\mathbf{x}_k - \mathbf{x}_0 = \sum_{i=0}^{k-1} \alpha_i \mathbf{p}_i, \tag{4.11}$$

where $\mathbf{x}_0$ is the initial (arbitrary) guess and

$$\alpha_i = \frac{(\mathbf{p}_i, \mathbf{r}_i)}{(\mathbf{p}_i, \mathbf{A}\mathbf{p}_i)}$$

as determined from the minimization of the quadratic form.

    Let us now consider the (unknown) solution $\mathbf{s}$ and express it in terms of the n A-orthogonal vectors that form the conjugate directions. This is possible because these vectors are *linearly independent* owing to the A-orthogonality. Specifically, we offset the solution by the initial guess and then expand it as follows:

$$\mathbf{s} - \mathbf{x}_0 = \sum_{j=0}^{n-1} \gamma_j \mathbf{p}_j,$$

where from the orthogonality again we can compute the coefficients

$$\gamma_j = \frac{(\mathbf{p}_j, \mathbf{A}(\mathbf{s} - \mathbf{x}_0))}{(\mathbf{p}_j, \mathbf{A}\mathbf{p}_j)}.$$

Next, we consider the coefficient γ_k and subtract the scalar

$$\frac{(\mathbf{p}_k, \mathbf{A}(\mathbf{x}_k - \mathbf{x}_0))}{(\mathbf{p}_k, \mathbf{A}\mathbf{p}_k)},$$

which is zero from Equation (4.11). We can then combine the two to get

$$
\begin{aligned}
\gamma_k &= \frac{(\mathbf{p}_k, \mathbf{A}(\mathbf{s} - \mathbf{x}_0))}{(\mathbf{p}_k, \mathbf{A}\mathbf{p}_k)} - \frac{(\mathbf{p}_k, \mathbf{A}(\mathbf{x}_k - \mathbf{x}_0))}{(\mathbf{p}_k, \mathbf{A}\mathbf{p}_k)} \\
&= \frac{(\mathbf{p}_k, \mathbf{A}(\mathbf{s} - \mathbf{x}_k))}{(\mathbf{p}_k, \mathbf{A}\mathbf{p}_k)} \\
&= \frac{(\mathbf{p}_k, \mathbf{r}_k)}{(\mathbf{p}_k, \mathbf{A}\mathbf{p}_k)},
\end{aligned}
$$

where we have used the definition of the residual, that is, $\mathbf{r}_k = \mathbf{b} - \mathbf{A}\mathbf{x}_k = \mathbf{A}(\mathbf{s} - \mathbf{x}_k)$.

By comparing the coefficients γ_k and α_k we see that they are identical and therefore the n-term expansion of the conjugate direction iteration $(\mathbf{x}_k - \mathbf{x}_0)$ is identical to the exact solution $(\mathbf{s} - \mathbf{x}_0)$. This result is indeed remarkable!

Although the theorem of conjugate directions is valid for any set of conjugate directions, efficiency is what distinguishes the conjugate gradient algorithm. For example, the use of the eigenvectors of $\mathbf{A}$ would be prohibitively expensive as it takes much more computational work to compute the eigenvectors of the matrix than to solve the linear system! Another approach would be to use the Gram–Schmidt algorithm to obtain conjugate directions, but this is also very expensive and would amount to $\mathcal{O}(n^4)$ work.

To this end, the idea of Hestenes and Stiefel [55] to *compute iteratively* the search directions $\mathbf{p}$ is the keystone of this method. It is very efficient and requires the storage of only two or three vectors. Initially, we set $\mathbf{p}_0 = \mathbf{r}_0$, and then we iterate

$$
\mathbf{p}_{k+1} = \mathbf{r}_{k+1} + \beta_k \mathbf{p}_k,
$$

where we need to determine the scalar β_k by using the A-conjugate property of the search directions $\mathbf{p}_k$. For this, we take the inner product of the previous equation with $\mathbf{p}_k^T$ and impose A-orthogonality on the left-hand-side:

$$
0 = (\mathbf{p}_k, \mathbf{A}\mathbf{p}_{k+1}) = (\mathbf{p}_k, \mathbf{A}\mathbf{r}_{k+1}) + \beta_k (\mathbf{p}_k, \mathbf{A}\mathbf{p}_k).
$$

This leads to

$$
\beta_k = -\frac{(\mathbf{p}_k, \mathbf{A}\mathbf{r}_{k+1})}{(\mathbf{p}_k, \mathbf{A}\mathbf{p}_k)} = -\frac{(\mathbf{r}_{k+1}, \mathbf{A}\mathbf{p}_k)}{(\mathbf{p}_k, \mathbf{A}\mathbf{p}_k)},
$$

which can always be computed because the denominator is guaranteed to be nonzero. The last equality is valid since $\mathbf{A}$ is symmetric.

Next, we prove some useful relationships between the orthogonal directions and the residual that can be used to reduce even further the computational complexity of the conjugate gradient algorithm. First, it is clear that using its definition we can also compute the residual iteratively as

$$
\begin{aligned}
\mathbf{r}_{k+1} &= \mathbf{b} - \mathbf{A}\mathbf{x}_{k+1} \\
&= \mathbf{b} - \mathbf{A}(\mathbf{x}_k + \alpha_k \mathbf{p}_k) \\
&= (\mathbf{b} - \mathbf{A}\mathbf{x}_k) - \alpha_k \mathbf{A}\mathbf{p}_k \\
&= \mathbf{r}_k - \alpha_k \mathbf{A}\mathbf{p}_k.
\end{aligned}
$$

Using these equation we now show that

$$(\mathbf{r}_i, \mathbf{p}_j) = 0, \quad i \neq j, \tag{4.12}$$

$$(\mathbf{r}_i, \mathbf{p}_i) = (\mathbf{r}_i, \mathbf{r}_i), \tag{4.13}$$

$$(\mathbf{r}_i, \mathbf{r}_j) = 0, \quad i \neq j. \tag{4.14}$$

This is shown by induction, that is, by assuming that the first of these equations is valid we will also show that $(\mathbf{r}_{i+1}, \mathbf{p}_j) = 0$. We substitute $\mathbf{r}_{i+1}$ from the iteration equation and then it becomes obvious; we proceed similarly for the other two equations.

Based on these relations, we can also prove that β_k is the ratio of the square of the magnitudes of two successive gradients, that is,

$$\beta_k = -\frac{(\mathbf{p}_k, \mathbf{A}\mathbf{r}_{k+1})}{(\mathbf{p}_k, \mathbf{A}\mathbf{p}_k)} = \frac{(\mathbf{r}_{k+1}, \mathbf{r}_{k+1})}{(\mathbf{r}_k, \mathbf{r}_k)} \, .$$

We now finalize the **CG algorithm for linear systems of equations:**

CONJUGATE GRADIENT ALGORITHM

Initialize: Choose $\mathbf{x}_0 \Rightarrow \mathbf{p}_0 = \mathbf{r}_0 = \mathbf{b} - \mathbf{A}\mathbf{x}_0$.
Begin Loop: for $k = 1$ to n

$$\alpha_k = \frac{(\mathbf{r}_k, \mathbf{r}_k)}{(\mathbf{p}_k, \mathbf{A}\mathbf{p}_k)}$$

$$\mathbf{x}_{k+1} = \mathbf{x}_k + \alpha_k \mathbf{p}_k$$

$$\mathbf{r}_{k+1} = \mathbf{r}_k - \alpha_k \mathbf{A}\mathbf{p}_k$$

$$\beta_k = \frac{(\mathbf{r}_{k+1}, \mathbf{r}_{k+1})}{(\mathbf{r}_k, \mathbf{r}_k)}$$

$$\mathbf{p}_{k+1} = \mathbf{r}_{k+1} + \beta_k \mathbf{p}_k$$

endfor

End Loop

This code represents the ideal algorithm that terminates after exactly n iterations; it assumes that the orthogonality of the conjugate directions is preserved independently of the matrix $\mathbf{A}$, i.e., of its size and its structure. In practice, however round-off errors may destroy such orthogonality, resulting in incomplete convergence. The convergence process then is controlled by the condition number of $\mathbf{A}$ as discussed in Chapter 9, where preconditioning techniques for convergence acceleration are also presented.

The simplicity of the CG algorithm both in terms of coding as well as in terms of computational complexity is amazing! We only need to perform one matrix–vector product (i.e., $\mathbf{A}\mathbf{p}_k$), one dot product, and three *daxpy* operations, all of which can be implemented very efficiently using the BLAS routines discussed in Section 2.2.7.

PUTTING IT INTO PRACTICE

Here we provide our implementation of a nonpreconditioned conjugate gradient routine. We also use a stopping criterion for convergence in anticipation of round-off errors. Our program can then be terminated before or after n iterations, depending on the matrix **A** and the tolerance level we use. For this implementation, we are using *classes* from the *software suite*, namely, *SCVector* and *SCMatrix*.

The beautiful thing about the implementation here is that by using classes (and all the mechanics that are available for using classes in C++), the CG method can be described succinctly in a few lines of code. Next, we present our implementation

```
SCVector ConjugateGradient(SCMatrix A, SCVector b,
    SCVector x0){
  int dim = x0.Dimension();
  const double tolerance = 1.0e-14;
  SCVector x(dim),r(dim),v(dim),z(dim);
  double c,t,d;

  x = x0;
  r = b - A*x;
  v = r;
  c = dot(r,r);

  for(int i=0;i<dim;i++){
    if(sqrt(dot(v,v))<tolerance){
      cerr << "Error in ConjugateGradient: execution "
      cerr << "of function terminated" << endl;
      break;
    }
    z = A*v;
    t = c/dot(v,z);
    x = x + t*v;
    r = r - t*z;
    d = dot(r,r);
    if(sqrt(d) < tolerance)
      break;
    v = r + (d/c)*v;
    c = d;
  }

  return x;
}
```

In this function, we have used classes for encapsulating the ideas of a vector and a matrix, and we have used the idea of *overloaded operators* to perform the mathematical operations necessary. Notice that we are using operators like "+", "−", and "∗" *between* variables of type *SCVector* and *SCVector*, and between *SCMatrix* and *SCVector*. As we discussed in Section 3.1.8, this is accomplished by overloading the operators, that is, by extending the definition of these operators to include operations between our newly created data types.

We now present a simple main driving program that uses this function.

```
#include <iostream.h>
#include "SCmathlib.h"
#include "SCchapter4.h"

int main(int argc, char * argv[]){
  int dim = 4;
  SCVector x(dim),b(dim),x0(dim);
  SCMatrix A(dim);

  // Set our initial guess
  x0(0) = x0(1) = x0(2) = x0(3) = 1.0;

  for(int i=0;i<dim;i++){
    for(int j=0;j<dim;j++){
      A(i,j) = 1+(i+1)*(j+1);

      /* We do this to make sure that the symmetric matrix that
         we create has a determinant that is nonzero */

      if(i==3 && j == 2)
        A(i,j) = 12;
      if(i==2 && j == 3)
        A(i,j) = 12;
    }
  }

  cout << "The Matrix A that we are using: " << endl;
  A.Print();
  cout << endl;

  SCVector y(dim);
  y(0) = 2.;
  y(1) = -3.;
  y(2) = 5.43;
  y(3) = -22.56;

  cout << "The exact solution is: " << endl;
  y.Print();
  cout << endl;

  b = A*y;

  cout << "The right-hand side, b, of Ax=b: " << endl;
  b.Print();
  cout << endl;

  x = ConjugateGradient(A,b,x0);
```

```
    cout << "The approximate solution using CG is: " << endl;
    x.Print();
    cout << endl;

}
```

4.2 NUMERICAL INTEGRATION METHODS

Approximate integration of a function is a very old subject. It was first performed rigorously by Archimedes, who used the method of inscribed and circumscribed polygons to obtain lower and upper bounds for the value of the area of a circle. He also computed the center of mass and center of buoyancy for many complicated figures, a task that requires accurate integration. Simpson suggested a very accurate formula in the mid-eighteenth century, and Gauss proposed his famous quadrature rules in the early part of the nineteenth century. Numerical discretization methods such as finite elements and boundary elements, in particular, depend critically on efficient numerical integration procedures. There exist both simple quadrature rules as well as more advanced approaches, which we present next. More details on integration can be found in the books of Davis and Rabinowitz [23] and Ghizzetti and Ossicini [43].

4.2.1 Simple Integration Algorithms

The simplest quadrature formulas are based on either piecewise constant approximations of a function in the interval of interest,

$$I = \int_a^b f(x)dx,$$

as shown schematically in Figure 4.3 (right), or on piecewise linear approximations (Figure 4.3, left). Assuming that h is the size of each of the n equal cells involved in the discretization, we obtain the following approximations:

- *Midpoint-Rectangle Rule*:

$$I \approx R(h) = h \sum_{i=1}^{n} f_{i-1/2}.$$ (4.15)

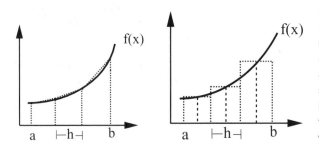

Figure 4.3: Trapezoid (left) versus midpoint-rectangle (right) rule: The accuracy is of the same order, $\mathcal{O}(h^2)$ for both, but surprisingly the midpoint-rectangle wins by a factor of 2.

This is implemented in the code that follows.

PUTTING IT INTO PRACTICE

We present a functional implementation of the midpoint rule. Notice that we are continuing to use the concept of passing functions to functions.

```
double MidpointRule(int level, double xleft, double xright,
                    double (*func)(double)){

   int i, nsteps = (int) pow(2.0,level)-1;
   double h = (xright-xleft)/pow(2.0,level);
   double sum = 0.0;

   for(i=0;i<=nsteps;i++)
     sum += func(xleft + (i+0.5)*h);
   sum *= h;

   return sum;
}
```

- *Trapezoid Rule*:

$$I \approx T(h) = h[\frac{1}{2} f_0 + f_1 + \cdots + f_{n-1} + \frac{1}{2} f_n] .$$ (4.16)

This is implemented in the code that follows.

PUTTING IT INTO PRACTICE

We present a functional implementation of the trapezoidal rule. Observe the use of shorthand operators in the function. We are able to use such operators for both addition and multiplication.

```
double TrapezoidRule(int level, double xleft, double xright,
                     double (*func)(double)){
   int i, nsteps = (int) pow(2.0,level)-1;
   double h = (xright-xleft)/pow(2.0,level);
   double sum = 0.0;

   for(i=1;i<=nsteps;i++)
     sum += func(xleft + i*h);
   sum *= 2;

   /* Add the first and the last point to the summation */
   sum += func(xleft) + func(xright);
   sum *= 0.5*h;

   return sum;
}
```

Note that, by definition, the following identity applies:

$$T(h) = \frac{1}{2}[T(2h) + R(2h)],$$

so we can easily relate the two formulas. Intuitively, one would guess that the trapezoid rule may be more accurate than the midpoint-rectangle rule because of the higher order approximation involved (i.e., linear versus constants). However, as we will see in a moment, the quadrature error in the trapezoid rule is twice the quadrature error in the midpoint-rectangle rule!

Quadrature Error

To obtain the quadrature error for these two methods we assume that $f''(x)$ is continuous in $[a, b]$. We then consider a grid consisting of the $(m + 1)$ points

$$[x_0, x_1, \ldots, x_m]$$

and construct the unique polynomial

$$p(x) = c_0 + c_1(x - x_0) + c_2(x - x_0)(x - x_1) + \cdots + c_m(x - x_0)(x - x_1) \cdots (x - x_{m-1}), \quad (4.17)$$

so that $p(x_i) = f(x_i)$, $i = 0, 1, \ldots, m$. This is Newton's formula of approximating $f(x)$ in the interval $[a, b]$, where $x_0 = a$ and $x_m = b$. Then, if $f(x)$ possesses continuous derivatives of order at least $(m + 1)$, we obtain

$$f(x) - p(x) = \frac{f^{(m+1)}(\xi)}{(m + 1)!}(x - x_0)(x - x_1) \ldots (x - x_m) \qquad (4.18)$$

for some point $\xi \in [a, b]$. We can then obtain the quadrature error by simply integrating the right-hand side of Equation (4.18) and by providing an upper bound for the magnitude of the $(m + 1)$ derivative.

For the trapezoid rule we obtain on each cell i

$$\epsilon_i^T = T_i(h) - \int_{x_{i-1}}^{x_i} f(x)dx = -\int_{x_{i-1}}^{x_i} \frac{f''(\xi)}{2}(x - x_{i-1})(x - x_i)dx, \quad \xi \in [x_{i-1}, x_i],$$

and thus

$$\epsilon_i^T \approx -\frac{1}{2} f''(\xi_i) \int_{x_{i-1}}^{x_i} (x - x_{i-1})(x - x_i)dx.$$

Let

$$x = x_{i-1} + hs, \quad \epsilon_i^T \approx -\frac{1}{2} f''(\xi_i) \int_0^1 hs\, h(s - 1)h\, ds = \frac{h^3 f''(\xi_i)}{12}.$$

This is the *local quadrature error* on the cell i. We can easily obtain the *global error* by summing over all the cells i, that is,

$$\epsilon^T = \sum_{i=1}^n \epsilon_i^T \approx f''(\xi)\frac{(b - a)h^2}{12},$$

where

$$b - a = \sum_{i=1}^{n} h.$$

Therefore, the trapezoid rule results in a second-order convergence rate $[\mathcal{O}(h^2)]$ for the global error.

For the midpoint-rectangle rule we need to expand the function around the midpoint $x_0 = (x_{i-1} + x_i)/2$ in the cell i:

$$f(x) \approx f(x_0) + (x - x_0) f'(x_0) + \frac{(x - x_0)^2}{2} f''(\xi),$$

where $\xi \in [a, b]$. Then the error for the integral $R_i(h)$ is

$$\epsilon_i^R = R_i(h) - \int_{x_{i-1}}^{x_i} f(x)dx = -\int_{x_{i-1}}^{x_i} f'(x_0)(x - x_0)dx - \int_{x_{i-1}}^{x_i} \frac{f''(\xi)}{2}(x - x_0)^2 dx$$

$$= f''(\xi)\frac{h^3}{24}.$$

This is the *local quadrature error* on the cell i. We can easily obtain the *global error* by summing over all the cells i, that is,

$$\epsilon^R = \sum_{i=1}^{n} \epsilon_i^R \approx f'(\xi)\frac{(b - a)h^2}{24}.$$

Comparing now the global quadrature errors ϵ^R and ϵ^T we see that, surprisingly, the midpoint-rectangle rule approximates the integral I better, as its corresponding error is half of that for the trapezoid rule!

Better Trapezoid Rules

We present here two efficient ways of improving the second-order accuracy of the trapezoid rule:

1. by correcting the end values and
2. by subdividing the interval.

First, the **corrected trapezoid rule** is based on a trigonometric interpolation of the function, unlike the Newton linear approximation used for the standard trapezoid [Equation (4.17) with $m = 1$]. It adds a correction term at the ends to the standard trapezoid formula, that is,

$$T_C(h) = h[\frac{1}{2} f_0 + f_1 + \cdots + f_{n-1} + \frac{1}{2} f_n] + \frac{h^2}{12}[f'(a) - f'(b)], \qquad (4.19)$$

with corresponding quadrature error

$$\epsilon^{TC} \approx \frac{h^4}{720} \times [f'''(b) - f'''(a)].$$

Clearly, for functions that are *periodic* in the interval $[a, b]$, a very high degree of accuracy is achieved without the addition of the extra correction terms.

Another efficient method to increase the formal order of accuracy of the trapezoid rule is **Romberg's method**. This method, which is also called extrapolation to the limit, is a systematic procedure of using subdivision of intervals with the trapezoid rule. It is based on Richardson's extrapolation idea, which is used most often in numerical differentiation.

Let us define a series of trapezoid sums

$$T_0, \quad T_1, \quad T_2, \ldots$$

by successively bisecting the interval of integration:

$$T_0 = \frac{h_0}{2}[f(x_0) + f(x_0 + h_0)]$$

$$T_1 = \frac{h_1}{2}[f(x_o) + 2f(x_0 + h_1) + f(x_0 + 2h_1)]$$

$$\vdots \quad \vdots$$

$$T_k = \frac{h_k}{2}[f(x_0) + 2\sum_{i=1}^{2^k-1} f(x_0 + ih_k) + f(x_0 + 2^k h_k)].$$

Then the error on each grid (k) is $\epsilon_k = I - T_k$, where I is the exact value of the integral. Because of the quadratic convergence, we have

$$\epsilon_{k+1} \approx \frac{1}{4}\epsilon_k.$$

We also have for $k = 0, 1, \ldots$

$$I = T_0 + \epsilon_0,$$

$$I = T_1 + \epsilon_1 \simeq T_1 + \frac{1}{4}\epsilon_0 = T_1 + \frac{1}{4}(I - T_0) \Rightarrow I \simeq \frac{4T_1 - T_0}{3}.$$

In general, we have by induction

$$I_k^1 = \frac{4T_k - T_{k-1}}{3},$$

which defines a *one-step correction*. Expanding T_k and T_{k-1} and substituting into this formula we obtain a quadrature error for I_k^1 that is proportional to h^4, competitive with Simpson's rule (see next subsection). Thus, the error in successive terms of I_k^1 is reduced by a factor of $1/16$ and we obtain a *two-step correction*:

$$I_k^2 = \frac{16I_k^1 - I_{k-1}^1}{15}.$$

Continuing this process m times, we get the recurrence formula

$$I_k^m = \frac{4^m I_k^{m-1} - I_{k-1}^{m-1}}{4^m - 1}, \quad m \geq 1, k \geq m. \tag{4.20}$$

To completely define the recursive process, we also need to specify the initial conditions, that is,

$$I_k^0 = T_k, \quad I_{k-1}^0 = T_{k-1}.$$

The corresponding quadrature error in Romberg's method is

$$\epsilon_k^m \sim h^{2m+2} \cdot f^{(2m+2)}(\xi).$$

This method uses a fine grid (k) and a coarse grid ($k-1$) and extrapolates the standard trapezoid rule. The reason why this algorithm works is because we know that the error structure has the polynomial form

$$c_1 h^2 + c_2 h^4 + c_3 h^6 + \cdots$$

for the trapezoid rule. So the idea of the method is to use more than one grid, a *fine grid* and a *coarse grid*, and then at the first correction level construct the extrapolant, at the second correction level construct the extrapolant of the extrapolant, and so on. By weighting appropriately these successive constructs, we can extrapolate the resulting quadrature values to higher accuracy.

In theory, Romberg's method gives arbitrarily high convergence rate, but in practice round-off error slows down convergence and accuracy.

Software Suite

PUTTING IT INTO PRACTICE

We present a functional implementation of Romberg's integration. Notice that this implementation consists of two components:

1. an implementation of the trapezoid rule and
2. a recursive definition for Romberg integration.

In the case presented here, the stopping condition for the recursion is when the variable *m* is equal to zero. When this is true, we execute the trapezoid rule. For all other valid values of *m* we recursively call the Romberg function with appropriately changed arguments.

```
double Romberg(int m, int k, double xleft, double xright,
               double (*func)(double)){
  double RI,I1,I2;
  double coeff = pow(4.0,m);

  if(k < m){
    cerr << "ROMBERG::Value of k must be >= m; setting k=m\n";
    k = m;
  }

  if(m==0){
    RI = TrapezoidRule(k,xleft,xright,func);
  }
  else{
    I1 = Romberg(m-1,k,  xleft,xright,func);
```

```
    I2 = Romberg(m-1,k-1,xleft,xright,func);
    RI = (coeff*I1 - I2)/(coeff-1.0);
  }

  return RI;
}
```

Simpson's Rule

The idea in Simpson's rule of integration is to connect three consecutive ordinates by a parabola and use Newton's approximation formula to obtain the quadrature error. The standard or **1/3 Simpson's rule** employs an even number of cells. For the i cell defined by $[x_{i-1}, x_i, x_{i+1}]$ we obtain

$$\int_{i-1}^{i+1} f(x)dx \approx S_i(h) = \frac{h}{3}[f_{i-1} + 4f_i + f_{i+1}], \tag{4.21}$$

and the Simpson quadrature for the entire interval $[a, b]$ is

$$S(h) = \frac{h}{3}[f_0 + 4f_1 + 2f_2 + \cdots + 4f_{m-1} + f_m], \tag{4.22}$$

where *m is an even number.*

To obtain the error in Simpson's formula we employ Equation (4.17) with $m = 2$. Then

$$\epsilon_i^S = h\int_0^2 \frac{t(t-1)(t-2)}{6}h^3 f'''(\xi)dt = 0,$$

and thus the leading term in the error is zero, so we have to integrate the next term

$$\epsilon_i^S = h\int_0^2 \frac{t(t-1)(t-2)(t-3)}{24}h^4 f^{(4)}(\xi)dt = -\frac{h^5}{90}f^{(4)}(\xi),$$

and so the local error is $\mathcal{O}(h^5)$. The *global error* can be easily obtained by replacing $h = (b-a)/2$, giving

$$\epsilon^S = -\frac{(b-a)}{180}h^4 f^{(4)}(\xi).$$

It is interesting to note that in Simpson's rule we obtain $\mathcal{O}(h^4)$ convergence with a quadratic polynomial fit as we take advantage of the *even* number of cells and the corresponding cancellation in the error terms. In fact, a cubic polynomial fit in Equation (4.17) leads to the **3/8 rule**

$$S_i(h) = \frac{3}{8}h[f_{i-2} + 3f_{i-1} + 3f_i + f_{i+1}]$$

with an error

$$\epsilon_i^S = -\frac{3h^5}{80}f^{(4)}(\xi),$$

which is larger than the local error of the 1/3 Simpson's rule corresponding to a lower order polynomial approximation. However, this rule is useful when an *odd number of cells* is required in the integration, which can be broken up into two subintervals: The first one consists of three cells (3/8 rule), and the second one consists of the rest, which corresponds to an even number of cells where we apply the standard 1/3 Simpson's rule.

Software
Suite

EXAMPLE

As an example, we put into practice several of the functions implemented here (see *software suite*). We are attempting to approximate the integral of x^4 on the interval [0, 1], for which we know the exact value to be 0.2. In the program, we compute the midpoint rule, trapezoid rule, and Simpson's rule approximation for ten levels. The output of the program is the following table:

Level	Midpoint	Trapezoidal	Simpson's
0	1.375000e-01	3.000000e-01	8.333333e-03
1	3.984375e-02	8.125000e-02	5.208333e-04
2	1.030273e-02	2.070312e-02	3.255208e-05
3	2.597046e-03	5.200195e-03	2.034505e-06
4	6.505966e-04	1.301575e-03	1.271566e-07
5	1.627326e-04	3.254890e-04	7.947286e-09
6	4.068837e-05	8.137822e-05	4.967053e-10
7	1.017242e-05	2.034493e-05	3.104406e-11
8	2.543125e-06	5.086255e-06	1.940226e-12
9	6.357825e-07	1.271565e-06	1.212364e-13

From these data, we observe the following:

- The trapezoid rule has, in fact, an error that is about twice that of the midpoint rule, just as predicted by the theory
- Both the midpoint rule and the trapezoid rule exhibit second-order convergence, as predicted by the theory
- For Simpson's rule, we obtain fourth-order convergence, as predicted by the theory

Key Concept

Theoretical results should be used to test the validity of your implementation.

4.2.2 Advanced Quadrature Rules

All integration methods in the previous section are based on Newton's formula and low-order polynomial approximation. We can extend these methods to high-order polynomial interpolation using Lagrangian interpolation (see Section 3.1). The objective is to maximize the order of accuracy for a fixed number of points whose locations are allowed to vary. This leads us to **Gauss quadrature**. For example, suppose that we want to evaluate the integral

$$\int_0^1 \frac{1+x}{\sqrt{x}} dx,$$

the exact value of which is 8/3. We can only use $n = 2$ quadrature points and Gauss integration to compute this integral exactly!

The important difference from the methods of the previous section is the location of the quadrature points. These are special points, as we will explain, and typically they are *roots of an appropriate orthogonal polynomial*. The Legendre polynomial is the most-often used but Chebyshev, Laguerre, and Hermite polynomials are also used. For the aforementioned integral, the two special points are determined from the roots of the second-order Legendre polynomial

$$P_2(s) = \frac{1}{2}(3s^2 - 1), \quad s \in [-1, 1]$$

(i.e., $s_{\pm} = \pm 1/\sqrt{3}$). These special points need to be mapped in the interval of integration $[a, b]$, so we obtain

$$x = \frac{a+b}{2} + \frac{b-a}{2}s, \quad \text{where} \quad x \in [a, b] \quad \text{and} \quad s \in [-1, 1].$$

Let us now derive the general Gauss quadrature. We assume that the values

$$f(x_1), \ f(x_2), \ldots, \ f(x_n)$$

cannot provide sufficient information for determining $f(x)$. Let $x = x_k$ and correspondingly $y_k \equiv f(x_k)$, and determine the polynomial $p_{n-1}(x)$ that fits the coordinates $y_1, y_2, \ldots, y_n$. We can employ Lagrange's interpolation by constructing the fundamental polynomial

$$F_n(x) = (x - x_1)(x - x_2)\ldots(x - x_n)$$

and define

$$h_i(x) = \frac{1}{F_n'(x_i)} \frac{F_n(x)}{x - x_i}, \quad i = 1, 2, \ldots, n,$$

$$h_i(x_k) = 0, \quad h_i(x_i) = 1, \quad \text{by construction.}$$

We then obtain the polynomial

$$p_{n-1}(x) = y_1 h_1(x) + y_2 h_2(x) + \cdots + y_n h_n(x),$$

where

$$p_{n-1}(x_k) = y_k.$$

The Gauss integral can then be approximated as

$$I_G = \int_{-1}^{+1} p_{n-1}(x)dx = \sum_{k=1}^{n} y_k \int_{-1}^{1} h_k(x)dx = \sum_{k=1}^{n} y_k w_k,$$

where

$$w_k \equiv \int_{-1}^{+1} h_k(x)dx$$

are the weights of integration, which are independent of the integrand.

Gauss's idea is then to add an extra point x_{n+1} without changing x_k, $k \leq n$, or equivalently to add the term

$$h_{n+1}(x) = \frac{F_n(x)}{F'_{n+1}(x_{n+1})},$$

and thus the $(n+1)$ weight is

$$w_{n+1} \sim \int_{-1}^{1} F_n(x)dx.$$

Similarly, if we add m new points

$$\underbrace{x_{n+1}, \, x_{n+2}, \ldots, \, x_{n+m}}_{m \text{ points}}$$

then the $(n+1)$th weight is obtained from

$$w_{n+1} = \int_{-1}^{+1} F_n(x)G^i_{m-1}(x)dx,$$

where $G^i_{m-1}(x)$ is a polynomial of order $(m-1)$. Now, if we impose that all moments of $F_n(x)$ up to $(m-1)$ are zero, that is,

$$\int_{-1}^{1} F_n(x)x^k dx, \quad k = 0, 1, \ldots, m-1,$$

then orthogonality leads to

$$\int_{-1}^{+1} F_n(x)G^i_{m-1}(x)dx = 0,$$

since G is a linear combination of powers x^k. We can add up to n points to the original grid, and thus we can effectively *double the number of points* considered with only half the weights!

Therefore, the Gauss formula

$$I_G = \sum_{k=1}^{n} y_k w_k$$

that employs a grid of n points results in quadrature accuracy equivalent to a grid corresponding to $2n$ coordinates using the simple rules of the previous section.

Jacobi Polynomials

Jacobi polynomials $P_n^{\alpha,\beta}(x)$ are a family of polynomial solutions to the singular Sturm–Liouville problem. A significant feature of these polynomials is that they are orthogonal in the interval $[-1, 1]$ with respect to the function $(1-x)^\alpha(1+x)^\beta$ ($\alpha, \beta > -1$). We have already presented the Chebyshev polynomials in Section 3.1.5 – they are a subset of Jacobi polynomials for the special case that $\alpha = \beta = -\frac{1}{2}$. A detailed account of their properties can be found in Abramowitz and Stegun [1, Chapter 22] and also in Ghizzetti and Ossicini [43, Chapter 3.4].

DIFFERENTIAL EQUATION. Jacobi polynomials are solutions to the following differential equation:

$$(1-x)(1+x)\frac{d^2y(x)}{dx^2} + (\beta - \alpha - (\alpha + \beta + 2)x)\frac{dy(x)}{dx} = -\lambda_n y(x) \tag{4.23}$$

or

$$\frac{d}{dx}\left[(1-x)^{1+\alpha}(1+x)^{1+\beta}\frac{dy(x)}{dx}\right] = -\lambda_n(1-x)^{\alpha}(1+x)^{\beta}y(x), \tag{4.24}$$

$$\lambda_n = n(n+\alpha+\beta+1),$$

$$y(x) = P_n^{\alpha,\beta}(x).$$

SPECIAL CASES. Two important special cases are Legendre polynomials ($\alpha = \beta = 0$):

$$P_n(x) = P_n^{0,0}(x)$$

and Chebychev polynomials ($\alpha = \beta = -\frac{1}{2}$):

$$T_n(x) = \frac{2^{2n}(n!)^2}{(2n)!}P_n^{-\frac{1}{2},-\frac{1}{2}}(x).$$

RECURSION RELATIONS. The recursion relations for Jacobi polynomials are as follows:

$$P_0^{\alpha,\beta}(x) = 1,$$

$$P_1^{\alpha,\beta}(x) = \frac{1}{2}[\alpha - \beta + (\alpha + \beta + 2)x],$$

$$a_n^1 P_{n+1}^{\alpha,\beta}(x) = (a_n^2 + a_n^3 x)P_n^{\alpha,\beta}(x) - a_n^4 P_{n-1}^{\alpha,\beta}(x), \tag{4.25}$$

$$a_n^1 = 2(n+1)(n+\alpha+\beta+1)(2n+\alpha+\beta),$$

$$a_n^2 = (2n+\alpha+\beta+1)(\alpha^2-\beta^2),$$

$$a_n^3 = (2n+\alpha+\beta)(2n+\alpha+\beta+1)(2n+\alpha+\beta+2),$$

$$a_n^4 = 2(n+\alpha)(n+\beta)(2n+\alpha+\beta+2);$$

$$b_n^1(x)\frac{d}{dx}P_n^{\alpha,\beta}(x) = b_n^2(x)P_n^{\alpha,\beta}(x) + b_n^3(x)P_{n-1}^{\alpha,\beta}(x), \tag{4.26}$$

$$b_n^1(x) = (2n+\alpha+\beta)(1-x^2),$$

$$b_n^2(x) = n[\alpha - \beta - (2n+\alpha+\beta)x],$$

$$b_n^3(x) = 2(n+\alpha)(n+\beta).$$

SPECIAL VALUES. Jacobi polynomials have certain special values:

$$P_n^{\alpha,\beta}(1) = \binom{n+\alpha}{n} = \frac{(n+\alpha)!}{\alpha!n!}, \tag{4.27}$$

$$P_n^{\alpha,\beta}(-x) = (-1)^n P_n^{\beta,\alpha}(x). \tag{4.28}$$

ORTHOGONALITY RELATIONS. The orthogonality relations for Jacobi polynomials are

$$\int_{-1}^{1} (1-x)^{\alpha}(1+x)^{\beta} P_n^{\alpha,\beta}(x) P_m^{\alpha,\beta}(x) dx = 0, \qquad n \neq m, \qquad (4.29)$$

$$\int_{-1}^{1} (1-x)^{\alpha}(1+x)^{\beta} P_n^{\alpha,\beta}(x) P_n^{\alpha,\beta}(x) dx$$

$$= \frac{2^{\alpha+\beta+1}}{2n+\alpha+\beta+1} \frac{\Gamma(n+\alpha+1)\Gamma(n+\beta+1)}{n!\Gamma(n+\alpha+\beta+1)}.$$

Evaluation of the Zeros of Jacobi Polynomials

The formulas for the *weights* of the general Jacobi polynomials (see Table 4.3 for the Legendre case) have a closed form in terms of the grid points x_i. In general, however, there are no explicit formulas for the grid points. These are defined in terms of the roots of the Jacobi polynomial such that

$$x_i = x_{i,m}^{\alpha,\beta},$$

$$P_m^{\alpha,\beta}(x_{i,m}^{\alpha,\beta}) = 0, \qquad i = 0, 1, \ldots, m-1.$$

The zeros $x_{i,m}^{\alpha,\beta}$ can be numerically evaluated using an iterative technique, such as the Newton–Raphson method we studied in Section 4.1.3. However, we note that the zeros of the Chebychev polynomial ($\alpha = \beta = -\frac{1}{2}$) do have an explicit form,

$$x_{i,m}^{-\frac{1}{2},-\frac{1}{2}} = -\cos\left(\frac{2i+1}{2m}\pi\right), \qquad i = 0, \ldots, m-1,$$

and so we can use $x_{i,m}^{-\frac{1}{2},-\frac{1}{2}}$ as an initial guess to the iteration.

To ensure that we find a new root at each search we can apply *polynomial deflation* or reduction, where the known roots are factored out of the initial polynomial once they have been determined. This means that the root-finding algorithm is applied to the polynomial

$$f_{m-n}(x) = \frac{P_m^{\alpha,\beta}(x)}{\prod_{i=0}^{n-1}(x-x_i)},$$

where x_i ($i = 0, \ldots, n-1$) are the known roots of $P_m^{\alpha,\beta}(x)$.

Noting that

$$\frac{f_{m-n}(x)}{f_{m-n}'(x)} = \frac{P_m^{\alpha,\beta}(x)}{[P_m^{\alpha,\beta}(x)]' - P_m^{\alpha,\beta}(x)\sum_{i=0}^{n-1}[1/(x-x_i)]},$$

we can write a root-finding algorithm to determine the m roots of $P_m^{\alpha,\beta}(x)$ using the Newton–Raphson iteration with polynomial

Table 4.3: Zeros of Legendre polynomials $P_n(x)$ and corresponding weights.

n	Abscissas x_j	Weights w_j
2	$\pm 0.577350 = \pm\dfrac{1}{\sqrt{3}}$	1
3	0	8/9
	± 0.774597	5/9
4	± 0.339981	0.652145
	± 0.861136	0.347855
5	0	0.568889
	± 0.538469	0.478629
	± 0.906180	0.236927

deflation:

for $k = 0, m - 1$
$\quad r = x_{k,m}^{-\frac{1}{2},-\frac{1}{2}}$
$\quad$ if $(k > 0)r = (r + x_{k-1})/2$
$\quad$ For $j = 1$, stop

$$s = \sum_{i=0}^{k-1} \frac{1}{(r-x_i)}$$

$$\delta = -\frac{P_m^{\alpha,\beta}(r)}{[P_m^{\alpha,\beta}(r)]' - P_m^{\alpha,\beta}(r)s}$$

$$r = r + \delta$$

$\quad\quad$ if $(\delta < \epsilon)$ exit loop

$\quad\quad$ endfor

$\quad\quad x_k = r$

endfor

Here ϵ is a specified tolerance. Numerically, we find that a better approximation for the initial guess is given by the average of $r = x_{k,m}^{-\frac{1}{2},-\frac{1}{2}}$ and x_{k-1}. The values of $P_m^{\alpha,\beta}(x)$ and $[P_m^{\alpha,\beta}(x)]'$ can be generated using the recursion relationships (4.25) and (4.26).

In the following, we first use these formulas to compute the Jacobi polynomials and its derivatives, and subsequently we implement the root-finding algorithm.

PUTTING IT INTO PRACTICE

Here we present an implementation of the Jacobi polynomials. Observe that our definition relies on the recursive nature of these polynomials and that we have specifically implemented the three-term recurrence relation immediately into the code.

```
double JacobiPoly(int degree, double x, double alpha,
                  double beta){
  double value;
  double tmp,degm1;
  double a1=0.,a2=0.,a3=0.,a4=0.;

  switch(degree){
  case 0:
    value = 1.0;
    break;
  case 1:
    value = 0.5*(alpha-beta+(alpha+beta+2.0)*x);
    break;
  default:
    degm1 = degree-1.0;
    tmp = 2.0*degm1+alpha+beta;
    a1= 2.0*(degm1+1)*(degm1+alpha+beta+1)*tmp;
```

Software

Suite

```
      a2= (tmp+1)*(alpha*alpha-beta*beta);
      a3= tmp*(tmp+1.0)*(tmp+2.0);
      a4= 2.0*(degm1+alpha)*(degm1+beta)*(tmp+2.0);

      value = ((a2+a3*x)*JacobiPoly(degree-1,x,alpha,beta)-
        a4*JacobiPoly(degree-2,x,alpha,beta))/a1;
   }

   return value;

}
```

Similarly, for the derivatives of the Jacobi polynomials, we rely on the three-term recurrence relation to provide us with a fast way of implementing the derivative.

```
double JacobiPolyDerivative(int degree, double x,
                            double alpha, double beta){
   double value;
   double tmp;
   double b1,b2,b3;

   switch(degree){
   case 0:
     value = 0.0;
     break;
   default:
     tmp = 2.0*degree+alpha+beta;
     b1 = tmp*(1.0-x*x);
     b2 = degree*(alpha-beta-tmp*x);
     b3 = 2.0*(degree+alpha)*(degree+beta);

     value = (b2*JacobiPoly(degree,x,alpha,beta) +
              b3*JacobiPoly(degree-1,x,alpha,beta))/b1;
   }
   return value;
}
```

To compute the zeros of the Jacobi polynomials, we use a reduction technique. In the code that follows, you will notice that we use two primary concepts:

• We rely on our previous function definitions for the Jacobi polynomials and their derivatives.
• We rely on using Newton–Raphson iteration for obtaining the root.

```
void JacobiZeros(int degree, double *z, double alpha,
                 double beta){
   int i,j,k;
   const int maxit = 30;
```

```
const double EPS = 1.0e-14;
double    dth = M_PI/(2.0*degree);
double    poly,pder,rlast=0.0;
double    sum,delr,r;
double one = 1.0, two = 2.0;

// If the degree of the polynomial is zero (or less),
// then there are no roots
if(degree<=0)
  return;

for(k = 0; k < degree; k++){
  r = -cos((two*k + one) * dth);
  if(k) r = 0.5*(r + rlast);

  for(j = 1; j < maxit; ++j){
    poly = JacobiPoly(degree,r,alpha,beta);
    pder = JacobiPolyDerivative(degree,r,alpha,beta);

    sum = 0.0;
    for(i = 0; i < k; ++i)
      sum += one/(r - z[i]);

    delr = -poly / (pder - sum * poly);
    r    += delr;
    if( fabs(delr) < EPS ) break;
  }
  z[k]  = r;
  rlast = r;
}

return;
}
```

Combining everything that we have done so far, we can now implement one function that, when called, returns the zeros and the weights of the Jacobi polynomial of your choice. Notice in this function that we assume that both arrays z and w have already been allocated.

```
void JacobiZW(int degree, double * z, double *w,
              double alpha, double beta){
  int i;
  double fac, one = 1.0, two = 2.0, apb = alpha + beta;

  JacobiZeros(degree, z, alpha, beta);

  for(i=0;i<degree;i++)
    w[i] = JacobiPolyDerivative(degree,z[i],alpha,beta);
```

```
fac   = pow(two,apb + one)*GammaF(alpha + degree + one)*
        GammaF(beta + degree + one);
fac /= GammaF(degree + one)*GammaF(apb + degree + one);

for(i = 0; i < degree; ++i)
  w[i] = fac/(w[i]*w[i]*(one-z[i]*z[i]));

return;
}
```

We note that the orthogonality conditions are satisfied automatically by the Legendere polynomials $P_n(x)$. The zeros of these polynomials will then determine the locations of the special points x_j. Some values are shown in Table 4.3; these values were computed using the *JacobiZW* function presented here with both the *alpha* and *beta* arguments set to zero.

Also, the *fast convergence* in the error in Gauss quadrature is due to the fast convergence of the Legendre interpolation. In addition, the computational advantage results from our employing only half of the $(2n)$ coordinates explicitly. Equidistant interpolation is not a well-convergent process, as we have seen in Section 3.1.4, and for functions with singularities inside the "oval region" (see Section 3.1.4) convergence is not guaranteed. The convergence in Legendre distribution is always guaranteed.

EXAMPLE. Let us compare the Gauss quadrature with the trapezoid rule for the integral evaluation

$$\int_0^4 xe^x dx = 3e^4 + 1 \cong 164.79445.$$

Using the trapezoid with rule nine equidistant coordinates we obtain

$$T(h) = (1/2)\left(\frac{1}{2}0 + 0.824361 + \cdots + \frac{1}{2}218.3926\right) = 170.42826$$

with error

$$\epsilon^{\mathrm{T}} = 5.63381.$$

Next, we employ Gauss quadrature using five coordinates obtained from Legendre's zeros,

$$x_k = 2 + 2s_k, \quad s_k \in [-1, 1],$$

which in the domain of interest are

$$2(1 \pm 0.906179846),$$
$$2(1 \pm 0.538469310).$$

Table 4.4 lists the fives coordinates in physical space and also the corresponding weights, which also need to be corrected as follows:

$$w_k \times \frac{b-a}{2}$$

because

$$\int_a^b f(x)dx = \frac{b-a}{2} \int_{-1}^1 f(s)ds.$$

The result is

$$I_G = \sum_1^5 y_k w_k = 1.64794290,$$

with error

$$\epsilon^G = 1.5981 \times 10^{-4},$$

which is four orders of magnitude less than the result obtained with the trapezoid rule. We, therefore, find that the good interpolation with ninth-order Legendre polynomials leads to good integration with effectively nine total coordinates.

Table 4.4: Five Gauss–Legendre coordinates and corresponding weights in the interval $x \in [0,4]$.

x_k	w_k
0.18764031	0.47385377
0.9230618	0.95725734
2	1.13777778
3.07693862	0.95725734
3.81235969	0.47385377

Gauss Quadrature Error

The error in Gaussian quadrature is relatively difficult to obtain. The standard formula employs the $(2n)$th derivative (see Lanczos [66]), that is,

$$\epsilon^G \sim \left[\frac{(n!)^2}{(2n)!} \right]^2 \frac{2^{2n+1}}{2n+1} \frac{f^{(2n)}(\xi)}{(2n)!}, \tag{4.30}$$

where $\xi \in [-1, 1]$. However, such an error cannot be easily computed, and also this bound is not very sharp as it is based on the evaluation of a very high order derivative.

An alternative estimate proposed by Lanczos is obtained as follows: Let us start with the identity

$$\int_{-1}^1 [xf(x)]'dx = \int_{-1}^1 xf'dx + \int_{-1}^1 f(x)dx$$

$$= f(1) + f(-1).$$

Then, if we consider the error ϵ^* in the Gauss quadrature of the function (xf') we have that it is equal to the quadrature error of the function $(xf)'$ minus the quadrature error in f because $(xf)' = xf' + f$. Therefore,

$$\epsilon^* = f(1) + f(-1) - I_G - \sum_{k=1}^n w_k \xi_k f'(\xi_k).$$

In the case of a general interval $[a, b]$ instead of $[-1, 1]$ we have

$$\epsilon^* = \frac{b-a}{2}[f(b) + f(a)] - I_G - \left(\frac{b-a}{2} \right)^2 \sum_{k=1}^n w_k \xi_k f'(x_k).$$

The next key step relies on the assumption that we integrate a function $f(x)$ that is relatively smooth, and thus we can assume that the unknown point is at $\xi \approx 0$.

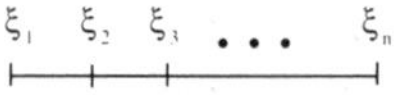

ξ₁ ξ₂ ξ₃ . . .   ξₙ

Figure 4.4: Grid to compute the weights.

Then the term in the Taylor expansion of the error [Equation (4.30)] is approximately equal to the coefficient ξ^{2n} in, the Taylor expansion around the origin $\xi = 0$. However, the expansion of $[\xi f'(\xi)]$ is identical to the original expansion except for the shift in coefficients and thus the a_{2n} coefficient is multiplied by $(2n+1)$. By comparison then we can obtain that

$$\epsilon^G \approx \frac{1}{2n+1}\epsilon^*,$$

which relates the Gauss quadrature error to the first derivative of the function. If the function $f(x)$ does not meet the smoothness criterion, this estimate overpredicts the quadrature error. If $f'(x)$ changes sign in the interval $[a, b]$, this procedure breaks down completely.

Weights and Weighted Moments

Let us consider the grid of Figure 4.4. On this grid, all powers

$$1, x, x^2, \ldots, x^{n-1}$$

are interpolated exactly, and thus the corresponding quadrature associated with all these powers will also be exact. Let us compute the kth moment

$$u_k = \int_a^b \rho(x)x^k dx = \sum_{m=1}^n w_m f(\xi_m),$$

where $\rho(x)$ is a weight function. Thus, we can obtain the weights from the known moments,

$$w_1 + w_2 + \cdots + w_n = u_0,$$

$$w_1\xi_1 + w_2\xi_2 + \cdots + w_n\xi_n = u_1,$$

$$w_1\xi_1^{n-1} + w_2\xi_2^{n-1} + \cdots + w_n\xi_n^{n-1} = u_{n-1},$$

by solving this system. Alternatively, we can compute the weights directly from

$$w_k = \int_{-1}^1 h_k(x)dx.$$

THEOREM: *The weights w_k in the Gauss quadrature are positive.*

PROOF. The formula is exact for $f(x) = h_k^2(x)$, since this is a polynomial of degree $2n$. But $h_k(x_j) = \delta_{ij}$, $k \neq j$. Thus,

$$\int_a^b [h_k(x)]^2 dx = w_k(h_k(x_k))^2 \Rightarrow w_k = \int_a^b [h_k(x)]^2 dx > 0.$$

Gaussian Quadrature over Infinite Intervals

The two general strategies in dealing with such important applications of numerical integration are as follows:

1. Use knowledge of the integrand to bound the magnitude of the integral from some finite value to infinity by a positive constant, and then use a quadrature formula for the remaining finite interval.
2. Use a quadrature formula especially developed for the infinite interval.

LAGUERRE INTEGRATION. Following the second approach here we introduce a weight function

$$w(x) = e^{-x}, \quad x \in [0, \infty],$$

where we employ the Laguerre polynomial $L_n(x)$ defined by

$$L_0(x) = 1,$$

$$L_1(x) = 1 - x,$$

$$(n+1)L_{n+1}(x) = -xL_n(x) + (2n+1)L_n(x) - nL_{n-1}(x)$$

and its derivative defined by

$$L'_{n+1}(x) = L'_n(x) - L_n(x).$$

Software

Suite

The corresponding quadrature points are defined by the roots of the Laguerre polynomial (see Table 4.5 and corresponding *software suite*). Specifically, the weights are given by

$$w_j = \frac{(n!)^2}{L'_n(x_j)L_{n+1}(x_j)}.$$

Then we approximate the integral

$$\int_0^\infty e^{-x} f(x) = \sum_{j=1}^n w_j f_j + \epsilon^L,$$

and the error is

$$\epsilon^L = \frac{(n!)^2}{(2n)!} f^{(2n)}(\xi).$$

EXAMPLE. Taking $n = 3$ we can compute the interval

$$\int_0^\infty e^{-x} x^7 dx \cong (0.711093)(0.415774)^7$$

$$+(0.278518)(2.294280)^7$$

$$+ (0.010389)(6.289945)^7 = 4139.9$$

Table 4.5: Zeros of Laguerre polynomials and corresponding weights.

n	Abscissas x_j	Weights w_j
2	0.585786	0.853553
	3.414214	0.146447
3	0.415775	0.711093
	2.294280	0.278518
	6.289945	0.010389
4	0.322548	0.603154
	1.745761	0.357419
	4.536620	0.038888
	9.395071	0.000539
5	0.263560	0.521756
	1.413403	0.398667
	3.596426	0.074942
	7.085810	0.003612
	12.640801	0.000023

using the values of Table 4.5. The exact value is 5,040, and thus substantial errors occur because $f^{(6)}(x)$ is not bounded. Note, however, that for $n = 4$, $f^{(8)}(x) \equiv 0$, and thus we obtain the exact result!

In the *software suite* we present the code necessary to compute the zeros and the weights of the Laguerre polynomials. Four functions are provided:

1. the polynomial definition (using recursion) – the function *LaguerrePoly*,
2. the derivative definition (using recursion) – the function *LaguerrePolyDerivative*,
3. the computation of zeros (using reduction and Newton–Raphson iteration) – the function *LaguerreZeros*, and
4. the combination to get zeros and weights – the function *LaguerreZW*.

HERMITE INTEGRATION. Here the weight function is

$$w(x) = e^{-x^2},$$

and we can use the Hermite polynomials that are associated with this weight to perform this integration efficiently. We can then compute integrals of the form

$$\int_{-\infty}^{\infty} e^{-x^2} f(x)\,dx = \sum_{j=1}^{n} w_j\, f(x_j) + \epsilon^{H},$$

with the Hermite polynomial $H_n(x)$ defined by

$$H_0(x) = 1,$$

$$H_1(x) = 2x,$$

$$H_{n+1}(x) = 2x H_n(x) - 2n H_{n-1}(x),$$

and its derivative defined by

$$H'_{n+1}(x) = 2(n+1) H_n(x).$$

The corresponding weights are given by

$$w_j = \frac{2^{n+1} n! \sqrt{\pi}}{[H'_n(x_j)]^2},$$

and the error is

$$\epsilon^{H} = \frac{n! \sqrt{\pi}}{2^n (2n)!}\, f^{2n}(\xi).$$

In Table 4.6 we present the zeros of the Hermite polynomials and corresponding weights for n up to 5.

In the *software suite* we present the code necessary to compute the zeros and the weights of the Hermite polynomials. Four functions are provided:

1. the polynomial definition (using recursion) – the function *HermitePoly*,
2. the derivative definition (using recursion) – the function *HermitePolyDerivative*,
3. the computation of zeros (using reduction and Newton–Raphson iteration) – the function *HermiteZeros*, and
4. the combination to get zeros and weights – *HermiteZW*.

Software

Suite

Gauss–Chebyshev Quadrature

The Gauss–Chebyshev quadrature uses the weight function $w(x) = (1 - x^2)^{-1/2}$ in the interval $x \in [-1, 1]$, that is,

$$\int_{-1}^{1} \frac{f(x)}{\sqrt{1 - x^2}} dx = \sum_{k=1}^{n} w_k f_k + \epsilon^{C},$$

where the quadrature points are the zeros of the Chebyshev polynomial obtained from

$$T_n(x) = \cos(n \cos^{-1} x) = 0,$$

and thus

$$x_j = \cos \frac{(2j - 1)\pi}{2n}, \quad j = 1, \dots, n,$$

$$w_j = \frac{\pi}{n}.$$

The corresponding quadrature error is

$$\epsilon^{C} = \frac{2\pi}{2^{2n}(2n)!} f^{(2n)}(\xi).$$

Table 4.6: Zeros of Hermite polynomials and corresponding weights.

n	Abscissas a_j	Weights H_j
2	± 0.707107	0.886227
3	0	1.181636
	± 1.224745	0.295409
4	± 0.524648	0.804914
	± 1.650680	0.081313
5	0	0.945309
	± 0.958572	0.393619
	± 2.020183	0.019953

Singular Integrals

We can also follow a weight-function approach to deal with singular integrals. Let us consider integrands with singularities at the end points of the interval and write the general problem as

$$\int_{a}^{b} \rho(x) f(x) dx = \sum_{j=1}^{k} w_k f(x_k) + \epsilon,$$

where $\rho(x)$ is a weight function, which may be *singular* at one end point or at both. Accordingly, we distinguish the following cases:

CASE 1. Here the weight function is $\rho(x) = (1 - x^2)^{1/2}$ on $[-1, 1]$. Then, we will employ Chebyshev polynomials of the second kind defined as

$$U_n(x) = \frac{\sin[(n + 1) \cos^{-1} x]}{\sin(\cos^{-1} x)},$$

which gives the following quadrature points:

$$x_j = \cos \frac{j\pi}{n + 1}, \quad j = 1, \dots, n,$$

with corresponding weights

$$w_j = \frac{\pi}{n + 1} \sin^2 \frac{j\pi}{n + 1}.$$

The error in this quadrature is

$$\epsilon = \frac{\pi}{2^{2n+1}(2n)!} f_{(\xi)}^{(2n)} \; .$$

CASE 2. Here the weight function is $\rho(x) = 1/\sqrt{x}$ on $[0, 1]$. The appropriate polynomial is defined as

$$p_n(x) = P_{2n}(\sqrt{x}),$$

where P_{2n} is the Legendre polynomial. Then the quadrature points are the roots of $p_n(x)$ and the appropriate weights are twice the weights corresponding to $P_{2n}(x)$.

The quadrature error is

$$\epsilon = \frac{2^{4n+1}[(2n)!]^3}{(4n+1)[(4n)!]} f^{(2n)}(\xi).$$

EXAMPLE. We now return to the integral we mentioned in the introduction of this section, that is,

$$\int_0^1 \frac{1+x}{\sqrt{x}} dx,$$

and we use $n = 2$. From Table 4.3 we obtain the Legendre points

$$x_1 = (0.339981)^2, \quad x_2 = (0.861136)^2$$

and

$$w_1 = 1.304290, \quad w_2 = 0.695710.$$

Therefore,

$$\int_0^1 \frac{1+x}{\sqrt{x}} dx \cong 2.66666,$$

which is equal to the exact value $(8/3)$!

CASE 3. Here the weight function is $\rho(x) = \sqrt{x}$ on $[0, 1]$. The appropriate polynomial has singularities in the derivative and is defined based on the Legendre polynomial

$$p_n(x) = \frac{1}{\sqrt{x}} P_{2n+1}(\sqrt{x}).$$

The roots x_j of $p_n(x)$ determine the quadrature points and they are then related to the roots of the Legendre polynomial (X_j) by $x_j = X_j^2$. Correspondingly, the appropriate weights are

$$w_j = 2W_j X_j^2,$$

where W_j are the Legendre weights.

The quadrature error is given by

$$\epsilon = \frac{2^{4n+3}[(2n+1)!]^4}{(4n+3)[(4n+2)!](2n)!} f^{(2n)}(\xi).$$

CASE 4. Here the weight function is $\rho(x) = [x/(1-x)]^{1/2}$ on [0, 1]. The appropriate polynomial is defined in terms of the Chebyshev polynomial, that is,

$$p_n(x) = \frac{1}{\sqrt{x}} T_{2n+1}(\sqrt{x}).$$

This has a singularity at one point and a derivative singularity at another point. Here the set of quadrature points, weights, and error, respectively, are given by

$$x_j = \cos^2 \frac{(2j-1)\pi}{4n+2},$$

$$w_j = \frac{2\pi}{2n+1} W_j,$$

$$\epsilon = \frac{\pi}{2^{4n+1}(2n)!} f^{(2n)}(\xi),$$

where W_j refers to the corresponding Chebyshev weights.

REMARK: More details on Gauss quadrature based on Jacobi polynomials, which includes both Chebyshev and Legendre polynomials, can be found in Ghizzetti and Ossicini [43] and in Karniadakis and Sherwin [63]. In particular, there exist three different approaches in distributing the quadrature points:

- In *Gauss integration* the end points are not included, and the locations of the quadrature points are determined by the zeros of the Jacobi polynomials.
- In *Gauss–Lobatto integration* both end points are included and the interior quadrature points are determined by the zeros of the first derivative of the Jacobi polynomials.
- In *Gauss–Radau integration* only one point is included and the interior points are determined by the zeros of the Jacobi polynomials with mixed weights.

4.2.3 Multidimensional Integration

Numerical integration in two or three dimensions can be accomplished similarly following the algorithms presented in the previous section, where *direction splitting* is applied.

We show here how to compute, using Simpson's rule, a two-dimensional integral over a rectangular region as well as a more general region. To this end, we consider the integral

$$Q \equiv \int_{X_1^L}^{X_1^R} \int_{X_2^L}^{X_2^R} f(x_1, x_2) dx_1 dx_2$$

and subdivide the two directions of integration as follows:

$$x_1 = X_1^L + ih_1, \quad i = 0, 1, \dots, 2I,$$

$$x_2 = X_2^L + jh_2, \quad j = 0, 1, \dots, 2J,$$

where

$$h_1 = \frac{X_1^R - X_1^L}{2I} \quad \text{and} \quad h_2 = \frac{X_2^R - X_2^L}{2J}.$$

We apply Simpson's rule direction by direction; that is, we first compute

$$Q_2 \equiv \int_{X_2^L}^{X_2^R} f(x_1, x_2)dx_2,$$

so

$$Q_2 \approx \frac{h_2}{3}\left[f(x_1, x_2^0) + 2\sum_{j=1}^{J-1} f(x_1, x_2^{2j}) + 4\sum_{j=1}^{J} f(x_1, x_2^{2j-1}) + f(x_1, x_2^{2J}) \right].$$

Then, the two-dimensional integral is approximated as

$$Q \approx \frac{h_2}{3}\left[\int_{X_1^L}^{X_1^R} f(x_1, x_2^0)dx_1 + 2\sum_{j=1}^{J-1} \int_{X_1^L}^{X_1^R} f(x_1, x_2^{2j})dx_1 \right.$$

$$\left. + 4\sum_{j=1}^{J} \int_{X_1^L}^{X_1^R} f(x_1, x_2^{2j-1})dx_1 + \int_{X_1^L}^{X_1^R} f(x_1, x_2^{2J})dx_1 \right].$$

Next, we need to integrate each one of these terms along the x_1-direction using again Simpson's rule. This will give

$$Q \approx \frac{h_1 h_2}{9}\left\{ \left[f(x_1^0, x_2^0) + 2\sum_{i=1}^{I-1} f(x_1^{2i}, x_2^0) + 4\sum_{i=1}^{I} f(x_1^{2i-1}, x_2^0) + f(x_1^{2I}, x_2^0) \right] \right.$$

$$+ 2\left[\sum_{j=1}^{J-1} f(x_1^0, x_2^{2j}) + 2\sum_{j=1}^{J-1}\sum_{i=1}^{I-1} f(x_1^{2i}, x_2^{2j}) + 4\sum_{j=1}^{J-1}\sum_{i=1}^{I} f(x_1^{2i-j}, x_2^{j}) \right.$$

$$\left. + \sum_{j=1}^{J-1} f(x_1^{2I}, x_2^{2j}) \right]$$

$$+ 4\left[\sum_{j=1}^{J} f(x_1^0, x_2^{2j-1}) + 2\sum_{j=1}^{J}\sum_{i=1}^{I-1} f(x_1^{2j}, x_2^{2j-1}) + 4\sum_{j=1}^{J}\sum_{j=1}^{I} f(x_1^{2i-1}, x_2^{2j-1}) \right.$$

$$\left. + \sum_{j=1}^{J} f(x_1^{2I}, x_2^{2j-1}) \right]$$

$$\left. + \left[f(x_1^0, x_2^{2J}) + 2\sum_{i=1}^{I-1} f(x_1^{2i}, x_2^{2J}) + 4\sum_{i=1}^{I} f(x_1^{2i-1}, x_2^{2J}) + f(x_1^{2I}, x_2^{2J}) \right] \right\}.$$

The error is additive if the partial fourth-order derivate is continuous along both directions; thus

$$\epsilon^S = -\frac{L_1 L_2}{18}\left[h_1^4 \frac{\partial^4 f(\xi_1, \zeta_1)}{\partial x_1^4} + h_2^4 \frac{\partial^4 f(\xi_2, \zeta_2)}{\partial x_2^4}\right],$$

where (ξ_i, ζ_i) for $i = 1, 2$ are some unknown points inside the region of integration.

In many applications the region of integration is not rectangular. To this end, we can either use domain decomposing or employ variable step size integration. For example, if we consider the case with $X_2^L(x_1)$ and $X_2^R(x_1)$ then

$$Q = \iint\limits_{\Omega} f(x_1, x_2)dx_1 dx_2,$$

where Ω is a general, non-Cartesian region. In this case, we can proceed as before by allowing the step size

$$h_2(x_1) = \frac{X_2^R(x_1) - X_2^L(x_1)}{2J}.$$

Therefore, for each fixed x_1 location we integrate along x_2 with fixed h_2 step size, as before.

For Gaussian quadrature, we can also form tensor-product interpolations of the integrand as was discussed in Section 3.1. This is straightforward for Cartesian (orthogonal) domains. For triangular domains the barycentric coordinates (l_1, l_2, l_3) can also be used, and for linear approximations the following exact relations hold:

$$\int_A l_1^m l_2^n l_3^k dA = m!n!k!\frac{2A}{(m+n+k+2)!},$$

$$\int_{L_e} l_1^m l_2^n ds = m!n!\frac{L_e}{(m+n+1)!},$$

where A is the area of the triangular region and L_e is the length of the edge of the triangle.

For integrals in multiple dimensions (greater than three) or for integrands that are not very smooth it is more efficient to resort to Monte Carlo integration. The convergence of this approach is very slow (e.g., $\mathcal{O}(N^{-1/2})$ compared to $\mathcal{O}(N^{-2})$ for the trapezoid rule or $\mathcal{O}(N^{-4})$ for Simpson's rule), and thus it is very inefficient for one- two- or three-dimensional integrals. Convergence acceleration is used in practice following standard algorithms such as *importance sampling* or *control variate*; see [15] for more details.

4.3 BACK TO PARALLEL COMPUTING: REDUCTION

The concept of numerical integration lends itself to a discussion of *domain decomposition*. Suppose that you want to integrate a function numerically on multiple processors. From our knowledge of calculus, we know that we can write an integral over a interval $[a, b]$ as the sum of the integrals over a disjoint partition of subintervals of $[a, b]$.

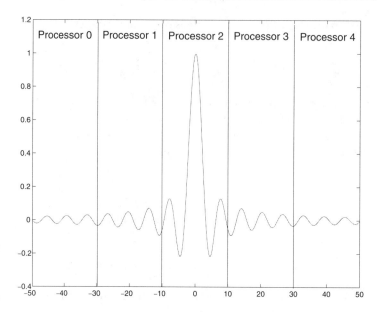

Figure 4.5: Plot of the Lanczos filter $(\sin x)/x$ and processor assignment.

For the purposes of this explanation, let us integrate the function $f(x) = (\sin x)/x$ on the interval $[-50, 50]$. This is a very important function often used in computer graphics as a filtering function – the Lanczos filter (see Section 3.2).

Suppose that we have *five* processors across which we can partition this integral operation. First, we must partition the problem into five processes so that each is doing roughly the same amount of work. This step is graphically accomplished in Figure 4.5. Notice that we partition the entire domain $[-50, 50]$ into five equal-length subdomains:

$$[-50, -30], [-30, -10], [-10, 10], [10, 30], [30, 50].$$

As we have expressed before, we can now use our numerical integration routines discussed previously in this chapter to accomplish the integration on our local interval. Once this is accomplished, we can add up the integral components from each processor. How can this be accomplished? Recall from our previous discussions that the classical way of accomplishing this would be for each process to send its result to one process (process 0), and then for process 0 to accumulate all the results from the individual processes and to print out a result. This type of operation is so common in scientific computing that MPI has a function built in to accomplish all of this in one function call!

| Key Concept | If it seems like a collection of operations is repeatedly done, in all likelihood a function to accomplish those operations already exists to simplify your life. |

The function is called *MPI_Reduce* and combines the sending of information with one operation. The admissible operations are given in Table 4.7.

In our case, we are interested in the *MPI_SUM* operation; that is, we want to take a piece of information from each processor, and we want the sum of all the pieces to be given to process 0 for printing the result. This type of operation is graphically depicted in Figure 4.6.

Here, we present the function syntax, argument list description, usage examples, and some remarks for both **MPI_Reduce** and **MPI_Allreduce**. The functions are very similar. *MPI_Reduce* takes information from all processes and sends the result of the MPI operation to only one process. *MPI_Allreduce* sends the results of the operation back to all processes; it is useful when all processes need the value of the joint operation.

Table 4.7: Summary of MPI commands for reduction operations.

Operation name	Meaning
MPI_MAX	Maximum
MPI_MIN	Minimum
MPI_SUM	Sum
MPI_PROD	Product
MPI_LAND	Logical and
MPI_BAND	Bitwise and
MPI_LOR	Logical or
MPI_BOR	Bitwise or
MPI_LXOR	Logical exclusive or
MPI_BXOR	Bitwise exclusive or
MPI_MAXLOC	Maximum and location of maximum
MPI_MINLOC	Minimum and location of minimum

MPI_Reduce

FUNCTION CALL SYNTAX

```
int MPI_Reduce(
        void*           operand     /*  in   */,
        void*           result      /*  out  */,
        int             count       /*  in   */,
        MPI_Datatype    datatype    /*  in   */,
        MPI_Op          operator    /*  in   */,
        int             root        /*  in   */,
        MPI_Comm        comm        /*  in   */)
```

UNDERSTANDING THE ARGUMENT LIST

- *operand* – starting address of the send buffer.
- *result* – starting address of the receive buffer.
- *count* – number of elements in the send buffer.
- *datatype* – data type of the elements in the send/receive buffer.
- *operator* – reduction operation to be executed.
- *root* – rank of the root process obtaining the result.
- *comm* – communicator.

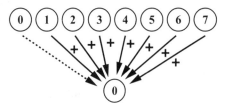

Figure 4.6: Reduction (*MPI_Reduce*) combines fanning-in within a single operation.

MPI

EXAMPLE OF USAGE

```
int mynode, totalnodes;
int datasize; // number of data units over which
              //    reduction should occur
int root;     // process to which reduction will occur

MPI_Init(&argc,&argv);
MPI_Comm_size(MPI_COMM_WORLD, &totalnodes);
MPI_Comm_rank(MPI_COMM_WORLD, &mynode);

// Determine datasize and root

double * senddata = new double[datasize];
double * recvdata = NULL;
if(mynode == root)
   recvdata = new double[datasize];

// Fill in senddata on all processes

MPI_Reduce(senddata,recvdata,datasize,MPI_DOUBLE,MPI_SUM,
           root,MPI_COMM_WORLD);

// At this stage, the process root contains the result
// of the reduction (in this case MPI_SUM) in the
// recvdata array
```

MPI

REMARKS

- The *recvdata* array only needs to be allocated on the process of rank root (since root is the only processor receiving data). All other processes may pass NULL in the place of the *recvdata* argument.
- Both the *senddata* array and the *recvdata* array must be of the same data type. Both arrays should contain at least *datasize* elements.

MPI_Allreduce

MPI

FUNCTION CALL SYNTAX

```
int MPI_Allreduce(
        void*         operand    /* in  */,
        void*         result     /* out */,
        int           count      /* in  */,
        MPI_Datatype  datatype   /* in  */,
        MPI_Op        operator   /* in  */,
        MPI_Comm      comm       /* in  */)
```

MPI

UNDERSTANDING THE ARGUMENT LIST

- *operand* – starting address of the send buffer.
- *result* – starting address of the receive buffer.

- *count* – number of elements in the send/receive buffer.
- *datatype* – data type of the elements in the send/receive buffer.
- *operator* – reduction operation to be executed.
- *comm* – communicator.

EXAMPLE OF USAGE

```
int mynode, totalnodes;
int datasize; // number of data units over which
              //       reduction should occur

MPI_Init(&argc,&argv);
MPI_Comm_size(MPI_COMM_WORLD, &totalnodes);
MPI_Comm_rank(MPI_COMM_WORLD, &mynode);

// Determine datasize and root

double * senddata = new double[datasize];
double * recvdata = new double[datasize];

// Fill in senddata on all processes

MPI_Allreduce(senddata,recvdata,datasize,MPI_DOUBLE,
              MPI_SUM,MPI_COMM_WORLD);

// At this stage, all processes contain the result
// of the reduction (in this case MPI_SUM) in the
// recvdata array
```

REMARKS

- In this case, the *recvdata* array needs to be allocated on all processes since all processes will be receiving the result of the reduction.
- Both the *senddata* array and the *recvdata* array must be of the same data type. Both arrays should contain at least *datasize* elements.

We present a sample MPI code that accomplishes the integration of $f(x) = (\sin x)/x$ on the interval $[-50, 50]$ across multiple processes, the number of which is specified by the user, that is, *totalnodes* in the example code that follows.

```
#include<iostream.h>
#include<math.h>
#include<mpi.h>
#include "SCchapter4.h"

double func(double x);

int main(int argc, char * argv[]){
  int mynode, totalnodes;
  const double global_a = -50.0;
  const double global_b =  50.0;
```

```
  const int levels = 10;
  double local_a,local_b,local_sum,answer;

  MPI_Init(&argc,&argv);
  MPI_Comm_size(MPI_COMM_WORLD, &totalnodes);
  MPI_Comm_rank(MPI_COMM_WORLD, &mynode);

  local_a = global_a + mynode    *(global_b-global_a)/
     totalnodes;
  local_b = global_a + (mynode+1)*(global_b-global_a)/
     totalnodes;

  local_sum = MidpointRule(levels, local_a, local_b, func);

  MPI_Reduce(&local_sum,&answer,1,MPI_DOUBLE,
           MPI_SUM,0,MPI_COMM_WORLD);

  if(mynode == 0){
    cout << "The value of the integral is: " << answer << endl;
  }

  MPI_Finalize();
}

double func(double x){
  return(sin(x)/x);
}
```

We would like to draw your attention to the following points:

- Observe that every process has the same *global_a* and *global_b* variable, here defined as a constant (by using the keyword *const* in the declaration of the variable), however, every process must maintain its own version of *local_a* and *local_b*. This is a very important concept to understand: There exists a global domain, which in this case is the interval $[-50, 50]$, and each processor must keep track of its "computational responsibility" on this domain.
- Notice the use of the operator "& ." In this case, you can translate "&" to mean "the address of." Hence &local_sum is equivalent to saying "the address of local_sum." Why do we do this? Recall that for this particular argument position, MPI expects us to provide it with a pointer variable (which, if you recall, is an address variable). However, we did not allocate an array; we merely had one value. Instead of creating an array that contained only one element, copying the value of *local_sum* into that array element, and then passing the pointer variable to *MPI_Reduce*, we used a neat programming feature of C++. Recall from Section 3.1.2 the programming feature "&," which is an operator that allows you to obtain the address of a variable (and hence you can "pass it off" as a pointer). In this example you should be mindful that

```
  MPI_Reduce(local_sum,answer,1,MPI_DOUBLE,
           MPI_SUM,0,MPI_COMM_WORLD);
```

is invalid, because *MPI_Reduce* will expect pointer (address) variables in the argument positions for *local_sum* and *answer*, and hence you must use

```
MPI_Reduce(&local_sum,&answer,1,MPI_DOUBLE,
           MPI_SUM,0,MPI_COMM_WORLD);
```

- Each process puts the result of its local integration in the first argument of *MPI_Reduce*, and immediately following this call on process 0 (because in the sixth argument we have placed a "0," denoting that process zero is to be the recipient of the reduction) the variable answer contains the sum of all the information contained in the *local_sum* variables across all the processes. If we were to do an *MPI_Allreduce*, then we would not specify which processor the reduction was going to (because all processes would obtain the result of the reduction), and on each process their local copy of the variable "answer" would contain the sum of all *local_sum* variables.

4.4 HOMEWORK PROBLEMS

4.4.1 Homework Problems for Section 4.1

1. Consider the iteration

$$x_{n+1} = ax_n - ax_n^2.$$

Plot the converged solution for different values of a, that is, $a = 1, 2, 3, 3.3, 3.5, 3.7, 3.8$, etc.

What do you observe?

2. Write a C++ program to compute the first dozen roots of $\tan x = x$.

3. Modify the function *NewtonRaphson* given in the text so that it does not accomplish unnecessary reevaluations of the function (per the remarks made in the text).

4. Write a function similar to *NewtonRaphson* that implements the secant method. Your function should allow the user to input an arbitrary function (just as the *NewtonRaphson* function does).

5. Find all the intersection points of the functions

$$f(x) = e^x \quad \text{and} \quad g(x) = 2x^2.$$

What is the convergence rate that you observed?

6. Write a C++ code to find the intersection of the circle

$$x^2 + y^2 = 1$$

with the ellipse

$$\frac{x^2}{4} + 16y^2 = 1$$

to within double precision ($\epsilon = 10^{-14}$).

7. Prove that we can compute $\sqrt{C}$ with cubic rate of convergence from the formula

$$x_{n+1} = x_n \frac{x_n^2 + 3C}{3x_n^2 + C}.$$

8. Let us replace the equation $\mathbf{A}\mathbf{x} = \mathbf{0}$ (which has the trivial solution $\mathbf{x} = \mathbf{0}$) with the iteration

$$\mathbf{x}_{n+1} - \mathbf{x}_n = -\mathbf{A}\mathbf{x}_n,$$

where $\mathbf{x}_0$ is arbitrary.

(a) What is the appropriate test on the matrix $\mathbf{A}$ to check convergence?

(b) We want to apply the steepest descent method to minimize $P = x_1^2 - x_1 x_2 + x_2^2$ and we set the step size $\alpha = 1$. First, obtain an expression for the vector $\mathbf{x}_{n+1}$. Do the iterations converge to the bottom point of P (at $x = 0$)? Sketch the quadratic $P(x_1, x_2)$ and follow the first iteration graphically starting from an initial vector $\mathbf{x}_0 = (1, 1)$ and $\mathbf{x}_0 = (1, -1)$.

9. Use the method of steepest descent to obtain the solutions of the following systems:

(i)

$$x_1^2 + x_2^2 = 2,$$
$$-\cosh x_1 + x_2 = 0;$$

(ii)

$$x_3 = e^{x_1} + e^{x_2},$$
$$x_2^2 = 4 + 2x_1 x_3,$$
$$x_1 x_3 = x_1^3 + x_1^2 x^2 + 6$$

to within tolerances (a) $\epsilon = 10^{-2}$ and (b) $\epsilon = 10^{-5}$.

How does the number of iterations scale with the tolerance level?

Can you solve this system using Newton's method? What is the relative gain in iteration number versus computational work?

10. **Halley's method:** Show that the iteration

$$x_{n+1} = x_n - \frac{f_n f_n'}{(f_n')^2 - (f_n f_n'')/2}$$

finds the roots of $f(x) = 0$ and estimate the convergence rate. Here $f_n = f(x_n)$.

(*Hint:* Set $\phi(x) \equiv f/\sqrt{f'}$ and use the Newton–Raphson formula for $\phi(x)$).

11. **Mueller's method:** In this method a quadratic approximation of the given function is assumed given three pairs of data points: (x_1, y_1), (x_2, y_2), (x_3, y_3), as follows:

$$f(x) \approx y_3 + y'(x - x_3) + y''(x - x_3)(x - x_2),$$

where

$$y' = \frac{y_3 - y_2}{x_3 - x_2}, \quad y_1' = \frac{y_2 - y_1}{x_2 - x_1}$$

and

$$y'' = \frac{y' - y_1'}{x_3 - x_1}, \quad z = y' = y''(x_3 - x_2).$$

Show that we can solve approximately for the root

$$s = x_3 - \frac{2y_3}{z + \text{sign}(z)\sqrt{z^2 - 4y_3 y''}}.$$

In the next update we set

$$x_1 = x_2, \ x_2 = x_3, \ x_3 = s,$$

and so on, until convergence to specified tolerance.

The rate of convergence of Mueller's method is $m \approx 1.84$ and requires only function evaluations, just like the secant method. It can also be used to find both complex and real roots.

Practice this method by solving the equation

$$f(x) = 2x^{10} - 1 = 0.$$

12. The natural frequencies of the vibrations of a beam structure depend on the boundary conditions (i.e., the type of support of the structure).

    (a) If the beam is pinned at one end and free at the other end, the eigenfrequencies are solutions of the equation

    $$\tan \omega - \tanh \omega = 0.$$

    (b) If the beam is clamped at one end and free at the other end, the equation is

    $$\tan \omega - \tanh \omega + 1 = 0.$$

    Here ω is a nondimensional frequency that depends on the length of the beam, its density, and its flexural rigidity.

    Obtain the eigenfrequencies for both cases for *single* and *double* precision and compare the corresponding computational work for each case.

13. Consider the iteration

    $$y_i = x_i - \frac{f(x_i)}{f'(x_i)}, \quad x_{i+1} = y_i - \frac{f(y_i)}{f'(x_i)}.$$

    This is the Newton–Raphson iteration with the derivative computed only every second step.

    (a) Show that if the iteration converges,

    $$\lim_{i \to \infty} \frac{x_{i+1} - \alpha}{(y_i - \alpha)(x_i - \alpha)} = \frac{f''(\alpha)}{f'(\alpha)} \quad \text{as } x_i \to \alpha.$$

$$\begin{bmatrix} 4+\mu & -1 & & -1 & -1 & & & & & & & -1 \\ -1 & 4+\mu & -1 & & & -1 & & & & & & & -1 \\ & -1 & 4+\mu & -1 & & & -1 & & & & & & & -1 \\ -1 & & -1 & 4+\mu & & & & -1 & & & & & & & -1 \\ -1 & & & & 4+\mu & -1 & & -1 & -1 & & & & \\ & -1 & & & -1 & 4+\mu & -1 & & & -1 & & & \\ & & -1 & & & -1 & 4+\mu & -1 & & & -1 & & \\ & & & -1 & -1 & & -1 & 4+\mu & & & & -1 & \\ & & & & -1 & & & & 4+\mu & -1 & & -1 & -1 \\ & & & & & -1 & & & -1 & 4+\mu & -1 & & & -1 \\ & & & & & & -1 & & & -1 & 4+\mu & -1 & & & -1 \\ & & & & & & & -1 & -1 & & -1 & 4+\mu & & & & -1 \\ -1 & & & & & & & & -1 & & & & 4+\mu & -1 & & -1 \\ & -1 & & & & & & & & -1 & & & -1 & 4+\mu & -1 \\ & & -1 & & & & & & & & -1 & & & -1 & 4+\mu & -1 \\ & & & -1 & & & & & & & & -1 & -1 & & -1 & 4+\mu \end{bmatrix} * \begin{bmatrix} u[0][0] \\ u[1][0] \\ u[2][0] \\ u[3][0] \\ u[0][1] \\ u[1][1] \\ u[2][1] \\ u[3][1] \\ u[0][2] \\ u[1][2] \\ u[2][2] \\ u[3][2] \\ u[0][3] \\ u[1][3] \\ u[2][3] \\ u[3][3] \end{bmatrix} = \begin{bmatrix} q[0][0] \\ q[1][0] \\ q[2][0] \\ q[3][0] \\ q[0][1] \\ q[1][1] \\ q[2][1] \\ q[3][1] \\ q[0][2] \\ q[1][2] \\ q[2][2] \\ q[3][2] \\ q[0][3] \\ q[1][3] \\ q[2][3] \\ q[3][3] \end{bmatrix}$$

Figure 4.7: Matrix system $Au = q$ for $N = 4$.

(b) Thus conclude that

$$\lim_{i \to \infty} \frac{x_{i+1} - \alpha}{(x_i - \alpha)^3} = \frac{1}{2}\left[\frac{f''(\alpha)}{f'(\alpha)}\right]^2.$$

(c) If the cost of computing $f(x)$ is 1 and $f'(x)$ is C, for what values of C is the method more efficient than (i) the Newton–Raphson method or (ii) the secant method?

14. Write a C++ program to calculate the wavenumber corresponding to a given angular frequency for gravity water waves in finite depth, including surface tension effects. Plot κ versus ω for various depths, assuming that for water

$$\tau = 70 \text{ mN/m}, \rho = 1,000 \text{ kg/m}^3, g = 9.81 \text{ m/s}^2.$$

The dispersion relation for finite depth, including surface tension is

$$(g\kappa + \frac{\tau}{\rho}\kappa^3)\tanh(\kappa h) = \omega^2.$$

15. Write an MPI code to accomplish a parallel CGM. Assume that the matrix is distributed by rows across each process.

(a) Given that the matrix is partitioned by rows across each process, outline the parallel decomposition of the CG algorithm. What operations can be done concurrently, and when will parallel calls be required?

(b) It is necessary to determine how many calls to make to *MPI_Reduce/ MPI_Allreduce*. What operations within the CG algorithm require reduction?

(c) Where will *MPI_Send/MPI_Recv* be required? Why?

(d) Define $h = 1/N$, $\mu = h^2$, and $q[i][j] = (8\pi^2 + 1)h^2\sin(2\pi hi)\sin(2\pi hj)$, where $i, j = 0, \ldots, N-1$. Let $\mathbf{A}$ be of the form given in Figure 4.7. Solve the matrix system $\mathbf{Au} = \mathbf{q}$ for u for both $N = 4$ and $N = 20$. Notice that this definition uses two-dimensional arrays, which we will go over in the next chapter. Implement the concept of a two-dimensional array using only a one-dimensional array construction. What indexing is required?

(e) When you run the program on different numbers of processors, is there a noticeable difference in the performance time?

4.4.2 Homework Problems for Section 4.2

1. Ramanujan proposed that the number of numbers between a and b that are either squares or sums of two squares is given approximately by the integral

$$0.764 \int_a^b \frac{dx}{\sqrt{\log_e x}}.$$

Use Gauss quadrature to test numerically this hypothesis for $a = 1, b = 30$.

2. Evaluate the sine integral

$$Si(x) = \int_0^x \frac{\sin z}{z} dz$$

using Simpson's, Romberg's, and Gauss's method for $x = 2$. What do you observe?

3. Use Simpson's formula to find the length of the ellipse

$$\frac{x^2}{a^2} + \frac{y^2}{b^2} = 1.$$

Plot the error versus the number of quadrature points, and verify the fourth-order convergence of the method.
(*Hint*: Describe the ellipse parametrically using

$$x(\theta) = a \cos \theta,$$

$$y(\theta) = b \sin \theta, \theta \in [0, 2\pi]$$

and obtain the length using the formula

$$\int \sqrt{dx^2 + dy^2} .)$$

4. Compute the error function

$$\text{Erf}(x) = \frac{2}{\sqrt{\pi}} \int_0^x e^{-t^2} dt$$

for $x = 1/2$, 1, 2, and 4 using the trapezoid rule and using the appropriate Gauss quadrature for $n = 6$ and 12 quadrature points. Using the formula for the error bounds, obtain an estimate of errors for the two cases.

5. Use a four-level Romberg integration to compute the integral

$$I = \int_1^5 \frac{1}{x^2} dx .$$

How many quadrature points are required to achieve accuracy of 10^{-6}?

6. Use Simpson's rule and Gaussian quadrature to compute the multidimensional integrals

   (a)
   $$\int_0^\pi \int_0^\pi (y^2 \sin x + x^2 \cos^2 y) dx dy,$$

   (b)
   $$\int_0^1 \int_0^1 \int_{-xy}^{xy} e^{x^2 + y^2} dx dy dz$$

   with $n = 4$ quadrature points in each direction.

7. Compute the integrals

   (a)
   $$\int_{-\infty}^\infty \frac{dx}{1 + x^2},$$

   (b)
   $$\int_0^\infty e^{-x} \sin x dx$$

   with $n = 5$ quadrature points, and compute the quadrature error in each case.

5

Explicit Discretizations

In this chapter we consider explicit discretizations of space and time derivatives. In such discretizations we can express directly a derivative at one grid point in terms of function values at adjacent grid points (spatial discretizations) or in terms of previous time levels (temporal discretizations). This, in turn, implies that there is no implicit coupling, and thus no matrix inversion is involved; instead, only simple *daxpy* type operations are required.

The material in this chapter is relatively easy to program both on serial as well as on parallel computers. It is appropriate for demonstrating fundamental concepts of discretization and primary constructs of the C++ language and of the MPI library. Specifically, we will demonstrate the use of loops, arrays, functions, and passing functions to functions. In addition to presenting *MPI_Send* and *MPI_Recv* implementations for finite differences, we also introduce *MPI_Sendrecv* and *MPI_Sendrecv_replace* as alternative advanced MPI function calls for parallelizing finite differences discretizations.

5.1 EXPLICIT SPACE DISCRETIZATIONS

5.1.1 Basics

The formulation of derivatives based on function values on a set of points, which we call the *grid*, dates back to Euler in the beginning of the eighteenth century. However, advances have of course been made since then. In this section, we will formulate ways to compute first- and higher order derivatives of a function using discrete data points. The key idea is to use Taylor expansions at a subset of adjacent points of the grid, as shown in Figure 5.1.

Assuming that we have an equidistant grid [i.e., the distance $\Delta x \equiv x_{i+1} - x_i$ is constant for every grid point (i)], then using Taylor's expansion for the smooth function $u(x)$ around the point (i), we obtain

$$u_{i\pm1} = u(x \pm \Delta x) = u(x) \pm \Delta x u_x(x) + \frac{\Delta x^2}{2} u_{xx}(x) \pm \ldots .$$

Here the x subscript denotes differentiation and the i subscript refers to the index of data points; also Δx^2 means $(\Delta x)^2$.

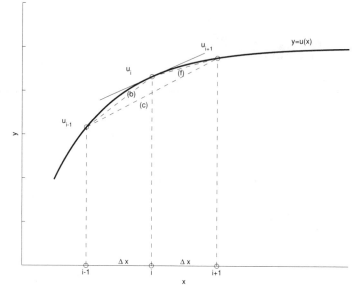

Figure 5.1: A stencil of
two or three points is
required to define the
discrete first
derivative: (c)
corresponds to central
difference; (b)
corresponds to
backward difference;
and (f) corresponds to
forward difference.

We can now form three types of differences from these expansions:

$$Forward: (u_x)_i = \frac{u_{i+1} - u_i}{\Delta x} + \underbrace{\mathcal{O}(\Delta x)}_{-1/2(u_{xx})_i \Delta x} \,,$$

$$Backward: (u_x)_i = \frac{u_i - u_{i-1}}{\Delta x} + \underbrace{\mathcal{O}(\Delta x)}_{+1/2(u_{xx})_i \Delta x} \quad (upwind),$$

$$Central: (u_x)_i = \frac{u_{i+1} - u_{i-1}}{2\Delta x} + \underbrace{\mathcal{O}(\Delta x^2)}_{-1/6(u_{xxx})_i \Delta x^2} \,.$$

The accuracy of each finite difference approximation depends on the last term. Therefore, the forward and backward differences are first order [i.e., $\mathcal{O}(\Delta x)$], whereas the
central difference is of second order [i.e., $\mathcal{O}(\Delta x^2)$]. We also note that the backward and
forward differences are actually $\mathcal{O}(\Delta x^2)$ approximations to derivatives at the half-point
$(i \pm 1/2)$, respectively; for example,

$$(u_x)_{i+1/2} = \frac{u_{i+1} - u_i}{\Delta x} + \mathcal{O}(\Delta x^2).$$

To obtain a second-order-accurate formula for the second derivative we simply add the
two Taylor expansions formed at the $(i \pm 1)$ points:

$$(u_{xx})_i \approx \frac{u_{i+1} - 2u_i + u_{i-1}}{\Delta x^2} - \frac{1}{12}(u_{xxxx})_i \Delta x^2.$$

The basic subset of grid points, the *stencil*, consists of two or three adjacent points for

these discrete derivatives. From the parallel computing standpoint, this implies that *local* computations
are involved. In particular, these are **explicit** formulas, in that the derivative at a point is computed in
terms of function values at adjacent points in the same
stencil. Therefore, there are no other derivatives invol-

Left End Point   Right End Point

$i = 1$ $i = 2$ $i = N-3$ $i = N-2$

$i = 0$ $i = N-1$

**Figure 5.2: Interior
and end (boundary)
points in an interval.**

ved in the discretization besides the derivative at point *i*. In Chapter 6, we will see
implicit formulas in which other derivatives are involved in the discretization.

PUTTING IT INTO PRACTICE

Explicit formulas are also easy to program. Here we demonstrate with the next C++
example how *first derivatives* can be approximated for both nonperiodic and periodic
intervals.

Software

Suite

In this first example, we demonstrate how finite differencing can be done for a
nonperiodic interval (see Figure 5.2). Notice that we cannot use the central difference
formula to calculate an approximation of the derivatives at the end points because we
have no information from outside the interval! Hence, as in this case, we use what
are called "one-sided" approximations, which use information only from inside the
interval. Observe that this requires us to break the approximation process into three
stages:

1. Compute the approximation for the interior points ($i = 1, \ldots, N - 2$).
2. Compute the approximation for the left end point ($i = 0$).
3. Compute the approximation for the right end point ($i = N - 1$).

```
void SO_FirstDeriv_1D (int npts, double dx, double *u,
                       double *u_x){
  double two_invdx = 1.0/(2.0*dx);

  for(int i=1;i<npts-1;i++)
    u_x[i] = (u[i+1]-u[i-1])*two_invdx;

  // Forward Differencing
  u_x[0] = (-3.0*u[0] + 4.0*u[1] - u[2])*two_invdx;

  // Backward Differencing
  u_x[npts-1] = (3.0*u[npts-1] - 4.0*u[npts-2] +
                u[npts-3])*two_invdx;

  return;
}
```

For *periodic* boundary conditions, we can use the central approximation for the end
points; however, care must be taken to properly index the array. Notice that we cannot
access the array at the value −1, and hence we must explicitly treat the end points
so that the appropriate values are taken. Once again, we break the computation into

three stages:

1. Compute the approximation for the interior points ($i = 1, \ldots, N - 2$).
2. Compute the approximation for the left end point ($i = 0$).
3. Compute the approximation for the right end point ($i = N - 1$).

```
void SO_FirstDeriv_1Dper (int npts, double dx, double *u,
                          double *u_x){
  double two_invdx = 1.0/(2.0*dx);

  for(int i=1;i<npts-1;i++)
    u_x[i] = (u[i+1]-u[i-1])*two_invdx;

  // Left Endpoint
  u_x[0] = (u[1]-u[npts-1])*two_invdx;
  // Right Endpoint
  u_x[npts-1] = (u[0]-u[npts-2])*two_invdx;

  return;
}
```

Let us point out, at this stage, a small optimization hint that may be of use in the future. Notice in our examples that at the beginning of the function we explicitly calculate the value of the variable *two_invdx*, and then we continue to use this variable throughout the function. We do this because we observed that the value of *dx* is not changing inside any of the loops within this function, and hence computing $2.0 * dx$ needs to be done only once. Consequently, we can do it up front (at the beginning of the function) instead of repeatedly doing it within the loop. We have chosen to go ahead and do the division because on many machines division is more expensive than multiplication, and then multiplying within the loop instead of dividing is the most efficient choice.

Key Concept	If something is not dependent on the looping variable, then do not do it in the loop!

5.1.2 Uniform Grids

In the following we show how we can systematically obtain finite difference formulas on one-dimensional grids, assuming that the spacing between the grid points is constant. The objective is to develop formulas for high-order approximations for interior points as well as for boundary points.

Method of Undetermined Coefficients

The key idea in this method is to consider the Taylor expansions as functions of Δx and obtain equations for the weights (unknown coefficients) by equating the coefficients of powers of Δx. We demonstrate this by an example.

EXAMPLE. We want to obtain a one-sided, second-order finite difference for $(u_x)_i$, that is,

$$(u_x)_i = \frac{au_i + bu_{i-1} + cu_{i-2}}{\Delta x} + \mathcal{O}(\Delta x^2),$$

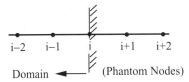

Figure 5.3: Grid at the right boundary of the domain.

as shown in the sketch of Figure 5.3, to handle a boundary condition on the right end of the computational domain. One approach is to employ phantom or ghost nodes outside the domain and construct central difference schemes but this would require extra information about the physics of the problem. The more general approach is to construct one-sided differences extracting information from the interior of the domain.

As before, we expand the function at the different points around the point of interest to obtain

$$c: u_{i-2} = u_i - 2\Delta x(u_x)_i + 2\Delta x^2(u_{xx})_i - \frac{(2\Delta x)^3}{6}(u_{xxx})_i + \dots,$$

$$b: u_{i-1} = u_i - \Delta x(u_x)_i + \frac{\Delta x^2}{2}(u_{xx})_i - \frac{\Delta x^3}{6}(u_{xxx})_i + \dots,$$

$$a: u_i = u_i.$$

Upon substitution in the assumed expression for $(u_x)_i$ we obtain

$$(\Delta x)(u_x)_i = au_i + bu_{i-1} + cu_{i-2} + \mathcal{O}(\Delta x^3)$$

$$= (a + b + c)u_i - \Delta x(2c + b)(u_x)_i + \frac{\Delta x^2}{2}(4c + b)(u_{xx})_i + \mathcal{O}(\Delta x^3).$$

Therefore, solving a 3×3 system we find the values for the coefficients

$$\left.\begin{cases} a + b + c = 0 \\ 2c + b = -1 \\ 4c + b = 0 \end{cases}\right\} \Rightarrow a = 3/2,\ b = -2,\ c = 1/2,$$

and the final formula is

$$(u_x)_i = \frac{3u_i - 4u_{i-1} + u_{i-2}}{2\Delta x} + \mathcal{O}(\Delta x^2).$$

This is a second-order *upwind difference* for the first derivative with truncation error $T \approx \Delta x^2/3$.

In general, a first-order derivative at mesh point (i) can be made of order of accuracy (p) by an explicit formula involving $(p + 1)$ points. However, this is not true for implicit discretizations (see Chapter 6), where on a two-point stencil we can obtain second-order accuracy for the first derivative.

Difference Operators

The method of difference operators is based on symbolic manipulation. We first define the operators that will be acting on functions assigned to grid points, as follows:

Displacement: $\quad E^n u_i \equiv u_{i+n}$,

Forward: $\quad\quad\; \delta^+ u_i \equiv u_{i+1} - u_i \Rightarrow \delta^+ = E - 1$,

Backward: $\quad\; \delta^- u_i \equiv u_i - u_{i-1} \Rightarrow \delta^- = 1 - E^{-1}$,

Half-central: $\;\; \delta u_i \equiv u_{i+1/2} - u_{i-1/2} \Rightarrow \delta = E^{1/2} - E^{-1/2}$,

Central: $\quad\quad \bar{\delta} u_i \equiv (1/2)(u_{i+1} - u_{i-1}) \Rightarrow \bar{\delta} = (1/2)(E - E^{-1})$,

Average: $\quad\quad \mu u_i \equiv (1/2)(u_{i+1/2} + u_{i-1/2}) \Rightarrow \mu = (1/2)(E^{1/2} + E^{-1/2})$,

Derivative: $\quad Du \equiv \partial u / \partial x$.

The symbolic manipulations are straightforward; for example,

$$\delta^{+2} = \delta^+ \delta^+ = (E - 1)(E - 1) = E^2 - 2E + 1,$$

and similarly, $\mu \delta = \bar{\delta}$, etc. We can also write the Taylor expansion in operator form by considering the expansion

$$u(x + \Delta x) = u(x) + \Delta x u_x + \frac{\Delta x^2}{2!} u_{xx} + \frac{\Delta x^3}{3!} u_{xxx} + \dots.$$

The corresponding operator form is

$$E u(x) = \left[1 + \Delta x D + \frac{(\Delta x D)^2}{2!} + \frac{(\Delta x D)^3}{3!} + \dots \right] u(x)$$

or

$$E u(x) = e^{\Delta x D} u(x) \Rightarrow E = e^{\Delta x D} \Rightarrow \Delta x D = \ln(E). \tag{5.1}$$

This last equation is very useful and will be used repeatedly in the following.

• *Forward Differences*: Starting from Equation (5.1) we have

$$\Delta x D = \ln(E) = \ln(1 + \delta^+) \text{ [because } \delta^+ = E - 1]$$

$$= \delta^+ - \frac{\delta^{+2}}{2} + \frac{\delta^{+3}}{3} - \frac{\delta^{+4}}{4} + \dots,$$

where the first neglected term gives the truncation error. For example, if we keep two terms,

$$\Delta x (Du)_i = \delta^+ u_i - \frac{\delta^{+2}}{2} u_i$$

$$= (u_{i+1} - u_i) - \frac{1}{2} (E^2 - 2E + 1) u_i$$

$$= (u_{i+1} - u_i) - \frac{1}{2} (u_{i+2} - 2u_{i+1} + u_i),$$

we obtain a one-sided, second-order formula, similar to the one we obtained before using the method of undetermined coefficients:

$$Du_i = (u_x)_i = \frac{-3u_i + 4u_{i+1} - u_{i+2}}{2\Delta x} + \underbrace{\frac{\Delta x^2}{3}(u_{xxx})_i}_{\text{truncation error}} \quad .$$

Here the coefficients have the opposite sign compared to the formula before because this formula is for the left boundary (*downwind difference*).

• *Backward Differences*: Similarly, we can obtain formulas for backward differences starting from

$$\Delta x D = \ln(E) = -\ln(1 - \delta^-)$$

or

$$\ln E = \delta^- + \frac{\delta^{-2}}{2} + \frac{\delta^{-3}}{3} + \frac{\delta^{-4}}{4} + \dots.$$

• *Central Differences*: Here we can use either the *half-central* or the *central* operators to derive appropriate formulas. To this end,

$$\delta u_i = u_{i+1/2} - u_{i-1/2} = (E^{1/2} - E^{-1/2})u_i$$

$$\Rightarrow \delta = e^{\Delta x D/2} - e^{-\Delta x D/2} = 2\sinh\frac{\Delta x D}{2}$$

$$\Rightarrow \Delta x D = 2\sinh^{-1}(\delta/2) = 2\left[\delta/2 - \frac{1}{2\cdot 3}\left(\frac{\delta}{2}\right)^3 + \frac{1\cdot 3}{2\cdot 4\cdot 5}(\delta/2)^5\right.$$

$$\left. -\frac{1\cdot 3\cdot 5}{2\cdot 4\cdot 6\cdot 7}(\delta/2)^7 + \dots\right].$$

Therefore, we obtain again

$$\Delta x D = \delta - \frac{\delta^3}{24} + \frac{3\delta^5}{640} - \frac{5\delta^7}{7168} + \dots.$$

If we only keep the first term, we derive a second-order formula

$$Du_i = \frac{u_{i+1/2} - u_{i-1/2}}{\Delta x} - \frac{\Delta x^2}{24}(u_{xxx})_i + \dots;$$

however, now we need values at Δx half-integer grid points. This will be suitable for staggered grids where both half-integer and integer grid points are employed.

i − 2   i − 1   i   i + 1   i + 2...

Figure 5.4: A five-point stencil for explicit discretization of the first derivative with fourth-order accuracy.

To involve function values at the integer grid points we employ the central operator

$$\bar{\delta} = \frac{1}{2}(E - E^{-1}) = \frac{1}{2}(e^{\Delta x Dx} - e^{-\Delta x D}) = \sinh(\Delta x D)$$

$$\Rightarrow \Delta x D = \sinh^{-1}\bar{\delta}$$

$$= (\bar{\delta} - \frac{\bar{\delta}^3}{6} + \frac{3}{2 \cdot 4 \cdot 5}\bar{\delta}^5 + \ldots).$$

To achieve *second-order* accuracy we keep the first term only, that is,

$$Du_i = \bar{\delta}/\Delta x = \frac{u_{i+1} - u_{i-1}}{2\Delta x} - \frac{\Delta x^2}{6}(u_{xxx})_i + \ldots.$$

To achieve *fourth-order* accuracy we need to also keep the term $\bar{\delta}^3$, but this will lead to a relatively long stencil, that is, a seven-point stencil because of the index $(i \pm 3)$. In general, a fourth-order accuracy for approximating the first derivative should not require more than a five-point stencil, as shown in Figure 5.4. To achieve this requires doing some extra work by involving the average operator:

$$\mu^2 = 1 + \delta^2/4 \Rightarrow \mu(1 + \delta^2/4)^{-1/2} = 1$$

$$\Rightarrow \mu(1 - \frac{\delta^2}{8} + \frac{3\delta^4}{128} - \frac{5\delta^6}{1024} + \ldots) = 1.$$

However, we have already presented the expansion for the half-central operator, and using it we obtain after multiplying both sides by unity

$$1 \times [\Delta x D] = \left[\delta - \delta^3/24 + \frac{3\delta^5}{640} - \frac{5\delta^7}{7168}\right] \times 1$$

$$= \mu(\delta - \frac{1}{3!}\delta^3 + \frac{1^2 2^2}{5!}\delta^5 - \ldots)$$

$$= \bar{\delta}(1 - \frac{\delta^2}{3!} + \frac{2^2}{5!}\delta^4 - \frac{2^2 3^2}{7!}\delta^6 + \ldots).$$

Therefore, the fourth-order formula for the first derivative on a five-point stencil (see Figure 5.4) is

$$(u_x)_i = \frac{-u_{i+2} + 8u_{i+1} - 8u_{i-1} + u_{i-2}}{12\Delta x} + \frac{\Delta x^4}{30}\left(\frac{\partial^5 u}{\partial x^5}\right).$$

HIGHER ORDER DERIVATIVES. To compute higher derivatives we proceed in a similar way except we need to expand symbolically binomials as shown in the following:

• *Forward:*

$$\left(\frac{\partial^n u}{\partial x^n}\right)_i = D^n u_i = \frac{1}{\Delta x^n}[\ln(1 + \delta^+)]^n u_i$$

$$= \frac{1}{\Delta x^n} \left[\delta^{+n} - \frac{n}{2} \delta^{+(n+1)} + \frac{n(3n+5)}{24} \delta^{+(n+2)} \right.$$

$$\left. - \frac{n(n+2)(n+3)}{48} \delta^{+(n+3)} + \dots \right] u_i, \tag{5.2}$$

- *Backward:*

$$\left(\frac{\partial^n u}{\partial x^n} \right)_i = -\frac{1}{\Delta x^n} [\ln(1 - \delta^-)]^n u_i$$

$$= \frac{1}{\Delta x^n} \left(\delta^- + \frac{\delta^{-2}}{2} + \frac{\delta^{-3}}{3} + \dots \right)^n u_i$$

$$= \frac{1}{\Delta x^n} \left[\delta^{-n} + \frac{n}{2} \delta^{-(n+1)} + \frac{n(3n+5)}{24} \delta^{-(n+2)} \right. \tag{5.3}$$

$$\left. + \frac{n(n+2)(n+3)}{48} + \delta^{-(n+3)} + \dots \right] u_i, \tag{5.4}$$

- *Central:*

$$D^n u_i = \left(\frac{2}{\Delta x} \sinh^{-1} \frac{\delta}{2} \right)^n u_i = \frac{1}{\Delta x^n} \left[\delta - \frac{\delta^3}{24} + \frac{3\delta^5}{640} - \frac{5\delta^7}{7168} + \dots \right]^n u_i$$

$$= \frac{1}{\Delta x^n} \delta^n \left[1 - \frac{n}{24} \delta^2 + \frac{n}{64} \left(\frac{22 + 5n}{90} \right) \delta^4 \right.$$

$$\left. - \frac{n}{45} \left(\frac{5}{7} + \frac{n-1}{5} + \frac{(n-1)(n-2)}{35} \right) \delta^6 + \dots \right] u_i. \tag{5.5}$$

REMARK: For n even, function values at integer grid points are required.

SECOND DERIVATIVE. The formulas for the second derivative are simplified as follows

- *Forward:* $(u_{xx})_i = \frac{1}{\Delta x^2} \left(\delta^{+2} - \delta^{+3} + \frac{11}{12} \delta^{+4} - \frac{5}{6} \delta^{+5} + \dots \right) u_i,$
- *Backward:* $(u_{xx})_i = \frac{1}{\Delta x^2} \left(\delta^{-2} + \delta^{-3} + \frac{11}{12} \delta^{-4} + \frac{5}{6} \delta^{-5} + \dots \right) u_i,$
- *Central:* $(u_{xx})_i = \frac{1}{\Delta x^2} \left(\delta^2 - \frac{\delta^4}{12} + \frac{\delta^6}{90} - \frac{\delta^8}{560} + \dots \right) u_i.$

Note that because of symmetry, the central discretization leads to higher order accuracy by maintaining only the first term.

EXAMPLE. We can derive useful formulas by keeping only two terms in the expansions, as follows:

- *Forward:* $(u_{xx})_i = \frac{1}{\Delta x^2} (2u_i - 5u_{i+1} + 4u_{i+2} - u_{i+3}) + \frac{11}{12} \Delta x^2 \left(\frac{\partial^4 u}{\partial x^4} \right),$
- *Backward:* $(u_{xx})_i = \frac{1}{\Delta x^2} (2u_i - 5u_{i-1} + 4u_{i-2} - u_{i-3}) - \frac{11}{12} \Delta x^2 \left(\frac{\partial^4 u}{\partial x^4} \right),$
- *Central:* $(u_{xx})_i = \frac{1}{12\Delta x^2} (-u_{i+2} + 16u_{i+1} - 30u_i + 16u_{i-1} - u_{i-2}) + \frac{\Delta x^4}{90} \left(\frac{\partial^6 u}{\partial x^6} \right).$

These two one-sided formulas are important in handling boundary points. In the code example that follows, we implement these formulas for the left boundary, the right boundary, and the interior respectively, assuming the index i runs from left to right.

Software

Suite

PUTTING IT INTO PRACTICE

Just as with the first-derivative approximations, we break the approximation process into three stages:

1. Compute the approximation for the interior points ($i = 1, \ldots, N - 2$).
2. Compute the approximation for the left end point ($i = 0$).
3. Compute the approximation for the right end point ($i = N - 1$).

Here we present the second-derivative finite difference approximation for a *nonperiodic* interval. Observe that at the end points we use the four-point one-sided approximation already derived.

```
void SO_SecondDeriv_1D(int npts, double dx, double *u,
                       double *u_xx){
   int i;
   double inv_dx2 = 1.0/(dx*dx);

   // Forward differencing
   u_xx[0] = (2.0*u[0]-5.0*u[1]+4.0*u[2]-u[3])*inv_dx2;

   // Central differencing
   for(i=1;i<npts-1;i++)
     u_xx[i] = (u[i+1]-2.0*u[i]+u[i-1])*inv_dx2;

   // Backward differencing
   u_xx[npts-1] = (2.0*u[npts-1]-5.0*u[npts-2]+4.0*
                  u[npts-3]-u[npts-4])*inv_dx2;

   return;
}
```

As before, for the *periodic* interval approximation, we can use the central approximation for every point, being mindful that we must take special care when computing the end points to make sure that we do not overrun the arrays.

```
void SO_SecondDeriv_1Dper (int npts, double dx, double *u,
                           double *u_xx){
   int i;
   double inv_dx2 = 1.0/(dx*dx);

   u_xx[0] = (u[1]-2.0*u[0]+u[npts-1])*inv_dx2;

   // Central differencing
   for(i=1;i<npts-1;i++)
     u_xx[i] = (u[i+1]-2.0*u[i]+u[i-1])*inv_dx2;

   u_xx[npts-1] = (u[0]-2.0*u[npts-1]+u[npts-2])*inv_dx2;

   return;
}
```

How do we use these functions? Next we provide codes for testing both the non-periodic and periodic first- and second-derivative approximations. One thing we would like to point out is our selection of dx. Notice that if we have N points and we want these points to be uniformly spaced throughout the interval *including the end points*, then we must chose dx to be the length of the interval divided by $(N-1)$.

```cpp
#include <iostream.h>
#include <iomanip.h>
#include "SCchapter5.h"

double func(double x);
double func_first_der(double x);
double func_second_der(double x);

int main(int argc, char * argv[]){
  const int levels = 10; //number of levels to test
  const double a = 0.0;   //left end point of domain
  const double b = 1.0;   //right end point of domain
  int i,j,npts;
  double dx,dxp,ux_error,uxx_error;
  double *u,*u_x,*u_xx;

  cout << "npts\tError (First Deriv)\tError (Second Deriv)\n";
  for(i=2;i<levels+2;i++){
    npts = (int) pow(2.0,i); //number of grid points is equal
                             // to 2^level
    dx = 1.0/(npts-1); //set dx based on number of points

    // Allocate storage dynamically
    u = new double[npts];
    u_x = new double[npts];
    u_xx = new double[npts];

    for(j=0;j<npts;j++)
      u[j] = func(j*dx); // set function value

    SO_FirstDeriv_1D  (npts,dx,u,u_x); //calc. 1st deriv.
    SO_SecondDeriv_1D (npts,dx,u,u_xx); //calc. 2nd deriv.

    // Computation of the L2 error
    ux_error=0.0;
    uxx_error=0.0;
    for(j=0;j<npts;j++){
      ux_error  += dx*pow((u_x[j]-func_first_der(j*dx)),2);
      uxx_error += dx*pow((u_xx[j]-func_second_der(j*dx)),2);
    }

    cout << setprecision(10) << setiosflags(ios::scientific);
    cout << npts << "\t" << sqrt(ux_error);
```

```
        cout << "\t" << sqrt(uxx_error) << endl;

        //Deallocation of dynamic memory
        delete[] u;
        delete[] u_x;
        delete[] u_xx;
    }

}

double func(double x){
  return(x*x*x*x);
}

double func_first_der(double x){
  return(4*x*x*x);
}

double func_second_der(double x){
  return(12*x*x);
}
```

After compilation and execution of this program, the following results are printed:

npts	Error (First Deriv)	Error (Second Deriv)
4	4.4854079320e-01	2.0041110013e+00
8	6.9622902770e-02	2.4294654992e-01
16	1.3089009760e-02	3.6721619875e-02
32	2.7619740848e-03	6.1646753898e-03
64	6.2730612749e-04	1.1069179087e-03
128	1.4891039346e-04	2.1107879261e-04
256	3.6234744984e-05	4.2896354790e-05
512	8.9342897099e-06	9.2915223897e-06
1024	2.2180019754e-06	2.1242917384e-06
2048	5.5255279205e-07	5.0463557743e-07

According to the theory, both of these methods should be second-order accurate. If this were true, then doubling the number of grid points used should lead to a reduction in the error by a factor of 4. Notice the convergence rate – it is just as predicted by the theory! Every time we increase the number of points by a factor of 2, the error decreases by about a factor of 4; hence we have second-order convergence.

The code that follows is a slight modification of the preceding one, in which we now demonstrate the use of the periodic interval functions. Observe that since we have N points and we want points to be uniformly spaced throughout the interval *including only the left end point*, then we must chose dx to be the length of the interval divided by N. Why do we use only the left end point? Recall that we want the domain to be periodic. Hence, the last point value should not be the right-hand end of the domain because this value is periodic with the left-hand value. So we chose dx to be the length of the interval divided by N and not by $(N-1)$. The following code demonstrates the use of the periodic differencing functions:

```cpp
#include <iostream.h>
#include <iomanip.h>
#include "SCchapter5.h"

double func(double x);
double func_first_der(double x);
double func_second_der(double x);

int main(int argc, char * argv[]){
  const int levels = 10; //number of levels to test
  const double a = 0.0;  //left end point of domain
  const double b = 1.0;  //right end point of domain
  int i,j,npts;
  double dx,dxp,ux_error,uxx_error;
  double *u,*u_x,*u_xx;

  cout << "npts\tError (First Deriv)\tError (Second Deriv)\n";
  for(i=2;i<levels+2;i++){
    npts = (int) pow(2.0,i); //number of grid points is equal
                             // to 2^level
    dx = 1.0/(npts); //set dx based on number of points

    // Allocate storage dynamically
    u = new double[npts];
    u_x = new double[npts];
    u_xx = new double[npts];

    for(j=0;j<npts;j++)
      u[j] = func(j*dx); // set function value

    SO_FirstDeriv_1Dper (npts,dx,u,u_x); //calc. 1st deriv.
    SO_SecondDeriv_1Dper(npts,dx,u,u_xx); //calc. 2nd deriv.

    // Computation of the L2 error
    ux_error=0.0;
    uxx_error=0.0;
    for(j=0;j<npts;j++){
      ux_error  += dx*pow((u_x[j]-func_first_der(j*dx)),2);
      uxx_error += dx*pow((u_xx[j]-func_second_der(j*dx)),2);
    }

    cout << setprecision(10) << setiosflags(ios::scientific);
    cout << npts << "\t" << sqrt(ux_error) << "\t";
    cout << << sqrt(uxx_error) << endl;
```

```
        //Deallocation of dynamic memory
        delete[] u;
        delete[] u_x;
        delete[] u_xx;
    }

}

double func(double x){
  return(sin(2.0*M_PI*x));
}

double func_first_der(double x){
  return(2.0*M_PI*cos(2.0*M_PI*x));
}

double func_second_der(double x){
  return(-4.0*M_PI*M_PI*sin(2.0*M_PI*x));
}
```

After compilation and execution of this program above, the following results are printed:

npts	Error (First Deriv)	Error (Second Deriv)
4	1.6144558134e+00	5.2880398006e+00
8	4.4288293816e-01	1.4057888067e+00
16	1.1331413699e-01	3.5690383940e-01
32	2.8492869631e-02	8.9570538385e-02
64	7.1335237874e-03	2.2414226421e-02
128	1.7840256502e-03	5.6049069655e-03
256	4.4604671517e-04	1.4013111524e-03
512	1.1151419784e-04	3.5033306453e-04
1024	2.7878706903e-05	8.7583596378e-05
2048	6.9696865656e-06	2.1895920354e-05

Notice the convergence rate – it is again just as predicted by the theory! Just as in the previous example, every time we increase the number of points by a factor of 2, the error decreases by about a factor of 4; hence we have second-order convergence.

5.1.3 MPI Parallel Implementation of Finite Differences

To implement these differencing functions in MPI, we will first partition our domain among the processors. Assuming that the domain has been properly partitioned, it is the responsibility of each processor to compute the finite differences necessary for all points contained on that processor. Where do we need MPI? On each subdomain, the end points of the domain need information that is not resident to the processor; such information resides on a different processor. Hence, we must use *MPI_Send* and *MPI_Recv*

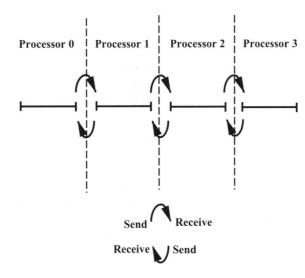

Send ⌒ Receive

Receive ⌄ Send

Figure 5.5: MPI send–receive pattern for finite differencing across processors.

to transmit the information from one processor to another, as demonstrated in Figure 5.5.

Next we present our implementation of one-dimensional (1D) first-derivative finite differencing for a nonperiodic interval.

Software ⊙ *Suite*

1D First-Derivative Parallel Code: MPI_Send/MPI_Recv for a Nonperiodic Interval

```
void SO_FirstDeriv_1DP(int npts, double dx, double *u,
                       double *u_x, int mynode,
                       int totalnodes){
  double two_invdx = 1.0/(2.0*dx);
  double mpitemp;
  MPI_Status status;

  if(mynode == 0)
    u_x[0] = (-3.0*u[0] + 4.0*u[1] - u[2])*two_invdx;

  if(mynode == (totalnodes-1))
    u_x[npts-1] = (3.0*u[npts-1] - 4.0*u[npts-2] +
                  u[npts-3])*two_invdx;

  for(int i=1;i<npts-1;i++)
    u_x[i] = (u[i+1]-u[i-1])*two_invdx;

  if(mynode == 0){
    mpitemp = u[npts-1];
    MPI_Send(&mpitemp,1,MPI_DOUBLE,1,1,MPI_COMM_WORLD);

    MPI_Recv(&mpitemp,1,MPI_DOUBLE,1,1,MPI_COMM_WORLD,
             &status);
```

```
    u_x[npts-1] = (mpitemp - u[npts-2])*two_invdx;
}
else if(mynode == (totalnodes-1)){
  MPI_Recv(&mpitemp,1,MPI_DOUBLE,mynode-1,1,
          MPI_COMM_WORLD, &status);
  u_x[0] = (u[1]-mpitemp)*two_invdx;

  mpitemp = u[0];
  MPI_Send(&mpitemp,1,MPI_DOUBLE,mynode-1,1,
          MPI_COMM_WORLD);
}
else{
  MPI_Recv(&mpitemp,1,MPI_DOUBLE,mynode-1,1,
          MPI_COMM_WORLD, &status);
  u_x[0] = (u[1]-mpitemp)*two_invdx;
  mpitemp = u[0];
  MPI_Send(&mpitemp,1,MPI_DOUBLE,mynode-1,1,
          MPI_COMM_WORLD);

  mpitemp = u[npts-1];
  MPI_Send(&mpitemp,1,MPI_DOUBLE,mynode+1,1,
          MPI_COMM_WORLD);
  MPI_Recv(&mpitemp,1,MPI_DOUBLE,mynode+1,1,
          MPI_COMM_WORLD, &status);
  u_x[npts-1] = (mpitemp-u[npts-2])*two_invdx;
}

return;
}
```

Observe the following cases that need special attention:

1. Process 0 contains the left end point, and hence special one-sided differences must be employed.
2. Process *(totalnodes-1)* contains the right end point, and hence special one-sided differencing must be employed.
3. For any other process, differencing for interior points can be done, and communication with neighbors to obtain information concerning adjacent points should be performed.

Care must be taken to guarantee that when one process is sending information, another process is ready to receive information. Notice the careful staggering of *MPI_Send* and *MPI_Recv*. If two processors were to call *MPI_Send* at the same time, with messages intended for each other, then we would arrive at what is referred to as a *race-condition*, and both processors would sit forever waiting for the other to call *MPI_Recv*!

Key Concept

Care must be taken to avoid *race-conditions*. Recall that for every *send*, there must be a *receive* ready to accept the information.

Notice that in every case in this example, we are "exchanging" information; that is, every process wants to "swap information" with its adjacent process. We have implemented this code using a combination of sends and receives; however, MPI provides us with the functions *MPI_Sendrecv* and *MPI_Sendrecv_replace*, which can help to automate this process. We now present the function syntax, argument list, usage examples, and remarks for *MPI_Sendrecv* and *MPI_Sendrecv_replace*.

MPI_Sendrecv/MPI_Sendrecv_replace

FUNCTION CALL SYNTAX

MPI

```
int MPI_Sendrecv(
        void*           sendbuf     /*   in    */,
        int             sendcount   /*   in    */,
        MPI_Datatype    sendtype    /*   in    */,
        int             dest        /*   in    */,
        int             sendtag     /*   in    */,
        void*           recvbuf     /*   out   */,
        int             recvcount   /*   in    */,
        MPI_Datatype    recvtype    /*   in    */,
        int             source      /*   in    */,
        int             recvtag     /*   in    */,
        MPI_Comm        comm        /*   in    */,
        MPI_Status*     status      /*   out   */)

int MPI_Sendrecv_replace(
        void*           buffer      /*   in    */,
        int             count       /*   in    */,
        MPI_Datatype    sendtype    /*   in    */,
        int             dest        /*   in    */,
        int             sendtag     /*   in    */,
        int             source      /*   in    */,
        int             recvtag     /*   in    */,
        MPI_Comm        comm        /*   in    */,
        MPI_Status*     status      /*   out   */)
```

UNDERSTANDING THE ARGUMENT LISTS

MPI

- *sendbuf* – starting address of the send buffer.
- *sendcount* – number of elements in the send buffer.
- *sendtype* – data type of the elements in the send buffer.

- *dest* – process rank of destination.
- *sendtag* – send message tag.
- *recvbuf* – starting address of the receive buffer.
- *recvcount* – number of elements in the receive buffer.
- *recvtype* – data type of the elements in the receive buffer.
- *source* – process rank of source process.
- *sendtag* – send message tag.
- *comm* – communicator.
- *status* – status object.
- *buffer* – starting address of the send/recv buffer (replace case).
- *count* – number of elements in the send/recv buffer (replace case).

MPI

EXAMPLE OF USAGE

```
int mynode, totalnodes;
int datasize;  // number of data units to be sent/recv
int process1, process2;  //process rank of two
                         //  processes to exchange data
int tag1,tag2; // integer message tag

MPI_Status status; // variable to contain status information

MPI_Init(&argc,&argv);
MPI_Comm_size(MPI_COMM_WORLD, &totalnodes);
MPI_Comm_rank(MPI_COMM_WORLD, &mynode);

// Determine datasize, process1, process2

double * sendbuffer = new double[datasize];
double * recvbuffer = new double[datasize];
double * buffer     = new double[datasize];

if(mynode == process1){

  // The call below sends the contents of sendbuffer to
  //    process2 and obtains from process2 data placed
  //    into recvbuffer

  MPI_Sendrecv(sendbuffer,datasize,MPI_DOUBLE,process2,
               tag1,recvbuffer,datasize,MPI_DOUBLE,process2,
               tag2,MPI_COMM_WORLD,&status);

  // The call below will 'swap' the contents of buffer with
  //    process2; note the corresponding call to
  //    MPI_Sendrecv_replace below

  MPI_Sendrecv_replace(buffer,datasize,MPI_DOUBLE,process2,
                       tag1,process2,tag2,MPI_COMM_WORLD,
                       &status);
```

```
}
if(mynode == process2){

    // The call below sends the contents of sendbuffer to
    //    process1 and obtains from process1 data placed
    //    into recvbuffer

    MPI_Sendrecv(sendbuffer,datasize,MPI_DOUBLE,process1,
                tag2,recvbuffer,datasize,MPI_DOUBLE,process1,
                tag1,MPI_COMM_WORLD,&status);

    // The call below will 'swap' the contents of buffer
    //    with process1; note the corresponding call to
    //    MPI_Sendrecv_replace above

    MPI_Sendrecv_replace(buffer,datasize,MPI_DOUBLE,process1,
                    tag2,process1,tag1,MPI_COMM_WORLD,
                    &status);

}

// At this point, process1 has in its recvbuffer the contents
// of process1's sendbuffer, process2 has in its recvbuffer
// the contents of process1's sendbuffer, and process1
// and process2's buffer arrays have been exchanged with
// each other.
```

REMARKS

MPI

- *MPI_Sendrecv* allows us to send to one process and receive from another process (or from the same process to which we are sending) in one function call. This type of MPI function is ideal for swapping or shifting information among a collection of processes.
- *MPI_Sendrecv_replace* allows us the functionality of *MPI_Sendrecv* with the additional caveat that the information that is being sent is overwritten by the received information. MPI guarantees that the "sending" is accomplished before the "receiving."
- For both *MPI_Sendrecv* and *MPI_Sendrecv_replace*, the sending and receiving processes do not have to be the same. For instance, *process 1* can send data to *process 2* while obtaining data from *process 0*.
- For *MPI_Sendrecv*, *MPI_Recv* can be used on the receiving process to obtain the information being sent. Similarly, *MPI_Sendrecv* can receive data from a process using *MPI_Send* to send.
- In most cases the *sendtype* and *recvtype* are identical.
- The tag can be any integer between 0 and 32,767.

We implement again the finite differencing function previously given, now using *MPI_Sendrecv_replace* as opposed to *MPI_Send/MPI_Recv*. Notice that the "race-condition" problem is handled by MPI, and not by us!

Software

Suite

Key Concept

If you find yourself repeating some pattern of *MPI_Send* and *MPI_Recv* calls, it is very likely that an MPI function already exists that combines the pattern into one MPI call.

1D First-Derivative Parallel Code: MPI_Sendrecv_replace for a Nonperiodic Interval

```
void SO_FirstDeriv_1DP(int npts, double dx, double *u,
                       double *u_x,int mynode,
                       int totalnodes){
  double two_invdx = 1.0/(2.0*dx);
  double mpitemp;
  MPI_Status status;

  if(mynode == 0)
    u_x[0] = (-3.0*u[0] + 4.0*u[1] - u[2])*two_invdx;

  if(mynode == (totalnodes-1))
    u_x[npts-1] = (3.0*u[npts-1] - 4.0*u[npts-2] +
                   u[npts-3])*two_invdx;

  for(int i=1;i<npts-1;i++)
    u_x[i] = (u[i+1]-u[i-1])*two_invdx;

  if(mynode == 0){
    mpitemp = u[npts-1];
    MPI_Sendrecv_replace(&mpitemp,1,MPI_DOUBLE,1,1,1,1,
                         MPI_COMM_WORLD, &status);
    u_x[npts-1] = (mpitemp - u[npts-2])*two_invdx;
  }
  else if(mynode == (totalnodes-1)){
    mpitemp = u[0];
    MPI_Sendrecv_replace(&mpitemp,1,MPI_DOUBLE,mynode-1,
                         1,mynode-1,1, MPI_COMM_WORLD,
                         &status);
    u_x[0] = (u[1]-mpitemp)*two_invdx;
  }
  else{
    mpitemp = u[0];
    MPI_Sendrecv_replace(&mpitemp,1,MPI_DOUBLE,mynode-1,
                         1,mynode-1,1, MPI_COMM_WORLD,
                         &status);
    u_x[0] = (u[1]-mpitemp)*two_invdx;

    mpitemp = u[npts-1];
    MPI_Sendrecv_replace(&mpitemp,1,MPI_DOUBLE,mynode+1,
```

```
                          1,mynode+1,1, MPI_COMM_WORLD,
                          &status);
      u_x[npts-1] = (mpitemp-u[npts-2])*two_invdx;
  }

  return;
}
```

In the *software suite* we present a C++ program that uses the MPI differencing functions provided here. It is very similar to the scalar programs shown earlier. Also, we use the *MPI_Reduce* function, which was discussed earlier, for collecting the error information from all the processors and supplying it to process 0.

We also include several C++/MPI implementations for first and second derivatives on periodic and nonperiodic domains using *MPI_Send/MPI_Recv* and also using *MPI_Sendrecv_replace*.

Software

Suite

Variable Coefficient

A situation that often arises in applications is a second-order derivative term with variable coefficient, which is a function of the location and thus may vary along the grid points. To maintain the desired accuracy in this case we have to symmetrize the discretization as follows:

$$\frac{\partial}{\partial x}[\nu(x)\frac{\partial}{\partial x}]u_i = \frac{1}{\Delta x^2}\delta^-(\nu_{i+1/2}\delta^+)u_i + \mathcal{O}(\Delta x^2) = \frac{1}{\Delta x^2}\delta^+(\nu_{i-1/2}\delta^-)u_i + \mathcal{O}(\Delta x^2).$$

Thus,

$$\frac{\partial}{\partial x}[\nu(x)\frac{\partial}{\partial x}]u_i = \frac{\nu_{i+1/2}(u_{i+1} - u_i)}{\Delta x^2} - \frac{\nu_{i-1/2}(u_i - u_{i-1})}{\Delta x^2} + \mathcal{O}(\Delta x^2).$$

Many diffusion problems with space-dependent diffusivity are formulated in this fashion.

5.1.4 Multidimensional Arrays in C++

As the level of complexity of our programs increases, we will increasingly find that single-indexed (one-dimensional) arrays do not fulfill all our programming needs. This is not to say that we cannot use single arrays for doing all of our work, but rather that sometimes the algorithm naturally breaks itself down into what we refer to as multidimensional arrays (for example, matrices, which can be considered an $N \times M$ array). Just as with single-dimension arrays, there are two ways to allocate multidimensional arrays: *statically* and *dynamically*.

Static Allocation of Multidimensional Arrays

Just as with single-indexed arrays, we can allocate multidimensional arrays statically as follows: Suppose that we want to declare an array of *double* that is 20×20 in size. We would use the following array declaration:

```
double x[20][20];
```

We have now declared an array x that contains 20×20 doubles, which can be indexed $i = 0, 19$ in the first index and $j = 0, 19$ in the second index. Hence if we wanted item (3,4), we would access $x[3][4]$.

If we want more than two dimensions, we can continue to append dimensions as follows:

```
double x[20][20][20][20];
```

which is a $20 \times 20 \times 20 \times 20$ array! All of the previous rules introduced with single-indexed arrays still apply.

Dynamic Allocation of Multidimensional Arrays

Dynamic allocation of multidimensional arrays is very similar to that of single-dimension arrays. Suppose, once again, that we now want to dynamically allocate an array of 10×10 elements. This can be done as follows:

```
int npts = 10;
double ** x;

x = new double*[npts];
for(i=0;i<npts;i++)
    x[i] = new double[npts];
```

To delete the allocated memory, we would use the following reversal of the process:

```
for(int i=0;i<npts;i++)
    delete[] x[i];
delete[] x;
```

The key points to get from this are the following:

• For a single-dimension array, we used a double*. For a two-dimensional array, we use a double**. For a three-dimensional array, we use a double***, and so on. This is because at each successive level, we are declaring an "array of arrays." A two-dimensional array is an array of one-dimensional arrays. A three-dimensional array is an array of two-dimensional arrays, which, in turn, are arrays of one-dimensional arrays.
• Observe that when declaring a two-dimensional array, we first must declare the array of double* variables, and then we assign to each double* variable an allocation of a single-dimensional array. A schematic of this is shown in Figure 5.6.

- Creating arrays in this fashion does not create contiguous blocks! This means that what we have shown you here gives the most freedom to the operating system to decide how to fit things into memory.
- Observe that when deleting the dynamic allocation, we must reverse the allocation process. First, we must deallocate the single-dimension arrays that we assigned, and then we must delete the original array.

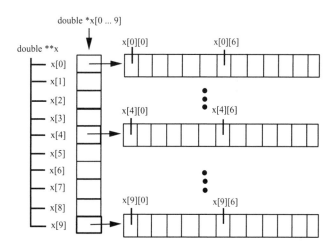

Figure 5.6: Diagram showing conceptual picture of two-dimensional array memory allocation.

Dynamic Allocation of Multidimensional Arrays in Contiguous Blocks

In some instances when using BLAS or MPI it may be necessary to allocate multidimensional arrays as a contiguous block of memory, which is different than what was previously shown. This is because both BLAS and MPI act on contiguous blocks of memory. To create a two-dimensional array in which the allocation is a continuous block of memory, we allocate the block of memory and index the pointer array ourselves. We will first present a sample code to accomplish this and then we will comment on this code.

```
int N = size; //size is the specified size of the
    matrix (N x N)
double ** x;

x = new double*[N]; //allocate double* indexing array

x[0] = new double[N*N]; //allocate storage as a
                        //contiguous block
for(int i=1;i<N;i++)
  x[i] = x[0]+i*N;
```

Observe that after allocating our indexing array, we allocate a contiguous block of memory equal to the total size that we need and then assign the leading address of that block of memory to the first indexed position of our indexing array. We then loop through the remainder of the indexing array and assign to each position the appropriately offset amount, as shown in Figure 5.7. With this type of memory allocation we are certain that $x[0]$ points to a contiguous block of memory representing the entire $N \times N$ matrix. Hence, in MPI, if we wanted to send this matrix to another process, we could pass $x[0]$ as the starting pointer and send $N \times N$ doubles to a receiving process.

Row-Major Order versus Column-Major Order

Previously we mentioned that there is a difference between row-major order and column-major order. In this section we will explain the differences between these two orderings and explain why they are significant.

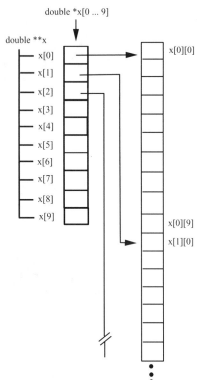

Figure 5.7: Diagram showing conceptual picture of two-dimensional array memory allocation with contiguous memory.

Multidimensional arrays require us to derive a mapping from the multidimensional ordering of the array to a linearly addressable ordering used for accessing memory. In Figure 5.8 we present a diagram demonstrating the difference between a row-major ordering and a column-major ordering.

Observe that in a row-major ordering, we map the array row by row into the linearly addressed memory, whereas in a column-major ordering we map the array column by column. It is important to be mindful of row-major ordering and column-major ordering for the following reasons:

- When using BLAS (or ATLAS), by default matrices are assumed to be stored in *column-major order* (consistent with FORTRAN) instead of *row-major order* (consistent with C/C++). You may be required to manually reorder your matrix to accommodate BLAS. Another option provided by BLAS that enables you to forgo manual reordering is to specify that you are passing the transpose of the matrix (the transpose of a row-major ordered matrix is a column-major ordered matrix). Care must be taken though when interpreting the results of the BLAS call. The resulting operation will be in column-major order.
- Whether a matrix is stored in column-major order or row-major order determines the most efficient way to access the array entries. Suppose we needed to print the contents of a matrix, and we wanted to access memory in the most efficient way possible. Consider the following looping example:

```
// Optimal for column-major ordering
for(int i=0;i<N;i++)
  for(int j=0;j<N;j++)
    cout << A[j][i] << endl;

// Optimal for row-major ordering
for(int i=0;i<N;i++)
  for(int j=0;j<N;j++)
    cout << A[i][j] << endl;
```

C++ uses row-major ordering; the latter example shows the optimal means of accessing the contents of the multidimensional array *A*. We design the loops so that the *innermost loop* runs over the *outermost index*.

5.1.5 Nonuniform Grids

Because there are steep gradients in the solution in some regions and smooth variation in other regions, we often need to compute derivatives on a nonuniform grid. Such solution behavior is present in boundary layers, but it may also be dictated by the geometry of the problem or because of semi-infinite or infinite computational domains. Here, we present two different ways of handling nonuniform grids, first using *Lagrangian interpolation* and second using *mappings*.

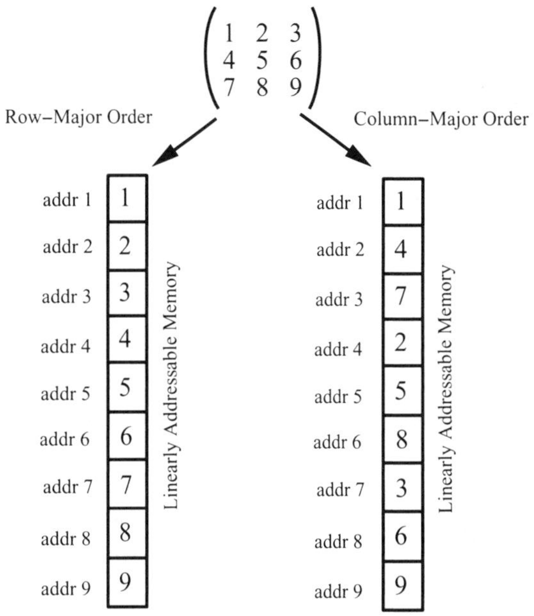

Lagrangian Interpolation and Nonuniform Grids

So far we have obtained discretizations of the first and second derivatives on uniforms grids. Next, we assume that we have an arbitrary distribution of grid points denoted by $(\alpha_0, \alpha_1, \ldots, \alpha_N)$, as shown in Figure 5.9. We will look for approximations of the mth-order derivative on a stencil consisting of n points, where $n \geq m$. We allow $m = 0$, which is the degenerate case for interpolation. This method was first proposed by Fornberg, and here we have adopted his notation [37].

Let us consider the function $f(x)$ and look for the approximation of the mth-order derivative at the point x_0:

$$\frac{d^m f}{dx^m}\Big|_{x=x_0} = \sum_{\nu=0}^{n} c_{n,\nu}^m f(\alpha_\nu), \quad \begin{aligned} m &= 0, 1, \ldots, M, \\ n &= m, m+1, \ldots, N. \end{aligned} \tag{5.6}$$

The question is then: How do we compute $c_{n,\nu}^m$ efficiently for any point in the interval $x \in [\alpha_0, \alpha_N]$? The key idea here is to use *Lagrangian interpolation*.

For simplicity, let us consider the point $x_0 = 0$. We then define

$$F_n(x) \equiv \Pi_{k=0}^{n}(x - \alpha_k),$$

and thus the nth-degree Lagrangian polynomial is

$$h_\nu^n(x) \equiv \frac{F_n(x)}{F_n'(\alpha_\nu)(x - \alpha_\nu)}, \quad h_\nu^n(\alpha_k) = \delta_{\nu k}.$$

Then we can perform Lagrangian interpolation for $f(x)$, that is,

$$f(x) \approx \sum_{\nu=0}^{n} h_\nu^n(x) f(\alpha_\nu). \tag{5.7}$$

Now by comparing Equation (5.6) and the mth-order derivative of the Lagrangian representation in Equation (5.7), we obtain

$$c_{n,\nu}^m = \frac{d^m}{dx^m} h_\nu^n(x)\Big|_{x=0}.$$

$$\begin{pmatrix} 1 & 2 & 3 \\ 4 & 5 & 6 \\ 7 & 8 & 9 \end{pmatrix}$$

Row–Major Order   Column–Major Order

Figure 5.8: Diagram showing a conceptual picture of row-major order versus column-major order for the contiguous allocation of a two-dimensional array. Observe that both orderings require the same quantity of linearly addressable memory; however, the distributions of the two-dimensional array elements differ based upon which ordering is used.

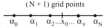

(N + 1) grid points

$\alpha_0 \quad \alpha_1 \quad \alpha_2 ... x_0 ... \alpha_\nu \quad \alpha_N$

Figure 5.9: The grid points are distinct but arbitrarily distributed in the domain.

Inversely, the nth-degree polynomial $h_\nu^n(x)$ can be expressed using a Taylor expansion of the form

$$h_\nu^n(x) = \sum_{m=0}^{n} \frac{c_{n,\nu}^m}{m!} x^m.$$

The next step is to obtain recurrence formulas for $h_\nu^n(x)$ so that they can be computed efficiently, and subsequently to compute $c_{n,\nu}^m$ recursively. To this end,

$$F_n(x) = (x - \alpha_n)F_{n-1}(x),$$

$$F_n'(x) = (x - \alpha_n)F_{n-1}'(x) + F_{n-1}(x).$$

This recursive function calling is implemented in the following example. We assume that the array *alpha[i]* contains the grid coordinates as shown in Figure 5.9.

```
double F(int n, double x, double *alpha){
  double answer;

  if(n==0)
    answer = x - alpha[n];
  else
    answer = (x-alpha[n])*F(n-1,x,alpha);

  return answer;
}
```

The recursion for the Lagrangian polynomials is then obtained from

$$\nu \neq n: \ h_\nu^n(x) = \frac{F_n(x)}{F_n'(\alpha_\nu)(x - \alpha_\nu)} = \frac{(x - \alpha_n)F_{n-1}(x)}{(\alpha_\nu - \alpha_n)F_{n-1}'(\alpha_\nu)(x - \alpha_\nu)}$$

$$= \frac{x - \alpha_n}{\alpha_\nu - \alpha_n} \frac{F_{n-1}(x)}{F_{n-1}'(\alpha_\nu)(x - \alpha_\nu)}$$

$$= \frac{x - \alpha_n}{\alpha_\nu - \alpha_n} h_\nu^{n-1}(x),$$

$$\nu = n: \ h_n^n(x) = \frac{F_{n-1}(x)}{F_{n-1}(\alpha_n)} = \frac{F_{n-2}(\alpha_{n-1})}{F_{n-1}(\alpha_n)}(x - \alpha_{n-1})h_n^{n-1}(x).$$

By equating coefficients in the expansion for $h_\nu^n(x)$ we obtain

$$x_0 = 0 \begin{cases} n \neq \nu: \ c_{n,\nu}^m = \dfrac{1}{\alpha_n - \alpha_\nu}(\alpha_n c_{n-1,\nu}^m - m c_{n-1,\nu}^{m-1}), \\[2ex] n = \nu: \ c_{n,n}^m = \dfrac{F_{n-2}(\alpha_{n-1})}{F_{n-1}(\alpha_n)}(m c_{n-1,n-1}^{m-1} - \alpha_{n-1} c_{n-1,n-1}^m). \end{cases}$$

We can also use

$$\sum_{v=0}^{n} c_{n,v}^{m} = \begin{cases} 1, m = 0, \\ 0, m \neq 0; \end{cases}$$

however, this formula should not be used because it may induce round-off error.

Note that for $x_0 \neq 0$ we replace

$$\begin{cases} \alpha_n \to (\alpha_n - x_0), \\ \alpha_{n-1} \to (\alpha_{n-1} - x_0) \end{cases}$$

and that there is no restriction on x_0 coinciding with any α_v.

PUTTING IT INTO PRACTICE

The following code computes the weights in the *Fornberg method* and gives us the opportunity to introduce a triple array, which can be viewed as an array of two-dimensional arrays. Notice that we use a double***! The indexing of this array is just as we discussed earlier.

```
void FornbergWeights(double xi, double *x, int m, int n,
                     double ***C){
  int i,j,k,mn;
  double C1,C2,C3;

  C[0][0][0] = 1.0;
  C1 = 1.0;

  for(j=1;j<=n;j++){
    if(j<m)
      mn = j;
    else
      mn = m;
    C2 = 1.0;

    for(k=0;k<=(j-1);k++){
      C3 = x[j]-x[k];
      C2 = C2*C3;
      if(j<=m) C[j][j-1][k]=0.;
      C[0][j][k] = (x[j]-xi)*C[0][j-1][k]/C3;
      for(i=1;i<=mn;i++)
        C[i][j][k] = ((x[j]-xi)*C[i][j-1][k]-i*
                     C[i-1][j-1][k])/C3;
    }

    C[0][j][j] = -C1*(x[j-1]-xi)*C[0][j-1][j-1]/C2;

    for(i=1;i<=mn;i++)
      C[i][j][j] = C1*(i*C[i-1][j-1][j-1]-
                   (x[j-1]-xi)*C[i][j-1][j-1])/C2;
```

Software o *Suite*

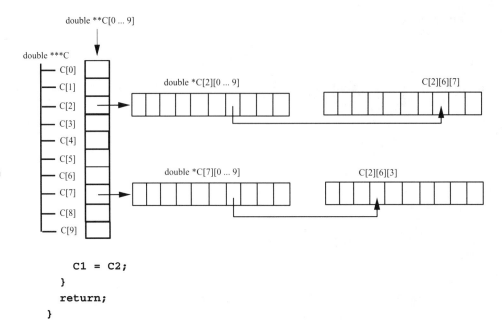

Figure 5.10: Diagram showing conceptual picture of three-dimensional array memory allocation.

```
        C1 = C2;
    }
    return;
}
```

REMARK 1: The triple indexing of the *double* $***$ array C follows the same rules as previously discussed for double-indexed arrays. A diagram showing a conceptual picture of the three-dimensional array is given in Figure 5.10. The first index i of $C[i][j][k]$ denotes which *double* $**$ array is selected. The second index j of $C[i][j][k]$ denotes which *double* $*$ array is selected. The third index k of $C[i][j][k]$ denotes which *double* is selected.

REMARK 2: Pay careful attention to the required size of the array C. It is the calling functions responsibility to allocate appropriate space for C. The routine given here does allocate memory; it assumes that the three-dimensional array C has already been declared. By examining the loops within this routine, it is possible to deduce a required size for C given the parameters m and n.

Mappings and Nonuniform Grids

It is common practice to transform nonuniform grids to uniform grids (if possible), and then on the uniform grid to compute the discrete derivatives. This is because the formal accuracy (e.g., second order) of the scheme is maintained on the uniform grid whereas only first-order accuracy can be achieved on the original (nonuniform) grid. However, the actual accuracy depends strongly on the transformation between the nonuniform grid $[x]_i$ and the uniform grid $[\xi]_i$, and thus it is not always clear which is the better grid to compute discrete derivatives. We analyze this next, following the work of Hoffman [58].

Let us assume that the two grids are related by the transformation

$$x = \phi(\xi) \Rightarrow \xi = \phi^{-1}(x). \tag{5.8}$$

On the uniform grid (ξ_i) the first derivative of the function $u(x)$ is

$$u_x = u_\xi \phi_x^{-1},$$

and a central difference approximation at point (i) is

$$(u_x)_i^\xi = (\phi_x^{-1})_i \frac{u_{i+1} - u_{i-1}}{\xi_{i+1} - \xi_{i-1}}.$$

From Taylor expansion we can also obtain that

$$(u_x)_i^\xi = (\phi_x^{-1})_i (u_\xi)_i + \mathcal{O}(\Delta \xi^2). \tag{5.9}$$

It is now clear from Equation (5.9) that the approximation of the first derivative on a uniform grid is of second-order. However, a central difference formula for the first derivative on a non-uniform grid produces a first-order accurate approximation of the form

$$(u_x)_i^x = (u_x)_i + \frac{1}{2}(u_{xx})_i(\Delta x_+ - \Delta x_-) + \mathcal{O}(\Delta x_\pm^2), \tag{5.10}$$

where $\Delta x_+ \equiv x_{i+1} - x_i$ and $\Delta x_- \equiv x_i - x_{i-1}$. Thus if $\Delta x_\pm$ is halved by doubling the number of grid points, then the error decreases only by a *factor of 2*, which corresponds to first-order accuracy. However, it is also possible to redistribute the points during refinement so that by doubling the number of grid points the term $(\Delta x_+ - \Delta x_-)$ quarters. In this case, second-order accuracy is achieved even on a nonuniform grid. A procedure to obtain this was derived by Hoffman [58] by expanding the coordinate transformation $x = \phi(\xi)$ in a Taylor series

$$\Delta x_+ - \Delta x_- = \phi_{\xi\xi}\Delta \xi^2 + \mathcal{O}(\Delta \xi^4).$$

This equation suggests that if we half the grid spacing on the uniform grid, then the effective spacing on the nonuniform grid is quartered, and thus we recover second-order-type behavior for the approximation error. The corresponding truncation errors on the two grids are also related by

$$(u_x)_i^x = (u_x)_i^\xi + \mathcal{O}(\Delta \xi^2).$$

In the special case that the transformation $\phi(\xi)$ is a polynomial of second order or less, the two derivative approximations are identical because the truncation error in this equation is identically zero.

Similar conclusions can be drawn for higher derivatives. For example, for the second derivative the difference in the approximation on the two grids is zero if the transformation is a first-order polynomial.

Some commonly used mappings include the following:

• **Exponential Stretching:**

$$x = L(e^{a\xi} - 1),$$

with the purpose of increasing resolution around $x = 0$, where L is the length of the domain and $\xi \in [0, 1]$. The parameter a determines the exact point distribution.

- **Semi-Infinite Domain:**
  1. Algebraic mapping: $x = L\frac{1+\xi}{1-\xi}$, $x \in [0, \infty] \to \xi \in [-1, 1]$.
  2. Logarithmic mapping: $x = -L \ln\left(\frac{1-\xi}{2}\right)$, $[0, \infty] \to [-1, 1]$.
- **Infinite Domain:**
  1. Exponential mapping: $x = L \tanh^{-1}, \xi$ $x \in [-\infty, \infty] \to \xi \in [-1, 1]$.
  2. Algebraic mapping: $x = L\frac{\xi}{\sqrt{1-\xi^2}}$, $x \in [-\infty, \infty] \to \xi \in [-1, 1]$.

5.1.6 One-Dimensional Boundary Value Problem

Next we apply the discretization of the second derivative for the one-dimensional boundary value problem of the form

$$
\begin{cases}
\theta'' = -\sin 2\pi x, \\
\theta_0 = \theta_N = 0
\end{cases}
$$

subject to homogeneous boundary conditions. The exact solution, obtained analytically, is

$$
\Theta(x) = \frac{1}{4\pi^2} \sin 2\pi x.
$$

THE DIFFERENCE EQUATION is obtained by discretizing the second derivative and applying the equation at the node (i) neglecting the truncation error:

$$
\frac{1}{\Delta x^2}(\theta_{i-1} - 2\theta_i + \theta_{i+1}) = -\sin 2\pi x_i, \quad \theta_0 = \theta_N = 0.
$$

THE EQUIVALENT DIFFERENTIAL EQUATION is obtained by including on the right-hand side of the differential equation the truncation terms, that is,

$$
\hat{\theta}'' = -\sin 2\pi x - \underbrace{\overbrace{\frac{\Delta x^2}{12}\hat{\theta}^{(iv)}}^{T_i} + \dots}_{\text{truncation error}}.
$$

We note that $T_i \to 0$ as $\Delta x \to 0$, and therefore our discretization is *consistent* as we recover the original differential equation when the discretization parameter approaches zero. This condition is called *consistency* and it is the key to convergence for boundary value problems (derived from the Lax theorem [77]).

We can now proceed to solve the difference equation analytically by assuming a solution of the form

$$
\theta_i = A \sin 2\pi i \Delta x \quad (i = 0, N \Rightarrow \theta_i = 0).
$$

Therefore,

$$
\frac{A}{\Delta x^2}[\sin 2\pi(i-1)\Delta x - 2\sin 2\pi i \Delta x + \sin 2\pi(i+1)\Delta x] = -\sin 2\pi i \Delta x,
$$

or

$$\frac{A}{\Delta x^2} \sin 2\pi i \Delta x (\cos 2\pi \Delta x - 2 + \cos 2\pi \Delta x) = -\sin 2\pi i \Delta x$$

$$\Rightarrow A = \frac{\Delta x^2}{2(1 - \cos 2\pi \Delta x)} = \frac{\Delta x^2}{2[1 - (1 - \frac{(2\pi)^2 \Delta x^2}{2} + \frac{(2\pi)^4 \Delta x^4}{24}) + \ldots]}$$

$$= \frac{\Delta x^2}{(2\pi)^2 \Delta x^2 - \frac{(2\pi)^4 \Delta x^4}{12} + \ldots}$$

$$= \frac{1}{4\pi^2 \left[1 - \frac{(2\pi)^2 \Delta x^2}{12} + \ldots\right]}$$

$$= \frac{1}{4\pi^2} \left[1 + \frac{(2\pi)^2 \Delta x^2}{12} + \ldots\right].$$

Finally, the solution of the *difference equation* is

$$\theta_i = \underbrace{\frac{1}{4\pi^2} \sin 2\pi x_i}_{\Theta \text{ exact}} + \frac{\Delta x^2}{12} \sin 2\pi x_i + \ldots.$$

We have shown directly that the approximation of the second derivative with second-order accuracy leads to a solution that is second-order accurate.

To solve the *equivalent differential equation* we use perturbation expansions while taking Δx^2 as a small parameter:

$$\hat{\theta} = \hat{\theta}_0 + \Delta x^2 \hat{\theta}_2 + \Delta x^4 \hat{\theta}_4 + \ldots.$$

By matching successive powers of Δx we obtain

$$\Delta x^0: \left. \begin{array}{l} \hat{\theta}_0'' = -\sin 2\pi x, \\ \hat{\theta}_0(0) = \hat{\theta}_0(1) = 0 \end{array} \right\} \Rightarrow \hat{\theta}_0 = \Theta = \frac{1}{4\pi^2} \sin 2\pi x,$$

$$\Delta x^2: \left. \begin{array}{l} \hat{\theta}_2'' = -\frac{1}{12}\hat{\theta}_0^{(iv)} = -\frac{(2\pi)^4}{12(4\pi^2)} \sin 2\pi x, \\ \hat{\theta}_2(0) = \hat{\theta}_2(1) = 0 \end{array} \right\} \Rightarrow \hat{\theta}_2 = \frac{1}{12} \sin 2\pi x,$$

and so

$$\hat{\theta}(x) = \frac{1}{4\pi^2} \sin 2\pi x + \frac{\Delta x^2}{12} \sin 2\pi x + \ldots.$$

Notice that $\hat{\theta}(x_i) = \theta_i$, in other words $\hat{\theta}(x)$, the solution of the equivalent differential equation, collocates the solution at the nodes.

- Thus, the numerical solution is an "exact" solution at the nodes of the corresponding *equivalent* differential equation but not of the differential equation itself.

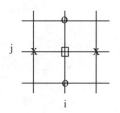

Figure 5.11: Sketch of the five-point molecule.

5.1.7 Multidimensional Discretizations

Similar to multidimensional interpolation and integration, multidimensional differentiation is obtained by *splitting directions*, that is, by differentiating one direction engaging points only in that direction while fixing the other direction, in a Cartesian fashion. For example, we can use Taylor expansions again to obtain discrete derivatives in a five-point stencil or "molecule" (see Figure 5.11).

At the marked points we obtain

$$\times: \ (u_x)_{ij} = \frac{u_{i+1,j} - u_{i-1,j}}{2\Delta x} - \frac{\Delta x^2}{12}\left(\frac{\partial^4 u}{\partial x^4}\right),$$

$$O: \ (u_{yy})_{ij} = \frac{u_{i,j+1} - 2u_{ij} + u_{i,j-1}}{\Delta y^2} - \frac{\Delta y^2}{12}\left(\frac{\partial^4 u}{\partial y^4}\right).$$

Similarly, we can obtain the discrete Laplacian

$$\nabla^2 u_{ij} = (u_{xx} + u_{yy})_{ij} = \underbrace{\frac{u_{i-1,j} - 2u_{ij} + u_{i+1,j}}{\Delta x^2} + \frac{u_{i,j-1} - 2u_{ij} + u_{i,j+1}}{\Delta y^2}}_{\nabla^2_+ + \mathcal{O}(\Delta x^2, \Delta y^2)}, \qquad (5.11)$$

where we have introduced the Cartesian discrete Laplacian operator ∇^2_+, and thus in symbolic form we can write

$$\nabla^2_+ u_{ij} = \left(\frac{\delta_x^2}{\Delta x^2} + \frac{\delta_y^2}{\Delta y^2}\right) u_{ij},$$

where δ_x and δ_y are the central difference operators defined in Section 5.1.2.

PUTTING IT INTO PRACTICE

In the following example we present a C++ code that implements the Laplacian five-point molecule for the interior points. We assume that the boundary values of the differentiation are handled elsewhere in the code. The key thing to notice in this example is how easily the finite difference formulas translate into C++ code once you have a handle on how arrays work. In this example, we assume that we have already allocated double arrays for both u and u_xx_yy; we merely need to index the arrays properly to obtain the desired result.

```
void CD_SecondDeriv(int npts, double dx, double dy, double **u,
                    double **u_xx_yy){

    double inv_dx2 = 1.0/(dx*dx);
    double inv_dy2 = 1.0/(dy*dy);

    for(int i=1;i<npts-1;i++)
      for(int j=1;j<npts-1;j++){
```

```
    u_xx_yy[i][j] = (u[i-1][j]-2.0*u[i][j] +u[i+1][j])
                        *inv_dx2
                  + (u[i][j-1]-2.0*u[i][j] +u[i][j+1])
                        *inv_dy2;
  }

  return;
}
```

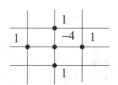

Figure 5.12: Five-point molecule and corresponding weights for a uniform grid.

This formula can be simplified for **equidistant grids** in both x- and y-directions; that is, for $\Delta x = \Delta y$ we obtain the simple molecule of Figure 5.12. The numbers at the grid points are the corresponding weights in the discrete Laplacian, and thus

$$\nabla^2_+ u_{ij} = \frac{u_{i-1,j} + u_{i+1,j} - 4u_{ij} + u_{i,j-1} + u_{i,j+1}}{\Delta x^2}.$$

Also, using symbolic notation we can derive the consistent second-order discrete Laplacian with a **variable coefficient**:

$$\nabla \cdot (\nu \nabla u)_{ij} = \frac{1}{\Delta x^2} \delta^-_x (\nu_{i+1/2,j} \delta^+_x) u_{ij} + \frac{1}{\Delta y^2} \delta^-_y (\nu_{i,j+1/2} \delta^+_y) u_{ij} + \mathcal{O}(\Delta x^2, \Delta y^2).$$

An alternative approach to the Cartesian direction splitting we followed to derive the discrete operator ∇^2_+ is to use **diagonal splitting**. In this case we derive the following discrete Laplacian operator:

$$\begin{aligned}
\nabla^2_x u_{ij} &= \left[\frac{(\mu_y \delta_x)^2}{\Delta x^2} + \frac{(\mu_x \delta_y)^2}{\Delta y^2} \right] u_{ij} \\
&= \frac{1}{4\Delta x^2} [(E_y + E_y^{-1} + 2)(E_x + E_x^{-1} - 2)] u_{ij} \\
&\quad + \frac{1}{4\Delta y^2} \left[(E_x + E_x^{-1} + 2)(E_y + E_y^{-1} - 2) \right] u_{ij},
\end{aligned}$$

which for $\Delta x = \Delta y$ has the simpler form

$$\nabla^2_x = \frac{1}{2\Delta x^2} [E_x E_y + E_x^{-1} E_y^{-1} + E_x^{-1} E_y + E_x E_y^{-1} - 4].$$

Figure 5.13: Weights for the diagonal splitting for a uniform grid.

The corresponding stencil is shown diagrammatically in Figure 5.13 with the appropriate weights.

However, there is a problem with diagonal splitting: It leads to two independent stencils, as shown in Figure 5.14, which in turn will produce *odd–even oscillations* in the odd-numbered and even-numbered grid points.

To overcome this difficulty we define a new operator that combines both approaches (i.e., Cartesian and diagonal splitting) using appropriate

1/2 x

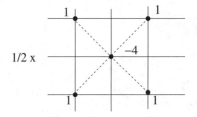

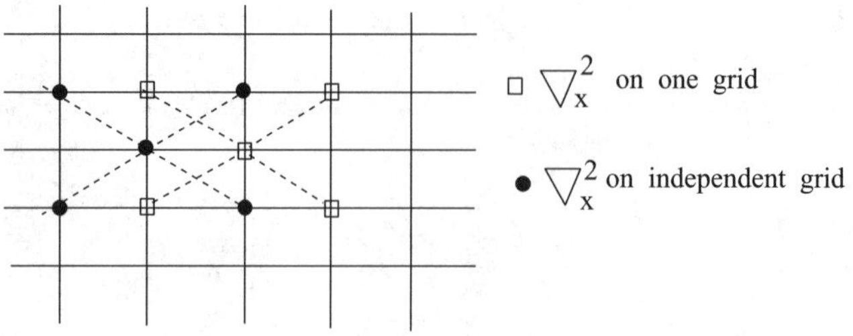

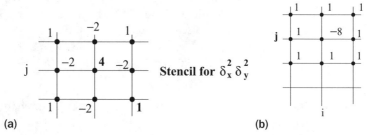

Figure 5.14: Decoupling of the discrete Laplacian operator induced by diagonal splitting.

$\square \ \nabla_x^2$ on one grid

$\bullet \ \nabla_x^2$ on independent grid

Figure 5.15: (a) Stencil for the product $\delta_x^2\delta_y^2$. (b) Stencil for $b = 2/3$.

Stencil for $\delta_x^2\,\delta_y^2$

weights. To this end, we write

$$\nabla_*^2 u_{ij} = (a\nabla_+^2 + b\nabla_x^2)u_{ij}, \quad a + b = 1.$$

If we now substitute for ∇_+^2 and ∇_x^2 and also use $a = 1 - b$, assuming a uniform grid ($\Delta x = \Delta y$), we obtain

$$\nabla_*^2 = \frac{1}{\Delta x^2}(\delta_x^2 + \delta_y^2) + \frac{b}{\Delta x^2}[(\mu_y\delta_x)^2 + (\mu_x\delta_y)^2 - (\delta_x^2 + \delta_y^2)]$$

$$= \frac{1}{\Delta x^2}\left\{(\delta_x^2 + \delta_y^2) + \frac{b}{2}\left[2\delta_x^2(\mu_y^2 - 1) + 2\delta_y^2(\mu_x^2 - 1)\right]\right\},$$

but

$$2\delta_x^2(\mu_y^2 - 1) = 2(E_x + E_x^{-1} - 2)\left[\frac{1}{4}(E_y + E_y^{-1} + 2) - 1\right]$$

$$= \frac{1}{2}(E_x + E_x^{-1} - 2)(E_y + E_y^{-1} - 2)$$

$$= \frac{1}{2}\delta_x^2\delta_y^2.$$

By symmetry the second term $(2\delta_y^2(\mu_x^2 - 1))$ is the same as the above, and therefore we have

$$\nabla_*^2 = \frac{1}{\Delta x^2}\left[(\delta_x^2 + \delta_y^2) + \frac{b}{2}\delta_x^2\delta_y^2\right] = \nabla_+^2 + \frac{b}{2}\delta_x^2\delta_y^2 \cdot \frac{1}{\Delta x^2}.$$

It is clear that we can now construct a family of two-dimensional stencils for the discrete Laplacian by selecting different values for $b \in (0, 1)$. In Figure 5.15 we first construct the weights for the product $\delta_x^2\delta_y^2$, and subsequently we construct a stencil for $b = 2/3$. This stencil is similar to a nine-node quadrilateral finite element [59].

Another useful construction is the **Dahlquist–Bjorck stencil** corresponding to $b = 1/3$ (see Figure 5.16). In this case we get

$$\nabla_*^2 u_{ij} = \nabla^2 u_{ij} + \frac{\Delta x^2}{12} \underbrace{\left[\frac{\partial^4 u}{\partial x^4} + \frac{\partial^4 u}{\partial y^2} + 6 \cdot \frac{1}{3} \frac{\partial^4 u}{\partial x^2 \partial y^2} \right]}_{\text{truncation error}}.$$

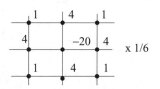

Figure 5.16: Stencil for the Dahlquist–Bjorck stencil.

From this construction and from the preceding definitions we can derive

$$\nabla_*^2 u_{ij} = \nabla^2 u_{ij} + \frac{\Delta x^2}{12} \nabla^4 u.$$

This form suggests that in solving the eigenvalue problem $\nabla^2 u = \lambda u$ the truncation error is $-\frac{\Delta x^2}{12}(\lambda^2 u)$, and thus by ejecting its opposite on the right-hand side as follows:

$$\nabla_*^2 u_{ij} = (\lambda + \frac{\lambda^2 \Delta x^2}{12})u,$$

we obtain a discretization with a fourth-order truncation error although the discrete operators were all of second order. This is called the *method of corrected differences*, or the *booster* method, and it is used often in scientific computing to enhance the formal accuracy of the method.

We can proceed similarly to discretize **mixed derivatives**

$$\frac{\partial^2 u}{\partial x \partial y}.$$

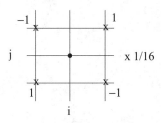

Figure 5.17: Stencil and corresponding weights for a mixed second derivative.

Using symbolic notations and operators defined previously we obtain

$$u_{xy} = \frac{1}{\Delta x \Delta y} \mu_x \delta_x \left[(1 - \frac{\delta_x^2}{6}) + \mathcal{O}(\Delta x^4) \right] \mu_y \delta_y \left[\left(1 - \frac{\delta_y^2}{6}\right) + \mathcal{O}(\Delta y^4) \right] u_{ij}.$$

From this we can construct the second-order-accurate stencil

$$u_{xy} = \frac{1}{\Delta x \Delta y} \mu_x \delta_x \mu_y \delta_y u_{ij} + \mathcal{O}(\Delta x^2, \Delta y^2),$$

which is shown diagrammatically in Figure 5.17. More explicitly,

$$(u_{xy})_{ij} = \frac{1}{4 \Delta x \Delta y} \left[u_{i+1,j+1} - u_{i+1,j-1} - u_{i-1,j+1} + u_{i-1,j-1} \right] + \mathcal{O}(\Delta x^2),$$

and we see that the (ij) point is not employed; that is, there is no element on the diagonal corresponding to u_{ij}. This will lead to algebraic systems with loss of diagonal dominance and thus substantial computational complexity.

PUTTING IT INTO PRACTICE

The following C++ function example is an implementation of the aforementioned cross-type molecule. Note that for writing the function, it is better to expand the symbolic operators first, which leads to an immediate translation into C++ array indexing. Once again, the key thing to notice in this example is how easily the finite difference

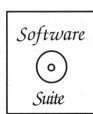

Software

Suite

formulas translate into C++ code once you have a handle on how arrays work. In this example, we assume that we have already allocated double arrays for both *u* and *u_xy*; we merely need to index the arrays properly to obtain the desired result.

```
void CrossDerivative(int npts, double dx, double dy,
                     double **u, double **u_xy){
  double inv_dxdy = 1.0/(4.0*dx*dy);

  for(int i=1;i<npts-1;i++)
    for(int j=1;j<npts-1;j++){
      u_xy[i][j] = inv_dxdy*(u[i+1][j+1]-u[i+1][j-1]-
                   u[i-1][j+1]+u[i-1][j-1]);
    }

  return;
}
```

To restore *diagonal dominance* we proceed as follows. We first observe that in the formula for the mixed derivative if we omit the average operator μ we lose an order of accuracy, that is,

$$(u_{xy})_{ij} = \frac{1}{4\Delta x \Delta y}(\mu_x \delta_x \delta_y^+)u_{ij} + \mathcal{O}(\Delta x^2, \Delta y).$$

Therefore, a first-order-accurate stencil in both Δx *and* Δy is

$$(u_{xy})_{ij} = \frac{1}{\Delta x \Delta y}\delta_x^+ \delta_y^+ u_{ij} + \mathcal{O}(\Delta x, \Delta y).$$

This is a *forward differencing* for the mixed derivative (see Figure 5.18a). Similarly, we can construct a backward difference stencil. We can then combine the two stencils to produce a symmetric stencil (see Figure 5.18b), with a nonzero coefficient in the diagonal. This has the form

Figure 5.18: Stencils for forward (a) and symmetric (b) differentiation of a mixed derivative.

$$(u_{xy})_{ij} = \frac{1}{2\Delta x \Delta y}[\delta_x^+ \delta_y^+ + \delta_x^- \delta_y^-],$$

and this symmetric stencil is now of second order on a uniform grid.

5.2 EXPLICIT TIME DISCRETIZATIONS

In this section we apply finite difference operations to discretize the time variable in time-dependent differential equations. To this end, we consider the initial

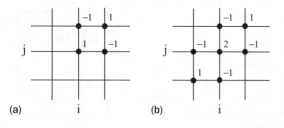

value problem (IVP)

$$\frac{dU}{dt} = \mathcal{F}(U, t), \tag{5.12}$$

with prescribed initial conditions $U(t = 0) = U_0$. If $\mathcal{F}(U)$ only, that is, the right-hand side does not depend explicitly on time, then this is an *autonomous* ordinary differential equation for which very efficient algorithms can be constructed. To analyze the stability of various discretizations it is convenient to employ the corresponding eigenvalue model problem

$$\frac{dU}{dt} = \lambda U, \quad \lambda \in \mathbf{C}, \quad \mathrm{Re}(\lambda) < 0; \tag{5.13}$$

that is, λ is a complex number with negative real part.

5.2.1 Multistep Schemes

In this discretization there are several time steps involved, and the discrete analog of Equation (5.12) has the general form

$$\frac{U^{n+1} - U^{n-k}}{(k+1)\Delta t} = \mathcal{F}(t, U^{n+1}, U^n, U^{n-1}, \ldots) \quad \text{for } k \geq 0, \tag{5.14}$$

where $U^n \equiv U(n\Delta t)$. An *implicit scheme* corresponds to a right-hand side $\mathcal{F}$ that depends on U^{n+1}; otherwise it is *explicit*. A multistep scheme has $\mathcal{F}$ depending on several previous time levels of the solution (i.e., U^n, U^{n-1}, U^{n-2}, etc.). The simplest member of the class of discretization derived from Equation (5.14) is the **Euler-forward**, which is a one-sided backward finite difference, that is,

$$\frac{U^{n+1} - U^n}{\Delta t} = \mathcal{F}(t, U^n) \Rightarrow U^{n+1} = U^n + \Delta t \mathcal{F}(t, U^n).$$

Another example is the **leap-frog scheme**, which is a two-step explicit scheme. For the model eigenvalue problem it has the form

$$\frac{U^{n+1} - U^{n-1}}{2\Delta t} = \lambda U^n.$$

Clearly, it is of second-order accuracy since the first derivative is represented by central differencing.

More generally, **multistep schemes** can be either explicit or implicit. The general formula for a k-step scheme is

$$\sum_{j=0}^{k} a_j U^{n+1-j} = \Delta t \sum_{j=0}^{k} \beta_j \mathcal{F}^{n+1-j},$$

where $\alpha_0 = 1$ for normalization, and $\beta_0 = 0$ corresponds to an explicit scheme. The physical analog is a "recursive digital filter."

Example: The Adams Family

The first member of the family is the Euler-forward scheme. The other two (explicit) members are

- second-order Adams–Bashforth: $\frac{U^{n+1}-U^n}{\Delta t} = \frac{3}{2}\mathcal{F}^n - \frac{1}{2}\mathcal{F}^{n-1}$,
- third-order Adams–Bashforth: $\frac{U^{n+1}-U^n}{\Delta t} = \frac{23}{12}\mathcal{F}^n - \frac{16}{12}\mathcal{F}^{n-1} + \frac{5}{12}\mathcal{F}^{n-2}$.

Multisteps schemes require lower order schemes in the first few steps; this may affect their accuracy. In the following C++ code we implement first-, second-, and third-order Adams–Bashforth schemes. As mentioned previously, we are confronted with the decision between optimality and generality. In this case, we choose to be general; that is, we have created a function that uses a *switch* statement to interpret which order Adams–Bashforth scheme the user wants to employ.

One additional point to make in this example is the use of the default within the *switch* statement. Notice in the following example that the default is Euler-forward, which is also the case 1 option. Instead of printing an error and terminating if someone were to ask for an Adams–Bashforth scheme of order higher than three, we default to first order. These types of decisions are constantly being made by programmers: How will the function respond if given unexpected input? In this case, if order is not given as either one, two, or three, then the action is still well defined: The function will "default" to first-order integration.

Software *Suite*

PUTTING IT INTO PRACTICE

Next we present a C++ function for accomplishing time integration using the Adams–Bashforth methods. This function takes as arguments the order, the old value, the time step, and the saved right-hand sides (stored in an array called *RHS*).

```cpp
double AdamsBashforth(int order, double u_old,
                      double dt, double * RHS){
  double answer;

  switch(order){
  case 1: /* 1st Order Adams-Bashforth -- Euler-forward */
    answer = u_old + dt*RHS[0];
    break;
  case 2: /* 2nd Order Adams-Bashforth */
    answer = u_old + dt*(1.5*RHS[0] - 0.5*RHS[1]);
    break;
  case 3: /* 3rd Order Adams-Bashforth */
    answer = u_old + dt*( (23./12.)*RHS[0] - (4./3.)*
            RHS[1] + (5./12.)*RHS[2]);
    break;
  default: /* default is Euler-forward */
    answer = u_old + dt*RHS[0];
  }

  return answer;

}
```

REMARK 1: Observe that we use a *switch* statement to distinguish among the different cases. We have written the *switch* statement so that the default case is Euler-forward, which is first order.

REMARK 2: Observe that this function can easily be modified to handle an array of points to integrate in time (such as would be used for time marching a finite difference scheme).

As programmers, we are always confronted with a balance between generality and optimality.

Key Concept

5.2.2 Convergence: Consistency and Stability

There exists a connection between consistency and convergence for boundary value problems, as we have briefly discussed in the previous section. This condition, first proposed by Lax, is necessary but not sufficient for initial value problems, and we need to introduce the concept of stability, as we will do next. However, we first need to show that the explicit multistep schemes are *consistent*, and to this end we need to consider the *equivalent differential equation* for the IVP given by Equation (5.12). For simplicity, let us consider the Euler-forward scheme. From Taylor's expansion we obtain

$$\left(\frac{dU^n}{dt} - \mathcal{F}^n \right) = \Delta t \left(-\frac{1}{2} \frac{d^2 U^n}{dt^2} \right)$$

$$+ \Delta t^2 \left(-\frac{1}{6} \frac{d^3 U^n}{dt^3} \right) + \ldots.$$

Clearly, this satisfies the consistency requirement as the right-hand side is zero as $\Delta t \to 0$, and thus we recover the original initial value problem. We can also obtain the accuracy of the method by examining the *truncation error*, which is the forcing term in the equivalent differential equation. From the leading error term in this equation we see that the Euler-forward scheme is first order.

Unlike boundary value problems (BVPs) for which consistency is sufficient to prove convergence, in initial value problems (IVP) we also need to prove *stability*. This is explained graphically in Figure 5.19. With time integration there may be an accumulation of error, which will eventually lead to catastrophic instabilities!

Next, we introduce the concept of stability by defining the error as

$$\epsilon \equiv U_{\text{ex}}^n - U^n.$$

We define the following:

- *General stability* occurs if

$$|\epsilon^n| < f(t_n),$$

where $t_n = n\Delta t$. In other words, errors are bounded at a fixed time by a function that may depend on time ($t_n = $ fixed, $\Delta t \to 0, n \to \infty$).

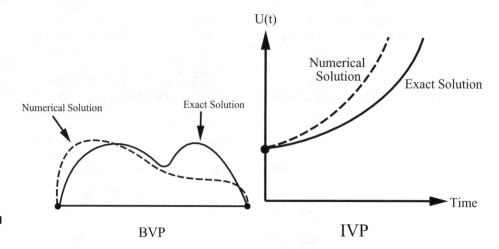

Figure 5.19: Comparison of boundary value (BVP) and initial value (IVP) problems.

- *Absolute stability* occurs if

$$|\epsilon^{n+1}| \le |\epsilon^n|.$$

Here the equality implies *weak* stability whereas the nonequality implies *strong* stability. The interpretation here is that for absolute stability all components of error should be uniformly bounded.

EXAMPLE. Let us examine the stability of the Euler-forward scheme for the eigenvalue model problem $\frac{dU}{dt} = \lambda U, \lambda < 0$.

Then, the error satisfies: $\epsilon^{n+1} = \epsilon^n(1 + \lambda \Delta t)$. But

$$|1 + \lambda \Delta t| < |1 - \lambda \Delta t| < e^{-\lambda \Delta t};$$

thus

$$|\epsilon^{(n+1)}| < e^{-\lambda \Delta t}|\epsilon^n| \le (e^{-\lambda \Delta t})^n|\epsilon^0| \Rightarrow |\epsilon| < e^{-\lambda(n\Delta t)}|\epsilon^1|.$$

According to the definition for general stability, this scheme is then stable! However, consider the counterexample for the IVP:

$$\frac{dU}{dt} = -U, \quad U(0) = 1,$$

with $U_{ex} = e^{-t}$. Then, for $\Delta t = 3$ we obtain $U^{n+1} = -2U^n$, and we produce the sequence

$$(1, -2, 4, -8, 16, \ldots),$$

which obviously does not converge to e^{-t} for $t = 12$.

General stability is limited in practice, and instead we need to apply the concept of absolute stability. Proceeding as before we need to bound the error, so we impose

$$|1 + \lambda \Delta t| \le 1 \Rightarrow \Delta t \le -2/\lambda.$$

Notice that we have violated this condition in our example by taking $\Delta t = 3$.

The key points to remember are the following:

- General stability is useful for *short-time* integration only.
- Stability is the property of a *difference equation* and not of the differential equation.

LAX'S EQUIVALENCE THEOREM: *If a (linear) difference equation is consistent with a differential equation and stable, its solution will converge as* $\Delta t \to 0$ *to that of the differential equation.*

This condition is sufficient as well as necessary [77]. The equivalence theorem of Lax shows that to analyze an initial value problem, two tasks have to be performed:

1. *The consistency condition must be analyzed.* This leads to determining the order of accuracy of the scheme and the corresponding truncation error.
2. *The stability condition must be analyzed.* This leads to determining the frequency distribution of the error (e.g., eigenvalue-type analysis).

REMARK: A stronger version of this theorem was developed by Dahlquist [20]. It applies to both linear and nonlinear IVPs, and it states that a *multistep* scheme is convergent *if and only if* it is consistent and stable. The Lax equivalence theorem, which was formulated for partial differential equations, requires linearity.

5.2.3 Stability and Characteristic Polynomials

A very effective method for studying the stability of time discretizations is to examine the properties of their corresponding characteristic polynomials. To this end, we propose a construction by associating two polynomials $\rho(z)$ and $\sigma(z)$ to the k-step scheme

$$\sum_{j=0}^{k} \alpha_j U^{n+1-j} = \Delta t \sum_{j=0}^{k} \beta_j \mathcal{F}^{n+1-j}.$$

For the left-hand side we have

$$\rho(z) = \sum_{j=0}^{k} \alpha_j z^{k-j},$$

and for the right-hand side we have

$$\sigma(z) = \sum_{j=0}^{k} \beta_j z^{k-j}.$$

The degree of the polynomial $\rho(z)$ is k, and the degree of the polynomial $\sigma(z) \leq k$, with the equal sign valid for *implicit* schemes (see Chapter 6). We can normalize the coefficients by imposing that

$$\sum_{j=0}^{k} \beta_j = 1.$$

Examples

- The *leap-frog* scheme has $\rho(z) = \frac{z^2-1}{2}$, $\sigma(z) = z$; it is explicit since $\sigma(z)$ is a linear polynomial but $\rho(z)$ is quadratic.
- The *Crank–Nicolson* scheme, which is an implicit scheme (see Section 6.2) has $\rho(z) = z - 1$, $\sigma(z) = \frac{1}{2}(z+1)$. Both polynomials are linear.

Based on the characteristic polynomials several properties of multistep schemes can be deduced, and the interested reader should consult the book by Gear [42].

RATIONAL APPROXIMATION THEOREM: *A multistep scheme with $\sigma(1) \neq 0$ has order of accuracy p if and only if, as $z \to 1$,*

$$\frac{\rho(z)}{\sigma(z)} = \log z + \mathcal{O}((z-1)^{p+1})$$

$$= [(z-1) - \frac{1}{2}(z-1)^2 + \frac{1}{3}(z-1)^3 - \ldots]$$

$$+ \mathcal{O}((z-1)^{p+1}).$$

It is a consistent scheme if and only if

$$\begin{cases} \rho(1) = 0 \quad (\Rightarrow p \geq 0), \\ \rho'(1) = \sigma(1) \quad (\Rightarrow p \geq 1). \end{cases}$$

EXAMPLE 1. The Crank–Nicolson is a consistent scheme since

$$\sigma(1) = \frac{1}{2}(z+1)|_{z=1} \neq 0, \rho(1) = (z-1) = 0, \rho'(1) = 1 = \sigma(1).$$

To examine its accuracy we consider the ratio

$$\frac{\rho(z)}{\sigma(z)} = \frac{z-1}{\frac{1}{2}(z+1)} = \frac{z-1}{1 + \frac{1}{2}(z-1)} = (z-1)\left[1 - \frac{z-1}{2} + \frac{(z-1)^2}{4} - \ldots\right]$$

$$= (z-1) - \frac{(z-1)^2}{2} + \frac{(z-1)^3}{4} - \ldots.$$

Note that the last term is not equal to $(z-1)^3/3$ (as in the *log* expansion), and thus it represents the truncation error. Therefore, we conclude that $p = 2$ and the Crank–Nicolson scheme is second-order accurate.

EXAMPLE 2. Let $\rho(z) = z^2 - z$ and $k = 2$; then

$$\sigma(z) = \frac{z^2 - z}{\log z} + \mathcal{O}((z-1))^3) = \frac{z(z-1)}{(z-1) - \frac{1}{2}(z-1)^2 + \frac{1}{3}(z-1)^3} + \mathcal{O}((z-1)^3)$$

$$= \frac{z}{1 - \frac{1}{2}(z-1) + \frac{1}{3}(z-1)^2 - \ldots} + \mathcal{O}((z-1)^3)$$

$$= z\left[1 + \frac{1}{2}(z-1) - \frac{1}{3}(z-1)^2 + \frac{1}{4}(z-1)^4)\right] + \mathcal{O}(\ldots)$$

$$= \frac{5}{12}z^2 + \frac{8}{12}z - \frac{1}{12} = \sigma(z).$$

Thus, we obtain the third-order (implicit) Adams–Moulton scheme (see also Section 6.2).

EXAMPLE 3. Consider a multistep formula based purely on extrapolation of previous values, for example

$$U^{n+1} = 2U^n - U^{n-1},$$

for which $\rho(z) = (z-1)^2$ and $\sigma(z) = 0$. We have that $\rho(1) = 0$ and $\rho'(1) = \sigma(1) = 0$. Notice that we need $\sigma(1) \neq 0$ to satisfy the rational approximation theorem. Obviously, such a formula cannot converge because we do not use any differential equation!

ROOT CONDITION FOR STABILITY : *A multistep scheme is stable* if and only if *all the roots of* $\rho(z)$ *satisfy* $|z| \leq 1$, *and any root with* $|z| = 1$ *is simple.*

PROOF. The polynomial $\rho(z)$ has a total of k roots for which we can write (if they are distinct)

$$U^n = z^n,$$

where on the left-hand side n denotes superscript while on the right-hand side it denotes an exponent. For stability we require that the entire sequence

$$\{U^n, n = 1, 2, \ldots\}$$

be bounded, and thus $|z| \leq 1$. However, for multiple roots, say of multiplicity m, we have the roots

$$U^n = nz^n, n^2 z^n, \ldots, n^{m-1} z^n.$$

In this case the requirement for boundness of the sequence U^n is $|z| < 1$.

An alternative proof can be formulated based on matrices as follows:

$$
\begin{bmatrix} U^{n+2-k} \\ U^{n+3-k} \\ \vdots \\ U^{n+1} \end{bmatrix}
=
\underbrace{\begin{bmatrix} 0 & 1 & & & \\ & 0 & 1 & & \\ & & \ddots & \ddots & \\ & & & & 1 \\ -\alpha_k & & -\alpha_2 & -\alpha_1 \end{bmatrix}}_{\mathbf{A}}
\begin{bmatrix} U^{n+1-k} \\ U^{n+2-k} \\ \vdots \\ U^n \end{bmatrix},
$$

or

$$\mathbf{U}^{n+1} = \mathbf{A}\,\mathbf{U}^n.$$

Notice that the eigenvalues of $\mathbf{A}$ are roots of the polynomial $\rho(z)$. Thus, for boundness of $\mathbf{U}^{n+1}$, we require that the eigenvalues of $\mathbf{A}$ be smaller than 1 and those equal to 1 be simple. A rigorous proof requires the transformation of $\mathbf{A}$ to its Jordan canonical form (e.g., see [42]).

EXAMPLE 4. Let us consider an Adams–Bashforth scheme of kth order:

$$\rho(z) = z^k - z^{k-1} = z^{k-1}(z-1),$$

with roots $\{1, 0, 0, \ldots\}$. Therefore, this scheme is stable.

EXAMPLE 5. We can construct the most accurate two-step explicit scheme corresponding to $p = 3$ from

$$U^{n+1} = -4U^n + 5U^{n-1} + \Delta t(4\mathcal{F}^n + 2\mathcal{F}^{n-1}).$$

Therefore, $\rho(z) = z^2 + 4z - 5$ with roots $\{1, -5\}$, which, according to the root condition, corresponds to an unstable scheme! Note that this scheme violates the **first Dahlquist Stability Barrier** theorem (see Section 6.2.1), which states that the order of accuracy p of any explicit multistep scheme (k steps) cannot exceed the number of steps (i.e. $p \leq k$).

EXAMPLE 6. Similarly, we can construct a three-step scheme from

$$U^{n+1} = -\frac{3}{2}U^n + 3U^{n-1} - \frac{1}{2}U^{n-2} + 3\Delta t \cdot f^n$$

with corresponding polynomial

$$\rho(z) = 2z^3 + 3z^3 - 6z + 1 = (z - 1)(2z^2 + 5z - 1),$$

which has the roots 1.0, 0.186, and -2.686. Therefore, this scheme is unstable!

EXAMPLE 7. Based on the root condition, we can also prove that all one-step methods of the form

$$U^{n+1} = U^n + \Delta t \mathcal{F}^n$$

are stable because $\rho(z) = z - 1$. Therefore, the root is 1 and simple, and thus the root condition for stability is satisfied.

REMARK: We note here that in all the preceding examples stability was interpreted according to the general definition. In the following, we introduce the requirements for *absolute stability*. According to the **Second Dahlquist Stability Barrier** theorem (see Section 6.2.1), an explicit multistep scheme cannot be absolutely stable for arbitrary values of the time step Δt.

Stability Regions and Absolute Stability

Let us consider the linear ordinary differential equation

$$\frac{dU}{dt} = \lambda U + q(t), \quad \lambda \in \mathbf{C}, \ \mathrm{Re}(\lambda) < 0.$$

The corresponding error, ϵ^n, at the time level $(n\Delta t)$ satisfies the equation

$$\sum_{j=0}^{k}(\alpha_j - \Delta t \lambda \beta_j)\epsilon^{k-j} = 0,$$

independently of the inhomogeneity $q(t)$.

To compute the solution of this difference equation, we introduce $\epsilon^n = z^n$ (where n on the left-hand side denotes superscript but on the right-hand side denotes an exponent), and thus

$$\sum_{j=0}^{k}(\alpha_j - \Delta t\lambda\beta_j)z^{k-j} = 0.$$

Therefore, the z are roots of the polynomial

$$\Pi(z) \equiv \rho(z) - \lambda\Delta t \cdot \sigma(z) = 0,$$

which we denote as z_j.

If all the roots are distinct, then the general solution for the error ϵ^n is

$$\epsilon^n = \sum_{j=1}^{k} c_j z_j^n$$

(assuming k roots). If z_j is an m-fold root, then the term

$$(c_j + c_{j+1}n + c_{j+2}n^2 + \cdots + c_{j+m-1}n^{m-1})z_j^n$$

is present. Therefore, for any $|z_j| \geq 1$, disturbances are amplified irrespective of Δt, and the corresponding scheme is unstable.

In general, the roots depend on Δt [i.e., $z_j = z_j(\lambda\Delta t)$]. Therefore, if

$$|z_j(0)| < 1 \Rightarrow \exists\,\Delta t^*\colon |z_j(\lambda\Delta t)| \leq 1$$

in the neighborhood around 0 with radius Δt^* (see sketch in Figure 5.20). Expanding $z_j(\lambda\Delta t)$ in a Taylor series around 0 we obtain

$$z_j(\lambda\Delta t) = z_j(0) + \mathcal{O}(\Delta t\lambda).$$

Thus,

$$|z_j^n(\lambda\Delta t)| \leq |z_j(0) + C\Delta t|^n \leq |1 + C\Delta t|^n \leq e^{Cn\Delta t} \leq e^{Ct};$$

that is, if $|z_j(0)| \leq 1$ then the roots of $\Pi(z)$ are less than 1, which implies stability. This explains also how the roots of $\rho(z) = \Pi(0)$ are related to stability of the scheme (see the previous theorem on root condition). For *strong stability* we require that the roots of $\Pi(z)$ are ≤ 1 in absolute value; that is, we have to find

$$\lambda\Delta t\colon \quad |z_j(\lambda\Delta t)| \leq 1,$$

and this constraint determines the *regions of absolute stability* of a time-discretization scheme. We illustrate this in the following examples.

EXAMPLE 1 – EULER-FORWARD. We first construct the polynomial

$$\Pi_{\text{EF}} = (z - 1) - \lambda\Delta t \cdot 1 = z - (1 + \lambda\Delta t)$$

and obtain the roots $z = 1 + \lambda\Delta t$. We now require that

$$-1 \leq 1 + \lambda t \leq 1 \Rightarrow |\lambda\Delta t - (-1)| \leq 1$$

$$\Rightarrow \Delta t \leq -2/\lambda, \quad \lambda \in \mathbf{C},\ \text{Re}(\lambda) < 0.$$

Figure 5.20: Sketch showing the neighborhood around 0.

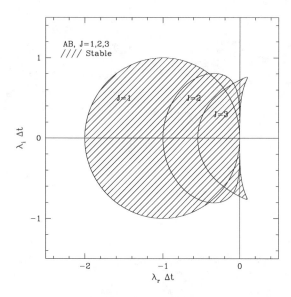

Note that for physical stability, we have also considered that $\lambda \Delta t \leq 0$ for the exact modes to decay. The region of stability in the complex plane is shown in Figure 5.21 for $J = 1$. Note that it touches the imaginary axis (which represents advection) only at one point, and thus this scheme is only marginally stable for advection problems.

EXAMPLE 2 - LEAP-FROG. We construct the polynomial

$$\Pi_{\mathrm{LF}} = z^2 - 2\lambda \Delta t z - 1$$

and obtain the two roots whose product is $z_1 \cdot z_2 = 1$. Therefore, we have that

$$|z_1| \leq 1, \ |z_2| \geq 1.$$

For stability the only possibility is $|z_1| = |z_2| = 1$, and thus the region of stability is the region on the imaginary axis between $-i$ and i. Therefore, the leap-frog scheme is a good candidate for problems with purely imaginary eigenvalues, for example, advection in a periodic domain, discretized by a nondissipative scheme. Even slight dissipation, however, will introduce real eigenvalues that will lead to instabilities.

In general, to obtain the stability regions of multistep schemes we construct the curve

$$\lambda \Delta t = \frac{\rho(z)}{\sigma(z)},$$

with $z = e^{i\theta}, \theta \in [0, 2\pi]$ in the complex $\lambda \Delta t$ plane. Using this approach we have obtained the stability regions for the (explicit) Adams family and the results ares shown in Figure 5.21. Note that the third-order scheme has a stability region with a substantial intersection with the imaginary (advection) axis.

5.2.4 Runge–Kutta Methods

Unlike the Adams family, Runge–Kutta methods – developed by Runge (1895), Heun (1900), and Kutta (1901) – are single-step methods, and in particular they are *multistage methods*. The basic idea is to create a weighted sum of corrections ΔU^k to the solution at several stages within the same time step, that is,

$$U^{n+1} = U^n + C_1 \Delta U^1 + C_2 \Delta U^2 + C_3 \Delta U^3 + \ldots.$$

The coefficients C_k are determined by matching this expansion with the corresponding expansion by Taylor series. Other parameters are also introduced to accommodate different stages, for example,

$$\Delta U^1 = \Delta t \mathcal{F}^n(t^n, U^n) \quad \textit{(Euler-forward)},$$

$$\Delta U^2 = \Delta t \mathcal{F}(t^n + \alpha \Delta t, U^n + \beta \Delta U^1).$$

Runge–Kutta methods tend to be *nonunique* because of the large number of parameters introduced. In modern versions the objective has been to minimize storage levels, as shown in the following examples. For hyperbolic systems it is important to produce Runge–Kutta schemes that are total variation diminishing (TVD) or total variation bounded (TVB) – see for example [50]. TVD and TVB schemes do not allow any spurious oscillation to appear in the numerical solution, and this is a highly desirable property. In the following, we present representative algorithms of some of the most popular versions.

SECOND-ORDER ALGORITHM (RK2) WITH TWO LEVELS OF STORAGE

Set:

$$X = U^n$$

$$Y = \mathcal{F}(U, t^n)$$

Compute:

$$X = X + \alpha \cdot \Delta t Y$$

$$Y = aY + \mathcal{F}(X, t^n + \alpha \Delta t)$$

Update: $\quad U^{n+1} = X + \frac{\Delta t}{2\alpha} Y,$
where $a = -1 + 2\alpha - \alpha^2$.

Note that for $\alpha = 1/2$ we obtain the modified Euler method and for $\alpha = 1$ we obtain the classical Heun method.

CLASSICAL FOURTH-ORDER ALGORITHM (RK4)

Compute:

$$X_1 = \mathcal{F}(U^n, t^n)$$

$$X_2 = \mathcal{F}(U^n + \frac{1}{2}X_1 \Delta t, t^n + \frac{1}{2}\Delta t)$$

$$X_3 = \mathcal{F}(U^n + \frac{1}{2}X_2 \Delta t, t^n + \frac{1}{2}\Delta t)$$

$$X_4 = \mathcal{F}(U^n + X_3 \Delta t, t^n + \Delta t)$$

Update:

$$U^{n+1} = U^n + \frac{1}{6}\Delta t[X_1 + 2X_2 + 2X_3 + X_4]$$

An *alternative implementation* requires only three levels of storage, as follows (due to Blum [9]):

Stage I: $X = U^n; Y = X; Z = \mathcal{F}(X, t^n)$
Stage II: $X = X + \frac{1}{2}\Delta t Z; Y = Z; Z = \mathcal{F}(X, t^n + \frac{1}{2}\Delta t)$
Stage III: $X = X + \frac{1}{2}\Delta t(Z - Y); Y = \frac{1}{6}Y; Z = \mathcal{F}(X, t^n + \frac{1}{2}\Delta t) - \frac{1}{2}Z$

Stage IV: $X = X + \Delta t Z; Y = Y - Z; Z = \mathcal{F}(X, t^n + \Delta t) + 2Z$
Update:

$$U^{n+1} = X + \Delta t \left(Y + \frac{1}{6} Z \right)$$

Software

Suite

PUTTING IT INTO PRACTICE

Next we provide a C++ implementation of these algorithms. Notice that we are re-using two previously discussed concepts: that of passing a function to a function and that of using static declaration of an array. In this function, we pass the *rkfunc* function (which is the right-hand side of our ODE) into the Runge–Kutta function so that it can be evaluated (in this case, being evaluated four times). We store the intermediate stages within the statically allocated array *hold*, which we explicitly declare to contain four values since there are four stages to this method.

One key issue to point out is that it would be perfectly legitimate for us to dynamically allocate the space for the array *hold*. However, in this case, it is more efficient to allocate the space for *hold* statically at the beginning of the function. A convenience of static allocation in this case is that deallocation is handled automatically! Recall that there is no need to explicitly deallocate the static declaration. All of this is possible because we know ahead of time the number of items that *hold* will need to contain (in this case, four items), and hence we can explicitly declare how much memory we will need to properly implement this function.

```
double RungeKutta4(double uold, double time, double dt,
                   double (*rkfunc)(double,double)){
  int i;
  double unew, hold[4];

  hold[0] = rkfunc(uold,time);
  hold[1] = rkfunc(uold+0.5*hold[0],time+0.5*dt);
  hold[2] = rkfunc(uold+0.5*hold[1],time+0.5*dt);
  hold[3] = rkfunc(uold+hold[2],time+dt);

  unew = uold + (1.0/6.0)*(hold[0]+2.0*(hold[1]+
                           hold[2])*hold[3]);

  return unew;
}
```

AUTONOMOUS ODE. An autonomous ODE it is defined by the right-hand side being

$$\mathcal{F} = \mathcal{F}(U)$$

only.

The following version is due to Jameson et al. [60], and it produces a Runge–Kutta method of order p with only three levels of storage.

Set: $X = U^n$
  For $k = p, 1, -1$

$$X = U^n + \frac{1}{k}\Delta t \mathcal{F}(X)$$

  End For
Update: $U^{n+1} = X$

PUTTING IT INTO PRACTICE

The algorithm presented here is implemented in the following example code. Here we show how this method easily translates into a C++ function. We want to draw your attention to one particular item within this function: the looping index. In previous examples, we have started at a value for the incrementor and have consistently *added* to that value. In this example, we decrement! Careful attention should be placed on the stopping condition. Notice that we want the value of k to start at *order* and to decrement to $k = 1$ inclusive.

Software

Suite

```
double RungeKutta(int order, double dt, double uold,
                  double (*rkfunc)(double)){
  double unew = uold;

  for(int k=order;k>=1;k--)
    unew = uold + (dt/k)*rkfunc(unew);

  return unew;
}
```

PROGRAMMER BEWARE!

• Think carefully about your loop-ending condition.

Warning

5.2.5 Stability of Runge–Kutta Methods

As an example let us consider the equation

$$\frac{dU}{dt} = \lambda U$$

and examine the stability of RK4. We compute

$$X_1 = \lambda U^n,$$

$$X_2 = \lambda(U^n + \frac{1}{2}\lambda U^n \Delta t)$$

$$\vdots$$

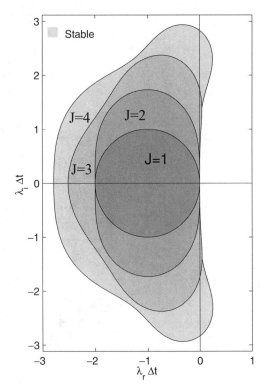

Figure 5.22: Stability diagrams for the Runge–Kutta methods of order one to four.

and therefore

$$U^{n+1} = U^n + \frac{1}{6}\Delta t[X_1 + X_2 + 2X_3 + X_4],$$

or

$$U^{n+1} = U^n \left[1 + \lambda\Delta t + \frac{\lambda^2 \Delta t^2}{2} + \frac{\lambda^3 \Delta t^3}{6} + \frac{\lambda^4 \Delta t^4}{24} \right].$$

The growth factor is then

$$G = \left[1 + \cdots + \frac{\lambda^4 \Delta t^4}{24} \right]$$

and we require

$$|G| \leq 1.$$

By setting $\mu \equiv \lambda\Delta t$, we solve

$$1 + \mu + \frac{\mu^2}{2} + \frac{\mu^3}{6} + \frac{\mu^4}{24} = e^{i\theta}, \quad \theta \in [0, 2\pi],$$

and determine (numerically) $\mu(\theta)$. In Figure 5.22 we plot the stability regions of the Runge–Kutta methods. We notice that unlike the multistep methods, in Runge–Kutta methods the stability regions increase with order!

5.3 HOMEWORK PROBLEMS

1. Use the method of undetermined coefficients to obtain a third-order finite difference approximation for one-sided (upwind-type) first and second (one-dimensional) derivatives.

2. Use the half-central and the central difference operators to derive approximations of second and fourth order of accuracy approximations for the fourth (one-dimensional) derivative.

3. Finite differencing as we have presented it can be formulated as a matrix multiplication operation. Each explicit finite difference operator yields a *differentiation matrix*, which can be formed during a preprocessing stage before computations are accomplished. Each time differentiation is needed, premultiplication by the differentiation matrix yields an approximation of the derivative.

   (a) Formulate a one-dimensional second-order first-derivative differentiation matrix and a one-dimensional second-order second-derivative differentiation matrix assuming a periodic domain.

   (b) What is the bandwidth of the matrix?

(c) Write C++ functions that generate these matrices (using individual functions per matrix).

(d) Write a C++ function that implements differentiation by matrix multiplication. The function should take as input the size of the differentiation matrix, the differentiation matrix (as a double ** array), an array containing the values on which to operate, and an array for storing the result.

(e) Verify your routines by comparing results with the functions SO_FirstDeriv_1Dper and SO_SecondDeriv_1Dper. Demonstrate second-order convergence as shown in the text.

4. Write a C++ function to implement a five-point stencil for explicit discretization of the first derivative. Assume that the domain is periodic. Verify that you obtain fourth-order convergence.

5. Write an MPI program using *MPI_Sendrecv* that implements a parallel version of the previous function just described. For number of processors $P = 2, 4$, and 6, verify that you obtain the same convergence rate as the previous function.

6. Write an MPI program using *MPI_Sendrecv_replace* that implements a parallel version of the previous function just described. Compared with the previous program, how many MPI function calls are necessary? For number of processors $P = 2, 4$, and 6, verify that you obtain the same convergence rate as the previous program.

7. Obtain numerical solutions to the the ordinary differential equation

$$\frac{dy}{dt} = 2\sqrt{y}$$

in the interval $[0, 1]$, with initial conditions

$$y = 0.1, \ y = 0.01, \ y = 0.001, \ y = 0.0001, \ y = 0.$$

Compare the Runge–Kutta scheme of second order to the Adams–Bashforth scheme of secon l order. What do you observe?

8. **Period doubling and chaos:**
Sometimes numerical instabilities appear as numerical chaos, similar to the physical response that we encounter in dynamical systems. This is demonstrated here with the ordinary differential equation

$$\frac{dy}{dt} = 10y(1 - y), \quad y(0) = 0.1.$$

(a) Solve this problem analytically and show that $y(t) \to 1$ as $t \to \infty$.

(b) Show that using the Euler-forward method with step size $h = \Delta t$ we obtain

$$y^{n+1} = (1 + 10h)y^n - 10h(y^n)^2, \quad y^0 = 0.1.$$

(c) For $h = 0.18$, 0.23, 0.25, and 0.3 show that the first 40 iterations of the Euler-forward scheme appear to converge to 1; jump between 1.18 and 0.69; jump among 1.23, 0.54, 1.16, and 0.70; and display no discernible pattern, respectively, for all cases. Produce a plot of y^n versus h for $n = 1,001$ to $2,000$ and $h = 0.1$ to 1.

(d) Approximate the solution with the fourth-order Runge–Kutta scheme and compute the first 60 iterations using $h = 0.3$. Repeat with $h = 0.325$ and $h = 0.35$. Which values of h, if any, give the correct approximation to the solution and why?

(*Note*: The transitions from convergence to jumping between two numbers, to among four numbers, and so on are called *period doubling* whereas the phenomenon exhibited when $h = 0.3$ is *chaos*.)

9. Obtain the stability curves of Figures 5.21 and 5.22 for the Adams–Bashforth and the Runge–Kutta methods, respectively.

10. **Evolution of an ecosystem:**
In this problem we model and solve competition between different species in an attempt to quantify Darwin's thoughts! Vito Volterra, an Italian mathematician, was the first to do this in the 1920s.

Consider an ecological system that contains a predator and a prey species. Prey, whose concentration is denoted by x, multiplies autonomously but is consumed by the predator, whose concentration is denoted by y. The evolution of the population of the prey follows the ordinary differential equation (ODE)

$$\frac{dx}{dt} = ax - Axy, \tag{5.15}$$

where a is positive birth rate constant (determined by the societal norms) and A is another positive constant that expresses how often predator catches prey. The evolution of the predator, in contrast, follows the differential equation

$$\frac{dy}{dt} = -by + A\epsilon xy, \tag{5.16}$$

where b is a death constant owing to starvation and ϵ is a share constant that indicates how many individual predators are necessary to eat up one individual prey.

These two equations comprise the Lotka–Volterra system. There are two obvious steady-state solutions (fixed points), denoted by (x^*, y^*): the trivial one $(x^*, y^*) = (0, 0)$ and a nontrivial one, which is found by setting the right-hand side of these equations equal to zero and solving the resulting system of nonlinear algebraic equations for x and y.

Consider a system with $\epsilon = 1$, $a = 0.400$, $b = 0.450$, and $A = 0.50$. Calculate the nontrivial steady concentrations (x^*, y^*), and then integrate the Lotka–Volterra system using the *explicit third-order Adams–Bashforth method* subject to the initial conditions $x(t = 0) = 0.10$, $y(t = 0) = 0.20$. Carry the integration for a long enough time so that you can assess the asymptotic behavior of the system at very long times. Plot $x(t)$ versus $y(t)$ and discuss the trajectories of this solution as $t \to \infty$.

11. **Stochastic ODE:**
    Consider the first-order linear ODE

$$\frac{dy}{dt} = -ky \quad \text{with } y\,(t = 0) = y_0 \text{ and } t \in [0, T]\,, \tag{5.17}$$

where k is a stochastic process of second order such that

$$k = \bar{k} + v\,(t, \omega)\,. \tag{5.18}$$

Here $\bar{k}$ is the mean value of k and $v\,(t, \omega)$ represents a random variable depending on time and random space. We assume that the probability distribution function (PDF) remains the same for all ks and takes the form of a Gaussian distribution with constant variance. The PDF of k at time t is

$$f\,(k\,(t)) = \frac{1}{\sigma\sqrt{2\pi}} e^{-\frac{1}{2}\frac{(k(t)-\bar{k})^2}{\sigma^2}}\,, \tag{5.19}$$

where $\bar{k}$ is the mean value of k and σ^2 is the variance of k.

Random values of k, generated in time every Δt_s, can be mutually independent, partially correlated, or fully correlated. To this end, we consider the following cases:
Case 1: The PDF of the solution for the *mutually independent* case takes the form

$$f\,(y\,(t)) = \frac{1}{\sigma y\sqrt{2\pi t \Delta t_s}} e^{-\frac{1}{2}\frac{\left(\ln\frac{y}{y_0} - \bar{k}t\right)^2}{\sigma^2 t \Delta t_s}}\,. \tag{5.20}$$

Case 2: The PDF of the solution for the partially correlated case takes the form

$$f\,(y\,(t)) = \frac{1}{\sigma \Delta t_s S y\sqrt{2\pi}} e^{-\frac{1}{2}\frac{\left(\ln\frac{y}{y_0} - \bar{k}t\right)^2}{(\sigma \Delta t_s S)^2}}\,, \quad \Delta t_s \ll T, \tag{5.21}$$

and

$$S = \left(N\frac{(1+C)}{(1-C)} - 2C\frac{(1-C^N)}{(1-C)^2} \right)^{\frac{1}{2}}\,, \tag{5.22}$$

where $C = e^{-\frac{\Delta t_s}{A}}$, $N = \frac{T}{\Delta t_s}$, and A is the correlation length of the random process.
Case 3: In the fully correlated case, the random process k becomes a random variable and the PDF of the solution takes the form

$$f\,(y\,(t)) = \frac{1}{\sigma t y\sqrt{2\pi}} e^{-\frac{1}{2}\frac{\left(\ln\frac{y}{y_0} - \bar{k}t\right)^2}{(\sigma t)^2}}\,. \tag{5.23}$$

An easy way to write the *first moment* (i.e., mean) in a general form for all cases is to express it in a logarithmic form:

$$\ln\left(\frac{E\,(y)}{y_0}\right) = -\bar{k}t + \frac{1}{2}\sigma^2\Gamma, \tag{5.24}$$

where $\Gamma = t\Delta t_s$ for Case 1, $\Gamma = t^2$ for Case 3, and $\Gamma = \Delta t_s \left(t\frac{(1+C)}{(1-C)} - 2C\Delta t_s\frac{(1-C^N)}{(1-C)^2} \right)$ for Case 2.

The *second moment* (i.e., variance) for all cases can be obtained from the expressions of the mean:

$$E\left(y^2\right) = \left(e^{\sigma^2 \Gamma} - 1\right) E^2\left(y\right), \tag{5.25}$$

where $\Gamma = t\Delta t_s$ for Case 1, $\Gamma = t^2$ for Case 3, and $\Gamma = t\Delta t_s \left(t\frac{(1+C)}{(1-C)} - 2C\Delta t_s \frac{(1-C^N)}{(1-C)^2}\right)$ for Case 2.

(a) Use a multistep or a multistage ODE solver of various orders to obtain solutions and corresponding errors for the *mean* and *variance* response corresponding to $\bar{k} = 0$ and $\sigma = 1$, respectively, and final time of integration $T = 1$. To do this you need to follow a **Monte Carlo** approach in which $v(t, \omega)$ is obtained from a Gaussian PDF corresponding to $\sigma = 1$. The correlation length for Case 2 is assumed to be $A = 0.1$.

(b) Does the accuracy of the numerical solutions you obtained increase with the formal solver of the time-stepping scheme you used as expected? Explain.

12. We presented in the text a function for time marching using Adams–Bashforth on a single ODE. Modify the function to handle a system of ODEs.

(a) What changes to the arguments must occur?

(b) Which is more efficient, looping over the switch or placing loops within the switch statement? Verify your answer by creating an example problem and report the timing results you find.

6

Implicit Discretizations

In this chapter we consider implicit discretizations of space and time derivatives. Unlike the explicit discretizations presented in the previous chapter, here we express a derivative at one grid point in terms of function values as well as *derivative values* at adjacent grid points (spatial discretization) or in terms of previous and *current* time levels (temporal discretization). This, in turn, implies that there is implicit coupling, and thus matrix inversion is required to obtain the solution.

The material of this chapter serves to introduce solutions of tridiagonal systems and correspondingly parallel computing of sparse linear systems using MPI. We also introduce two new MPI functions: *MPI_Barrier*, used for synchronizing processes, and *MPI_Wtime*, used for obtaining the wall-clock timing information.

6.1 IMPLICIT SPACE DISCRETIZATIONS

The discretizations we present here are appropriate for any order spatial derivative involved in a partial differential equation, but they are particularly useful when *high-order accuracy* and *locality of data* is sought. The explicit finite differences could also lead to high accuracy but at the expense of long stencils, and this, in turn, implies coupling involving many grid points and consequently a substantial communications overhead. In contrast, the implicit finite differences employ very compact stencils and guarantee *locality*, which is the key to success of any parallel implementation. We only consider discretizations on uniform (i.e., equidistant) grids, as we assume that a mapping of the form presented in the previous chapter is always available to transform a nonuniform grid to a uniform one. We also present discretizations only for one-dimensional grids since multidimensional discretizations are accomplished using *directional splitting*, as before.

6.1.1 Difference Operators

We can employ the same difference operators defined in the previous chapter to obtain compact formulas for first- and higher order derivatives.

First Derivative

We begin with the expansion

$$\Delta x D = \mu(\delta - \frac{\delta^3}{3!} + \frac{1^2 2^2}{5!}\delta^5 - \ldots),$$

and for *fourth-order accuracy* we truncate as follows:

$$\Delta x D = \mu\delta(1 - \frac{\delta^2}{6}) + \mathcal{O}(\Delta x^5).$$

What makes the implicit approach different than the explicit one is the treatment of the operator in parentheses for the first term on the right-hand side. To this end, we approximate it as a geometric series expansion employing the *Padé approximation* to obtain

$$\Delta x D \approx \frac{\mu\delta}{1 + \frac{\delta^2}{6}} + \mathcal{O}(\Delta x^5),$$

which we rewrite as

$$(1 + \delta^2/6)D = \frac{\mu\delta}{\Delta x} + \mathcal{O}(\Delta x^4). \qquad (6.1)$$

We can further simplify the term on the right-hand side to get

$$\mu\delta u_i = \mu[u_{i+1/2} - u_{i-1/2}] = \frac{1}{2}[u_{i+1} + u_i - u_i - u_{i-1}],$$

and therefore the right-hand side of Equation (6.1) is equal to

$$\text{RHS} = \frac{1}{2}\frac{u_{i+1} - u_{i-1}}{\Delta x} + \mathcal{O}(\Delta x^4).$$

Similarly, we can work on the left-hand side of Equation (6.1):

$$\left(1 + \frac{\delta^2}{6}\right)Du_i = \left[(u_x)_i + \frac{1}{6}(E + E^{-1} - 2)(u_x)_i\right]$$

$$= (u_x)_i + \frac{1}{6}[(u_x)_{i+1} + (u_x)_{i-1} - 2(u_x)_i]$$

$$= \frac{1}{6}[(u_x)_{i+1} + 4(u_x)_i + (u_x)_{i-1}].$$

Figure 6.1: (a) Three-point stencil for implicit discretization of the first derivative with fourth-order accuracy. (b) Corresponding five-point stencil for explicit discretization.

Upon substitution in Equation (6.1), we obtain

$$\frac{1}{6}[(u_x)_{i+1} + 4(u_x)_i + (u_x)_{i-1}] = \underbrace{\frac{u_{i+1} - u_{i-1}}{2\Delta x}}_{\text{2nd order}} + \mathcal{O}(\Delta x^4). \qquad (6.2)$$

Equation (6.2) indicates that we need to employ a three-point stencil (Figure 6.1a) to discretize the first derivative with fourth-order accuracy. In contrast, to obtain fourth-order accuracy with explicit discretization we need to employ a five-point stencil as follows (see Figure 6.1b):

$$(u_x)_i = \frac{-u_{i+2} + 8u_{i+1} - 8u_{i-1} + u_{i-2}}{12\Delta x} + \frac{\Delta x^4}{30}\frac{\partial^5 u}{\partial x^5}.$$

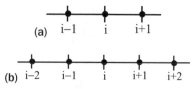

The graphical comparison of Figure 6.1 of the two stencils involved in the implicit and explicit discretization indicates the locality of the computations in implicit approaches.

This derivation of the first derivative on a three-point stencil can be represented by the general scheme

$$\beta(u_x)_{i-1} + \alpha(u_x)_i + \beta(u_x)_{i+1} = \frac{u_{i+1} - u_{i-1}}{2\Delta x} + \mathcal{O}(\Delta x^p)$$

and can be extended to a longer stencil to match any order (p). In other words, on the left-hand side we have a linear symmetric coupling of the derivative approximated at the points of the grid and on the right-hand side we have a lower order (here second-order) approximation. In the next section we will discuss methods for computing the weights (coefficients α, β, and γ) more systematically. Notice that Equation (6.2) is implicit and requires the solution of a tridiagonal linear system.

One of the useful properties of implicit discretizations as we have discussed here is its *compactness*. This is demonstrated clearly with the **two-point stencil** for discretizing the first derivative. We begin again with

$$\Delta x D = \ln E = \ln(1 + \delta^+),$$

or

$$\Delta x D = \delta^+ - \frac{\delta^{+2}}{2} + \underbrace{\frac{\delta^{+3}}{3} - \frac{\delta^{+4}}{4}}_{\mathcal{O}(\Delta x^3)} + \cdots$$

$$= \delta^+ \left(1 - \frac{\delta^+}{2}\right) + \mathcal{O}(\Delta x^3)$$

$$= \delta^+ \frac{1}{1 + \frac{\delta^+}{2}} + \mathcal{O}(\Delta x^3),$$

where in the last equation we employ the geometric series approximation. We then proceed as follows:

$$\left(1 + \frac{\delta^+}{2}\right) D = \frac{\delta^+}{\Delta x} + \mathcal{O}(\Delta x^2),$$

or

$$\{(u_x)_i + \frac{1}{2}[(u_x)_{i+1} - (u_x)_i]\} = \frac{u_{i+1} - u_i}{\Delta x} + \mathcal{O}(\Delta x^2),$$

which leads to a second-order formula for the first derivative, that is,

$$\frac{1}{2}[(u_x)_{i+1} + (u_x)_i] = \frac{u_{i+1} - u_i}{\Delta x} + \mathcal{O}(\Delta x^2). \tag{6.3}$$

This formula is also implicit but one-sided, and it involves the solution of a linear bidiagonal system.

Second Derivative

The method to compute second- or higher order derivatives is similar to that for first-order ones. The starting point here is to employ the appropriate expansion given by the expansion of $D^n u_i$ [see Equations (5.2),(5.4),(5.5)] and subsequently to use the Padé approximation in the truncation of the series. For example, we can apply this approach to obtain a fourth-order-accurate approximation for the second derivative using central differencing, as follows:

$$(u_{xx})_i = \frac{1}{\Delta x^2}\left[\delta^2 - \frac{\delta^4}{12} + \frac{\delta^6}{90} - \frac{\delta^8}{560} + \dots\right] u_i$$

$$= \frac{\delta^2}{\Delta x^2}\left[1 - \frac{\delta^2}{12}\right] u_i + \mathcal{O}(\Delta x^4)$$

$$= \frac{1}{\Delta x^2}\frac{\delta^2 u_i}{1 + \delta^2/12} + \mathcal{O}(\Delta x^4).$$

From this we obtain

$$\left(1 + \frac{\delta^2}{12}\right)(u_{xx})_i = \frac{1}{\Delta x^2}\delta^2 u_i + \mathcal{O}(\Delta x^4),$$

which leads to the formula

$$\frac{1}{12}[(u_{xx})_{i+1} + 10(u_{xx})_i + (u_{xx})_{i-1}] = \frac{1}{\Delta x^2}[u_{i+1} - 2u_i + u_{i-1}] + \mathcal{O}(\Delta x^4). \qquad (6.4)$$

We thus obtained fourth-order accuracy on the three-point stencil, unlike the explicit discretization, which leads to second-order accuracy on the same stencil. The price to pay here is that we need to obtain the derivative values at the grid points by solving the tridiagonal system

$$\frac{1}{12}\begin{bmatrix} \ddots & \ddots & \ddots & 0 \\ & 1 & 10 & 1 \\ 0 & \ddots & \ddots & \ddots \end{bmatrix}[(u_{xx})_i]$$

with a known right-hand side given by the function values at the grid points.

6.1.2 Method of Undetermined Coefficients

We now present a more general approach to constructing compact implicit finite difference schemes on uniform grids for first-, second-, third-, and fourth-order derivatives. It is based on the method of undetermined coefficients that we first encountered in the previous chapter (see Section 5.1). However, unlike the explicit constructions, in the implicit approach we employ two different grids. Here, we follow the derivations of Lele [68].

First Derivative

We consider two grids and appropriate corresponding stencils for the discretization expressed by the following equation:

$$\beta(u_x)_{i-2} + \alpha(u_x)_{i-1} + (u_x)_i + \alpha(u_x)_{i+1} + \beta(u_x)_{i+2}$$

$$= c\frac{u_{i+3} - u_{i-3}}{6\Delta x} + b\frac{u_{i+2} - u_{i-2}}{4\Delta x} + a\frac{u_{i+1} - u_{i-1}}{2\Delta x}.$$

5/7 Stencil:

LHS

RHS

Figure 6.2: Two grids employed for the implicit discretization of the first derivative.

The key idea here is to approximate the left-hand side of this equation on the grid and corresponding five-point stencil shown in Figure 6.2 (upper) and the right-hand side on the seven-point stencil of Figure 6.2 (lower). In particular, on the former we assign derivative values at the grid points whereas on the latter we form explicit central differences on substencils formed by the entire stencil. These explicit differences are of lower order (here second-order) accuracy.

The unknowns on these equations are the weight coefficients on both sides, that is, a total of five unknowns:

$$\{\alpha, \beta, c, b, a\}.$$

Note that if $\beta = 0$ then the computational complexity of obtaining the derivative values at the grid points is equivalent to solving a tridiagonal system, whereas if $\beta \neq 0$ then we have to solve a pentadiagonal system. Therefore, β defines the implicit stencil related to the right-hand side. Similarly, the extent of the right-hand side stencil is dictated by the coefficients a, b, and c, and this selection is important for parallel computations as it dictates *locality* of data.

The method to obtain these unknown coefficients is similar to the one presented in the previous chapter, and it based on matching the Taylor expansions for $(u_x)_{i\pm1}$, $u_{i\pm1}$, etc. The difference, however, is that now we need to expand both the function as well as the first derivative around the central point (i). The first unmatched coefficient will give the *truncation error*.

Based on this matching we obtain the following constraints:

$$a + b + c = 1 + 2\alpha + 2\beta, \quad \mathcal{O}(\Delta x^2),$$

$$a + 2^2b + 3^2c = 2\frac{3!}{2!}(\alpha + 2^2\beta), \quad \mathcal{O}(\Delta x^4),$$

$$a + 2^4b + 3^4c = 2\frac{5!}{4!}(\alpha + 2^4\beta), \quad \mathcal{O}(\Delta x^6),$$

$$a + 2^6b + 3^6c = 2\frac{7!}{6!}(\alpha + 2^6\beta), \quad \mathcal{O}(\Delta x^8),$$

$$\vdots$$

We first consider **tridiagonal schemes**, corresponding to $\beta = 0$ and requiring $5N$ operations, where N is the number of the grid points in the grid. In such triagonal

Figure 6.3: The 3/5 dual stencil for discretizing the first derivative.

3/5 Stencil:

Figure 6.4: The 3/7 dual stencil for discretizing the first derivative.

3/7 Stencil:

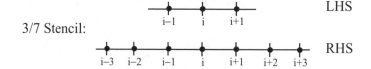

schemes we can have either 3/5 stencils or 3/7 stencils, corresponding to $c = 0$ and $c \neq 0$, respectively. Here the first number (3) refers to the bandwidth of the stencil of the first grid, and the second number (5 or 7) to the bandwidth of the stencil of the second grid.

In the *3/5 stencil* (see Figure 6.3) we employ only two equations, and thus the truncation error is $\mathcal{O}(\Delta x^4)$. We also have that

$$c = 0 \Rightarrow a = \frac{2}{3}(\alpha + 2), \quad b = \frac{1}{3}(4\alpha - 1).$$

Specifically, the truncation error is

$$T'_{3/5} = \frac{4}{5!}(3\alpha - 1)\Delta x^4 \left(\frac{\partial^5 u}{\partial x^5}\right)_i,$$

which is a function of the free parameter α, which can be chosen arbitrarily.

Therefore, we can construct an α-*family* of schemes. Some typical members of the α-family correspond to the following:

- $\alpha = 1/4$: This implies $b = 0$, and therefore this is a 3/3 stencil, the most compact scheme of the family. It is often called the *Padé scheme*, and it is of $\mathcal{O}(\Delta x^4)$ accuracy although it uses an identical three-point stencil as its explicit counterpart of $\mathcal{O}(\Delta x^2)$.
- $\alpha = 1/3$: This choice leads to cancellation of the leading term in the truncation error, and thus it produces an $\mathcal{O}(\Delta x^6)$ scheme.
- $\alpha \to 0$: Here we recover the explicit central difference of $\mathcal{O}(\Delta x^2)$.

To construct a *3/7 stencil* we employ three constraints and obtain schemes of (at least) *sixth-order* accuracy. The corresponding stencils are shown in Figure 6.4.

The corresponding coefficients are obtained from

$$a = \frac{1}{6}(\alpha + 9), \quad b = \frac{1}{15}(32\alpha - 9), \quad c = \frac{-3\alpha + 1}{10},$$

so again we have an α-family of schemes. We can obtain eighth-order accuracy $[\mathcal{O}(\Delta x^8)]$ by setting $\alpha = 3/8$, which zeros out the leading term in the truncation error. This scheme provides the highest order of the α-family.

Next, we consider **pentadiagonal schemes**, corresponding to $\beta \neq 0$ and requiring $11N$ operations, where N is the total number of grid points. This reflects the computational complexity of inverting a pentadiagonal matrix using Gaussian elimination (see Section 9.1).

5/5 Stencil:

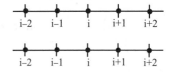

A 5/5 *stencil* (see Figure 6.5) can be obtained by setting $c = 0$ with corresponding sixth-order accuracy. All coefficients are then defined in terms of α as follows:

5/7 Stencil:

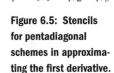

$$a = \frac{2}{9}(8 - 3\alpha), \quad \beta = \frac{-1 + 3\alpha}{12}, \quad b = \frac{-17 + 57\alpha}{18},$$

and the corresponding truncation error is

Figure 6.5: Stencils for pentadiagonal schemes in approximating the first derivative.

$$T'_{5/5} = \frac{4}{7!}(9\alpha - 4)\Delta x^6 \left(\frac{\partial^7 u}{\partial x^7}\right).$$

Similarly, on a 5/7 *stencil* (see Figure 6.5), where $c \neq 0$, we can obtain eighth-order accuracy from the set of coefficients

$$a = \frac{12 - 7\alpha}{6}, \ b = \frac{568\alpha - 183}{150}, \ \beta = \frac{-3 + 8\alpha}{20}, \ c = \frac{9\alpha - 4}{50}.$$

We can even obtain *tenth-order* accuracy for the proper choice of α:

$$T'_{5/7} = \frac{144}{9!}(2\alpha - 1)\Delta x^8 \frac{\partial^9 u}{\partial x^9},$$

if we set $\alpha = 1/2$. This is the highest possible order of accuracy in this family.

We note that in contrast the corresponding explicit difference scheme would require an eleven-point stencil!

Second Derivative

Here we employ a general dual symmetric stencil of the 5/7 type as shown in Figure 6.6.

The general form of the discretization is

$$\beta(u_{xx})_{i-2} + \alpha(u_{xx})_{i-1} + (u_{xx})_i + \alpha(u_{xx})_{i+1} + \beta(u_{xx})_{i+2}$$
$$= a\frac{u_{i+1} - 2u_i + u_{i-1}}{\Delta x^2} + b\frac{u_{i+2} - 2u_i + u_{i-2}}{4\Delta x^2} + c\frac{u_{i+3} - 2u_i + u_{i-3}}{9\Delta x^2}.$$

5/7 Stencil:

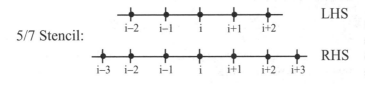

Figure 6.6: A 5/7 dual stencil for implicit discretization of the second derivative.

We use Taylor expansions for the terms on both sides, and upon substitution into this equation we obtain the following constraints:

$$a + b + c = 1 + 2\alpha + 2\beta, \quad \mathcal{O}(\Delta x^2),$$

$$a + 2^2 b + 3^2 c = \frac{4!}{2!}(\alpha + 2^2 \beta), \quad \mathcal{O}(\Delta x^4),$$

$$a + 2^4 b + 3^4 c = \frac{6!}{4!}(\alpha + 2^4 \beta), \quad \mathcal{O}(\Delta x^6),$$

$$a + 2^6 b + 3^6 c = \frac{8!}{6!}(\alpha + 2^6 \beta), \quad \mathcal{O}(\Delta x^8),$$

$$a + 2^8 b + 3^8 c = \frac{10!}{8!}(\alpha + 2^8 \beta), \quad \mathcal{O}(\Delta x^{10})$$

$$\vdots$$

or in general form, for truncation error up to (Δx^p),

$$a + 2^{p-2} b + 3^{p-2} c = \frac{p!}{(p-2)!}(\alpha + 2^{p-2}\beta), \quad p = 4, 6, \ldots.$$

As before, we can now construct either a 3/5 or a 5/7 stencil, the former corresponding to a *one-parameter* family of schemes and the latter to a *two-parameter* family.

For the *3/5 stencil* we have that $c = \beta = 0$ and for fourth-order accuracy we employ the first two constraints to obtain

$$a = \frac{4}{3}(1 - \alpha), \quad b = \frac{1}{3}(-1 + 10\alpha),$$

with truncation error

$$T_{3/5}'' = -\frac{4}{6!}(11\alpha - 2)\Delta x^4 \frac{\partial^6 u}{\partial x^6}.$$

We thus have an α-family of schemes with typical members:

- $\alpha = 1/10$: This leads to $b = 0$, which corresponds to the classical 3/3 Padé scheme.
- $\alpha = 2/11$: This leads to truncation error of order $\mathcal{O}(\Delta x^6)$.
- $\alpha \to 0$: This recovers the explicit central difference scheme.

The longer *5/7 stencil* leads to a *two-parameter family* for schemes of sixth-order accuracy $[\mathcal{O}(\Delta x^6)]$ with free parameters α and β. Specifically, the truncation error has the form

$$T_{5/7}'' = -\frac{8}{8!}(9 - 38\alpha + 214\beta)\Delta x^6 \frac{\partial^8 u}{\partial x^8},$$

and the coefficients of the right-hand side are

$$a = \frac{6 - 9\alpha - 12\beta}{4}, \quad b = \frac{-3 + 24\alpha - 6\beta}{5}, \quad c = \frac{2 - 11\alpha + 124\beta}{20}.$$

If we require $\mathcal{O}(\Delta x^8)$ accuracy, then we will employ four constraints while having five unknowns, and thus a *one-parameter family* of schemes is obtained, the α-family.

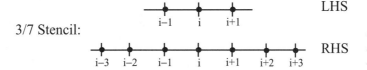

3/7 Stencil:

LHS

RHS

Figure 6.7: A 3/7 stencil for implicit discretization of the third derivative.

The corresponding coefficients are

$$\beta = \frac{38\alpha - 9}{214}, \quad a = \frac{696 - 1191\alpha}{428}, \quad b = \frac{2454\alpha - 294}{530},$$

with truncation error

$$T''_{5/7} = \frac{899\alpha - 334}{2,696,400} \Delta x^8 \frac{\partial^{10} u}{\partial x^{10}}.$$

Therefore, we can obtain very high order accuracy [i.e., $\mathcal{O}(\Delta x^{10})$] for $\alpha = 334/899$!

Third Derivative

To approximate the third derivative with fourth-order accuracy on a 3/7 stencil (see Figure 6.7), we need second-order approximations at both the integer and half grid points. On the integer grid points we have

$$(u_{xxx})_i = \frac{1}{2\Delta x^3}(u_{i+2} - 2u_{i+1} + 2u_{i-1} - u_{i-2}) - \frac{1}{4}\Delta x^2(u^{(iv)}),$$

whereas on the half grid points we have

$$(u_{xxx})_i = \frac{1}{\Delta x^3}(u_{i+3/2} - 3u_{i+1/2} + 3u_{i-1/2} - u_{i-3/2}) - \frac{\Delta x^2}{8}(u^{(v)}).$$

We then employ the equation

$$\alpha(u_{xxx})_{i-1} + (u_{xxx})_i + \alpha(u_{xxx})_{i+1} = b\frac{u_{i+3} - 3u_{i+1} + 3u_{i-1} - u_{i-3}}{8\Delta x^3}$$

$$+ a\frac{u_{i+2} - 2u_{i+1} + 2u_{i-1} - u_{i-2}}{2\Delta x^3}$$

to obtain the coefficients

$$a = 2, \quad b = 2\alpha - 1,$$

with truncation error

$$T'''_{3/7} = \frac{42}{7!}(16\alpha - 7)\Delta x^4 \frac{\partial^7 u}{\partial x^7}.$$

We can now deduce some special members of this α-family:

- For $\alpha = 1/2$, we obtain $b = 0$, which shows that the 3/5 stencil is the most compact $\mathcal{O}(\Delta x^4)$ scheme.
- For $\alpha = 7/16$, the leading term in the truncation error is zero, and thus we obtain $\mathcal{O}(\Delta x^6)$, which gives the highest possible accuracy for this family.

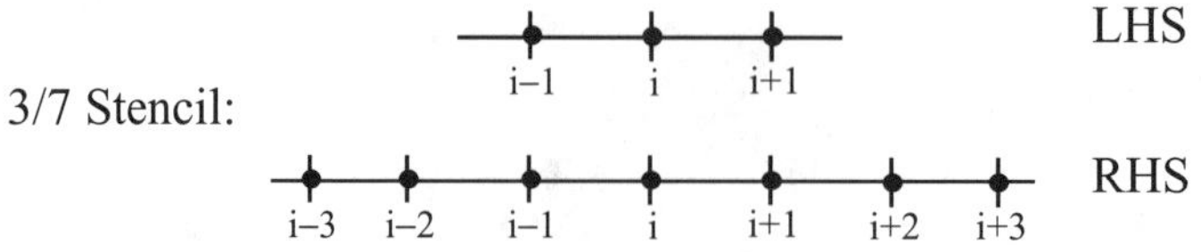

**Figure 6.8: A 3/7
stencil for the implicit
discretization of the
fourth derivative.**

3/7 Stencil:

LHS

RHS

Fourth Derivative

From the many possible variations, here we present only the 3/7 stencil shown in Figure 6.8. The corresponding matching of Taylor expansions leads to

$$\alpha u_{i-1}^{iv} + u_i^{iv} + \alpha u_{i+1}^{iv} = b\frac{u_{i+3} - 9u_{i+1} + 16u_i - 9u_{i-1} + u_{i-3}}{6\Delta x^4}$$
$$+ a\frac{u_{i+2} - 4u_{i+1} + 6u_i - 4u_{i-1} + u_{i-2}}{\Delta x^4}.$$

For a fourth-order accurate scheme we obtain the coefficients

$$a = 2(1 - \alpha), \quad b = 4\alpha - 1,$$

with the following best members:

- For $\alpha = 1/4$, we obtain the most compact (3/5) stencil of $\mathcal{O}(\Delta x^4)$.
- For $\alpha = 7/26$, the leading term of the truncation error is zero and we obtain accuracy of $\mathcal{O}(\Delta x^6)$.

Boundary Conditions

Next we obtain one-sided formulas for implicit discretization of the first and second derivative on a five-point stencil as shown in Figure 6.9.

For the **first derivative**, the equation generating the coefficients is

$$(u_x)_1 + \alpha(u_x)_2 = \frac{1}{\Delta x}(au_1 + bu_2 + cu_3 + du_4),$$

and depending on the required accuracy we can construct a specific formula or a family of schemes, as follows:

- $\mathcal{O}(\Delta x^2)$: $a = -\frac{3+\alpha+2d}{2}$, $b = 2 + 3d$, $c = \frac{1-\alpha+6d}{2}$.
- $\mathcal{O}(\Delta x^3)$: $a = -\frac{11+2\alpha}{6}$, $b = \frac{6-\alpha}{2}$, $c = \frac{2\alpha-3}{2}$, $d = \frac{2-\alpha}{6}$.
- $\mathcal{O}(\Delta x^4)$: $\alpha = 3$, $a = -17/6$, $b = 3/2$, $d = -1/6$.

**Figure 6.9: A five-
point stencil for
implicit discretization
of the first and second
derivatives.**

For the **second derivative** we obtain similarly as before

$$(u_{xx})_1 + 11(u_{xx})_2 = \frac{1}{\Delta x^2}(13u_1 - 27u_2 + 15u_3 - u_4) + \frac{\Delta x^3}{12}\left(\frac{\partial^5 u}{\partial x^5}\right)_1,$$

which is of third-order accuracy. It is instructive to compare this with the corresponding explicit one-sided formula:

$$(u_{xx})_1 = \frac{1}{\Delta x^2}\left(\frac{35}{12}u_1 - \frac{26}{3}u_2 + \frac{19}{2}u_3 - \frac{14}{3}u_4 + \frac{11}{12}u_5\right) + \frac{5}{6}\Delta x^3\left(\frac{\partial^5 u}{\partial x^5}\right)_1.$$

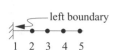

left boundary

1 2 3 4 5

We see that the truncation error of the explicit difference is *ten times* larger than the corresponding third-order compact scheme!

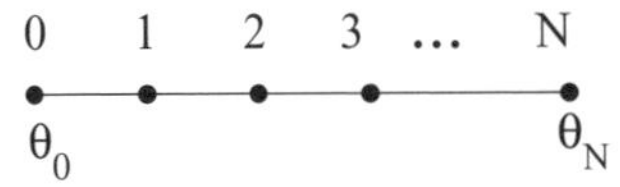

REMARK: We note here that in applications it is often possible to mix the order of discretization accuracy in the interior and at the boundary, with the latter being of lower order. This may be required for stability of the approximation, (e.g., in hyperbolic systems) or for computational efficiency (e.g., in elliptic problems). Theoretical justification for this can be obtained by a theorem (e.g., see [65]).

Figure 6.10: Grid for the one-dimensional boundary value problem.

6.1.3 One-Dimensional Boundary Value Problem

Let us revisit the one-dimensional boundary value problem BVP that we first encountered in Section 5.1.6:

$$\begin{cases} \theta'' = q(x), \\ \theta_0 = \theta_N = 0. \end{cases}$$

We will apply different discretizations to this simple problem on the grid of Figure 6.10 to illustrate the computational complexity involved in each approach.

We start with *explicit second-order*, $\mathcal{O}(\Delta x^2)$, differencing:

$$\frac{1}{\Delta x^2}(\theta_{i+1} - 2\theta_i + \theta_{i-1}) = q_i, \quad i = 1, \ldots, N-1.$$

We can cast these equations into matrix form as follows (recall that each equation is a row in the matrix):

$$\underbrace{\begin{bmatrix} 1 & & & & \\ 1/\Delta x^2 & -2/\Delta x^2 & 1/\Delta x^2 & & \mathbf{0} \\ & \ddots & \ddots & \ddots & \\ \mathbf{0} & & 1/\Delta x^2 & -2/\Delta x^2 & 1/\Delta x^2 \\ & & & & 1 \end{bmatrix}}_{\mathbf{A}} \underbrace{\begin{bmatrix} \theta_0 \\ \theta_1 \\ \vdots \\ \theta_{N-1} \\ \theta_N \end{bmatrix}}_{\theta} = \underbrace{\begin{bmatrix} q_0 \\ q_1 \\ \vdots \\ q_{N-1} \\ q_N \end{bmatrix}}_{\mathbf{q}}.$$

We can also write this in compact form as

$$\mathbf{A}\theta = \mathbf{q},$$

where $\mathbf{A}$ is a sparse tridiagonal matrix.

We now employ *matrix condensation* to impose Dirichlet boundary conditions for this system. Assuming that the columns of matrix $\mathbf{A}$ are denoted by $\mathbf{a}_i$ then we have

$$\sum_{i=1}^{N-1} \theta_i \mathbf{a}_i = \mathbf{q} - \theta_0 \mathbf{a}_0 - \theta_N \mathbf{a}_N.$$

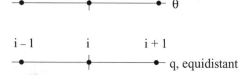

Figure 6.11: Dual 3/3 stencil for discretization of the second derivative in the BVP.

This is an efficient approach as it effectively reduces the rank of the matrix we need to invert.

REMARK: Note here that it will be extremely inefficient to obtain the solution by multiplying the right-hand side by the inverse of matrix $\mathbf{A}$, because the inverse is a full matrix! This can be heuristically justified by a physical analog. Consider, for example, that we solve a steady-state heat equation on a rod, which is governed by the previous one-dimensional BVP. Let us now denote the columns of $\mathbf{A}^{-1}$ by $\mathbf{b}_i^{-1}$; then the solution can be written as

$$\theta = \mathbf{A}^{-1}\mathbf{q} \Rightarrow \theta = \sum_{i=0}^{N} q_i \mathbf{b}_i^{-1}.$$

Now consider that we apply a discrete unit heat source at node (i), that is,

$$q_i = 1, \quad q_j = 0, \quad j \neq i.$$

Then

$$\theta = \mathbf{b}_i^{-1}.$$

In other words the elements of the column vector $\mathbf{b}^{-1}$ are the temperature values at the nodes resulting from a unit heat source at node i. Thus, they should be *nonzero* because of the ellipticity property and the fact that we imposed zero values at the end points.

Next we employ a *compact scheme* on a 3/3 stencil (Figure 6.11) for the discretization of the one-dimensional BVP. We could write down directly the discretization but here we repeat the derivation of the formulas using Taylor expansions and the method of undetermined coefficients. To this end, we have to expand

$$\theta_{i\pm1} = \theta_i \pm \Delta x^2 \theta_i' + \frac{\Delta x^2}{2}\theta_i'' \pm \frac{\Delta x^4}{24}\theta_i^{iv} + \dots$$

and use the model

$$\alpha\theta_{i-1} + \beta\theta_i + \alpha\theta_{i+1} = aq_{i-1} + bq_i + aq_{i+1} + T_i.$$

Notice here that instead of expanding the second derivative we expand the right-hand side. However, we have that

$$\theta'' = q \Rightarrow q_{i\pm1} = q_i \pm \Delta x q_i' + \frac{\Delta x^2}{2}\theta^{(iv)} + \mathcal{O}(\Delta x^4).$$

Proceeding as before, we obtain the coefficients

$$\alpha = 1/\Delta x^2, \quad \beta = -2/\Delta x^2, \quad a = 1/12, \quad b = 5/6.$$

Thus, upon substitution in the BVP we obtain

$$\frac{1}{\Delta x^2}(\theta_{i-1} - 2\theta_i + \theta_{i+1}) = \frac{1}{12}(q_{i-1} + 10q_i + q_{i+1}) + \mathcal{O}(\Delta x^4).$$

This rather simple example helps us to understand the difference between *explicit* and *implicit* discretization. Specifically, here following the implicit discretization we have effectively modified the right-hand side (RHS) through a *mass matrix*; that is, we have distributed the forcing around the node of interest, just like in finite element methods (e.g., see [59]). Therefore, for the RHS we have

$$
\frac{1}{12}
\underbrace{
\begin{bmatrix}
\ddots & \ddots & \ddots & & O \\
 & 1 & 10 & 1 & \\
O & & \ddots & \ddots & \ddots
\end{bmatrix}
}_{\text{mass matrix}}
\begin{bmatrix}
\vdots \\
q_{i-1} \\
q_i \\
q_{i+2} \\
\vdots
\end{bmatrix}.
$$

Note that what we have obtained by expanding the RHS in this particular BVP is identical to the most compact scheme of $\mathcal{O}(\Delta x^4)$ for $\alpha = 1/10$, that is,

$$
\frac{1}{10}\underbrace{(\theta_{xx})_{i-1}}_{q_{i-1}} + \underbrace{(\theta_{xx})_i}_{q_i} + \frac{1}{10}\underbrace{(\theta_{xx})_{i+1}}_{q_{i+1}} = \frac{12}{10}\frac{\theta_{i+1} - 2\theta_i + \theta_{i+1}}{\Delta x^2} + \mathcal{O}(\Delta x^4).
$$

This formula is exactly what we have derived previously in Equation (6.4).

6.1.4 Thomas Algorithm for Tridiagonal Systems

Three-point stencils lead to second-order accuracy and fourth-order accuracy for explicit and implicit discretizations of second-order boundary value problems, respectively. As we have seen from the previous example, solution of such BVPs reduces to solving the linear system

$$
\mathbf{A}\mathbf{x} = \mathbf{q},
$$

where the matrix $\mathbf{A}$ is tridiagonal if the boundary conditions are Dirichlet. In the following, we demonstrate how to solve this system using the *Thomas algorithm*, which is a special case of Gaussian elimination (see also Section 9.1). This method consists of three main steps:

- the LU decomposition of matrix $\mathbf{A}$, that is, its factorization into a lower triangular matrix $\mathbf{L}$ and an upper triangular matrix $\mathbf{U}$ (note that because this factorization maintains the bandwidth, both matrices $\mathbf{L}$ and $\mathbf{U}$ are bidiagonal),
- the forward substitution where the matrix $\mathbf{L}$ is involved, and
- the final backward substitution, where the matrix $\mathbf{U}$ is involved.

More specifically, we have

$$
\underbrace{\begin{bmatrix}
a_1 & c_1 & & & \\
b_2 & a_2 & c_2 & & \mathbf{0} \\
 & b_3 & a_3 & c_3 & \\
 & & \ddots & \ddots & \ddots & \ddots & c_{N-1} \\
\mathbf{0} & & & & b_N & a_N
\end{bmatrix}}_{\mathbf{A}}
=
\underbrace{\begin{bmatrix}
1 & & & \\
\ell_2 & 1 & & \mathbf{0} \\
 & \ell_3 & 1 & \\
 & & \ddots & \ddots \\
\mathbf{0} & & & \ell_N & 1
\end{bmatrix}}_{\mathbf{L}}
\underbrace{\begin{bmatrix}
d_1 & u_1 & & \\
 & d_2 & u_2 & \mathbf{0} \\
 & & d_3 & u_3 \\
 & \mathbf{0} & & \ddots & \ddots \\
 & & & & d_N
\end{bmatrix}}_{\mathbf{U}}
$$

STEP 1: LU DECOMPOSITION. $(\mathbf{A} = \mathbf{LU})$. We determine the elements of matrices $\mathbf{L}$ and $\mathbf{U}$ in three stages, separating the end points from the interior points as follows:

$$d_1 = a_1, \quad u_1 = c_1,$$

$$
i\text{th} \begin{cases}
\ell_i d_{i-1} = b_i \Rightarrow \ell_i = b_i/d_{i-1} & (N \text{ multiplications}), \\
\ell_i u_{i-1} + d_i = a_i \Rightarrow d_i = a_i - \ell_i u_{i-1} & (N \text{ multiplications}, N \text{ additions}), \\
u_i = c_i,
\end{cases}
$$

$$
N\text{th} \begin{cases}
\ell_N d_{N-1} = b_N \Rightarrow \ell_N = b_N/d_{N-1}, \\
\ell_N u_{N-1} + d_N = a_N \Rightarrow d_N = a_N - \ell_N u_{N-1}.
\end{cases}
$$

Therefore, we see that the total *computational complexity* for an LU decomposition of a tridiagonal matrix corresponds to $2N$ multiplications and N additions.

STEP 2: FORWARD SUBSTITUTION. $(\mathbf{Ly} = \mathbf{q})$ The intermediate vector $\mathbf{y}$ is determined from

$$
\begin{bmatrix}
1 & & & \\
\ell_2 & 1 & & \mathbf{0} \\
 & \ell_3 & 1 & \\
\mathbf{0} & & \ddots & \ddots \\
 & & & \ell_N & 1
\end{bmatrix}
\begin{bmatrix}
y_1 \\ y_2 \\ y_3 \\ \vdots \\ y_N
\end{bmatrix}
=
\begin{bmatrix}
q_1 \\ q_2 \\ q_3 \\ \vdots \\ q_N
\end{bmatrix}
\Rightarrow
\begin{cases}
y_1 = q_1, \\
\ell_i y_{i-1} + y_i = q_i \Rightarrow y_i = q_i - \ell_i y_{i-1}.
\end{cases}
$$

Here the operation count is N multiplications and N additions.

STEP 3: BACKWARD SUBSTITUTION $(\mathbf{Ux} = \mathbf{y})$. In the final step we have

$$
\begin{bmatrix}
d_1 & u_1 & & \\
 & d_2 & u_2 & \mathbf{0} \\
 & & d_3 & u_3 \\
 & \mathbf{0} & & \ddots & \ddots \\
 & & & & d_N
\end{bmatrix}
\begin{bmatrix}
x_1 \\ x_2 \\ x_3 \\ \vdots \\ x_N
\end{bmatrix}
=
\begin{bmatrix}
y_1 \\ y_2 \\ y_3 \\ \vdots \\ y_N
\end{bmatrix},
$$

and the final solution is obtained from

$$\begin{cases} x_N = y_N/d_N, \\ d_i x_i + u_i x_{i+1} = y_i \Rightarrow x_i = (y_i - u_i x_{i+1})/d_i, \quad i = N-1, \dots, 1. \end{cases}$$

The corresponding operation count is $2N$ multiplications and N additions.

We can now summarize the operation count:

LU:	$2N$ multiplications,	N additions
Forward:	N multiplications,	N additions
Backward:	$2N$ multiplications,	N additions

Total:	$5N$ multiplications,	$3N$ additions

REMARK: It can be shown that the Thomas algorithm will always converge if the tridiagonal system is diagonally dominant, that is, if

$$|a_k| \geq |b_k| + |c_k|, \quad k = 2, \dots, N-1,$$

$$|a_1| > |c_1|, \text{ and } |a_N| > |b_N|.$$

Also, if a, b, c are matrices instead of scalars we will have a *block-tridiagonal* system and the same algorithm can be applied.

PROGRAMMER BEWARE!

- Think carefully about indexing. Simple mistakes can cause major headaches

Warning

PUTTING IT INTO PRACTICE

Next we present a serial C++ implementation of the Thomas algorithm.

Software
Suite

```
void ThomasAlgorithm(int N, double *b, double *a, double *c,
                     double *x, double *q){
  int i;
  double *l,*u,*d,*y;

  l = new double[N];
  u = new double[N];
  d = new double[N];
  y = new double[N];

  /* LU Decomposition */
  d[0] = a[0];
  u[0] = c[0];
  for(i=0;i<N-2;i++){
    l[i] = b[i]/d[i];
```

```
      d[i+1] = a[i+1] - l[i]*u[i];
      u[i+1] = c[i+1];
   }
   l[N-2] = b[N-2]/d[N-2];
   d[N-1] = a[N-1] - l[N-2]*u[N-2];

   /* Forward Substitution [L][y] = [q] */
   y[0] = q[0];
   for(i=1;i<N;i++)
      y[i] = q[i] - l[i-1]*y[i-1];

   /* Backward Substitution [U][x] = [y] */
   x[N-1] = y[N-1]/d[N-1];
   for(i=N-2;i>=0;i--)
      x[i] = (y[i] - u[i]*x[i+1])/d[i];

   delete[] l;
   delete[] u;
   delete[] d;
   delete[] y;
   return;
}
```

COMMON PROGRAMMING TRICK. Notice that every time we call this routine we must *allocate* and *deallocate* memory. Suppose that we are calling this routine over and over, using the same size allocation each time. We are wasting a lot of time just allocating and deallocating! What can be done? One common trick is to use *static*. When a variable is declared static, it is allocated only once (in the static part of a program's memory), and it remains allocated throughout the duration of the program. Hence, if you declare a pointer variable as static within the routine, and allocate an array of memory the first time that the routine is called, then you can dispense with allocating/deallocating each time. This is demonstrated in the following modified code.

```
void ThomasAlgorithm(int N, double *b, double *a, double *c,
                     double *x, double *q){
   int i;
   static double *l=NULL,*u=NULL,*d=NULL,*y=NULL;

   if(l == NULL){
      l = new double[N];
      u = new double[N];
      d = new double[N];
      y = new double[N];
   }

   /* LU Decomposition */
   d[0] = a[0];
   u[0] = c[0];
   for(i=0;i<N-2;i++){
```

```
      l[i] = b[i]/d[i];
      d[i+1] = a[i+1] - l[i]*u[i];
      u[i+1] = c[i+1];
   }
   l[N-2] = b[N-2]/d[N-2];
   d[N-1] = a[N-1] - l[N-2]*u[N-2];

   /* Forward Substitution [L][y] = [q] */
   y[0] = q[0];
   for(i=1;i<N;i++)
      y[i] = q[i] - l[i-1]*y[i-1];

   /* Backward Substitution [U][x] = [y] */
   x[N-1] = y[N-1]/d[N-1];
   for(i=N-2;i>=0;i--)
      x[i] = (y[i] - u[i]*x[i+1])/d[i];

   return;
}
```

REMARK: In this example, the pointer variables are declared static and are initialized to NULL *the first time that the routine is run*. Since the pointer is NULL, the memory is allocated the first time the routine is run; however, for all subsequent calls, the value of the pointer *l* is not NULL (it contains some address value), and hence memory is not allocated. Of course, in this implementation we have assumed that the value of *N* is always less than or equal to the first value of *N* passed to this routine. More complex schemes can be devised to make allocations and deallocations only when the size changes. This methodology is a common trick and is valid with respect to the language, but it despised by many as unclean programming!

You need not recompute things that do not change	**Key Concept**

Instead of using static allocations, one preferred way of increasing code reuse is to move the memory allocation outside of the Thomas algorithm routines and to break the algorithm into two functions:

1. *ThomasAlgorithmLU* accomplishes the LU decomposition of the matrix **A**. This routine needs to be called only once per matrix **A**.
2. *ThomasAlgorithmSolve* accomplishes the forward and back substitution. This routine needs to be called every time the right-hand-side value **b** changes.

The memory allocation is moved outside of these functions; the calling function is responsible for memory allocation. We now present both of these functions.

```
void ThomasAlgorithmLU(int N, double *b, double *a, double *c,
                  double *l, double *u, double *d){
```

```
    int i;

    /* LU Decomposition */
    d[0] = a[0];
    u[0] = c[0];
    for(i=0;i<N-2;i++){
      l[i] = b[i]/d[i];
      d[i+1] = a[i+1] - l[i]*u[i];
      u[i+1] = c[i+1];
    }
    l[N-2] = b[N-2]/d[N-2];
    d[N-1] = a[N-1] - l[N-2]*u[N-2];

    return;
}

void ThomasAlgorithmSolve(int N, double *l, double *u,
                          double *d, double *x, double *q){
    int i;
    double *y = new double[N];

    /* Forward Substitution [L][y] = [q] */
    y[0] = q[0];
    for(i=1;i<N;i++)
      y[i] = q[i] - l[i-1]*y[i-1];

    /* Backward Substitution [U][x] = [y] */
    x[N-1] = y[N-1]/d[N-1];
    for(i=N-2;i>=0;i--)
      x[i] = (y[i] - u[i]*x[i+1])/d[i];

    delete[] y;
    return;
}
```

Figure 6.12: Domain for solving the steady heat equation in a ring.

REMARK: Notice that the function that accomplishes the forward solve and the back solve does not require the matrix arrays a, b, and c; it requires only the l, u, and d arrays, which contain the LU decomposition of **A**. Once the LU decomposition has been accomplished, and if the matrix **A** is not needed for any other purpose, the arrays a, b, and c can be deallocated.

Thomas Algorithm for Periodic Tridiagonal Systems

The boundary value problem (BVP) we considered in the preceding example employed Dirichlet boundary conditions, but often *periodic boundary conditions* are required. This could be a case, for example, where an infinite domain is simulated or the physics of the problem dictates it, as in solving an elliptic problem on a ring (see Figure 6.12). In this case, despite the sparsity of the matrix resulting from the discretization and its almost tridiagonal form everywhere, the bandwidth is actually equal to the

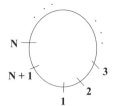

order of the matrix in the following form:

$$
\begin{bmatrix}
a_1 & c_1 & & & b_1 \\
b_2 & a_2 & c_2 & & \mathbf{0} \\
& \ddots & \ddots & \ddots & \\
& & \ddots & \ddots & c_N \\
c_{N+1} & \mathbf{0} & & b_{N+1} & a_{N+1}
\end{bmatrix}
\begin{bmatrix}
x_1 \\
x_2 \\
\vdots \\
x_N \\
x_{N+1}
\end{bmatrix}
= \begin{bmatrix} q \end{bmatrix},
$$

where we assume that b_1 and c_{N+1} are coefficients corresponding to the periodic boundary conditions, (e.g., equal to 1 in the preceding example).

We can solve this system by first "condensing" the matrix, that is, eliminating the last row and the last column, to arrive at

$$
\underbrace{\begin{bmatrix}
a_1 & c_1 & & & \\
b_2 & a_2 & c_2 & & \mathbf{0} \\
& \ddots & \ddots & \ddots & \\
& & & & c_{N-1} \\
\mathbf{0} & & & b_N & a_N
\end{bmatrix}}_{\mathbf{A}^c}
\begin{bmatrix}
x_1 \\
x_2 \\
\vdots \\
\\
x_N
\end{bmatrix}
= \mathbf{q} - \begin{bmatrix}
b_1 \\
0 \\
\vdots \\
0 \\
c_N
\end{bmatrix} x_{N+1}.
$$

Now we use the linear property and propose a superposition of the form

$$
\mathbf{x} = \mathbf{x}^{(1)} + \mathbf{x}^{(2)} \cdot x_{N+1},
$$

where $\mathbf{x}^{(1)}$ and $\mathbf{x}^{(2)}$ are solutions of the tridiagonal "condensed" system with N unknowns, that is,

$$
\mathbf{A}^c \mathbf{x}^{(1)} = \mathbf{q},
$$

$$
\mathbf{A}^c \mathbf{x}^{(2)} = \begin{bmatrix}
-b_1 \\
0 \\
\vdots \\
0 \\
-c_N
\end{bmatrix}.
$$

We finally compute x_{N+1} from the last equation in the original system by back substitution, yielding

$$
c_{N+1}(x_1^{(1)} + x_{N+1} x_1^{(2)}) + b_{N+1}(x_N^{(1)} + x_{N+1} x_N^{(2)}) + a_{N+1} x_{N+1} = q_{N+1},
$$

and we solve for x_{N+1} to get

$$
x_{N+1} = \frac{q_{N+1} - c_{N+1} x_1^{(1)} - b_{N+1} x_N^{(1)}}{a_{N+1} + c_{N+1} x_1^{(2)} + b_{N+1} x_N^{(2)}}.
$$

PUTTING IT INTO PRACTICE

In the following we present a serial C++ implementation of the Thomas algorithm for *periodic systems*. As was discussed, the Thomas algorithm for periodic systems requires us to accomplish LU solves on *condensed systems*. Note that we accomplish this

Software

Suite

by reusing the Thomas algorithm functions that we previously presented on the condensed system.

```
void ThomasAlgorithm-per(int N, double *b, double *a,
                         double *c, double *x, double *q){
  int i;
  double *x1,*x2,*q2;

  x1 = new double[N-1];
  x2 = new double[N-1];
  q2 = new double[N-1];

  /* Prepare secondary q */
  for(i=0;i<N-1;i++)
    q2[i] = 0.0;
  q2[0] = -b[N-1];
  q2[N-2] = -c[N-2];

  ThomasAlgorithm(N-1,b,a,c,x1,q);
  ThomasAlgorithm(N-1,b,a,c,x2,q2);

  x[N-1] = (q[N-1] - c[N-1]*x1[0] - b[N-2]*x1[N-2])/
    (a[N-1] + c[N-1]*x2[0] + b[N-2]*x2[N-2]);

  for(i=0;i<N-1;i++)
    x[i] = x1[i] + x2[i]*x[N-1];

  delete[] x1;
  delete[] x2;
  delete[] q2;
}
```

Key Concept

Code reuse is important. If you have already invested the time to make sure that a routine is well written and correctly implemented, then you can use the routine as a component in new routines.

6.1.5 Parallel Algorithm for Tridiagonal Systems

In seeking a parallelization strategy for solving triagonal systems, we will once again examine the structure of the LU decomposition as we did in formulating the Thomas algorithm. By exploiting the recursive nature of the LU decomposition, we will devise a *full-recursive-doubling* procedure for solving for the unknown LU coefficients. For a more detailed description of the algorithm that follows we refer the reader to [24].

As before, we seek an LU decomposition of the tridiagonal matrix $\mathbf{A}$ as follows:

$$
\underbrace{\begin{bmatrix}
a_1 & c_1 & & & \\
b_2 & a_2 & c_2 & & \text{\Large 0} \\
 & b_3 & a_3 & c_3 & \\
 & & \ddots & \ddots & \ddots & c_{N-1} \\
\text{\Large 0} & & & b_N & a_N
\end{bmatrix}}_{\mathbf{A}}
=
\underbrace{\begin{bmatrix}
1 & & & & \\
\ell_2 & 1 & & \text{\Large 0} & \\
 & \ell_3 & 1 & & \\
 & & \ddots & \ddots & \\
\text{\Large 0} & & & \ell_N & 1
\end{bmatrix}}_{\mathbf{L}}
\underbrace{\begin{bmatrix}
d_1 & u_1 & & & \\
 & d_2 & u_2 & \text{\Large 0} & \\
 & & d_3 & u_3 & \\
\text{\Large 0} & & & \ddots & \ddots & u_{N-1} \\
 & & & & d_N
\end{bmatrix}}_{\mathbf{U}}.
$$

Upon examination of this expression, we see that we can formulate recurrence relations for the unknown coefficients d_j, u_j, and l_j as follows:

$$a_1 = d_1, \tag{6.5}$$

$$c_j = u_j, \tag{6.6}$$

$$a_k = d_k + l_k u_{k-1}, \tag{6.7}$$

$$b_k = l_k d_{k-1}, \tag{6.8}$$

where $j = 1, \ldots, N$ and $k = 2, \ldots, N$. Given Equation (6.6), we can immediately solve for all the unknown coefficients u_j. To solve for d_j and l_j, we rely on the recursive nature of these equations. Substituting Equations (6.6) and (6.8) into Equation (6.7) and rearranging terms yields the following rational recursion relationship for the unknown coefficient d_j:

$$
\begin{aligned}
d_j &= a_j - l_j u_{j-1} \\
&= a_j - \frac{b_j}{d_{j-1}} u_{j-1} \\
&= \frac{a_j d_{j-1} - b_j c_{j-1}}{d_{j-1} + 0}.
\end{aligned}
$$

We can then inductively solve for all the coefficients d_j and use this information along with Equation (6.8) to solve for l_j.

To parallelize this procedure, we make use of a full-recursive-doubling procedure on the sequence of 2×2 matrices given by

$$
\mathbf{R}_0 = \begin{bmatrix} a_0 & 0 \\ 1 & 0 \end{bmatrix}
$$

and

$$
\mathbf{R}_j = \begin{bmatrix} a_j & -b_j c_{j-1} \\ 1 & 0 \end{bmatrix}
$$

Table 6.1: Full-recursive-doubling communication pattern. The number of stages is equal to $\log_2 M$, where M is the number of processes. In this case, $M = 8$ and hence there are three stages of communication.

for $j = 1, \ldots, N$. Using the Möbius transformations

$$\mathbf{T}_j = \mathbf{R}_j \mathbf{R}_{j-1} \ldots \mathbf{R}_0$$

we have that

$$d_j = \frac{\begin{pmatrix} 1 \\ 0 \end{pmatrix}^t \mathbf{T}_j \begin{pmatrix} 1 \\ 1 \end{pmatrix}}{\begin{pmatrix} 0 \\ 1 \end{pmatrix}^t \mathbf{T}_j \begin{pmatrix} 1 \\ 1 \end{pmatrix}}.$$

Stage 1	Stage 2	Stage 3
$P_0 \rightarrow P_1$	$P_0 \rightarrow P_2$	$P_0 \rightarrow P_4$
$P_1 \rightarrow P_2$	$P_1 \rightarrow P_3$	$P_1 \rightarrow P_5$
$P_2 \rightarrow P_3$	$P_2 \rightarrow P_4$	$P_2 \rightarrow P_6$
$P_3 \rightarrow P_4$	$P_3 \rightarrow P_5$	$P_3 \rightarrow P_7$
$P_4 \rightarrow P_5$	$P_4 \rightarrow P_6$	
$P_5 \rightarrow P_6$	$P_5 \rightarrow P_7$	
$P_6 \rightarrow P_7$		

To explain how this information can be used for parallelization, we will examine a specific example. Suppose that we are given a tridiagonal matrix $\mathbf{A}$ of size 40 and we want to solve the problem using 8 processes. Assume that all processes have a copy of the original matrix $\mathbf{A}$. We first partition the matrix such that each process is responsible for five rows: Process P_0 is responsible for rows 0–4, P_1 is responsible for rows 5–9, etc. We then accomplish the following steps:

1. On each process P_j, form the matrices $\mathbf{R}_k$, where k corresponds to the row indices for which the process is responsible and ranges between k_min and k_max.
2. On each process P_j, form the matrix $\mathbf{S}_j = \mathbf{R}_{k\_max} \mathbf{R}_{k\_max-1} \ldots \mathbf{R}_{k\_min}$.
3. Using the full-recursive-doubling communication pattern as given in Table 6.1, distribute and combine the $\mathbf{S}_j$ matrices as given in Table 6.2.
4. On each process P_j, calculate the local unknown coefficients d_k ($k\_min \le k \le k\_max$) using local $\mathbf{R}_k$ and matrices obtained from the full-recursive-doubling.
5. For processes P_0 through P_6, send the local d_{k_max} to the process 1 process id up (i.e., P_0 sends to P_1; P_1 sends to P_2; etc.).
6. On each process P_j, calculate the local unknown coefficients l_k ($k\_min \le k \le k\_max$) using the local d_k values and the value obtained in the previous step.
7. Distribute the d_j and l_j values across all processes so that each process has all the d_j and l_j coefficients.
8. On each process P_j, perform a local forward and backward substitution to obtain the solution.

Software
Suite

PUTTING IT INTO PRACTICE

We now present a *parallel Thomas algorithm function* that uses the full-recursive-procedure. This function assumes that the MPI initialization has already been accomplished by the calling function, and it requires that the number of processes used is a *power of 2*. It takes as input its process *id number*, the total number of processes being used, the size of the matrix, the matrix **A** stored in the arrays *a*, *b*, and *c* as before, and the right-hand-side vector **q** stored in the array *q*. The output of this function on all processes is the solution vector contained within the array *x*. We first present the function definition and then present some remarks on the code.

```
void ThomasAlgorithm_P(int mynode, int numnodes, int N,
    double *b, double *a, double *c, double *x, double *q){
  int i,j,k,i_global;
  int rows_local,local_offset;
  double S[2][2],T[2][2],s1tmp,s2tmp;
  double *l,*d,*y;
  MPI_Status status;

  l = new double[N];
  d = new double[N];
  y = new double[N];

  for(i=0;i<N;i++)
    l[i] = d[i] = y[i] = 0.0;

  S[0][0] = S[1][1] = 1.0;
  S[1][0] = S[0][1] = 0.0;

  rows_local = (int) floor(double N/numnodes);
  local_offset = mynode*rows_local;

  // Form local products of R_k matrices
  if(mynode==0){
    s1tmp = a[local_offset]*S[0][0];
    S[1][0] = S[0][0];
    S[1][1] = S[0][1];
    S[0][1] = a[local_offset]*S[0][1];
    S[0][0] = s1tmp;
    for(i=1;i<rows_local;i++){
      s1tmp = a[i+local_offset]*S[0][0] -
              b[i+local_offset-1]*c[i+local_offset-1]*S[1][0];
      s2tmp = a[i+local_offset]*S[0][1] -
              b[i+local_offset-1]*c[i+local_offset-1]*S[1][1];
      S[1][0] = S[0][0];
      S[1][1] = S[0][1];
      S[0][0] = s1tmp;
      S[0][1] = s2tmp;
    }
  }
  else{
    for(i=0;i<rows_local;i++){
      s1tmp = a[i+local_offset]*S[0][0] -
```

Table 6.2: Distribution and combination pattern of the S_j matrices for each stage. The interpretation of the table is as follows: Given the communication pattern as given in Table 6.1, in stage one P_0 sends S_0 to P_1, which P_1 combines with its local S_1 to form the product $S_1 S_0$. Similarly, in stage one, P_1 sends S_1 to P_2, etc. In stage two, P_0 sends S_0 to P_2, which P_2 combines with its local product $S_2 S_1$ to form $S_2 S_1 S_0$. Similarly, P_1 sends $S_1 S_0$ to P_3, which is then combined on P_3 to form $S_3 S_2 S_1 S_0$. In stage three, the final communications occur such that each process j stores locally the product $S_j S_{j-1} \ldots S_0$.

Process	Stage 0	Stage 1	Stage 2	Stage 3
P_0	S_0			
P_1	S_1	$S_1 S_0$		
P_2	S_2	$S_2 S_1$	$S_2 S_1 S_0$	
P_3	S_3	$S_3 S_2$	$S_3 S_2 S_1 S_0$	
P_4	S_4	$S_4 S_3$	$S_4 S_3 S_2 S_1$	$S_4 S_3 S_2 S_1 S_0$
P_5	S_5	$S_5 S_4$	$S_5 S_4 S_3 S_2$	$S_5 S_4 S_3 S_2 S_1 S_0$
P_6	S_6	$S_6 S_5$	$S_6 S_5 S_4 S_3$	$S_6 S_5 S_4 S_3 S_2 S_1 S_0$
P_7	S_7	$S_7 S_6$	$S_7 S_6 S_5 S_4$	$S_7 S_6 S_5 S_4 S_3 S_2 S_1 S_0$

```
                    b[i+local_offset-1]*c[i+local_offset-1]*S[1][0];
        s2tmp = a[i+local_offset]*S[0][1] -
                    b[i+local_offset-1]*c[i+local_offset-1]*S[1][1];
      S[1][0] = S[0][0];
      S[1][1] = S[0][1];
      S[0][0] = s1tmp;
      S[0][1] = s2tmp;
    }
  }

// Full-recursive-doubling algorithm for distribution
for(i=0; i<=log2(numnodes);i++){
  if(mynode+pow(2.0) < numnodes)
    MPI_Send(S,4,MPI_DOUBLE,int(mynode+pow(2.0)),0,
            MPI_COMM_WORLD);
  if(mynode-pow(2.0)>=0){
    MPI_Recv(T,4,MPI_DOUBLE,int(mynode-pow(2.0)),0,
            MPI_COMM_WORLD,&status);
    s1tmp = S[0][0]*T[0][0] + S[0][1]*T[1][0];
    S[0][1] = S[0][0]*T[0][1] + S[0][1]*T[1][1];
    S[0][0] = s1tmp;
    s1tmp = S[1][0]*T[0][0] + S[1][1]*T[1][0];
    S[1][1] = S[1][0]*T[0][1] + S[1][1]*T[1][1];
    S[1][0] = s1tmp;
  }
}

//Calculate last d_k first so that it can be distributed,
//and then do the distribution.
d[local_offset+rows_local-1] = (S[0][0] + S[0][1])/
                                (S[1][0] + S[1][1]);
if(mynode == 0){
  MPI_Send(&d[local_offset+rows_local-1],1,MPI_DOUBLE,
          1,0,MPI_COMM_WORLD);
```

```
  }
  else{
    MPI_Recv(&d[local_offset-1],1,MPI_DOUBLE,mynode-1,0,
              MPI_COMM_WORLD,&status);
    if(mynode != numnodes-1)
      MPI_Send(&d[local_offset+rows_local-1],1,MPI_DOUBLE,
                mynode+1,0,MPI_COMM_WORLD);
  }

  // Compute in parallel the local values of d_k and l_k
  if(mynode == 0){
    l[0] = 0;
    d[0] = a[0];
    for(i=1;i<rows_local-1;i++){
      l[local_offset+i] = b[local_offset+i-1]/
                          d[local_offset+i-1];
      d[local_offset+i] = a[local_offset+i] -
                          l[local_offset+i]*c[local_offset+
                                                    i-1];
    }
    l[local_offset+rows_local-1] = b[local_offset+
                                    rows_local-2]/
                                    d[local_offset+
                                    rows_local-2];
  }
  else{
    for(i=0;i<rows_local-1;i++){
      l[local_offset+i] = b[local_offset+i-1]/
                          d[local_offset+i-1];
      d[local_offset+i] = a[local_offset+i] -
                          l[local_offset+i]*c[local_offset+
                                                    i-1];
    }
    l[local_offset+rows_local-1] = b[local_offset+
                                    rows_local-2]/
                                    d[local_offset+
                                    rows_local-2];
  }

  /************************************************************/

  if(mynode>0)
    d[local_offset-1] = 0;

  // Distribute d_k and l_k to all processes

  double * tmp = new double[N];
```

```
for(i=0;i<N;i++)
  tmp[i] = d[i];
MPI_Allreduce(tmp,d,N,MPI_DOUBLE,MPI_SUM,MPI_COMM_WORLD);
for(i=0;i<N;i++)
  tmp[i] = l[i];
MPI_Allreduce(tmp,l,N,MPI_DOUBLE,MPI_SUM,MPI_COMM_WORLD);
delete[] tmp;

if(mynode ==0){
  /* Forward Substitution [L][y] = [q] */
  y[0] = q[0];
  for(i=1;i<N;i++)
    y[i] = q[i] - l[i]*y[i-1];

  /* Backward Substitution [U][x] = [y] */
  x[N-1] = y[N-1]/d[N-1];
  for(i=N-2;i>=0;i--)
    x[i] = (y[i] - c[i]*x[i+1])/d[i];

{

delete[] l;
delete[] y;
delete[] d;
return;
}
```

REMARK 1: Since we know that we are dealing with 2×2 matrices, we have chosen to allocate the 2×2 S array statically. It is important to note that when static allocation of arrays is used, the memory allocation is contiguous and in row-major order, as shown in Figure 6.13. We can use the contiguousness of the block of memory to our advantage

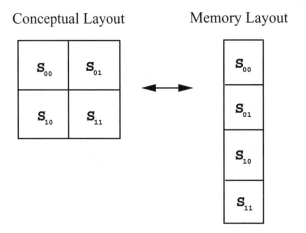

Figure 6.13: Memory layout of the matrix S. The double-indexed array S is stored in a contiguous block of memory in row-major order.

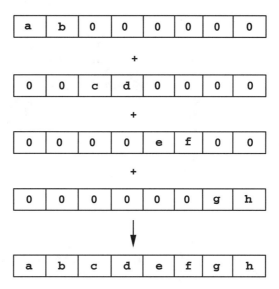

Figure 6.14: How to use the reduction operator to mimic the gathering process. In this example, we have four processes, each of which has two unique items to contribute. On each process, all other entries in the array are zeroed and then a sum is performed. The result is that the data are gathered into one array.

when using MPI. Since S is stored as one contiguous block in memory, we can send the entire array in one MPI call instead of having to send the array row by row (as in the case where each row was dynamically allocated using the **new** command).

REMARK 2: Sometimes it becomes advantageous to use the reduction operator to mimic a gathering operation. We pictorially demonstrate how this can be accomplished in Figure 6.14. In the previous code, we use this trick to gather all the d_j and l_j values across all processors.

MPI Implementation Issues

In the preceding sections, we presented serial and parallel versions of the Thomas algorithm. How can we time our parallel program to examine the speedup due to adding more processes? MPI provides two functions that allow us to accomplish this task: *MPI_Wtime* and *MPI_Wtick*. We will now present for these two functions the function call syntax, argument list explanation, usage example, and some remarks.

FUNCTION CALL SYNTAX

```
double MPI_Wtime(void);
double MPI_Wtick(void);
```

MPI

UNDERSTANDING THE ARGUMENT LISTS
MPI_Wtime and MPI_Wtick take no arguments.

MPI

MPI

EXAMPLE OF USAGE

```
int mynode, totalnodes;
double starttime, finaltime, precision;

MPI_Init(&argc,&argv);
MPI_Comm_size(MPI_COMM_WORLD, &totalnodes);
MPI_Comm_rank(MPI_COMM_WORLD, &mynode);

precision = MPI_Wtick();
starttime = MPI_Wtime();

// Execution of commands here

finaltime = MPI_Wtime();

if(mynode == 0){
  cout << "The execution time was : " << finaltime-starttime;
  cout << " sec. with a precision of " << precision;
  cout << " sec." << endl;
}
```

MPI

REMARKS

- These commands are very useful both for determining the parallel speedup of your algorithm and for determining the components of your program that are using the most time.
- These commands provide you with the wall-clock time (the physical time that has elapsed), not specifically the CPU time or communication time.

One question you may ask is: How do I know that all the processes are exactly at the same point (assuming that I am doing the timing only on process 0)? MPI provides a function for synchronizing all processes called *MPI_Barrier*. When *MPI_Barrier* is called, the function will not return until all processes have called *MPI_Barrier*. This functionality allows you to synchronize all the processes, knowing that all processes exit the *MPI_Barrier* call at the same time. We will now present the function call syntax, argument list explanation, usage example, and some remarks.

MPI_Barrier

MPI

FUNCTION CALL SYNTAX

```
int MPI_Barrier(
MPI_Comm  comm  /* in */,
```

MPI

UNDERSTANDING THE ARGUMENT LISTS

- *comm* – communicator.

EXAMPLE OF USAGE

```
int mynode, totalnodes;
```

```
MPI_Init(&argc,&argv);
MPI_Comm_size(MPI_COMM_WORLD, &totalnodes);
MPI_Comm_rank(MPI_COMM_WORLD, &mynode);

MPI_Barrier(MPI_COMM_WORLD);

// At this stage, all processes are synchronized
```

REMARKS

- This command is a useful tool to help ensure synchronization among processes. For example, you may want all processes to wait until one particular process has read in data from disk. Each process would call *MPI_Barrier* in the place in the program where the synchronization is required.

6.2 IMPLICIT TIME DISCRETIZATIONS

Unlike the explicit time discretizations of the previous chapter, here the solution at the current level cannot be expressed in terms of information from only previous time levels. Instead, the right-hand side for the first-order IVP

$$\frac{dU}{dt} = \mathcal{F}(U, t), \quad U(t = 0) = U_0, \tag{6.9}$$

is also evaluated at the *current time level*, resulting in an implicit expression for the solution.

The most popular schemes are derived from the θ-family, which are one-step schemes:

$$\frac{U^{n+1} - U^n}{\Delta t} = \theta \mathcal{F}(U^{n+1}, t^{n+1}) + (1 - \theta)\mathcal{F}(U^n, t^n). \tag{6.10}$$

- For $\theta = 1$, we obtain the *Euler-backward* scheme .
- For $\theta = 1/2$, we obtain the *Crank–Nicolson* scheme.

We note that θ can take any value in the range $[0, 1]$, and for $\theta = 0$ we obtain the Euler-forward method, an explicit scheme we encountered in Section 5.2.

The θ-family produces a *consistent discretization* of the IVP considered in the form

$$\left(\frac{dU^n}{dt} - \mathcal{F}^n\right) = \Delta t \left(\theta \frac{d\mathcal{F}^n}{dt} - \frac{1}{2}\frac{d^2 U^n}{dt^2}\right)$$

$$+ \Delta t^2 \left(\frac{\theta}{2}\frac{d^2 \mathcal{F}^n}{dt^2} - \frac{1}{6}\frac{d^3 U^n}{dt^3}\right) + \cdots.$$

As $\Delta t \to 0$, the right-hand side of this discretization goes to zero and thus we recover the original initial value problem of Equation (6.9). Specifically, for $\theta = 1$ or $\theta = 1/2$ the truncation error (right-hand side) asymptotes to zero with first- and second-order convergence rate, respectively. This convergence rate, which expresses the first- and second-order accuracy of the Euler-backward and Crank–Nicolson schemes, is consistent with the results on spatial discretization, as they correspond to one-sided and central-differencing schemes, respectively.

We now examine the *stability* of these schemes following the definitions established in the previous chapter. For a general θ-scheme we solve the linear eigenproblem

$$\frac{dU}{dt} = \lambda U, \quad \text{Re}(\lambda) < 0, \tag{6.11}$$

which is discretized as follows:

$$\frac{U^{n+1} - U^n}{\Delta t} = \theta \lambda U^{n+1} + (1 - \theta) \lambda U^n.$$

The solution error also satisfies this equation and thus

$$\epsilon^{n+1}(1 - \theta \lambda \Delta t) = \epsilon^n [1 + (1 - \theta) \lambda \Delta t],$$

so

$$\epsilon^{n+1} = \epsilon^n \frac{1 + (1 - \theta) \lambda \Delta t}{1 - \theta \lambda \Delta t}.$$

The scheme is *absolutely stable* if

$$|1 + (1 - \theta) \lambda \Delta t| \leq 1 - \theta \lambda \Delta t, \ (\text{Re}(\lambda) < 0),$$

or

$$\begin{cases} 0 \geq \lambda \Delta t \ \forall \ \Delta t \geq 0, \\[2mm] -1 + \theta \lambda \Delta t \leq 1 + (1 - \theta) \lambda \Delta t \\[2mm] \Rightarrow -(1 - 2\theta) \lambda \Delta t \leq 2. \end{cases}$$

- For $0 \leq \theta < 1/2$, we have $\Delta t \leq \frac{-2}{(1-2\theta)\lambda}$, which implies *conditional stability*.
- For $\theta \geq 1/2$ we obtain unconditional stability. Therefore, both the Crank–Nicolson ($\theta = 1/2$) and the Euler-backward ($\theta = 1$) are unconditionally stable schemes. The Euler-backward scheme converges monotonically and damps high-frequency components rapidly, whereas the Crank–Nicolson scheme converges in an oscillatory manner.

The stability regions of both the Euler-backward and Crank–Nicolson schemes include the entire left half of the complex plane, and such schemes are referred to as **A-stable**. This region can also be obtained using the theory of characteristic polynomials of Section 5.2. For example, for the Crank–Nicolson scheme, we construct the polynomial

$$\Pi_{\text{CN}} = (z - 1) - \frac{\lambda \Delta t}{2}(z + 1) = (1 - \frac{1}{2}\lambda \Delta t)z - (1 + \frac{1}{2}\lambda \Delta t),$$

or

$$z = \frac{1 + 1/2 \lambda \Delta t}{1 - 1/2 \lambda \Delta t} = \frac{2 + \lambda \Delta t}{2 - \lambda \Delta t}.$$

For Re $(\lambda) \leq 0$, we obtain absolute stability throughout the left half of the plane, as shown in Figure 6.15.

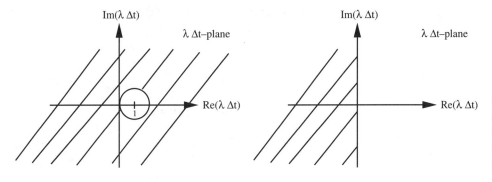

Figure 6.15: Regions of stability for the Euler-backward (left) and Crank–Nicolson (right) schemes.

Forward versus Backward Differentiation

In implicit temporal discretizations, it is possible either to construct the backward difference of the left-hand side of Equation (6.9) or to expand its right-hand side over several time levels. This is demonstrated in the next two examples.

- In the *third-order backward differentiation method*, we have

$$\frac{U^{n+1} - \frac{1}{11}(18U^n - 9U^{n-1} + 2U^{n-2})}{\Delta t} = \frac{6}{11}\mathcal{F}^{n+1}.$$

Here the left-hand side is expanded backward in time, whereas the right-hand side is evaluated at the current time level. In Section 6.2.2 we will see that such schemes have very interesting stability properties.

- In the *third-order Adams–Moulton method*, we have

$$\frac{U^{n+1} - U^n}{\Delta t} = \frac{5}{12}\mathcal{F}^{n+1} + \frac{8}{12}\mathcal{F}^n - \frac{1}{12}\mathcal{F}^{n-1}.$$

Here, the right-hand side is formed by evaluating it at the current as well as at previous time levels. Typically, the coefficients of the Adams–Moulton method are smaller than the coefficients of the Adams–Bashforth method that we presented in Section 5.2. This, in turn, means that they correspond to lower truncation error and lower round-off error. Also, for the same accuracy the Adams–Moulton family employs fewer points than the Adams–Bashforth family, but it is implicit and thus computationally more complex.

The region of stability for the implicit Adams–Moulton family can be constructed using its characteristic polymonial (see Section 5.2). By comparison of the plots in Figure 6.16 with the plots in Figure 5.21 we see that the stability regions of the Adams–Moulton family are larger by a factor of about 10 than that of the Adams–Bashforth family.

6.2.1 Fundamental Theorems for Multistep Methods

We summarize here without proof two basic theorems of multistep methods originally proposed by Dahlquist [20]. They relate accuracy, stability, and number of steps:

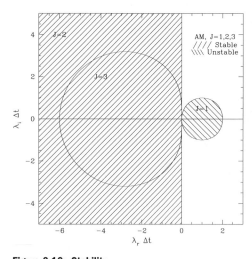

Figure 6.16: Stability diagrams for the first three members of the (implicit) Adams–Moulton family. Note that $J = 1$ corresponds to the Euler-backward discretization.

FIRST DAHLQUIST STABILITY BARRIER. *The order of accuracy p of a stable k-step (linear) multistep formula satisfies*

$$p \leq \begin{cases} k+2, & k \text{ even}, \\ k+1, & k \text{ odd}, \\ k, & \text{explicit form}. \end{cases}$$

For example, the four-step Adams–Moulton formula corresponds to sixth-order accuracy. Similarly, the Crank–Nicolson one-step method is of second-order accuracy, and the explicit three-step Adams–Bashforth method is of third-order accuracy. Notice that the highest order accuracy obtainable with a k-step method is $2k$, however, such a method is unstable.

SECOND DAHLQUIST STABILITY BARRIER. *The order of accuracy of an explicit A-stable multistep formula satisfies $p \leq 2$. An explicit multistep formula cannot be A-stable.*

Notice that of all second-order A-stable methods, the one with the smallest truncation error is the Crank–Nicolson scheme. It is also possible to get around the restriction $p \leq 2$ for A-stability by use of Richardson's extrapolation, which is similar to the Romberg procedure discussed in Section 4.2.

6.2.2 Stability of Stiff ODEs

A "stiff" equation has a slowly varying solution combined with rapidly decaying transients. Typically, of interest is the long-term (asymptotic) solution; however, the initial transients cause severe problems in stability. There are a plethora of physical problems in which such behavior is encountered (e.g., in most coupled-domain problems, such as aero-acoustics, combustion, flow–structure interactions, electric circuits, etc.). We illustrate this behavior with the following example:

$$\frac{dU}{dt} = -1000(U - t^3) + 3t^2, \quad U(0) = 1,$$

which has the exact solution

$$U_{\text{ex}}(t) = e^{-1000t} + t^3,$$

plotted in Figure 6.17. Notice that the boundary layer term is important only initially.

Let us first attempt to employ the Euler-forward explicit scheme

$$U^{n+1} = U^n - 1000\Delta t[U^n - (t^n)^3] + 3\Delta t(t^n)^2$$

with error

$$\epsilon^{n+1} = \epsilon^n(1 - 1000\Delta t).$$

If

$$\Delta t = 0.1 \Rightarrow \epsilon^{n+1} = 99\epsilon^n;$$

thus we lose two decimal points in each time step, yet the scheme is generally stable according to the corresponding definition, that is,

$$\epsilon^n = (1 - 1000\Delta t)^n \epsilon^0 < e^{1000\Delta t n}|\epsilon^0|,$$

or

$$\epsilon^n < e^{1000t}|\epsilon^0|, \quad \forall \Delta t.$$

However, the error bound constant is e^{1000t}, which is so large at $t = 1$ that this discretization is totally impractical even though it is stable!

For useful results we require absolute stability, that is,

$$|1 - 1000\Delta t| < 1 \Rightarrow \Delta t = 0.002;$$

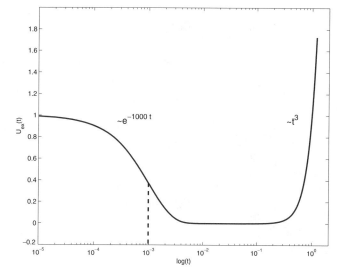

that is, we require a very small Δt to resolve the transient e^{-1000t} rather than the long-term solution t^3.

If we now employ the implicit Euler-backward scheme we obtain

$$U^{n+1} = U^n - 1000\Delta t(U^{n+1} - (t^{n+1})^3) + 3\Delta t(t^{n+1})^2$$

with error

$$\epsilon^{n+1} = \epsilon^n/(1 + 1000\Delta t).$$

If $\Delta t = 0.1$ then

$$\epsilon^{n+1} = \epsilon^n/101.$$

Therefore, the error in the Euler-backward scheme decreases as rapidly as it increases for the Euler-forward method. For large values of Δt the boundary layer is inaccurate but we capture the long-term solution. Clearly, an A-stable scheme would solve the stiffness problem, however, it is too restrictive. Ideally, for these problems we require (see Figure 6.18):

- absolute stability for the transient behavior and
- general stability for the long-term behavior.

To this end, following the work of Gear [42], we introduce a general stiffly stable scheme of order k of the form

$$U^{n+1} = \sum_{j=0}^{k} \alpha_{j+1} U^{n-j} + \Delta t \beta_0 \mathcal{F}^{n+1}$$

for the general initial value problem described by Equation (6.9). The coefficients are obtained by matching appropriate Taylor expansions and are given in Table 6.3.

For stiffly stable schemes *stability studies* are more complicated because the $\rho(z)$ polynomials are nontrivial. For example the third-order

Figure 6.17: Stiff solution of an ordinary differential equation. A boundary layer of thickness 0.001 is present. Notice the logarithmic horizontal scale.

Figure 6.18: Required region of stability for discretizations of stiff equations.

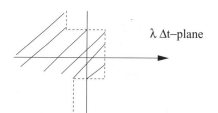

$\lambda \Delta t$–plane

Table 6.3: Weights for the first four stiffly stable schemes.

k	2	3	4
β_0	2/3	6/11	12/25
α_1	4/3	18/11	48/25
α_2	−1/3	−9/11	−36/25
α_3	−	2/11	16/25
α_4	−	−	−3/25

scheme corresponds to

$$\rho(z) = \frac{1}{11}(11z^3 - 18z^2 + 9z - 2),$$

$$\sigma(z) = \frac{6}{11}z^3.$$

They are stable for order $1 \leq k \leq 6$ and generally unstable for $6 < k < 12$ (with some exceptions); they are definitely unstable for $k \geq 12$ (see proof in [53]). Typical stability regions for the first three members of the family are plotted in Figure 6.19.

6.2.3 Second-Order Initial Value Problems

Next we consider second-order initial value problems of the form

$$U_{tt}(t) = \mathcal{F}(t, U(t), U_t(t)), \quad U(0) = U_0, \ U_t(0) = Z_0, \tag{6.12}$$

Figure 6.19: Region of stability for stiffly stable schemes for the first three members. Note that the first member corresponds to the Euler-backward scheme.

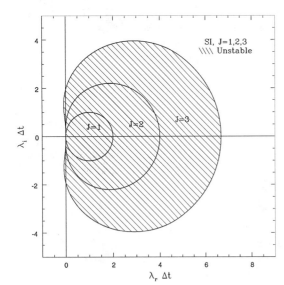

where U_0 and Z_0 are given. Such problems are encountered in flow–structure interactions, wave propagation, etc. They can be reduced to a first-order system by the simple substitution

$$U_t = Z, \quad Z_t = \mathcal{F}(t, U, Z),$$

and thus one of the explicit or implicit algorithms that we have presented previously can be used for this system.

A particularly successful approach is the **Newmark method**, which is second-order accurate and unconditionally stable for certain values of its parameters. We explain this method further, starting with the Taylor expansion of $U^{n+1} \equiv U(t + \Delta t)$, that is,

$$U^{n+1} = U^n + \Delta t U_t^n + \Delta t^2 \left(\beta U_{tt}^{n+1} + (\frac{1}{2} - \beta)U_{tt}^n \right) + \mathcal{O}(\Delta t^3),$$

where β is a parameter that determines the degree of implicit dependence. Upon substitution from Equation

(6.12), we obtain

$$U^{n+1} = U^n + \Delta t U_t^n + \Delta t^2 \left(\beta \mathcal{F}^{n+1} + (\tfrac{1}{2} - \beta)\mathcal{F}^n \right) + \mathcal{O}(\Delta t^2).$$

We also expand similarly the first derivative $U_t^{n+1} \equiv U_t(t + \Delta t)$ and substitute from Equation (6.12) to arrive at

$$U_t^{n+1} = U_t^n + \Delta t \left(\gamma \mathcal{F}^{n+1} + (1 - \gamma)\mathcal{F}^n \right) + \mathcal{O}(\Delta t^2),$$

where again γ is a parameter that determines the degree of implicit dependence.

We can now make the substitution

$$Z(t) = U_t(t)$$

to obtain the first-order system

$$U^{n+1} = U^n + \Delta t Z^n + \Delta t^2 \left(\beta \mathcal{F}^{n+1} + (\tfrac{1}{2} - \beta)\mathcal{F}^n \right) + \Delta t T_u,$$

$$Z^{n+1} = Z^n + \Delta t \left(\gamma \mathcal{F}^{n+1} + (1 - \gamma)\mathcal{F}^n \right) + \Delta t T_z.$$

The leading terms in the (local) truncation errors T_u and T_z are

$$T_u = (\tfrac{1}{6} - \beta)\Delta t^2 U_{ttt}^n + \mathcal{O}(\Delta t^3),$$

$$T_z = (\tfrac{1}{2} - \gamma)\Delta t U_{ttt}^n + \mathcal{O}(\Delta t^2).$$

Therefore, it is clear that to obtain a globally *second-order accurate* scheme we need to choose

$$\gamma = \frac{1}{2}.$$

If $\gamma \neq \tfrac{1}{2}$ then we have a scheme that is only first-order accurate. The choice of the parameter β will depend on the stability of the scheme. In particular, by considering the corresponding second-order linear oscillator

$$U_{tt} + \omega^2 U = 0,$$

we can obtain the stability requirements, which for $\gamma = \tfrac{1}{2}$ reduce to

$$\beta \geq \frac{1}{4}.$$

Finally, we can combine the two equations of this system to write a single statement for the Newmark scheme for the special case $\gamma = \tfrac{1}{2}$ and $\beta = \tfrac{1}{4}$:

$$U^{n+2} - 2U^{n+1} + U^n = \Delta t^2 \left(\frac{1}{4}\mathcal{F}^{n+2} + \frac{1}{2}\mathcal{F}^{n+1} + \frac{1}{4}\mathcal{F}^n \right).$$

In practice, it is more convenient to use the Newmark scheme in a system form instead of the single statement given here.

6.2.4 How to March in Time

We summarize here some of the most important features of the explicit and implicit time discretizations, based on which specific time integrator we decide to use in applications:

- The **Rung–Kutta** method is the easiest to use and is often a good choice, although it is somewhat inefficient. Low storage and total variation bounded schemes are useful in practice. Boundary conditions at intermediate stages may be an issue as they may affect accuracy.
- **Multistep** methods (e.g., Adams–Bashforth) are often used in discretizing convective contributions. They require substantial memory, but they are efficient. The high-order versions exhibit very low dispersion errors. In an unstable multistep time integration the error has oscillatory form.
- **Leap-frog** schemes are good for problems with complex eigenvalues.
- **Predictor–corrector** methods are good except when it is necessary to change the step size. It is also easy to estimate time errors with them. They are less stable than implicit methods.
- Stiff equations require implicit methods. For efficiency, **stiffly stable** methods (i.e., backward differentiation) are recommended.
- The truncation error of a k-order stiffly stable method is $1/k$ compared to the corresponding Adams–Moulton method.
- Typical instabilities appear in a spontaneous (explosive) way – it only takes a few time steps for the solution to blow up!

6.3 HOMEWORK PROBLEMS

1. Consider a three-point 1D stencil, consisting of the points (i) and $(i \pm 1)$. Construct the highest order difference formula of the second derivative at the point (i) that does not involve any other second-order derivatives. You may include first-order derivatives, however, as well as function values at the three points. Also, compute the truncation error. What is the computational work to compute such a derivative on an N-point grid with periodic boundary conditions?

2. Write a C++ program to compute first-order and second-order derivatives with high accuracy (greater than second order) using the implicit formulas. More specifically, design a computer library of one-dimensional implicit formulas according to the text in Section 6.1.2. For the families of different orders allow the user to input the proper parameter to select different members of the family.

3. Solve numerically the elliptic Helmholtz equation in the square domain $[-1, 1] \times [-1, 1]$, that is,

$$\nabla^2 U - \lambda U = \sin \frac{\pi x}{2} \sin \frac{\pi y}{2}, \quad \lambda = 1,000,$$

using the Padé scheme of fourth order. First use a uniform grids of 50×50 grid points and then an appropriate nonuniform grids of 25×25 grid points and 50×50 grid points. Compare the errors in the three solutions. What do you observe? Also, justify your particular selection of the nonuniform grid.

4. Solve numerically the elliptic Helmholtz equation in the wedge domain of Figure 6.20, that is,

$$\nabla^2 U - \lambda U = F(x, y), \quad \lambda = 1,$$

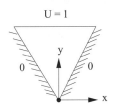

Figure 6.20: Wedge domain.

(a) using second-order finite difference explicit differentiation, and

(b) using fourth-order finite difference implicit differentiation. Consider different functions $F(x, y)$ and plot your results in terms of iso-contours of $U(x, y)$.

5. **Sherman–Morrison formula**
Prove that for a nonsingular matrix $\mathbf{T}$

$$(\mathbf{T} - \mathbf{a}_1\mathbf{a}_2^T)^{-1} = \mathbf{T}^{-1} - b^{-1}\mathbf{T}^{-1}\mathbf{a}_1\mathbf{a}_2^T\mathbf{T}^{-1},$$

where

$$b = 1 + \mathbf{a}_2^T\mathbf{T}^{-1}\mathbf{a}_1 \neq 0.$$

Now consider the Thomas algorithm for the problem with periodic boundary conditions (values c and d) and write

$$\mathbf{A} = \mathbf{T} + \mathbf{a}_1\mathbf{a}_2^T,$$

where $\mathbf{T}$ is the tridiagonal submatrix and $\mathbf{a}_1 = c\mathbf{e}_1 + d\mathbf{e}_2$ and also $\mathbf{a}_2 = \mathbf{e}_1 + \mathbf{e}_2$.

(a) Use the Sherman–Morrison formula to obtain the solution to $\mathbf{Ax} = \mathbf{b}$ using only tridiagonal solvers. What is the dominant cost to invert such matrices $\mathbf{A}$?

(b) Write the forward substitution and backward substitution using full-recursive-doubling (which will reduce the cost to $\mathcal{O}(\log n)$ for the solves).

6. Formulate a pentadiagonal solver using the same methodology as used for the Thomas algorithm.

(a) Write a C++ function to solve $\mathbf{Ax} = \mathbf{b}$, where $\mathbf{A}$ is pentadiagonal.

(b) Solve the one-dimensional heat equation

$$\frac{d^2 T}{ds^2} = \sin 2\pi s, \quad s \in [0, 1],$$

with $u(0) = u(1) = 0.0$ using a five-point explicit stencil.
Use more than one grid and compare convergence rates and computational times.

7. Add timing to the parallel Thomas algorithm function. Using the three-point stencil to approximate second derivatives, formulate the matrix $\mathbf{A}$ and use it to perform

the following tests:

(a) For $N = 10, 20, 30,$ and 100 compute the timings when using the serial version.

(b) Repeat this experiment using $P = 2, 4,$ and 8 processes.

(c) What is the parallel speedup? Does it change depending on the number of points (N) used? Explain your answer.

8. Find the parameter η for which the multistep implicit time-stepping scheme

$$\frac{U^{n+1} + \eta U^n - (1 + \eta)U^{n-1}}{\Delta t} = \frac{1}{2}[-\eta \mathcal{F}^{n+1} + (4 + 3\eta)\mathcal{F}^n]$$

is of second order and an A-stable discretization to $dU/dt = \mathcal{F}$.

9. Employ a third-order stiffly stable scheme to solve the system

$$\frac{dx}{dt} = -1000x + y,$$

$$\frac{dy}{dt} = 999x - 5y$$

assuming that $x(0) = 1$ and $y(0) = 0$. Is your solution stable for long-time integration for any Δt?

10. **Period doubling and chaos**: Consider the homework problem of Section 5.3 for *period doubling and chaos* and use the Crank–Nicolson method with step sizes $h = 0.3, 1,$ and 5 to obtain numerical solutions. Do you obtain the correct approximation to the solution for all the chosen values of h? Justify your answer.

11. Employ the method of undetermined coefficients that we studied in Sections 5.1.2 and 6.1.2 for deriving finite differences to obtain the fourth-order Adams-Bashforth scheme

$$\frac{U^{n+1} - U^n}{\Delta t} = \frac{1}{24}[55\mathcal{F}^n - 59\mathcal{F}^{n-1} + 37\mathcal{F}^{n-2} - 9\mathcal{F}^{n-3}],$$

and also the fourth-order Adams–Moulton scheme

$$\frac{U^{n+1} - U^n}{\Delta t} = \frac{1}{24}[9\mathcal{F}^{n+1} + 19\mathcal{F}^n - 5\mathcal{F}^{n-1} + \mathcal{F}^{n-2}].$$

12. Plot the stability region of the fourth-order Adams–Bashforth scheme and compare it with the stability region of the fourth-order Adams–Moulton scheme. What do you observe?

13. Plot the stability regions for stiffly stable schemes of order $p = 1$ to 6 and contrast them against the stability diagrams of Runge–Kutta schemes for order $p = 1$ to 4.

14. **Evolution of an ecosystem**: In this problem we revisit the Lotka–Volterra equations for the evolution of an ecosystem that we considered in Section 5.3 using explicit methods.

Can you solve this system by using an implicit scheme (e.g., Crank–Nicolson)? What do you observe? Compare and discuss your answers and also comment on the computational complexity of the implicit versus explicit approaches.

7

Relaxation: Discretization and Solvers

In this chapter we present discretizations for mixed initial value/boundary value problems (IVP/BVP) and for relaxation iterative solvers associated with such discretizations. The analogy between iterative procedures and equations of evolution, especially of parabolic type (diffusion), was realized about two centuries ago, but a rigorous connection was not established until the mid-1950s.

In the following, we first consider various mixed discretizations, and subsequently we derive some of the most popular iterative solvers. Our emphasis will be on parallel computing: *A good algorithm is not simply the one that converges faster but also the one that is parallelizable.* The Jacobi algorithm is such an example; forgotten for years in favor of the Gauss–Seidel algorithm, which converges twice as fast for about the same computational work, it was rediscovered during the past two decades as it is trivially parallelizable, and today it is used mostly as a preconditioner for multigrid methods. The Gauss–Seidel algorithm, although faster on a serial computer, is not parallelizable unless a special multicolor algorithm is employed, as we explain in Section 7.2.4. Based on these two basic algorithms, we present the multigrid method that exploits their good convergence properties but in a smart adaptive way.

On the parallel computing side, we introduce three new commands: *MPI_Gather*, *MPI_Allgather*, and *MPI_Scatter*. Both *MPI_Gather* and *MPI_Allgather* are used for gathering information from a collection of processes. *MPI_Scatter* is used to scatter data from one process to a collection of processes. In addition to providing syntax and usage information, we present the applicability of the gathering functions in the parallel implementation of the Jacobi method.

7.1 DISCRETE MODELS OF UNSTEADY DIFFUSION

We introduce here unsteady diffusion, a physical process, to model relaxation to equilibrium and thus convergence to a steady state, that is, a fixed point. Let us consider the one-dimensional *parabolic* equation

$$
\begin{cases}
\dfrac{\partial \Theta}{\partial t} = \kappa \dfrac{\partial^2 \Theta}{\partial x^2}, & 0 \le x \le 1, \\[2mm]
\Theta(0, t) = \Theta(1, t) = 0, \\[2mm]
\Theta(x, 0) = \sin \pi x = \Theta_0(x).
\end{cases}
\tag{7.1}
$$

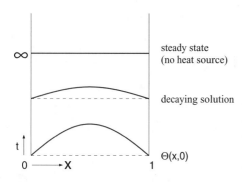

**Figure 7.1: The initial
solution specified at
$t = 0$ decays
exponentially to zero
(equilibrium state).**

Here we specify both initial conditions and boundary conditions since this is a *mixed* IVP/BVP. The dependent variable $\Theta(x, t)$ may represent the temperature and correspondingly κ can be interpreted as the thermal diffusivity. For the sinusoidal initial solution form specified, we can obtain the exact solution using separation of variables, that is,

$$\Theta(x, t) = e^{-\kappa \pi^2 t} \sin \pi x.$$

This solution decays to a steady state, which, in this particular case in the absence of any heat sources, is zero. This is shown graphically in the sketch of Figure 7.1.

We are dealing, therefore, with a continuous diffusion model that produces a solution that relaxes exponentially to the equilibrium state, that is, the steady state. Next, we will construct corresponding discrete models.

7.1.1 Temporal and Spatial Discretization

We first discretize the differential equation *in time* while keeping the spatial derivative continuous. Following a multistep discretization we obtain

$$\frac{\Theta^{n+1} - \Theta^n}{\theta \Delta t} = \mathcal{F}\left(\frac{\partial^2 \Theta^{n+1}}{\partial x^2}, \frac{\partial^2 \Theta^n}{\partial x^2}, \frac{\partial^2 \Theta^{n-1}}{\partial x^2}, \cdots\right).$$

Here $\mathcal{F}$ represents a linear combination of its arguments, and its form is determined by the time-stepping methods as in the discretization of ODEs in Sections 5.2 and 6.2. For example, following the θ-method we obtain the semidiscrete equation

$$\frac{\Theta^{n+1} - \Theta^n}{\kappa \Delta t} = \theta \frac{\partial^2 \Theta^{n+1}}{\partial x^2} + (1 - \theta) \frac{\partial^2 \Theta^n}{\partial x^2}.$$

Next, we can discretize each spatial derivative at all required time levels on the right-hand side of this equation to obtain

$$\frac{\Theta_j^{n+1} - \Theta_j^n}{\kappa \Delta t} = \theta \Delta_{xx} \Theta_j^{n+1} + (1 - \theta) \Delta_{xx} \Theta_j^n, \quad j = 1, \ldots, N - 1, \tag{7.2}$$

$$\Theta_0^{n+1} = 0 = \Theta_N^{n+1}, \tag{7.3}$$

$$\Theta_j^0 = \sin \pi x_j. \tag{7.4}$$

Specifically, we have employed the second-order three-point stencil

$$\Delta_{xx} \Theta_j \equiv \frac{1}{\Delta x^2}(\Theta_{j+1} - 2\Theta_j + \Theta_{j-1})$$

to approximate the second derivatives. The notation we adopt is as follows:

- *superscripts* denote time levels, and
- *subscripts* denote spatial location, unless otherwise stated explicitly.

In this discretization, we can obtain two fundamentally different time–space discretization stencils. Specifically,

- for $\theta = 0$ we obtain a *fully parallel* but *conditionally stable* scheme [see Figure 7.2 (left)], and
- for $\theta = 1$, we obtain a *partially parallel* but *unconditionally stable* scheme [see Figure 7.2 (right)].

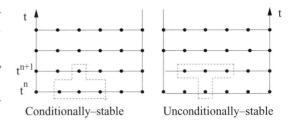

Conditionally–stable   Unconditionally–stable

Next, we will examine in some detail the properties of these and similar *time–space* stencils; we start with accuracy.

Figure 7.2:
Space–time explicit (left) and implicit (right) stencils.

7.1.2 Accuracy of Difference Equation

We will denote the convergence rate and correspondingly the accuracy of the time–space stencils using the notation

$$\mathcal{O}(\Delta t^p, \Delta x^q),$$

where p corresponds to *temporal* accuracy order and q to *spatial* accuracy order.

We rewrite the difference equation in the form

$$\frac{\Theta_j^{n+1} - \Theta_j^n}{\kappa \Delta t} - \theta \Delta_{xx}\Theta_j^{n+1} - (1-\theta)\Delta_{xx}\Theta_j^n = 0,$$

and we expand the time derivative using Taylor series as

$$\frac{\Theta_j^{n+1} - \Theta_j^n}{\Delta t} = \frac{\partial \Theta_j^n}{\partial t} + \frac{1}{2}\Delta t \frac{\partial^2 \Theta_j^n}{\partial t^2} + \mathcal{O}(\Delta t^2).$$

Next, we expand the space derivatives at time levels n and $(n+1)$ to get

$$\Delta_{xx}\Theta_j^n = \frac{\partial^2 \Theta_j^n}{\partial x^2} + \underbrace{\frac{\Delta x^2}{12}\frac{\partial^4 \Theta_j^n}{\partial x^4}}_{\mathcal{O}(\Delta x^2)} + \mathcal{O}(\Delta x^4),$$

$$\Delta_{xx}\Theta_j^{n+1} = \Delta_{xx}\Theta_j^n + \Delta t \Delta_{xx}\frac{\partial \Theta_j^n}{\partial t} + \mathcal{O}(\Delta t^2)$$

$$= \frac{\partial^2 \Theta^n}{\partial x^2} + \frac{\Delta x^2}{12}\frac{\partial^4 \Theta_j^n}{\partial x^4} + \Delta t \frac{\partial^2}{\partial x^2}\frac{\partial \Theta_j^n}{\partial t} + \mathcal{O}(\Delta t^2) + \mathcal{O}(\Delta t \Delta x^2) + \mathcal{O}(\Delta x^4).$$

Assuming it is permissible to perform the operation

$$\frac{\partial \Theta}{\partial t} = \kappa \frac{\partial^2 \Theta}{\partial x^2} \Rightarrow \frac{\partial^2 \Theta}{\partial t^2} = \kappa \frac{\partial^2}{\partial x^2}\frac{\partial \Theta}{\partial t} = \kappa \frac{\partial^4 \Theta}{\partial x^4},$$

and also setting $\kappa = 1$ for simplicity, we obtain the *difference equation*

$$\frac{\partial \Theta_j^n}{\partial t} + \frac{1}{2}\Delta t \frac{\partial^4 \Theta_j^n}{\partial x^4} + \mathcal{O}(\Delta t^2) - \theta \frac{\partial^2 \Theta_j^n}{\partial x^2} - \theta \frac{\Delta x^2}{12}\frac{\partial^4 \Theta_j^n}{\partial x^4} - \theta \Delta t \frac{\partial^4 \Theta_j^n}{\partial x^4} + \mathcal{O}(\Delta t^2) + \mathcal{O}(\Delta t^3)$$

$$- (1-\theta)\frac{\partial^2 \Theta_j^n}{\partial x^2} - (1-\theta)\frac{\partial^4 \Theta_j^n}{\partial x^4}\frac{\Delta x^2}{12} + \mathcal{O}(\Delta x^4) + \mathcal{O}(\Delta t \Delta x^2) = 0.$$

We can now collect all terms and substitute in the difference equation to obtain the *equivalent differential equation*:

$$\underbrace{\left(\frac{\partial \Theta_j^n}{\partial t} - \frac{\partial^2 \Theta_j^n}{\partial x^2}\right) - \Delta t(\theta - 1/2)\frac{\partial^4 \Theta_j^n}{\partial x^4}}_{T_j^n = \text{truncation error}}$$

$$+ \mathcal{O}(\Delta x^2) + \mathcal{O}(\Delta t^2) + \mathcal{O}(\Delta x^2, \Delta t^2) + \mathcal{O}(\Delta t \Delta x^2) = 0, \ \text{H.O.T.}$$

where H.O.T. denotes higher order terms. For *consistency* we require that the truncation error

$$T_j^n \to 0, \quad \text{for} \quad \Delta t, \Delta x \to 0,$$

which is true for this difference equation. The truncation error also reveals the order of accuracy. Specifically,

- for $\theta = 0$ or 1 the truncation error is

$T \sim \mathcal{O}(\Delta t, \Delta x^2),$

  as expected since this corresponds to the Euler-forward and Euler-backward time-stepping scheme, respectively, and
- for $\theta = 1/2$ the truncation error is

$T \sim \mathcal{O}(\Delta t^2, \Delta x^2),$

  which corresponds to a second-order (Crank–Nicolson) time-stepping scheme.

7.1.3 Stability of Difference Equation

The Lax *equivalence theorem* for linear partial differential equations (PDEs) states that if a difference equation is consistent with a PDE, that is,

$$\| T_i^n \|_2 \to 0, \quad \Delta t, \Delta x \to 0,$$

then *stability* of the difference equation is a sufficient and necessary condition for convergence.

We have already seen in Section 5.2 that for the difference equation resulting from an ODE of the form

$$\frac{dU}{dt} = \lambda U,$$

we need to march with a time step smaller than a critical value, that is,

$$\Delta t < \Delta t_c(\lambda),$$

where here in Equation (7.1), λ corresponds to the eigenvalues of the Laplacian operator since we can write

$$\frac{\partial^2 \Theta}{\partial^2 x} = \lambda \Theta,$$

and in general

$$\nabla^2\Theta = \lambda\Theta.$$

These eigenvalues depend on the spatial discretization parameter Δx, so we expect that for *conditional stability* we would have

$$\Delta t < \mathcal{F}(\Delta x).$$

The specific form of the right-hand side will depend on the spatial differential operator.

We can also use physical intuition to justify the constraint $\Delta t < \mathcal{F}(\Delta x)$. To this end, let us consider a semi-infinite plate of thermal diffusivity κ and model the heat propagation through this medium by Equation (7.1) (Figure 7.3). By performing dominance balance on this equation assuming a characteristic spacing Δx and characteristic time scale Δt_c we obtain

$$\frac{\Theta}{\Delta t_c} \sim \kappa \frac{\Theta}{\Delta x^2} \Rightarrow \Delta t_c \sim \frac{\Delta x^2}{\kappa}.$$

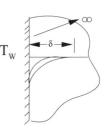

Figure 7.3: Propagation of heat in a semi-infinite medium.

To resolve that time scale we require that

$$\Delta t < \Delta t_c \Rightarrow \Delta t < C \frac{\Delta x^2}{\kappa},$$

where $C \sim \mathcal{O}(1)$, that is, C is a constant of *order one*. This inequality can be rewritten as

$$D \equiv \frac{\kappa \Delta t}{\Delta x^2} < C, \tag{7.5}$$

which simply states that the nondimensional left-hand side, termed *diffusion number*, should be less than a constant of *order unity* for proper temporal resolution of the heat propagation in this isotropic medium.

In the following, we will demonstrate three different ways of obtaining the exact stability constraint, that is, the value of the constant C. We will start from the more intuitive perturbation method, and we will proceed with the classical von Neumann analysis and a more general method based on matrices.

Discrete Perturbation Stability Analysis

This method is based on the physics of propagation of perturbation. A discrete perturbation in $\Theta(x, t)$ is introduced into the equation at an arbitrary point, and its effect is followed in time. Stability is indicated if the perturbation dies out [78].

To demonstrate this approach we employ for simplicity the Euler-forward timestepping scheme. Let us introduce a disturbance ϵ into the difference equation at time level n at grid point i, and follow its evolution in time, that is,

$$\frac{\Theta_i^{n+1} - (\Theta_i^n + \epsilon)}{\Delta t} = \underbrace{\kappa}_{\text{thermal diffusivity}} \frac{\Theta_{i+1}^n - 2(\Theta_i^n + \epsilon) + \Theta_{i-1}^n}{\Delta x^2}.$$

Let us also assume that at time level n we have $\Theta_i^n = 0$, and thus

$$\frac{\Theta_i^{n+1} - \epsilon}{\Delta t} = -2 \frac{\kappa \epsilon}{\Delta x^2}.$$

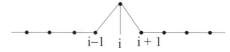

$i-1 \quad i \quad i+1$

Figure 7.4: Initial disturbance introduced at time level n.

The initial disturbance at time level n is shown schematically in Figure 7.4. The disturbance distribution at the next time level is determined by

$$\Theta_i^{n+1} = \epsilon(1 - 2D),$$

where D is the diffusion number [see Equation (7.5)]. We note here that Θ_i^{n+1} represents the evolving disturbance (since $\Theta_i^n = 0$) of the initial disturbance ϵ. We now require that

$$\left| \frac{\Theta_i^{n+1}}{\epsilon} \right| \leq 1 \Rightarrow -1 \leq 1 - 2D \leq 1, \tag{7.6}$$

and therefore

$$D \leq 1.$$

If we require that no *overshoots* or *undershoots* appear in the solution, that is, we want to prevent spurious oscillations, we will need to impose the *same sign* constraint,

$$\Theta_i^{n+1}/\epsilon \geq 0,$$

which in turn leads to a more strict upper limit for the diffusion number, that is,

$$D \leq 1/2.$$

At the $(n+1)$ time level we can obtain the new perturbation at all grid points from the difference equation: $\Theta_{i\pm1}^{n+1} = \epsilon D$; thus

$$\Theta_i^{n+2} = \Theta_i^{n+1} + D[\Theta_{i+1}^{n+1} + \Theta_{i-1}^{n+1} - 2\Theta_i^{n+1}]$$
$$= \epsilon(1 - 2D) + D[\epsilon D + \epsilon D - 2\epsilon(1 - 2D)],$$

and therefore

$$\Theta_i^{n+2} = \epsilon(1 - 4D + 6D^2).$$

We require also at this time level that disturbances do not grow; that is, we impose

$$\left| \frac{\Theta_i^{n+2}}{\epsilon} \right| \leq 1 \Rightarrow -1 \leq 1 - 4D + 6D^2 \leq 1,$$

which is satisfied for

$$D \leq 2/3.$$

Graphically, the evolution of disturbance for the first few time steps is described in Figure 7.5, and after many time steps the asymptotic spreading of a single perturbation approaches a $2\Delta x$ *wave*. Therefore, the most dangerous disturbance is produced asymptotically and corresponds to an amplitude ϵ'. The difference equation then gives

$$\Theta_i^{n+1} = \epsilon' + D(-\epsilon' - 2\epsilon' - \epsilon') = \epsilon'(1 - 4D).$$

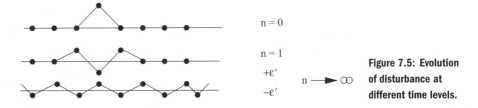

Figure 7.5: Evolution of disturbance at different time levels.

For stability we require that

$$\left| \frac{\Theta_i^{n+1}}{\epsilon'} \right| \le 1 \Rightarrow -1 \le 1 - 4D \le 1,$$

and from this we deduce that

$$D \le 1/2.$$

If we now compare this constraint on the diffusion number derived from the asymptotic spreading of the disturbance with the initial requirement of preventing spurious oscillations we come to the following conclusion:

- *The long-time stability requirement is equivalent to the requirement for zero overshoots for an isolated disturbance.*

The von Neumann Stability Analysis

This approach was developed by John von Neumann in the early 1940s at Los Alamos, and it is the most popular method. It assumes that the domain is infinite in extent or periodic and employs the discrete analog of Fourier series expansions in the form

$$\Theta_j^n = \sum_{k=1}^{N-1} a_k^n \sin \pi k x_j,$$

with $\Theta_0^n = \Theta_N^n = 0$ and $x_j = j \cdot \Delta x$; a_k^n are the Fourier sine coefficients. The main idea is to reduce the *difference* equation for Θ_j^n into an uncoupled ordinary difference equation for a_k^n and subsequently require that

$$|a_k^{n+1}| \le |a_k^n|$$

to guarantee *absolute stability*.

To proceed we use the general identity

$$\Theta_{j-1} - 2\Theta_j + \Theta_{j+1} = \sum_{k=1}^{N-1} a_k [\sin \pi k \Delta x (j-1) - 2 \sin \pi k \Delta x j + \sin \pi k \Delta x (j+1)]$$

$$= \sum_{k=1}^{N-1} a_k \sin \pi k \Delta x j (2 \cos \pi k \Delta x - 2)$$

$$= - \sum_{k=1}^{N-1} \sigma_k a_k \sin \pi k \Delta x j,$$

where $\Delta x = 1/N$ and

$$\sigma_k \equiv 2(1 - \cos \pi k \Delta x), \quad \text{where} \quad 0 < \sigma_\kappa < 4.$$

We analyze the time–space stencil corresponding to the θ-method again, and upon substitution in the difference equation (7.2) we obtain

$$\Theta_j^{n+1} - \Theta_j^n = \theta D(\Theta_{j-1}^{n+1} - 2\Theta_j^{n+1} + \Theta_{j+1}^{n+1}) + D(1 - \theta)(\Theta_{j-1}^n - 2\Theta_j^n + \Theta_{j+1}^n),$$

and therefore

$$\sum_{k=1}^{N-1} (a_k^{n+1} - a_k^n) \sin \pi k x_j = D\theta \sum_{k=1}^{N-1} -\sigma_k a_k^{n+1} \sin \pi k x_j + D(1 - \theta) \sum_{k=1}^{N-1} -\sigma_k a_k^n \sin k \pi x_j,$$

or

$$a_k^{n+1} - a_k^n = -D\theta \sigma_k a_k^{n+1} - D(1 - \theta)\sigma_k a_k^n,$$

and finally

$$a_k^{n+1} = a_k^n \left(\frac{1 - D(1 - \theta)\sigma_k}{1 + D\theta\sigma_k} \right). \tag{7.7}$$

We can now obtain specific forms for the three main members of the family:

- $\theta = 0$ corresponds to the *Euler-forward* scheme. We obtain

$$a_k^{n+1} = a_k^n(1 - D\sigma_k) \Rightarrow |1 - D\sigma_k| \le 1 \Rightarrow D \le 2/\sigma_k, \ \forall k.$$

  Since $\max \sigma_k = 4$, $\forall k$, we have that $D \le 1/2$, as before.
- $\theta = 1/2$ corresponds to the *Crank–Nicolson* scheme. Here we obtain

$$a_k^{n+1} = \frac{1 - \frac{D\sigma_k}{2}}{1 + \frac{D\sigma_k}{2}} a_k^n.$$

  This is an unconditionally stable scheme. It damps high-frequency components very weakly, although these components may (physically) decay very rapidly. However, for $\theta = 1/2 + \alpha \Delta t$, where α is a small positive constant, all components of the solution are damped and the method is still formally second-order accurate in time, that is, $\mathcal{O}(\Delta t^2)$.
- $\theta = 1$ corresponds to the *Euler-backward* scheme. We have

$$a_k^{n+1} = \frac{a_k^n}{1 + D\sigma_k}.$$

  This is also an unconditionally stable scheme, and it damps high-frequency components very rapidly.

The structure of the instability can be studied by examining the most dangerous mode, which corresponds to

$$k = N - 1 \Rightarrow \sigma_{k,\max} = 4,$$

and therefore

$$\epsilon \sim \sin \pi (N - 1)x$$

with wavelength

$$\frac{2\pi}{\pi(N-1)} \sim \frac{2}{N} = 2\Delta x.$$

Therefore, the error has a "sawtooth" form with wavelength $2\Delta x$, as our previous perturbation analysis also showed.

Matrix Methods for Stability Analysis

This is the most general method and is suitable for studying the effect of boundary conditions on the stability of the difference equation. The main idea is to follow the *method of lines*, where we discretize the space derivatives first while we keep the time derivatives continuous. For example, for the heat equation (7.1) we obtain the vector equation

$$\frac{d\Theta_j}{dt} = \mathbf{A}\Theta_j,$$

where $\mathbf{A}$ is the discrete operator

$$\mathbf{A} = \frac{\kappa}{\Delta x^2}(\mathbf{E} - 2\mathbf{I} + \mathbf{E}^{-1})$$

defined in terms of the displacement operator $\mathbf{E}$ (see Section 5.1). In this form, we can examine the eigenspectrum of the matrix obtained from the operator $\mathbf{A}$ to determine the stability of the difference equation.

Before we treat the effect of boundary conditions, however, we revisit the heat equation with periodic boundary conditions, and in this context we introduce the matrix stability analysis. To this end, we obtain the fully discrete form of Equation (7.1)

$$\Theta_j^{n+1} = \mathbf{C}\Theta_j^n, \quad \mathbf{C} = \mathbf{I} + \Delta t \cdot \mathbf{A} = \mathbf{I} + D(\mathbf{E} - 2\mathbf{I} + \mathbf{E}^{-1}),$$

where D is the diffusion number. This form corresponds to the Euler-forward scheme ($\theta = 0$) as before. We can recover the von Neumann analysis here by introducing a *single* harmonic perturbation

$$\Theta_j^n = \hat{\Theta}^n e^{ij\phi}, \quad \text{where} \quad \phi_\kappa = \phi = k\frac{\pi}{N}.$$

Upon substitution, we obtain

$$\hat{\Theta}^{n+1} = \underbrace{\mathbf{G}(\phi)}_{\text{amplification matrix}} \hat{\Theta}^n = [G(\phi)]^n \hat{\Theta}^1.$$

For stability $[\mathbf{G}(\phi)]^n$ has to be bounded, and thus the von Neumann necessary condition for stability is

$$\rho(\mathbf{G}) = \max_k |\lambda_k| \leq 1,$$

where $\rho(\mathbf{G})$ is the *spectral radius* of the matrix $\mathbf{G}$. (Actually, the more precise condition is $\leq 1 + \mathcal{O}(\Delta t)$; see [77]). If $\mathbf{G}$ is a *normal matrix* (i.e., it commutes with its Hermitian conjugate), then the condition $\rho(\mathbf{G}) \leq 1$ is also a *sufficient* condition.

EXAMPLE 1 – THE EULER-FORWARD SCHEME. We can clarify this matrix further by considering the Euler-forward scheme, which we have already analyzed with the previous two methods. We first introduce a single harmonic in the equation

$$\Theta_j^{n+1} = \Theta_j^n + \frac{\kappa \Delta t}{\Delta x^2}(\Theta_{j+1}^n - 2\Theta_j^n + \Theta_{j-1}^n),$$

and we have also defined $D \equiv \kappa \Delta t / \Delta x^2$. Here we have a scalar equation, and the amplification factor is

$$e^{ij\phi}G(\phi) = e^{ij\phi} + \frac{\kappa \Delta t}{\Delta x^2}(e^{i(j+1)\phi} - 2e^{ij\phi} + e^{i(j-1)\phi})$$

$$\Rightarrow G(\phi) = 1 + D(e^{i\phi} - 2 + e^{-i\phi})$$

$$\Rightarrow G(\phi) = 1 - 4D\sin^2(\phi/2).$$

Thus, we require that

$$|G(\phi)| \leq 1 \Rightarrow 0 \leq D \leq 1/2,$$

and we recover the condition derived previously with the other two methods.

For the Euler-forward scheme we can also use the amplification factor $G(\phi)$ to analyze the nature of the error. The exact solution we obtained can be rewritten as

$$\Theta^n = e^{-i\omega(n\Delta t)} \cdot e^{ikj\Delta x} \cdot \Theta_0^*(k),$$

where $\Theta_0^*(k)$ is the harmonic corresponding to initial data, so

$$\Theta^n = (e^{-i\omega\Delta t})^n e^{ikj\Delta x}\Theta_0^*(k) = G^n e^{ikj\Delta x}\Theta_0^*(k).$$

Thus, $G = e^{-i\omega\Delta t}$ is the exact amplification factor, where $\omega = \omega(k)$ defines the exact *dispersion relation*. Let

$$\omega = \omega_r + i\omega_i;$$

then

$$G = e^{\omega_i \Delta t} \cdot e^{-i\omega_r \Delta t} = |G|e^{-i\Phi},$$

where $\Phi = \omega_r \Delta t$ and $|G| = e^{\omega_i \Delta t}$. To compare the error in *amplitude*, we define

$$\epsilon_D = \frac{|G|}{e^{\omega_i \Delta t}}$$

for numerical *dissipation*. Similarly, to compare the error in *phase*, we define

$$\epsilon_\phi = \frac{\Phi}{\omega_r \Delta t},$$

for numerical *dispersion*. Specifically, for the Euler-forward time discretization of Equation (7.1) we have

$$\omega = -i\kappa k^2 = -iD\frac{\phi^2}{\Delta t}, \quad \text{where} \quad \phi = \frac{k\pi}{N} = k\Delta x.$$

Therefore, the dissipation error is

$$\epsilon_D^{\text{EF}} = \frac{1 - 4D\sin^2(\phi/2)}{e^{-D\phi^2}} = \frac{1 - D\phi^2 + D\phi^4/12 + \dots}{1 - D\phi^2 + (D^2\phi^4/2) + \dots}$$

or

$$\epsilon_D^{\text{EF}} \approx 1 - \frac{D^2\phi^4}{2} + \frac{D\phi^4}{12} + \dots \approx 1 - \frac{\kappa^2 k^4 \Delta t^2}{2} + \frac{\kappa k^4}{12}\Delta t\Delta x^2 - \dots.$$

Clearly, for *low frequencies* ($\phi \approx 0$) there are only small errors, and specifically for $D = 1/6$ we obtain a high-order scheme, that is, $\mathcal{O}(\Delta t^2, \Delta x^4)$!

EXAMPLE 2 - THE DUFORT-FRANKEL SCHEME. This is an example of an *inconsistent scheme*, which sometimes converges and sometimes does not, and this is a very dangerous practice. It involves two previous time levels, and so the amplification factor is now a matrix and not a scalar as before. We first apply the *leap-frog* scheme to Equation (7.1), that is,

$$\Theta_j^{n+1} - \Theta_j^{n-1} = 2D(\Theta_{j+1}^n - 2\Theta_j^n + \Theta_{j-1}^n).$$

Then, we average *in time* the term Θ_j^n on the right-hand side to obtain $\frac{1}{2}[\Theta_j^{n+1} + \Theta_j^{n-1}]$, and upon substitution into the previous expression, we have

$$\Theta_j^{n+1} - \Theta_j^{n-1} = 2D(\Theta_{j+1}^n - \Theta_j^{n+1} - \Theta_j^{n-1} + \Theta_{j-1}^n),$$

or

$$\Theta_j^{n+1}(1 + 2D) = \Theta_j^{n-1}(1 - 2D) + 2D(\Theta_{j+1}^n + \Theta_{j-1}^n).$$

Let us now introduce a new variable $z^n = \Theta^{n-1}$ and recast this equation into the system

$$\Theta_j^{n+1} = \frac{1 - 2D}{1 + 2D}z^n + \frac{2D}{1 + 2D}(\Theta_{j+1}^n + \Theta_{j-1}^n),$$

$$z_j^{n+1} = \Theta_j^n.$$

In matrix form, if we set $\mathbf{W} = \begin{bmatrix} \Theta_j^n \\ z_j^n \end{bmatrix}$, we have

$$\mathbf{W}^{n+1} = \mathbf{C}\mathbf{W}^n, \quad \text{where} \quad \mathbf{C} = \begin{bmatrix} \frac{2D(E+E^{-1})}{1+2D} & \frac{1-2D}{1+2D} \\ 1 & 0 \end{bmatrix}.$$

The corresponding amplification matrix becomes

$$\mathbf{G} = \begin{bmatrix} \frac{2D(e^{i\phi}+e^{-i\phi})}{1+2D} & \frac{1-2D}{1+2D} \\ 1 & 0 \end{bmatrix} = \begin{bmatrix} \frac{4D\cos\phi}{1+2D} & \frac{1-2D}{1+2D} \\ 1 & 0 \end{bmatrix}$$

with eigenvalues

$$\lambda_\pm = \frac{2D\cos\phi \pm \sqrt{1 - 4D^2\sin^2\phi}}{1 + 2D},$$

and for

$$D > 0 \Rightarrow |\lambda \pm| < 1, \quad \forall \phi.$$

This result, which implies unconditional stability for an explicit scheme, is suspicious! It clearly violates the second stability barrier of Dahlquist (see Section 6.2.1). To analyze this, we need to examine convergence, and thus we need to consider the consistency of this scheme. To this end, we obtain the *equivalent differential equation*

$$\Theta_t - \kappa \Theta_{xx} = -\frac{\Delta t^2}{6} \Theta_{tt} + \kappa \frac{\Delta x^2}{12} \left(\frac{\partial^4 \Theta}{\partial x^4} \right) + \frac{\kappa \Delta x^4}{360} \left(\frac{\partial^6 \Theta}{\partial x^6} \right)$$

$$- \kappa \frac{\Delta t^2}{\Delta x^2} \Theta_{tt} - \frac{\kappa \Delta t^4}{12 \Delta x^2} \left(\frac{\partial^4 \Theta}{\partial t^4} \right) + \dots .$$

In the limit as $\Delta t, \Delta x \to 0$ at the *same rate* the ratio $\Delta t / \Delta x$ is constant, and thus we solve a modified differential equation and not the original Equation (7.1). Specifically, we solve

$$\frac{\partial \Theta}{\partial t} + \underbrace{\kappa \left(\frac{\Delta t}{\Delta x} \right)^2 \frac{\partial^2 \Theta}{\partial t^2}}_{\text{extra term}} = \kappa \frac{\partial^2 \Theta}{\partial x^2}.$$

We have a clear violation of the consistency condition! However, in practice one can take the diffusion number $D = \kappa \Delta t / \Delta x^2$ to be constant, and then the DuFort–Frankel scheme is almost consistent since $\Delta t \to 0$ faster than $\Delta x \to 0$.

7.1.4 Spectrum of the Diffusion Operator

Next, we examine the eigenspectrum of the matrix

$$\mathbf{A} = \frac{\kappa}{\Delta x^2} (\mathbf{E} - 2\mathbf{I} + \mathbf{E}^{-1})$$

corresponding to different types of boundary conditions. Specifically, we consider the following:

- *Dirichlet boundary conditions*: Let us assume that $\Theta_0(0) = a$, $\Theta_N = b$. Then the equations for the end points are

$$\frac{d\Theta_1}{dt} = \frac{\kappa}{\Delta x^2} (a - 2\Theta_1 + \Theta_2)$$

and

$$\frac{d\Theta_{N-1}}{dt} = \frac{\kappa}{\Delta x^2} (b - 2\Theta_{N-1} + \Theta_{N-2}).$$

The corresponding linear system is

$$
\frac{d\Theta}{dt} = \frac{\kappa}{\Delta x^2}
\begin{bmatrix}
-2 & 1 & & & \\
1 & -2 & 1 & & \\
& 1 & -2 & 1 & \\
& & \ddots & \ddots & \ddots \\
& & & 1 & -2
\end{bmatrix}
\begin{bmatrix}
\Theta_1 \\ \vdots \\ \vdots \\ \vdots \\ \Theta_{N-1}
\end{bmatrix}
+
\begin{bmatrix}
\frac{\kappa a}{\Delta x^2} \\ \vdots \\ 0 \\ \vdots \\ \frac{\kappa b}{\Delta x^2}
\end{bmatrix}.
$$

- *Neumann boundary conditions*: We assume that $\frac{\partial \Theta}{\partial x}|_0 = a$ and $\Theta_N = b$. For the boundary point with the Neumann condition we have

$$
\frac{1}{\Delta x}(\Theta_1 - \Theta_0) = a \Rightarrow \Theta_0 = \Theta_1 - a\Delta x,
$$

and thus

$$
\frac{d\Theta_1}{dt} = \frac{\kappa}{\Delta x^2}(\Theta_0 - 2\Theta_1 + \Theta_2) = \frac{\kappa}{\Delta x^2}(-\Theta_1 + \Theta_2 - a\Delta x).
$$

The corresponding linear system is

$$
\frac{d\Theta}{dt} = \frac{\kappa}{\Delta x^2}
\begin{bmatrix}
-1 & 1 & & & \\
1 & -2 & 1 & & \\
& 1 & -2 & 1 & \\
& & & \ddots & \\
& & & 1 & -2
\end{bmatrix}
\begin{bmatrix}
\Theta_1 \\ \vdots \\ \vdots \\ \vdots \\ \Theta_{N-1}
\end{bmatrix}
+
\begin{bmatrix}
-\frac{\kappa a}{\Delta x} \\ \vdots \\ 0 \\ \vdots \\ \frac{\kappa b}{\Delta x^2}
\end{bmatrix}.
$$

- *Periodic boundary conditions*: We assume that $\Theta_0 = \Theta_N$ and $\Theta_{-1} = \Theta_{N-1}$. The equations for the boundary points are

$$
\frac{d\Theta_0}{dt} = \frac{\kappa}{\Delta x^2}(\Theta_{N-1} - 2\Theta_0 + \Theta_1),
$$

$$
\frac{d\Theta_{N-1}}{dt} = \frac{\kappa}{\Delta x^2}(\Theta_0 - 2\Theta_{N-1} + \Theta_{N-2}).
$$

Then

$$
\frac{d\Theta}{dt} = \frac{\kappa}{\Delta x^2}
\begin{bmatrix}
-2 & 1 & & & 1 \\
1 & -2 & 1 & & \\
& 1 & -2 & 1 & \\
& & & \ddots & \\
1 & & & 1 & -2
\end{bmatrix}
\begin{bmatrix}
\Theta_0 \\ \vdots \\ \\ \\ \Theta_{N-1}
\end{bmatrix}.
$$

It can be shown (see Section 7.3) that the eigenvalues of a general tridiagonal matrix $\mathbf{B}(a, b, c)$ of rank N determined from the condition $\det |\mathbf{B}(a, b - \lambda, c)| = 0$ are given

by

$$\lambda_j = b + 2\sqrt{(ac)} \cos \frac{j\pi}{N+1}, \ \ j = 1, \ldots, N,$$

and the corresponding eigenvectors are

$$\phi_m^{(j)} = C_j \left(\frac{a}{c}\right)^{(m-1)/2} \sin m \left(\frac{j\pi}{N+1}\right), \ \ m = 1, \ldots, N.$$

Notice that the eigenvectors do not depend on the diagonal element b and that C_j is arbitrary and is determined by normalization conditions.

Similarly, for the *periodic case* we have

$$\lambda_j = b + ae^{-i2\pi j/N} + ce^{i2\pi j/N},$$

$$\phi_m^j = C_j e^{i(2\pi j/N)m}, \ \text{ where } m = 1, \ldots, N,$$

which can be obtained directly from the properties of a *circulant* matrix.

Specifically now for the Diffusion operator we have the following:

- *Dirichlet boundary conditions*:

$$\lambda_j = \frac{-4\kappa}{\Delta x^2} \sin^2 \left(\frac{\pi j}{2(N+1)}\right), \ \ j = 1, \ldots, N.$$

- *Periodic boundary conditions*:

$$\lambda_j = \frac{-4\kappa}{\Delta x^2} \sin^2 \left(\frac{\pi j}{N}\right).$$

- *Neumann–Dirichlet boundary conditions*:

$$\lambda_j = \frac{-4\kappa}{\Delta x^2} \sin^2 \frac{(2j-1)\pi}{(2N+1)2}.$$

The important conclusion from inspecting these eigenvalues is that they grow as N^2 since $\Delta x \sim 1/N$. We also note that for the Euler-forward scheme we recover again

$$\Delta t < 2/|\lambda| \Rightarrow D \le 1/2$$

as before. Finally, we observe that all type of boundary conditions lead to stable discretizations, unlike the discrete *convection* equation (see Chapter 8). Stability here is satisfied if $\text{Re}(\lambda_j) \le 0$, $\forall \ j$. In addition, if $\lambda_j = 0$ it has to be a simple eigenvalue.

Experiments with Euler-Forward and Euler-Backward

Software

Suite

We will now consider both an Euler-forward and an Euler-backward time integration combined with the second-order finite difference spatial differentiation operator.

First, we present a C++ function that incorporates a central finite difference scheme with the Euler-forward time integration scheme. The function takes as input the number of points in the grid, the diffusion number DN, an array containing the current value of the solution *uold*, and an array *unew* into which to place the solution at the new time. Observe that we only update the interior points $1, \ldots, N-2$, leaving the boundary conditions to be handled separately.

```
void Diffusion_EF_CentralDifference(int N, double DN,
                                     double *uold, double
                                            *unew){

  for(int i=1;i<N-1;i++)
    unew[i] = uold[i] + DN*(uold[i+1] - 2.0*uold[i]
        + uold[i-1]);

  return;
}
```

Observe that this function is fully explicit, both in space and in time. Given the current value of the solution at a particular time, the solution at the next time step is obtained by finite differencing and explicit time marching. Compare this with the Euler-backward implementation, which uses implicit time marching.

We now present a C++ function that incorporates a central finite difference scheme with the Euler-backward time integration scheme. The function takes as input the number of points in the grid, the diffusion number *DN*, an array containing the current value of the solution *uold*, and an array *unew* into which to place the solution at the new time. To solve the Euler-backward problem, we use our Thomas algorithm tridiagonal solver. The tridiagonal system is formed by the second-order finite difference operator. Observe that we only update the interior points $1, \ldots, N-2$ [by passing only $(N-2)$ points to the *ThomasAlgorithm* function], leaving the boundary conditions to be handled separately.

Software

Suite

```
void Diffusion_EB_CentralDifference(int N, double DN,
                                     double *uold, double
                                            *unew){

  ThomasAlgorithm(N-2,-DN,1.0+2.0*DN,-DN,&unew[1],&uold[1]);

  return;
}
```

Notice the use of "&" in the preceding code. Recall what this means – the "&" operator gives us "the address of." So, in the preceding expression, we are passing to the *ThomasAlgorithm* routine the *address* of the second entry of the *uold* and the *unew* array. In Figure 7.6, we show the memory addressing for the *unew* array and how the "&" operator can be used to obtain memory addresses for elements of the *unew* array.

Programming Note

As a model problem for the Euler-forward and Euler-backward implementations presented here, we will examine the problem of finding the solution $\Theta(x, t)$ of Equation (7.1) on the interval [0, 1] with the boundary conditions $\Theta(0, t) = \Theta(1, t) = 0.0$. We

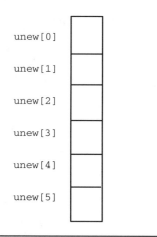

Array Indexing		Memory Indexing
&unew[0]	=	unew
&unew[1]	=	unew + 1
&unew[2]	=	unew + 2
....		....

Figure 7.6: Memory addressing for the array unew.

present a total of three numerical experiments, two cases using Euler-forward and one case using Euler-backward.

EXPERIMENT 1 – EULER-FORWARD WITH D = 0.7. For this experiment, we use the parameters as given in Table 7.1. The results are presented in Figure 7.7. This choice of the parameter D is clearly above the $D \leq 0.5$ necessary for stability. Observe in Figure 7.7 the $2\Delta x$ instability that renders the computation useless in very few iterations.

EXPERIMENT 2 – EULER-FORWARD WITH D = 0.4. For this experiment, we use the parameters as given in Table 7.2. The results are presented in Figure 7.8. This choice of the parameter D is clearly below the $D \leq 0.5$ necessary for stability. Observe in Figure 7.8 that the solution remains stable and agrees quite well with the exact solution for the three different times presented.

EXPERIMENT 3 – EULER-BACKWARD WITH D = 1.0. For this experiment, we use the parameters as given in Table 7.3. The results are presented in Figure 7.9. Because we now use an implicit method for the time integration, we are no longer bound by the $D \leq 0.5$ limit imposed for Euler-forward. Observe in Figure 7.9 that the solution remains stable and agrees quite well with the exact solution for the three time instances presented. Because of the use of a larger D, however, fewer iterations are necessary than in the Euler-forward case.

7.1.5 MultiDimensional Time–Space Stencils

We now turn to two-dimensional domains to demonstrate how we obtain discrete models of diffusion. Let us consider the unsteady diffusion equation in a domain Ω (see Figure 7.10) with heat sources $q(x, t)$, that is,

$$\frac{\partial \Theta}{\partial t} = \nabla^2 \Theta + q, \qquad (7.8)$$

$$\Theta(x, y, t) = 0 \text{ on } \partial\Omega, \qquad (7.9)$$

$$\Theta(x, y, 0) = \Theta_0(x, y) \text{ in } \Omega. \qquad (7.10)$$

We have assumed that we have homogeneous boundary conditions and that $\Theta_0(x, y)$ is a known function. We employ the θ-method to discretize this *in time* first, that is,

$$\frac{\Theta^{n+1} - \Theta^n}{\Delta t} = \theta(\nabla^2\Theta^{n+1} + q^{n+1})$$
$$+ (1-\theta)(\nabla^2\Theta^n + q^n).$$

Table 7.1: Parameters used for the simulations presented in Figure 7.7.

Parameter	Value
Method	Euler-forward central difference
Interval	[0, 1]
N	21
Δt	0.00175
D	0.7
Initial condition	$u(x, 0) = \sin(\pi x)$
Boundary conditions	$u(0, t) = u(1, t) = 0$

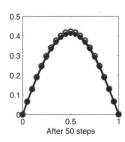
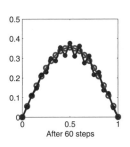
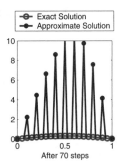

After 50 steps After 60 steps After 70 steps

Figure 7.7: Euler-forward/central difference versus exact solution at different times for $D = 0.7$.

We now use the Cartesian five-point stencil (see Section 5.1) to discretize in space,

$$\frac{\Theta_{ij}^{n+1} - \Theta_{ij}^{n}}{\Delta t} = \theta \left[\frac{\Theta_{i+1,j}^{n+1} - 2\Theta_{ij}^{n+1} + \Theta_{i-1,j}^{n+1}}{\Delta x^2} + \frac{\Theta_{i,j+1}^{n+1} - 2\Theta_{ij}^{n+1} + \Theta_{i,j-1}^{n+1}}{\Delta y^2} \right]$$
$$+ (1 - \theta) \left[\frac{\Theta_{i+1,j}^{n} - 2\Theta_{ij}^{n} + \Theta_{i-1,j}^{n}}{\Delta x^2} + \frac{\Theta_{i,j+1}^{n} - 2\Theta_{ij}^{n} + \Theta_{i,j-1}^{n}}{\Delta y^2} \right]$$
$$+ \theta q_{ij}^{n+1} + (1 - \theta) q_{ij}^{n} .$$

The accuracy of this discretization can be obtained by examining the truncation error, and as expected is as follows:

- For $\theta = 0$ or $\theta = 1$, the overall accuracy is $\mathcal{O}(\Delta t, \Delta x^2, \Delta y^2)$.
- For $\theta = 1/2$, the overall accuracy is $\mathcal{O}(\Delta t^2, \Delta x^2, \Delta y^2)$.

Directional Splitting Method

We consider again the diffusion equation (7.1) with $\kappa = 1$. One of the most economical approaches in solving this problem is to split directions and perform one-dimensional solves on corresponding and equivalent PDEs. The key to successful implementation of this idea is the construction of the new approximate equations. In the following, we demonstrate a few different ways of accomplishing this task.

Table 7.2: Parameters used for the simulations presented in Figure 7.8.

ALTERNATING-DIRECTION-IMPLICIT METHOD. In two dimensions, the alternating-direction-implicit (ADI) method solves implicitly along the x-direction first, and subsequently it solves implicitly along the y-direction. This is done in two steps as follows:

$$pass\ I: \quad \frac{\Theta_{i,j}^{*} - \Theta_{i,j}^{n}}{\Delta t} = \Theta_{xx}^{*} + \Theta_{yy}^{n} ,$$

$$pass\ II: \quad \frac{\Theta_{i,j}^{n+1} - \Theta_{i,j}^{*}}{\Delta t} = \Theta_{xx}^{*} + \Theta_{yy}^{n+1} .$$

Parameter	Value
Method	Euler-forward central difference
Interval	$[0, 1]$
N	21
Δt	0.001
D	0.4
Initial condition	$u(x, 0) = \sin(\pi x)$
Boundary conditions	$u(0, t) = u(1, t) = 0$

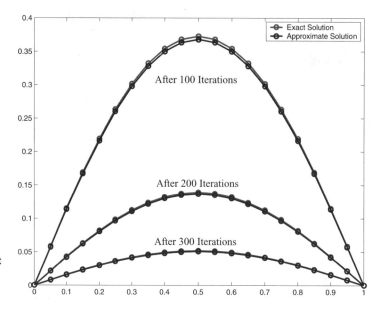

Figure 7.8:
Euler-forward/central
difference versus exact
solution at different
times for $D = 0.4$.

From pass I we obtain Θ^* and from pass II we obtain the final solution Θ^{n+1}. To avoid bias toward one direction, we can alternate the order in the $x-$ and y-directions every step. This method is $\mathcal{O}(\Delta t^2, \Delta x^2, \Delta y^2)$, and it is unconditionally stable. However, in the presence of time-dependent boundary conditions the two substeps introduce boundary errors of different orders, that is, $\mathcal{O}(\Delta t)$ and $\mathcal{O}(\Delta t^2)$, to the solution.

APPROXIMATE FACTORIZATION. We consider the time-discrete equation

$$\frac{\Theta_{ij}^{n+1} - \Theta_{ij}^n}{\Delta t} = \left(\frac{\partial^2}{\partial x^2} + \frac{\partial^2}{\partial y^2} \right) \Theta_{ij}^{n+1},$$

which is rewritten in Helmholtz operator form as

$$\left\{ 1 - \Delta t \left(\frac{\partial^2}{\partial x^2} + \frac{\partial^2}{\partial y^2} \right) \right\} \Theta_{ij}^{n+1} = \Theta_{ij}^n.$$

We then *approximate* this by the product of two *one-dimensional* operators:

$$\left(1 - \Delta t \frac{\partial^2}{\partial x^2} \right) \left(1 - \Delta t \frac{\partial^2}{\partial y^2} \right) \Theta_{ij}^{n+1} \approx \Theta_{ij}^n,$$

which can be solved in two passes:

$$pass\ I: \left(1 - \Delta t \frac{\partial^2}{\partial y^2} \right) \Theta_{i,j}^* = \Theta_{i,j}^n,$$

$$pass\ II: \left(1 - \Delta t \frac{\partial^2}{\partial x^2} \right) \Theta_{ij}^{n+1} = \Theta_{ij}^*.$$

Table 7.3: Parameters
used for the
simulations presented
in figure 7.9.

Parameter	Value
Method	Euler-backward central difference
Interval	$[0, 1]$
N	21
Δt	0.0025
D	1.0
Initial condition	$u(x, 0) = \sin(\pi x)$
Boundary conditions	$u(0, t) = u(1, t) = 0$

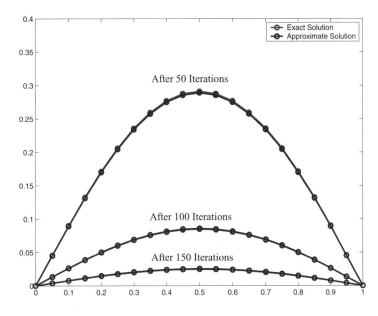

Figure 7.9: Euler-
backward/central
difference versus exact
solution at varying
times for $D = 1.0$.

Multiplying the two one-dimensional Helmholtz operators we obtain

$$\left\{ 1 - \Delta t \left(\frac{\partial^2}{\partial x^2} + \frac{\partial^2}{\partial y^2} \right) + \underbrace{\Delta t^2 \left(\frac{\partial^2}{\partial x^2} \frac{\partial^2}{\partial y^2} \right)}_{\text{extra term}} \right\} \Theta_{ij}^{n+1} = \Theta_{ij}^n.$$

Therefore, the factorization has introduced an extra term that is $\mathcal{O}(\Delta t^2)$ and is equal to the *local error* of the Euler-backward discretization.

EXAMPLE: ADI FACTORIZATION VERSUS CRANK–NICOLSON. We consider discretizations over a time interval of $2\Delta t$. We first construct a Crank–Nicolson time discretization

$$\Theta^{n+2} - \Theta^n = \frac{2\Delta t}{2} \left\{ \left(\Theta_{xx}^{n+2} + \Theta_{yy}^{n+2} \right) + \left(\Theta_{xx}^n + \Theta_{yy}^n \right) \right\}$$

$$\Rightarrow \left\{ 1 - \Delta t \left(\frac{\partial^2}{\partial x^2} + \frac{\partial^2}{\partial y^2} \right) \right\} \Theta^{n+2} = \left\{ 1 + \Delta t \left(\frac{\partial^2}{\partial x^2} + \frac{\partial^2}{\partial y^2} \right) \right\} \Theta^n$$

and an approximate factorization:

$$\left(1 - \Delta t \frac{\partial^2}{\partial x^2} \right) \Theta^{n+1} = \left(1 + \Delta t \frac{\partial^2}{\partial y^2} \right) \Theta^n,$$

$$\left(1 - \Delta t \frac{\partial^2}{\partial y^2} \right) \Theta^{n+2} = \left(1 + \Delta t \frac{\partial^2}{\partial x^2} \right) \Theta^{n+1},$$

where we have assumed that all these linear operators are commutative.

**Figure 7.10:
Two-dimensional
domain.**

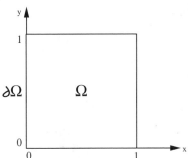

Therefore, for the factorization we obtain

$$\left(1 - \Delta t \frac{\partial^2}{\partial x^2}\right)\left(1 - \Delta t \frac{\partial^2}{\partial y^2}\right)\Theta^{n+2} = \left(1 + \Delta t \frac{\partial^2}{\partial x^2}\right)\left(1 + \Delta t \frac{\partial^2}{\partial y^2}\right)\Theta^n,$$

and expanding further we obtain

$$\left\{1 - \Delta t \left(\frac{\partial^2}{\partial x^2} + \frac{\partial^2}{\partial y^2}\right) + \Delta t^2 \left(\frac{\partial^2}{\partial x^2}\frac{\partial^2}{\partial y^2}\right)\right\}\Theta^{n+2}$$

$$= \left\{1 + \Delta t \left(\frac{\partial^2}{\partial x^2} + \frac{\partial^2}{\partial y^2}\right) + \Delta t^2 \left(\frac{\partial^2}{\partial x^2}\frac{\partial^2}{\partial y^2}\right)\right\}\Theta^n.$$

Comparing this ADI form and the Crank–Nicolson form we see that there is an extra term in the factorization, namely,

$$A = \Delta t^2 \left(\frac{\partial^2}{\partial x^2}\frac{\partial^2}{\partial y^2}\right)\left(\Theta^{n+2} - \Theta^n\right).$$

We can approximate

$$\frac{\partial \Theta^n}{\partial t} = \frac{\Theta^{n+2} - \Theta^n}{2\Delta t} + \mathcal{O}(\Delta t) \Rightarrow A \approx 2\Delta t^3 \left(\frac{\partial^2}{\partial x^2}\frac{\partial^2}{\partial y^2}\right)\frac{\partial \Theta^n}{\partial t},$$

which is an $\mathcal{O}(\Delta t^3)$ term and thus consistent with the local error in the Crank–Nicolson approximation. Therefore, the accuracy between the two approaches is comparable, but in the approximate factorization only one-dimensional solves are involved.

ADI FOR STATIONARY PROBLEMS. ADI methods can also be used to solve the system resulting from a stationary elliptic equation, that is,

$$\Theta_{xx} + \Theta_{yy} = q.$$

Assuming that we discretize with the three-point central difference in each direction we obtain

$$[\mathbf{A}_x + \mathbf{A}_y]\Theta = \mathbf{q}, \tag{7.11}$$

where $\mathbf{A}_x$ and $\mathbf{A}_y$ are the discrete operators in x- and y-directions, respectively. In the following, we present algorithms for two-dimensional and three-dimensional discretizations.

Peaceman–Rachford Algorithms for Two Dimensions

The idea here is to combine ADI with convergence acceleration tricks, that is,

$$(\mathbf{A}_x + \rho_n\mathbf{I})\Theta^* = (\rho_n\mathbf{I} - \mathbf{A}_y)\Theta^n + \mathbf{q},$$

$$(\mathbf{A}_y + \rho_n\mathbf{I})\Theta^{n+1} = (\rho_n\mathbf{I} - \mathbf{A}_x)\Theta^* + \mathbf{q},$$

where $\rho_n, n = 1, \ldots,$ is a sequence of positive acceleration parameters. Also, $\mathbf{I}$ is the identity operator.

For positive-definite systems, $\mathbf{A}_x$ and $\mathbf{A}_y$ have real eigenvalues and several theoretical results hold (see [89]). For example, if $\mathbf{A}_x$, $\mathbf{A}_y$ are positive-definite and symmetric, any sequence $\rho_n = C > 0$ will produce a convergent iteration. The rate of convergence of ADI can be greatly enhanced by a sequence ρ_n in *cyclic* order.

Douglas–Rachford Algorithm for Three Dimensions

Here we consider the three-dimensional analog of Equation (7.11) split in three directions as follows:

$$(\mathbf{A}_x + \rho_n\mathbf{I})\Theta^* = -(\mathbf{A}_x + 2\mathbf{A}_y + 2\mathbf{A}_z - \rho_n\mathbf{I})\Theta^n + 2\mathbf{q},$$

$$(\mathbf{A}_y + \rho_n\mathbf{I})\Theta^{**} = -(\mathbf{A}_x + \mathbf{A}_y + 2\mathbf{A}_z - \rho_n\mathbf{I})\Theta^n - \mathbf{A}_x\Theta^* + 2\mathbf{q},$$

$$(\mathbf{A}_z + \rho_n\mathbf{I})\Theta^{***} = -(\mathbf{A}_x + \mathbf{A}_y + \mathbf{A}_z - \rho_n\mathbf{I})\Theta^n - \mathbf{A}_x\Theta^* - \mathbf{A}_y\Theta^{**} + 2\mathbf{q}.$$

We note here that convergence is not always guaranteed for $\rho_n = C > 0$.

Stability Analysis

We can apply von Neumann analysis similarly to the one-dimensional case, that is,

$$\Theta_{ij}^n = \sum_k \sum_\ell a_{k\ell}^n \sin k\pi x_i \sin \ell\pi y_j.$$

We then substitute this expression into the *homogeneous* difference equation to obtain the uncoupled recursion for $a_{k\ell}^n$:

$$a_{k\ell}^{n+1} = a_{k\ell}^n \frac{1 - D(1-\theta)\sigma_{k\ell}}{1 + D\theta\sigma_{k\ell}},$$

$$\sigma_{k\ell} = 2[(1 - \cos k\pi \Delta x) + \delta^2(1 - \cos \ell\pi \Delta y)] > 0,$$

where $\delta = \Delta x/\Delta y$ and $D = \Delta t/\Delta x^2$ is the *diffusion number*. For the specific members of the θ-family the following are true:

- For $\theta = 1/2, 1$, we have unconditional stability.
- For $\theta = 0$, we have explicit time discretization; thus

$$-1 \leq 1 - D\sigma_{k\ell} \leq 1 \Rightarrow D \leq \frac{2}{\sigma_{k\ell}},$$

where

$$\max_{k,\ell} \sigma_{k\ell} = 4(1 + \delta^2).$$

Therefore, $D \leq \frac{1}{2(1+\delta^2)}$ and thus

$$\Delta t \leq \frac{1}{2} \frac{1}{2\left(\frac{1}{\Delta x^2} + \frac{1}{\Delta y^2}\right)}.$$

If $\Delta x = \Delta y$ then

$$\Delta t \leq \frac{\Delta x^2}{4}.$$

This condition is more restrictive than in the one-dimensional case where $\Delta t \leq \Delta x^2/2$!

REMARK 1: In three dimensions the diffusion number limit is 1/8 (obtained by similar analysis). Therefore, if we double the resolution in one-dimensional problems the cost is increased by a factor of 8, whereas if we double the resolution in three-dimensional problems the cost is increased by a factor of 32!

REMARK 2: Implicit time discretization requires the solution of a stationary elliptic equation of the Helmholtz type, since

$$\frac{\Theta^{n+1} - \Theta^n}{\Delta t} = \nabla^2 \Theta^{n+1} + q^{n+1}$$

and by rearranging we obtain

$$\left(\nabla^2 - \frac{1}{\Delta t}\right)\Theta^{n+1} = -\frac{\Theta^n}{\Delta t} - q^{n+1},$$

which is an A-stable scheme.

We can also apply **matrix methods** as in the one-dimensional case to analyze the stability of multidimensional difference equations. For example, for two-dimensional problems with *periodic boundary* conditions we consider a single harmonic component $e^{i\phi_x}e^{i\phi_y}$, then discretizing with the θ-family we obtain

$$G - 1 = \theta DG[(e^{i\phi_x} + e^{-i\phi_x} - 2) + \delta^2(e^{i\phi_y} + e^{-i\phi_y} - 2)]$$
$$+ (1 - \theta)D[(e^{i\phi_x} + e^{-i\phi_x} - 2) + \delta^2(e^{i\phi_y} + e^{-i\phi_y} - 2)],$$

and therefore

$$G = \frac{1 - 4D(1-\theta)[\sin^2\frac{\phi_x}{2} + \delta^2\sin^2\frac{\phi_y}{2}]}{1 + 4D\theta[\sin^2\frac{\phi_x}{2} + \delta^2\sin^2\frac{\phi_y}{2}]},$$

where $\delta \equiv \frac{\Delta x}{\Delta y}$. For the specific members of the family:

- For $\theta = 0$, we obtain

$$|1 - 4D(\sin^2\frac{\phi_x}{2} + \delta^2\sin^2\frac{\phi_y}{2})| \leq 1,$$

  which for $\Delta x = \Delta y$ leads to $D \leq \frac{1}{4}$ or $\Delta t \leq \frac{\Delta x^2}{4\kappa}$, as before.
- For $\theta = 1, 1/2$, we have unconditional stability $\forall\, D > 0$.

7.2 ITERATIVE SOLVERS

Discretization of the diffusion equation leads us naturally to iterative solutions of elliptic problems of the form

$$\nabla^2 \Theta + q = 0 \text{ on } \Omega, \quad \Theta(x, y) = 0 \text{ on } \partial\Omega, \tag{7.12}$$

where Ω and $\partial\Omega$ are the domain and the boundary of the domain, respectively (see Figure 7.11). Here we assume homogeneous boundary conditions for clarity in the presentation.

This connection becomes more clear by introducing a *pseudo-time derivative* to obtain

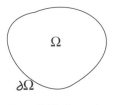

$$\frac{\partial \Theta}{\partial t} = \nabla^2 \Theta + q \text{ on } \Omega, \quad \Theta(x, y) = 0 \text{ on } \partial\Omega. \tag{7.13}$$

Figure 7.11: General two-dimensional domain Ω.

We then compute the sequence

$$\Theta_{ij}^0, \; \Theta_{ij}^1, \; \Theta_{ij}^2, \ldots, \; \Theta_{ij}^{n-1}, \; \Theta_{ij}^n, \ldots, \; \Theta_{ij}^{\infty}$$

from Equation (7.13) in the limit of many iterations. Therefore, Θ_{ij}^{∞} is the steady-state solution, which is different from the exact solution owing to *spatial* discretization error. Any other member of the sequence differs from the exact solution by the spatial discretization error as well as the solver convergence error; we will analyze the latter in the following.

7.2.1 Jacobi Algorithm

We now demonstrate how we can derive the algorithm for perhaps the oldest iterative solver, the Jacobi iterative method. We apply Euler-forward discretization to the diffusion equation (7.13) assuming that we have a two-dimensional domain Ω [such as in Figure 7.12 (left)] and taking $\Delta x = \Delta y$. We also assume that we are given some function q defined on the domain [such as in Figure 7.12 (right)]. We then have

$$\frac{\Theta_{ij}^{n+1} - \Theta_{ij}^n}{\Delta t} = q_{ij} + \frac{1}{\Delta x^2}(\Theta_{i+1,j}^n + \Theta_{i,j+1}^n - 4\Theta_{ij}^n + \Theta_{i,j-1}^n + \Theta_{i-1,j}^n),$$

or

$$\Theta_{ij}^{n+1} = \Delta t \cdot q_{ij} + D(\Theta_{i+1,j}^n + \Theta_{i,j+1}^n - 4\Theta_{ij}^n + \Theta_{i-1,j}^n + \Theta_{i,j-1}^n) + \Theta_{ij}^n,$$

Figure 7.12: Example domain (left) and function $q(x, y)$ (right) used to demonstrate the Jacobi algorithm.

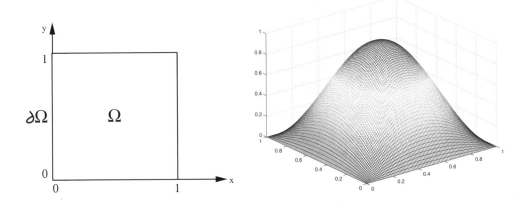

where $D = \Delta t/\Delta x^2$ is the diffusion number defined in Equation (7.5). To determine the *rate of convergence*, we write

$$\Theta_{ij}^n = \Theta_{ij}^\infty + \epsilon_{ij}^n,$$

where ϵ_{ij}^n is the deviation from the fixed point, that is, the steady state.

It is also clear that Θ_{ij}^∞ satisfies the difference equation

$$\frac{1}{\Delta x^2}(\Theta_{i+1,j}^\infty + \Theta_{i,j+1}^\infty - 4\Theta_{ij}^\infty + \Theta_{i-1,j}^\infty + \Theta_{i,j-1}^\infty) + q_{ij} = 0.$$

By subtracting these two difference formulas we obtain an equation for the convergence error:

$$\epsilon_{ij}^{n+1} = \epsilon_{ij}^n + D(\epsilon_{i+1,j}^n + \epsilon_{i,j+1}^n - 4\epsilon_{ij}^n + \epsilon_{i-1,j}^n + \epsilon_{i,j-1}^n).$$

Convergence is obtained if $|\epsilon^n| \to 0$, which is implied by absolute stability. Therefore, we require that $D \leq 1/4$ and specifically we take $D = 1/4$ for the fastest possible convergence.

Given this analysis we can now write the **Jacobi algorithm** for solving Equation (7.12) in the form

$$\Theta_{ij}^{n+1} = \frac{1}{4}(\Theta_{i+1,j}^n + \Theta_{i,j+1}^n + \Theta_{i-1,j}^n + \Theta_{i,j-1}^n + \Delta x^2 q_{ij})$$

for all the *interior points*. Appropriate modifications with one-sided differences may be required to construct similar equations applied at the boundary.

Software
Suite

PUTTING IT INTO PRACTICE

We now present a C++ implementation of the algorithm previously discussed. This function takes as input the number of points N, the grid spacing dx, the time step δt, the matrix **A** as a *double* $**$ array, the right-hand-side vector **q**, and a stopping tolerance.

```
int Diffusion_Jacobi(int N, double dx, double dt,
      double **A, double **q, double abstol){
  int i,j,k;
  int maxit = 100000;
  double sum;
  double ** Aold = CreateMatrix(N,N);

  double D = dt/(dx*dx);

  for(i=1; i<N-1; i++)
    for(j=1;j<N-1;j++)
      Aold[i][j] = 1.0;

  /* Boundary Conditions -- all zeros */
  for(i=0;i<N;i++){
    A[0][i] = 0.0;
    A[N-1][i] = 0.0;
```

```
      A[i][0] = 0.0;
      A[i][N-1] = 0.0;
  }

  for(k=0; k<maxit; k++){
    for(i = 1; i<N-1; i++){
      for(j=1; j<N-1; j++){
          A[i][j] = dt*q[i][j] + Aold[i][j] +
              D*(Aold[i+1][j] + Aold[i][j+1] - 4.0*Aold[i][j] +
                      Aold[i-1][j] + Aold[i][j-1]);
      }
    }

    sum = 0.0;
    for(i=0;i<N;i++){
      for(j=0;j<N;j++){
        sum += (Aold[i][j]-A[i][j])*(Aold[i][j]-A[i][j]);
        Aold[i][j] = A[i][j];
      }
    }

    if(sqrt(sum)<abstol){
      DestroyMatrix(Aold,N,N);
      return k;
    }

  }

  cerr << "Jacobi: Maximum Number of Interations Reached \n";
  DestroyMatrix(Aold,N,N);

  return maxit;

}
```

REMARK: Remember to free dynamically allocated memory when exiting a routine. Often programmers forget to free things when they exit a function after a particular tolerance is found. Observe in this code that if the tolerance is reached, we first free the dynamically allocated memory, and then we return the value k.

You must often decide which resource is more valuable – memory or computation. In this example, we expend extra memory to store boundary conditions, which are zero, so that the computational algorithm is simple. If we had to save memory, then we would need to explicitly write code, which takes into account the modification of the differencing stencil when we are computing along the edges and corners of the domain.

Programming Note

Convergence Rate

The convergence error ϵ^n satisfies the same equation as the $a_{k\ell}^n$ modes in the von Neumann equation (7.7) of the previous section, that is,

$$\epsilon_{k\ell}^{n+1} = \epsilon_{k\ell}^n \left\{ \frac{1 - \frac{1}{4}(1-\theta)\sigma_{k\ell}}{1 + \frac{\theta}{4}\sigma_{k\ell}} \right\},$$

where we set $\theta = 0$ for Euler-forward discretization and $\delta = 1$ since $\Delta x = \Delta y$. Therefore

$$\epsilon_{k\ell}^{n+1} = \epsilon_{k\ell}^n (1 - \frac{1}{4}\sigma_{k\ell}),$$

where

$$\sigma_{k\ell} = 2[(1 - \cos k\pi\,\Delta x) + (1 - \cos \pi\ell\,\Delta y)].$$

The minimum of $\sigma_{k\ell}$ corresponds to the most "resistant" error in decaying. This occurs for $k = \ell = 1$, and thus we obtain for an error estimate

$$\epsilon^{n+1} = \epsilon^n \left[1 - \frac{1}{2}[(1 - \cos \pi\,\Delta x) + (1 - \cos \pi\,\Delta x)] \right],$$

or

$$\epsilon^{n+1} = \epsilon^n [1 - (1 - \cos \pi\,\Delta x)],$$

which can be approximated as

$$\epsilon^{n+1} \approx \epsilon^n \left(1 - \frac{\pi^2 \Delta x^2}{2} \right).$$

We now define the *convergence rate* z_J of the Jacobi method as

$$z_J \equiv \frac{\epsilon^{n+1}}{\epsilon^n} = \left(1 - \frac{\pi^2 \Delta x^2}{2} \right);$$

therefore

$$\epsilon^n = z_J^n \epsilon^0,$$

where n on z_J^n is an exponent, whereas elsewhere it denotes iteration level.

To reduce ϵ^n to e^{-d}, that is, to obtain accuracy defined by $z_J^n = e^{-d}$, we have

$$n \ln z_J = -d \Rightarrow -n\frac{\pi^2 \Delta x^2}{2} \sim -d \Rightarrow n \sim \frac{2}{\pi^2}\frac{d}{\Delta x^2} \text{ iterations.}$$

Here $\Delta x = \frac{1}{N}$, and d is roughly equal to the number of correct digits in the solution. Therefore, the number of iterations is proportional to the total number of grid points in a two-dimensional grid $N \times N$, that is,

$$n \sim \mathcal{O}(N^2).$$

The corresponding computational work is

$$z_J * \mathcal{O}(N^2) \approx \mathcal{O}(N^4)$$

since we need at least one operation for each grid point. This corresponds to more work than $\mathcal{O}(N^3)$ required for a backsolve in Gaussian elimination, although to factorize the matrix by LU requires $\mathcal{O}(N^4)$ (see Section 9.1). These estimates assume that we solve the elliptic problem (7.12) on a grid $N \times N$ with center differencing resulting in a matrix with order N^2 and bandwidth $m = N$. The number of backsolve operations in the Gaussian elimination is then $\mathcal{O}(mN^2) = \mathcal{O}(N^3)$.

In the preceding analysis, we considered specifically the *discrete diffusion equation* to derive the Jacobi iteration algorithm. However, this is not necessary, and the Jacobi iteration can be employed to solve general linear systems of the form

$$\mathbf{A}\mathbf{x} = \mathbf{b}.$$

To this end, we decompose the matrix $\mathbf{A}$ as

$$\mathbf{A} = \underbrace{\mathbf{L}}_{\text{(strictly lower)}} + \underbrace{\mathbf{D}}_{\text{(diagonal)}} + \underbrace{\mathbf{U}}_{\text{(strictly upper)}}.$$

Denoting by n the iteration number, we formulate the following iteration procedure:

$$\mathbf{D}\mathbf{x}^{n+1} = \mathbf{b} - (\mathbf{L} + \mathbf{U})\mathbf{x}^n.$$

This is the general Jacobi algorithm, which does not requires matrix inversion as the diagonal matrix is trivially inverted, that is,

$$\mathbf{D}^{-1} = \frac{1}{\mathbf{D}},$$

assuming nonzero diagonal entries.

As an example, we can recover the Jacobi algorithm specific to diffusion equation from

$$\frac{-4}{\Delta x^2}\Theta_{ij}^{n+1} = -q_{ij} - \frac{1}{\Delta x^2}(\Theta_{i+1,j}^n + \Theta_{i,j+1}^n + \Theta_{i-1,j}^n + \Theta_{i,j-1}^n),$$

or

$$\Theta_{ij}^{n+1} = \frac{1}{4}(\Theta_{i+1,j}^n + \Theta_{i,j+1}^n + \Theta_{i-1,j}^n + \Theta_{i,j-1}^n + \Delta x^2 q_{ij})$$

as before.

The general Jacobi iteration converges if matrix $\mathbf{A}$ is strictly *row-diagonally dominant*. This means that the absolute value of each diagonal element of $\mathbf{A}$ is greater than the sum of absolute values of all the other entries in that row. However, this condition does not apply to the discrete diffusion equation considered here. Instead, a weaker condition is applied, by requiring that the matrix $\mathbf{A}$ is weakly row-diagonally dominant. This simply implies that some of the diagonal elements may be equal to the sum in each row but may be greater on at least one row. This condition needs to be strengthened with the condition of *irreducibility*.

The irreducibility condition is related to the *directed graph* of the matrix, which consists of a sequence of nodes with arrows connecting the nonzero entries of a matrix. If each node in the graph is accessible by any other node, then this is a strongly connected graph and the corresponding matrix is irreducible. Together the two conditions of weak row-diagonal dominance and of irreducibility guarantee that the Jacobi method will converge for systems resulting from central difference discretizations of the diffusion equation. Note that the cross-directional splitting of Section 7.1.5 leads to a matrix with a corresponding graph that is not strongly connected.

Programming Note

What tolerance should you use? This depends on the problem you are trying to solve. If the modeling error for your problem is $\mathcal{O}(10^{-4})$, there may not be a need to converge your solution to $\mathcal{O}(10^{-14})$. The bottom line is this: Know and understand the problem that you are trying to solve!

Software
Suite

In the *software suite* we implement the Jacobi algorithm again but this time we take into account the prespecified tolerance.

7.2.2 Parallel Jacobi Algorithm

In our implementation of the parallel Jacobi algorithm, we will use an MPI command not previously discussed: *MPI_Allgather*. *MPI_Gather* and *MPI_Allgather* provide us with the ability to assemble (gather) data from a collection of processes and combine them either on one specific process (*MPI_Gather*) or on all processes (*MPI_Allgather*). MPI also provides an inverse operation called *MPI_Scatter*, which distributes data from one process to a collection of processes. We will now present for these three functions the function call syntax, argument list explanation, usage example, and some remarks.

MPI_Gather

MPI

FUNCTION CALL SYNTAX

```
int MPI_Gather(
        void*        sendbuf     /* in  */,
        int          sendcount   /* in  */,
        MPI_Datatype sendtype    /* in  */,
        void*        recvbuf     /* out */,
        int          recvcount   /* in  */,
        MPI_Datatype recvtype    /* in  */,
        int          root        /* in  */,
        MPI_Comm     comm        /* in  */)
```

MPI

UNDERSTANDING THE ARGUMENT LIST

- *sendbuf* – starting address of the send buffer.
- *sendcount* – number of elements in the send buffer.
- *sendtype* – data type of the elements in the send buffer.
- *recvbuf* – starting address of the receive buffer.

- *recvcount* – number of elements for any *single* receive.
- *recvtype* – data type of the elements in the receive buffer.
- *root* – rank of the root process obtaining the result.
- *comm* – communicator.

EXAMPLE OF USAGE

```
int mynode, totalnodes;
int datasize; // number of data units to be gathered
              //    from each process
int root;     // process to which the data are gathered

MPI_Init(&argc,&argv);
MPI_Comm_size(MPI_COMM_WORLD, &totalnodes);
MPI_Comm_rank(MPI_COMM_WORLD, &mynode);

// Determine datasize and root

double * senddata = new double[datasize];
double * recvdata = NULL;
if(mynode == root)
  recvdata = new double[datasize*totalnodes];

// Fill in senddata array for each process

MPI_Gather(senddata,datasize,MPI_DOUBLE,recvdata,datasize,
          MPI_DOUBLE,root,MPI_COMM_WORLD);

// At this point, process root has received from each
// process the contents of senddata and stored them
// in recvdata according to the process ordering
```

MPI

REMARKS

MPI

- *MPI_Gather* allows us to "gather" to one specified process information from all processes with the communicator. This *collection* function allows us to retrieve from all processes information that may need to be acted upon in an assembled form. In Figure 7.13 we present a schematic demonstrating the results of a gather operation from all processes to process 0.

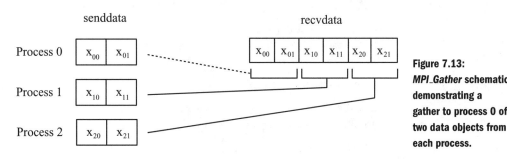

Figure 7.13: *MPI_Gather* schematic demonstrating a gather to process 0 of two data objects from each process.

- The array *recvbuf* is only relevant on the process of rank root. All other processes may pass NULL in place of the argument for *recvbuf*.
- In most cases the *sendtype* and *recvtype* are identical, and the value of *sendcount* and the value of *recvcount* are identical. MPI requires that the amount of data sent (sendcount times the size in bytes of the datatype sendtype) equals the amount of data received (recvcount times the size in bytes of the datatype recvtype) per process/root pair.
- The allocated size of *recvbuf* should be equal to at least the value of *recvtype* times the number of processes (*totalnodes*).

MPI_Allgather

MPI

FUNCTION CALL SYNTAX

```
int MPI_Allgather(
        void*         sendbuf     /*  in   */,
        int           sendcount   /*  in   */,
        MPI_Datatype  sendtype    /*  in   */,
        void*         recvbuf     /*  out  */,
        int           recvcount   /*  in   */,
        MPI_Datatype  recvtype    /*  in   */,
        MPI_Comm      comm        /*  in   */)
```

MPI

UNDERSTANDING THE ARGUMENT LIST

- *sendbuf* – starting address of the send buffer.
- *sendcount* – number of elements in the send buffer.
- *sendtype* – data type of the elements in the send buffer.
- *recvbuf* – starting address of the receive buffer.
- *recvcount* – number of elements for any *single* receive.
- *recvtype* – data type of the elements in the receive buffer.
- *comm* – communicator.

MPI

EXAMPLE OF USAGE

```
int mynode, totalnodes;
int datasize; // number of data units to be
              //      gathered from each process

MPI_Init(&argc,&argv);
MPI_Comm_size(MPI_COMM_WORLD, &totalnodes);
MPI_Comm_rank(MPI_COMM_WORLD, &mynode);

// Determine datasize and root

double * senddata = new double[datasize];
double * recvdata = new double[datasize*totalnodes];

// Fill in senddata array for each process
```

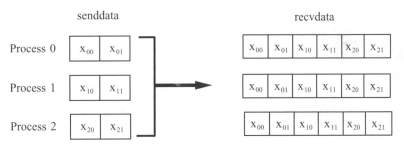

Figure 7.14:
MPI_Allgather
schematic
demonstrating an
"allgather" to all
processes of two data
objects from each
process.

```
MPI_Allgather(senddata,datasize,MPI_DOUBLE,recvdata,datasize,
              MPI_DOUBLE,MPI_COMM_WORLD);

// At this point, each process has received from every other
// process the contents of senddata and stored them
// in recvdata according to the process ordering
```

REMARKS

MPI

- *MPI_Allgather* allows us to "gather" to all processes information from all processes with the communicator. The action of "allgather" is as if we were to gather to one process using *MPI_Gather*, and then send from that process to all other processes the assembled information. In Figure 7.14 we present a schematic demonstrating the results of an "allgather" operation.
- Both the *sendbuf* and *recvbuf* arrays are relevant on all processes in the communicator.
- In most cases the *sendtype* and *recvtype* are identical, and the value of *sendcount* and the value of *recvcount* are identical. MPI requires that the amount of data sent (sendcount times the size in bytes of the datatype sendtype) equals the amount of data received (recvcount times the size in bytes of the datatype recvtype) per process/root pair.
- The allocated size of *recvbuf* should be at least equal to the value of *recvtype* times the number of processes (*totalnodes*).

MPI_Scatter

```
int MPI_Scatter(
        void*           sendbuf     /*  in   */,
        int             sendcount   /*  in   */,
        MPI_Datatype    sendtype    /*  in   */,
        void*           recvbuf     /*  out  */,
        int             recvcount   /*  in   */,
        MPI_Datatype    recvtype    /*  in   */,
        int             root        /*  in   */,
        MPI_Comm        comm        /*  in   */)
```

```
MPI
```

UNDERSTANDING THE ARGUMENT LIST

- *sendbuf* – starting address of the send buffer.
- *sendcount* – number of elements in the send buffer.
- *sendtype* – data type of the elements in the send buffer.
- *recvbuf* – starting address of the receive buffer.
- *recvcount* – number of elements for any *single* receive.
- *recvtype* – data type of the elements in the receive buffer.
- *root* – rank of the root process obtaining the result.
- *comm* – communicator.

```
MPI
```

EXAMPLE OF USAGE

```
int mynode, totalnodes;
int datasize; // number of data units to be scattered to
    each process
int root;        // process from which the data are scattered

MPI_Init(&argc,&argv);
MPI_Comm_size(MPI_COMM_WORLD, &totalnodes);
MPI_Comm_rank(MPI_COMM_WORLD, &mynode);

// Determine datasize and root

double * senddata = NULL;
if(mynode == root)
  senddata = new double[datasize*totalnodes];

double * recvdata = new double[datasize];

// Fill in senddata array on process root

MPI_Scatter(senddata,datasize,MPI_DOUBLE,recvdata,datasize,
            MPI_DOUBLE,root,MPI_COMM_WORLD);

// At this point, each process has received from root
// process the part of the contents of senddata which
// it is to receive (based on the process ordering)
```

```
MPI
```

REMARKS

- *MPI_Scatter* allows us to "scatter" from one specified process information to all processes with the communicator. This function allows us to distribute partitioned data to all processes. In Figure 7.15 we present a schematic demonstrating the results of a scatter operation from process 0 to all processes within the communicator.
- The array *sendbuf* is only relevant on the process of rank root. All other processes may pass NULL in place of the argument for *sendbuf*.

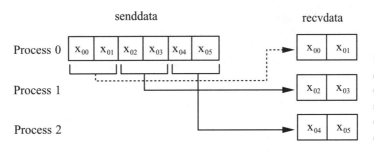

Figure 7.15: *MPI_Scatter* schematic demonstrating a scatter from process 0 of two data objects to each process.

- In most cases the *sendtype* and *recvtype* are identical, and the value of *sendcount* and the value of *recvcount* are identical. MPI requires that the amount of data sent (sendcount times the size in bytes of the datatype sendtype) equals the amount of data received (recvcount times the size in bytes of the datatype recvtype) per process/root pair.
- The allocated size of *sendbuf* should be at least equal to the value of *sendtype* times the number of processes (*totalnodes*).
- Each *recvdata* array should contain at least *datasize* elements.

PUTTING IT INTO PRACTICE

We now present a parallel implementation of the Jacobi method. This function assumes that the MPI initialization has already been accomplished by the calling function. It takes as input its process id number, the total number of processes being used, the size of the matrix, the matrix **A** as a *double**∗∗* array, an array *x* into which the solution is to be stored, an array *b* containing the right-hand side, and a stopping tolerance. On all processes other than the root process, the pointers *A*, *x*, and *b* should be NULL; process 0 distributes the matrix and right-hand side among the processes, and only process 0 returns the solution vector **x**. We first present the function definition and then present some remarks on the code.

```
int Jacobi_P(int mynode, int numnodes, int N, double **A,
             double *x, double *b, double abstol){
  int i,j,k,i_global;
  int maxit = 100000;
  int rows_local,local_offset,last_rows_local;
  int *count,*displacements;
  double sum1,sum2,*xold;
  double error_sum_local, error_sum_global;
  MPI_Status status;

  rows_local = (int) floor((double)N/numnodes);
  local_offset = mynode*rows_local;
  if(mynode == (numnodes-1))
    rows_local = N - rows_local*(numnodes-1);

  /*Distribute the Matrix and R.H.S. among the processors */
```

Software Suite

```
if(mynode == 0){
  for(i=1;i<numnodes-1;i++){
    for(j=0;j<rows_local;j++)
      MPI_Send(A[i*rows_local+j],N,MPI_DOUBLE,i,j,
               MPI_COMM_WORLD);

    MPI_Send(b+i*rows_local,rows_local,MPI_DOUBLE,i,
             rows_local, MPI_COMM_WORLD);
  }
  last_rows_local = N-rows_local*(numnodes-1);
  for(j=0;j<last_rows_local;j++)
    MPI_Send(A[(numnodes-1)*rows_local+j],N,MPI_DOUBLE,
             numnodes-1,j,MPI_COMM_WORLD);
  MPI_Send(b+(numnodes-1)*rows_local,last_rows_local,
           MPI_DOUBLE,numnodes-1,last_rows_local,
           MPI_COMM_WORLD);
}
else{
  A = CreateMatrix(rows_local,N);
  x = new double[rows_local];
  b = new double[rows_local];
  for(i=0;i<rows_local;i++)
    MPI_Recv(A[i],N,MPI_DOUBLE,0,i,MPI_COMM_WORLD,&status);
  MPI_Recv(b,rows_local,MPI_DOUBLE,0,rows_local,
           MPI_COMM_WORLD,&status);
}

xold = new double[N];
count = new int[numnodes];
displacements = new int[numnodes];

//set initial guess to all 1.0
for(i=0; i<N; i++){
  xold[i] = 1.0;
}

for(i=0;i<numnodes;i++){
  count[i] = (int) floor((double)N/numnodes);
  displacements[i] = i*count[i];
}
count[numnodes-1] = N - ((int)floor((double)N/numnodes))*
                    (numnodes-1);

for(k=0; k<maxit; k++){
  error_sum_local = 0.0;
  for(i = 0; i<rows_local; i++){
    i_global = local_offset+i;
    sum1 = 0.0; sum2 = 0.0;
```

```
      for(j=0; j < i_global; j++)
        sum1 = sum1 + A[i][j]*xold[j];
      for(j=i_global+1; j < N; j++)
        sum2 = sum2 + A[i][j]*xold[j];

      x[i] = (-sum1 - sum2 + b[i])/A[i][i_global];
      error_sum_local += (x[i]-xold[i_global])*
                          (x[i]-xold[i_global]);

    }

    MPI_Allreduce(&error_sum_local,&error_sum_global,1,
                  MPI_DOUBLE,MPI_SUM,MPI_COMM_WORLD);
    MPI_Allgatherv(x,rows_local,MPI_DOUBLE,xold,count,
                    displacements,MPI_DOUBLE,MPI_COMM_WORLD);

    if(sqrt(error_sum_global)<abstol){
      if(mynode == 0){
        for(i=0;i<N;i++)
          x[i] = xold[i];
      }
      else{
        DestroyMatrix(A,rows_local,N);
        delete[] x;
        delete[] b;
      }
      delete[] xold;
      delete[] count;
      delete[] displacements;
      return k;
    }
  }

  cerr << "Jacobi: Maximum Number of Interations Reached\n";
  if(mynode == 0){
    for(i=0;i<N;i++)
      x[i] = xold[i];
  }
  else{
    DestroyMatrix(A,rows_local,N);
    delete[] x;
    delete[] b;
  }
  delete[] xold;
  delete[] count;
  delete[] displacements;

  return maxit;
}
```

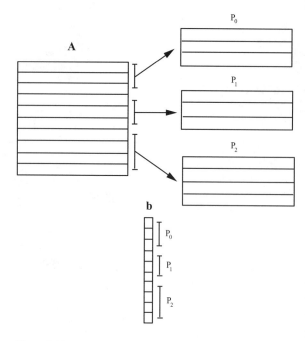

Figure 7.16: Distribution of matrix A across processes.

REMARK 1: The rows are distributed across processes as shown in Figure 7.16. Notice that in this routine we do not require that the number of processes equally divide the number of rows. This fact is taken into account using the *variable length* feature in MPI as discussed in the next remark.

REMARK 2: Observe that we use a slight modification to *MPI_Allgather; MPI_Allgatherv*. The function *MPI_Allgatherv* allows us to specify per process how much information is expected. Recall that in the standard *MPI_Allgather* it is assumed that each process is sending the same amount of data.

REMARK 3: As you can see, other than the initial distribution of the matrix **A** and the right-hand-side vector **b**, the Jacobi method is highly parallelizable. Only two MPI calls are needed per iteration – *MPI_Allreduce* to compute the error and *MPI_Allgatherv* to distribute the updated solution vector at the conclusion of an iteration.

7.2.3 Gauss–Seidel Algorithm

The Gauss–Seidel algorithm is usually twice as fast as the Jacobi algorithm but not as easily parallelizable. It is based on the observation that convergence usually is improved if we compute implicitly; hence in the Gauss–Seidel algorithm we use the most recently computed values. To illustrate this algorithm, we use the matrix version of the Jacobi algorithm, where instead of the diagonal on the left-hand side we employ the lower triangular matrix, that is,

$$(\mathbf{L} + \mathbf{D})\mathbf{x}^{n+1} = \mathbf{b} - \mathbf{U}\mathbf{x}^{n}.$$

We now apply this algorithm to the diffusion equation to obtain

$$\frac{1}{\Delta x^2}(\Theta_{i-1,j}^{n+1} + \Theta_{i,j-1}^{n+1} - 4\Theta_{ij}^{n+1}) = -q_{ij} - \frac{1}{\Delta x^2}(\Theta_{i+1,j}^{n} + \Theta_{i,j+1}^{n}),$$

or

$$\Theta_{ij}^{n+1} = \frac{1}{4}(\Theta_{i+1,j}^{n} + \Theta_{i,j+1}^{n} + \Theta_{i-1,j}^{n+1} + \Theta_{i,j-1}^{n+1} + \Delta x^2 q_{ij}).$$

We note that although on the right-hand side we use values at the $(n+1)$ time level, these values are already known because of the "sweep" process we choose, from left to right in the grid of Figure 7.17. Therefore, we use the newly computed information sooner than in the Jacobi method where we wait for a full cycle!

The *serial* Gauss–Seidel method is better than the *serial* Jacobi iteration because although the convergence criteria are similar the convergence rate for Gauss–Seidel is twice that of Jacobi, that is,

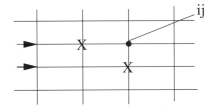

$$z_{GS} = z_J^2,$$

x – known information because of sweep direction!

in most cases (always when we have consistent ordering; see [95]).

Figure 7.17: Horizontal sweeping of the grid from left to right.

We can also use overwriting $\Theta_{ij}^{n+1} \leftrightarrow \Theta_{ij}^n$ to save in memory. However, the overall work is still $\mathcal{O}(N^4)$ on a grid with $N \times N$ points, so we have simply reduced the number of iterations by half but not the scaling with respect to the number of grid points. On a parallel computer, however, we need to use a special ordering of the unknowns on the grid to obtain an efficient algorithm because the standard Gauss–Seidel algorithm is inherently serial.

In the *software suite* we present implementations of the Gauss–Seidel algorithm for the diffusion equation and as a general iterative solver for the system $\mathbf{Ax} = \mathbf{b}$.

When examining the functions *Diffusion_GaussSeidel* and *GaussSeidel*, we draw your attention to the following:

- Observe that the function definitions for *Diffusion_GaussSeidel* and *GaussSeidel* are very similar to the definitions for *Diffusion_Jacobi* and *Jacobi*, respectively. Recall from our previous discussion that the only modification necessary to transform the Jacobi method into the Gauss–Seidel method is to modify the updating pattern, as seen in these coding examples.
- Observe that although in Gauss–Seidel we could directly update the solution array with the new values, we still maintain an "old" and "new" solution array. We do this so that at the end of one sweep we can compare the two solutions to determine when the solution has converged.

In Figure 7.18, we present the number of iterations necessary to converge to the solution for different mesh sizes using our Jacobi and Gauss–Seidel implementations for the diffusion equation example previously given. Observe that when solving for the same mesh size, the Gauss–Seidel method converges with half as many iterations has needed for the Jacobi method, just as the theory discussed here predicted.

7.2.4 Parallel (Black-Red) Gauss-Seidel Algorithm

The computational complexity of the Gauss–Seidel iteration

$$\mathbf{x}^{n+1} = (\mathbf{L} + \mathbf{D})^{-1}[-\mathbf{Ux}^n + \mathbf{b}]$$

consists of

- matrix–vector products for computing $\mathbf{Ux}^n$ and
- solution of the triangular system for $(\mathbf{L} + \mathbf{D})^{-1}$.

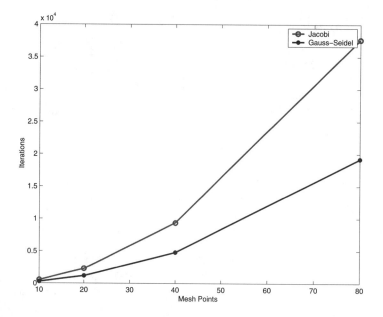

Figure 7.18:
Comparison of the
convergence rate for
the Jacobi and
Gauss–Seidel
algorithms.

In particular, the solution of the triangular system can cause limitations with respect to parallelism (see Chapter 9). However, we can apply a proper re-ordering of the difference equations to introduce more parallelism. This can be accomplished by a *multi-coloring scheme*, the simplest version of which is the *red–black* algorithm.

The key idea is to group the grid points into two groups, identified as *black* and *red* nodes, and observe that for Cartesian differencing the black nodes are surrounded by black nodes only, and the red nodes are surrounded by red nodes only. This is shown schematically in Figures 7.19 and 7.20 along with the corresponding matrices **A**. Using this grouping and denoting with subscripts (b) and (r) the black and red nodes, respectively, we can decompose the system as follows:

$$\begin{bmatrix} \mathbf{D}_r & \mathbf{U} \\ \mathbf{L} & \mathbf{D}_b \end{bmatrix} \begin{bmatrix} \mathbf{x}_r \\ \mathbf{x}_b \end{bmatrix} = \begin{bmatrix} \mathbf{b}_r \\ \mathbf{b}_b \end{bmatrix},$$

and using the Gauss–Seidel iteration, we obtain

$$\begin{bmatrix} \mathbf{D}_r & 0 \\ \mathbf{L} & \mathbf{D}_b \end{bmatrix} \begin{pmatrix} \mathbf{x}_r^{n+1} \\ \mathbf{x}_b^{n+1} \end{pmatrix} = \begin{bmatrix} 0 & -\mathbf{U} \\ 0 & 0 \end{bmatrix} \begin{pmatrix} \mathbf{x}_r^n \\ \mathbf{x}_b^n \end{pmatrix} + \begin{pmatrix} \mathbf{b}_r \\ \mathbf{b}_b \end{pmatrix},$$

or

$$\begin{cases} \mathbf{x}_r^{n+1} = \mathbf{D}_r^{-1}[-\mathbf{U}\mathbf{x}_b^n + \mathbf{b}_r], \\ \\ \mathbf{x}_b^{n+1} = \mathbf{D}_b^{-1}[-\mathbf{L}\mathbf{x}_r^{n+1} + \mathbf{b}_b]. \end{cases}$$

Thus, we no longer have to invert a triangular system. Instead, we need to perform matrix–vector products and vector scaling operations.

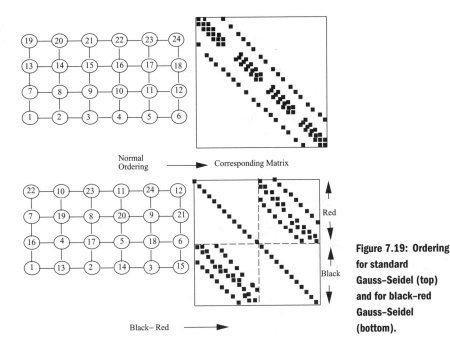

Normal Ordering ⟶ Corresponding Matrix

Black– Red ⟶

Figure 7.19: Ordering for standard Gauss-Seidel (top) and for black–red Gauss-Seidel (bottom).

An *alternative way* is to eliminate the red unknowns and solve for the black nodes first, that is,

$$(\mathbf{D}_b - \mathbf{U}\mathbf{D}_r^{-1}\mathbf{U})\mathbf{x}_b = \mathbf{b}_b + \mathbf{U}\mathbf{D}_r^{-1}\mathbf{b}_r,$$

with half as many unknowns. However, we need to solve a triangular system, which we can precondition with the diagonal for faster convergence (see Chapter 9).

REMARK 1: In general, the convergence rate depends on ordering unless it is a *consistent ordering* (see [95]). There have also been efforts to assign chaotic ordering (also known as *chaotic iteration*), but the convergence of such schemes is not guaranteed! A matrix $\mathbf{A} = \mathbf{L} + \mathbf{D} + \mathbf{U}$ is *consistently ordered* if the eigenvalues of the matrix

$$\mathbf{D}^{-1}(\alpha^{-1}\mathbf{L} + \alpha\mathbf{U})$$

do not depend on α for any $\alpha \neq 0$. A different definition was introduced by Young based on the permutations of the matrix $\mathbf{A}$ [95]. Specifically, the matrix is termed *2-cyclic* if there is a perturbation matrix $\mathbf{P}$ such that $\mathbf{P}\mathbf{A}\mathbf{P}^T$ can be written as a 2×2 matrix with the diagonal matrices being diagonal. For example, every block tridiagonal matrix with nonsingular diagonal blocks is consistently ordered and 2-cyclic.

Figure 7.20: Typical black (solid line) and red (dashed line) stencils for the parallel Gauss-Seidel algorithm.

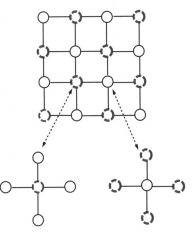

REMARK 2: The black–red Gauss–Seidel algorithm can be implemented in two parallel steps: one for updating the red points and one for the black points. This is equivalent to two parallel Jacobi steps per iteration. Therefore, the total number of parallel steps between the Jacobi algorithm and the black–red Gauss–Seidel algorithm is the same given that the latter converges twice as fast as the former. However, the black–red algorithm operates on half the number of points. Overall, communications and latency are the factors that will ultimately determine whether there is a substantial speedup factor using the black–red algorithm. A better approach is to use the black–red coloring idea with an overrelaxation method, as we discuss next.

7.2.5 Successive Over Relaxation – SOR

The convergence of the Gauss–Seidel method can be effectively accelerated if we introduce a relaxation procedure of the form

$$\Theta_{ij}^{n+1} = \Theta_{ij}^n + \omega d_{ij}^n, \quad d_{ij}^n \equiv \hat{\Theta}_{ij}^{n+1} - \Theta_{ij}^n, \tag{7.14}$$

where $\hat{\Theta}_{ij}^{n+1}$ is predicted by the standard Gauss–Seidel method. This intermediate answer is then corrected to obtain Θ_{ij}^{n+1}; such a method is called *predictor–corrector*. The displacement d_{ij}^n is given by

$$d_{ij}^n = \frac{1}{4}(\Theta_{i+1,j}^n + \Theta_{i,j+1}^n - 4\Theta_{ij}^n + \Theta_{i,j-1}^{n+1} + \Theta_{i-1,j}^{n+1} + \Delta x^2 q_{ij}).$$

Upon substitution in Equation (7.14), the corrected value is

$$\Theta_{ij}^{n+1} = \frac{\omega}{4}(\Theta_{i+1,j}^n + \Theta_{i,j+1}^n + \Theta_{i,j-1}^{n+1} + \Theta_{i-1,j}^{n+1} + \Delta x^2 q_{ij}) + (1 - \omega)\Theta_{ij}^n .$$

This method converges for $0 < \omega < 2$ assuming that the corresponding matrix **A** is positive-definite and symmetric.

- For $\omega = 1$, we recover the standard Gauss–Seidel;
- For $\omega > 1$, we have *overrelaxation* (SOR).
- For $\omega < 1$ we have *underrelaxation*.

The latter is not used often in practice because of its slow convergence. For the diffusion equation (7.12) we can obtain the *optimum* relaxation parameter that maximizes the convergence rate. For central differencing we have

$$\omega_{\text{opt}} = \frac{2}{(1 + \sqrt{1 - z_J^2})} \quad \text{and} \quad z_{\text{opt}} = \frac{z_J^2}{(1 + \sqrt{1 - z_J^2})^2},$$

where z_J is the convergence rate of the Jacobi method for the same discretization. In particular, for $\Delta x = \Delta y$ the Jacobi convergence rate is $z_J = \cos \pi \Delta x$, and thus we obtain

$$\omega_{\text{opt}} = \frac{2}{1 + \sin \pi \Delta x} \approx 2(1 - \pi \Delta x),$$

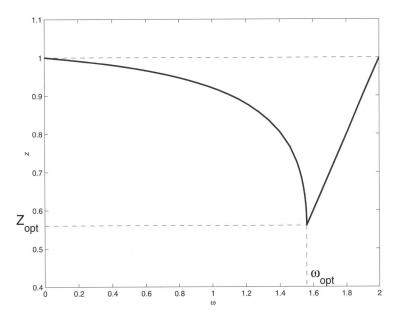

Figure 7.21: Convergence rate versus relaxation parameter for SOR.

and correspondingly

$$z_{opt} = \frac{\cos^2 \pi \Delta x}{(1 + \sin \pi \Delta x)^2} \approx 1 - 2\pi \Delta x.$$

This approximation provides an estimate for the number of iterations to reach convergence with accuracy of about d correct digits; thus

$$\text{number of SOR}(\omega)\text{ iterations:} \quad n \sim \frac{-d}{\ln z_{opt}} \sim N$$

since $\Delta x = 1/N$. This implies that for SOR(ω_{opt}) we have that $n \sim \mathcal{O}(N)$, and thus the computational work is $\mathcal{O}(N^3)$ versus $\mathcal{O}(N^4)$ for the standard Gauss–Seidel iteration assuming an $N \times N$ grid. We will revisit the issue of convergence rate of overrelaxation methods in Section 7.2.8.

REMARK: For general matrices $\mathbf{A}$ an estimate of the form $\omega_{opt} = 2 - \mathcal{O}(\Delta x)$, where Δx, the spacing, is a good initial guess. Subsequent numerical experiments can provide more refined values of the optimum relaxation parameter by comparing corresponding values of the convergence rate z and searching for a local minimum. Unfortunately, the minimum occurs over a quite narrow range in ω, as is shown in Figure 7.21.

PUTTING IT INTO PRACTICE

We now present a function SOR that performs successive overrelaxation to obtain the solution $\mathbf{x}$ to the system $\mathbf{Ax} = \mathbf{b}$. The function takes as input the relaxation parameter *omega*, the size of the system N, a double** array containing the matrix $\mathbf{A}$, an array

x into which the solution is to be placed, the right-hand side stored in the array *b*, and the convergence tolerance *abstol*.

```
void SOR(double omega, int N, double **A, double *x,
         double *b, double abstol){
  int i,j,k;
  int maxit = 10000;
  double sum1,sum2;
  double * xold = new double[N];

  //set initial guess
  for(i=0; i<N; i++){
    x[i] = 1.0e0;
    xold[i] = 1.0e0;
  }

  for(k=0; k<maxit; k++){
    for(i = 0; i<N; i++){
      sum1 = 0.0; sum2 = 0.0;
      for(j=0; j < i; j++)
        sum1 = sum1 + A[i][j]*x[j];
      for(j=i+1; j < N; j++)
        sum2 = sum2 + A[i][j]*xold[j];

      x[i] = (1.0-omega)*xold[i] + omega*
             (-sum1 - sum2 + b[i])/A[i][i];
    }

    if(sqrt(dot(N,x,xold))<abstol){
      delete[] xold;
      return;
    }

    for(i=0; i<N; i++)
      xold[i] = x[i];
  }

  cerr << "SOR: Maximum Number of Interations Reached\n";
  delete[] xold;

  return;
}
```

7.2.6 Symmetric Successive Acceleration Techniques – SSOR

The standard SOR method assumes a preferential direction as it sweeps the domain from left to right. This bias may cause error accumulation, but in addition the amplification matrix **G** of the SOR may have complex eigenvalues. This may not be desirable as certain acceleration schemes (e.g., Chebyshev acceleration, which we study next) require real eigenvalues. The idea of the *symmetric SOR* (SSOR) is then to sweep the domain in two passes, one from the left to right and subsequently from right to left. To this end, we write the standard SOR presented previously in matrix form,

$$(\mathbf{D} + \omega\mathbf{L})\hat{\mathbf{x}}^{n+1} = [(1 - \omega)\mathbf{D} - \omega\mathbf{U}]\mathbf{x}^n + \omega\mathbf{b},$$

to obtain the intermediate solution $\hat{\mathbf{x}}^{n+1}$.

The SOR iteration in the *reverse direction* is

$$(\mathbf{D} + \omega\mathbf{U})\mathbf{x}^{n+1} = [(1 - \omega)\mathbf{D} - \omega\mathbf{L}]\hat{\mathbf{x}}^{n+1} + \omega\mathbf{b},$$

to obtain the final solution $\mathbf{x}^{n+1}$ at the $(n+1)$-st iteration. The optimum relaxation parameter for SSOR is different than the ω_{opt} of SOR and it is not known exactly. An approximation proposed in [95] is

$$\omega_{opt} \approx \frac{2}{1 + \sqrt{2[1 - \rho(\mathbf{G})]}},$$

which leads to twice the convergence rate of the one-directional SOR; however, the number of operations is also doubled. For the diffusion model that we consider we then have that

$$z_{SSOR} \approx 1 - \pi\Delta x \approx 1 - \frac{\pi}{N}.$$

The corresponding amplification matrix is symmetric and has real eigenvalues with spectral radius

$$\rho_{SSOR}(\mathbf{G}) = 1 - \frac{\pi}{N}.$$

We will make use of this property of SSOR in the following section.

7.2.7 SSOR with Chebyshev Acceleration

What we have done so far is to convert the system $\mathbf{A}\mathbf{x} = \mathbf{b}$ to a fixed-point iteration of the form

$$\mathbf{x}^{n+1} = \mathbf{G}\mathbf{x}^n + \mathbf{c}.$$

It is often the case, as we have seen in the multistep schemes for temporal discretization, that a linear combination of the iterates $\{\mathbf{x}^n\}$ converges faster than the last iterate. This is the idea of Chebyshev acceleration, and in the following we will see how Chebyshev polynomials come into play in this context; we will basically exploit their *minimax property* (see Section 3.1.5). Let us define the linear combination

$$\mathbf{y}_n = \sum_{q=0}^{n} \gamma_n^q \mathbf{x}^q$$

and form the error with respect to the exact solution $\mathbf{x}$:

$$\mathbf{y}_n - \mathbf{x} = \sum_{q=0}^{n} \gamma_n^q (\mathbf{x}^q - \mathbf{x}) = \sum_{q=0}^{n} \gamma_n^q \mathbf{G}^q (\mathbf{x}^0 - \mathbf{x}) = p_n(\mathbf{G})(\mathbf{x}_0 - \mathbf{x}) .$$

Here we have defined the polynomial p_n of degree n with $p_n(1) = 1$ since the interpolation coefficients satisfy

$$\sum_{q=0}^{n} \gamma_n^q = 1.$$

To minimize the computational work we should choose the polynomial p_n carefully. We know (using the spectral mapping theorem) that the eigenvalues of $p_n(\mathbf{G})$ are given by $p_n[\lambda(\mathbf{G})]$. We then need to minimize these eigenvalues, or even simpler we need to minimize the maximum eigenvalue (spectral radius ρ). Owing to their *minimax property*, the polynomials that best satisfy this requirement are the *Chebyshev polynomials*. We have also assumed here that the eigenvalues of the amplification matrix $\mathbf{G}$ are real.

Let us then assume that $x \in [-\rho, \rho]$ and define the polynomial

$$p_n(x) \equiv \frac{T_n(x/\rho)}{T_n(1/\rho)} = \frac{T_n(x/\rho)}{C_n} ,$$

where the last equation defines the normalization constant C_n. We will now use the three-term recursive property of Chebyshev polynomials to obtain y_n recursively and construct the convergence acceleration algorithm. Note that C_n can also be obtained recursively in a similar way, that is,

$$C_n = \frac{2}{\rho} C_{n-1} - C_{n-2} .$$

For the error $(\mathbf{y}^n - \mathbf{x})$ we have

$$\begin{aligned}
\mathbf{y}^n - \mathbf{x} &= p_n(\mathbf{G})(\mathbf{x}^0 - \mathbf{x}) \\
&= C_n^{-1} T_n(\mathbf{G}/\rho)(\mathbf{x}^0 - \mathbf{x}) \\
&= C_n^{-1} [2 \cdot \mathbf{G}/\rho \cdot T_{n-1}(\mathbf{G}/\rho)(\mathbf{x}^0 - \mathbf{x}) - T_{n-2}(\mathbf{G}/\rho)(\mathbf{x}^0 - \mathbf{x})] \\
&= C_n^{-1} [2 \cdot \mathbf{G}/\rho \cdot C_{n-1} p_{n-1}(\mathbf{G}/\rho)(\mathbf{x}^0 - \mathbf{x}) - C_{n-2} p_{n-2}(\mathbf{G}/\rho)(\mathbf{x}^0 - \mathbf{x})] \\
&= C_n^{-1} [2 \cdot \mathbf{G}/\rho \cdot C_{n-1}(\mathbf{y}^{n-1} - \mathbf{x}) - C_{n-2}(\mathbf{y}^{n-2} - \mathbf{x})].
\end{aligned}$$

We can now write the recursive relation

$$\mathbf{y}^n = 2\frac{C_{n-1}}{C_n} \frac{\mathbf{G}}{\rho} \mathbf{y}^{n-1} - \frac{C_{n-2}}{C_n} \mathbf{y}^{n-2} + \mathbf{D}^n, \tag{7.15}$$

where we have defined

$$\mathbf{D}^n = \frac{2}{\rho} \frac{C_{n-1}}{C_n} \mathbf{c}$$

and we recall the iteration $\mathbf{x}^{n+1} = \mathbf{G}\mathbf{x}^n + \mathbf{c}$.

We now have a recursion relation but we still need to initialize the first guess and the normalization constants. From the definition we have that $C_0 = 1$ and $C_1 = 1/\rho$, and we set $\mathbf{y}^1 = \mathbf{G}\mathbf{x}^0 + \mathbf{c}$.

We can also estimate the number of iterations by observing that in this algorithm the error is multiplied in each iteration by the *inverse* of

$$C_n \equiv T_n(1/\rho).$$

For the SSOR algorithm we have that $\rho \approx 1 - \frac{\pi}{N}$ and thus $1/\rho \approx 1 + \frac{\pi}{N}$. Now, from the Chebyshev properties we have that

$$T_n(1 + \pi/N) \geq \frac{1}{2}(1 + n\sqrt{2\pi/N}).$$

To multiply the error by a factor less than 1, we need

$$\frac{2}{1 + n\sqrt{2\pi/N}} \leq 1,$$

and thus the number of iterations n scales as $n \propto \mathcal{O}(\sqrt{N})$. The total computational work for the SSOR with Chebyshev acceleration is therefore

$$\mathcal{O}(N^{5/2})$$

versus $\mathcal{O}(N^3)$ for SOR. We see that SSOR with Chebyshev acceleration beats even the direct solver, that is, Gaussian elimination, which is $\mathcal{O}(N^3)$ for the backsolve.

7.2.8 Convergence Analysis of Iterative Solvers

Basic Analysis

We have already discussed some of the conditions necessary for convergence of the basic iterative algorithms presented in this chapter. In general, if the coefficient matrix $\mathbf{A}$ is symmetric and positive-definite the Gauss–Seidel iteration converges to a unique solution for any initial vector $\mathbf{x}^0$, although for the Jacobi iteration a stronger condition is needed. We have also seen the relation between the time–space stencils for diffusion and the iteration algorithms. In this section, we provide some more details on the convergence of the basic iterative solvers.

We start by restating the analogy between iterative procedures and equations of evolution. This analogy was formulated rigorously by Garabedian [41], who considered the equation

$$K \frac{\partial \Theta}{\partial t} = \kappa \frac{\partial^2 \Theta}{\partial x^2} - U \frac{\partial \Theta}{\partial x}, \tag{7.16}$$

which is an advection–diffusion equation. By exploiting the properties of this PDE one can obtain information about the convergence of the discrete iterative algorithms. It can be shown, for example, that the smaller K is the more rapid the convergence is. Here, K depends on the specific iterative procedure considered. Convergence to steady solution is equivalent to existence of solutions of the PDE. A *necessary* condition for convergence is that Equation (7.16) be parabolic for $t > 0$. This condition implies that

- for Jacobi: $K_J = 2\kappa \frac{\Delta t}{\Delta x^2} > 0$,
- for Gauss–Seidel: $K_{GS} = \frac{\kappa \Delta t}{\Delta x^2} \left(1 - \frac{U \Delta x}{2\kappa}\right) > 0$ $(U \Delta x < 2\kappa)$, and
- for SOR: $K_{SOR} = \frac{\kappa \Delta t}{\Delta x^2} \left(\frac{2 - \omega}{\omega} - \frac{U \Delta x}{2\kappa}\right) > 0$.

However, $K > 0$ is not sufficient for convergence as we need to have a stable scheme too.

The case of $U \neq 0$ will be studied in the next chapter. Here by setting $U = 0$ we obtain

$$K_J = 2K_{GS} \quad \text{and} \quad \omega K_{SOR} = (2 - \omega) K_{GS}.$$

For the SOR iteration, convergence is obtained if

$$0 < \frac{2 - \omega}{\omega} < 1 \Rightarrow 2 - \omega < \omega \Rightarrow \omega > 1 \text{ and } \omega < 2.$$

We now generalize the iteration algorithms by introducing the concept of a *preconditioner*. Let us consider the system

$$\mathbf{A} \Theta = \mathbf{q},$$

where $\mathbf{A}$ is a stiffness matrix (e.g., the discrete Laplacian) as before. Then, we define the convergence (vector) error as

$$\epsilon^n = \Theta^n - \Theta^\infty,$$

which we will analyze in the following. We split the spatial discretization matrix as follows:

$$\mathbf{A} = \mathbf{M} + \mathbf{N}$$

and set up the iteration

$$\mathbf{M} \Theta^{n+1} = \mathbf{q} - \mathbf{N} \Theta^n,$$

or

$$\mathbf{M} \Delta \Theta^n = -\mathbf{r}^n, \quad \mathbf{r} \equiv \mathbf{A} \Theta - \mathbf{q},$$

where $\mathbf{r}$ is the *residual*. This residual equation above is derived from

$$\Delta \Theta^n \equiv \Theta^{n+1} - \Theta^n \Rightarrow \mathbf{M}(\Theta^{n+1} - \Theta^n) = \underbrace{\mathbf{q}^n - (\mathbf{M} + \mathbf{N})\Theta^n}_{-\mathbf{r}^n}.$$

We can recover all the schemes presented earlier by the proper choice of the preconditioner $\mathbf{M}$, that is,

- Jacobi: $\mathbf{M} = \mathbf{D}$,
- Gauss–Seidel: $\mathbf{M} = \mathbf{D} + \mathbf{L}$,
- SOR: $\mathbf{M} = \mathbf{D} + \omega \mathbf{L}$, and
- SSOR: $\mathbf{M} = (\mathbf{D} + \omega \mathbf{L})\mathbf{D}^{-1}(\mathbf{D} + \omega \mathbf{U})$.

Next, we obtain the error equation by subtracting the equations

$$\mathbf{M}\Theta^{n+1} = \mathbf{q}^n - \mathbf{N}\Theta^n,$$
$$(\mathbf{M} + \mathbf{N})\Theta^{\infty} = \mathbf{q}$$

to get

$$\mathbf{M}\epsilon^{n+1} = -\mathbf{N}\epsilon^n.$$

This leads us to the definition of the *amplification matrix*, which we have already used earlier:

$$\epsilon^{n+1} = -\mathbf{M}^{-1}\mathbf{N}\epsilon^n = (-\mathbf{M}^{-1}\mathbf{N})^n\epsilon^1$$
$$= \underbrace{(\mathbf{I} - \mathbf{M}^{-1}\mathbf{A})^n}_{\mathbf{G}:\text{ amplification matrix}}\epsilon^1.$$

Therefore

$$\epsilon^{n+1} = \mathbf{G}^{n+1}\epsilon^0. \tag{7.17}$$

For stability we require that the spectral radius of the amplification matrix be less than one, that is,

$$\rho(\mathbf{G}) \leq 1$$

since $\rho(\mathbf{A}) \leq \| \mathbf{A} \|$ for any matrix norm.

This condition can be applied effectively as it may be sufficient to know the eigenvalues of the matrices that comprise the original matrix $\mathbf{A}$. For example, for the Jacobi iteration we have

$$\mathbf{G}_J = \mathbf{I} - \mathbf{M}^{-1}\mathbf{A} \Rightarrow \lambda_J = 1 - (1/d_j)\lambda_j(\mathbf{A}),$$

where d_j are the diagonal elements of matrix $\mathbf{D}$, and we have made use of the spectral mapping theorem.

We can now derive the **error–residual** relationship by subtracting the equations

$$\mathbf{r}^n = -\mathbf{q}^n + (\mathbf{M} + \mathbf{N})\Theta^n,$$
$$0 = -\mathbf{q}^n + (\mathbf{M} + \mathbf{N}))\Theta^{\infty},$$

where the second equation is valid in steady state. Upon subtraction we obtain

$$\mathbf{r}^n = \mathbf{A}\epsilon^n,$$

which is a very useful equation relating the error and the residual.

REMARK 1: When the residual $\mathbf{r}^n$ is reduced to machine accuracy it does not mean that the solution Θ^n is within machine accuracy, because we still have to account for the discretization error.

REMARK 2: To compute the matrix–vector products in the iterations we can use either of two ways suggested by the equations

$$\mathbf{w} = \mathbf{M}^{-1}\mathbf{A}\mathbf{v} = \mathbf{M}^{-1}(\mathbf{M} + \mathbf{N})\mathbf{v} = \mathbf{v} + \mathbf{M}^{-1}\mathbf{N}\mathbf{v}.$$

That is, we compute $\mathbf{w}$ from

$$
\begin{cases}
\mathbf{r} = \mathbf{A}\mathbf{v}, \\
\mathbf{w} = \mathbf{M}^{-1}\mathbf{r}
\end{cases}
$$

or from

$$
\begin{cases}
\mathbf{r} = \mathbf{N}\mathbf{v}, \\
\mathbf{w} = \mathbf{M}^{-1}\mathbf{r}, \\
\mathbf{w} = \mathbf{v} + \mathbf{w}.
\end{cases}
$$

It is more efficient to use the second set as it involves matrix–vector multiplies with matrices, which are substantially less dense than the original matrix $\mathbf{A}$.

Fourier Representation of Convergence Error

We can decompose the convergence error into normal modes by considering the *eigenstructure* of the matrix $\mathbf{A}$. For clearer illustration of the main points, we will assume that the amplification matrix $\mathbf{G}$ shares eigenvectors with the coefficient matrix $\mathbf{A}$. This is true, for example, for the Jacobi algorithm on a discrete Laplacian but not for the Gauss–Seidel iteration. With this assumption we can represent the convergence error as

$$
\epsilon^n = \sum_j \lambda_j^n \epsilon_j^0 \Phi_j , \tag{7.18}
$$

where ϵ_j^0 is the initial error distribution and λ_j, Φ_j are associated with the matrices $\mathbf{G}$ and $\mathbf{A}$, respectively. In particular, Φ_j are the eigenvectors of the discrete diffusion operator. This representation is possible because the error behaves like the homogeneous part of the solution. The eigenvectors Φ_j are also eigenvectors of $\mathbf{G}$ only for special cases, for example, periodic boundary conditions and Jacobi iteration, but not for Gauss–Seidel, as stated above.

As n increases, the low λ_j (corresponding to high frequencies) will decay faster. Asymptotically, after a few iterations, we are left with the highest λ_j (which correspond to low frequencies). The convergence history of these methods would then have the form shown in Figure 7.22: A very fast decay is obtained initially followed by an extremely slow decay.

We can use Equation (7.18) for the error to obtain a measure of convergence of the iterative solvers. To this end, we recall the *error–residual* relationship and substitute the Fourier representation for the error:

$$
\mathbf{r}^n = \sum_j \lambda_j^n(\mathbf{G})\epsilon_j^0 \mathbf{A}\Phi_j = \sum_j \lambda_j^n(\mathbf{G})\epsilon_j^0 \underbrace{\lambda_j(\mathbf{A})}_{\text{eigenvalues of } A} \Phi_j .
$$

If the Φ_j are orthonormal eigenvectors, then we can obtain a simple expression for the L_2 norm of the residual, that is,

$$
\| \mathbf{r}^n \|_{L_2} = \left[\sum (\lambda_j^n(\mathbf{G})\lambda_j(\mathbf{A})\epsilon_j^0)^2 \right]^{1/2} .
$$

This scalar residual is typically used as a measure of convergence of iterative solvers.

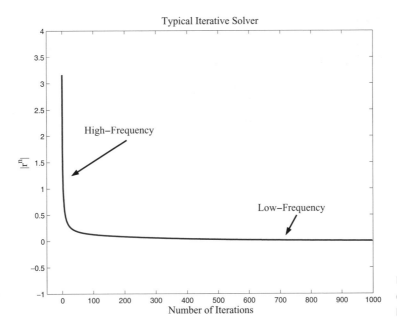

Figure 7.22: Typical convergence history of basic iterative solvers.

We can also use the eigenvalues of the amplification matrix to gain more insight into the convergence rate of individual modes (frequencies) for the iterative methods we presented. For example, in the *Jacobi* iteration

$$\lambda(\mathbf{G}_J) = 1 - (\sin^2(\phi_x/2) + \sin^2(\phi_y/2)) = \frac{1}{2}(\cos\phi_x + \cos\phi_y), \tag{7.19}$$

which is obtained from

$$\mathbf{G}_J = \mathbf{I} - \mathbf{M}^{-1}\mathbf{A}, \quad J = k + (\ell - 1)N, \quad \text{where} \quad \ell, m = 1, \dots, N-1$$

and $\phi_x = k\pi/N$, $\phi_y = \ell\pi/N$.

From Equation (7.19) we see that at low frequencies, $\phi_x \simeq 0$, $\phi_y \simeq 0$, the damping rate (i.e., convergence rate) is very poor as $\lambda \sim 1$. At intermediate frequencies ($k, \ell \sim N/2$), damping is very strong, and at high frequencies ($k, \ell \to N$), damping is very weak again. Specifically, the most resistant error corresponds to $k = \ell = 1$; thus

$$\rho(\mathbf{G}_J) = \cos\frac{\pi}{N} \Rightarrow \rho(\mathbf{G}_J) \cong 1 - \frac{\pi^2}{2N^2}.$$

This analysis suggests that the number of iterations is proportional to $\mathcal{O}(N^2)$, as we have already seen earlier.

Following a similar analysis, we obtain that for the Gauss–Seidel iteration we have

$$\lambda(\mathbf{G}_{GS}) = \frac{1}{4}(\cos\phi_x + \cos\phi_y)^2 = \lambda^2(\mathbf{G}_J), \tag{7.20}$$

which shows that the Gauss–Seidel iteration converges twice as fast as the Jacobi iteration.

7.2.9 Relaxed Jacobi and Gauss–Seidel

We can also apply the preceding analysis to relaxation or weighted methods. Let us first introduce the *relaxed Jacobi* algorithm:

$$\Theta_{ij}^{n+1} = \frac{\omega}{4}(\Theta_{i+1,j}^{n} + \Theta_{i,j+1}^{n} + \Theta_{i,j-1}^{n} + \Theta_{i-1,j}^{n} + q_{ij}^{n}) + (1-\omega)\Theta_{ij}^{n}.$$

Thus, the new amplification matrix is

$$\mathbf{G}_{J(\omega)} = (1-\omega)\mathbf{I} + \omega\mathbf{G}_J,$$

and its corresponding eigenvalues are

$$\lambda(\mathbf{G}_{J(\omega)}) = (1-\omega) + \omega\lambda(\mathbf{G}_J). \tag{7.21}$$

For convergence we require that

$$\rho(\mathbf{G}_{J(\omega)}) \leq |1-\omega| + \omega\rho(\mathbf{G}_J) < 1,$$

or

$$|1-\omega| < 1 - \omega\rho(\mathbf{G}_J) \Rightarrow -[1-\omega\rho(\mathbf{G}_J)] < 1 - \omega < 1 - \omega\rho(\mathbf{G}_J),$$

and thus

$$0 < \omega < \frac{2}{1+\rho(G_J)}.$$

Therefore, to damp high frequencies we should select $\omega < 1$ and ω toward $\lambda_{\min}$. To damp low frequencies we should select $\omega > 1$ and ω toward $\lambda_{\max}$.

To better understand this *selective damping* of the Fourier components of the error for the Jacobi method, we perform one-dimensional experiments. To this end, we revisit the Dirichlet problem

$$-\Theta_{j-1} + 2\Theta_j - \Theta_{j+1} = 0, \quad 1 \leq j \leq N-1,$$

$$\Theta_0 = \Theta_N = 0,$$

so the corresponding matrix $\mathbf{A}$ is tridiagonal with elements $(-1, 2, -1)$. The eigenvalues of this matrix are

$$\lambda_k(\mathbf{A}) = 4\sin^2\left(\frac{k\pi}{2N}\right), \quad 1 \leq k \leq N-1, \tag{7.22}$$

and the corresponding eigenvectors for the grid points $0 \leq j \leq N$ are

$$\Phi_j^k(\mathbf{A}) = \sin\left(\frac{jk\pi}{N}\right), \quad 1 \leq k \leq N-1. \tag{7.23}$$

We have already seen these results in Section 7.1.4 earlier in this chapter.

For the *relaxed Jacobi* algorithm we can derive from Equation (7.21) the following:

$$\lambda_k(\mathbf{G}_{J(\omega)}) = 1 - \frac{\omega}{2}\lambda_k(\mathbf{A}),$$

and thus

$$\lambda_k(\mathbf{G}_{J(\omega)}) = 1 - 2\omega \sin^2(\frac{k\pi}{2N}), \quad 1 \le k \le N-1. \qquad (7.24)$$

We can now examine what is the best value for ω, that is, the one that gives

$$|\lambda_k(\mathbf{G}_{J(\omega)})| = \text{minimum}, \quad \forall\, 1 \le k \le N-1.$$

By inspection we can see that the *smooth components* of the error (i.e., the modes corresponding to $1 \le k \le N/2$) are affected very little by ω. In contrast, the damping of the *rough components* corresponding to $N/2 \le k \le N-1$ are affected significantly. We thus seek an optimum value of ω for the rough modes by limiting this minimization to the upper half of the spectrum, that is, $N/2 \le k \le N-1$. This minimum is achieved if

$$\lambda_N(\mathbf{G}_{J(\omega)}) = -\lambda_{(N/2)}(\mathbf{G}_{J(\omega)}),$$

which gives the optimum $\omega = 2/3$ for the one-dimensional problem, The corresponding reduction of the error is

$$\lambda_k(\omega = 2/3) = 1/3,$$

which means that the rough components will be reduced by a *factor of 3* in each Jacobi iteration.

The effectiveness of this choice is shown in the next two figures. In Figure 7.23 we plot the evolution of the solution from the relaxed Jacobi algorithm starting from the initial condition

$$\frac{1}{2}(\Phi_2 + \Phi_{32})$$

after 10 and also after 100 iterations with the relaxed Jacobi algorithm and $\omega = 2/3$. We see that the initially very rough solution relaxes to the smooth *mode two*, which remains nearly the same. The correct solution is $\Theta_j = 0$, $j = 1, \ldots, N$, since we solve the homogeneous one-dimensional Laplace's equation with zero Dirichlet conditions. A more comprehensive picture is shown in Figure 7.24, where we record the number of relaxed Jacobi iterations to reduce the mean error by a factor of 100. Specifically, the initial condition here is a single Fourier mode, which coincides with the eigenmode of the Laplacian and the eigenmode of the relaxed Jacobi iteration matrix $\mathbf{G}_{J(\omega)}$. The choice of $\omega = 1$ is most effective for the intermediate range of modes whereas the choice $\omega = 2/3$ damps effectively the upper half of the spectrum. The actual number of iterations for the low modes is much higher than 100, in fact of the $\mathcal{O}(1,000)$, but here we set a maximum 100 iterations for clarity of the plot.

Next we analyze the *Gauss–Seidel overrelaxation* method. We use the matrix form

$$(\mathbf{D} + \omega\mathbf{L})\Delta\Theta^n = -\omega\mathbf{r}^n,$$

Figure 7.23: Jacobi algorithm with initial condition $(\Phi_2 + \Phi_{32})/2$. The curves correspond to the initial condition (large oscillations); results after 10 iterations (small oscillations); and results after 100 oscillations (smooth curve); $\omega = 2/3$.

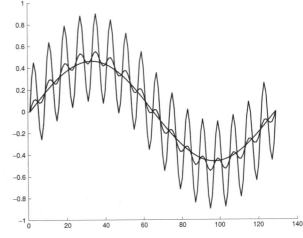

so the corresponding amplification matrix is

$$\mathbf{G}_{\text{SOR}}(\omega) = \mathbf{I} - \omega(\mathbf{D} + \omega\mathbf{L})^{-1}\mathbf{A},$$

or

$$\mathbf{G}_{\text{SOR}}(\omega) = \underbrace{(\mathbf{D} + \omega\mathbf{L})^{-1}}_{\text{triangular}}\underbrace{[(1-\omega)\mathbf{D} - \omega\mathbf{U}]}_{\text{triangular}}.$$

Since $\mathbf{G}_{\text{SOR}}(\omega)$ is a product of triangular matrices, its determinant is the product of its diagonal element. Thus

$$\det \mathbf{G}_{\text{SOR}}(\omega) = \det(\mathbf{I} + \omega\mathbf{D}^{-1}\mathbf{L})^{-1}\det[(1-\omega)\mathbf{I} - \omega\mathbf{D}^{-1}\mathbf{U}]$$

$$= 1 \cdot \det[(1-\omega) - \omega\mathbf{D}^{-1}\mathbf{U}]$$

$$= (1-\omega)^N.$$

But

$$\det \mathbf{G}_{\text{SOR}}(\omega) = \Pi_{i=1}^{N}\lambda_i \leq \rho^N(\mathbf{G}_{\text{SOR}}(\omega)),$$

so

$$|1-\omega| \leq \rho(\mathbf{G}_{\text{SOR}}(\omega)) < 1,$$

and so *for stability* we recover the result $0 < \omega < 2$, as before.

REMARK 1: For general symmetric $\mathbf{A}$ matrices we have that

$$\lambda(\omega) = 1 - \omega + \omega\lambda^{1/2}(\omega) \cdot \lambda(\mathbf{G}_J),$$

and for $\omega = 1 \Rightarrow \lambda(\omega = 1) = \lambda^2(\mathbf{G}_J)$, as before.

Figure 7.24: Number of Jacobi iterations to reduce the error 100 times for different values of ω. The initial condition is a single Laplace mode with wavenumber k.

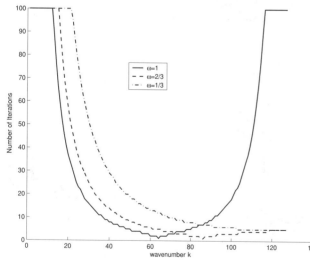

REMARK 2: Unlike the Jacobi method, the Gauss–Seidel method does not share the same eigenvectors with the Laplacian matrix $\mathbf{A}$. Specifically, the eigenfunctions of the Gauss–Seidel iteration matrix $\mathbf{G}_{\text{GS}}$ are

$$\Phi_j^k = [\cos(\frac{k\pi}{N})]^j \sin(\frac{jk\pi}{N}), \quad 1 \leq k \leq N-1.$$

It is interesting to observe that the Gauss–Seidel method damps the Laplacian modes in a fashion similar to that of the relaxed Jacobi method (i.e., the rough components are damped faster). In contrast, the Gauss–Seidel eigenmodes are damped in a fashion similar to that of the unrelaxed Jacobi method. This behavior is demonstrated in Figure 7.25, where the number of iterations to reduce the mean error by a factor of 100 is recorded.

The *selective damping* achieved by the Jacobi and Gauss–Seidel methods is a typical property of all relaxation schemes. The Fourier error modes are determined by the grid spacing or, equivalently, by the number of grid points. Therefore, a *rough* mode on a fine grid may appear as a *smooth* mode on a coarse grid. This simple observation along with the selective damping of relaxation schemes is exploited in the multigrid method, which is one of the most effective solvers and is presented next.

7.2.10 The Multigrid Method

The multigrid method is not really a new algorithm; rather, it is a procedure to make the relaxation algorithms effective at *all* wave-

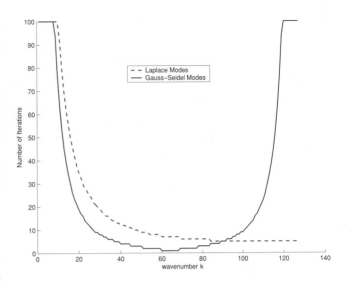

Figure 7.25: Number of Gauss–Seidel iterations to reduce the error 100 times for different initial conditions corresponding to single Laplace modes (dash line) and single Gauss–Seidel modes (solid line).

numbers, including the low wavenumbers. The main idea of the multigrid procedure is based on the observation that the classical iterations rapidly kill high-frequency (or wavenumber) errors but are slower for the low-frequency (i.e., largest) eigenvalues. Since this is all determined by the grid spacing, the idea of multigrid is to change the grid so that low frequencies on the fine grid look *higher* on the *coarser* grid. Conversely, errors that are invisible on the coarse grid are no problem on the fine grid. Figure 7.23 illustrates how the initial error consisting of both high (rough) and low (smooth) modes relaxes after a few iterations with a single grid discretization. The remaining low mode will appear as an intermediate or high mode in a discretization with a coarser grid. Relaxation on the new grid will effectively damp this mode as well.

This discussion also suggests that the relaxation scheme will be more effective if we employ an initial condition that does not include smooth components. This can be accomplished by first solving the problem on a coarse grid and subsequently transferring the solution to the finer grid. Alternatively, we can start on a fine grid and subsequently transfer the solution onto a coarser grid.

However, there is a further complication in these intergrid transfers that we have to take into account. When we transfer from a fine grid to a coarse grid, the smooth modes become rough modes, but also the initially rough modes, although reduced in amplitude, are transformed (at least some of them) into smooth modes. This is the phenomenon of *aliasing*, which results in misrepresentation of the rough modes in the coarse grid after a fine-to-coarse grid transfer.

To make these ideas more concrete let us introduce some notation. We will denote by h the fine grid and by H the coarse grid, and (in most cases) we will imply that we coarsen the grid by halving the number of points leading to grid spacing $H = 2h$. The question on how to *start* the intergrid transfers (i.e., from a coarse or fine grid) that we posed is also related to what exactly we should transfer from one grid to the other.

Should that be

- the system $\mathbf{A}\Theta = \mathbf{q}$ that we want to solve *or*
- the residual $\mathbf{r} = \mathbf{A}\Theta - \mathbf{q}$ that we want to minimize?

Both ideas have been explored in multigrid research and have been used in practice for different problems.

The idea of transferring the original system is combined with the use of the coarse grid solution as an initial start, and it is called *nested iteration*. It consists of the following steps:

NESTED ITERATION ALGORITHM.

1. Relax $\mathbf{A}_H\Theta_H = \mathbf{q}_H$ on a coarse grid to obtain an initial solution.
2. Transfer the solution Θ_H to the fine grid to obtain an initial condition Θ_h^0.
3. Relax $\mathbf{A}_h\Theta_h = \mathbf{q}_h$ using the initial condition Θ_h^0.
4. Test for convergence. If needed, go to step 1 and continue.

In this algorithm there can be several relaxation sweeps. Also, in each new execution of the algorithm the old fine grid is overwritten with the new coarse grid.

A second approach involves transferring the residual from one grid to the next, starting with the fine grid. This is the *correction* method and it consists of the following steps:

CORRECTION ALGORITHM.

1. On the fine grid, relax $\mathbf{A}_h\Theta_h = \mathbf{q}_h$.
2. Transfer the residual $\mathbf{r}_h$ to the coarser grid to obtain $\mathbf{r}_H$.
3. Obtain the correction $\delta\Theta_H$ by solving $\mathbf{A}_H(\delta\Theta_H) = \mathbf{r}_H$ at a reduced computational cost.
4. Transfer the correction to the fine grid to generate a new update $\Theta_h \leftarrow \Theta_h + \delta\Theta_H$.
5. Test for convergence. If needed, go to step 1 and continue.

Similar to the nested iteration, in this algorithm also several coarser grids can be involved.

These two algorithms make use of three important operations in multigrid:

- relaxation of the solution or correction (*smoother*),
- transfer to coarse grid (*restriction*), and
- transfer to fine grid (*prolongation*).

To define a specific multigrid method we need to specify the corresponding three operators named in this list (inside the parenthesis). We give details for each operator in the following.

The Smoother

To evaluate the smoothing properties of the relaxation method employed (e.g., relaxed Jacobi, Gauss–Seidel, or any other variant) we need to examine the eigenspectrum of the amplification matrix $\mathbf{G}$. We have already seen in the previous section that we cannot really affect the low modes, and the best we can do is to come up with a good choice on how to most effectively damp the upper half of the eigenspectrum of $\mathbf{G}$. With this in mind, we define the *smoothing factor* as

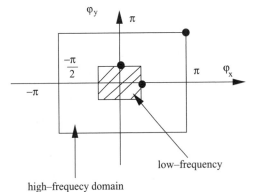

h: $\quad \Delta x = L/N \quad \varphi \in [\pi/N, \pi]$

H: $\quad 2\Delta x \quad \varphi \in [\pi/N, \pi/2]$

φ coarse grid

Figure 7.26:
Fine–coarse grids in
one-dimensional
domain.

$$\mu = \max |\lambda(\mathbf{G}(\phi))|, \quad \frac{\pi}{2} \le |\phi| \le \pi. \tag{7.25}$$

Here $\phi = k\pi/N$; in multidimensions we have to extend this definition to account for ϕ_x, ϕ_y, and ϕ_z, which will depend on the resolution in x, y, and z, respectively.

Values of $|\phi|$ close to zero correspond to low wavenumbers whereas values of $|\phi|$ close to π correspond to high wavenumbers. To appreciate this correspondence between the angular variable ϕ and the spacing in the physical domain we sketch in Figure 7.26 the one-dimensional discretization for a fine–coarse grid combination.

We have seen in the previous section that for the relaxed Jacobi method the eigenvalues are

$$\lambda_k(\mathbf{G}_{J(\omega)}) = 1 - 2\omega \sin^2(\phi/2),$$

and thus the smoothing factor for the *one-dimensional* problem is

$$\mu = \lambda(\pi/2) = 1/3 \quad \text{and} \quad \omega = 2/3.$$

In the *two-dimensional* case we also have to separate the domain into high frequency (wavenumber) and low frequency (wavenumber) and formulate a *minimax* problem for the smoother in the domain, as shown diagrammatically in Figure 7.27. We first note that the *standard* Jacobi algorithm has an eigenvalue of -1 at $\phi_x = \phi_y = \pi$ (in the high-frequency domain), and thus it is *not* a good smoother! However, the *relaxed* Jacobi can be used to damp high frequencies, as in the one-dimensional case.

In the high-frequency domain, the extreme eigenvalues of Jacobi are

Figure 7.27:
Frequency domain for
estimating the
smoother.

$$\lambda(\mathbf{G}_J) \begin{cases} -1 & \text{at} \quad (\pi, \pi), \\ +1/2 & \text{at} \quad (\pi/2, 0). \end{cases}$$

Then

$$\lambda(\mathbf{G}_{J(\omega)}) = [(1 - \omega) + \omega\lambda(G_J)]$$

and

$$\lambda(\mathbf{G}_{J(\omega)}) = \begin{cases} 1 - \omega + \omega/2 = 1 - \omega/2, \\ 1 - \omega - \omega = 1 - 2\omega. \end{cases}$$

This *minimax* problem can be solved graphically as shown in Figure 7.28; we obtain for the optimum $\omega = 4/5 = 0.8$, with the corresponding smoothing factor

$$\mu_J = \text{minmax} \{|1 - \omega/2|, |1 - 2\omega|\} = 0.6.$$

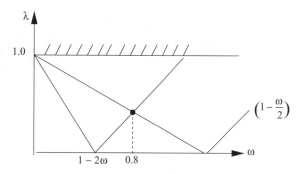

Figure 7.28: Estimation of the smoother for the two-dimensional Jacobi method.

REMARK 1: The total reduction of the error during the smoothing substep is proportional to μ^{n_1}, where n_1 is the number of relaxation sweeps.

REMARK 2: A similar but more elaborate analysis for Gauss–Seidel gives $\mu_{GS} = 0.5$ [92]. Therefore, the Gauss–Seidel smoother achieves an order of magnitude reduction in the high-frequency error after only three iterations.

REMARK 3: In multidimensions we can relax by *points*, *lines*, or *planes* or by alternating directions, and parallel versions such as the red–black coloring can be employed.

The Coarse-Grid Correction

The coarse-grid correction (CGC) stage is a very important operation and has to be done accurately and efficiently. To identify the main operations during this stage we define two grids, as shown in Figure 7.29. Assuming that on the fine grid we have obtained

$$\mathbf{P}(\delta\Theta_h) = \mathbf{r}_h,$$

where $\mathbf{P}$ is an operator to be determined later, we perform the following steps in CGC:

- Transfer the residual to the coarse grid via the *restriction operator*, $\mathbf{I}_h^H$, that is,

  $$\mathbf{r}_H = \mathbf{I}_h^H \mathbf{r}_h.$$

- Solve $\mathbf{A}_H(\delta\Theta_H) = \mathbf{r}_H$ at low cost.
- Transfer the correction $\delta\Theta_H$ to the fine mesh via the *prolongation operator*, $\mathbf{I}_H^h$, i.e.,

  $$\delta\Theta_h = \mathbf{I}_H^h(\delta\Theta_H).$$

Figure 7.29: Two-grid transfer. The fine grid spacing is denoted by h and the coarse grid spacing is denoted by H.

We have outlined these multigrid substeps at a high level, and we now need to define the restriction and prolongation operators more precisely. We do that for simple finite difference representations following the two-grid model.

The **restriction operator** involves a projection from N points to $N/2$ points. The finite difference expressions for the residuals on the fine and coarse grids, respectively, are

$$r_{h,i} = \frac{1}{h^2}(\Theta_{i+1} - 2\Theta_i + \Theta_{i-1}) - q_i,$$

$$r_{H,k} = \frac{1}{4h^2}(\Theta_{k-1} - 2\Theta_k + \Theta_{k+1}) - q_k,$$

where $i = 2k$.

Based on these residuals we can define a restriction operator that accomplishes the transfer; it is shown schematically in Figure 7.30. This projection is referred to as *full weighting*, in contrast to a simpler projection by *injection*, which would

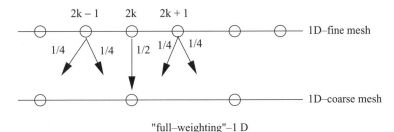

2k − 1   2k   2k + 1

1/4   1/4   1/2   1/4   1/4

1D–fine mesh

1D–coarse mesh

"full–weighting"–1 D

Figure 7.30: One-dimensional restriction operator (full weighting).

imply that $\Theta_k^H = \Theta_i^h$. We can define more precisely the full-weighting restriction operator for the one-dimensional case in matrix form as follows:

$$\mathbf{I}_h^H = \begin{array}{c} \\ k-1 \\ k \\ k+1 \end{array} \begin{array}{|ccc|} \multicolumn{3}{c}{2k-1 \ \ 2k \ \ 2k+1} \\ \hline 1/4 & 1/2 & 1/4 & & \\ & & 1/4 & 1/2 & 1/4 & \\ & & & & 1/4 & 1/2 & 1/4 \end{array} \right|,$$

which is an $(N/2) \times N$ matrix. The coarse grid residual is then obtained from

$$\mathbf{r}_H = \mathbf{I}_h^H \mathbf{r}_h \,.$$

Next, we explain how the restriction operator acts on the k modes of the Laplacian $\mathbf{A}_h$; these modes are given by

$$\Phi_{k,j}^h = \sin(\frac{jk\pi}{N}), \quad 0 \le j \le N \,.$$

In particular, the result is different depending on the mode, that is, whether it is a smooth or a rough mode. In the one-dimensional case for *smooth modes* we have that

$$\mathbf{I}_h^H \Phi_k^h = \cos^2(\frac{k\pi}{2N}) \, \Phi_k^H, \quad 1 \le k \le N/2 \,.$$

This equation simply states that the projected kth mode remains the kth mode on the coarse grid. An example is shown in Figure 7.31, where the $k = 4$ mode is projected onto a grid with 8 grid points from a grid of 16 points.

In contrast, for the high *rough* modes aliasing may transform them to smooth modes on the coarse grid according to

$$\mathbf{I}_h^H \Phi_k^h = -\sin^2(\frac{k\pi}{2N}) \, \Phi_{N-k}^H, \quad N/2 < k \le N \,.$$

This is shown schematically in Figure 7.32, where the $k = 12$ mode is projected onto a grid with 8 grid points from a grid of 16 points. It is clear that

Figure 7.31: Action of a full-weighting restriction operation on a *smooth* mode ($N = 16, k = 4$).

$$\mathbf{r}_H = \mathbf{I}_h^H \mathbf{r}_h \,.$$

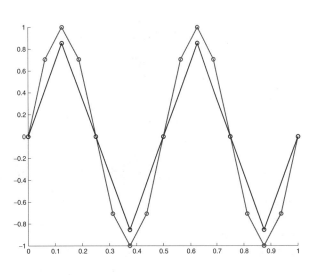

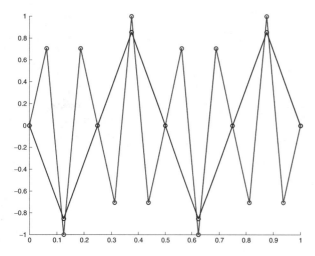

Figure 7.32: Action of a full-weighting restriction operation on a *rough* mode ($N = 16, k = 12$).

the projected mode is a $(16 - 12) = 4$ mode, that is, a smooth mode on the coarse grid.

In two or three dimensions, several choices for the restriction operator are possible, representing different ways of weighting the contribution from the fine grid nodes to the coarse grid nodes. Examples are shown in Figure 7.33. The full-weighting scheme is the most popular choice, as it leads to the following important property between the restriction and prolongation operators:

$$\mathbf{I}_h^H = C\,\mathbf{I}_H^h,$$

which means that the restriction and interpolation operators are *transposes* of each other apart from a constant C.

We now examine some of the properties of the interpolation or **prolongation operator** that we need to define to transfer quantities (e.g., the correction) from the coarse to fine grid.

The one-dimensional prolongation operation is defined as shown in Figure 7.34, the two-dimensional prolongation operation is sketched in Figure 7.35. They both involve *linear* interpolation, which is effective if the solution error is relatively smooth. A more accurate prolongation operator based on *cubic* interpolation has also been found to be very effective.

For the one-dimensional problem the *prolongation matrix* is defined as follows:

$$
\mathbf{I}_H^h =
\begin{vmatrix}
& k-1 & k & k+1 & \\
\ldots\ 0 & 1/2 & 1/2 & \ldots & 2k-1 \\
0 & 0 & 1 & 0 & 2k \\
& 1/2 & 1/2 & & 2k+1
\end{vmatrix}.
$$

To understand the action of the prolongation operator for the one-dimensional case, we examine how the modes of the Laplacian on the coarse grid are interpolated

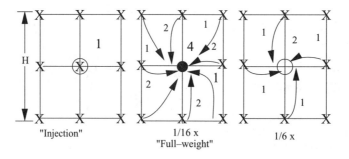

Figure 7.33: Three different schemes of restriction from fine to coarse grids.

onto the fine grid. Specifically, we find that

$$\mathbf{I}_H^h \Phi_k^H = [\cos^2(\frac{k\pi}{2N})]\Phi_k^h - [\sin^2(\frac{k\pi}{2N})]\Phi_{N-k}^h .$$

This equation provides considerable insight into the coarse-to-fine grid transfer. It states that the k mode is *not* preserved but is mixed up with the complimentary mode $(N-k)$, so the smooth mode

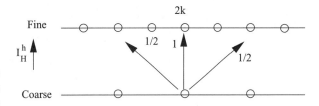

picks up some rough component as it is transferred onto the fine grid! This, in turn, suggests that after we transfer the correction $\delta\Theta_h$ to the fine grid we need to perform *additional* relaxation sweeps to get rid of this unwanted component. Fortunately, the rough component is of smaller magnitude compared to the smooth component, as indicated from the approximation to the previous equation,

Figure 7.34: Schematic for the one-dimensional prolongation operation.

$$\mathbf{I}_H^h \Phi_k^H = [1 - \mathcal{O}(\frac{k^2}{N^2})]\Phi_k^h - [\mathcal{O}(\frac{k^2}{N^2})]\Phi_{N-k}^h ,$$

which is valid for $k \ll N/2$.

We now return to the *coarse-grid correction operator* $\mathbf{P}_{\text{CGC}}$, which we will define by the following "backward" analysis. We begin with the correction at the fine grid and trace it back to the two-grid correction (see Figure 7.36) as follows:

$$\delta\Theta_h = \mathbf{I}_H^h(\delta\Theta_H)$$

$$= \mathbf{I}_H^h \mathbf{A}_H^{-1} \mathbf{r}_H$$

$$= \mathbf{I}_H^h \mathbf{A}_H^{-1} \mathbf{I}_h^H \mathbf{r}_h$$

$$\Rightarrow \underbrace{(\mathbf{I}_H^h \mathbf{A}_H^{-1} \mathbf{I}_h^H)^{-1}}_{\mathbf{P}_{\text{CGC}}} \delta\Theta_h = \mathbf{r}_h .$$

The corresponding *amplification matrix* or *two-grid correction* operator is then

$$\mathbf{G}_{\text{CGC}} = \mathbf{I} - \mathbf{P}_{\text{CGC}}^{-1}\mathbf{A}_h$$

$$= \mathbf{I} - \mathbf{I}_H^h \mathbf{A}_H^{-1} \mathbf{I}_h^H \mathbf{A}_h .$$

Figure 7.35: Schematic for the two-dimensional prolongation operation.

It is interesting again to examine what this operator does to the Laplacian modes, both smooth and rough. Combining the properties of the restriction and prolongation operators, we obtain

$$\mathbf{G}_{\text{CGC}}\Phi_k = [\sin^2(\frac{k\pi}{2N})]\Phi_k + [\sin^2(\frac{k\pi}{2N})]\Phi_{N-k},$$

$$\mathbf{G}_{\text{CGC}}\Phi_{N-k} = [\cos^2(\frac{k\pi}{2N})]\Phi_k + [\cos^2(\frac{k\pi}{2N})]\Phi_{N-k} .$$

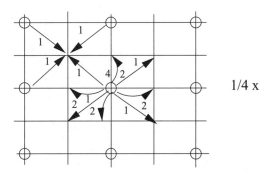

$1/4 \times$

These equations simply state that the coarse-grid correction operator *mixes up* the modes, irrespective of the mode (smooth or rough) to which it is applied, unlike, for

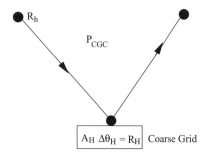

Figure 7.36:
Schematic of the
coarse-grid correction
stage.

example, the restriction operator. However, the amplitudes are different depending on whether the original mode is smooth or rough, and this is really what saves the day for multigrid! In particular, when $\mathbf{G}_{CGC}$ operates on smooth modes the amplitudes of the resulted smooth and rough modes are proportional to $\mathcal{O}(k^2/N^2)$ (for $k \ll N/2$), in contrast with the high modes whose resulted modes have amplitudes of $\mathcal{O}(1)$.

This analysis is useful as it also suggests the potential benefits of relaxation. To this end, we recall that most of the relaxation solvers do not mix up the modes. Assuming, for example, that we employ the relaxed Jacobi method as smoother, and we perform n_1 relaxation sweeps, then the amplification matrix is

$$\mathbf{G}_{CGC} \cdot \mathbf{G}_{J(\omega)}^{n_1} .$$

The corresponding action of this operator to the Laplacian modes is then given by

$$\mathbf{G}_{CGC} \cdot \mathbf{G}_{J(\omega)}^{n_1} \cdot \Phi_k = [\sin^2(\frac{k\pi}{2N})]\lambda_k^{n_1}\Phi_k + [\sin^2(\frac{k\pi}{2N})]\lambda_k^{n_1}\Phi_{N-k},$$

$$\mathbf{G}_{CGC} \cdot \mathbf{G}_{J(\omega)}^{n_1} \cdot \Phi_{N-k} = [\cos^2(\frac{k\pi}{2N})]\lambda_{N-k}^{n_1}\Phi_k + [\cos^2(\frac{k\pi}{2N})]\lambda_{N-k}^{n_1}\Phi_{N-k},$$

where λ_k are the eigenvalues of the Jacobi amplification matrix $\mathbf{G}_{J(\omega)}$, which are, of course, all less than one. Therefore, relaxation reduces significantly the already small amplitudes of the smooth modes, but the more significant effect is on the rough modes, since $\lambda_{N-k} < \lambda_k$ for small wavenumbers.

Multigrid Algorithm

We now have all the ingredients required to write the complete multigrid algorithm. Two popular choices of multigrid algorithms, corresponding to a *V-cycle* and a *W-cycle*, are shown schematically in Figure 7.37. They both start with a fine grid and transfer the residual down to the coarsest grid and then they interpolate back to a fine grid. The path of return to the fine grid is different for the V-cycle and the W-cycle, as illustrated in the figure.

For the V-cycle, in particular, we provide all the steps of the algorithm:

- Perform n_1 relation sweeps with smoother S_1 on solution Θ_h^n ($n_1 \sim 2$–4).
- Perform a coarse-grid correction, $\Theta_h^{n+1} = \Theta_h^n + \delta\Theta_h$.
- Perform n_2 relaxation sweeps with smoother S_2 on solution Θ_h^{n+1} ($n_2 \sim 2$–4).

The total amplification factor is then

$$\mathbf{G}_{h,H} = \mathbf{G}_{S_2}^{n_2} \cdot \mathbf{G}_{CGC} \cdot \mathbf{G}_{S_1}^{n_1} .$$

Figure 7.37:
Schematic of typical
V-cycle and W-cycle
multigrid algorithms.

n_1 n_2 V–cycle

n_1 n_2 W–cycle

REMARK 4: In this algorithm we have implemented the V-cycle for the correction scheme; it transfers the residual between grids. A similar algorithm can be obtained using nested iteration; it transfers the linear system from one grid to the other, starting from the coarse-grid solution. This is the *full multigrid cycle*; for more details, the reader is referred to [10, 11, 92].

Convergence and Computational Cost

The question of computational complexity of the multigrid method is related to the convergence rate of the method. The storage requirements are relatively simple to estimate. They are less than *twice* of that required on the fine grid in either one-dimensional or multidimensional problems.

The convergence rate of multigrid is defined by the spectral radius of the *total amplification matrix*, which is less than one, that is,

$$\rho(\mathbf{G}_{h,H}) < 1 \,.$$

Asymptotically, the multigrid algorithm is particularly effective for large-scale problems, since ρ is (in most cases) independent of the spacing h or equivalently the number of grid points N. The major cost is due to the smoother as the intergrid transfers cost about 15% of the entire cycle.

We can provide an estimate for the work required for a V-cycle assuming that we only perform one relaxation sweep per grid that costs δt_r. Assuming also that we employ m coarse grids, and since we visit twice each grid, then the total work is

$$W_V = 2[1 + 2^{-d} + 2^{-2d} + \cdots + 2^{-md}]\delta t_r = \frac{2}{1 - 2^{-d}}\delta t_r \,,$$

where d denotes space dimension. For example, in three dimensions ($d = 3$) we have that the work for the entire V-cycle, W_V, is slightly more than twice the work (time) required for one relaxation sweep, δt_r.

Next, we can estimate the number of required sweeps per levels n_1 and n_2. For simplicity, we assume that $n_1 = n_2 = n$ and that the spectral radius $\rho(\mathbf{G}_{h,H})$ is indeed independent of h. The multigrid V-cycle should reduce the algebraic error from $\mathcal{O}(1)$ to (at least) the level of the discretization error $\mathcal{O}(h^p) = \mathcal{O}(N^{-p})$, where p is the order of the finite difference discretization accuracy (e.g., $p = 2$). This condition implies that

$$\rho(\mathbf{G}_{h,H})^n = \mathcal{O}(N^{-p}) \Rightarrow n \approx \mathcal{O}(\log N).$$

The total cost of the V-cycle is then

$$W_V \approx n \times \mathcal{O}(N^d) \approx \mathcal{O}(N^d \log N),$$

where $\mathcal{O}(N^d)$ is the minimum number of operations for the N^d grid points involved in d space dimensions. In most problems the value of $n \sim \mathcal{O}(1)$ (for example $n = 4$) and thus, for two dimensions, the optimum cost is $\mathcal{O}(N^2)$ versus $\mathcal{O}(N^3)$ for direct solvers and $\mathcal{O}(N^4)$ for the Jacobi or the Gauss–Seidel solvers. These estimates assume an $N \times N$ grid. For preconditioned conjugate gradients (see Section 9.4) the work is $\mathcal{O}(N^{5/2})$. Therefore, the multigrid is indeed a very efficient method!

REMARK 5: We have presented here only the main elements of multigrid for linear systems. For more in-depth study of multigrid including applications to nonlinear systems the reader should consult the references [10, 11, 92]. A very good online resource is the site **www.MGNet.org**.

REMARK 6: The computational efficiency of the multigrid method depends critically on the parallel implementation of the smoother and the solution of the system on the coarse grid. Modern implementations of multigrid exploit the memory hierarchies of the processors and in particular the level 2 and level 1 cache (see [34]). In terms of available parallel multigrid software, the free C/MPI package **ParMGridGen** from the University of Minnesota generates an optimum sequence of successive coarse grids that are suitable for the multigrid algorithm.

7.3 HOMEWORK PROBLEMS

1. Use von Neumann analysis to show that leap-frog time differencing combined with central differencing to discretize

$$\frac{\partial u}{\partial t} = \frac{\partial^2 u}{\partial x^2}$$

leads to an unstable scheme. Verify your results with heuristic arguments using the corresponding equivalent differential equation.

2. Write a C++ code to implement the DuFort–Frankel scheme for solving

$$\frac{\partial u}{\partial t} = \frac{\partial^2 u}{\partial x^2}, \quad x \in [-1, 1],$$

with

$$u(-1, t) = 0, \quad u(1, t) = 1, \quad \text{and} \quad u(x, 0) = -(x + 1)/2.$$

Consider two grids with number of points $N = 20$ and $N = 40$, and advance the solution to time $t = 1$

(a) using a constant diffusion number D, and

(b) using a time step Δt that scales linearly with Δx.

What do you observe?

3. Show that the eigenvalues of the one-dimensional diffusion matrix obtained from second-order central differencing with Dirichlet boundary conditions are

$$\lambda_j = -\frac{4}{\Delta x^2} \sin^2 \left(\frac{j\pi}{2(N+1)} \right)$$

and that the corresponding eigenvectors are

$$\phi_j = [\sin(\frac{j\pi}{2(N+1)}), \ \sin(\frac{2j\pi}{2(N+1)}), \dots, \ \sin(\frac{Nj\pi}{2(N+1)})]^T.$$

4. Show that the eigenvalues of the partial differential equation

$$\frac{\partial^2 u}{\partial x^2} + \delta^2 \frac{\partial^2 u}{\partial y^2} = \lambda u,$$

with homogeneous Dirichlet boundary conditions are given by

$$-4\sin^2(\frac{i\pi}{2(N+1)}) - 4\delta^2 \sin^2(\frac{j\pi}{2(N+1)}) \quad \text{with} \quad i, j = 1, \ldots, N.$$

Also assume that the discretization is second-order central differencing and that $\Delta x = \Delta y = 1$.

5. Consider the diffusion equation with the "wrong sign" (negative diffusion)

$$\frac{\partial u}{\partial t} = -\frac{\partial^2 u}{\partial x^2}$$

with

$$u(-1, t) = u(1, t) = 0 \quad \text{and} \quad u(0, 0) = 1.$$

   (a) What is the solution $u(x, t)$ after times $t = 0.1$, 1 and also $t \to \infty$.

   (b) Use explicit time-stepping to advance the solution and observe a numerical instability developing. Is the physical solution stable?

6. Solve the nonlinear parabolic equation

$$\frac{\partial u}{\partial t} + u + u^3 = \frac{\partial^2 u}{\partial x^2} + \cos(\pi x)$$

with

$$u(0, t) = u(t, 1) = 0 \quad \text{and} \quad u(x, 0) = \sin(\pi x).$$

   (a) using an explicit method to obtain empirically an equivalent diffusion number for stability, and

   (b) implicitly using in addition Newton's method for the nonlinear equation.

7. Solve the one-dimensional heat equation

$$\frac{d^2 T}{ds^2} = \sin 2\pi s, \quad s \in [0, 1],$$

with periodic boundary conditions using

   (a) the Thomas algorithm,

   (b) the serial Jacobi method,

   (c) the parallel Jacobi method.

Use more than one grid and compare convergence rates as well as computational times.

8. Consider the Helmholtz equation

$$\frac{\partial^2 u}{\partial^2 x} + \frac{\partial^2 u}{\partial y^2} - \lambda^2 u = 0,$$

where $(x, y) \in [-1, 1] \times [-1, 1]$ and

$$u(-1, y) = 0, \ u(1, y) = 0, \ u(x, -1) = 0, \ u(x, 1) = 1.$$

Discretize this equation using central differencing and solve the corresponding algebraic system using the Jacobi and SOR methods. Experiment with $N_x = N_y = 10, 50, 100$ grid points.

    Is convergence of these iterative solvers guaranteed for all values of λ^2?

    What is the optimum value of the relaxation parameter ω?

9. Consider the 2×2 matrix with a constant value a in the main diagonal and b and $-b$ in the cross-diagonal. Determine the relationship between a and b so that the Jacobi, Gauss–Seidel, and SOR methods are guaranteed to converge.

10. Discretize the equation $\nabla^2 u = f$ with the exact solution

$$u(x, y) = \cos(\pi x) \sin(\pi y), \quad (x, y) \in [-1, 1] \times [-1, 1],$$

using the fourth-order compact (Padè) scheme. Use the ADI and Peaceman–Rachford methods to obtain the numerical solutions and determine the convergence rate of the solver as well as the spatial accuracy of the discretization.

    What do you observe?

11. Show that in the relaxed Jacobi algorithm, when ω is chosen to damp the smooth modes, then the rough modes are amplified.

12. Write a C++ code for the one-dimensional relaxed Jacobi and SOR. Then experiment with different initial modes and compare against the Laplacian modes.

13. Show that the prolongation operator (with linear interpolation) and the restriction operator (with full weighting) satisfy the transpose property, that is,

$$\mathbf{I}_H^h = C(\mathbf{I}_h^H)^T,$$

where C is a scaling constant.

14. Implement the multigrid V-cycle in two dimensions for the unsteady diffusion equation using second-order central differencing. Consider first a square domain and subsequently a rectangle with aspect ratio 25. Use a relaxed Jacobi for smoother and full weighting for the restriction operator.

    What is the convergence rate for the square domain and what is it for the large-aspect-ratio domain?

15. Implement an MPI version of the SOR algorithm. Solve the one-dimensional heat equation

$$\frac{d^2 T}{ds^2} = \sin 2\pi s, \quad s \in [0, 1],$$

with periodic boundary conditions using

(a) the relaxation parameter chosen so that the method becomes a Gauss–Seidel solver,

(b) using an optimal relaxation parameter.

Use more than one grid and compare convergence rates as well as computational times. Compare computational timing results (using *MPI_Wtime*) for these two methods against parallel Jacobi for $P = 2, 4$, and 8 processes.

16. Consider $\nabla^2 u = A \sin(2\pi x) \sin(2\pi y)$ on the unit square. Solve for $A = 1.0, 2.0, 3.0, 5.0$, and 10.0 using

(a) the serial Jacobi method,

(b) the serial SOR method,

(c) the parallel Jacobi method.

Use more than one grid and compare convergence rates and computational times. If you fix the number of grid points per direction to 20 and examine the number of iterations that each methods takes to converge, does this number of iterations vary as you change the value of A?

8

Propagation: Numerical Diffusion and Dispersion

In this chapter we continue with mixed discretizations for initial value problems and boundary value problems, but our emphasis is on advection equations and wave propagation with and without dissipation. Specifically, we introduce two important nondimensional numbers that define the accuracy and the stability of discretizations we present: the *Courant number* or CFL condition, first proposed by Courant in 1928, and the (grid) *Peclet number* for advection–diffusion systems. We also provide C++ functions and corresponding results that illustrate the effects of numerical diffusion and numerical dispersion in pure advection and in advection–diffusion systems. The advection equation is therefore a good yardstick by which we can measure these two fundamental properties of a numerical method.

On the parallel computing side, we introduce the concept of nonblocking communications, specifically the use of *MPI_Isend* and *MPI_Irecv*. Nonblocking communications may lead to a reduction in the computational time by allowing the programmer to appropriately intertwine computation and communication.

8.1 ADVECTION EQUATION

We consider as a prototype problem the linearized wave or advection equation

$$\frac{\partial \Theta}{\partial t} + U \frac{\partial \Theta}{\partial x} = 0 \quad \left(\text{or } \frac{D\Theta}{Dt} = 0\right), \tag{8.1}$$

which expresses the (passive) advection of heat or a species in one dimension by the flow with transport velocity $U(x, t)$. For a constant U this is a deceptively simple-looking equation, but it is perhaps one of the most difficult equations to resolve in scientific computing. The reason is that, as we will see below, it exhibits no physical diffusion or dispersion. However, there is no practical numerical method for the solution of Equation (8.1) that does not introduce at least some amount of either numerical diffusion or dispersion! This equation is therefore a good yardstick by which we can measure these two fundamental properties of a numerical method.

Let us assume that we have *periodic* boundary conditions, that is, $\Theta(0, t) = \Theta(1, t)$, and that the initial conditions are $\Theta(x, 0) = \Theta_0(x) = \sin 2\pi x$; then the exact solution is $\Theta = \Theta_0(x - Ut) = \sin 2\pi(x - Ut)$, which is a traveling wave of constant amplitude that propagates to the right in Figure 8.1, with constant velocity U. The exact solution can be verified by direct substitution in Equation (8.1). Any initial waveform (see Figure 8.2) is simply advected to the right without diffusion or dispersion.

8.1.1 Dispersion and Diffusion

We explain next the concepts of dispersion and diffusion that a partial differential equation may exhibit as we need to distinguish these from the
numerically induced ones. We can use complex arithmetic to write the solution of
Equation (8.1) as

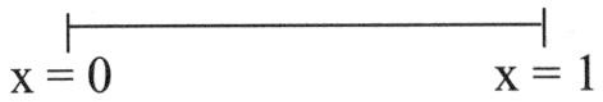

Figure 8.1: Domain for the one-dimensional linear advection equation.

$$\Theta = \text{Re}\left\{\left(e^{i2\pi kx}\right)\left(e^{-i2\pi\omega t}\right)\right\}$$

$$= \text{Re}\left\{e^{i2\pi k(x-\frac{\omega}{k}\cdot t)}\right\}$$

of constant amplitude; here, ω is the eigenvalue and it is related to the frequency of
the wave. The definition of *phase speed*, suggested by this expression, is

$$C_\phi = \omega/k,$$

and for the linear advection equation it is obtained upon substitution of the assumed
solution into Equation (8.1), that is,

$$\left.\begin{array}{c} \dfrac{\partial\Theta}{\partial t} = -i2\pi\omega\Theta \\[2mm] -U\dfrac{\partial\Theta}{\partial x} = -2\pi ki\Theta U \end{array}\right\} \Rightarrow \omega = kU \Rightarrow \frac{\omega}{k} = C_\phi = U.$$

Thus, the waveforms are not dispersed as time progresses, because the phase speed is
equal to the constant transport velocity U; they are also nondissipative, and thus we
obtain solutions as sketched in Figure 8.2.

In contrast, in the *diffusion equation*

$$\frac{\partial\Theta}{\partial t} = \frac{\partial^2\Theta}{\partial x^2}, \tag{8.2}$$

and assuming a solution of the form

$$\Theta = \text{Re}\{e^{\sigma t}e^{i\pi 2kx}\},$$

where σ is the eigenvalue, we obtain upon substitution in Equation (8.2)

$$\frac{\partial\Theta}{\partial t} = \sigma\Theta = -(2\pi k)^2\Theta = \frac{\partial\Theta}{\partial x^2}.$$

Figure 8.2: A wave-form advected with constant velocity to the right as described by Equation (8.1).

Therefore, we have dissipation of the waveform, and σ is the attenuation factor; that
is, the solution $\Theta(x, t)$ is dissipative.

Similarly, we consider a *third-order equation*

$$\frac{\partial\Theta}{\partial t} = \frac{\partial^3\Theta}{\partial x^3}, \tag{8.3}$$

and assuming a solution of the form

$$\Theta = \text{Re}\{e^{i2\pi kx}e^{-i2\pi\omega t}\},$$

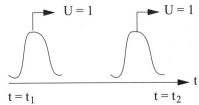

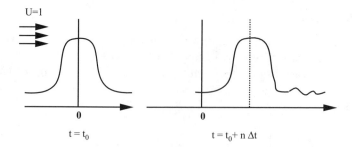

Figure 8.3: Dispersion leads to short waves leading the waveform.

upon substitution in Equation (8.3) we obtain

$$\frac{\partial \Theta}{\partial t} = -i2\pi\omega\Theta = -i(2\pi k)^3\Theta = \frac{\partial^3 \Theta}{\partial x^3},$$

and therefore

$$\frac{\omega}{k} = C_\phi = (2\pi k)^2.$$

This is the *dispersion equation* for the third-order partial differential equation with periodic boundary conditions. It shows that the phase speed depends on the wavenumber, with short waves traveling *quadratically* faster. Each wave corresponding to wavenumber k travels at a speed proportional to the square of its wavenumber, and we obtain solutions that graphically look like the sketch in Figure 8.3.

In summary, we have seen that the order of spatial derivative determines if a PDE exhibits *dispersion* or *diffusion*. Specifically,

    i. $\Theta_t = -\Theta_x$ leads to nondissipative, nondispersive solutions,
    ii. $\Theta_t = \Theta_{xx}$ leads to dissipative solutions,
    iii. $\Theta_t = \Theta_{xxx}$ leads to nondissipative but dispersive solutions, and
    iv. $\Theta_t = -\Theta_{xxxx}$ leads to dissipative solutions (similar justification as above).

Therefore, the *odd derivatives* (higher than first) are associated with dispersion, whereas the *even derivatives* are associated with dissipation. We will use this fact in the following to determine the numerical properties of a specific discretization by examining its corresponding *equivalent differential equation*.

8.1.2 Other Advection Equations

Burgers Equation

The nonlinear advection equation has the form

$$\frac{\partial \Theta}{\partial t} + \frac{1}{2}\Theta\frac{\partial \Theta}{\partial x} = 0. \tag{8.4}$$

It has been introduced by the fluid mechanician J. M. Burgers [12] to model quadratic nonlinearities that appear in many physical phenomena including turbulence and shock waves. In particular, the initial conditions are very important in determining the structure of solutions to this *inviscid* Burgers equation. The basic discretizations employed for the solution of Equation (8.1) can also be used to solve Equation (8.4) with appropriate treatment of the nonlinear terms.

Second-Order Wave Equation

The advection equation (8.1) is first order and admits one-directional wave solutions. Its second-order analogue has the form

$$\frac{\partial^2 \Theta}{\partial t^2} = c^2 \frac{\partial^2 \Theta}{\partial x^2} , \tag{8.5}$$

and admits left- and right-traveling waves with velocity c. This equation can be reduced to a system of first-order linear advection equations, similar to Equation (8.1), as follows:

$$\frac{\partial v}{\partial t} = c \frac{\partial \Theta}{\partial x} , \qquad \frac{\partial \Theta}{\partial t} = c \frac{\partial v}{\partial x} .$$

STOCHASTIC ADVECTION EQUATION. We assume that the transport velocity is a stochastic variable that can be decomposed into its mean and a fluctuation component as follows: $U = \bar{U} + u$. If the fluctuation component follows a Gaussian distribution with variance σ^2, its probability distribution function has the form

$$f(u) = \frac{1}{\sqrt{2\pi\sigma^2}} \exp[-\frac{u^2}{2\sigma^2}].$$

An exact expression can be obtained for the *mean solution*, that is,

$$\bar{\Theta} = \Theta_0(x - \bar{U}t) \exp[-\pi^2 \alpha t].$$

Here, $\Theta_0(x)$ is the initial (deterministic) condition, and α is an *effective diffusivity* resulting from random fluctuations given by

$$\alpha = \frac{\sigma^2 \tau}{2} ,$$

where τ is a time scale that determines the sampling rate. For example, if the initial distribution u is not updated during the time integration, then $\tau = t$, but if the fluctuation is updated every, say, ten time steps, then $\tau = 10\Delta t$. Note that numerical discretizations of Equation (8.1) can be employed for different distributions of u to obtain a statistically converged solution, which will be an approximation to the solution given here. This is the so-called Monte Carlo method, the efficiency of which depends on the efficiency of numerical solutions for the deterministic equation (8.1).

In the following, we consider first- and second-order discretizations of the linear advection equations. For other types of advection equations the same scheme applies.

8.1.3 First-Order Discrete Schemes

Most explicit schemes for the advection equation are conditionally stable and depend on a nondimensional number, that is, the Courant or CFL number. In the following, we first introduce some first-order schemes, which are useful for short-term integration

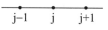

Figure 8.4: The EF/CD schemes employ a three-point stencil.

only, and subsequently we present second-order schemes that are suitable for both short-term and long-term time integration.

Euler-Forward/Center-Differencing Scheme

The Euler-forward/center-differencing (EF/CD) scheme is a straightforward discretization for Equation (8.1) on the stencil of Figure 8.4; it is not as useful in practice, but it brings out the subtleties associated with the numerical solution of hyperbolic equations. For simplicity, let us assume that $U = 1$ and we also define the first-order central difference

$$\Delta_x \Theta_j \equiv \frac{\Theta_{j+1} - \Theta_{j-1}}{2\Delta x}.$$

The discrete EF/CD scheme is

$$\frac{\Theta_j^{n+1} - \Theta_j^n}{\Delta t} + \frac{\Theta_{j+1}^n - \Theta_{j-1}^n}{2\Delta x} = 0, \ j = 1, \ldots N,$$

with periodic boundary conditions

$$\Theta_0^n = \Theta_N^n$$

and initial conditions given by

$$\Theta_j^0 = \sin 2\pi x_j.$$

The total truncation error is obtained by Taylor-expanding all terms to obtain

$$T_j = \frac{\Delta t}{2} \frac{\partial^2 \Theta^n}{\partial t^2} + \mathcal{O}(\Delta t^2, \Delta x^2) = \frac{\Delta t}{2} \cdot \frac{\partial}{\partial x} \left(\frac{\partial \Theta}{\partial x} \right) + \mathcal{O}(\Delta t^2, \Delta x^2).$$

Clearly, this is a consistent scheme of first-order accuracy in time and second-order accuracy in space as expected. The *equivalent differential equation* is obtained by the differential Equation (8.1) enhanced with the truncation term, that is,

$$\frac{\partial \hat{\Theta}}{\partial t} + \frac{\partial \hat{\Theta}}{\partial x} + T_j = 0 \Rightarrow \frac{\partial \hat{\Theta}}{\partial t} + \frac{\partial \hat{\Theta}}{\partial x} = -\frac{\Delta t}{2} \frac{\partial^2 \hat{\Theta}}{\partial x^2} + \mathcal{O}(\Delta t^2, \Delta x^2).$$

Therefore, we see that the equivalent differential equation introduces a second-order derivative, which, according to the previous discussion, indicates numerical dissipation. Moreover, the coefficient is negative (i.e., the numerical diffusivity is negative), which in turn implies *exponential growth*. Based on this heuristic argument we expect that this scheme is unstable at least for long-term integration.

A more rigorous analysis can be obtained based on the **von Neumann stability** method. Let us assume that

$$\Theta_j^n = \sum_{k=-\infty}^{\infty} a_k^n e^{2\pi i k x_j}$$

and form the difference

$$\Theta_{j+1} - \Theta_{j-1} = \sum a_k e^{2\pi i k x_j} (e^{2\pi i k \Delta x} - e^{-2\pi i k \Delta x})$$

$$= \sum a_k e^{2\pi i k x_j} \cdot 2i \sin 2\pi k \Delta x.$$

Upon substitution in the EF/CD scheme we obtain

$$\sum_k (a_k^{n+1} - a_k^n)e^{2\pi ikx_j} = -\frac{C}{2}\sum_k (2i\sin 2\pi k\Delta x)\cdot a_k^n e^{2\pi ikx_j},$$

where

$$C \equiv \frac{U\Delta t}{\Delta x}. \tag{8.6}$$

This nondimensional number is the **Courant number** or **CFL number** or condition, and it was first introduced in the work of Courant, Friedrichs, and Lewy (1928) [18].

We can now obtain the amplification factor of EF/CD from the magnitudes of the amplitudes

$$a_k^{n+1} = a_k^n(1 - iC\sin 2\pi k\Delta x),$$

or

$$|a_k^{n+1}| = |a_k^n||1 + C^2\sin^2 2\pi k\Delta x|^{1/2}.$$

This equation shows that the amplitudes grow in time, and thus the EF/CD scheme is *absolutely unstable*, irrespective of the value of the Courant number C (i.e., irrespective of the time step!).

It is interesting to note, however, that the EF/CD scheme is conditionally stable in the *general stability* sense. Let us examine the magnitude of the amplitude

$$|a_k^{n+1}| \le |a_k^n|(1 + C^2)^{1/2} \le |a_k^n|e^{C^2/2}$$
$$\le |a_k^0|e^{nC^2/2}.$$

Thus,

$$|a_k^n| \le |a_k^0|e^{\left(\frac{\Delta t}{2\Delta x^2}\right)(n\Delta t)},$$

and this inequality indicates general stability. In practice, this means that for $(n\cdot\Delta t)$ fixed we can get a stable result for

$$\frac{\Delta t}{\Delta x^2} < \text{constant as } \Delta t, \Delta x \to 0.$$

This condition is in fact as restrictive as the condition for diffusion analyzed in the previous chapter. For $U \ne 1$ it is equivalent to

$$D = \frac{U\Delta t}{\Delta x^2} < \mathcal{O}(1),$$

which is a condition on the diffusion number D! Clearly, this is not a practical scheme because the solution blows up after a few time periods, as shown in Figure 8.5; see corresponding parameters in Table 8.1. However, it can be used as a *starter* in multistep stable high-order explicit schemes.

It is also instructive to examine the stability of this scheme by investigating how the eigenspectrum of the advection operator fits into the stability region of the

Table 8.1: Parameters used for the solution shown in Figure 8.5.

Euler-forward scheme, which is a unit circle on the left complex plane (see Section 5.2). The eigenvalues are obtained from

$$\frac{a_k^{n+1} - a_k^n}{\Delta t} = \underbrace{\left(\frac{-i \sin 2\pi k \Delta x}{\Delta x}\right)}_{\lambda} a_k^n$$

Parameter	Value
Method	EF/CD
Interval	[0, 1]
N	20
Δt	0.005
C	0.1
Initial condition	$u(x, 0) = \sin(2\pi x)$
Boundary conditions	Periodic

and are purely imaginary. This means that there is only one point of contact between the stability region of EF and the eigenvalues, and thus the EF/CD is an unstable scheme. A successful scheme, however, would be one that employs *leap-frog* time integration (see Section 5.2), as its stability region is the imaginary axis. Thus, for $C \leq 1$ the leap-frog/CD scheme is absolutely stable.

PUTTING IT INTO PRACTICE

Next we present a C++ implementation of the advection equation using central differencing in space and Euler-forward in time. This function takes as input the number of grid points, the CFL number, and the values at the current time level stored in the array *uold*. This function updates the array *unew* with the new values at the next time level.

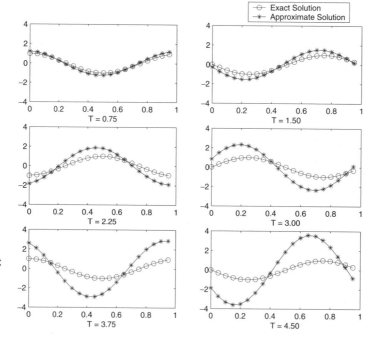

Figure 8.5: Euler-forward/central difference versus exact solution at various times T for the parameters listed in Table 8.1.

```
void EF_CentralDifference(int N, double CFL, double *uold,
                          double *unew){

  for(int i=1; i<N-1; i++){
    unew[i] = uold[i] - 0.5*CFL*(uold[i+1]-uold[i-1]);
  }

  unew[0] = uold[0] - 0.5*CFL*(uold[1]-uold[N-1]);
  unew[N-1] = uold[N-1] - 0.5*CFL*(uold[0]-uold[N-2]);

}
```

> Often boundary conditions are handled separately from interior points for looping simplicity.
>
> **Key Concept**

Propagation and the CFL Condition

The Courant number or CFL condition C has a physical meaning and a geometric interpretation that we present next. From an order-of-magnitude analysis of Equation (8.1) we have that

$$\frac{\Delta\Theta}{\Delta t} \propto U\frac{\Delta\Theta}{\Delta x} \quad \text{or} \quad C = \frac{U\Delta t}{\Delta x} \propto \mathcal{O}(1).$$

For the geometric interpretation we refer to Figure 8.6 and make use of the properties of characteristics (i.e., lines along which information is propagated). In our case the characteristic lines are defined by

$$\frac{dX}{dt} = U,$$

and they are straight lines for constant velocity U. In the figure we plot characteristics for both U and $-U$ for the point P. The points P_L and P_R are the locations of point P at time level ($n\Delta t$) if the wave was advected with velocity U and $-U$, respectively. By definition the lengths ($P_L B$) and ($P_R B$) are equal to the magnitude $U\Delta t$, and the region ($P P_L P_R$) is the domain of influence of the differential equation. We have already seen that $C \leq \mathcal{O}(1)$ and this simply means that the domain of dependence of the differential equation should be contained within the domain of dependence of the difference equation, the latter defined in Figure 8.6 by the region (PAC).

Euler-Forward/Upwind-Differencing Scheme (EF/UD)

The Euler-forward/central-differencing (EF/CD) scheme is inconsistent with the physics of the problem, which suggests that information is propagating from left to right. However, in the previous scheme we used information from the node ($j + 1$), which is downstream of node (j). Here, we present a scheme consistent with the

Figure 8.6: Time-space discretization in an explicit scheme. The lines PP_L and PP_R are the characteristics emanating from the point P.

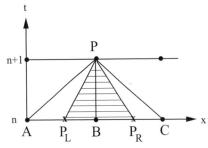

physics of the problem and employ an upwind derivative for spatial discretization. The discrete EF/UD scheme is

$$\frac{\Theta_j^{n+1} - \Theta_j^n}{\Delta t} + \frac{\Theta_j^n - \Theta_{j-1}^n}{\Delta x} = 0, \ \ j = 1, \dots, N,$$

which can be rewritten as

$$\Theta_j^{n+1} = \Theta_j^n - \frac{C}{2} \left(\Theta_{j+1}^n - \Theta_{j-1}^n \right) + \frac{C}{2} \left(\Theta_{j+1}^n - 2\Theta_j^n + \Theta_{j-1}^n \right).$$

In this form, we can see that the EF/UD scheme is similar to the EF/CD with the addition of an extra term on the right-hand side. This term is the discrete central difference second-order derivative, and thus it represents *numerical diffusion* added to the difference equation. Correspondingly, the equivalent differential equation is

$$\frac{\partial \hat{\Theta}}{\partial t} + \frac{\partial \hat{\Theta}}{\partial x} = \underbrace{\frac{1}{2} (\Delta x - U \Delta t) \frac{\partial^2 \hat{\Theta}_j}{\partial x^2} + \mathcal{O}(\Delta x^2, \Delta t^2)}_{T_j}.$$

We note that if $\Delta x = \Delta t$ then the Courant number is $C = 1$ and this scheme is exact; that is, $\Theta_j^{n+1} = \Theta_{j-1}^n$! This is because all high-order terms have the factor $(\Delta x - U \Delta t)$. With regards to stability, we can make the following statements:

- If $C < 1$, then $U \Delta t \le \Delta x$, and the equivalent differential equation has a positive numerical diffusivity, which in turn implies stability. However, the scheme is of first order, that is, $\mathcal{O}(\Delta t, \Delta x)$.
- If $C > 1$, then an instability occurs owing to negative diffusivity and associated exponential growth as before.

Figure 8.7: Stability region of the EF/UD scheme.

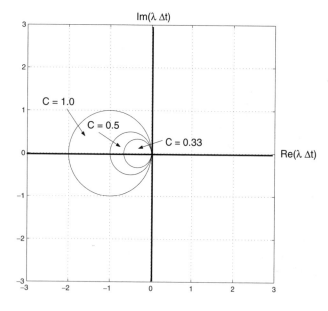

These results are confirmed from **von Neumann stability** analysis. Specifically, we obtain for the amplitude

$$a_k^n = a_k^n \left[1 - C(1 - e^{-2\pi i k \Delta x}) \right],$$

and taking its magnitude we have

$$|a_k^{n+1}| = |a_k^n| |1 - C(1 - e^{-2\pi i k \Delta x})|$$

$$= |a_k^n| \left[1 + 2(C^2 - C)(1 - \cos 2\pi k \Delta x) \right]^{1/2}.$$

For stability, we need to have attenuation of the amplitude, and thus we require

$$2C^2 - 2C \le 0 \Rightarrow C \le 1,$$

which is the same condition for stability as given by the equivalent differential equation.

We can also examine the region of stability in the *complex plane* by identifying the eigenspectrum for the UD scheme, that is,

$$\frac{a_k^{n+1} - a_k^n}{\Delta t} = \underbrace{-\frac{1 - e^{-2\pi i k \Delta x}}{\Delta x}}_{\lambda \text{ complex}} a_k^n,$$

and thus we obtain

$$\lambda \Delta t = -C(1 - e^{-2\pi i k \Delta x}) = -C(1 - \cos 2\pi k \Delta x) - iC \sin 2\pi k \Delta x.$$

In the complex $\lambda \Delta t$ plane, the curves described here are circles enclosed within the unit circle for $C \leq 1$, and thus stability is ensured (see Figure 8.7). In contrast to the EF/CD scheme, here the damping due to upwinding brings the $\lambda \Delta t$ into the stability region of the Euler scheme (the $C = 1$ curve). Therefore, with regards to stability the EF/UD is the opposite of the EF/CD. In fact it is too stable! This is suggested by reexamining the equivalent differential equation and writing it in the form

$$\frac{\partial \hat{\Theta}}{\partial t} + U \frac{\partial \hat{\Theta}}{\partial t} = \nu_{\text{eff}} \frac{\partial^2 \hat{\Theta}}{\partial x^2} + \dots,$$

where

$$\nu_{\text{eff}} = \frac{U \Delta x}{2}(1 - C) \sim U \Delta x.$$

The numerical solution will be so damped in time that the initial waveform will disappear after some time. This is shown in Figure 8.8, where the parameters of Table 8.2 are used.

We now present a C++ implementation of the advection equation using first-order upwinding in space and Euler-forward in time. This function takes as input the number of grid points, the CFL number, and the values at the current time level stored in the array *uold*. This function updates the array *unew* with the new values at the next time level.

```
void EF_FirstOrderUpwind(int N, double CFL, double *uold,
                         double *unew){

  for(int i=1; i<N; i++)
    unew[i] = uold[i] - CFL*(uold[i]-uold[i-1]);

  unew[0] = uold[0] - CFL*(uold[0]-uold[N-1]);
}
```

PUTTING IT INTO PRACTICE

Software

Suite

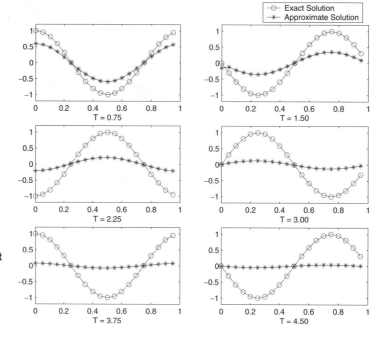

Figure 8.8:
Euler-forward/upwind
difference versus exact
solution at various
times *T* for the
parameters listed in
Table 8.2.

Programming
Note

A sign mistake can make all the difference. Take for instance this upwind scheme. The sign of the last term (`CFL*(uold[i]-uold[i-1])`) determines which way the wave is moving. If the sign is correct for upwinding, then the scheme is stable. If not, your code will blow up. The bottom line is this: Check your signs carefully.

Table 8.2: Parameters
used for the solution
shown in Figure 8.8.

REMARK: Numerical discretization of propagation problems should have the *transportive property* according to Roache [78]. This means that the effect of a perturbation is advected only in the direction of the velocity. Therefore, the upwind scheme is transportive but the central difference scheme is nontransportive. For a *variable* transport velocity U the following algorithm has been suggested by Roache:

1. *First order*:

$$\frac{\partial \Theta}{\partial t} + U \frac{\partial \Theta}{\partial x} \Rightarrow \frac{\Delta \Theta_j}{\Delta t} = - \frac{U_j \Theta_j - U_{j-1} \Theta_{j-1}}{\Delta x}.$$

This scheme is transportive but not conservative when U changes sign.

Parameter	Value
Method	EF/UD
Interval	[0, 1]
N	20
Δt	0.005
c	0.1
Initial condition	$u(x, 0) = \sin(2\pi x)$
Boundary conditions	Periodic

2. *Second order*: If the spatial derivative is discretized as

$$-\frac{U_R \Theta_R - U_L \Theta_L}{\Delta x},$$

where

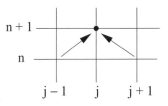

Figure 8.9:
Time–space stencil for
the Lax–Friedrichs
scheme.

$$U_R = \frac{1}{2}(U_{j+1} + U_j), \quad U_L = \frac{1}{2}(U_{j-1} + U_j),$$

$$\Theta_R = \Theta_j, \, U_R > 0,$$

$$\Theta_L = \Theta_{j-1}, \, U_L > 0$$

then this scheme is transportive, conservative, and (almost) second order.

Lax-Friedrichs Scheme and Tadmor's Correction

The idea of the Lax–Friedrichs (LF) scheme is to stabilize the EF/CD scheme by replacing the contribution from node j (i.e., the value Θ_j^n) by its average, as shown in Figure 8.9. Thus, the discrete scheme is

$$\Theta_j^{n+1} = \underbrace{\frac{1}{2}(\Theta_{j+1}^n + \Theta_{j-1}^n)}_{\text{average for } \Theta_j^n} - \frac{C}{2}(\Theta_{j+1}^n - \Theta_{j-1}^n). \tag{8.7}$$

This can be considered as a correction to the *unstable* EF/CD scheme as can be seen by rewriting this equation as

$$\Theta_j^{n+1} - \Theta_j^n = \underbrace{\frac{1}{2}(\Theta_{j+1}^n - 2\Theta_j^n + \Theta_{j-1}^n)}_{\text{fixed dissipation}} - \frac{C}{2}(\Theta_{j+1}^n - \Theta_{j-1}^n).$$

The **von Neumann analysis** shows that

$$a_k^{n+1} = a_k^n[\cos 2\pi k \Delta x - iC \sin 2\pi k \Delta x],$$

and thus stability is obtained for $C \leq 1$. For $C = 1$ we obtain $|a^{n+1}| = |a^n|$, which implies that there are no dissipation errors. In general, however, this scheme is *overly dissipative*, in fact more dissipative than the first-order upwind scheme. This is shown from the analysis of the *equivalent differential equation*

$$\frac{\partial \hat{\Theta}}{\partial t} + U \frac{\partial \hat{\Theta}}{\partial x} = \frac{\Delta x^2}{2\Delta t}(1 - C^2)\hat{\Theta}_{xx} + \frac{U \Delta x^2}{3}(1 - C^2)\hat{\Theta}_{xxx} + \cdots.$$

The numerical viscosity is

$$\nu_{\text{eff}} = \frac{U}{2C} \Delta x (1 - C^2)$$

$$= \frac{U \Delta x}{2}(1 - C)\frac{(1 + C)}{C}.$$

Therefore, the diffusion of this scheme is higher than the numerical viscosity of EF/UD by the factor $\left(\frac{1+C}{C}\right)$.

The *phase errors* are measured by

$$\epsilon_\phi \equiv \frac{\omega/k}{U}, \quad \phi = 2\pi k \Delta x,$$

the exact value of which is $\epsilon_\phi = 1$ for Equation (8.1). For $C = 1$ there are no dispersion errors but in general

$$\epsilon_\phi = \frac{\omega/k}{U} \approx 1 + \frac{\phi^2}{3}(1 - C^2) + \mathcal{O}(\Delta x^4),$$

and since $\epsilon_\phi > 1$ we have *leading* phase errors.

The Lax–Friedrichs scheme is of first order, but a *second-order version* has been proposed more recently by Tadmor (see [71]). It employs piecewise linear interpolation instead of constant values within the cell for the standard Lax–Friedrichs scheme. For the nonlinear case the scheme can be written as a predictor–corrector procedure (see the homework problems), but for the linear advection equation we consider here, it can be performed in a single step as follows:

$$\Theta_j^{n+1} = \frac{1}{2}[\Theta_{j+1}^n + \Theta_{j-1}^n] + \frac{1 - C^2}{4}[\Theta_{j-1}' - \Theta_{j+1}'] - \frac{C}{2}[\Theta_{j+1}^n - \Theta_{j-1}^n]. \tag{8.8}$$

The Tadmor correction therefore introduces the extra (middle) term Equation (8.8). Here, the first derivatives are computed properly so that they are of second-order accuracy, but they also satisfy nonoscillatory reconstruction procedures. To this end, we have

$$\Theta_j' = \text{MinMod}[\Delta\Theta_{j+1/2}^n, \Delta\Theta_{j-1/2}^n],$$

where we define

$$\text{MinMod}[x, y] = \frac{1}{2}[\text{sgn}(x) + \text{sgn}(y)]\text{Min}[|x|, |y|]$$

and also

$$\Delta\Theta_{j+1/2}^n \equiv \Theta_{j+1}^n - \Theta_j^n.$$

This is just one of several possible ways of computing Θ_j'. An alternative way that may lead to crisper discontinuities has also been suggested in [71]; it has the form

$$\Theta_j' = \text{MinMod}[\alpha\Delta\Theta_{j+1/2}^n, \frac{1}{2}(\Theta_{j+1}^n - \Theta_{j-1}^n), \alpha\Delta\Theta_{j-1/2}^n]. \tag{8.9}$$

The free parameter α is chosen so that a steeper slope near discontinuities is obtained. It is in the range $\alpha \in [1, 4)$ to satisfy the CFL condition and monotonicity constraints.

Software

○

Suite

EXAMPLE. To demonstrate the difference between the Lax–Friedrichs scheme and Tadmor's correction, we have implemented both Equation (8.7) and Equation (8.8) with Θ_j' defined as in Equation (8.9). The implementations can be found in the *software suite*. For this experiment, we will compare the exact solution versus the LF scheme, LF with Tadmor's correction using $\alpha = 1$, and LF with Tadmor's correction using $\alpha = 3$.

Table 8.3: Parameters for the solutions shown in Figure 8.10.

Parameter	Value
Method	Lax–Friedrichs/Tadmor's correction
Interval	[0, 1]
N	1,000
Δt	0.0005
C	0.5
Steps N	10,000
Final time T	5.0
Initial condition	$u(x, 0) = \begin{cases} 100(x - 0.4)(0.6 - x) & \text{if } 0.4 \leq x \leq 0.6 \\ 0 & \text{otherwise} \end{cases}$
Boundary conditions	Periodic

The parameters used for these experiments are presented in Table 8.3 with a parabola as initial condition.

In Figure 8.10, we present the results of our numerical experiments. The exact solution to this problem is for the initial condition to be advected with speed *one* through the periodic domain. Observe that although the Lax–Friedrichs solution has reasonably maintained the correct phase, the numerical solution is highly dissipated compared to the exact solution. Using Tadmor's correction with $\alpha = 1$, we see a significant improvement in the dissipation error. By setting $\alpha = 3$, we see slight improvement over the $\alpha = 1$ case; however, this improvement is at the cost of the solution being slightly more dispersive. Observe that for $\alpha = 3$ we see slight trailing wiggles

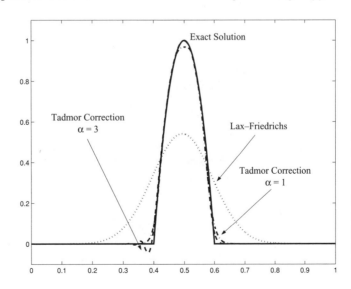

Figure 8.10: Comparison of exact solution (solid), Lax–Friedrichs scheme (dotted), Lax–Friedrichs with Tadmor correction for $\alpha = 1$ (dot-dashed), and Lax–Friedrichs with Tadmor correction for $\alpha = 3$ (dashed). Details of the numerical experiment are given in the text; the parameters are listed in Table 8.3.

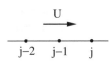

Figure 8.11: Stencil for second-order upwind scheme.

in the solution, indicating the dominance of the dispersion error over the dissipation error.

In the following, we present other high-order schemes suitable for propagation problems.

8.1.4 High-Order Discrete Schemes

Second-Order Upwind Scheme (EF/UD2)

The second-order upwind (EF/UD2) scheme was introduced by Warming and Beam [91] to correct the first-order upwind scheme EF/UD. It is applied on the stencil of Figure 8.11 and has the form

$$\Theta_j^{n+1} = \Theta_j^n - \underbrace{C(\Theta_j^n - \Theta_{j-1}^n)}_{\text{first-order upwind}} + \frac{1}{2}C(C-1)\underbrace{(\Theta_j^n - 2\Theta_{j-1}^n + \Theta_{j-2}^n)}_{\text{dissipation at } (j-1)}.$$

Therefore, it adds to the upwind node $(j-1)$ positive or negative dissipation depending on the value of C. The corresponding equivalent differential equation

$$\hat{\Theta}_t + U\hat{\Theta}_x = \frac{U}{6}\Delta x^2(1-C)(2-C)\hat{\Theta}_{xxx} - \frac{C}{8}\Delta x^3(1-C)^2(2-C)\left(\frac{\partial^4\hat{\Theta}}{\partial x^4}\right) + \cdots$$

shows that there is no second-order derivative and therefore dissipation is reduced compared to the first-order upwind scheme.

The precise stability condition is determined from **von Neumann analysis** as follows:

$$a_k^{n+1} = a_k^n \left\{1 - 2C[1-(1-C)\cos\phi]\sin^2\phi/2 - iC\sin\phi[1+2(1-C)\sin^2\phi/2]\right\},$$

and we can obtain

$$\left|\frac{a_k^{n+1}}{a_k^n}\right|^2 = 1 - 4C(1-C^2)(2-C)\sin^4\phi/2.$$

For stability, we require that $C \leq 2$.

Analysis of **phase errors** shows that

$$\epsilon_\phi = \frac{\omega/k}{U} \approx 1 + \frac{1}{6}(1-C)(2-C)\phi^2 + \mathcal{O}(\phi^4),$$

which suggests that the phase errors are leading errors for $C < 1$ and lagging error for $C > 1$. This is demonstrated in Figure 8.12; the parameters for the solution are in Table 8.4.

Software

Suite

PUTTING IT INTO PRACTICE

In the following we present a C++ implementation of the advection equation using second-order upwinding in space and Euler-forward in time. This function takes as input the number of grid points, the CFL number, and the values at the current time

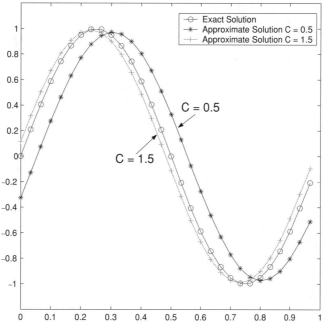

Figure 8.12: Euler-forward/second-order upwind difference versus exact solution at $T = 10.0$ for $C = 0.5$ and 1.5; the parameters are listed in Table 8.4.

level stored in the array *uold*. This function updates the array *unew* with the new values at the next time level.

```
void EF_SecondOrderUpwind(int N, double CFL, double *uold,
                          double *unew){

  for(int i=2; i<N; i++){
    unew[i] = (1.0e0 - CFL*((3.0/2.0) - CFL/2.0))*uold[i] +
             CFL*(2.0-CFL)*uold[i-1] +
             (CFL/2.0)*(CFL-1.0)*uold[i-2];
  }

  unew[0] = (1.0 - CFL*((3.0/2.0) - CFL/2.0))*uold[0] +
           CFL*(2.0-CFL)*uold[N-1] +
           (CFL/2.0)*(CFL-1.0)*uold[N-2];

  unew[1] = (1.0 - CFL*((3.0/2.0) - CFL/2.0))*uold[1] +
           CFL*(2.0-CFL)*uold[0] +
           (CFL/2.0)*(CFL-1.0)*uold[N-1];

}
```

REMARK: Unlike in previous examples, second-order upwinding, owing to its stencil, requires us to handle separately the first two values (**unew[0]** and **unew[1]**) instead of the two end points of the domain (**unew[0]** and **unew[N-1]**).

Parameter	Value
Method	Euler-forward 2nd-order UD
Interval	$[0, 1]$
N	30
Δt	0.01667 and 0.05
c	0.5 and 1.5
T	10.0
Initial condition	$u(x, 0) = \sin(2\pi x)$
Boundary conditions	Periodic

Lax–Wendroff Scheme

Like the previous EF/UD2, the Lax–Wendroff Scheme (EF/LW) is second-order. In fact, these two schemes are the only single-step schemes that achieve second-order accuracy on a three-point stencil. The key idea is somewhat different: Instead of substituting the Taylor expansions of all derivatives in Equation (8.1), we first expand in time the numerical solution and subsequently replace the time derivatives with the first- and second-order wave equations.

We start with

$$\Theta_j^{n+1} = \Theta_j^n + \Delta t(\Theta_t)_j + \frac{\Delta t^2}{2}(\Theta_{tt})_j^n + \mathcal{O}(\Delta t^3)$$

and replace the first-order time derivative from Equation (8.1) and also the second-order time derivative from

$$\Theta_{tt} = U^2 \Theta_{xx} \quad \text{(second-order wave equation)};$$

thus,

$$\Theta_j^{n+1} = \Theta_j^n - U\,\Delta t(\Theta_x)_j + \frac{U^2 \Delta t^2}{2}(\Theta_{xx})_j + \mathcal{O}(\Delta t^3),$$

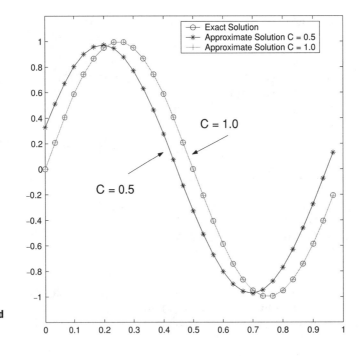

Figure 8.13: Lax-Wendroff versus exact solution at $T = 10.0$ for $C = 0.5$ and 1.0; parameters are listed in Table 8.5.

or

$$\Theta_j^{n+1} = \Theta_j^n - \frac{C}{2}(\Theta_{j+1}^n - \Theta_{j-1}^n)$$

$$+ \frac{C^2}{2}\underbrace{(\Theta_{j+1}^n - 2\Theta_j^n + \Theta_{j-1}^n)}_{\text{dissipation}}.$$

The last term is a high-order numerical dissipation contribution because it scales with C^2, that is, with $(\Delta t)^2$.

The corresponding *equivalent differential equation* is

$$\hat{\Theta}_t + U\hat{\Theta}_x = -\frac{U}{6}\Delta x^2(1 - C^2)\hat{\Theta}_{xxx} - \frac{U\Delta x^3}{8}$$

$$\cdot C(1 - C^2)\hat{\Theta}_{xxxx} + \mathcal{O}(\Delta x^4),$$

which shows predominantly *phase errors* since the dominant term in the truncation error is a third-order derivative.

The **von Neumann** stability analysis shows that

$$a_k^{n+1} = a_k^n[1 - iC\sin 2\pi k\Delta x - C^2(1 - \cos 2\pi k\Delta x)],$$

and thus for stability we require that $C \leq 1$.

The phase errors are *lagging* in this scheme since

$$\epsilon_\phi \approx 1 - \frac{1}{6}(1 - C^2)\phi^2 + \mathcal{O}(\phi^4),$$

with the largest phase errors present at high frequencies. This behavior of the Lax–Wendroff scheme is demonstrated in Figure 8.13, which is obtained based on the parameters of Table 8.5.

Table 8.5: Parameters used for the solutions of Figure 8.13.

Parameter	Value
Method	Lax–Wendroff
Interval	[0, 1]
N	30
Δt	0.01667 and 0.0333
C	0.5 and 1.0
T	10.0
Initial condition	$u(x, 0) = \sin(2\pi x)$
Boundary conditions	Periodic

PUTTING IT INTO PRACTICE

We now present a C++ implementation of the advection equation using the Lax–Wendroff scheme. This function takes as input the number of grid points, the CFL number, and the values at the current time level stored in the array *uold*. This function updates the array *unew* with the new values at the next time level. The following code was used to produce the results shown in Figure 8.13.

Software Suite

```
void LaxWendroff(int N, double CFL, double *uold,
                double *unew){

  for(int i=1; i<N-1; i++){
    unew[i] = uold[i] - (CFL/2.0)*(uold[i+1]-uold[i-1])+
              (CFL*CFL/2.0)*(uold[i+1]-2.0*uold[i]+uold[i-1]);
  }
```

```
unew[0] = uold[0] - (CFL/2.0)*(uold[1]-uold[N-1])+
          (CFL*CFL/2.0)*(uold[1]-2.0*uold[0]+uold[N-1]);

unew[N-1] = uold[N-1] - (CFL/2.0)*(uold[0]-uold[N-2])+
            (CFL*CFL/2.0)*(uold[0]-2.0*uold[N-1]+uold[N-2]);

}
```

REMARK 1: Grouping terms to reduce operations can increase computational efficiency. Take the example here. Observe that uold[$i + 1$] is used twice on the right-hand-side expression. The scheme could be rewritten as **unew[i] =c1*uold[i]+c2*uold[i+1]+ c3*uold[i-1]***, where $c1 = 1.0 - CFL * CFL$, $c2 = CFL(-1.0 + CFL)/2.0$, and $c3 = CFL$ $(1.0 + CFL)/2.0$. Since $c1$, $c2$, and $c3$ do not change with respect to i, we can compute them ahead of time and merely use them within the loop. A good compiler will attempt to optimize this for you, but the programmer should always be mindful of such things. The bottom line is this: If you can save the computer time by thinking a little, then you should try thinking a little.

REMARK 2: Given that the EF/UD2 and EF/LW schemes have leading and lagging errors, respectively, in the range $0 < C \leq 1$, we can construct *hybrid schemes* by combining the two second-order schemes to obtain fourth-order accuracy in the phase properties. This is important especially for long-time integration.

Adams–Bashforth/Center-Differencing Scheme (AB/CD)

So far we have considered single-step explicit schemes, but higher order schemes can be easily achieved using either multistage schemes such as Runge–Kutta or multistep schemes such as Adams–Bashforth. Here we present results for the latter; specifically first we present a second-order Adams–Bashforth scheme and subsequently a third-order Adams–Bashforth scheme. The previous stable single-step schemes can be employed in the initial steps.

The **second-order** scheme is

$$\frac{\Theta_j^{n+1} - \Theta_j^n}{\Delta t} + \frac{3}{2}\Delta_x \Theta_j^n - \frac{1}{2}\Delta_x \Theta_j^{n-1} = 0,$$

with corresponding *equivalent differential equation*

$$\frac{\partial \hat{\Theta}}{\partial t} + \frac{\partial \hat{\Theta}}{\partial x} = \left(\frac{5\Delta t^2}{12} - \frac{\Delta x^2}{6}\right)\frac{\partial^3 \hat{\Theta}}{\partial x^3} + \dots.$$

The term on the right-hand side indicates that the dominant errors are phase errors. Note that unlike the previous cases, here the terms Θ_{xxxx}, Θ_{vi}, ... are *not* all zero, and thus we have amplitude errors as well but they are subdominant.

The **von Neumann stability** analysis leads to

$$a_k^{n+1} + a_k^n\left(-1 + \frac{3}{2}iC\sin 2\pi k\Delta x\right) + a_k^{n-1}\left(-\frac{iC}{2}\sin 2\pi k\Delta x\right) = 0.$$

Let us define

$$\mu \equiv \frac{a_k^{n+1}}{a_k^n} \Rightarrow \mu^2 + \mu\left(-1 + \frac{3}{2}i\sin 2\pi k\Delta x\right) + \left(\frac{-iC}{2}\sin 2\pi k\Delta x\right) = 0,$$

where μ is complex. For $C \ll 1$ we can obtain approximate expressions for the two roots: The larger one

$$\mu_+ = 1 - iC\sin 2\pi k\Delta x - \frac{C^2}{2}\sin^2 2\pi k\Delta x - \frac{1}{4}iC^3\sin^3 2\pi k\Delta x - \frac{1}{8}C^4\sin^4 2\pi k\Delta x + \ldots$$

corresponds to the physical mode because it is approximately 1, whereas the smaller root

$$\mu_- = -\frac{1}{2}iC\sin 2\pi k\Delta x + \frac{1}{2}C^2\sin^2 2\pi k\Delta x + \ldots$$

is a spurious (numerical) mode.

Note that both roots μ_+, μ_- depend on the initial conditions and that the numerical mode is damped relatively to the physical mode. For C small we have that $\to |\mu_-| \ll 1$.

The root corresponding to the physical mode can be bounded from above as shown by performing leading order analysis:

$$|\mu_+| = \left(1 + \frac{1}{2}C^4\right)^{1/2} + \mathcal{O}(C^n),$$

$$|a_k^n| \approx |a_k^0|(1 + \frac{1}{2}C^4)^{n/2}$$

$$\leq |a_k^0|e^{\frac{C^4 n}{4}} = |a_k^0|e^{\frac{\Delta t^3(n\cdot\Delta t)}{4\Delta x^4}}.$$

The last inequality shows that the second-order Adams–Bashforth/center-differencing (AB2/CD) scheme is *generally* stable. More specifically, the scheme is similar to EF/CD, but here the growth is proportional to C^4, not C^2, and requires only $\Delta t^3 < \Delta x^4$, and not $\Delta t < \Delta x^2$ as in the EF/CD scheme.

Therefore, we see that this is a stable scheme in practice, so we have the case of an unstable scheme, which however is usable for C small. The phase errors for this scheme (shown in Figure 8.14, which is obtained from the parameters in Table 8.6) are large for long time integration.

Figure 8.14: Second-order Adams–Bashforth/central difference versus exact solution at various times *T* ; parameters are listed in Table 8.6.

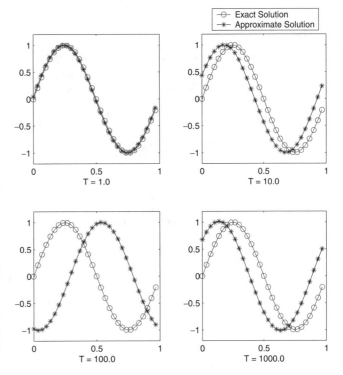

Table 8.6: Parameters used for the solutions of Figure 8.14.

Parameter	Value
Method	2nd order Adams–Bashforth/CD
Interval	[0, 1]
N	30
Δt	0.003333
C	0.1
Initial condition	$u(x, 0) = \sin(2\pi x)$
Boundary conditions	Periodic

A better scheme is the **third-order Adams-Bashforth/CD** scheme

$$\frac{\Theta^{n+1} - \Theta_j^n}{\Delta t} + \frac{23}{12}\Delta_x\Theta_j^n - \frac{16}{12}\Delta_x\Theta_j^{n-1}$$

$$+ \frac{5}{12}\Delta_x\Theta_j^{n-2} = 0.$$

Its corresponding *equivalent differential equation* is

$$\frac{\partial\hat{\Theta}^2}{\partial t} + \frac{\partial\hat{\Theta}}{\partial x} = \underbrace{\frac{-\Delta x^2}{6}\frac{\partial^3\hat{\Theta}}{\partial x^3}}_{\text{dispersive}}$$

$$\underbrace{+\, \mathcal{O}(\Delta t^3)\frac{\partial^4\hat{\Theta}}{\partial x^4}}_{\text{diffusive}} + \mathcal{O}(\Delta t\Delta x^2).$$

Therefore, the phase errors are second order, and if high-order spatial discretization is used this scheme will exhibit very small dispersion. It is conditionally stable, and the Courant number limit is given by considering the imaginary eigenvalues

$$\lambda\Delta t = -iC\sin 2\pi k\Delta x < 0.723i.$$

For stability, we require that $C \leq 0.723$.

In the homework problems we investigate the phase errors for short-time as well as long-time integration.

Crank–Nicolson/Center-Differencing Scheme (CN/CD)

We now study an *implicit* scheme to discretize Equation (8.1), the Crank–Nicolson/center-differencing (CN/CD) scheme as follows:

$$\frac{\Theta_j^{n+1} - \Theta_j^n}{\Delta t} + \frac{1}{2}\Delta_x\Theta_j^{n+1} + \frac{1}{2}\Delta_x\Theta_j^n = 0.$$

The **von Neumann stability** analysis leads to

$$a_k^{n+1} = \left(\frac{1 - \frac{iC}{2}\sin 2\pi k\Delta x}{1 + \frac{iC}{2}\sin 2\pi k\Delta x}\right) a_k^n \Rightarrow |a_k^{n+1}| = |a_k^n| \quad \forall C, k,$$

so we have neutral stability, more specifically absolute but weak stability. The eigenvalues

$$\lambda\Delta t = \frac{-\frac{C^2}{4}\sin^2 2\pi k\Delta x - \frac{iC}{2}\sin 2\pi k\Delta x}{1 - \frac{C^2}{4}\sin^2 2\pi k\Delta x}$$

are on the left half-plane for any positive value of C.

Although there are no amplitude errors there are *phase errors*, which are determined from the *equivalent differential equation*

$$\frac{\partial\hat{\Theta}}{\partial t} + \frac{\partial\hat{\Theta}}{\partial x} = \left(-\frac{1}{12}\Delta t^2 - \frac{1}{6}\Delta x^2\right)\frac{\partial^3\hat{\Theta}}{\partial x^3},$$

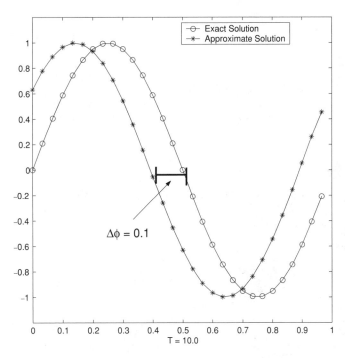

Figure 8.15: Crank–Nicolson/central difference versus the exact solution at $T = 10.0$; parameters are listed in Table 8.7.

where all Θ_{xx}, Θ_{xxxx}, and so on vanish. Let us now assume that

$$\hat{\Theta} = \mathrm{Re}\left\{e^{2\pi i k x}e^{-2\pi i \omega t}\right\}.$$

Then we can obtain the approximate dispersion relationship

$$-2\pi i \omega = -2\pi i k - \left(\frac{1}{12}\Delta t^2 + \frac{1}{6}\Delta x^2\right)(-i)(2\pi k)^3,$$

and therefore

$$\epsilon_\phi = 1 - \underbrace{\left(\frac{1}{12}\Delta t^2 + \frac{1}{6}\Delta x^2\right)(2\pi k)^2}_{\text{phase error}}.$$

Thus, the *phase errors* are $\Delta\phi = -\left(\frac{1}{12}\Delta t^2 + \frac{1}{6}\Delta x^2\right)(2\pi k)^2$, which lead to errors in period and peak as shown in Figure 8.16; the parameters used in the solution are listed in Table 8.7 and corresponding results in Figure 8.15.

In general, the largest errors correspond to high wavenumbers, but for $k = N/2$ in particular, we have that

$$\Theta \sim \mathrm{Re}\left\{e^{2\pi i k \Delta x \cdot j}\right\} = \mathrm{Re}\left\{e^{2\pi i \frac{N}{2}\frac{j}{N}}\right\} = \mathrm{Re}\left\{e^{\pi i j}\right\},$$

and thus

$$\frac{\Theta_{j+1} - \Theta_{j-1}}{2\Delta x} = 0.$$

Table 8.7: Parameters used for the solutions of Figure 8.15.

Parameter	Value
Method	Crank–Nicolson/central difference
Interval	[0, 1]
N	30
Δt	0.0333
C	1.0
T	10.0
Initial condition	$u(x, 0) = \sin(2\pi x)$
Boundary conditions	Periodic

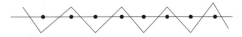

Figure 8.16:
Stationary mode
develops a 2 Δx wave
pattern for the CN/CD
scheme.

Software
Suite

Therefore, this mode never moves, although it should be traveling with speed $C_\phi = 1$! Instead, it develops a standing wave with wavelength $2\Delta x$, as shown in Figure 8.16.

PUTTING IT INTO PRACTICE

In the following we present a C++ implementation of the advection equation using central differencing in space and Crank–Nicolson in time. This function takes as input the number of grid points, the CFL number and the values at the current time level stored in the array *uold*. This function updates the array *unew* with the new values at the next time level.

```
void CrankNicolson_CentralDifference(int N, double CFL,
                          double *uold, double *unew){

   double c = 0.25*CFL;
   double *q = new double[N];

   for(int i=1; i<N-1; i++)
     q[i] = uold[i] - 0.25*CFL*(uold[i+1]-uold[i-1]);

   q[0] =   uold[0] - 0.25*CFL*(uold[1]-uold[N-1]);
   q[N-1] = uold[N-1] - 0.25*CFL*(uold[0]-uold[N-2]);

   ThomasAlgorithm_per(N,-c,1.0e0,c,unew,q);

   delete[] q;

}
```

Key
Concept

Reuse of code is important. Notice how easily Crank–Nicolson can be implemented once we know that we have our Thomas algorithm tridiagonal solver.

REMARK: The computational complexity of this algorithm is determined from the work required in solving the linear system, that is, the implicit part, which includes the terms

$$\frac{1}{\Delta t}\Theta_j^{n+1} + \frac{1}{4\Delta x}(\Theta_{j+1}^{n+1} - \Theta_{j-1}^{n+1}).$$

This is a triadigonal system and it requires linear work if no pivoting is required. This is guaranteed if we have diagonal dominance, which here means that

$$\frac{1}{4\Delta x} + \frac{1}{4\Delta x} < \frac{1}{\Delta t},$$

and this condition is satisfied if

$$C < 2.$$

- In other words for stability any value of C leads to a stable scheme for CN/CD. However, for linear work we should have $C < 2$; otherwise pivoting is required, which may lead to quadratic or even cubic work!

8.1.5 Effects of Boundary Conditions

So far we have considered periodic boundary conditions, essentially avoiding complications in the discretization resulting from the boundaries. In general, hyperbolic equations like Equation (8.1) are very sensitive to boundary conditions, compared, for example, to the parabolic equations we studied in the previous chapter.

To illustrate this effect, let us revisit the linear advection problem but enforce Dirichlet boundary conditions on the left boundary, that is,

$$\frac{\partial \Theta}{\partial t} + U \frac{\partial \Theta}{\partial x} = 0, \; \Theta(x, t = 0) = \sin 2\pi x, \tag{8.10}$$

$$0 < x < 1, \quad \Theta(x = 0, t) = -\sin 2\pi t. \tag{8.11}$$

Physically, we have that the left boundary located at $x = 0$ generates the information that is then propagated through the domain. Note that no boundary conditions are needed at the right boundary (outflow) located at $x = 1$.

To proceed, we first consider the **Crank–Nicolson** scheme, which for the periodic case was absolutely stable. The new discretization should include the boundary conditions as follows:

$$\frac{\Theta_j^{n+1} - \Theta_j^n}{\Delta t} + \frac{1}{2} \left(\frac{\Theta_{j+1}^{n+1} - \Theta_{j-1}^{n+1}}{2\Delta x} + \frac{\Theta_{j+1}^n - \Theta_{j-1}^n}{2\Delta x} \right) = 0, \; j = 1, \dots, N-1,$$

$$\Theta_0^{n+1} = -\sin 2\pi t^{n+1}, \quad \Theta_j^0 = \sin 2\pi x_j.$$

Here we have excluded node $j = N$, as we cannot write the central difference for the first-order spatial derivative. To this end, we add a fictitious node at $j = N+1$ (see Figure 8.17) and obtain Θ_{N+1} by linear extrapolation as follows:

$$\Theta_{N+1} = \Theta_N + \Delta x \frac{\Theta_N - \Theta_{N-1}}{\Delta x} = 2\Theta_N - \Theta_{N-1},$$

which can be rewritten as

$$\frac{\Theta_{N+1} - \Theta_N}{\Delta x} = \frac{\Theta_N - \Theta_{N-1}}{\Delta x},$$

so at the outflow node we employ a first-order, one-sided derivative. This will affect the accuracy locally, but overall we still obtain $\mathcal{O}(\Delta x^2)$ because errors are advected to the right and are propagated outside the domain. Therefore, at node $j = N$ we have

$$\frac{\Theta_N^{n+1} - \Theta_N^n}{\Delta t} + \frac{1}{2} \left(\frac{\Theta_N^{n+1} - \Theta_{N-1}^{n+1}}{\Delta x} + \frac{\Theta_N^n - \Theta_{N-1}^n}{\Delta x} \right) = 0.$$

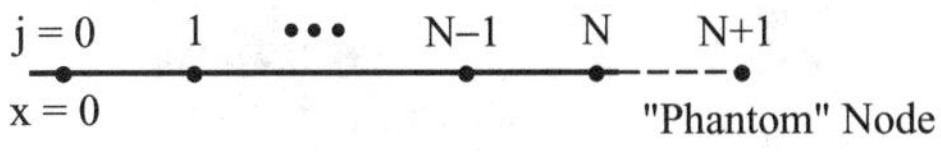

Figure 8.17: An extra node is added at the outflow to compute the derivative at the node N.

The addition of the upwind derivative does not adversely influence the stability of the CN scheme as it produces eigenvalues in the left half-plane.

In contrast, if we consider **explicit schemes** the outflow condition influences very strongly their stability. For example, the EF/CD scheme, which was unstable in the periodic case, now becomes stable owing to the dissipation of the upwind derivative at this outflow, which makes the corresponding eigenvalues land in the left half-plane instead of the imaginary axis as in the periodic case. Let us examine what happens with the second-order Adams–Bashforth scheme we presented earlier. The discrete equation at the outflow node $j = N$ is

$$\frac{\Theta_N^{n+1} - \Theta_N^n}{\Delta t} + \underbrace{\frac{3}{2}\left(\frac{\Theta_N^n - \Theta_{N-1}^n}{\Delta x}\right) - \frac{1}{2}\left(\frac{\Theta_N^{n-1} - \Theta_{N-1}^{n-1}}{\Delta x}\right)}_{\text{dissipative}} = 0.$$

In the following we first implement this equation and subsequently we perform numerical experiments to study its behavior.

Software

Suite

PUTTING IT INTO PRACTICE

Next we present a C++ implementation of the advection equation using central differencing in space and second-order Adams–Bashforth in time. This function takes as input the number of grid points, the CFL number, and the values at the current time level stored in the array *uold*. This function updates the array *unew* with the new values at the next time level.

```
void AB2_CentralDifferenceNP(int N, double CFL, double **uold,
                             double *unew){

  for(int i=1; i<N-1; i++){
    unew[i] = uold[0][i] - 0.75*CFL*(uold[0][i+1]-uold[0]
              [i-1]) + 0.25*CFL*(uold[1][i+1]-uold[1][i-1]);
  }

  unew[N-1] = uold[0][N-1] - 1.5*CFL*(uold[0][N-1]-uold[0]
              [N-2]) + 0.5*CFL*(uold[1][N-1]-uold[1][N-2]);

}
```

REMARK: This function assumes that the left-hand boundary condition (**unew[0]**) is handled by the calling function. For the numerical results presented in Figure 8.18, the exact solution was used at the inflow. The corresponding parameters are listed in Table 8.8. There is some small error at the outflow; however, we obtain a stable result.

We now turn to the **leap-frog** scheme, which was a stable scheme for the periodic case, but it now becomes unstable owing to the effects of dissipation at the outflow

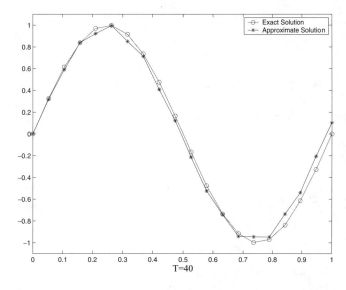

Figure 8.18: Second-order Adams–Bashforth/central difference at $T = 40.0$ for $C = 0.1$, $N = 20$; parameters are listed in Table 8.8.

node. The scheme is given by

$$\frac{\Theta_j^{n+1} - \Theta_j^{n-1}}{2\Delta t} + \frac{\Theta_{j+1}^n - \Theta_{j-1}^n}{2\Delta x} = 0, \quad j = 1, \ldots, N-1,$$

$$\frac{\Theta_N^{n+1} - \Theta_N^{n-1}}{2\Delta t} + \frac{\Theta_N^n - \Theta_{N-1}^n}{\Delta x} = 0.$$

This is an unstable scheme, as we ask you to verify in the homework problems.

8.2   ADVECTION–DIFFUSION EQUATION

We now introduce physical dissipation by including a second-order derivative (in space) to the linearized advection equation (8.1). The initial waveform is both advected and diffused at the same time, as shown in Figure 8.19.

This simple model describes, for example, advection and diffusion of dye by a uniform stream and has the form

$$\frac{\partial \Theta}{\partial t} + U \frac{\partial \Theta}{\partial x} = \alpha \frac{\partial^2 \Theta}{\partial x^2}, \quad -\infty < x < \infty, \quad (8.12)$$

where α is the diffusion coefficient and depends on the material. The ratio

$$\frac{U\Theta_x}{\alpha \Theta_{xx}} \sim \frac{U \frac{\Delta\Theta}{a}}{\alpha \cdot \frac{\Delta\Theta}{a^2}} \sim \frac{U \cdot a}{\alpha} = Pe$$

Table 8.8: Parameters used for the solutions of Figure 8.18.

Parameter	Value
Method	2nd-order Adams–Bashforth/CD
Interval	[0, 1]
N	40
Δt	0.005
C	0.1
T	40.0
Initial condition	$u(x, 0) = \sin(2\pi x)$
Boundary conditions	Nonperiodic

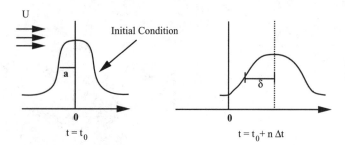

Figure 8.19: Advection and diffusion of an initial waveform by a uniform airstream.

is defined as the (physical) Peclet number of the process and expresses the relative importance of advection compared to diffusion. Here a is the characteristic length scale of the problem.

In practice, we need to truncate the domain to finite limits and thus the interval of interest is

$$-L_{\mathrm{I}} \text{ (inflow) } \leq x \leq L_{\mathrm{O}} \text{ (outflow).}$$

Later, we will discuss how to choose the size of the truncated domain defined by L_{I} and L_{O} and what are the appropriate boundary conditions to impose there.

8.2.1 Discrete Schemes

We present next representative discretizations of fully implicit, fully explicit, semi-implicit, and semi-Lagrangian schemes. By this we refer to the time-stepping algorithms involved in handling the advection and diffusion terms, which may or may not be identical for each contribution.

Fully Implicit Discretization

A typical second-order fully implicit scheme is one based on Crank–Nicolson time stepping with central differencing in space. Defining the central discrete first- and second-derivative operators Δ_x and Δ_{xx} respectively, as before, we have

$$\frac{\Theta_j^{n+1} - \Theta_j^n}{\Delta t} = \frac{1}{2}(\alpha \Delta_{xx}\Theta_j^{n+1} - U\Delta_x\Theta_j^{n+1}) + \frac{1}{2}(\alpha \Delta_{xx}\Theta_j^n - U\Delta_x\Theta_j^n),$$

which can be recast in a form that leads more easily to constructing the algebraic system

$$\left(\Delta_{xx} - \frac{U}{\alpha}\Delta_x - \frac{2}{\alpha\Delta t}\right)\Theta_j^{n+1} = -\frac{2}{\alpha\Delta t}\Theta_j^n - \left(\Delta_{xx} - \frac{U}{\alpha}\Delta_x\right)\Theta_j^n.$$

From von Neumann analysis we obtain the amplitude relation

$$a_k^{n+1} = a_k^n\left(\frac{1 - \frac{\lambda\Delta t}{2}}{1 + \frac{\lambda\Delta t}{2}}\right),$$

where the eigenvalues are complex:

$$\lambda = -\frac{i\sin 2\pi k\Delta x \cdot U}{\Delta x} - \alpha\overbrace{\frac{(1 - \cos 2\pi k\Delta x)}{\Delta x^2}}^{\sigma_k}.$$

Combining these two equations, we can conclude that the scheme is stable with no amplitude errors but that it suffers from dispersion (phase) errors, as we have seen before in the previous section.

Fully Explicit Discretization

Here we use an Euler-forward time-stepping algorithm combined with central differencing; a higher order scheme for time discretization could be employed in practice (e.g., third-order Adams–Bashforth). However, the issue of stability associated with explicit discretization for an advection–diffusion system are more clearly demonstrated with the first-order scheme

$$\frac{\Theta_j^{n+1} - \Theta_j^n}{\Delta t} = \alpha \Delta_{xx} \Theta_j^n - U \Delta_x \Theta_j^n.$$

This scheme has the following *equivalent differential equation*:

$$\frac{\partial \hat{\Theta}}{\partial t} + U \frac{\partial \hat{\Theta}}{\partial x} = \left(\alpha - \frac{1}{2} \Delta t \cdot U^2 \right) \frac{\partial^2 \hat{\Theta}}{\partial x^2} + \cdots + \mathcal{O}(\Delta t^2, \Delta x^2) \cdot \frac{\partial^3 \hat{\Theta}}{\partial x^3}.$$

For stability we require that the modified diffusion coefficient be positive, and thus

$$\frac{1}{2} \Delta t \cdot U^2 \leq \alpha \Rightarrow \Delta t < \frac{2\alpha}{U^2}.$$

REMARK: For $\alpha = \frac{1}{2} \Delta t \cdot U^2$, we recover the Lax–Wendroff scheme presented in the previous section for the linear advection equation (8.1).

A more rigorous **von Neuman** stability analysis leads to

$$\frac{a_k^{n+1} - a_k^n}{\Delta t} = \lambda a_k^n$$

with complex eigenvalues

$$\lambda = \frac{-i \sin 2\pi k \Delta x U}{\Delta x} - \frac{\sigma_k \alpha}{\Delta x^2},$$

where $\sigma_k = 2(1 - \cos 2\pi k \Delta x)$ as before. It is clear that as $\Delta x \to 0$, the second (diffusive) term dominates, and thus we require that

$$\Delta t \leq \frac{\Delta x^2}{2\alpha},$$

or

$$\Delta t \lambda_{\text{diff}} > -2 \Rightarrow -\frac{\sigma_k \alpha}{\Delta x^2} \cdot \Delta t > -2,$$

so we recover the limit for the diffusion number, that is, $D \leq \frac{1}{2}$ as before. We note here that the highest derivative "governs" the stability of the advection–diffusion equation, which is true for other systems as well. In Figure 8.20 we present the stability diagram in the $\lambda \Delta t$ plane.

Figure 8.20: Stability diagram and eigenvalues of the EF/CD scheme for the advection-diffusion equation.

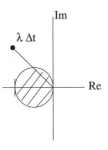

In summary, to guarantee stability of the EF/CD scheme, we have obtained two independent upper limits for the maximum allowable time step, that is,

$$\Delta t \leq \frac{\Delta x^2}{2\alpha}$$

and

$$\Delta t \leq \frac{2\alpha}{U^2}.$$

The question then becomes which of the two limits we should use. If we *assume* that

$$\frac{\Delta x^2}{2\alpha} < \frac{2\alpha}{U^2}$$

then we obtain that

$$Pe_g \equiv \frac{U \Delta x}{\alpha} < 2.$$

This equation defines the *grid Peclet number*, which should be less than 2 to obtain a stable explicit scheme if we only satisfy the diffusion limit.

This statement is *not* equivalent to the previous two conditions; that is, it is not a necessary condition, but it is sufficiently restrictive. In fact, it imposes a restriction on the mesh size (for stability) independent of the time step Δt, which is somewhat strange. The condition $Pe_g \leq 2$ has been used for a long time in simulations although it does not present the true stability limit for advection–diffusion as we will see next. However, because the numerical solution develops spatial oscillations for $Pe_g > 2$, it was assumed that it was the correct stability criterion.

We now reexamine more carefully the stability of the the EF/CD scheme for Equation (8.12) by following the analysis presented in [56].

If we rewrite the amplitude equation from the von Neumann analysis in terms of the Courant (C) and diffusion (D) numbers, we have

$$a_k^{n+1} = a_k^n [1 + 2D(\cos \phi - 1) - iC \sin \phi].$$

We can now construct the polar plot in the complex plane shown in Figure 8.21. By inspection of the plot, from first glance we see that stability is obtained if the ellipse is within the unit circle of stability, that is,

$$C \leq 2D \leq 1.$$

However, this is not quite correct, and in fact we recover the same condition as before, that is, the overly restrictive limit on the grid Peclet number! The correct analysis computes exactly the possible intersection points of the ellipse with the circle [56]. We first write the equations for each curve: for the circle, we have

$$\xi^2 + \eta^2 = 1;$$

for the ellipse, we have

$$\frac{[\xi - (1 - 2D)]^2}{4D^2} + \frac{\eta^2}{C^2} = 1.$$

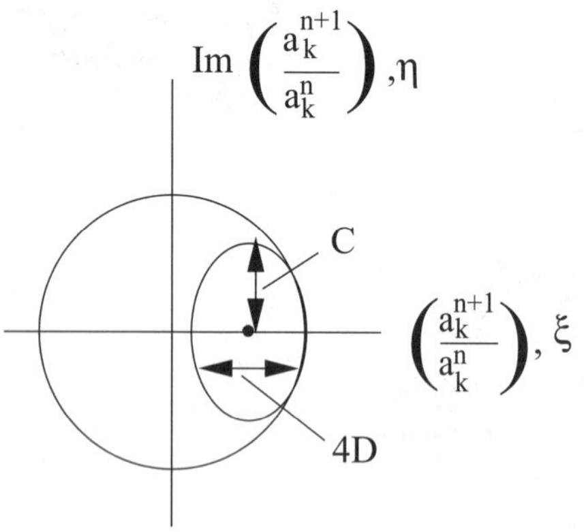

Figure 8.21: Polar plot in the complex plane of the EF/CD scheme.

To ensure that we have stability (i.e., $|a_k^{n+1}/a_k^n| \leq 1$) we have to ensure that there is no intersection next to the point $(1,0)$. To this end, we compute the (hypothetical) second intersection point from

$$\begin{cases} \xi = \dfrac{(1-4D)C^2 + 4D^2}{C^2 - 4D^2}, \\ \eta^2 = 1 - \xi^2. \end{cases}$$

To avoid intersection inside the circle and next to the point $(1,0)$, we require that $\xi \geq 1$. This leads to the condition

$$C^2 \leq 2D,$$

which is different from the previous condition (i.e., $C \leq 2D$). Note that we still need to satisfy the diffusion limit (i.e., $2D \leq 1$), and thus finally we have

$$C^2 \leq 2D \leq 1 \Rightarrow C \leq \frac{Pe}{2} \leq \frac{1}{C}$$

or

$$C \leq \frac{2}{Pe} \leq \frac{1}{C}.$$

This is the *necessary* and *sufficient* condition for stability. It is equivalent to what we derived heuristically initially using the equivalent differential equation.

REMARK: Note that as $\alpha \to 0$ we recover the unconditionally unstable scheme for convection as before. Thus, diffusion (physical here) stabilizes the difference EF/CD equation, leading to conditional stability.

Do Not Suppress the Wiggles!

We now demonstrate that for $Pe_g > 2$, the numerical solution develops *spatial oscillations*, although we may have a stable scheme and thus convergence, if the aforementioned two stability criteria are satisfied. To proceed, we need to introduce a more general type of analysis that examines amplification both in time and space. In particular, we can use the time–space normal mode analysis introduced by Godunov and Ryabenkii to analyze the advection–diffusion equation [44]. Similar to having a *time* amplification factor z, we now have a *space* amplification factor κ. We write

$$\Theta_j^n = \tilde{\Theta} z^n \kappa^j,$$

where the tilde variable denotes amplitude. When introduced into a numerical scheme, including the boundary conditions, we obtain a quadratic equation for κ with two solutions κ_1, κ_2, that is,

$$\Theta_j^n = \tilde{\Theta} z^n (A\kappa_1^j + B\kappa_2^j).$$

The constants A and B are determined from the boundary conditions, and thus we can also investigate the effects of boundary conditions on the stability.

To examine the effect of $Pe_g > 2$ in the advection–diffusion equation, we consider the stationary problem $\left(\frac{\partial}{\partial t} = 0\right)$

$$U\frac{\partial \Theta}{\partial x} = \alpha \frac{\partial^2 \Theta}{\partial x^2}, \quad 0 \leq x \leq L,$$

$$\Theta(0) = \Theta_0, \quad x = 0,$$

$$\Theta(L) = \Theta_L, \quad x = L.$$

The corresponding difference equation is

$$U\frac{\Theta_{j+1} - \Theta_{j-1}}{2\Delta x} = \alpha \frac{\Theta_{j+1} - 2\Theta_j + \Theta_{j-1}}{\Delta x^2},$$

or

$$(2 - Pe)\Theta_{j+1} - 4\Theta_j + (2 + Pe)\Theta_{j-1} = 0.$$

We now introduce the mode $\Theta_j = \kappa^j$ and obtain the quadratic algebraic equation

$$(2 - Pe)\kappa^2 - 4\kappa + (2 + Pe) = 0$$

with roots

$$\kappa_1 = 1 \text{ and } \kappa_2 = \frac{2 + Pe}{2 - Pe},$$

with the general solution

$$\Theta_j = A\kappa_1^j + B\kappa_2^j,$$

or

$$\Theta_j = A + B\left(\frac{2 + Pe}{2 - Pe}\right)^j.$$

From the boundary conditions we determine that

$$A = \frac{\Theta_0 \kappa_2^n - \Theta_L}{\kappa_2^N - 1} \quad \text{and} \quad B = \frac{\Theta_L - \Theta_0}{\kappa_2^N - 1},$$

where N is the total number of grid points, and thus the solution is

$$\Theta_j = \Theta_0 + (\Theta_L - \Theta_0)\frac{\kappa_2^j - 1}{\kappa_2^N - 1}.$$

We note that for $U > 0$ then $\kappa_2 < 0$ for $Pe > 2$. Therefore, the numerical solution will alternate in sign from one grid point to the next, producing an oscillatory behavior. If it is stable, the amplitude of the oscillation will be decreasing as $\Delta x \to 0$.

In terms of accuracy, the exact solution is given by

$$\Theta_{ex}(x) = \Theta_0 + (\Theta_L - \Theta_0)\frac{e^{Pe\frac{x}{L}} - 1}{e^{Pe} - 1},$$

and so the numerical solution is a second-order approximation to it.

Semi-Implicit Discretization

Semi-implicit discretizations allow us to treat the advection contribution differently from the diffusion terms. Specifically, since the diffusion limits the time step more severely than the advection, we will treat the former implicitly whereas we will treat the latter explicitly. To show this, let us integrate Equation (8.12) in time with $t \in [t_n, t_{n+1}]$, that is,

$$\int_{t_n}^{t_{n+1}} d\Theta + \int_{t_n}^{t_{n+1}} U \frac{\partial \Theta}{\partial x} dt = \int_{t_n}^{t_{n+1}} \alpha \frac{\partial^2 \Theta}{\partial x^2} dt.$$

It is clear that we can approximate these integrals differently. Here we choose to use Adams–Bashforth of second-order to compute the second integral on the left while we use Euler-backward to compute the integral on the right-hand side. It is more convenient to do this in two steps by *splitting* this equation as follows:

$$Step \ I: \quad \frac{\bar{\Theta}_j^{n+1} - \Theta_j^n}{\Delta t} = -\frac{3}{2} U \Delta_x \Theta_j^n + \frac{1}{2} \Delta_x \Theta_j^{n-1}, \tag{8.13}$$

$$Step \ II: \quad \frac{\Theta_j^{n+1} - \bar{\Theta}_j^{n+1}}{\Delta t} = \alpha \Delta_{xx} \Theta_j^{n+1}. \tag{8.14}$$

This discretization is $\mathcal{O}(\Delta t^2)$ in the advection but only $\mathcal{O}(\Delta t)$ in the diffusion term, but a Crank–Nicolson scheme can be employed in the second substep, if uniform second-order convergence is desired. However, it is useful to have a high order (e.g., third-order Adams–Bashforth or fourth-order Runge–Kutta) in the convection scheme to reduce phase errors, which are crucial in propagation phenomena, whereas second-order accuracy for amplitude errors may suffice. With regards to stability, a semi-implicit scheme has typically the same stability characteristics as the explicit scheme employed. This is true if the implicit step for diffusion is up to second order and thus unconditionally stable. For higher order treatment of the diffusion, however, the time step limit of the semi-implicit scheme is determined as the minimum of the two limits for advection and diffusion. A useful criterion in practice in this case is

$$\Delta t \le \frac{1}{\frac{1}{\Delta t_{conv}} + \frac{1}{\Delta t_{diff}}},$$

which is an empirical rule.

Semi-Lagrangian Discretization

The Semi-Lagrangian discretization scheme, which has been used very effectively in metereology simulations, allows the use of a *very large time step* as it bypasses, in effect, the CFL limit by introducing a *variable stencil* defined by the characteristics of wave propagation. It is a semi-implicit scheme with the diffusion treated implicitly but with the advection handled in semi-Lagrangian manner. The Lagrangian form of Equation (8.12) in multidimensions is

$$\frac{D\Theta}{Dt} = \alpha \nabla^2 \Theta,$$

$$\frac{D\boldsymbol{x}}{Dt} = \mathbf{U}(\boldsymbol{x}, t).$$

The idea of a true Lagrangian scheme is to solve the first equation along the characteristics defined by the second equation. This leads to an effective decoupling of the advection and diffusion terms and an *unconditionally stable* scheme. However, a moving grid is involved, which, if distorted substantially, may lead to great inaccuracies. To this end, regridding is typically performed but that may mean a substantial overhead to the computation.

The idea of a semi-Lagrangian scheme is to use a fixed grid with the arrival points (along the characteristics) coinciding with the grid points. The departure points are obtained by backward extrapolation, and they typically do not coincide with the grid points; instead, they are obtained by interpolation. The second-order Crank–Nicolson semi-Lagrangian form for the multidimensional advection–diffusion equation is

$$\frac{\Theta^{n+1} - \Theta_d^n}{\Delta t} = \alpha \nabla^2 \left(\frac{\Theta^{n+1} + \Theta^n}{2} \right),$$

$$\frac{D\boldsymbol{x}}{Dt} = \mathbf{U}(\boldsymbol{x}, t), \quad \boldsymbol{x}^{n+1} = \boldsymbol{x}_a.$$

Here Θ_d^n denotes the numerical solution at the *departure point* $\boldsymbol{x}_d$ whereas $\boldsymbol{x}_a$ is the location of the *arrival point*, which is a grid point. The characteristic equation is solved backward to obtain $\boldsymbol{x}_d^n$ given the initial condition $\boldsymbol{x}^{n+1} = \boldsymbol{x}_a$.

The *backward integration* could be either explicit or implicit, as we show next for second-order accuracy. First, we use a predictor–corrector method to obtain

$$\hat{\boldsymbol{x}} = \boldsymbol{x}_a - \frac{\Delta t}{2} \mathbf{U}(\boldsymbol{x}_a, t^n),$$

$$\boldsymbol{x}_d = \boldsymbol{x}_a - \Delta t \mathbf{U}(\hat{\boldsymbol{x}}, t^n + \frac{\Delta t}{2}).$$

By defining

$$\beta \equiv \boldsymbol{x}_a - \boldsymbol{x}_d$$

we can rewrite the explicit scheme as

$$\beta = \Delta t \mathbf{U}(\boldsymbol{x}_a - \frac{\Delta t}{2} \mathbf{U}(\boldsymbol{x}_a, t^n), t^n + \frac{\Delta t}{2}).$$

If instead we employ implicit integration we obtain

$$\hat{\boldsymbol{x}} = \boldsymbol{x}_a - \frac{\Delta t}{2} \mathbf{U}(\hat{\boldsymbol{x}}, t^n + \frac{\Delta t}{2}),$$

and finally for the difference β we have

$$\beta = \Delta t \mathbf{U}(\boldsymbol{x}_a - \frac{\beta}{2}, t^n + \frac{\Delta t}{2}).$$

Although both the explicit and implicit integration algorithms shown here are of second order, better results have been achieved with the implicit scheme, which can be solved using the Newton–Raphson method.

This semi-Lagrangian scheme requires extra searching and interpolation algorithms to obtain the departure points and these may be expensive in multidimensional computations. However, the scheme is stable for any time step, and it has accuracy

$$\mathcal{O}(\Delta^k + \frac{\Delta x^{p+1}}{\Delta t}),$$

where k is the time-integration order (e.g., here $k = 2$) and p is the spatial discretization (e.g., for standard central differencing $p = 2$). For small time steps the second contribution to the overall error typically dominates, but for larger time steps the first term dominates. These two competing contributions create a plateau in the error versus time step, which can be exploited in practice to perform computations with large time step while maintaining high accuracy.

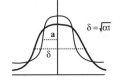

Figure 8.22: Advection–diffusion of a Gaussian waveform. Here a is the initial width and δ is the width after time t.

8.2.2 Effects of Boundary Conditions

In advection–diffusion systems the solution is advected while at the same time its amplitude is decreasing. Therefore, the concept of periodic boundary conditions cannot be employed here. Instead, boundary conditions that allow the solution to leave the domain without upstream effects are required. In general, we have *proper* boundary conditions, that is, mathematically required physical boundary conditions at a physical boundary. However, in a simulation we may also need *artificial* boundary conditions, which are introduced by discretization and the domain truncation but are not required by the continuous mathematics or physics. Such boundary conditions are application specific, but some generalizations can be made. Let us revisit the advection–diffusion problem of advecting a Gaussian waveform to the right in the sketch shown in Figure 8.22.

From an energy balance budget assuming an initial amplitude of unity and width of a, we can obtain the amplitude at time $t = t_f$:

$$\left.\begin{array}{l} \text{initial: } 1 \cdot a \\ \text{Later: } \overline{\Theta} \cdot \delta \\ \quad \delta \sim \sqrt{\alpha t} \end{array}\right\} \Rightarrow \overline{\Theta} = \frac{1}{\sqrt{\alpha t}}.$$

The waveform is advected in time t by $d = Ut$. For the mean temperature to decay to $\overline{\Theta} = 0.1$ (say) it takes

$$t_f \sim \frac{\delta^2}{\alpha} = \frac{(10a)^2}{\alpha} = 100\frac{a^2}{\alpha},$$

$$d_f = 100\frac{Ua^2}{\alpha},$$

and thus

$$\frac{d_f}{a} \sim 100 Pe.$$

From this simple analysis we see that for high Peclet number, which implies faster advection, the required domain should be larger. In general, we first need to obtain such estimates based on conservation laws to decide on the extent of the domain.

Table 8.9: Parameters for the solutions of Figure 8.23.

Parameter	Value
Method	Crank–Nicolson/ central difference
Interval	$[-3, 3]$
N	31
Δt	0.2
c	1.0
D	0.05
Initial condition	$\Theta(x, 0) = e^{-2x^2}$
Boundary conditions	$\Theta(-3, t) = 0$; $\frac{\partial \Theta}{\partial x}(3, t) = 0$

In addition to selecting the size of the domain, we need to provide boundary conditions at the truncated boundaries consistent with the physics of the problem. However, imposing Dirichlet boundary conditions leads to artificial *normal boundary layers* that may render the solution erroneous. Instead, weaker boundary conditions that do not affect the solution substantially are preferable (e.g., Neumann boundary conditions or radiation-type boundary conditions), as we explain next.

We revisit the steady-state advection–diffusion problem that we encountered earlier for which we obtained the following exact solution for *Dirichlet* boundary conditions:

$$\Theta_1(x) = \Theta_0 + (\Theta_L - \Theta_0) \frac{e^{Pe \frac{x}{L}} - 1}{e^{Pe} - 1}.$$

Next, we assume that on the right boundary we impose a Neumann boundary condition, that is,

$$\frac{\partial \Theta}{\partial x}(x = L) = \Theta'_L,$$

with corresponding exact solution

$$\Theta_2(x) = \Theta_0 + e^{Pe} \frac{\Theta'_L L}{Pe} [e^{Pe \frac{x}{L}} - 1].$$

By examining these two solutions, we see that the left (Dirichlet) boundary condition affects the solution independent of Pe. However, for small Peclet number (i.e., $Pe \ll 1$), the right boundary condition affects the entire solution, whereas for $Pe \gg 1$, it affects the solution in a region proportional to $\mathcal{O}(L/Pe)$ for the Dirichlet case and only $\mathcal{O}(1/Pe)$ for the Neumann case. In other words, the *normal boundary layer* developed at the downstream boundary caused by truncation of the domain can be minimized at high Peclet number if a Neumann boundary condition is employed there.

Table 8.10: Parameters for the solutions of Figure 8.24.

Parameter	Value
Method	Crank-Nicolson/ central difference
Interval	$[-3, 6]$
N	46
Δt	0.2
c	1.0
D	0.05
Initial condition	$\Theta(x, 0) = e^{-2x^2}$
Boundary conditions	$\Theta(-3, t) = 0$; $\frac{\partial \Theta}{\partial x}(6, t) = 0$

For propagation problems, specifically, a radiation-type boundary condition is similar to the linearized advection equation, that is,

$$\frac{\partial \Theta}{\partial t} + c \frac{\partial \Theta}{\partial x} = 0,$$

which leads to $\Theta(x, y, t) = \Theta(x - ct, y)$. In two-dimensional problems it works effectively; it is important, however, to choose the advection velocity c properly. This can be done following, for example, a mass-conservation principle, locally. However, even this boundary condition has been shown to reflect waves, especially oblique waves in the x–y plane. To this end, it has been found in [35] that when solving

$$\Theta_{tt} = c^2[\Theta_{xx} + \Theta_{yy}], \quad t, x \geq 0,$$

where at the $x = 0$ boundary the boundary condition

$$c\frac{\partial^2 \Theta}{\partial x \partial t} - \frac{\partial^2 \Theta}{\partial t^2} + \frac{1}{2}c^2\frac{\partial^2 \Theta}{\partial y^2} = 0$$

is employed, reflections are substantially reduced. For example, it was reported that the amplitudes of the reflections of 450 incident waves were reduced from 17% to only 3%.

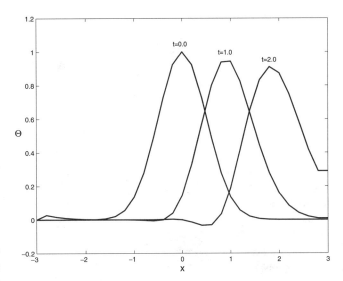

Figure 8.23: Crank–Nicolson/central difference at various times t for the parameters of Table 8.9 (short domain).

EXAMPLE. We present the results from the CN/CD discretization presented earlier with Dirichlet and Neumann boundary conditions employed downstream for two different truncations of the domain:

$$\left.\begin{array}{l} \Theta_t + \Theta_x = \dfrac{1}{100}\Theta_{xx}, \\ I.C. \ \Theta(x, t = 0) = e^{-2x^2}, \\ \Theta(-3, t) = 0, \quad \dfrac{\partial \Theta}{\partial x}(L_0, t) = 0. \end{array}\right\} \text{outflow errors}$$

The discrete parameters are described in Tables 8.9 and 8.10, and the corresponding results are shown in Figures 8.23 and 8.24 for a short domain and a longer domain. We verify that in the latter case more accurate results are produced as the outflow errors do not influence the results as much.

PUTTING IT INTO PRACTICE

In the following we present a C++ implementation of the advection–diffusion equation using central differencing in space and Crank–Nicolson in time. This function takes as input the number of grid points, the CFL number, the diffusion number, and the values at the current time level stored in the array *uold*. This function updates the array *unew* with the new values at the next time level.

```
void CrankNicolson_CentralDifference_AdvectionDiffusion(int N,
          double CFL,double DN, double *uold, double *unew){
  double c1 = 0.25*CFL - 0.5*DN,
    c2 = -0.25*CFL - 0.5*DN;
  double *q = new double[N-1];
```

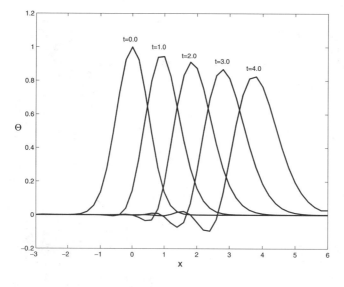

Figure 8.24: Crank-Nicolson/central difference at various times t for the parameters of Table 8.10 (long domain).

```
for(int i=1; i<N-1; i++)
  q[i-1] = uold[i] - 0.25*CFL*(uold[i+1]-uold[i-1])+
      0.5*DN*(uold[i+1] - 2.0*uold[i] + uold[i-1]);

ThomasAlgorithm_per(N-1,c2,1.0e0+DN,c1,&unew[1],q);

unew[N-1] = unew[N-2];

delete[] q;
}
```

REMARK: Notice the use of "&" in this code. Recall what this means – the "&" operator gives us "the address of." Hence, in the preceding expression we are passing to the ThomasAlgorithm_per routine the *address* of the second entry of the unew array. The following would have been equally valid:

```
ThomasAlgorithm_per(N-1,c2,1.0e0+DN,c1,unew+1,q);
```

which would use pointer arithmetic to pass the address held by *unew* incremented by one addressable unit, which is the address of *unew*[1].

8.3 MPI: NONBLOCKING COMMUNICATIONS

In Chapter 5 we presented MPI implementations for finite differencing similar to the central differencing function presented here. To accomplish the parallel implementation, we used either *MPI_Send/MPI_Recv* or *MPI_Sendrecv_replace* commands to exchange information. As was discussed, these functions require some level of synchronization for associating the corresponding sends and receives on the appropriate processes.

MPI_Send and *MPI_Recv* are *blocking communications*, which means that they will not return until it is safe to modify or use the contents of the send/recv buffer respectively. MPI also provides *nonblocking versions* of these functions called *MPI_Isend* and *MPI_Irecv*, where the "I" stands for immediate. These functions allow a process to post that it wants to send to or receive from a process, and then later allows it to call a function (*MPI_Wait*) to complete the sending/receiving. These functions are useful in that they allow the programmer to appropriately stagger computation and communication to minimize the total waiting time resulting from communication.

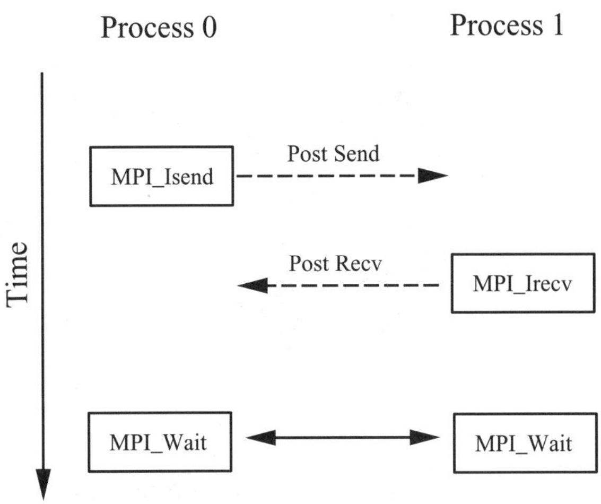

The basic idea behind *MPI_Isend* and *MPI_Irecv* is as follows. Suppose process 0 needs to send information to process 1, but owing to the particular algorithms that these two processes are running, the programmer knows that there will be a mismatch in the synchronization of these processes. Process 0 initiates an *MPI_Isend* to process 1 (posting that it wants to send a message) and then continues to accomplish things *that do not require the contents of the buffer to be sent*. At the point in the algorithm where process 0 can no longer continue without being guaranteed that the contents of the sending buffer can be modified, process 0 calls MPI_Wait to wait until the transaction is completed. On process 1, a similar situation occurs, with process 1 posting via *MPI_Irecv* that it is willing to accept a message. When process 1 can no longer continue without having the contents of the receive buffer, it too calls *MPI_Wait* to wait until the transaction is complete. At the conclusion of the *MPI_Wait*, the sender may modify the send buffer without compromising the send, and the receiver may use the data contained within the receive buffer; see Figure 8.25 for a diagram of this process.

To further expand on these two functions, we will now present the function call syntax, argument list explanation, usage examples, and some remarks.

Figure 8.25:
MPI_Isend/MPI_Irecv
schematic
demonstrating the
communication
between two
processes.

MPI_Isend/MPI_Irecv/MPI_Wait

FUNCTION CALL SYNTAX

MPI

```
int MPI_Isend(
        void*          message     /* in   */,
        int            count       /* in   */,
        MPI_Datatype   datatype    /* in   */,
        int            dest        /* in   */,
        int            tag         /* in   */,
        MPI_Comm       comm        /* in   */,
        MPI_Request*   request     /* out  */)
```

```
int MPI_Irecv(
        void*          message     /*  out  */,
        int            count       /*  in   */,
        MPI_Datatype   datatype    /*  in   */,
        int            source      /*  in   */,
        int            tag         /*  in   */,
        MPI_Comm       comm        /*  in   */,
        MPI_Request*   request     /*  out  */)

int MPI_Wait(
        MPI_Request*   request     /*  in/out  */
        MPI_Status*    status      /*  out     */)
```

MPI

UNDERSTANDING THE ARGUMENT LISTS

- *message* – starting address of the send/recv buffer.
- *count* – number of elements in the send/recv buffer.
- *datatype* – data type of the elements in the send buffer.
- *source* – process rank to send the data.
- *dest* – process rank to receive the data.
- *tag* – message tag.
- *comm* – communicator.
- *request* – communication request.
- *status* – status object.

EXAMPLE OF USAGE

```
int mynode, totalnodes;
int datasize;   // number of data units to be sent/recv
int sender;     // process number of the sending process
int receiver;   // process number of the receiving process
int tag;        // integer message tag

MPI_Status status;    // variable to contain status
                      //       information
MPI_Request request;  // variable to maintain
                      //       isend/irecv information

MPI_Init(&argc,&argv);
MPI_Comm_size(MPI_COMM_WORLD, &totalnodes);
MPI_Comm_rank(MPI_COMM_WORLD, &mynode);

// Determine datasize

double * databuffer = new double[datasize];
```

```
// Fill in sender, receiver, tag on sender/receiver
      processes,
// and fill in databuffer on the sender process.

if(mynode==sender)
  MPI_Isend(databuffer,datasize,MPI_DOUBLE,receiver,tag,
          MPI_COMM_WORLD,&request);

if(mynode==receiver)
  MPI_Irecv(databuffer,datasize,MPI_DOUBLE,sender,tag,
          MPI_COMM_WORLD,&request);

// The sender/receiver can be accomplishing various things
// which do not involve the databuffer array

MPI_Wait(&request,&status); //synchronize to verify
                            //   that data are sent

// Send/Recv complete
```

REMARKS

MPI

- In general, the *message* array for both the sender and receiver should be of the same type and both of size at least *datasize*.
- In most cases the *sendtype* and *recvtype* are identical.
- After the *MPI_Isend* call and before the *MPI_Wait* call, the contents of *message* should not be changed.
- After the *MPI_Irecv* call and before the *MPI_Wait* call, the contents of *message* should not be used.
- An *MPI_Send* can be received by an *MPI_Irecv/MPI_Wait*.
- An *MPI_Recv* can obtain information from an *MPI_Isend/MPI_Wait*.
- The tag can be any integer between 0 and 32,767.
- *MPI_Irecv* may use for the tag the wildcard *MPI_ANY_TAG*. This allows an *MPI_Irecv* to receive from a send using any tag.
- *MPI_Isend* cannot use the wildcard *MPI_ANY_TAG*. A specific tag must be specified.
- *MPI_Irecv* may use for the source the wildcard *MPI_ANY_SOURCE*. This allows an *MPI_Irecv* to receive from a send from any source.
- *MPI_Isend* must specify the process rank of the destination. No wildcard exists.

8.4 HOMEWORK PROBLEMS

1. Use von Neumann analysis to demonstrate that leap-frog time differencing combined with *central differencing* of

$$\frac{\partial \Theta}{\partial t} + \frac{\partial \Theta}{\partial x} = 0$$

(with periodic boundary conditions) leads to a conditionally stable scheme. Can you draw the same conclusion from the corresponding equivalent differential equation?

2. Use von Neumann analysis to analyze the stability of leap-frog time differencing combined with *upwind differencing* of

$$\frac{\partial \Theta}{\partial t} + \frac{\partial \Theta}{\partial x} = 0$$

(with periodic boundary conditions). Compare your findings with heuristic arguments derived from the corresponding differential equation.

3. Use a third-order Adams–Bashforth/central-differencing scheme with parameters similar to the ones in Table 8.6 but with $N = 30$ as well as $N = 100$ points to obtain solutions to the one-dimensional linear advection equation. Compare your solutions with the solutions of Figure 8.14 corresponding to the second-order Adams–Bashforth/central-differencing scheme.

4. Use a leap-frog/central difference scheme with $C = 0.2$ and $N = 30$ to obtain a solution of the one-dimension advection equation for periodic as well as nonperiodic boundary conditions. Are both solutions stable?

5. Solve numerically the one-dimensional advection–diffusion equation

$$\Theta_t + \Theta_x = \frac{1}{100} \Theta_{xx}$$

with the initial condition

$$\Theta(x, t = 0) = e^{-2x^2}$$

and boundary conditions

$$\Theta(-3, t) = 0, \quad \frac{\partial \Theta}{\partial x}(L, t) = 0$$

for $L = 3$ and $L = 10$.

Use center differencing for spatial derivatives and Euler explicit in time. You can choose your grid so that

(a) $\Delta x = 0.01$,

(b) $\Delta x = 0.1$.

Compare your solutions at time $t = 2$ and time $t = 5$.

6. **Nonlinear Lax–Friedrichs scheme and Tadmor's correction**: In this problem we are interested in solving the inviscid Burgers equation

$$\frac{\partial \Theta}{\partial t} + \frac{\partial F(\Theta)}{\partial x} = 0,$$

where here $F(\Theta) = \frac{1}{2}\Theta^2(x, t)$ and the initial conditions are

$$\Theta(x, 0) = \sin(\pi x), \quad x \in [-1, 1].$$

The solution of this problem develops a shock discontinuity at time $t_s \approx 0.31$, and we are interested in comparing the numerical solutions obtained with the Lax–Friedrichs scheme and the Tadmor correction before and after the shock is formed at times $t = 0.2$ and $t = 0.4$, respectively. Specifically, we want to obtain both the L_1 norm and the L_2 norm of errors for grids with $N = 50, 100, 200$, and 400 points.

The nonlinear versions of these schemes are as follows:

The standard Lax–Friedrichs scheme for the nonlinear hyperbolic law is

$$\Theta_j^{n+1} = \frac{1}{2}(\Theta_{j+1}^n + \Theta_{j-1}^n) - \frac{C}{2}[F(\Theta_{j+1}^n) - F(\Theta_{j-1}^n)].$$

The second-order version introduced in [71] consists of a *predictor*

$$\Theta_j^{n+1/2} = \Theta_j^n - \frac{1}{2}CF_j'$$

and a *corrector*

$$\Theta_j^{n+1} = \frac{1}{2}[\Theta_{j+1}^n + \Theta_{j-1}^n] + \frac{1}{4}[\Theta_{j-1}' - \Theta_{j+1}'] - \frac{C}{2}[F(\Theta_{j+1}^{n+1/2}) - F(\Theta_{j-1}^{n+1/2})].$$

In Section 8.1.3 we have defined all quantities except the derivative of the flux, which is chosen so that the scheme is free of spurious oscillations. This is given by

$$F_j' = \frac{\partial F}{\partial x}|_j \Theta_j'.$$

Obtain the convergence rate for each scheme and identify the free parameter α (see Section 8.1.3) that gives the best results in the aforementioned norms.

7. Rewrite the *EF_FirstOrderUpwind* function to be a parallel function using *MPI_Isend* and *MPI_Irecv*. Verify your code by replicating the numerical example given in the text. Modify your function to solve $u_t + au_x = 0$, where a is a nonzero constant that can be positive or negative. What must change in your MPI code if the direction of the wave propagation changes (i.e., should things change based on whether a is positive or negative)?

8. Modify the *CrankNicolson_CentralDifference* function so that instead of Crank–Nicolson it uses Euler-backward. Repeat the example from Table 8.7 for the new Euler-backward routine and compare results with those of Crank–Nicolson.

9. Create a new Crank–Nicolson C++ function that uses a fourth-order compact scheme for the space differentiation (instead of the second-order central difference scheme presented in the text). Repeat the example from Table 8.7. How much of a difference does the extra accuracy in space make?

10. **Gaussian-cone problem**: Consider the advection–diffusion equation with spatially varying advection velocity given by

$$u = +y, \qquad v = -x$$

and initial condition

$$u(x, y, 0) = e^{-[(x-x_0)^2 + (y-y_0)^2]/2\lambda^2}.$$

The exact solution is

$$u(x, y, t) = \frac{\lambda^2}{\lambda^2 + 2vt} e^{-[\hat{x}^2 + \hat{y}^2]/2(\lambda^2 + 2vt)},$$

where

$$\hat{x} = x - x_0 \cos t - y_0 \sin t, \qquad \hat{y} = y + x_0 \sin t - y_0 \cos t.$$

The constants are fixed at $\lambda = \frac{1}{8}$, $v = 10^{-4}$, and $(x_0, y_0) = (-\frac{1}{2}, 0)$.

Consider second-order central differencing on a grid consisting of 100×100 grid points, and perform time integration for *one revolution* corresponding to $t = 2\pi$.

(a) Obtain a numerical solution following the Eulerian approach and Second-order Adams–Bashforth/Crank–Nicolson time stepping. Use Courant number $C = 0.01$ and diffusion number $D = 0.5$.

(b) Repeat (a) using a semi-Lagrangian approach with backward integration based on the explicit midpoint rule.

(c) Repeat (b) but with time step Δt ten and twenty times larger, and compare the new results with the results in (b). What do you observe?

11. Repeat the previous problem but with a new initial condition, that is,

$$u(x, y, t = 0) = \begin{cases} -16 \left[r_0^2 - \frac{1}{16} \right] & \text{if } r_0 < \frac{1}{4}, \\ 0 & \text{elsewhere}, \end{cases}$$

where $r_0^2 = (x - x_0)^2 + (y - y_0)^2$ and (x_0, y_0) is the initial center position of the cone. The transport velocity field is the same as used in the previous example. The initial condition is a parabolic cone, which has a discontinuity in the derivatives, unlike the previously tested smooth Gaussian cone.

Compare the results from the Eulerian and semi-Lagrangian approaches in terms of contour plots and in terms of the L_2 error. What do you observe?

9
Fast Linear Solvers

We have already discussed how to solve tridiagonal linear systems of equations using direct solvers (the Thomas algorithm) in Chapter 6 and some iterative solvers (Jacobi, Gauss–Seidel, SOR, and multigrid) in Chapter 7. We have also discussed solutions of nonlinear and linear systems and have introduced the conjugate gradient method in Chapter 4. In the current chapter we revisit this subject and present general algorithms for the *direct* and *iterative* solution of large linear systems. We start with the classical Gaussian elimination (which is a fast solver) and then proceed with more sophisticated solvers and preconditioners for symmetric and nonsymmetric systems.

In parallel computing, we introduce the broadcasting command *MPI_Bcast* and demonstrate its usefulness in the context of Gaussian elimination. In addition, we reiterate the use of *MPI_Send*, *MPI_Recv*, *MPI_Allgather*, and *MPI_Allreduce* through example implementations of algorithms presented in this chapter.

9.1 GAUSSIAN ELIMINATION

Gaussian elimination is one of the most effective ways to solve the linear system

$$\mathbf{Ax} = \mathbf{b}.$$

The Thomas algorithm (see Section 6.1.4) is a special case of Gaussian elimination for tridiagonal systems.

The computational complexity of Gaussian elimination is associated with the size and structure of the $n \times n$ matrix $\mathbf{A}$, and so is its accuracy. It is based on the "superposition principle" for linear systems, that is, the fact that we can replace equations of the original system with equivalent equations formed as linear combinations of the rows of $\mathbf{A}$ and corresponding values of $\mathbf{b}$. In its simplest form it states the following:

- Take each row and subtract a multiple of it from subsequent rows to zero out the element of $\mathbf{A}$ below the diagonal.

We demonstrate this by the following example.

EXAMPLE. Consider the 3×3 system

$$\boxed{x_1} + \frac{1}{2}x_2 + \frac{1}{3}x_3 = 3, \tag{9.1}$$

$$\boxed{\frac{1}{2}x_1} + \frac{1}{3}x_2 + \frac{1}{4}x_3 = 2, \tag{9.2}$$

$$\boxed{\frac{1}{3}x_1} + \frac{1}{4}x_2 + \frac{1}{5}x_3 = 1. \tag{9.3}$$

We will solve this (3×3) system in two stages of elimination.

Stage 1. In the first stage we target the first terms (placed in boxes) in Equations (9.1)–(9.3). To this end, we select the *pivot* $a_{11} = 1$ and also the multipliers

$$\ell_{21}^{(1)} = \frac{a_{21}}{a_{11}} = \frac{1/2}{1} = 1/2 \quad \text{and} \quad \ell_{31}^{(1)} = \frac{a_{31}}{a_{11}} = \frac{1}{3}.$$

We then multiply Equation (9.1) by $\ell_{21}^{(1)}$ and subtract it from Equation (9.2). We also multiply Equation (9.1) by $\ell_{31}^{(1)}$ and subtract it from Equation (9.3). The resulting two new equations replace (9.2) and (9.3), that is,

$$x_1 + \frac{1}{2}x_2 + \frac{1}{3}x_3 = 3,$$

$$\boxed{\frac{1}{12}x_2} + \frac{1}{12}x_3 = 1/2, \tag{9.4}$$

$$\boxed{\frac{1}{12}x_2} + \frac{4}{45}x_3 = 0. \tag{9.5}$$

Stage 2. Next, we target the x_2 term and choose a new pivot and new multipliers, respectively, as

$$a_{22}^{(1)} = \frac{1}{12}, \qquad \ell_{32}^{(2)} = \frac{1/12}{1/12} = 1,$$

and proceed as before by multiplying Equation (9.4) by $\ell_{32}^{(2)}$ and subtracting it from Equation (9.5), obtaining

$$x_1 + \frac{1}{2}x_2 + \frac{1}{3}x_3 = 3,$$

$$\frac{1}{12}x_2 + \frac{1}{12}x_3 = \frac{1}{2}, \tag{9.6}$$

$$\frac{1}{180}x_3 = -\frac{1}{2}. \tag{9.7}$$

We now see that the system of Equations (9.1), (9.6), and (9.7) can be solved easily by back substitution starting from Equation (9.7), then Equation (9.6), and finally Equation (9.1) to obtain

$$x_3 = -90,$$

$$x_2 = 12\left[\frac{1}{2} - \frac{1}{12}(-90)\right] = 96,$$

$$x_1 = 3 - \frac{1}{2}(96) - \frac{1}{3}(-90) = -15.$$

In matrix form, the system of Equation (9.7) is

$$
\begin{bmatrix} 1 & \frac{1}{2} & \frac{1}{3} \\ 0 & \frac{1}{12} & \frac{1}{12} \\ 0 & 0 & \frac{1}{180} \end{bmatrix} \begin{bmatrix} x_1 \\ x_2 \\ x_3 \end{bmatrix} = \begin{bmatrix} 3 \\ \frac{1}{2} \\ -\frac{1}{2} \end{bmatrix},
$$

so the coefficient matrix is *upper triangular*; we will denote this matrix by $\mathbf{U}$. We also collect all the multipliers $\ell_{ij}^{(k)}$ we have calculated to form the following *lower triangular* matrix $\mathbf{L}$:

$$
\mathbf{L} = \begin{bmatrix} 1 & 0 & 0 \\ \frac{1}{2} & 1 & 0 \\ \frac{1}{3} & 1 & 1 \end{bmatrix},
$$

where we have placed 1s in the diagonal. We can verify that

$$
\mathbf{A} = \begin{bmatrix} 1 & \frac{1}{2} & \frac{1}{3} \\ \frac{1}{2} & \frac{1}{3} & \frac{1}{4} \\ \frac{1}{3} & \frac{1}{4} & \frac{1}{5} \end{bmatrix} = \begin{bmatrix} 1 & 0 & 0 \\ \frac{1}{2} & 1 & 0 \\ \frac{1}{3} & 1 & 1 \end{bmatrix} \begin{bmatrix} 1 & \frac{1}{2} & \frac{1}{3} \\ 0 & \frac{1}{12} & \frac{1}{12} \\ 0 & 0 & \frac{1}{180} \end{bmatrix} = \mathbf{L} \cdot \mathbf{U}.
$$

Therefore, the two first stages of Gaussian elimination resulted in the *factorization* of $\mathbf{A}$ into an $\mathbf{LU}$ product. Both $\mathbf{L}$ and $\mathbf{U}$ are special matrices, and this leads to substantial reduction in computational complexity.

REMARK: The matrix $\mathbf{A}$ employed in this example is a special matrix that has elements $a_{ij} = \frac{1}{i+j-1}$, so the nth row is the vector

$$
\left(\frac{1}{n}, \ \frac{1}{n+1}, \ \frac{1}{n+2}, \ \cdots, \ \frac{1}{2n-1} \right)^T.
$$

For n large (e.g., $n = 1{,}000$), the entries of the last row are about three orders of magnitude smaller than the entries of the first row. This large disparity leads to many difficulties because of the *ill-conditioning* of this matrix. This matrix was first introduced by the famous mathematician David Hilbert, and it is called the *Hilbert matrix*; it is an example of an ill-conditioned matrix. Its condition number is large (e.g., greater than 10^5 for $n \geq 5$).

9.1.1 LU Decomposition

We now generalize the Gaussian elimination procedure to an $n \times n$ system

$$
\begin{aligned}
a_{11}x_1 + a_{12}x_2 + \cdots + a_{1n}x_n &= b_1, \\
a_{21}x_1 + a_{22}x_2 + \cdots + a_{2n}x_n &= b_2, \\
\vdots \qquad\qquad \vdots \qquad\qquad \vdots \qquad\ \ \vdots \\
a_{n1}x_1 + a_{n2}x_2 + \cdots + a_{nn}x_n &= b_n.
\end{aligned}
$$

In the general case we need $(n-1)$ stages of elimination to arrive at the upper triangular system. We will assume that all the pivots at every stage k are $a_{(ii)}^{(k)} \neq 0$, but we will remove this constraint later when we discuss algorithms that involve row and/or column pivoting.

The *first stage* of elimination leads to

$$
\begin{aligned}
a_{11}x_1 + a_{12}x_2 + \cdots + a_{1n}x_n &= b_1, \\
a_{22}^{(1)}x_2 + \cdots + a_{2n}^{(1)}x_n &= b_2^{(1)}, \\
&\vdots \qquad\qquad \vdots \quad\vdots \\
a_{n2}^{(1)}x_2 + \cdots + a_{nn}^{(1)}x_n &= b_n^{(1)}.
\end{aligned}
$$

Here the intermediate coefficients $a_{ij}^{(1)}$ are defined by

$$
a_{ij}^{(1)} = a_{ij} - a_{1j}\ell_{i1}^{(1)}, \quad \ell_{i1}^{(1)} = \frac{a_{i1}}{a_{11}},
$$

and the entries on the right-hand side are

$$
b_i^{(1)} = b_i - b_1 \frac{a_{i1}}{a_{11}}.
$$

Similarly, the second stage of elimination produces $a_{ij}^{(2)}$ and $b_i^{(2)}$, and so on, until the $(n-1)$th stage, where we obtain $a_{nn}^{(n-1)}$ and $b_n^{(n-1)}$.

This procedure is the forward substitution and gives both matrices $\mathbf{L}$ and $\mathbf{U}$. In particular, we replace $\mathbf{Ax} = \mathbf{b}$ by

$$
\mathbf{L}\underbrace{\mathbf{Ux}}_{\mathbf{y}} = \mathbf{b} \Rightarrow \mathbf{Ly} = \mathbf{b},
$$

where

$$
\mathbf{Ux} = \mathbf{y}.
$$

We can now summarize the solution procedure, which consists of three main steps, as follows:

1. **LU** decomposition: $\mathbf{A} = \mathbf{L} \cdot \mathbf{U}$,
2. forward solve for **y**: $\mathbf{Ly} = \mathbf{b}$,
3. backward solve for **x**: $\mathbf{Ux} = \mathbf{y}$.

The pseudo-code for steps (1) and (2) is as follows:

$$
\begin{aligned}
&\text{for } k = 1, n-1 \\
&\quad \text{for } i = k+1, n \\[4pt]
&\qquad \ell_{ik} = \frac{a_{ik}}{a_{kk}} \text{ (assuming } a_{kk} \neq 0) \\[4pt]
&\qquad \text{for } j = k+1, n \\
&\qquad\quad a_{ij} = a_{ij} - \ell_{ik}a_{kj} \\
&\qquad \text{endfor} \\
&\qquad\quad b_i = b_i - \ell_{ik}b_k \\
&\qquad \text{endfor} \\
&\quad \text{endfor}
\end{aligned}
$$

COMPUTATIONAL COST. The *operation count* for this code is obtained by considering first the innermost loop j and then the loop i, and finally adding operations from all elimination stages: $k = 1$ to $n - 1$. Thus, we have

$$W_{LU} = 2 \sum_{k=1}^{n-1} (n-k) \cdot (n-k) = 2 \sum_{m=1}^{n-1} m^2 = 2 \frac{(n-1)n(2n-1)}{6} \approx \frac{2}{3} n^3,$$

where the factor 2 accounts for one addition and one multiplication. If only multiplications are counted then

$$W_{LU} \approx \frac{n^3}{3},$$

which is the operation count often quoted in the literature.

The *third step* in the solution is the *backward substitution*, which yields first

$$x_n = \frac{b_n^{(n-1)}}{a_{nn}^{(n-1)}}$$

and marching backward all the way to the first entry, we have

$$x_1 = \frac{b_1 - a_{12}x_2 \ldots - a_{1n}x_n}{a_{11}}.$$

The following pseudo-code represents this back solve:

$$\begin{aligned}
&\text{for } k = n, 1 \text{ (\textit{reverse ordering})} \\
&\quad x_k = b_k \text{ (\textit{initialization})} \\
&\quad \text{for } i = k + 1, n \\
&\qquad x_k = x_k - a_{ki} x_i \\
&\quad \text{endfor} \\
&\quad x_k = x_k / a_{kk} \\
&\text{endfor}
\end{aligned}$$

We conclude that the operation count for the backward/forward substitution is $\mathcal{O}(n^2)$.

REMARK 1: In the preceding pseudo-code, steps (1) and (2) are accomplished together for computational efficiency. Solving for $\mathbf{y}$ amounts to adding the ($b_i = b_i - \ell_{ik}b_k$) line in the appropriate place. At the conclusion of this algorithm, the matrix $\mathbf{A}$ has been overwritten with the upper triangular matrix $\mathbf{U}$, and the vector $\mathbf{b}$ has been overwritten with the solution of $\mathbf{Ly} = \mathbf{b}$. All that remains is to accomplish the backsolve for $\mathbf{Ux} = \mathbf{y}$.

REMARK 2: Note that in both of the preceding pseudo-codes we have attempted to minimize the required memory by overwriting onto the same memory locations. However, this should be avoided in cases where we are interested in using the matrix $\mathbf{A}$ again somewhere else in our program. In these codes both the entries of matrix $\mathbf{A}$ and the entries of the right-hand side are overwritten.

REMARK 3: We have already discussed the *Thomas algorithm* in Section 6.1.4, which is a subcase of the LU decomposition presented here with bandwidth $m = 1$. In general for a banded matrix with order n and (semi-) bandwidth m the operation count is as follows:

- for LU decomposition: $\mathcal{O}(m^2 n)$, $m \ll n$,
- for Backsolve: $\mathcal{O}(mn)$, $m \ll n$.

REMARK 4: The Gram–Schmidt QR factorization of a matrix presented in Chapter 2 produces an upper triangular matrix **R** but the **Q** matrix is an orthogonal *full* matrix. The Gram–Schmidt algorithm costs $\mathcal{O}(2n^3)$ (including addition and multiplications); that is, it is *three times* more expensive than the LU algorithm. However, the QR decomposition can also be achieved by the *Householder method*, which is only twice as expensive; that is, it costs $\mathcal{O}(\frac{4}{3}n^3)$ (see Section 9.3).

REMARK 5: (*Cramer versus Gauss*) We compare here the cost for solving $\mathbf{Ax} = \mathbf{b}$ using the Cramer method of determinants (time t_C), which is $\mathcal{O}(n!)$, with that of the Gaussian elimination method (time t_G), which is $\mathcal{O}\left(\frac{2n^3}{3}\right)$. We assume that we use a processor with sustained speed of 1 Gflops:[1]

$$n = 3 \begin{cases} t_C \approx \dfrac{3!}{10^9} \text{ seconds } \approx 6 \text{ nanoseconds,} \\[2mm] t_G \approx \dfrac{2}{3}\dfrac{3^3}{10^9} \text{ seconds } \approx 18 \text{ nanoseconds,} \end{cases}$$

$$n = 10 \begin{cases} t_C \approx \dfrac{10!}{10^9} \text{ seconds } \approx 3 \text{ milliseconds,} \\[2mm] t_G \approx \dfrac{210^3}{3 \cdot 10^9} \text{ seconds } \approx 0.6 \text{ microseconds,} \end{cases}$$

$$n = 20 \begin{cases} t_C \approx \dfrac{20!}{10^9} \text{ seconds } \approx 675{,}806 \text{ hours } \approx 28{,}1585 \text{ days } \approx 80 \text{ years,} \\[2mm] t_G \approx \dfrac{2}{3}\dfrac{20^3}{10^9} \text{ seconds } \approx 5 \text{ microseconds} \end{cases}$$

Clearly, Gauss wins by years! In Figure 9.1 we plot the growth in computational work of Cramer's method versus the Gaussian elimination method.

REMARK 6: Gaussian elimination offers an efficient way of computing the determinant of **A**, because

$$\det(\mathbf{A}) = \det(\mathbf{L}) \det(\mathbf{U})$$

$$= 1 \cdot [u_{11} \cdot u_{22} \ldots u_{nn}],$$

where u_{ii}, $i = 1, \ldots, n$, are the diagonal elements of the upper triangular matrix **U**. We recall that the determinant of any triangular matrix is simply the product of its diagonal elements.

---

[1] The terahertz processor is already on the horizon; it will consist of about one billion transistors!

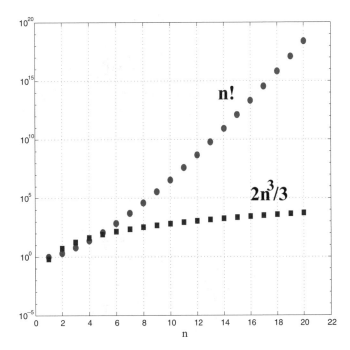

Figure 9.1: Comparison of the growth of computational work in Cramer's method, $n!$, versus Gaussian elimination method, $\frac{2}{3}n^3$.

REMARK 7: Gaussian elimination can be used to explicitly construct the inverse $\mathbf{A}^{-1}$ by setting the columns of the identity matrix $\mathbf{I} = \mathbf{A}\mathbf{A}^{-1}$ as

$$\mathbf{b}_i = (0\ldots 0 \underbrace{1}_{\text{index } i} 0\ldots 0)^T,$$

with only the ith entry being nonzero, and solving

$$\mathbf{A}\mathbf{x}_i = \mathbf{b}_i, \ i = 1, \ldots, n.$$

The solution vector $\mathbf{x}_i$ forms the ith column of the inverse $\mathbf{A}^{-1}$. Note that this involves only one LU decomposition and n backsolves of $\mathcal{O}(n^2)$, and the total cost is *still* $\mathcal{O}(n^3)$.

9.1.2 To Pivot or Not to Pivot?

So far we have conveniently assumed that all the pivoting elements are nonzero, that is,

$$a_{ii}^{(k)} \neq 0,$$

but this is not guaranteed for all problems! In practice, these pivots may be zero or very small numbers so that the multipliers $\ell_{ij}^{(k)}$ can potentially be very large numbers. To understand the effect of this, let us consider the 2×2 matrix

$$\mathbf{A} = \begin{bmatrix} \epsilon & 1 \\ 1 & 1 \end{bmatrix},$$

where $\epsilon \ll 1$. The condition number of $\mathbf{A}$ is $\kappa_2(\mathbf{A}) \to 2.6180$ as $\epsilon \to 0$ so this is a well-conditioned matrix. We now obtain the LU decomposition of $\mathbf{A}$: The $\mathbf{L}$ matrix is

$$\mathbf{L} = \begin{bmatrix} 1 & 0 \\ \epsilon^{-1} & 1 \end{bmatrix},$$

and the $\mathbf{U}$ matrix is

$$\mathbf{U} = \begin{bmatrix} \epsilon & 1 \\ 0 & 1 - \epsilon^{-1} \end{bmatrix}.$$

For ϵ sufficiently small, $1 - \epsilon^{-1} \approx -\epsilon^{-1}$ and thus

$$\mathbf{U} \approx \begin{bmatrix} \epsilon & 1 \\ 0 & -\epsilon^{-1} \end{bmatrix},$$

so

$$\mathbf{L} \cdot \mathbf{U} = \begin{bmatrix} \epsilon & 1 \\ 1 & 0 \end{bmatrix},$$

which is different from the original matrix $\mathbf{A}$ in the $(2, 2)$ entry, because

$$\mathbf{A} = \begin{bmatrix} \epsilon & 1 \\ 1 & 1 \end{bmatrix}.$$

We note that for any value of $a_{22} \neq 1$ (of order one) we get the same answer, which is obviously wrong! This is an example of a *numerical instability*. It occurs because the condition number of $\mathbf{L}$ and $\mathbf{U}$ is extremely large, unlike the condition number of the matrix $\mathbf{A}$, which is order one. This problem can be avoided if we simply reverse the order of the equations, that is, interchange the rows, and work with the reordered matrix

$$\mathbf{A} = \begin{bmatrix} 1 & 1 \\ \epsilon & 1 \end{bmatrix},$$

as now the multiplier is $\epsilon < 1$.

We can generalize this result and apply row interchange, which is also called *partial pivoting*, to obtain multipliers

$$|\ell_{ij}| < 1.$$

The following pseudo-code (an extension of the code we described earlier in the forward solve) describes Gaussian elimination with partial pivoting:

$$\text{for } k = 1, n - 1$$
$$|a_{mk}| = \max\{|a_{kk}|, |a_{k+1k}|, \ldots, |a_{nk}|\}$$
$$p = m$$
$$\text{for } q = k, n$$
$$\quad c = a_{kq}$$
$$\quad a_{kq} = a_{pq}$$
$$\quad a_{pq} = c$$
$$\text{endfor}$$
$$\text{for } i = k + 1, n$$
$$\quad \ell_{ik} = a_{ik}/a_{kk}$$
$$\quad \text{for } j = k + 1, n$$
$$\quad\quad a_{ij} = a_{ij} - \ell_{ik}a_{kj}$$
$$\quad \text{endfor}$$
$$\text{endfor}$$
$$\text{endfor}$$

We note that for the system $\mathbf{Ax} = \mathbf{b}$ we also need to interchange appropriately the right-hand side. Unlike the standard Gauss elimination, in the partial pivoting case we have

$$\mathbf{A} \neq \mathbf{LU},$$

but $\mathbf{A} = \mathbf{P}^{-1}\mathbf{LU}$ is true, where $\mathbf{P}$ is a permutation matrix describing the partial pivoting.

Although partial (row-pivoting) works effectively in practice, there are a few pathological cases where even this may break down. In these cases, we can perform an additional similar pivoting by columns, searching for a maximum pivot along both rows and columns. In general, indications of an ill-conditioned matrix are provided by the small magnitude of the pivot or the large magnitude of the solution compared to the right-hand side, although there are matrices that do not have these properties, but they are still ill-conditioned.

REMARK 1: For banded matrices, (e.g., the tridiagonal systems involved in Thomas algorithms; see Section 6.1.4), partial pivoting and complete pivoting result in increasing the bandwidth and even producing *full* matrices. Therefore, the computational work instead of being linear as in the Thomas algorithm may become $\mathcal{O}(n^2)$ or $\mathcal{O}(n^3)$ for row or row/column pivoting, respectively.

PUTTING IT INTO PRACTICE

The following function is an implementation of both the pivot and nonpivot versions of Gaussian elimination by LU decomposition. Three arguments are required: the matrix $\mathbf{A}$, the vector $\mathbf{b}$, and an integer parameter *pivotflag* denoting whether the pivoting should be enabled (zero for no pivoting and one for pivoting).

```
void GaussElimination(SCMatrix &A, SCVector &b, int pivotflag){
  int k, pivot;
  int N = A.Rows();
```

```
/* NOTE: The values contained in both the matrix A and
   the vector b are modified in this routine. Upon
   returning, A contains the upper triangular matrix
   obtained from its LU decomposition, and b contains
   the solution of the system Ax=b*/

// Steps (1) and (2) (decomposition and solution of Ly = b)
switch(pivotflag){
case 1: // Case in which pivoting is employed

  for(k=0; k < N-1; k++){
    pivot = A.MaxModInColumnindex(k,k);
    A.RowSwap(pivot,k);
    Swap(b(pivot),b(k));
    for(int i=k+1;i<N;i++){
      double l_ik = A(i,k)/A(k,k);
      for(int j=k;j<N;j++)
        A(i,j) = A(i,j) - l_ik*A(k,j);
      b(i) = b(i) - l_ik*b(k);
    }
  }
  break;

case 0:  // Case 0/default in which no pivoting is used
default:

  for(k=0; k < N-1; k++){
    for(int i=k+1;i<N;i++){
      double l_ik = A(i,k)/A(k,k);
      for(int j=k;j<N;j++)
        A(i,j) = A(i,j) - l_ik*A(k,j);
      b(i) = b(i) - l_ik*b(k);
    }
  }
}

// Step (3) (backsolving to solve Ux=y)
b(N-1) = b(N-1)/A(N-1,N-1);
for(k=N-2;k>=0;k--){
  for(int j=k+1;j<N;j++)
    b(k) -= A(k,j)*b(j);
  b(k) = b(k)/A(k,k);
}
}
```

REMARK 2: In the preceding implementation we use a *switch* statement to partition the different cases. There are two advantages of doing this: code readability and the ease of adding another condition. Suppose that we decided to implement a new pivoting algorithm; within the current function we could merely add another case to denote the new pivoting functionality. Notice that it is not required that case "0" go before case "1". Recall that the switch statement evaluates the validity of the switch in the order given in the code; hence in this case the switch statement first checks to see if case "1" is valid, and if not it checks for case "0". Also notice that we use a "default" case. If neither a *zero* nor a *one* is given in the switch input, the default will be executed. In this example, the default case and case "0" are identical.

REMARK 3: In the preceding code, we utilize two *matrix class* methods:

1. Matrix::MaxModInColumnindex(...) and
2. Matrix::Rowswap(...).

The first method implements the maximum modulus in a column operation needed for pivoting. The second method swaps two rows of the matrix **A**. The advantage of using these two methods is that from this level in the code the implementation details of how these two functions are accomplished are not our concern. At the level of this code we merely need to know the input, output, and contract for the methods.

REMARK 4: Notice that in the preceding code we both declare and initialize the iterating value (such as `int k=0`) within the *for* loops. Recall that C++ does not require us to declare all variables at the beginning of the function. In this function we have made liberal use of this ability by declaring and initializing each iterating value with its respective *for* loop.

The need for pivoting is dictated by the properties of the matrix **A**. There are two special categories of matrices for which we *do not need* to pivot. These matrices are

- diagonally dominant or
- positive-definite.

A *strictly diagonally dominant* matrix has the property

$$|a_{ii}| > \sum_{j=1}^{n} |a_{ij}|, \ i = 1, \ldots, n, \quad j \neq i,$$

and it is guaranteed to be nonsingular.

A *positive-definite* matrix is defined by the condition

$$\forall \mathbf{x} \neq 0, \quad \mathbf{x}^T \mathbf{A} \mathbf{x} > 0,$$

which guarantees that the matrix **A** is nonsingular. In addition, these properties guarantee that there will be no numerical instabilities in systems where such matrices are involved.

Fortunately, many of the algebraic systems resulting from PDEs that describe physical phenomena (presented in Chapters 6 and 7) have these desirable properties. In particular, the matrix obtained from the discretization of d^2u/dx^2 (see Chapter 6) is tridiagonal with diagonals $(1, -2, 1)$. Although it does not satisfy strictly the diagonal dominance condition, it is an *irreducible matrix*, that is, its associated directed graph is strongly connected, and this condition is equivalent to diagonal dominance.

The special matrices we have described are guaranteed to be nonsingular but they are also far from being even approximately singular. Clearly, if a matrix **A** is singular, then Gaussian elimination cannot be applied as $\mathbf{A}^{-1}$ does not exist. However, in practice many matrices are *almost singular*, and this is the condition we should investigate, as it leads to numerical instabilities. The value of the determinant, if the matrix is scaled properly, can give us an indication of whether the matrix is almost singular or *ill-conditioned*. However, computing determinants is costly and at least equivalent in computational complexity to an LU decomposition, the stability of which we investigate in first place! Only for special matrices can the computation of the determinant be employed.

Another approach is to employ the condition number $\kappa(\mathbf{A})$ for matrix **A**, that is,

$$\kappa(\mathbf{A}) \equiv \| \mathbf{A} \| \cdot \| \mathbf{A}^{-1} \| .$$

As we have seen in Chapter 2 it relates the perturbation of data to the changes in the solution, that is,

$$\frac{\| \mathbf{Ax} \|}{\| \mathbf{x} \|} \leq \kappa(\mathbf{A}) \frac{\| \mathbf{Ab} \|}{\| \mathbf{b} \|} .$$

The condition number is always computed with respect to some norm. We will use the notation $\kappa_i(\mathbf{A})$ to denote the condition number of **A** with respect to the $\| \cdot \|_i$ norm. When no subscript is given, we assume that the $\| \cdot \|_2$ norm is used. We can define relationships between different norm-based condition numbers using the equivalence relations between the norms.

By definition the condition number $\kappa(\mathbf{A})$ is greater than or equal to one, but we are interested in extremely large values of $\kappa(\mathbf{A})$, because it acts as an amplifier in the propagation of disturbance (noise) from the input to output (solution).

For symmetric matrices we have that

$$\kappa_2(\mathbf{A}) = \frac{|\lambda_{max}|}{|\lambda_{min}|} ,$$

and we have computed the eigenvalues λ_i for several cases in Chapter 6; see also Chapter 10. For general matrices, however, it is difficult to compute the condition number economically so approximate estimation algorithms are employed. Here we will present the estimator proposed by Hager [52]; see also [26]. The algorithm[2] obtains a lower bound on the inverse matrix in the one norm. However, we note that $\mathbf{A}^{-1}$ is not constructed explicitly as this is costly; in fact it requires an $\mathcal{O}(n^3)$ operation! Instead, the

---

[2] This algorithm is available in LAPACK, routines **sgesvx** and **slacon**.

matrix–vector products $\mathbf{A}^{-1}\mathbf{x}$ are computed on-the-fly:

Initialize: $\mathbf{x} : \| \mathbf{x} \|_1 = 1$

Begin Loop: $\mathbf{y} = \mathbf{A}^{-1}\mathbf{x}$
$\quad\quad\quad\quad\ \ \mathbf{z} = \text{sign}(\mathbf{y})$
$\quad\quad\quad\quad\ \ \mathbf{q} = (\mathbf{A}^{-1})^T\mathbf{z}$
$\quad\quad\quad\quad\ \ $ if $\ \| \mathbf{q} \|_\infty \le \mathbf{q}^T\mathbf{x}$ return $\ \| \mathbf{y} \|_1$
$\quad\quad\quad\quad\quad\quad\ \ $ elseif $\mathbf{x} = \mathbf{e}_j \text{sign}(q_j)$ with $|q_j| = \| \mathbf{q} \|_\infty$
$\quad\quad\quad\quad\ \ $ endif
$\quad\quad$*End Loop*

Here $\mathbf{e}_j = (0, 0, \dots, 1, \dots 0)^T$ is the jth column of the identity matrix. The condition number is then estimated from

$$\kappa \approx \| \mathbf{A} \|_1 \cdot \| \mathbf{y} \|_1 .$$

We note that $\| \mathbf{y} \|_1$ is a local maximum to $\| \mathbf{A}^{-1}\mathbf{x} \|_1$ and that this method is based on computing the gradient of $f(x) \approx \| \mathbf{A}^{-1}\mathbf{x} \|_1$; for a detailed explanation of the algorithm see [52].

REMARK 5: The accuracy degradation of the solution, if the condition number is large, can be estimated as follows: Assuming that the condition number is $\kappa(\mathbf{A}) \approx 10^p$, then the number of accurate digits in the solution is $(q - p)$ if the solution is computed in *q-digit* arithmetic.

9.1.3 Parallel LU Decomposition

The efficient parallel implementation of decomposing a nonsingular matrix $\mathbf{A}$ into its LU factorization requires that we address two main issues:

1. how to split the matrix $\mathbf{A}$ among the processors and
2. how to organize the triple loop so that efficient BLAS operations can be employed.

We consider here distributed memory computers and so only parts of the matrix $\mathbf{A}$ are stored in each processor. The obvious ways to split the matrix $\mathbf{A}$ are by rows or by columns, but it may also be beneficial to split it in blocks. A better layout, often used in practice, is *interleaved storage* either by row or by column. We examine these different cases in some detail in the following.

With regards to organizing the triple nested loop – recall that we deal with an $\mathcal{O}(n^3)$ operation – there are six ways of permutating the indices (ijk), just as in the matrix–matrix multiplication we discussed in Chapter 2. In Table 9.1 we present all six versions and basic operations involved.

We have defined the basic operation in Table 9.1 as the operation involved in the innermost loop. In four versions this is a *daxpy* operation [i.e., double a (scalar) $\mathbf{x}$ (vector) plus $\mathbf{y}$ (vector)], whereas in the other two versions (ijk and jik) it is a *ddot* (i.e.,

Table 9.1: Six different ways of writing the LU triple loops.

1. ijk Loop: A – by column (ddot)	2. ikj Loop: A – by row (daxpy)

for $i = 2, n$
  for $j = 2, i$
    $\ell_{i,j-1} = a_{i,j-1}/a_{j-1,j-1}$
    for $k = 1, j-1$
      $a_{ij} = a_{ij} - \ell_{ik}a_{kj}$
    endfor
  endfor
  for $j = i+1, n$
    for $k = 1, i-1$
      $a_{ij} = a_{ij} - \ell_{ik}a_{kj}$
    endfor
  endfor
endfor
	for $i = 2, n$
	  for $k = 1, i-1$
	    $\ell_{ik} = a_{ik}/a_{kk}$
	    for $j = k+1, n$
	      $a_{ij} = a_{ij} - \ell_{ik}a_{kj}$
	    endfor
	  endfor
	endfor

3. jik Loop: A – by column (ddot)	4. jki Loop: A – by column (daxpy)

for $j = 2, n$
  for $p = j, n$
    $\ell_{p,j-1} = a_{p,j-1}/a_{j-1,j-1}$
  endfor
  for $i = 2, j$
    for $k = 1, i-1$
      $a_{ij} = a_{ij} - \ell_{ik}a_{kj}$
    endfor
  endfor
  for $i = j+1, n$
    for $k = 1, j-1$
      $a_{ij} = a_{ij} - \ell_{ik}a_{kj}$
    endfor
  endfor
endfor
	for $j = 2, n$
	  for $p = j, n$
	    $\ell_{p,j-1} = a_{p,j-1}/a_{j-1,j-1}$
	  endfor
	  for $k = 1, j-1$
	    for $i = k+1, n$
	      $a_{ij} = a_{ij} - \ell_{ik}a_{kj}$
	    endfor
	  endfor
	endfor

5. kij Loop: A – by row (daxpy)	6. kji Loop: A – by column (daxpy)

for $k = 1, n-1$
  for $i = k+1, n$
    $\ell_{ik} = a_{ik}/a_{kk}$
    for $j = k+1, n$
      $a_{ij} = a_{ij} - \ell_{ik}a_{kj}$
    endfor
  endfor
endfor
	for $k = 1, n-1$
	  for $p = k+1, n$
	    $\ell_{pk} = a_{pk}/a_{kk}$
	  endfor
	  for $j = k+1, n$
	    for $i = k+1, n$
	      $a_{ij} = a_{ij} - \ell_{ik}a_{kj}$
	    endfor
	  endfor
	endfor

double dot product). These are both BLAS1 operations and cannot easily take advantage of *cache blocking* or *data reuse* (see Section 2.2.6). Thus, appropriate modifications of these basic loops are required to be able to employ BLAS2 and BLAS3 routines. This will depend on the specific way we lay out the matrix **A** to also maximize parallel efficiency. We examine this issue in more detail next.

Access by Rows

Let us first assume that the matrix **A** is accessed by rows as in the (kij) loop of Table 9.1 (see Figure 9.2 for a schematic explanation). Let us also assume that the first processor P_1 holds the first row $\mathbf{a}_1^T$, P_2 holds $\mathbf{a}_2^T$, and so on.

During the *first* elimination stage, the processor P_1 needs to send its row to all other processors so that processors $P_2, \ldots, P_n$ will simultaneously update their columns. Therefore, the operations

$$\left. \begin{array}{l} \ell_{i1} = \frac{a_{i1}}{a_{11}}, \\ a_{ij} = a_{ij} - \ell_{i1}a_{1j} \end{array} \right\} \begin{array}{l} j = 2, \ldots n, \\ P_2, \ldots, P_n \end{array}$$

can be performed *in parallel*. During this first stage, processor P_1 remains essentially idle after it communicates with the rest of the processors.

The *second* stage also starts with a communication step as P_2 needs to broadcast its new row to all other processors $P_3, \ldots, P_n$. It too remains idle after that, while $P_3, \ldots, P_n$

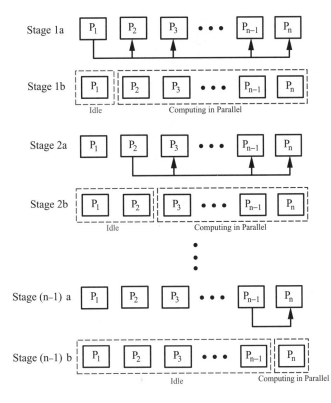

Figure 9.2: Schematic of communication (a) and computation (b) pattern when a matrix is partitioned such that each processor contains one row.

update their rows in parallel, and so on for the remaining stages. The computations of the multiplications as well as the updates are done in parallel, but after the kth stage, k processors $(P_1, \ldots, P_k)$ remain idle. This approach significantly reduces the parallel efficiency.

Some improvements can be made by *overlapping* communication with computation. For example, the broadcasting of the row of processor P_k can be done immediately after it is computed, so that the other processors receive it while they are updating their rows during the kth stage of elimination. This overlapping of computation and communication is called a *send-ahead* operation and it is quite common in distributed memory parallel computers. Another improvement would come about if we manage to increase the work done in parallel relative to communications. In general, the parallel efficiency improves as the ratio of computations to communications becomes larger. Thus, for given required communication the local work is increased as many rows are stored in each processor, so we have one, say, send-ahead operation every 100 rows on a $P = 10$ processor system and a matrix of $n = 1,000$.

Figure 9.3: Schematic of communication (a) and computation (b) pattern when a matrix is partitioned with an interleaved layout.

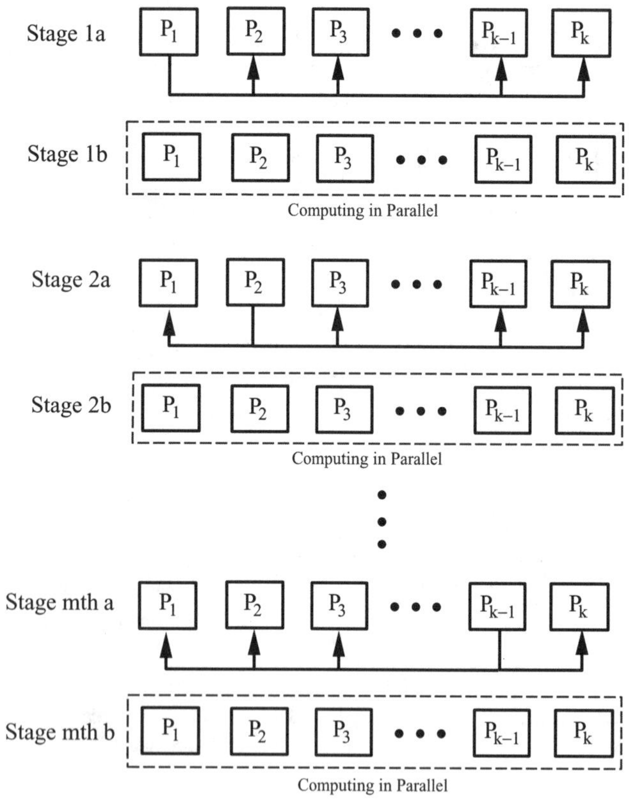

Blocked Layout

The row-blocked layout of the matrix $\mathbf{A}$ suggests that the practical way of storing $\mathbf{A}$ is by rows, and it extends also to a column-blocked layout (e.g., in the kji algorithm described in Table 9.1). In this case, the multiplications ℓ_{ij} are computed on the processor P_j (or its corresponding number for blocked storage), and then the ℓ_{ij} are broadcast to all other (active) processors.

Partial pivoting in the row-blocked and column-blocked parallel versions is handled differently. In the latter version, a search for the maximum pivot is performed within the processor whereas in the former (kij loop) the searching is across processors; this requires a fan-in algorithm for the *max* operator, as discussed in Chapter 2.

Another improvement of the row-blocked or column-blocked layout schemes is the introduction of a *cyclic* or *interleaved* layout (see Figure 9.3). For example, assuming that we have available $k = 10$ processors for a 100×100 matrix $\mathbf{A}$, then we pursue the following storage scheme:

$$P_1: \text{rows } 1, 11, 21, \ldots, 91,$$
$$P_2: \text{rows } 2, 12, 22, \ldots, 92,$$
$$\vdots$$
$$P_{10}: \text{rows } 10, 20, \ldots, 100,$$

and similarly in a column-oriented storage

scheme. Examining Figure 9.3, we observe that during stage 1a processor 1 communicates row 1 to all other processors, and then in stage 1b all processors are active accomplishing row reduction. In comparison to the previous block setup in which rows 1–10 would be assigned to processor 1, rows 11–20 to processor 2, etc., row 2 is now located on processor 2. Hence in stage 2a, processor 2 communicates row 2 to all other processors, and in stage 2b all processors accomplish row reduction concurrently. In this manner, for the first $m = 90$ stages all the processors remain active both in communication and computation. Some inefficiencies may occur during the last few stages, however, as the final row assigned to a processor is eliminated, hence retiring the processor from service for the elimination.

An even better option is to employ a block of rows (or columns) and assign these blocks in a cyclic or interleaved manner. The advantages of this approach are that no processor retires early and that BLAS2 and BLAS3 routines can be used because of the blocking. All processors see roughly the same amount of work, proportioned to $1/P$, although the first processors work less (e.g., after they compute their first block).

Finally, a combination of row- and column-blocked interleaved storage of matrix **A** can be pursued. In this case we can imagine a mapping of b size blocks of **A** in a cyclic manner (of cycle length C) onto a *mesh-type* parallel computer consisting of $P = P_r \times P_c$ processors. Schematically, this arrangement is shown in Figure 9.4.

1	2	1	2	1	2	1	2
3	4	3	4	3	4	3	4
1	2	1	2	1	2	1	2
3	4	3	4	3	4	3	4
1	2	1	2	1	2	1	2
3	4	3	4	3	4	3	4
1	2	1	2	1	2	1	2
3	4	3	4	3	4	3	4

Figure 9.4: Two-dimensional block interleaved mapping of a 16×16 matrix on $P = 4$ processors; here $b = 2$ and $C = 2$, and the processor id used is given by $S_i + 2S_j + 1$. Here S_i and S_j have the values 0 or 1.

This mapping can be established by setting

$$S_i = F(i, b) \text{ and } S_j = F(j, b),$$

with $i = 0, \ldots, n-1$ and $j = 0, \ldots, n-1$ (N being the size of **A**), where the value of the (S_i, S_j) pair defines the processor in the mesh architecture. The function F is defined as

```
function F(i, b)
    floor (i/b) modulo C
return;
```

where we assume that we deal with a square matrix and that $C^2 = P$. In the example of Figure 9.4, we have $P = 4$ and $C = 2$. We have also assumed here for simplicity that the computer (mesh array) is symmetric, but that may not be advantageous in practice, that is, we may want to have $P_r > P_c$ (more rows than columns). The advantage of this approach, in addition to its good parallel performance, is that it can make use of the BLAS3 routines, which provide high efficiency. The main steps of computing pivots, send-ahead, and parallel work on each processor that we presented earlier are also utilized here.

The plot of Figure 9.5 shows a graphical representation of LU decomposition using BLAS3. The new entries to be computed are in the shaded area in the right lower corner of the matrix **A**. The submatrix $\mathbf{A}_s$ that is currently shown to be computed has a size $b \times b$, that is, the size of the block of rows and columns. This implementation is included in ScaLAPACK software for distributed computers; see **www.netlib.org/scalapack**.

9.1.4 Parallel Back Substitution

We first present an *ideal* algorithm for parallel back substitution that provides a lower bound for its computational complexity. Although the lower bound may be

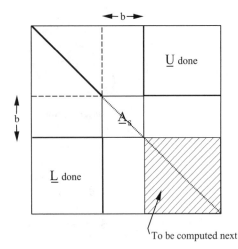

To be computed next

Figure 9.5: LU decomposition of a matrix A using two-dimensional block interleaved storage. BLAS2 and BLAS3 can be effectively employed in this algorithm.

unattainable given hardware constraints, it provides us with the "best-case" scenario that the algorithm can provide given unrestricted resources. By understanding the concept that yields the lower bound result, we hope that after incorporating relevant constraints we will obtain a reasonable algorithm. The ideal algorithm for parallel back substitution is based on a *divide-and-conquer* algorithm for inverting triangular matrices.

Let us consider the lower triangular matrix **L**, which we decompose into submatrices of half size $\mathbf{L}_1 \mathbf{L}_2$ and $\mathbf{L}_3$ as follows:

$$\mathbf{L} = \begin{bmatrix} \mathbf{L}_1 & 0 \\ \mathbf{L}_2 & \mathbf{L}_3 \end{bmatrix}.$$

We assume that $n = 2^k$ and that k is an integer. This is shown schematically in the plot of Figure 9.6.

It is clear that $\mathbf{L}_1$ and $\mathbf{L}_2$ are themselves lower triangular matrices. We can prove that

$$\mathbf{L}^{-1} = \begin{bmatrix} \mathbf{L}_1^{-1} & 0 \\ -\mathbf{L}_3^{-1}\mathbf{L}_2\mathbf{L}_1^{-1} & \mathbf{L}_3^{-1} \end{bmatrix}$$

and take advantage of this equation to set up a divide-and-conquer algorithm for inverting the matrix **L** of size n.

The main steps are shown in the following pseudo-code:

```
Function InvTriangular(L)
    if size(L)= 1 return 1/L
    else
        Set L1 top triangular part of L
        Set L2 square part of L
        Set L3 bottom triangular part of L

        InvL1 =InvTriangular(L1)
        InvL3 =InvTriangular(L3)
        UpdateL2 = - InvL3 * L2 * InvL1
```

$$\text{return } L = \begin{vmatrix} InvL1 & 0 \\ UpdateL2 & InvL3 \end{vmatrix}$$

```
    endif
```

We can perform the inversion of $\mathbf{L}_1$ and $\mathbf{L}_2$ in parallel, so the cost C is

$$C[\text{InvTriangular}(n)] = C[\text{InvTriangular}(n/2) + C[mxm(n/2)],$$

where by *mxm* we denote the matrix multiplication. The ideal time for this matrix multiplication (assuming we employ n^3 processors) is $\mathcal{O}(\log n)$, and thus the ideal cost for inverting triangular matrices is $\mathcal{O}(\log^2 n)$. Unfortunately, this cost is impossible to realize in practice.

The $\mathcal{O}(\log^2 n)$ time estimate is based on the equation

$$t(n) = t(n/2) + \mathcal{O}(\log n).$$

We set $k = \log_2 n$, and thus

$$t(k) = t(k-1) + \mathcal{O}(k)$$
$$= t(k-2) + \mathcal{O}(k) + \mathcal{O}(k-1)$$
$$= t(1) + \mathcal{O}(k) + \mathcal{O}(k-1) + \cdots + 1$$
$$\approx \frac{k(k-1)}{2} \sim \mathcal{O}(k^2/2) \sim \mathcal{O}(\log^2 n).$$

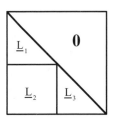

Figure 9.6: Decomposition of a lower triangular matrix L. Matrices L_1 and L_3 are also lower triangular.

Note that the $\mathcal{O}(\log n)$ ideal estimate for the matrix multiplication is based on the fact that all entries of the product matrix can be computed in parallel on $P = n^3$ processors and then summed up using a fan-in algorithm, which is $\mathcal{O}(\log n)$. This is of course unattainable at the moment since the $n = 1,000$ size (ideally parallel) matrix multiplication would require more than one billion processors, more than what we currently have on this planet!

We now discuss how the *back substitution* step $\mathbf{Ux} = \mathbf{y}$, which is also a triangular system, can be performed in parallel. The algorithm proceeds by computing first

$$x_n = \frac{b_n^{(n-1)}}{a_{nn}^{(n-1)}},$$

while all other unknowns are computed from

$$\forall i = n-1, \ldots, 1:$$
$$x_i = \frac{b_i^{(i-1)} - a_{ii}^{(i-1)} x_{i+1}}{a_{i,i}^{i-1}} = \frac{b_i - u_{i,i+1} x_{i+1} - u_{i,i+2} x_{i+2} - \ldots u_{in} x_{in}}{u_{ii}},$$

where u_{ij} denote entries of the matrix $\mathbf{U}$.

The most obvious implementation of this is the following:

```
for j = n, 1
    for j = i + 1, n
        b_i = b_i - u_ij x_j
    endfor
    x_i = b_i / u_ii
endfor
```

This assumes that $\mathbf{U}$ is stored by rows, which are accessed in the innermost loop j. More specifically, the matrix $\mathbf{U}$ is stored in blocks of rows assigned to each processor. The corresponding operation employs the BLAS1 *ddot* routine, which implements the inner (dot) product of the innermost loop. However, if $\mathbf{U}$ is stored in blocks of columns per processor, then the (ij) loop of the preceding *ddot* product implementation has to be reversed as follows:

$$
\begin{aligned}
&\text{for } j = n, 1 \\
&\quad x_j = b_j / u_{jj} \\
&\quad \text{for } i = 1, j - 1 \\
&\qquad b_i = b_i - u_{ij} x_j \\
&\quad \text{endfor} \\
&\text{endfor}
\end{aligned}
$$

Here the innermost loop (i) generates updates of the numerators for the final answer x_j while the outer loop (j) sweeps the matrix **U** by columns starting from right to left. This is sometimes referred to as *left-looking* access of **U**, and it involves *daxpy* operations in the innermost loop.

Software Suite

PUTTING IT INTO PRACTICE

Prior to presenting a parallel implementation of Gaussian elimination, we will first discuss one new MPI function not introduced previously: *MPI_Bcast*. This function allows us to distribute to all processes within the communicator an identical piece of data. In the case of Gaussian elimination, *MPI_Bcast* will allow us to "broadcast" to all processes a particular row being used in the elimination. We will now present the function call syntax, argument list explanation, usage example, and some remarks.

MPI_Bcast

MPI

FUNCTION CALL SYNTAX

```
int MPI_Bcast(
        void*          buffer      /*  in/out  */,
        int            count       /*  in      */,
        MPI_Datatype   datatype    /*  in      */,
        int            root        /*  in      */,
        MPI_Comm       comm        /*  in      */)
```

MPI

UNDERSTANDING THE ARGUMENT LIST

- *buffer* – starting address of the send buffer.
- *count* – number of elements in the send buffer.
- *datatype* – data type of the elements in the send buffer.
- *root* – rank of the process broadcasting its data.
- *comm* – communicator.

MPI

EXAMPLE OF USAGE

```
int mynode, totalnodes;
int datasize; // number of data units to be broadcast
int root;     // process that is broadcasting its data
```

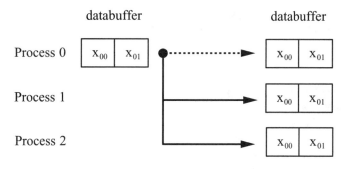

Figure 9.7: *MPI_Bcast* schematic demonstrating a broadcast of two data objects from process 0 to all other processes.

```
MPI_Init(&argc,&argv);
MPI_Comm_size(MPI_COMM_WORLD, &totalnodes);
MPI_Comm_rank(MPI_COMM_WORLD, &mynode);

// Determine datasize and root

double * databuffer = new double[datasize];

// Fill in databuffer array with data to be broadcast

MPI_Bcast(databuffer,datasize,MPI_DOUBLE,root,MPI_COMM_WORLD);

// At this point, every process has received into the
// databuffer array the data from process root
```

REMARKS

MPI

• Each process will make an identical call of the *MPI_Bcast* function. On the broadcasting (root) process, the *buffer* array contains the data to be broadcast. At the conclusion of the call, all processes have obtained a copy of the contents of the *buffer* array from process root (see Figure 9.7).

We now present a parallel implementation of Gaussian elimination with back substitution. As a model problem, we solve for the interpolating polynomial of the Runge function (see Section 3.1.4) by forming a Vandermonde matrix based on the Chebyshev points. Recall that the goal is to find the polynomial coefficients by solving the system $\mathbf{Ax} = \mathbf{b}$, where $\mathbf{A}$ is the Vandermonde matrix and $\mathbf{b}$ is the function of interest evaluated at the interpolation points.

To better explain the code, we have broken the entire program into six parts, as follows:

1. Part 1 – MPI initialization/setup and initial memory allocations.
2. Part 2 – Generation of the matrix rows local to each process.
3. Part 3 – Gaussian elimination of the augmented matrix.
4. Part 4 – Preparation for back substitution.
5. Part 5 – Back substitution to find the solution.
6. Part 6 – Program finalization and cleanup.

For each part, we will first present the code and then present a collection of remarks elucidating the salient points within each part.

```
MPI
```

PART 1 - MPI INITIALIZATION

```cpp
#include <iostream.h>
#include <iomanip.h>
#include "SCmathlib.h"
#include "SCchapter3.h"
#include<mpi.h>

void ChebyVandermonde(int npts, double *A, int row);

// Global variable to set size of the system
const int size = 10;

int main(int argc, char *argv[]){
  int i,j,k,index;
  int mynode, totalnodes;
  double scaling;
  MPI_Status status;

  MPI_Init(&argc,&argv);
  MPI_Comm_size(MPI_COMM_WORLD, &totalnodes);
  MPI_Comm_rank(MPI_COMM_WORLD, &mynode);

  int numrows = size/totalnodes;
  double **A_local = new double*[numrows];
  int * myrows = new int[numrows];
```

REMARK 1: Notice that for this program we use a global constant variable to denote the size of the matrix system. By placing the variable declaration outside of the main function, the declaration is global to all functions (including the main function).

REMARK 2: We have made the assumption that the size of the matrix is evenly divisible by the number of processors we are using. If this were not the case, we would have to properly take this into account by having different numbers of rows per processor.

```
MPI
```

PART 2 - GENERATION OF MATRIX ROWS

```cpp
/* PART 2 */
double * xpts = new double[size];
ChebyshevPoints(size,xpts);

for(i=0;i<numrows;i++){
  A_local[i] = new double[size+1];
  index = mynode + totalnodes*i;
  myrows[i] = index;
  ChebyVandermonde(size,A_local[i],index);
```

```
      // Set-up right-hand side as the Runge function
      A_local[i][size] = 1.0/(1.0+25.0*xpts[index]*xpts[index]);
   }
   delete[] xpts;

   double * tmp = new double[size+1];
   double * x = new double[size];
```

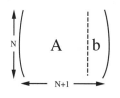

Figure 9.8: The augmented matrix consists of the original matrix A with the right-hand-side vector b appended as an additional column.

REMARK 1: Notice that we allocate for each row $(size + 1)$ columns. Recall that in Gaussian elimination it is necessary for us to act on the right-hand side (the vector **b**) as we do the row reduction. We can eliminate the extra communication cost that would come by handling the right-hand side separately by forming an augmented matrix as shown in Figure 9.8.

As you will see in the next section, all row-reduction steps will be accomplished on $(size + 1)$ columns so that both the matrix and right-hand side are updated properly.

REMARK 2: To keep track of which rows a processor possesses, we store the indices of the rows in an array named *myrows*. This array contains *numrows* entries, each entry denoting which rows in the matrix the processor is responsible for

PART 3 – GAUSSIAN ELIMINATION

MPI

```
/* PART 3 */
/* Gaussian elimination of the augmented matrix */
int cnt = 0;
for(i=0;i<size-1;i++){
  if(i == myrows[cnt]){
    MPI_Bcast(A_local[cnt],size+1,MPI_DOUBLE,
              mynode,MPI_COMM_WORLD);
    for(j=0;j<size+1;j++)
  tmp[j] = A_local[cnt][j];
    cnt++;
  }
  else{
    MPI_Bcast(tmp,size+1,MPI_DOUBLE,i%totalnodes,
              MPI_COMM_WORLD);
  }
  for(j=cnt;j<numrows;j++){
    scaling = A_local[j][i]/tmp[i];
    for(k=i;k<size+1;k++)
      A_local[j][k] = A_local[j][k] - scaling*tmp[k];
  }
}
```

REMARK 1: We use the integer variable *cnt* to keep track of how many rows *on each processor* have been reduced. Recall that each processor has its own copy of the variable *cnt*, and hence on each processor *cnt* can be used to keep track of which row is active.

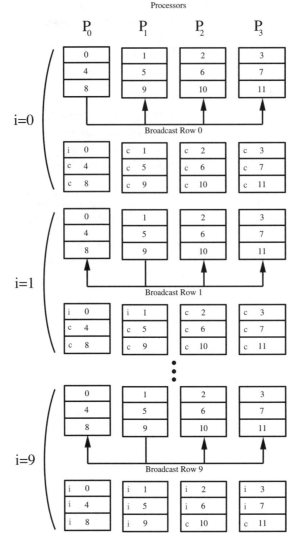

Figure 9.9: Schematic of the communication and computation pattern for a four-processor run executed on a $size = 12$ system. Iterations $i = 0$, $i = 1$, and $i = 9$ are shown. The letter i denotes an idle row; c denotes a computing row.

REMARK 2: We have chosen the *cyclic distribution* discussed earlier. A schematic of the communication and computation pattern for a four-processor run executed on a $size = 12$ system is shown in Figure 9.9.

MPI

PART 4 - PREPARATION FOR BACK SUBSTITUTION

```
/* PART 4 */

/* On each processor, initialize the value of x as equal to
   the modified (by Gaussian elimination) right-hand side if
```

```
      that information is on the processor; otherwise initialize
      to zero.
*/

cnt = 0;
for(i=0;i<size;i++){
  if(i==myrows[cnt]){
    x[i] = A_local[cnt][size];
    cnt++;
  }
  else
    x[i] = 0;
}
```

REMARK: To accomplish the back substitution, we first initialize the solution by setting the array entry $x[i]$ equal to the last column of the augmented matrix (which contains the modified right-hand side) for those rows for which a processor is responsible, and equal to zero for all rows for which a particular processor is not responsible.

PART 5 - BACK SUBSTITUTION

MPI

```
/* PART 5 */
/* Backsolve to find the solution x */
cnt = numrows-1;
for(i=size-1;i>0;i--){
  if(cnt>=0){
    if(i == myrows[cnt]){
      x[i] = x[i]/A_local[cnt][i];
      MPI_Bcast(x+i,1,MPI_DOUBLE,mynode,MPI_COMM_WORLD);
      cnt--;
    }
    else
      MPI_Bcast(x+i,1,MPI_DOUBLE,i%totalnodes,MPI_COMM_WORLD);
  }
  else
    MPI_Bcast(x+i,1,MPI_DOUBLE,i%totalnodes,MPI_COMM_WORLD);

  for(j=0;j<=cnt;j++)
    x[myrows[j]] = x[myrows[j]] - A_local[j][i]*x[i];
}

if(mynode==0){
  x[0] = x[0]/A_local[cnt][0];
  MPI_Bcast(x,1,MPI_DOUBLE,0,MPI_COMM_WORLD);
}
else
  MPI_Bcast(x,1,MPI_DOUBLE,0,MPI_COMM_WORLD);
```

REMARK 1: Observe that the variable *cnt* is initialized to (*numrows* − 1) and is decremented in this loop. Recall that we want to traverse back up the rows (hence the name back substitution). As a processor computes the solution for a row for which it is responsible, it then broadcasts the result to all the other processors.

REMARK 2: Why do we check for *cnt* ≥ 0? If you examine this loop carefully, you will notice that at some point the variable *cnt* is equal to −1. This occurs when all the solution components on a processor have been computed. We must verify that *cnt* ≥ 0 prior to attempting to access myrows[cnt]; otherwise we are performing an illegal memory access, and hence the process may fail. We know, however, that once a processor's value of *cnt* is equal to −1 it merely needs to obtain the updated values from other processors, and hence we can immediately proceed to an *MPI_Bcast* call to obtain the solution from another processor.

REMARK 3: Observe in the *MPI_Bcast* arguments that we use pointer arithmetic for updating the address that is passed to the function. Recall that *x* is a pointer (and hence has as its value an address). The expression $(x + i)$ is equivalent to the expression $\&x[i]$, which can be read as "the address of the array element $x[i]$."

MPI

PART 6 – PROGRAM FINALIZATION

```
/* PART 6 */

if(mynode==0){
  for(i=0;i<size;i++)
    cout << x[i] << endl;
}

delete[] tmp;
delete[] myrows;
for(i=0;i<numrows;i++)
  delete[] A_local[i];
delete[] A_local;

MPI_Finalize();

}

void ChebyVandermonde(int npts, double *A, int row){
  int i,j;
  double * x = new double[npts];

  ChebyshevPoints(npts,x);

  for(j=0;j<npts;j++)
    A[j] = pow(x[row],j);

  delete[] x;
}
```

REMARK: We conclude the program by printing the solution from the first processor ($mynode = 0$). If we were not to put the *if* statement there, all processors would print the solution.

9.1.5 Gaussian Elimination and Sparse Systems

Many linear systems that arise from discretization of partial differential equations, as we have seen in Chapters 6 and 7, are sparse and more specifically banded. Assuming that we deal with symmetrically banded systems of semibandwidth m, we can modify accordingly the (ijk) loops of Table 9.1 to account for this sparsity. For example, the kij loop is modified as follows:

$$
\begin{aligned}
&\text{for } k = 1, n-1 \\
&\quad \text{for } i = k+1, \ \min(k+m, n) \\
&\quad\quad \ell_{ik} = a_{ik}/a_{kk} \\
&\quad\quad \text{for } j = k+1, \ \min(k+m, n) \\
&\quad\quad\quad a_{ij} = a_{ij} - \ell_{ik}a_{kj} \\
&\quad\quad \text{endfor} \\
&\quad \text{endfor} \\
&\text{endfor}
\end{aligned}
$$

The computational complexity of this algorithm is significantly less on a serial computer than on a parallel computer. The operation count for LU decomposition is about $\mathcal{O}(nm^2)$ for an $n \times n$ matrix with bandwidth m, and for the backsolve it is $\mathcal{O}(nm)$. However, on a parallel computer a straightforward implementation of this algorithm would result in large inefficiencies. For example, the row- and column-blocked interleaved scheme discussed earlier becomes very inefficient when $m < P$, where P is the total number of processors, because only m processors are effectively used. Clearly, the case with $m = 1$ (i.e., the tridiagonal system) is the most difficult case and needs to be handled differently; we study this case next.

9.1.6 Parallel Cyclic Reduction for Tridiagonal Systems

Several algorithms have been developed over the years for the parallel solution of tridiagonal linear systems, including *recursive doubling* [82], *cyclic reduction* [13], *domain decomposition* [90], and their many variants. Here we present the cyclic reduction method, which has been one of the most successful approaches.

The main idea of cyclic reduction is to group the unknowns in *even-* and *odd-numbered* entries, just as in black–red Gauss–Seidel (see Section 7.2.4), and successively eliminate the odd-numbered entries. Most of the operations in this process can be done in parallel. We present here some details by considering a specific small system to illustrate how we manipulate the equations.

Let us consider the tridiagonal system

$$
a_i x_{i-1} + b_i x_i + c_i x_{i+1} = F_i, \qquad i = 1, \dots, n, \tag{9.8}
$$

where a_i, b_i, c_i, and F_i are given, and we also assume that $n = 2^p - 1$. If $n \neq 2^p - 1$ then we add additional trivial equations of the form $x_i = 0$, $i = n+1, \ldots, 2^p - 1$.

The key idea is then to combine linearly the equations to eliminate the odd-numbered unknowns

$$x_1, x_3, x_5, \ldots, x_n$$

in the first stage. We then reorder (i.e., renumber) the unknowns and repeat this process until we arrive at a single equation with one unknown. Upon solution of that equation, we march backward to obtain the rest of the unknowns. To do this we combine the equations in triplets.

Next, we demonstrate this for the case of $n = 7 = 2^3 - 1$ unknowns for which we have three triplets. We start by forming the first triplet from the first three equations. To this end, we multiply by the parameters α_2, β_2, and γ_2 to get

$$\alpha_2 b_1 x_1 + \alpha_2 c_1 x_2 = \alpha_2 F_1,$$

$$\beta_2 a_2 x_1 + \beta_2 b_2 x_2 + \beta_2 c_2 x_3 = \beta_2 F_2,$$

$$\gamma_2 a_3 x_2 + \gamma_2 b_3 x_3 + \gamma_2 c_3 x_4 = \gamma_2 F_3.$$

To eliminate x_1 and x_3, we add the equations and choose

$$\beta_2 = 1,$$

$$\alpha_2 b_1 + \beta_2 a_2 = 0,$$

$$\beta_2 c_2 + \gamma_2 b_3 = 0,$$

resulting in

$$\underbrace{(\alpha_2 c_1 + \beta_2 b_2 + \gamma_2 a_3)}_{\hat{b}_2} x_2 + \underbrace{\gamma_2 c_3}_{\hat{c}_2} x_4 = \underbrace{\alpha_2 F_1 + \beta_2 F_2 + \gamma_2 F_3}_{\hat{F}_2}.$$

Similarly, combining the third, fourth, and fifth equations obtained from Equation (9.8) we form the second triplet, from which we obtain

$$\underbrace{\alpha_4 a_3}_{\hat{a}_4} x_2 + \underbrace{(\alpha_4 c_3 + \beta_4 b_4 + \gamma_4 a_5)}_{\hat{b}_4} x_4 + \underbrace{\gamma_4 c_5}_{\hat{c}_4} x_6 = \underbrace{a_4 F_3 + \beta_4 F_4 + \gamma_4 F_5}_{\hat{F}_4},$$

and α_4, β_4, and γ_4 are determined from

$$\beta_4 = 1,$$

$$\alpha_4 b_3 + \beta_4 a_4 = 0,$$

$$\beta_4 c_4 + \gamma_4 b_5 = 0.$$

Finally, for the third triplet we obtain, as before, the only surviving equation

$$\hat{a}_6 x_4 + \hat{b}_6 x_6 = \hat{F}_6,$$

where the parameters α_6, β_6, and γ_6 involved in the definition of $\hat{a}_6$, $\hat{b}_6$, and $\hat{F}_6$ are determined by solving

$$\alpha_6 b_5 + \beta_6 a_6 = 0,$$

$$\beta_6 c_6 + \gamma_b b_7 = 0.$$

We see that the three resulting equations also form a tridiagonal system, that is,

$$\hat{b}_2 x_2 + \hat{c}_2 x_4 = \hat{F}_2, \tag{9.9}$$

$$\hat{a}_4 x_2 + \hat{b}_4 x_4 + \hat{c}_4 x_6 = \hat{F}_4, \tag{9.10}$$

$$\hat{a}_6 x_4 + \hat{b}_6 x_6 = \hat{F}_6. \tag{9.11}$$

We can repeat the same elimination process as before; that is, we first multiply those equations by α_4', β_4', and γ_4', respectively, and choose

$$\alpha_4' \hat{b}_2 + \beta_4' \hat{a}_4 = 0,$$

$$\beta_4' \hat{c}_4 + \gamma_4' \hat{b}_6 = 0,$$

which leads to only one equation:

$$\alpha_4^* x_4 = F_4^*.$$

Using back substitution, after we obtain x_4 from the preceding equation, we can compute x_2 from the reduced Equation (9.9) and x_6 from Equation (9.11). Finally, we use the original equations to obtain x_1, x_3, x_5, and x_7.

In summary, we perform the following steps:

1. Compute

$$(\alpha_2, \beta_2, \gamma_2),$$

$$(\alpha_4, \beta_4, \gamma_4),$$

$$(\alpha_6, \beta_6, \gamma_6).$$

2. Compute

$$(\hat{b}_2, \hat{c}_2, \hat{F}_2),$$

$$(\hat{a}_4, \hat{b}_4, \hat{c}_4, \hat{F}_4),$$

$$(\hat{a}_6, \hat{b}_6, \hat{F}_6).$$

3. Compute

$$(\alpha_4', \beta_4', \gamma_4'),$$

$$(a_4^*, F_4^*).$$

4. Solve for x_4, x_2, x_6, x_1, x_3, x_5, and x_7.

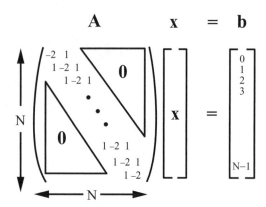

$$\mathbf{A} \qquad \mathbf{x} = \mathbf{b}$$

Figure 9.10: Tridiagonal system used as a model problem for cyclic reduction.

REMARK: There exist nonsingular matrices for which this method will terminate early with the solution. The number of levels used here is the worst-case scenario. For some matrices, the depth of reduction can be truncated because the solution can be obtained for one of the variables. Immediately, back substitution can begin.

The operation count is $\mathcal{O}(13n)$ multiplications compared to $\mathcal{O}(5n)$ for the standard LU decomposition. But this is the serial work and many of the preceding computations can be done in parallel. For example, let us assume that we have

$$P = \frac{n-1}{2}$$

processors and we store each triplet on one processor. The work for eliminating the odd-numbered unknowns can be done in parallel, and at the end of this stage each processor holds one reduced equation. To proceed, the processors need to exchange data. This can be done by nearest neighbor communications, for example, P_2 will receive data from P_1 and P_3, P_4 will receive data from P_3 and P_5, and so on. This implies that about half of the processors (e.g., all the odd-numbered $P_1, P_3, \ldots$) will remain idle. After $(p-1)$ reduction stages (where $n = 2^p - 1$) only one processor will solve the final equation. However, the rest of the processors are not quite retired yet, as in the back substitution they will all be called to duty again!

Software ⊙ *Suite*

PUTTING IT INTO PRACTICE

We now present implementations of cyclic reduction for tridiagonal systems. Owing to the complex nature of the indexing involved, we will present both the serial and then the parallel version. As pointed out earlier, the serial version of this algorithm is rarely used because it is actually more expensive than standard LU; we present it, however, because it is easier to understand the complex indexing in the serial setting without the additional complexity of the parallelization.

As a model problem, we solve for the system given in Figure 9.10. Notice that the matrix **A** is of the form found in discretizations of the Laplace's equation with second-order finite difference schemes.

To better explain the code, we have broken the entire program into multiple parts. The serial code is broken down into three parts as follows:

1. Part 1 – Memory allocation and generation of the matrix **A**.
2. Part 2 – Cyclic reduction stages.
3. Part 3 – Cyclic reduction back substitution to recover the solution.

For each part, we will first present the code and then present a collection of remarks elucidating the salient points within each part.

MPI

SERIAL

```
#include <iostream.h>
#include <iomanip.h>
```

```
#include "SCmathlib.h"

const int size = 15;

void main(){
  int i,j,k;
  int index1,index2,offset;
  double alpha,gamma;
```

PART 1 - MEMORY ALLOCATION AND GENERATION OF MATRIX

MPI

```
/* Part 1 */
double * x = new double[size];
for(i=0;i<size;i++)
  x[i] = 0.0;
double * F = new double[size];
double ** A = new double*[size];

for(i=0;i<size;i++){
  A[i] = new double[size];
  for(j=0;j<size;j++)
    A[i][j] = 0.;
  F[i] = (double)i;
}

A[0][0] = -2.0; A[0][1] = 1.0;
A[size-1][size-2] = 1.0; A[size-1][size-1] = -2.0;

for(i=1;i<size-1;i++){
  A[i][i] = -2.0;
  A[i][i-1] = 1.0;
  A[i][i+1] = 1.0;
}
```

REMARK 1: Observe that in this program we use more memory than necessary. Because we know that we are operating on a tridiagonal system, the memory required is greatly reduced from that which would be needed if **A** were full. Here we allocate memory as if **A** is a full matrix; we leave it as an exercise to modify this program to use only the necessary amount of memory.

PART 2 - CYCLIC REDUCTION

MPI

```
/* Part 2 */
for(i=0;i<log2(size+1)-1;i++){
  for(j=pow(2,i+1)-1;j<size;j=j+pow(2,i+1)){
    offset = pow(2,i);
    index1 = j - offset;
    index2 = j + offset;
```

```
    alpha = A[j][index1]/A[index1][index1];
    gamma = A[j][index2]/A[index2][index2];

    for(k=0;k<size;k++){
      A[j][k] -= (alpha*A[index1][k] + gamma*A[index2][k]);
    }
    F[j] -= (alpha*F[index1] + gamma*F[index2]);
  }
}
```

REMARK 2: In the preceding code section, the first *for* loop (over *i*) iterates through the levels of reduction that occur; the second *for* loop (over *j*) indexes which rows at each level are to be acted upon. Notice that both loops and the variables *index1* and *index2* are based on powers of 2.

MPI

PART 3 - BACK SUBSTITUTION

```
/* Part 3 */
int index = (size-1)/2;
x[index] = F[index]/A[index][index];

for(i=log2(size+1)-2;i>=0;i--){
  for(j=pow(2,i+1)-1;j<size;j=j+pow(2,i+1)){
    offset = pow(2,i);
    index1 = j - offset;
    index2 = j + offset;

    x[index1] = F[index1];
    x[index2] = F[index2];
    for(k=0;k<size;k++){
      if(k!= index1)
        x[index1] -= A[index1][k]*x[k];
      if(k!= index2)
        x[index2] -= A[index2][k]*x[k];
    }

    x[index1] = x[index1]/A[index1][index1];
    x[index2] = x[index2]/A[index2][index2];
  }
}

for(i=0;i<size;i++){
  cout << x[i] << endl;
}

delete[] x;
delete[] F;
for(i=0;i<size;i++)
```

```
      delete[] A[i];
    delete[] A;
}
```

REMARK 3: Once the full reduction has occurred, we must traverse back up the reduction tree. Note that the two *for* loops accomplish this traversal.

PARALLEL

We now present the parallel version of the serial code just presented. We assume that given P processors, we will accomplish cyclic reduction on a matrix of size $2^{\log_2(P+1)+1} - 1$. This amounts to associating three rows per processor during the first stage. The parallel code is broken down into four parts as follows:

1. Part 1 – MPI initialization and both memory allocation and generation of the matrix **A**.
2. Part 2 – Parallel cyclic reduction stages.
3. Part 3 – Parallel cyclic reduction back substitution to distribute necessary information.
4. Part 4 – Solution for the odd rows for which each process is responsible.

For each part, we will first present the code and then present a collection of remarks elucidating the salient points within each part.

PART 1 - MPI INITIALIZATION

```
#include <iostream.h>
#include <iomanip.h>
#include "SCmathlib.h"
#include<mpi.h>

int main(int argc, char *argv[]){
  int i,j,k,size,index;
  int index1,index2;
  int mynode, totalnodes;
  double alpha,gamma;
  const int numrows = 5;
  MPI_Status status;

  MPI_Init(&argc,&argv);
  MPI_Comm_size(MPI_COMM_WORLD, &totalnodes);
  MPI_Comm_rank(MPI_COMM_WORLD, &mynode);

  size = (int) pow(2.0,log2(totalnodes+1)+1)-1;

  double ** A = new double*[numrows];
  for(i=0;i<numrows;i++){
    A[i] = new double[size+1];
    for(j=0;j<size+1;j++)
```

MPI

MPI

```
                        A[i][j] = 0.0;
       }

       if(mynode==0){
         A[0][0] = -2.0; A[0][1] = 1.0;
         A[1][0] = 1.0; A[1][1] = -2.0; A[1][2] = 1.0;
         A[2][1] = 1.0; A[2][2] = -2.0; A[2][3] = 1.0;
       }
       else if(mynode==(totalnodes-1)){
         index = 2*mynode;
         A[0][index-1] = 1.0; A[0][index] = -2.0;
         A[0][index+1] = 1.0;
         index = 2*mynode+1;
         A[1][index-1] = 1.0; A[1][index] = -2.0;
         A[1][index+1] = 1.0;
         A[2][size-2] = 1.0; A[2][size-1] = -2.0;
       }
       else{
         for(i=0;i<3;i++){
           index = i + 2*mynode;
           A[i][index-1] = 1.0;
           A[i][index]   = -2.0;
           A[i][index+1] = 1.0;
         }
       }

       for(i=0;i<3;i++)
         A[i][size] = 2*mynode+i;

       int numactivep = totalnodes;
       int * activep = new int[totalnodes];
       for(j=0;j<numactivep;j++)
         activep[j] = j;

       for(j=0;j<size+1;j++){
         A[3][j] = A[0][j];
         A[4][j] = A[2][j];
       }
```

REMARK 1: Just as in the parallel Gaussian elimination code, we augment the matrix **A** with the right-hand side (appending **A** with an extra column). This helps to minimize the communication by allowing us to communicate both the row and right-hand-side information simultaneously.

MPI

PART 2 - CYCLIC REDUCTION

```
/* Part 2 */

for(i=0;i<log2(size+1)-1;i++){
```

```
    for(j=0;j<numactivep;j++){
      if(mynode==activep[j]){
        index1 = 2*mynode + 1 - pow(2,i);
        index2 = 2*mynode + 1 + pow(2,i);

        alpha = A[1][index1]/A[3][index1];
        gamma = A[1][index2]/A[4][index2];

        for(k=0;k<size+1;k++)
          A[1][k] -= (alpha*A[3][k] + gamma*A[4][k]);

        if(numactivep>1){
          if(j==0){
    MPI_Send(A[1],size+1,MPI_DOUBLE,activep[1],0,
                    MPI_COMM_WORLD);
  }
  else if(j==numactivep-1){
    MPI_Send(A[1],size+1,MPI_DOUBLE,activep[numactivep-2],
                    1,MPI_COMM_WORLD);
  }
  else if(j%2==0){
    MPI_Send(A[1],size+1,MPI_DOUBLE,activep[j-1],
                    1,MPI_COMM_WORLD);
    MPI_Send(A[1],size+1,MPI_DOUBLE,activep[j+1],
                    0,MPI_COMM_WORLD);
  }
  else{
    MPI_Recv(A[3],size+1,MPI_DOUBLE,activep[j-1],0,
                    MPI_COMM_WORLD,&status);
    MPI_Recv(A[4],size+1,MPI_DOUBLE,activep[j+1],1,
                    MPI_COMM_WORLD,&status);
  }
        }
      }
    }

  numactivep = 0;
  for(j=activep[1];j<totalnodes;j=j+pow(2,i+1)){
    activep[numactivep++]=j;
  }
}
```

REMARK 2: The communication is accomplished through a series of *MPI_Send* and *MPI_Recv* calls. Each processor is communicating (either sending or receiving) from at most two other processors. To keep track of whom is to be sending/receiving, we maintain an active processor list within the integer array *activep*. A communication schematic for cyclic reduction using seven processors is given in Figure 9.11.

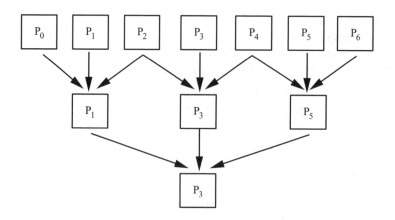

Figure 9.11: Cyclic reduction commu- nication pattern for seven-processor case.

```
MPI
```

PART 3 - BACK SUBSTITUTION

```
/* Part 3 */
  double * x = new double[totalnodes];
  for(j=0;j<totalnodes;j++)
    x[j] = 0.0;

  if(mynode==activep[0]){
    x[mynode] = A[1][size]/A[1][(size-1)/2];
  }

  double tmp;
  for(i=log2(size+1)-3;i>=0;i--){
    tmp = x[mynode];
    MPI_Allgather(&tmp,1,MPI_DOUBLE,x,1,MPI_DOUBLE,
                  MPI_COMM_WORLD);
    numactivep = 0;
    for(j=activep[0]-pow(2.0,i);j<totalnodes;j=j+pow(2.0,i+1)){
      activep[numactivep++]=j;
    }

    for(j=0;j<numactivep;j++){
      if(mynode == activep[j]){
        x[mynode] = A[1][size];
        for(k=0;k<totalnodes;k++){
          if(k!=mynode)
            x[mynode] -= A[1][2*k+1]*x[k];
        }
        x[mynode] = x[mynode]/A[1][2*mynode+1];
      }
    }
  }
```

```
tmp = x[mynode];
MPI_Allgather(&tmp,1,MPI_DOUBLE,x,
     1,MPI_DOUBLE,MPI_COMM_WORLD);
```

REMARK 3: A schematic for the backward solve communication is given in Figure 9.12. Notice that it varies slightly from that of the forward part of the reduction. After a processor has found the solution for its row and has communicated that information to the appropriate processors, it is no longer active. This can be observed in Figure 9.12, where we see that processor P_3 no longer has things to compute in the second and third levels.

REMARK 4: We use the *MPI_Allgather* command so that at any given level all the processors have the available solution up to that point. This all-inclusive communication could be replaced by *MPI_Send/MPI_Recv* pairs where only those processors requiring particular information would be updated.

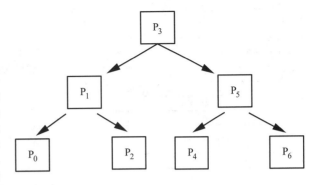

Figure 9.12: A schematic for the backward solve communication when seven processors are used.

MPI

PART 4 – SOLVING FOR ODD ROWS

```
/* Part 4 */
  for(k=0;k<totalnodes;k++){
    A[0][size] -= A[0][2*k+1]*x[k];
    A[2][size] -= A[2][2*k+1]*x[k];
  }
  A[0][size] = A[0][size]/A[0][2*mynode];
  A[1][size] = x[mynode];
  A[2][size] = A[2][size]/A[2][2*mynode+2];

  delete[] activep;
  for(i=0;i<numrows;i++)
    delete[] A[i];
  delete[] A;
  delete[] x;

  MPI_Finalize();
}
```

REMARK 5: The program concludes with each processor computing the solution for the odd rows for which it was responsible. If the total solution vector were needed on all processors, *MPI_Allgather* could be used to collect the solution on each processor. Note that some additional logic would be necessary to properly take into account the overlap in row distribution (i.e., both processor 0 and processor 1 solve for the solution of matrix row number 3), as shown in Figure 9.13.

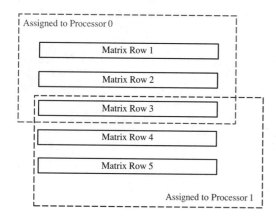

Figure 9.13: Overlap in row solutions for two-processor case.

9.2 CHOLESKY FACTORIZATION

A special case of the LU decomposition for a *symmetric positive-definite* matrix $\mathbf{A}$ can be obtained in the form

$$\mathbf{A} = \mathbf{L}\,\mathbf{L}^{T}.$$

Here, the matrix $\mathbf{U}$ is equal to the transpose of $\mathbf{L}$ because of symmetry. There are many possibilities for $\mathbf{L}$ but this factorization is unique if we require that all diagonal elements of $\mathbf{L}$ be positive. We note that in this case $\mathbf{L}$ is different from the matrix we obtain in the LU decomposition, where all *diagonal elements* are equal to one.

Instead of following the standard LU decomposition, we can obtain explicitly the elements ℓ_{ij} of $\mathbf{L}$ by setting

$$\begin{bmatrix} a_{11} & a_{12} & \dots & a_{1n} \\ \vdots & & & \\ \vdots & & & \\ \vdots & & & \\ a_{n1} & \dots & \dots & a_{nn} \end{bmatrix} = \begin{bmatrix} \ell_{11} & & & \mathbf{O} \\ \ell_{12} & \ell_{22} & & \\ \vdots & \vdots & \ddots & \\ \vdots & \vdots & & \ddots \\ \ell_{n1} & \ell_{n2} & \dots & \ell_{nn} \end{bmatrix} \begin{bmatrix} \ell_{11} & \ell_{21} & \dots & \ell_{n1} \\ & \ell_{22} & & \ell_{n2} \\ & & \ddots & \vdots \\ \mathbf{O} & & & \ddots \\ & & & \ell_{nn} \end{bmatrix}.$$

Next, we equate elements on both sides to obtain

$$a_{i1} = \ell_{i1}\ell_{11} \quad \text{and} \quad a_{11}^{2} = \ell_{11}^{2}$$

for the entire first column ($i = 1, \dots, n$), and similarly for the other columns. The following pseudo-code summarizes the Cholesky algorithm:

for $j = 1, n$

$$\ell_{jj} = \sqrt{a_{jj} - \sum_{k=1}^{j-1} \ell_{jk}^{2}}$$

for $i = j + 1, n$

$$\ell_{ij} = \frac{a_{ij} - \sum_{k=1}^{j-1} \ell_{ik}\ell_{jk}}{\ell_{jj}}$$

endfor
endfor

REMARK 1: The Cholesky factorization algorithm is stable and thus it does not require pivoting [25].

REMARK 2: The Cholesky algorithm requires about half the memory and about half the operations of the LU decomposition.

REMARK 3: The positive-definite property is important in obtaining the ℓ_{ij} without partial pivoting. In fact, partial pivoting can destroy the symmetry of a matrix $\mathbf{A}$.

REMARK 4: In some cases an *incomplete* or *approximate* Cholesky decomposition is required (e.g., as a preconditioner in accelerating the convergence of iterative solvers; see Section 9.4.2). This is achieved by simply filling in with zeros the entries of $\mathbf{L}$, which have corresponding zero entries in the original (presumably sparse) matrix $\mathbf{A}$.

9.3 QR FACTORIZATION AND HOUSEHOLDER TRANSFORMATION

The LU factorization is not the only way of factoring a matrix $\mathbf{A}$. The Householder transformation we present here is the basis of an efficient factorization of a general matrix

$$\mathbf{A} = \mathbf{QR},$$

where $\mathbf{Q}$ is an orthogonal matrix and $\mathbf{R}$ is an upper triangular matrix. We have already studied in Section 2.2.9 how to achieve such a QR decomposition by orthogonalizing vectors via the Gram–Schmidt procedure, but the procedure we present here is always stable and much more efficient.

We start by considering the following important operation in scientific computing:

- *how to take a full vector and produce a special vector with only one of its entries nonzero.*

This is accomplished efficiently in terms of the (*orthogonal*) Householder matrix, which is defined by

$$\mathbf{H} = \mathbf{I} - 2\frac{\mathbf{w}\mathbf{w}^T}{\mathbf{w}^T\mathbf{w}}, \quad \forall \mathbf{w} \neq 0.$$

Of particular interest is the vector

$$\alpha\mathbf{e}_1 = (\alpha, 0, 0, \ldots, 0)^T,$$

which can be created from an arbitrary vector $\mathbf{x}$ if the vector $\mathbf{w}$ is computed appropriately. To this end, we set $\mathbf{w}$ such that

$$\mathbf{H}\,\mathbf{x} = \left(\mathbf{I} - 2\frac{\mathbf{w}\mathbf{w}^T}{\mathbf{w}^T\mathbf{w}}\right)\mathbf{x} = \begin{bmatrix} \alpha \\ 0 \\ 0 \\ \vdots \\ 0 \end{bmatrix} = \alpha\mathbf{e}_1.$$

The solution to this problem is simple, and it is given by

$$\mathbf{w} = \mathbf{x} + \text{sign}(x_1) \cdot \|\mathbf{x}\|_2 \mathbf{e}_1,$$

where x_1 is the first entry of the vector $\mathbf{x}$. This transformation from $\mathbf{H}\mathbf{x} \to (\alpha, 0, 0, \ldots, 0)^T$ is called the *Householder transformation*.

First, we summarize the algorithm that describes the Householder transformation in the following pseudo-code:

$$x_m = \max\{|x_1|, |x_2|, \ldots, |x_n|\}$$
$$\text{for } k = 1, n$$
$$\qquad w_k = x_k / x_m$$
$$\text{endfor}$$
$$\alpha = \text{sign}(w_1)[w_1^2 + w_2^2 + \cdots + w_n^2]^{1/2}$$
$$w_1 = w_1 + \alpha$$
$$\alpha = -\alpha x_m$$

Then, the desired vector is $(\alpha, 0, 0, \ldots, 0)^T$. The number of operations is proportional to $\mathcal{O}(n)$; that is, it takes only *linear work* to accomplish this important operation.

EXAMPLE. Consider the vector

$$\mathbf{x} = \begin{pmatrix} 1 \\ 2 \\ -3 \end{pmatrix}.$$

Then $x_m = 3$, and the intermediate values of the components of $\mathbf{w}$ are

$$w_1 = \frac{1}{3}, \quad w_2 = \frac{2}{3}, \quad w_3 = -1.$$

Also, the intermediate value of α is

$$\alpha = +\sqrt{\frac{1}{3^2} + \frac{2^2}{3^2} + (-1)^2} = 1.2472.$$

The updated values are then

$$w_1 = \frac{1}{3} + 1.2472 = 1.5805, \quad w_2 = \frac{2}{3}, \quad w_3 = -1,$$

and

$$\alpha = -1.2472 \cdot 3 = -3.7416$$

and so the desired vector is

$$\mathbf{H}\mathbf{x} = \begin{pmatrix} -3.7416 \\ 0 \\ 0 \end{pmatrix}.$$

REMARK 1: The matrix–vector product with a Householder matrix

$$\mathbf{H} = \mathbf{I} - 2\frac{\mathbf{w}\mathbf{w}^T}{\mathbf{w}^T\mathbf{w}}$$

is only an $\mathcal{O}(n)$ operation compared to $\mathcal{O}(n^2)$ for a general matrix–vector product. This can be achieved from the relation

$$\mathbf{H}\,\mathbf{x} = \mathbf{x} - \beta\mathbf{w}(\mathbf{w}^T\mathbf{x}),$$

where $\beta^{-1} = \mathbf{w}^T\mathbf{w}/2$ is a scalar. We note that the right-hand side is computed within one loop

$$x_i = x_i - \beta \cdot \gamma \cdot w_i, \; i = 1, \dots, n,$$

where $\gamma = \mathbf{w}^T\mathbf{x}$ is also scalar.

Clearly, we do not need to explicitly construct $\mathbf{H}$ in this case – that cost would lead to an $\mathcal{O}(n^2)$ operation!

To accomplish the QR factorization of a square general $n \times n$ matrix $\mathbf{A}$, we consider its columns and apply successively the Householder transformation to zero out the subdiagonal entries of each column. We do this in $(n-1)$ stages, just as in LU decomposition.

STAGE 1. We consider the *first column* of $\mathbf{A}$ and determine a Householder matrix $\mathbf{H}_1$ so that

$$\mathbf{H}_1 \begin{bmatrix} a_{11} \\ a_{21} \\ \vdots \\ a_{n1} \end{bmatrix} = \begin{bmatrix} \alpha_1 \\ 0 \\ \vdots \\ 0 \end{bmatrix}.$$

To determine $\mathbf{H}_1$ we simply need to apply the Householder transformation algorithm to obtain $\mathbf{w}_1$ of length n. After the first stage we overwrite $\mathbf{A}$ by $\mathbf{A}_1$, where

$$\mathbf{A}_1 = \begin{pmatrix} \alpha_1 & a_{12}^* & \dots & a_{1n}^* \\ 0 & a_{22}^* & \dots & \dots \\ \vdots & \vdots & & \\ 0 & a_{n2}^* & \dots & a_{nn}^* \end{pmatrix} = \mathbf{H}_1\mathbf{A},$$

which has all new elements (denoted by star) after the first column.

STAGE 2. Next we consider the *second column* of the updated matrix

$$\mathbf{A} \equiv \mathbf{A}_1 = \mathbf{H}_1\mathbf{A}$$

and take only the part below the diagonal to obtain

$$\mathbf{H}_2^* \begin{bmatrix} a_{22}^* \\ a_{32}^* \\ \vdots \\ a_{n2}^* \end{bmatrix} = \begin{bmatrix} \alpha_2 \\ 0 \\ \vdots \\ 0 \end{bmatrix},$$

which yields a vector $\mathbf{w}_2$ of length $(n-1)$. This vector defines uniquely the Householder matrix

$$\mathbf{H}_2^* = \mathbf{I} - 2\frac{\mathbf{w}_2\mathbf{w}_2^T}{\mathbf{w}_2^T\mathbf{w}_2}.$$

Unlike $\mathbf{H}_1$, here we first need to "inflate" $\mathbf{H}_2^*$ to $\mathbf{H}_2$ and then overwrite $\mathbf{A}$ by $\mathbf{H}_2\mathbf{A}_1$, where

$$\mathbf{H}_2 = \begin{pmatrix} 1 \cdots & 0 \\ 0 & \mathbf{H}_2^* \end{pmatrix}.$$

STAGE K. In the kth stage of the QR procedure we produce a vector $\mathbf{w}_k$ of length $(n-k+1)$ by solving

$$\mathbf{H}_k^* \begin{bmatrix} a_{kk}^* \\ a_{k+1,k}^* \\ \vdots \\ a_{nk}^* \end{bmatrix} = \begin{bmatrix} \alpha_k \\ 0 \\ \vdots \\ 0 \end{bmatrix}.$$

Here again, we overwrite $\mathbf{A}$ by

$$\mathbf{A}_k = \mathbf{H}_k\mathbf{A}_{k-1},$$

and subsequently we "inflate" $\mathbf{H}_k^*$ as

$$\mathbf{H}_k = \begin{bmatrix} \mathbf{I}_{k-1} & 0 \\ 0 & \mathbf{H}_k^* \end{bmatrix}.$$

REMARK 2: The efficiency of the Householder algorithm is based on the efficient multiplication

$$\mathbf{A}_{k+1} = \mathbf{H}_{k+1} \cdot \mathbf{A}_k,$$

which should not be performed explicitly but rather using the $\mathcal{O}(n)$ matrix–vector product algorithm we presented previously; that is, we compute

$$(\mathbf{I} - \beta\mathbf{w}_{n-k}\mathbf{w}_{n-k}^T)[\mathbf{a}_{kj}],$$

where

$$\beta^{-1} = \mathbf{w}_{n-k}^T \cdot \mathbf{w}_{n-k}/2$$

and $\mathbf{a}_{kj}$ denotes the columns of $\mathbf{A}_k$ with $j = k+1, \ldots, n-k$. The determination of $\mathbf{H}_k^*$ requires $(n-k)$ operations because the unknown vector $\mathbf{w}$ is of length $(n-k)$.

Throughout the following, the subscript for the vector $\mathbf{w}$ will denote the current size of the vector; hence $\mathbf{w}_{n-k}$ denotes the vector of size $(n-k)$. In the algorithm to be presented, the notation w_{ij} denotes the ith entry of the vector $\mathbf{w}_j$.

After a total of $(n-1)$ stages we obtain an upper triangular matrix $\mathbf{R}$ with diagonal elements the α_k $(k = 1, \ldots, n)$ and the other entries computed from

$$r_{ij} = a_{ij} - \gamma w_{ik},$$

where $n \geq i$, $j \geq k$, and

$$\gamma = \beta \sum_{i=k}^{n} w_{ik} a_{ij},$$

$$\beta^{-1} = (\mathbf{w}_{n-k+1}^T \cdot \mathbf{w}_{n-k+1})/2.$$

We note that these formulas compute all the entries above the diagonal but also the r_{nn} entry.

Then, the matrix $\mathbf{R}$ is

$$\mathbf{R} = \begin{bmatrix} \alpha_1 & r_{12} & r_{13} & \cdots & \cdots & r_{1n} \\ & \alpha_2 & r_{23} & \cdots & \cdots & r_{2n} \\ & & \alpha_3 & \cdots & \cdots & r_{3n} \\ & & & \ddots & & \\ & \mathbf{O} & & & \alpha_{n-1} & \\ & & & & & r_{nn} \end{bmatrix}.$$

This matrix can be constructed by forming an equivalent Householder matrix $\mathbf{H}_k$ of size n at each stage from the $\mathbf{H}_k^*$ that has order $(n - k + 1)$. To this end, we simply set

$$\mathbf{H}_k = \begin{bmatrix} \mathbf{I}_{k-1} & O \\ O & \mathbf{H}_k^* \end{bmatrix},$$

and we also compute:

$$\mathbf{A}_k = \mathbf{H}_k \mathbf{A}_{k-1}$$

with

$$\mathbf{A}_1 \equiv \mathbf{A}.$$

The upper triangular matrix is then

$$\mathbf{R} = \mathbf{A}_{n-1} = \mathbf{H}_{n-1} \mathbf{A}_{n-2} = \ldots = \mathbf{H}_{n-1} \mathbf{H}_{n-2} \ldots \mathbf{H}_1 \mathbf{A}.$$

We can invert this equation if we set

$$\mathbf{Q}^T = \mathbf{H}_{n-1} \mathbf{H}_{n-2} \ldots \mathbf{H}_1;$$

then

$$\mathbf{Q}^{-1} = \mathbf{Q}^T$$

because the $\mathbf{H}_k$ are all orthogonal. Thus, $\mathbf{Q} \cdot \mathbf{R} = \mathbf{Q}\mathbf{Q}^T \mathbf{A} \Rightarrow \mathbf{A} = \mathbf{Q}\mathbf{R}$. We can now compute the orthogonal matrix $\mathbf{Q}$; that is, $\mathbf{Q} = \mathbf{H}_1^T \mathbf{H}_2^T \ldots \mathbf{H}_{n-1}^T$.

We have thus obtained a QR decomposition of an $n \times n$ matrix $\mathbf{A}$, similar to the Gram–Schmidt procedure but at *reduced cost*, since we are operating with shorter and shorter vectors in each stage. We first provide the pseudo-code for the Householder QR decomposition and then we will compute the exact operation count. The pseudo-code returns only the value of $\mathbf{R}$. The matrix $\mathbf{Q}$ can be formed from the preceding equation using the matrix $\mathbf{H}_i$ formed by its vector $\mathbf{w}$ from the Householder transformation.

HOUSEHOLDER ALGORITHM

Begin Loop: $k = 1, \ldots, n-1$ (number of stages)

$$Solve \ \mathbf{H}_k^* \begin{bmatrix} a_{kk}^* \\ a_{k+1,k}^* \\ \vdots \\ a_{nk}^* \end{bmatrix} = \begin{bmatrix} \alpha_k \\ 0 \\ \vdots \\ 0 \end{bmatrix} \ (\text{obtain } \mathbf{w}_{n-k+1})$$

$r_{kk} = \alpha_k$

Compute $\beta^{-1} = \mathbf{w}_{n-k+1}^T \cdot \mathbf{w}_{n-k+1}/2$

Zero a_{ik}: $i = k+1, \ldots, n$

Begin Loop: $j = k+1, \ldots, n$

   $\gamma_j = 0$

   Begin Loop: $q = k, \ldots n$

   $\gamma_j = \gamma_j + \beta w_{q-k+1,k} a_{qj}$

   End Loop

   Begin Loop: $i = k, \ldots, n$

   $r_{ij} = a_{ij} - \gamma_j w_{i-k+1,k}$
   $a_{ij} = r_{ij}$
   End Loop
   End Loop
End Loop

EXAMPLE. Let us consider the 3×3 Hilbert matrix

$$\mathbf{A} = \begin{bmatrix} 1 & \dfrac{1}{2} & \dfrac{1}{3} \\ \dfrac{1}{2} & \dfrac{1}{3} & \dfrac{1}{4} \\ \dfrac{1}{3} & \dfrac{1}{4} & \dfrac{1}{5} \end{bmatrix}$$

and apply the Householder QR algorithm.

- In the *first stage* ($k = 1$) we solve

$$\mathbf{H}_1 \begin{bmatrix} 1 \\ 1 \\ 2 \\ \frac{1}{3} \end{bmatrix} = \begin{bmatrix} \alpha_1 \\ 0 \\ 0 \end{bmatrix} \Rightarrow \mathbf{w}_1 = \begin{bmatrix} 2.1666 \\ 0.5 \\ 0.3333 \end{bmatrix},$$

and also $r_{11} = \alpha_1 = -1.1666$ and

$$\beta = \frac{2}{\mathbf{w}_1^T \mathbf{w}_1} = 0.3956.$$

Then, for $j = 2$, we calculate

$$\gamma_2 = \beta[w_{11}a_{12} + w_{21}a_{22} + w_{31}a_{32}] = 0.5274,$$

and thus

$$a_{12} := r_{12} = a_{12} - \gamma_2 w_{11} = -0.6429,$$
$$a_{22} := r_{22} = a_{22} - \gamma_2 w_{21} = 0.0696,$$
$$a_{32} := r_{32} = a_{32} - \gamma_2 w_{31} = 0.0795.$$

In the next iteration, $j = 3$, we calculate similarly

$$\gamma_3 = \beta[w_1 a_{13} + w_2 a_{23} + w_3 a_{33}] = 0.3615,$$

and thus

$$a_{13} := r_{13} = a_{13} - \gamma_3 w_{11} = -0.4500,$$
$$a_{23} := r_{23} = a_{23} - \gamma_3 w_{21} = 0.0692,$$
$$a_{33} := r_{33} = a_{33} - \gamma_3 w_{31} = 0.0795.$$

Also, we have that $a_{21} = a_{31} = 0$.

- In the *second stage* ($k = 2$) we solve

$$\mathbf{H}_2^* \begin{bmatrix} 0.0696 \\ 0.0795 \end{bmatrix} = \begin{bmatrix} \alpha_2 \\ 0 \end{bmatrix} \Rightarrow \mathbf{w}_2 = \begin{bmatrix} 2.3095 \\ 1.0000 \end{bmatrix}.$$

Also, $r_{22} = \alpha_2 = -0.1017$, and

$$\beta = 2/(\mathbf{w}_2^T \cdot \mathbf{w}_2) = 0.315759.$$

Then, for $j = 3$, we calculate

$$\gamma_3 = \beta[w_{22}a_{23} + w_{32}a_{33}] = 0.0756,$$
$$r_{23} = a_{23} - \gamma_3 w_{22} = -0.1053,$$
$$r_{33} = a_{33} - \gamma_3 w_{32} = 0.0039,$$

where we note that a_{23} and a_{33} are the updated values, which were modified in the first stage.

At the conclusion of this example, we now have the resulting **R** matrix of the **QR** decomposition, and we also have the Householder transformation vectors **w** from which we can form **Q**.

COMPUTATIONAL COST. The computational complexity of the QR decomposition, as described here, is determined by the cost of computing the matrix $\mathbf{H}_k^*$, which is $\mathcal{O}(n-k)$, and also of computing $\mathbf{A}_k$ from $\mathbf{A}_k = \mathbf{H}_k \mathbf{A}_{k-1}$, which requires $\mathcal{O}((n-k)^2)$ operations. Thus, the combined cost is

$$\sum_{k=1}^{n-1}(n-k) + \sum_{k=1}^{n-1}(n-k)^2 = \frac{(n-1)(n)}{2} + \frac{(n-1)(n)(2n-1)}{6} \approx \frac{n^3}{3}.$$

Calculating the constant factor more carefully and accounting for both additions and multiplications we have

$$\mathcal{O}\left(\frac{4}{3}n^3\right) \text{ for QR versus } \mathcal{O}\left(\frac{2}{3}n^3\right) \text{ for LU decomposition.}$$

REMARK 3: After we obtain the QR factorization of **A** we can solve a linear system $\mathbf{Ax} = \mathbf{b}$ as follows:

$$\mathbf{Ax} = \mathbf{b} \Rightarrow \mathbf{QRx} = \mathbf{b} \Rightarrow \mathbf{Q}^T\mathbf{QRx} = \mathbf{Q}^T\mathbf{b} \Rightarrow \mathbf{Rx} = \mathbf{Q}^T\mathbf{b}.$$

This is an upper triangular system and can be solved by back substitution.

REMARK 4: It can be shown that the QR decomposition based on the Householder transformation is always stable (see [47]).

REMARK 5: The Householder QR decomposition is about *twice* as expensive as the LU decomposition and it also expands the bandwidth of a sparse matrix **A**. In contrast, the LU decomposition preserves the bandwidth but it may be susceptible to numerical instabilities as demonstrated earlier. However, even with partial pivoting the LU decomposition is more efficient than the QR decomposition for large matrices **A**.

REMARK 6: A third way of obtaining the QR decomposition of a matrix **A** (in addition to Gram–Schmidt and Householder) is to employ the *Givens rotation matrix*

$$\mathbf{R}(\theta) \equiv \begin{bmatrix} \cos\theta & \sin\theta \\ -\sin\theta & \cos\theta \end{bmatrix},$$

which is orthonormal. By setting

$$\mathbf{R}(\theta) \cdot \begin{bmatrix} x \\ y \end{bmatrix} = \begin{bmatrix} (x^2 + y^2)^{1/2} \\ 0 \end{bmatrix}$$

we obtain

$$\cos\theta = \frac{x}{\sqrt{x^2 + y^2}}, \quad \sin\theta = \frac{y}{\sqrt{x^2 + y^2}}.$$

Based on this idea we construct a general *rotation* matrix

$$\mathbf{R}(\theta; i, j) = \begin{bmatrix} 1 & & \overset{i\text{th}}{\vdots} & \overset{j\text{th}}{\vdots} & & \\ & \ddots & \vdots & \vdots & & \\ & & \cos\theta & \sin\theta & & \mathbf{O} \\ & & -\sin\theta & \cos\theta & & \\ & \mathbf{O} & & & \ddots & \\ & & & & & 1 \end{bmatrix} \begin{matrix} \\ \\ \dots i\text{th} \\ \dots j\text{th} \\ \\ \end{matrix}$$

that can be employed to zero out *one entry* in each iteration cycle instead of a column as in the Householder transformation. However, the Givens rotation is *twice as expensive* the Householder and *four times* as expensive as the LU. It is not used in solving *square* linear systems but it is used in solutions of *least-squares* linear systems and also in eigensolvers.

REMARK 7: The stability of the Householder method (also the Givens rotation) results from the $\mathbf{Q}$ matrix being a product of orthogonal matrices, which have condition number equal to one.

Hessenberg and Tridiagonal Reduction

We now consider the transformation of a matrix $\mathbf{A}$ to an upper triangular matrix that also has the first lower diagonal *nonzero*. Specifically, this matrix has the form

$$\mathbf{H_e} \equiv \begin{bmatrix} * & * & * \dots * \\ * & * & \dots * \\ & \ddots \ddots & \vdots \\ & & * & * \\ \mathbf{O} & & * & * \end{bmatrix},$$

and it is called an *upper Hessenberg matrix*.

The Householder transformation procedure can also be used to obtain this for general matrices. If the matrix is also *symmetric* then the resulting matrix is tridiagonal.

The reduction algorithm involves $(n-2)$ stages of elimination. We want to obtain

$$\mathbf{H_e} = \mathbf{H} \cdot \mathbf{A} \cdot \mathbf{H}^T,$$

where the matrix $\mathbf{H} = \mathbf{H}_{n-2} \cdot \mathbf{H}_{n-1} \dots \mathbf{H}_1$. These are Householder matrices, which are computed from zeroing out subcolumns of $\mathbf{A}$ and its updated versions, that is,

$$\mathbf{H}_1 = \begin{bmatrix} \mathbf{I}_1 & 0 \\ 0 & \mathbf{H}_1^* \end{bmatrix},$$

where

$$\mathbf{H}_1^* \begin{bmatrix} a_{21} \\ a_{31} \\ \vdots \\ a_{n1} \end{bmatrix} = \begin{bmatrix} \alpha_1 \\ 0 \\ \vdots \\ 0 \end{bmatrix}$$

and

$$\mathbf{A}_1 = \mathbf{H}_1 \mathbf{A} \mathbf{H}_1^T$$

and so on.

Clearly, $\mathbf{A}$ has a new first column with $a_{11} \neq 0$ and $a_{21} \neq 0$, but all other entries are equal to zero.

EXAMPLE. We consider again the 3×3 Hilbert matrix

$$\mathbf{A} = \begin{bmatrix} 1 & \dfrac{1}{2} & \dfrac{1}{3} \\[2mm] \dfrac{1}{2} & \dfrac{1}{3} & \dfrac{1}{4} \\[2mm] \dfrac{1}{3} & \dfrac{1}{4} & \dfrac{1}{5} \end{bmatrix},$$

which we transform into an upper Hessenberg matrix in one stage. Since $\mathbf{A}$ is also symmetric we expect a tridiagonal matrix $\mathbf{H_e}$.

In the *first stage* ($k = 1$) we solve

$$\mathbf{H}_1^* \begin{bmatrix} \dfrac{1}{2} \\[2mm] \dfrac{1}{3} \end{bmatrix} = \begin{bmatrix} \alpha \\ 0 \end{bmatrix},$$

which gives

$$\mathbf{w}_2 = \begin{bmatrix} 2.2019 \\ 0.6666 \end{bmatrix}$$

and $\alpha = -0.6009$.

We then obtain the new entries of $\mathbf{A}$ using $a_{ij} = a_{ij} - \gamma_i w_j$:

$$\mathbf{H_e} = \mathbf{H}_1 \mathbf{A} \mathbf{H}_1^T = \begin{bmatrix} 1 & 0 & 0 \\ 0 & -0.8321 & -0.5547 \\ 0 & -0.5547 & 0.8321 \end{bmatrix},$$

$$
\begin{bmatrix} 1 & \frac{1}{2} & \frac{1}{3} \\[2mm] \frac{1}{2} & \frac{1}{3} & \frac{1}{4} \\[2mm] \frac{1}{3} & \frac{1}{4} & \frac{1}{5} \end{bmatrix}
\begin{bmatrix} 1 & 0 & 0 \\ 0 & -0.8321 & -0.5547 \\ 0 & -0.5547 & 0.8321 \end{bmatrix}
=
\begin{bmatrix} 1.0 & -0.6009 & 0.0 \\ -0.6009 & 0.5231 & -0.0346 \\ 0.0 & -0.0346 & 0.0103 \end{bmatrix}.
$$

REMARK 1: The solution of the Hessenberg linear system

$$\mathbf{H_e} \cdot \mathbf{x} = \mathbf{b}$$

can be obtained with Gaussian elimination with partial pivoting, and it is guaranteed to be stable [94]. The computational complexity of this, including the partial pivoting cost, is $\mathcal{O}(n^2)$.

PUTTING IT INTO PRACTICE

We now present a function for computing the upper Hessenberg matrix given a matrix **A**. The function takes as input the matrix **A** and upon completion returns the upper Hessenberg matrix in place of the matrix **A**.

Software
Suite

```
void Hessenberg(SCMatrix &A){
  int i,j,k,q;
  double beta,gamma;
  int N = A.Rows();
  SCVector *x = new SCVector(N),
    *w = new SCVector(N);

  for(k=0;k<N-2;k++){
    A.GetColumn(k,*x,k+1);
    A(k+1,k) = HouseholderTrans(*x,*w);
    beta = 2.0/dot(N-k-1,*w,*w);
    for(i=k+2;i<N;i++)
      A(i,k) = (*w)(i-k);
    for(j=k+1;j<N;j++){
      gamma = 0.0;
      for(q=k+1;q<N;q++)
        gamma += beta*(*w)(q-k-1)*A(q,j);
      for(i=k+1;i<N;i++){
        A(i,j) = A(i,j) - gamma*(*w)(i-k-1);
      }
    }
    for(i=0;i<N;i++){
      gamma = 0.0;
      for(q=k+1;q<N;q++)
        gamma += beta*(*w)(q-k-1)*A(i,q);
```

```
        for(j=k+1;j<N;j++){
          A(i,j) = A(i,j) - gamma*(*w)(j-k-1);
        }
      }
    }

    delete x;
    delete w;
  }
```

REMARK 2: Observe that we pass the reference to the matrix **A** (denoted by the "SCMatrix &A" in the argument list.) We do this because we want to replace the values in **A** with the new upper Hessenberg matrix. If we were to omit the "&" and hence pass by value, the modifications made to the matrix **A** within the function would be lost when the function returns to the calling program.

REMARK 3: Inside the function, we dynamically allocate two new SCVectors and assign them to the two pointers w and x. To use the "( )" operator associated with the SCVector class, we first use the unitary operator "*" to retrieve the object to which the pointer points. Hence, the expression (*w) yields the object to which the pointer w points. The extra parentheses around this expression are used to guarantee that the "*" is carried out before the "( )" operator.

9.4 PRECONDITIONED CONJUGATE GRADIENT METHOD – PCGM

9.4.1 Convergence Rate of CGM

We have already introduced the conjugate gradient method (CGM) in Section 4.1.7 for the linear system

$$\mathbf{Ax} = \mathbf{b}.$$

By defining the residual of the kth iteration

$$r_{\mathbf{k}} \equiv \mathbf{b} - \mathbf{Ax}_k,$$

the solution and search directions are computed from

$$\mathbf{x}_{k+1} = \mathbf{x}_k + \alpha_k \mathbf{p}_k, \tag{9.12}$$

$$\mathbf{p}_{k+1} = \mathbf{r}_{k+1} + \beta_k \mathbf{p}_k, \tag{9.13}$$

while the residual can also be computed iteratively, that is,

$$\mathbf{r}_{k+1} = \mathbf{r}_k - \alpha_k \mathbf{Ap}_k. \tag{9.14}$$

We can derive a three-term recurrence formula by substituting in Equation (9.12) the vector $\mathbf{p}_k$ from Equation (9.13) and also using the residual definition to obtain

$$\mathbf{x}_{k+1} = (1 + \gamma_k)\mathbf{x}_k + \alpha_k(\mathbf{b} - \mathbf{Ax}_k) - \gamma_k \mathbf{x}_{k-1},$$

where we have defined

$$\gamma_k \equiv \frac{\alpha_k \beta_{k-1}}{\alpha_{k-1}}.$$

This is sometimes referred to as the *Rutishauser* formula. Symmetry and orthogonality together lead to the familiar three-term *magic formula* as we have seen many times in this book.

We have mentioned in Section 4.1.7 that the CGM is equivalent to minimizing a properly defined quadratic form. In fact, it can be proved that if $\mathbf{s}$ is the exact solution, then the conjugate gradient iterate $\mathbf{x}_k$ minimizes the norm $||\mathbf{s} - \mathbf{x}||_A$ over the Krylov subspace of dimension k. This space is defined based on powers of $\mathbf{A}$ with the orthogonal directions, that is,

$$\mathcal{K}_k(\mathbf{A}, \mathbf{p}) = \text{span} \{\mathbf{p}, \mathbf{A}\mathbf{p}, \mathbf{A}^2\mathbf{p}, \ldots, A^{k-1}\mathbf{p}\}.$$

The Rutishauser formula is similar to the Lanczos three-term formula (see Section 10.3.6), and so CGM and Lanczos are related – they both use the same Krylov subspace and have three-term recurrence formulas. More specifically, a tridiagonal matrix $\mathbf{T}_j$ can be constructed for CGM from

$$\mathbf{T}_j = \mathbf{P}^T \mathbf{A} \mathbf{P}.$$

Here $\mathbf{P} = \mathbf{R}\mathbf{D}^{-1}$, where $\mathbf{D}$ is a diagonal matrix containing the magnitudes of residuals. Also, $\mathbf{R}$ is the product of two matrices, the first formed by the columns of the orthogonal search directions $\mathbf{p}_j$ whereas the second is a bidiagonal matrix with 1s in the diagonal and the scalars β_j above the main diagonal.

With regards to convergence, Reid [76] has observed that in practice CGM produces very good answers even before the total number of iterations reaches n, where $n \times n$ is the size of the symmetric positive-definite matrix $\mathbf{A}$. We recall that the fundamental theorem on conjugate directions, stated in Section 4.1.7, guarantees that the exact solution will be achieved after n iterations. More specifically, if matrix $\mathbf{A}$ has only $m \leq n$ distinct eigenvalues then convergence will be achieved in m iterations. Round-off errors and corresponding loss of orthogonality are responsible for deviation from the theory, although round-off errrors are not as severe as in the Lanczos method, as we discuss in Section 10.3.6.

In practice, we always use a *stopping criterion* for convergence instead of having a loop with n iterations. To this end, it is important that the tolerance ϵ in the convergence test be proportional to the relative reduction of the initial residual or in some cases for it to be normalized with the right-hand side, for example,

$$\| r_{k+1} \|_2 \leq \epsilon \| b \|_2 .$$

Here $\epsilon \approx 10^{-d}$ where d is the number of digits of desired accuracy. The computation of $\| \mathbf{r}_{k+1} \|^2 = (\mathbf{r}_{k+1}, \mathbf{r}_{k+1})$ requires no extra work because this quantity is used in the numerator of the formula for β_k. Also, we note that the residual $\| \mathbf{r}_{k+1} \|_2$ may not be decreasing *monotonically*, although the solution error $\| \mathbf{s} - \mathbf{x}_k \|_2$ decreases monotonically. This is because in the minimization procedure it is the *error* of the solution that is targeted directly, not the residual. Direct minimization of the residual is more common in solvers for nonsymmetric systems, as we discuss in Section 9.5. However, the $\mathbf{A}^{-1}$ residual norm, $(\mathbf{r}^T \mathbf{A}^{-1} \mathbf{r})$, decreases monotonically.

Because of finite arithmetic, the convergence rate of CGM is controlled by the condition number of matrix $\mathbf{A}$, which we denote by $\kappa_2(\mathbf{A})$. Specifically, the following estimate holds (see [26, 46]):

$$\frac{\parallel \mathbf{s} - \mathbf{x}_k \parallel_2}{\parallel \mathbf{s} - \mathbf{x}_0 \parallel_2} \leq 2\gamma^k \sqrt{\kappa_2(\mathbf{A})},$$

where

$$\kappa_2(\mathbf{A}) = \frac{\lambda_{\max}}{\lambda_{\min}} \quad \text{and} \quad \gamma = \frac{\sqrt{\kappa_2(\mathbf{A})} - 1}{\sqrt{\kappa_2(\mathbf{A})} + 1}.$$

For large values of κ_2 we have that $\gamma \to 1$, and thus the number of iterations for convergence of CGM is proportional to $\sqrt{\kappa_2(\mathbf{A})}$. For example, for the Poisson equation discretized on an $N \times N$ grid using second-order finite difference discretization (see Chapter 6) we have that $\kappa_2(\mathbf{A}) \propto N^2$, and thus the number of iterations is proportional to N. The computational cost of CGM is then similar to that of SOR assuming for the latter an optimum relaxation parameter.

9.4.2 Preconditioners

To accelerate the convergence of CGM we employ preconditioners (see also Section 7.2.8). That is, we transform the linear system $\mathbf{Ax} = \mathbf{b}$ to

$$\mathbf{M}^{-1}\mathbf{Ax} = \mathbf{M}^{-1}\mathbf{b}$$

by multiplying by the *preconditioner* (nonsingular) matrix $\mathbf{M}$. We have already seen in Section 7.2.8 some of the desired properties of the preconditioner: It should be

- spectrally close to matrix $\mathbf{A}$ so that the condition number

  $\kappa_2(\mathbf{M}^{-1}\mathbf{A}) \ll \kappa_2(\mathbf{A})$

  and also
- inexpensive to invert since the solution of $\mathbf{Mx} = \mathbf{b}$ will be required.

In addition, since we consider here a symmetric positive-definite matrix $\mathbf{A}$, then $\mathbf{M}$ also has to be symmetric and positive-definite.

The objective is to modify the original CG algorithm only slightly to "correct" the search directions but not to increase the computational complexity significantly. To this end, we first need to symmetrize the preconditioned system because $\mathbf{M}^{-1}\mathbf{A}$ is not a symmetric matrix. We then express $\mathbf{M}$ in terms of its eigenvectors and eigenvalues, that is,

$$\mathbf{M} = \mathbf{V}\Lambda\mathbf{V}^T \Rightarrow \mathbf{M}^{1/2} \equiv \mathbf{V}\Lambda^{1/2}\mathbf{V}^T.$$

Next we multiply $\mathbf{M}^{-1}\mathbf{A}\mathbf{x} = \mathbf{M}^{-1}\mathbf{b}$ by $\mathbf{M}^{1/2}$ to arrive at

$$(\mathbf{M}^{-1/2}\mathbf{A}\mathbf{M}^{-1/2})\,(\mathbf{M}^{1/2}\mathbf{x}) = \mathbf{M}^{-1/2}\mathbf{b}$$

$$\Rightarrow \mathbf{B}\mathbf{y} = \mathbf{f},$$

where

$$\mathbf{B} \equiv \mathbf{M}^{-1/2}\mathbf{A}\mathbf{M}^{-1/2},\ \mathbf{y} \equiv \mathbf{M}^{1/2}\mathbf{x}, \quad \text{and} \quad \mathbf{f} \equiv \mathbf{M}^{-1/2}\mathbf{b}.$$

This defines the new system (i.e., $\mathbf{B}$, $\mathbf{y}$, $\mathbf{f}$) to be solved using the original CGM. We note that

$$\mathbf{M}^{-1/2}\mathbf{B}\mathbf{M}^{1/2} = \mathbf{M}^{-1/2}(\mathbf{M}^{-1/2}\mathbf{A}\mathbf{M}^{-1/2})\mathbf{M}^{1/2} = \mathbf{M}^{-1}\mathbf{A},$$

and thus $\mathbf{B}$ and $\mathbf{M}^{-1}\mathbf{A}$ are similar, so they have the same eigenvalues.

The following PCG algorithm is derived by applying the standard CG algorithm to the new system

$$\mathbf{B}\mathbf{y} = \mathbf{f},$$

as defined here. The important thing is that we do not need to explicitly take the square root of $\mathbf{M}$ – this would have been costly!

PRECONDITIONED CONJUGATE GRADIENT ALGORITHM

Initialize:

    Choose $\mathbf{x}_0 \Rightarrow \mathbf{r}_0 = \mathbf{b} - \mathbf{A}\mathbf{x}_0$

    Solve $\mathbf{M}\tilde{\mathbf{r}}_0 = \mathbf{r}_0 \Rightarrow \mathbf{p}_0 = \tilde{\mathbf{r}}_0$

Begin Loop: for $k = 1, \ldots$

$$\alpha_k = \frac{(\tilde{\mathbf{r}}_k, \mathbf{r}_k)}{(\mathbf{p}_k, \mathbf{A}\mathbf{p}_k)}$$

$$\mathbf{x}_{k+1} = \mathbf{x}_k + \alpha_k \mathbf{p}_k$$

$$\mathbf{r}_{k+1} = \mathbf{r}_k - \alpha_k \mathbf{A}\mathbf{p}_k$$

$$\mathbf{M}\tilde{\mathbf{r}}_{k+1} = \mathbf{r}_{k+1}$$

    If $(\tilde{\mathbf{r}}_{k+1}, \mathbf{r}_{k+1}) \leq \epsilon$

    If $(\mathbf{r}_{k+1}, \mathbf{r}_{k+1}) \leq \epsilon$

return

$$\beta_k = \frac{(\tilde{\mathbf{r}}_{k+1}, \mathbf{r}_{k+1})}{(\tilde{\mathbf{r}}_k, \mathbf{r}_k)}$$

$$\mathbf{p}_{k+1} = \tilde{\mathbf{r}}_{k+1} + \beta_k \mathbf{p}_k$$

    endfor

End Loop

REMARK 1: The *stopping criterion* is based on the actual residual $\mathbf{r}$ and not on the modified residual $\tilde{\mathbf{r}}$. However, checking the latter first saves some computational time as it is readily available whereas the former requires explicit calculation.

The question is still open as to what is the *best preconditioner* since in most cases it is problem dependent. For matrices with diagonal elements that are very different in magnitude, using

$$\mathbf{M} = \text{diag}(a_{11}, a_{22}, \ldots, a_{nn})$$

is very effective as it reduces the condition number of **B** by a factor of n of its minimum value [26]. This is called *diagonal scaling* and corresponds to Jacobi preconditioning. An extension of this idea is to build **M** as a block-diagonal matrix out of block submatrices of **A**. Similarly, the Gauss–Seidel method can be used as preconditioner but it needs to be symmetrized first. To this end, the symmetric SOR we presented in Section 7.2.6 can be a more effective block preconditioner.

Diagonal scaling fails if all diagonal elements are equal, such as in the matrices resulting from finite difference discretization of diffusion problems on uniforms grids (see Chapter 7) or other Toeplitz-type matrices (see next section). One of the most effective and popular preconditioners for such problems is based on the **incomplete Cholesky factorization** of the matrix **A**. We have already presented the Cholesky factorization of **A** in Section 9.2, which is feasible for symmetric positive-definite matrices, like the ones we consider here. The problem with Cholesky is that it fills in the zero entries of **A** in the LL^T decomposition, and in some cases it may totally destroy the possible sparsity initially present in **A**.

To obtain an incomplete Cholesky factorization of **A** we can simply suppress the fill-in entries (i.e., zero out the entries corresponding to the zero entries of the original matrix). Alternatively, to avoid computing these entries in **L** and simply place zeros at the corresponding locations, we can modify the Cholesky algorithm so that

- if $a_{ij} \neq 0$, compute l_{ij},
- elseif $l_{ij} = 0$.

We note that the two approaches are not the same, as can be easily verified in the following example. Let us consider the (4×4) matrix

$$\mathbf{A} = \begin{bmatrix} 4 & -1 & -1 & 0 \\ -1 & 4 & 0 & -1 \\ -1 & 0 & 4 & -1 \\ 0 & -1 & -1 & 4 \end{bmatrix}.$$

We first perform a standard Cholesky decomposition, which yields the following triangular matrix:

$$\mathbf{L}_c = \begin{bmatrix} 2.0000 & 0 & 0 & 0 \\ -0.5000 & 1.9365 & 0 & 0 \\ -0.5000 & -0.1291 & 1.9322 & 0 \\ 0 & -0.5164 & -0.5521 & 1.8516 \end{bmatrix}.$$

We note that the (3,2) entry, which was initially zero in **A**, has become nonzero in $\mathbf{L}_c$.

The first version of incomplete Cholesky would then be

$$
\mathbf{L}_{i1} = \begin{bmatrix} 2.0000 & 0 & 0 & 0 \\ -0.5000 & 1.9365 & 0 & 0 \\ -0.5000 & 0 & 1.9322 & 0 \\ 0 & -0.5164 & -0.5521 & 1.8516 \end{bmatrix} .
$$

However, the second version, where we do not compute the l_{ij} at all if the corresponding $a_{ij} = 0$, is

$$
\mathbf{L}_{i2} = \begin{bmatrix} 2.0000 & 0 & 0 & 0 \\ -0.5000 & 1.9365 & 0 & 0 \\ -0.5000 & 0 & 1.9365 & 0 \\ 0 & -0.5164 & -0.5164 & 1.8619 \end{bmatrix} ,
$$

which is different than $\mathbf{L}_{i1}$ in the entries (3,3), (4,3), and (4,4).

In practice, we can replace the second code statement in our bulleted list by setting a *threshold value* on the Cholesky entry as follows:

- elseif $|l_{ij}| \leq \epsilon$ then $l_{ij} = 0$,

so that only significantly large entries are retained. Clearly, the incomplete Cholesky decomposition can be performed only initially (i.e., before the iteration loop) and stores $\mathbf{M} = \mathbf{L}\mathbf{L}^T$ or simply stores $\mathbf{L}$.

REMARK 2: Although Cholesky factorization of a symmetric positive-definite matrix is always feasible, incomplete factorization may not be possible in some cases. This complication may manifest itself as a square root of a negative number to compute the l_{ii}. In this case, a positive large number should over-write the appropriate element, which can be chosen either arbitrarily or as a sum of the adjoint diagonal entries or even as a sum of absolute values of the rest of the entries in the row; the latter will ensure diagonal dominance.

REMARK 3: *Domain decomposition* is another way of preconditioning partial differential equations. The idea is to break up the domain of interest into subdomains, which can also overlap, and subsequently solve the PDE approximately but fast in each of the subdomains. This can also be done independently for each domain in an *embarrassingly parallel* fashion. The preconditioner matrix $\mathbf{M}$ is constructed by piecing together the solutions to subproblems leading to a block diagonal $\mathbf{M}$ if the subdomains do not overlap or to a product of block diagonal submatrices if the subdomains overlap.

9.4.3 Toeplitz Matrices and Circulant Preconditioners

A special preconditioner the circulant matrix, is very effective for Toeplitz matrices. Topeplitz matrices have constant diagonals and are encountered in signal processing and in a wide range of other problems that are invariant in time and space. A circular matrix $\mathbf{C}$ is a Toeplitz matrix but its entries also satisfy

$$c_k = c_{k+n},$$

where $n \times n$ is the size of the matrix $\mathbf{C}$.

A general Toeplitz matrix has $(2n - 1)$ independent entries, which are determined by the first row and column. In contrast, a general circulant matrix has only n independent entries. Assuming symmetry, then a Toeplitz matrix has n independent entries (the first column) whereas a circulant matrix has $[n/2] + 1$. More clearly, the differences between a general Toeplitz and a general circulant matrix are as follows:

$$\mathbf{A} = \begin{bmatrix} a_0 & a_{-1} & \dots & \dots & a_{1-n} \\ a_1 & a_0 & a_{-1} & \dots & \vdots \\ \vdots & a_1 & a_0 & \dots & a_{-1} \\ a_{n-1} & \vdots & \vdots & a_1 & a_0 \end{bmatrix}$$

and

$$\mathbf{C} = \begin{bmatrix} c_0 & c_{n-1} & \dots & \dots & c_1 \\ c_1 & c_0 & c_{n-1} & \dots & \vdots \\ \vdots & c_1 & c_0 & \dots & c_{n-1} \\ c_{n-1} & \vdots & \vdots & c_1 & c_0 \end{bmatrix}.$$

Assuming we want to solve the system $\mathbf{Ax} = \mathbf{b}$, where $\mathbf{A}$ is a *symmetric Toeplitz* matrix, the suggestion, first proposed in [83], is to precondition it with a corresponding circulant matrix. To this end, we recall that in most applications the main diagonal and its neighbors are strongly dominant and thus we can use them to construct an appropriate circulant preconditioner $\mathbf{C}$. The entries $c_1 = a_1$ appear both next to the main diagonal but also in the extreme corners as shown in the preceding equations. It turns out that these relatively large entries control the eigenspectrum of $\mathbf{C}^{-1}\mathbf{A}$, which in turn controls the convergence rate of PCGM. The rest of the eigenvalues are clustered around one; this is demonstrated in the homework problems (see Section 10.7). Typically, we copy a few of the main diagonals from the Toeplitz matrix onto the circulant matrix, but of course not all! In the homework problems of Section 9.8 we ask you to experiment with different circulant preconditioners. As you will see, the speedup is substantial.

9.4.4 Parallel PCGM

The parallelization of the preconditioned conjugate gradient is fairly straight-forward. Assuming that the matrix $\mathbf{A}$ has been distributed by rows across processes, the conjugate gradient component of the algorithm can be accomplished with only four MPI calls: three calls to *MPI_Allreduce* to accomplish *dot products*, and one call to *MPI_Allgather*. We can eliminate one of the reduction calls if we decide to use the *dot product* of the residual with the modified residual for the stopping criterion. Depending on the choice of preconditioner, however, additional MPI calls may be required to accomplish the preconditioning. In the case of a diagonal preconditioner, no MPI calls are necessary since diagonal preconditioning can be accomplished locally on all rows contained in a process. Other preconditioners such as incomplete Cholesky may require additional MPI calls, the cost of which should be considered when determining which preconditioner to use. In Figure 9.14 we provide a schematic of the iterative part of the parallel PCG algorithm with annotations denoting the BLAS and MPI operations that should be used. Note that in Figure 9.14 we use the modified residual for the stopping criterion, and hence we only have three MPI calls.

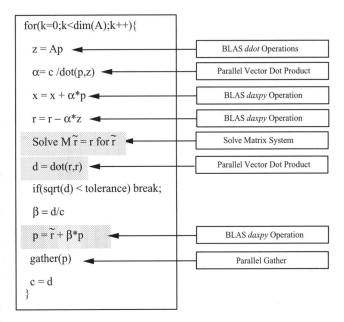

We now present an MPI program demonstrating the PCGM with a diagonal preconditioner. As a sample problem, we will solve (using second-order finite differences) the following equation:

$$\frac{d^2 u(x)}{dx^2} - c_2 e^{c_1(x-0.5)^2} u(x) = -\sin(2\pi x)(4\pi^2 - c_2 e^{c_1(x-0.5)^2}) \tag{9.15}$$

in the interval $x \in [0, 1]$ with boundary conditions $u(0) = u(1) = 0$ and constants $c_1 = 20.0$ and $c_2 = 1000.0$. The exact solution is $u(x) = \sin(2\pi x)$.

Figure 9.14: Iterative part of the PCG algorithm.

We have chosen the constants c_1 and c_2 so that there is a large disparity in the values along the diagonal. This will allow us to see the difference between the CGM and the PCGM with a diagonal preconditioner.

Since we have chosen to use a second-order finite difference method to approximate the derivative operator, we expect that the error should decrease by a factor of 4 when we double the number of grid points used. In Figure 9.15 we show a log–log plot of the L_2 error versus the number of grid points used. The magnitude of the slope of the line is approximately 2, consistent with the fact that our approximation is second order.

In Figure 9.16 we plot the inner product of the residual (r, r) for both the CGM and the PCGM. As predicted, PCGM converges much faster than the standard CGM.

To better explain the code, we have broken the entire program into four parts, as follows:

1. Part 1 – MPI initialization, initial memory allocation, and generation of grid and right-hand-side vector.
2. Part 2 – Memory allocation and generation of the matrix **A**.
3. Part 3 – PCGM initialization.
4. Part 4 – PCGM main iteration loop.

For each part, we will first present the code and then present a collection of remarks elucidating the salient points within each part.

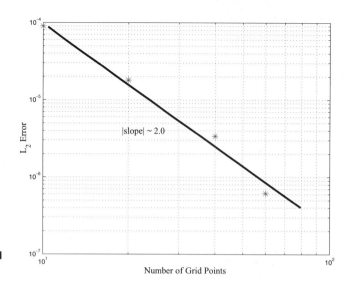

Figure 9.15: L_2 error versus the number of grid points for the PCGM example defined in Equation (9.15).

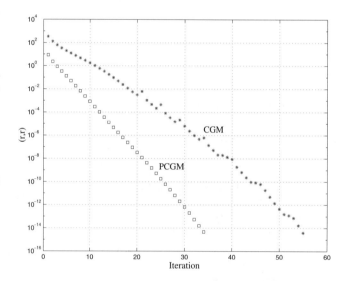

Figure 9.16: Inner product of the residual for both the CG and PCG methods applied to the PCGM example defined in Equation (9.15).

MPI

PART 1 - MPI INITIALIZATION

```
#include <iostream.h>
#include <iomanip.h>
#include "SCmathlib.h"
#include<mpi.h>

const int rows_per_proc = 40;
const double c1 = 20.0;
const double c2 = 1000.0;
const double tol = 1.0e-14;
```

```
int main(int argc, char *argv[]){
  int i,j,k;
  int mynode, totalnodes, totalsize, offset;
  MPI_Status status;
  double sum,local_sum,c,d,alpha,beta;
  double ** A, *q, *x, *grid;

  double *p,*z,*r,*mr;

  MPI_Init(&argc,&argv);
  MPI_Comm_size(MPI_COMM_WORLD, &totalnodes);
  MPI_Comm_rank(MPI_COMM_WORLD, &mynode);

  totalsize = totalnodes*rows_per_proc;

  p = new double[totalsize];
  z = new double[rows_per_proc];
  r = new double[rows_per_proc];
  mr = new double[rows_per_proc];

  x = new double[rows_per_proc];
  q = new double[rows_per_proc];
  grid = new double[rows_per_proc];

  double dx = 1.0/(totalsize+1);
  for(i=0;i<rows_per_proc;i++){
    grid[i] = dx*(1+rows_per_proc*mynode+i);
    q[i] = -dx*dx*sin(2.0*M_PI*grid[i])*
      (-4.0*M_PI*M_PI - c2*exp(c1*(grid[i]-0.5)*
        (grid[i]-0.5)));
    x[i] = 1.0;
  }
```

REMARK 1: We have four global variables in this program. The variable *rows_per_proc* gives the number of rows per processor. In this program we have decomposed the matrix by associating rows to processors. The two constants $c1$ and $c2$ are specific to the problem we are solving. The last global constant variable *tol* specifies the tolerance to which we should converge.

REMARK 2: Observe that with the exception of the array p all other arrays need only be of size *rows_per_proc* and not of size *totalsize*. Each processor need only maintain its part of the residual, modified residual, and solution vector; however, each processor must have a copy of the entire p vector.

PART 2 – MEMORY ALLOCATION AND GENERATION OF MATRIX

```
/* Part 2 */

A = new double*[rows_per_proc];
for(i=0;i<rows_per_proc;i++){
```

MPI

```
    A[i] = new double[totalsize];
    for(j=0;j<totalsize;j++)
      A[i][j] = 0.0;
}

if(mynode==0){
  A[0][0] = 2.0 + dx*dx*c2*exp(c1*(grid[0]-0.5)*
      (grid[0]-0.5));
  A[0][1] = -1.0;
  for(i=1;i<rows_per_proc;i++){
    A[i][i] = 2.0 + dx*dx*c2*exp(c1*(grid[i]-0.5)*
                (grid[i]-0.5));
    A[i][i-1] = -1.0;
    A[i][i+1] = -1.0;
  }
}
else if(mynode == (totalnodes-1)){
  A[rows_per_proc-1][totalsize-1] = 2.0 +
      dx*dx*c2*exp(c1*(grid[rows_per_proc-1]-0.5)*
      (grid[rows_per_proc-1]-0.5));
  A[rows_per_proc-1][totalsize-2] = -1.0;
  for(i=0;i<rows_per_proc-1;i++){
    offset = rows_per_proc*mynode + i;
    A[i][offset] = 2.0 + dx*dx*c2*exp(c1*(grid[i]-0.5)*
                (grid[i]-0.5));
    A[i][offset-1] = -1.0;
    A[i][offset+1] = -1.0;
  }
}
else{
  for(i=0;i<rows_per_proc;i++){
    offset = rows_per_proc*mynode + i;
    A[i][offset] = 2.0 + dx*dx*c2*exp(c1*(grid[i]-0.5)*
        (grid[i]-0.5));
    A[i][offset-1] = -1.0;
    A[i][offset+1] = -1.0;
  }
}
```

REMARK 3: We break the matrix setup into three cases. We have to carefully handle the first and last processors because they contain the first and last rows, respectively.

MPI

PART 3 - PCGM INITIALIZATION

```
/* Part 3 */

offset = mynode*rows_per_proc;
```

```
for(i=0;i<totalsize;i++)
  p[i] = 1.0;

for(i=0;i<rows_per_proc;i++){
  r[i] = q[i] - dot(totalsize,A[i],p); //calculation
                                            of residual
  mr[i] = r[i]/A[i][offset+i];   //calculation of
                                      modified residual

}

local_sum = dot(rows_per_proc,mr,r);
MPI_Allreduce(&local_sum,&sum,1,MPI_DOUBLE,MPI_SUM,
            MPI_COMM_WORLD);
c = sum;

MPI_Allgather(mr,rows_per_proc,MPI_DOUBLE,p,rows_per_proc,
            MPI_DOUBLE,MPI_COMM_WORLD);
```

REMARK 4: We have chosen our initial vector as the vector of all 1s. Because we have to calculate the initial residual, we require that all processors have the entire initial guess. Notice that we temporarily use the p array to accomplish this instead of allocating a new vector. Because p is not in use until after the modified residual is calculated, we can use the allocated space with no adverse effect.

PART 4 - PCGM MAIN ITERATION LOOP

```
MPI
```

```
/* Part 4 */

 for(k=0;k<totalsize;k++){

   for(i=0;i<rows_per_proc;i++)
     z[i] = dot(totalsize,A[i],p);

   local_sum = dot(rows_per_proc,z,p+offset);

   MPI_Allreduce(&local_sum,&sum,1,MPI_DOUBLE,MPI_SUM,
               MPI_COMM_WORLD);

   alpha = c/sum;

   for(i=0;i<rows_per_proc;i++){
     x[i] = x[i] + alpha*p[offset+i];
     r[i] = r[i] - alpha*z[i];
   }

   /* Preconditioning Stage */
   for(i=0;i<rows_per_proc;i++)
     mr[i] = r[i]/A[i][offset+i];

   local_sum = dot(rows_per_proc,mr,r);

   MPI_Allreduce(&local_sum,&sum,1,MPI_DOUBLE,MPI_SUM,
               MPI_COMM_WORLD);
```

```
    d = sum; //contains inner product of
              //residual and modified residual

    local_sum = dot(rows_per_proc,r,r);

    MPI_Allreduce(&local_sum,&sum,1,MPI_DOUBLE,MPI_SUM,
              MPI_COMM_WORLD);

    //sum now contains inner product of residual and residual
    if(mynode == 0){
      cout << k << "\t" << "dot(mr,r) = " << d << "\t";
      cout << "dot(r,r) = " << sum << endl;
    }

    if(fabs(d) < tol) break;
    if(fabs(sum) < tol) break;

    beta = d/c;

    for(i=0;i<rows_per_proc;i++)
      z[i] = mr[i] + beta*p[i+offset];

    MPI_Allgather(z,rows_per_proc,MPI_DOUBLE,p,rows_per_proc,
              MPI_DOUBLE,MPI_COMM_WORLD);

    c = d;

  }

  delete[] p;
  delete[] z;
  delete[] r;
  delete[] mr;
  delete[] x;
  delete[] q;
  delete[] grid;
  for(i=0;i<rows_per_proc;i++)
    delete[] A[i];
  delete[] A;

  MPI_Finalize();
}
```

REMARK 5: Observe that we only require four MPI calls: three to *MPI_Allreduce* and one to *MPI_Allgather*. The three reductions are used to obtain the inner product across all processors; the *Allgather* is used so that all processors have the updated value of p.

REMARK 6: Because we are using diagonal preconditioning, no additional communication is required for the preconditioner. If we were to use incomplete Cholesky as a preconditioner, additional communication similar to what was accomplished in the parallel Gaussian elimination solver would have to be used. The factorization would be accomplished before the iteration loop, and only the cost of two parallel backsolves would be incurred within the iteration loop.

9.5 NONSYMMETRIC SYSTEMS

The conjugate gradient algorithm assumes that the matrix $\mathbf{A}$ is symmetric and positive-definite. To deal with the nonsymmetric system

$$\mathbf{Ax} = \mathbf{b}$$

we need to come up with new solvers or transform the nonsymmetric system into a symmetric one as follows:

$$\mathbf{A}^T\mathbf{Ax} = \mathbf{A}^T\mathbf{b} \quad \text{(CGNR)}.$$

Clearly, this transformation produces a symmetric positive-definite matrix $\mathbf{B} \equiv \mathbf{A}^T\mathbf{A}$ and thus we can apply PCGM to it. This is called the conjugate gradient normal residual (CGNR) algorithm and it is an acceptable method for matrices that are well conditioned, although we have to pay extra to include matrix–vector multiplications with both $\mathbf{A}^T$ and $\mathbf{A}$. However, the condition number of $\mathbf{B}$ is the *square* of the condition number of $\mathbf{A}$ and thus for ill-conditioned matrices an extremely large number of iterations is required for convergence.

We now compare the CG and CGNR algorithms by considering which quantity we *minimize* in these minimization-based solvers. We have already seen in Section 4.1.7 that the solution with CG is equivalent to minimizing the quadratic form

$$P_{\text{CG}}(\mathbf{x}) = \frac{1}{2}(\mathbf{x}, \mathbf{Ax}) - (\mathbf{b}, \mathbf{x}).$$

We can rewrite this form in terms of the error $\mathbf{e} \equiv \mathbf{x} - \mathbf{s}$, where $\mathbf{s}$ is the exact solution, as follows:

$$2P_{\text{CG}}(\mathbf{x}) = (\mathbf{x}, \mathbf{Ax}) - 2(\mathbf{x}, \mathbf{As}) + (\mathbf{s}, \mathbf{As})$$

$$= \mathbf{e}^T\mathbf{Ae}$$

$$= ||\mathbf{e}||_A.$$

This equation above simply states that searching for the solution using the CG algorithm is equivalent to minimizing the *error* in the A norm. In contrast, the CGNR algorithm minimizes the residual in the L_2 norm, and thus the corresponding quadratic form is

$$2P_{\text{CGNR}}(\mathbf{x}) = ||\mathbf{b} - \mathbf{Ax}||_2$$

$$= (\mathbf{b} - \mathbf{Ax}, \mathbf{b} - \mathbf{Ax})$$

$$= (\mathbf{Ax}, \mathbf{Ax}) - 2(\mathbf{b}, \mathbf{Ax}) + (\mathbf{b}, \mathbf{b}).$$

Therefore, the minimization of P_{CGNR} corresponds to applying CG to the system

$$\mathbf{B}\mathbf{x} = \mathbf{f},$$

where $\mathbf{B} = \mathbf{A}^T\mathbf{A}$ and $\mathbf{f} = \mathbf{A}^T\mathbf{b}$.

The literature describes several *conjugate residual* algorithms, which are based on the minimization of the residual in different forms. A significant difference between such algorithms and the CG for symmetric systems is that the loss of symmetry results in the loss of the three-term magic recurrence formula, which keeps the matrices sparse and leads to efficiency both in memory and cost. Instead of two or three vectors, in the nonsymmetric conjugate algorithms we typically need to store the entire sequence of conjugate directions, which is prohibitively expensive for very large n. However, in practice a subset of the last k vectors may work or the algorithm can be *restarted* after k steps.

In the following, instead of presenting all variants of conjugate gradient residual algorithms we concentrate on one that makes use of an iterative procedure to simplify the original matrix, namely the *Arnoldi iteration*. Based on this procedure, we can solve, relatively efficiently, nonsymmetric systems as we demonstrate. We can also compute eigenvalues of nonsymmetric matrices, as we discuss in Section 10.5 in the next chapter.

9.5.1 The Arnoldi Iteration

The Arnoldi method is an orthogonal projection onto a Krylov subspace $\mathcal{K}_m$ for non-symmetric matrices $\mathbf{A}(n \times n)$; usually $m \ll n$. It reduces the matrix $\mathbf{A}$ to a *Hessenberg form*; that is, it accomplishes what Householder does for the entire matrix $\mathbf{A}$ but here we have the option of only going halfway. Arnoldi, who introduced this algorithm in the early 1950s [3], suggested that it leads to good approximations for some of the eigenvalues of $\mathbf{A}$ even if we terminate prematurely! In practice, it is a useful technique for obtaining the eigenvalues of *large sparse* matrices. It is useful to think of this as an extension of the Lanczos method (see Section 10.3.6) to nonsymmetric matrices. It has the same iterative and approximate form, although a separate version of Lanczos exists for nonsymmetric matrices [79].

Let us begin by considering the similarity transformation

$$\mathbf{A} = \mathbf{V}^T\mathbf{H}\mathbf{V},$$

where we define the matrix $\mathbf{V}$ or $\mathbf{V}_m$ with orthonormal columns

$$\mathbf{V}_m = [\,\mathbf{v}_1 \,|\, \mathbf{v}_2 \,|\, \ldots \,|\, \mathbf{v}_m\,],$$

and $\mathbf{H}_m$ is the Hessenberg matrix $(m \times m)$. We also define the extended matrix $\tilde{\mathbf{H}}_m$ of dimension $(m+1) \times m$ as follows:

$$\tilde{\mathbf{H}}_m = \begin{bmatrix} h_{11} & h_{12} & \ldots & & h_{1m} \\ h_{21} & h_{22} & \ldots & & h_{2m} \\ & \ddots & \ddots & & \vdots \\ & & h_{m,m-1} & & h_{mm} \\ & & & & h_{m+1,m} \end{bmatrix},$$

and we can write

$$\tilde{\mathbf{H}}_m = \mathbf{H}_m + h_{m+1,m}\mathbf{v}_{m+1}\mathbf{e}_m^T,$$

where $\mathbf{v}_{m+1}$ is defined as orthonormal; that is, it has unit norm.

The Arnoldi iteration process satisfies

$$\mathbf{AV}_m = \mathbf{V}_{m+1}\tilde{\mathbf{H}}_m, \tag{9.16}$$

and correspondingly, the mth column of this equation reads

$$\mathbf{Av}_m = h_{1m}\mathbf{v}_1 + h_{2m}\mathbf{v}_2 + \cdots + h_{mm}\mathbf{v}_m + h_{m+1,m}\mathbf{v}_{m+1},$$

which is an $(m+1)$-term recurrence formula, instead of the three-term formula in symmetric systems.

The basic algorithm of Arnoldi iteration implements this formula in a straightforward manner, as follows:

BASIC ARNOLDI ALGORITHM

Initialize: Choose a vector $\mathbf{x}_0 \Rightarrow \mathbf{v}_1 = \frac{\mathbf{x}_0}{\|\mathbf{x}_0\|}$

Begin Loop: $for\ j = 1, 2, \ldots, m$

$for\ i = 1, \ldots, j$

$h_{ij} = (\mathbf{Av}_j, \mathbf{v}_i)$

endfor

$\mathbf{w}_j = \mathbf{Av}_j - \sum_{i=1}^{j} h_{ij}\mathbf{v}_i$

$h_{j+1,j} = \|\mathbf{w}_j\|_2$

$\mathbf{v}_{j+1} = \mathbf{w}_j / h_{j+1,j}$

End Loop: endfor

This algorithm is basically the standard Gram–Schmidt orthogonalization procedure applied to the Krylov space $\mathcal{K}_m$.

We note that in each iteration we compute the entire j column, including the entry $h_{j+1,j}$ below the main diagonal. In particular, if $h_{j+1,j} = 0$ then the Arnoldi iteration stalls. But this is in fact good news because such a breakdown usually implies that we have achieved convergence and the iteration should be terminated. If we want to continue, we can *restart* the process with a new orthonormal vector $\mathbf{v}_{j+1}$, which can be selected arbitrarily.

The implementation of the Arnoldi algorithm given here is straightforward, although it suffers from round-off errors, just as is the case of the basic Gram–Schmidt algorithm. To this end, we can apply the *more stable* modified Gram–Schmidt orthogonalization procedure to the Krylov space to come up with a better code for the Arnoldi iteration, as follows:

MODIFIED ARNOLDI ALGORITHM

Initialize: Choose $\mathbf{x}_0 \Rightarrow \mathbf{v}_1 = \frac{\mathbf{x}_0}{\|\mathbf{x}_0\|_2}$.

$$\text{Begin Loop: for } j = 1, \ldots, m$$

$$\mathbf{w} = \mathbf{A}\mathbf{v}_j$$

$$\text{for } i = 1, \ldots, j$$

$$h_{ij} = (\mathbf{w}, \mathbf{v}_i)$$

$$\mathbf{w} = \mathbf{w} - h_{ij}\mathbf{v}_i$$

$$\text{endfor}$$

$$h_{j+1,j} = \| \mathbf{w} \|_2$$

$$\mathbf{v}_{j+1} = \mathbf{w}/h_{j+1,j}$$

$$\text{End Loop: } \quad \text{endfor}$$

This is a much more stable algorithm, but even this version needs further treatment sometimes, so an extra orthogonalization may be required occasionally. For robustness, we can apply the Householder algorithm periodically for extra orthogonalization.

Software
Suite

PUTTING IT INTO PRACTICE

Next we present a *function* for computing the Arnoldi decomposition using the *modified algorithm* presented earlier. The function takes four arguments: the integer value m denoting the dimension of the Krylov space onto which we are projecting, a SCMatrix A of size $N \times N$ on which the decomposition is to be accomplished, and two SCMatrix variables H and V for storing the resulting $\tilde{\mathbf{H}}$ and $\tilde{\mathbf{V}}$ from the decomposition. Note that H must be a SCMatrix of size $(m+1) \times m$ and V must be a SCMatrix of size $N \times (m+1)$. The initial direction vector x defaults to the first unit vector.

```
void ModifiedArnoldi(int m, const SCMatrix &A, SCMatrix &H,
                     SCMatrix &V){
  SCVector v(A.Rows()),w(A.Rows());
  v.Initialize(0.0);
  v(0) = 1.0;

  V.PutColumn(0,v);
```

```
for(int j=0;j<m;j++){
  w = A*v;
  for(int i=0;i<=j;i++){
    V.GetColumn(i,v);
    H(i,j) = dot(w,v);
    w = w - H(i,j)*v;
  }
  H(j+1,j) = w.Norm_l2();
  v = w/H(j+1,j);
  V.PutColumn(j+1,v);
}
}
```

REMARK 1: Once again we pass all three SCMatrix variables by reference (denoted by the "&" symbol) as opposed to by the default case of passing by value. For the variables H and V, the reason is as before – we want to change the values within the matrices, and we want those changes to remain valid after the function has returned (i.e., not be lost in the "pass by value" copy of the variable discarded when the function returns). However, in the case of the matrix A, this is not the case. We do not want to modify the values of A. Why then do we pass by reference as opposed to passing by value? In this case, we do so because we assume that A is very large, and therefore we do not wish to allocate space for a copy of A when the function is called. We instead pass the matrix by reference so that no additional memory must be allocated; the original memory from the calling function is used. We do, however, want to guarantee that the matrix A does not change within the function; hence why we add the **const** in the appropriate place within the argument list. The "const SCMatrix &A" allows us to pass the matrix A by reference, but not to update its values within the function *ModifiedArnoldi*.

REMARK 2: We introduced two new SCMatrix methods:

1. SCMatrix::PutColumn(int col, const SCVector &v) and
2. SCMatrix::GetColumn(int col, SCVector &v).

The first function copies the contents of the vector v into the *col* column of the matrix. The second function copies the contents of the *col* column from the matrix into the vector v.

EXAMPLE. As an example of the use of this code, we revisit our old friend the Hilbert matrix of size three:

$$\mathbf{A} = \begin{bmatrix} 1 & 1/2 & 1/3 \\ 1/2 & 1/3 & 1/4 \\ 1/3 & 1/4 & 1/5 \end{bmatrix}.$$

The goal is to find the decomposition when $m = 2$. We input into our function $m = 2$, the Hilbert matrix $\mathbf{A}$ as given, and two SCMatrix variables H and V, which are of size 3×2 and 3×3 respectively. As output we obtain $\tilde{\mathbf{H}}$ and $\tilde{\mathbf{V}}$ contained within the SCmatrix variables H and V respectively. The decomposition for the 3×3 Hilbert matrix given here is

$$
\tilde{\mathbf{V}} = \begin{bmatrix} 1.0000 & 0.0000 & 0.0000 \\ 0.0000 & 0.8321 & -0.5547 \\ 0.0000 & 0.5547 & 0.83205 \end{bmatrix}
$$

and

$$
\tilde{\mathbf{H}} = \begin{bmatrix} 1.00000 & 0.60093 \\ 0.60093 & 0.52308 \\ 0.00000 & 0.03462 \end{bmatrix}.
$$

9.5.2 GMRES

GMRES stands for "generalized minimum residual" and is one of the most effective solvers for nonsymmetric systems

$$
\mathbf{Ax} = \mathbf{b},
$$

where $\mathbf{A}$ is an $n \times n$ square but nonsymmetric matrix; $\mathbf{A}$ is also assumed to be nonsingular since we look for the solution $\mathbf{A}^{-1}\mathbf{b}$.

The main idea of GMRES is to minimize the residual $\| \mathbf{b} - \mathbf{Ax}_m \|_2$ at the mth iteration. Specifically, $\mathbf{x}_m$ is a vector in the Krylov space

$$
\mathcal{K}_m = \{\mathbf{v}, \mathbf{Ab}, \dots, \mathbf{A}^{m-1}\mathbf{b}\},
$$

and it can be determined by solving a least-squares problem; here $m < n$. At the point $m = n$ we are attempting to minimize the residual $\| \mathbf{b} - \mathbf{Ax}_n \|_2$ and hence obtain the solution $\mathbf{x}$.

Such a minimization is equivalent to performing a QR decomposition to the matrix of *least-squares coefficients* $\mathbf{C}$ (see Section 3.1.7). We illustrate this point next.

Let us assume that in matrix form we seek to find

$$
\| \mathbf{Ca} - \mathbf{f} \|_2 = \text{minimum}
$$

with respect to $\mathbf{a}$. Then, we need to QR-decompose $\mathbf{C}$, which is a nonsquare matrix $p \times q$, $p > q$.

The idea is to apply Householder transformation to the extended matrix $\mathbf{C}$ of $p \times p$ but stop when we have completed zeroing out the entries in the first q columns. We then write

$$
\mathbf{C} = \mathbf{Q} \begin{bmatrix} \mathbf{R} \\ 0 \end{bmatrix},
$$

where $\mathbf{R}$ is a $q \times q$ upper triangular matrix. Since $\| \mathbf{Q} \| = \| \mathbf{Q}^{-1} \| = 1$, we also have

$$
\| \mathbf{Ca} - \mathbf{f} \|_2 = \| \mathbf{Q}^{-1}(\mathbf{Ca} - \mathbf{f}) \|_2 = \| \tilde{\mathbf{R}}\mathbf{a} - \tilde{\mathbf{f}} \|_2,
$$

where we have defined $\tilde{\mathbf{R}} = \begin{bmatrix} \mathbf{R} \\ 0 \end{bmatrix}$ and also $\tilde{\mathbf{f}} = \mathbf{Q}^{-1}\mathbf{f}$.

But

$$\tilde{\mathbf{R}}\mathbf{a} - \tilde{\mathbf{f}} = \begin{bmatrix} \mathbf{R} \\ 0 \end{bmatrix}\mathbf{a} - \begin{bmatrix} \tilde{\mathbf{f}}_1 \\ \tilde{\mathbf{f}}_2 \end{bmatrix} = \begin{bmatrix} \mathbf{R}\mathbf{a} - \tilde{\mathbf{f}}_1 \\ -\tilde{\mathbf{f}}_2 \end{bmatrix},$$

where we split $\tilde{\mathbf{f}}$ into $\tilde{\mathbf{f}}_1$ of length q and $\tilde{\mathbf{f}}_2$ of length $(p - q)$. Then,

$$\| \mathbf{Ca} - \mathbf{f} \|_2^2 = \| \mathbf{Ra} - \tilde{\mathbf{f}}_1 \|_2^2 + \| \tilde{\mathbf{f}}_2 \|_2^2 .$$

Therefore, the least-squares problem is equivalent to solving

$$\mathbf{Ra} = \tilde{\mathbf{f}}_1,$$

which minimizes the entire residual, since $\tilde{\mathbf{f}}_2$ is fixed with respect to $\mathbf{a}$.

The problem, however, in directly applying this QR procedure to

$$\| \mathbf{Ax}_m - \mathbf{b} \|_2 = \text{minimum}$$

involved in GMRES is that it leads to numerical instabilities. This is exactly where the Arnoldi iteration comes in! The idea is to replace

$$\mathbf{x}_m = \mathbf{V}_m\mathbf{y}$$

and seek to find

$$\| \mathbf{AV}_m\mathbf{y} - \mathbf{b} \|_2 = \text{minimum}.$$

Here $\mathbf{V}_m$ is the matrix containing as columns the orthonormal vectors produced by the Arnoldi iteration. Notice that we still use the Krylov iteration but we basically orthonormalize them first via Arnoldi.

We can simplify this problem since $\mathbf{AV}_m = \mathbf{V}_{m+1}\tilde{\mathbf{H}}_m$, where $\tilde{\mathbf{H}}_m$ is the extended Hessenberg matrix we have encountered before. Therefore, we seek to find

$$\| \mathbf{V}_{m+1}\tilde{\mathbf{H}}_m\mathbf{y} - \mathbf{b} \|_2 = \text{minimum}$$

and after multiplying by $\mathbf{V}_{m+1}^T$ (whose norm is unity), we have

$$\| \tilde{\mathbf{H}}_m\mathbf{y} - \mathbf{V}_{m+1}^T\mathbf{b} \|_2 = \text{minimum}.$$

Finally, since $\mathbf{V}_{m+1}^T\mathbf{b} = \| \mathbf{b} \|_2 \, \mathbf{e}_1$ by construction of the first orthogonal vector $\mathbf{v}_1$, the minimization problem is

$$\| \tilde{\mathbf{H}}_m\mathbf{y} - \| \mathbf{b} \|_2 \, \mathbf{e}_1 \|_2 = \text{minimum}.$$

Applying QR to this problem now involves the Hessenberg matrix $\tilde{\mathbf{H}}_m$, so

$$\mathbf{Q}_m\tilde{\mathbf{H}}_m = \tilde{\mathbf{R}}_m = \begin{bmatrix} \mathbf{R}_m \\ 0 \end{bmatrix},$$

where $\mathbf{R}_m$ is an $m \times m$ upper triangular matrix, and $\mathbf{Q}_m$ is an $(m + 1) \times (m + 1)$ orthogonal matrix.

We can exploit the structure of the Hessenberg matrix and use Givens rotations for accomplishing the decomposition. Recall that the Hessenberg matrix contains an off-diagonal below the main diagonal. This set of entries can easily by modified to zero by the appropriate Givens rotations, yielding an upper triangular matrix $\mathbf{R}$.

Following the preceding discussion on least squares, we can compute $\mathbf{y}_m$ from

$$\mathbf{R}_m \mathbf{y} = \| \mathbf{b} \| \, \mathbf{q}_1,$$

where $\mathbf{q}_1$ is the *first column* of $\mathbf{Q}_m$ excluding the last entry (i.e., $\mathbf{q}_1$ is a vector of length m). Finally, we compute $\mathbf{x}_m$ from

$$\mathbf{x}_m = \mathbf{V}_m \mathbf{y}.$$

For convergence purposes we need to compute the residual $\mathbf{r}_m$. This is done efficiently as follows:

$$\| \mathbf{r}_m \|_2 = \| \tilde{\mathbf{H}}_m \mathbf{y} - \| \mathbf{b} \|_2 \, \mathbf{e}_1 \|_2$$

$$= \| \mathbf{Q}_m(\tilde{\mathbf{H}}_m \mathbf{y} - \| \mathbf{b} \|_2 \, \mathbf{e}_1) \|_2$$

$$= \| \mathbf{R}_m \mathbf{y} - \| \mathbf{b} \| \, \tilde{\mathbf{q}}_1 \|_2$$

$$= \| \underbrace{(\mathbf{R}_m y - \| \mathbf{b} \| \, \mathbf{q}_1)}_{0} + \| \mathbf{b} \| \, (\mathbf{q}_1 - \tilde{\mathbf{q}}_1) \|_2$$

$$= \| \mathbf{b} \| \times (\text{last entry of} |\tilde{\mathbf{q}}_1|),$$

where $\tilde{\mathbf{q}}_1$ is the extended $(m+1)$ vector produced by Arnoldi. This formula then gives a very inexpensive way to compute the residual and check convergence.

REMARK 1: Unlike CGM, in GMRES the residuals decrease monotonically, that is,

$$\| \mathbf{r}_{m+1} \|_2 < \| \mathbf{r}_m \|_2,$$

because the corresponding Krylov spaces are nested and the *residual* is minimized directly. We recall that in CGM the *error* is minimized instead, and thus reduction of the residual in the L_2 norm is not guaranteed.

REMARK 2: From Arnoldi, we can check the value of $h_{m+1,m}$ to tell us when the iteration can be terminated. When the condition $h_{m+1,m} = 0$ is satisfied, we know that the solution $\mathbf{x}$ lies within the Krylov space $\mathcal{K}_m$. This being the case, the least-squares problem over the Krylov space will produce the exact solution.

EXAMPLE. We now present an example to demonstrate the GMRES process. Consider the matrix

$$\mathbf{A} = \begin{bmatrix} 1.0 & 2.0 & 3.0 \\ 2.0 & 5.0 & 7.0 \\ 3.0 & 8.0 & 9.0 \end{bmatrix}$$

and right-hand-side vector

$$\mathbf{b} = \begin{bmatrix} 0.0 \\ 1.0 \\ 2.0 \end{bmatrix}.$$

We will assume that our initial guess is $\mathbf{x}_0 = \mathbf{0}$. Using our modified Arnoldi solver with $m = 3$ we obtain the extended Hessenberg matrix

$$\tilde{\mathbf{H}}_m = \begin{bmatrix} 14.2000 & 4.8652 & -0.8305 \\ 4.3081 & 1.0414 & 0.3855 \\ 0.0000 & 0.3855 & -0.2414 \\ 0.0000 & 0.0000 & 0.0000 \end{bmatrix}$$

and corresponding matrix

$$\mathbf{V}_{m+1} = \begin{bmatrix} 0.0000 & 0.8305 & 0.5571 & 0.4082 \\ 0.4472 & 0.4983 & -0.7428 & 0.8165 \\ 0.8944 & -0.2491 & 0.3714 & 0.4082 \end{bmatrix}.$$

Both of these matrices will be used. A linear combination of the first three columns of $\mathbf{V}_{m+1}$ will be used to form the solution. To determine the proper combination, we now want to solve the following problem:

$$\| \tilde{\mathbf{H}}_m \mathbf{y} - \| \mathbf{b} \|_2 \, \mathbf{e}_1 \|_2 = \text{minimum},$$

where $\| \mathbf{b} \|_2 \, \mathbf{e}_1 = (\sqrt{5} \ 0 \ 0 \ 0)^T$.

To solve the minimization problem, we accomplish QR decomposition using Givens rotations. For this problem, the three rotation matrices $\mathbf{G}_0$, $\mathbf{G}_1$, and $\mathbf{G}_2$ are

$$\mathbf{G}_0 = \begin{bmatrix} 0.0645 & 0.0196 & 0 & 0 \\ -0.0196 & 0.0645 & 0 & 0 \\ 0 & 0 & 1.0000 & 0 \\ 0 & 0 & 0 & 1.0000 \end{bmatrix},$$

$$\mathbf{G}_1 = \begin{bmatrix} 1.0 & 0.0 & 0.0 & 0.0 \\ 0.0 & -0.1876 & 2.5802 & 0.0 \\ 0.0 & -2.5802 & -0.1876 & 0.0 \\ 0.0 & 0.0 & 0.0 & 1.0000 \end{bmatrix},$$

$$\mathbf{G}_2 = \begin{bmatrix} 1.0 & 0.0 & 0.0 & 0.0 \\ 0.0 & 1.0 & 0.0 & 0.0 \\ 0.0 & 0.0 & -16.4509 & 0.0 \\ 0.0 & 0.0 & 0.0 & -16.4509 \end{bmatrix}.$$

Each successive Givens rotation matrix is formed based upon the updated matrix. Hence, $\mathbf{G}_0$ is formed based upon the entries of $\tilde{\mathbf{H}}_m$, $\mathbf{G}_1$ is formed based upon the entries of $\mathbf{G}_0\tilde{\mathbf{H}}_m$, and $\mathbf{G}_2$ is formed based upon the entries of $\mathbf{G}_1\mathbf{G}_0\tilde{\mathbf{H}}_m$. Applying the Givens rotations to both the right- and left-hand sides yields a modified matrix

$$\mathbf{R}_m = \begin{bmatrix} 1.0000 & 0.3341 & -0.0460 \\ 0.0000 & 1.0000 & -0.6305 \\ 0.0000 & 0.0000 & 1.0000 \end{bmatrix}$$

and a modified right-hand-side vector

$$\mathbf{z} = \begin{bmatrix} 0.1442 \\ 0.0082 \\ -1.8569 \end{bmatrix}.$$

Here we have omitted the last row of both the matrix and right-hand-side vector because all the entries are zero as expected. We now solve the system $\mathbf{R}_m\,\mathbf{y} = \mathbf{z}$ using back substitution. We obtain the vector

$$\mathbf{y} = \begin{bmatrix} 0.4472 \\ -1.1626 \\ -1.8569 \end{bmatrix},$$

which provides us with the coefficients for the linear combination of the vectors of $\mathbf{V}_{m+1}$. Taking the linear combination of the first three columns of $\mathbf{V}_{m+1}$ (since $m = 3$), we obtain

$$0.4472 \begin{bmatrix} 0.0000 \\ 0.4472 \\ 0.8944 \end{bmatrix} - 1.1626 \begin{bmatrix} 0.8305 \\ 0.4983 \\ -0.2491 \end{bmatrix} - 1.8569 \begin{bmatrix} 0.5571 \\ -0.7428 \\ 0.3714 \end{bmatrix} = \begin{bmatrix} -2.000 \\ 1.000 \\ 0.000 \end{bmatrix},$$

which is the exact solution.

9.5.3 GMRES(k)

The problem with the GMRES is that it requires storing all the vectors $\mathbf{v}_m$, which can become very expensive. To save storage and also computational cost we can run the GMRES process only for k steps and subsequently *restart it* with the vector $\mathbf{x}_k$ as an initial guess. This is the *GMRES(k)* version of the generalized minimum residual method. The choice of k is crucial, as a value too small may lead to divergence whereas a large value results in extra computations.

PUTTING IT INTO PRACTICE

In the following we present a serial implementation of GMRES(m). This function takes as input the integer m denoting the size of the Krylov subspace to be used, the matrix $\mathbf{A}$, the right-hand-side vector $\mathbf{b}$, and the result vector $\mathbf{x}$. We automatically set the initial direction to $(1, 0, \ldots, 0)^T$. Two constants can be found within the function:

maxit, which specifies the maximum number of iterations before terminating, and *tol*, which specifies the stopping tolerance.

```
void GMRES(int m, const SCMatrix &A, const SCVector &b,
           SCVector &x){
  int i,j,k,ll,nr;
  int N = A.Rows();
  SCMatrix H(m+1,m),V(N,m+1);
  SCVector w(N),r(N),y(m+1),z(N);
  double * c = new double[m+1];
  double * s = new double[m+1];
  const int maxit = 1000;
  const double tol = 1.0e-7;
  double delta,rho,tmp;

  x.Initialize(0.0);

  r = b - A*x;

  for(j=0;j<maxit;j++){
    y.Initialize(0.0);
    y(0) = r.Norm_l2();
    r.Normalize();

    ModifiedArnoldi(m,r,A,H,V);

    /* Givens rotation to accomplish QR factorization */
    for(i=0;i<m;i++){
      for(k=1;k<=i;k++){
        tmp = H(k-1,i);
        H(k-1,i) = c[k-1]*H(k-1,i) + s[k-1]*H(k,i);
        H(k,i) = -s[k-1]*tmp + c[k-1]*H(k,i);
      }

      delta = sqrt(H(i,i)*H(i,i)+H(i+1,i)*H(i+1,i));
      c[i] = H(i,i)/delta;
      s[i] = H(i+1,i)/delta;

      H(i,i) = c[i]*H(i,i) + s[i]*H(i+1,i);

      for(k=i+1;k<m+1;k++)
        H(k,i) = 0.0;

      y(i+1) = -s[i]*y(i);
      y(i)   =  c[i]*y(i);
      rho = fabs(y(i+1));
      if(rho < tol){
        nr = i;
        break;
```

```
    }
  }

  /* Backsolve to obtain coefficients */
  z.Initialize(0.0);
  if(i>=(m-1)){
    nr = m;
    z(nr-1) = y(nr-1)/H(nr-1,nr-1);
  }

  for(k=nr-2;k>=0;k--){
    z(k) = y(k);
    for(ll=k+1;ll<nr;ll++)
      z(k) -= H(k,ll)*z(ll);
    z(k) = z(k)/H(k,k);
  }

  /* Linear combination of basis vectors
     of the Krylov space                 */
  for(i=0;i<nr;i++){
    V.GetColumn(i,r);
    x = x + z(i)*r;
  }

  if(rho<tol)
    break;

  r = b - A*x;
  }
  delete[] c;
  delete[] s;
}
```

REMARK 1: Observe that this function requires the storage of both **H** and **V**, both of which may be of the same size as the original matrix **A**. This fact is one of the primary motivations for introducing the restart parameter so that smaller Krylov spaces (and hence less storage) can be used.

REMARK 2: Instead of forming the Givens matrices explicitly as we did in this the example, we can take advantage of the structure of the matrices so that we need not store the rotation matrices. Instead, we can loop through the appropriate positions, updating as we go.

9.5.4 Preconditioning GMRES

GMRES is used in practice when the matrix **A** is not well conditioned. This means that convergence is typically slow and appropriate preconditioners should be employed.

Similar to preconditioning of symmetric matrices where incomplete Cholesky was found to be effective, here we use *incomplete LU (ILU)*. Specifically, we employ the preconditioner

$$\mathbf{M} = \mathbf{LU},$$

where $\mathbf{L}$ and $\mathbf{U}$ are the lower and upper triangular matrices corresponding to $\mathbf{A}$ but with no fill-ins at the entries $a_{ij} = 0$. Note that the preconditioner should not be constructed explicitly, but rather it should be incorporated in the Arnoldi iteration process. To this end, we need to insert the following code:

$$\vdots$$

$$\mathbf{My} = \mathbf{v}_j$$

$$\mathbf{w} = \mathbf{Ay}$$

$$\text{for } i = 1, \ldots, j$$

$$h_{ij} = (\mathbf{w}, \mathbf{v}_i)$$

$$\mathbf{w} = \mathbf{w} - h_{ij}\mathbf{v}_i$$

$$\vdots$$

in the modified Arnoldi iteration algorithm previously presented.

REMARK: GMRES employs long vectors to obtain orthogonality, unlike the three-term recurrence formula associated with symmetric systems. For nonsymmetric systems it is also possible to use three-term recurrence formulas, as done in the biconjugate gradient (BiCG) method, employing *two* mutually orthogonal sequences of vectors. A more stable version of BiCG is the quasi-minimal residual (QMR) method, which avoids possible breakdowns and converges faster (i.e., as fast as GMRES [39]). Both BiCG and QMR solve tridiagonal systems corresponding to the three-term recurrence sequences. Details of implementation for both methods can be found in [5].

9.5.5 Parallel GMRES

One immediate complication when attempting to parallelize the serial algorithm previously presented is attempting to parallelize the modified Arnoldi component. The brute-force implementation leads to very poor scalability. Similarly to what we did for the parallel PCG algorithm, we can also use blocked operations to increase the efficiency and parallelism. One way proposed in [64] is to first produce the following basis for the Krylov space:

$$\mathbf{v}_1, \mathbf{Av}_1, \ldots, \mathbf{A}^k\mathbf{v}_1$$

and subsequently to orthogonalize the entire set. In contrast, in the standard GMRES method each new vector is immediately orthogonalized to all previous vectors. This approach significantly increases *data locality*.

Another approach is to employ BLAS2 routines as much as possible in GMRES instead of the obvious BLAS1, which is the least efficient. An algorithm proposed in [79] is to replace the modified Gram–Schmidt with the standard Gram–Schmidt but apply it twice. The double orthogonalization has been shown to reduce the numerical instability associated with the classical Gram–Schmidt method. In the context of more efficient computation, we can now compute all the *dot products* in parallel.

9.6 WHICH SOLVER TO CHOOSE?

The question of which solver and which preconditioner to choose is a complex one, and in many cases there are several good candidates. From the algorithmic point of view, we have to consider the properties of the matrix $\mathbf{A}$ and examine

- whether $\mathbf{A}$ is symmetric or nonsymmetric,
- whether $\mathbf{A}$ is positive-definite,
- whether both $\mathbf{A}$ and $\mathbf{A}^T$ are available,
- whether $\mathbf{A}$ is sparse,
- whether $\mathbf{A}$ is ill-conditioned or not, and
- whether a good preconditioner exists.

In addition, we have to consider the computational requirements and resources, namely,

- parallel or serial computation,
- vector or scalar processor,
- multithreading,
- reuse of data in cache,
- indirect addressing, and
- memory size.

Table 9.2: Main operations and storage for iterative solvers; n is the matrix order and j denotes the iteration number. The storage shown does not include the matrix storage.

These lists are indicative but not exhaustive of the issues that need to be considered in the decision regarding the choice of solver. What is obviously a faster code for serial computations is not necessarily faster on a parallel computer. In Table 9.2 we list the main operations in terms of BLAS routines of the iterative solvers we studied in this book. Algorithms that employ *dgemv*, (i.e., the matrix–vector multiplication) are typically more efficient as this operation can be done efficiently both in a serial and in a parallel environment.

For problems involving differential equations, the type of differential equation we have to deal with and the corresponding

Method	ddot	daxpy	dgemv	Storage
Jacobi			1	$3n$
SOR		1	1	$2n$
CGM	2	3	1	$6n$
GMRES	$j+1$	$j+1$	1	$(j+5)n$
QMR	2	12	2	$16n$

discretization we choose defines the linear system we solve. For Poisson and Helmholtz equations we obtain symmetric systems. Typical order-of-magnitude costs in computational work and storage for various direct and iterative solvers are shown in Table 9.3. The lower bound is of the same order of magnitude as the multigrid method. This clear advantage of multigrid, however, can easily be lost on a parallel computer because very sparse systems that need to be solved at the coarsest level of multigrid are not easily parallelizable. Hence, multigrid is not necessarily the fastest and Jacobi is not the slowest as the estimate for the serial work suggests. Similarly, the most effective (in terms of its spectrum and serial cost) preconditioner may not be the best overall preconditioner. Typically, the more sophisticated preconditioners are more complex and *simplicity* is the rule in parallel computing.

For large size problems the associated memory considerations suggest the use of iterative solvers. A possible decision tree for this case is as follows (see Figure 9.17):

Table 9.3: Computational work and storage for solution of a Poisson equation on a $N \times N$ finite difference grid; $n = N^2$. I stands for iterative and D for direct solver.

Method	Direct/iterative	Work	Storage
Multigrid	I	n	n
SSOR/Chebyshev	I	$n^{5/4}$	n
SOR	I	$n^{3/2}$	n
CGM	I	$n^{3/2}$	n
Gauss–Seidel	I	n^2	n
Jacobi	I	n^2	n
Gauss elimination/sparse	D	$n^{3/2}$	$n \cdot \log n$
Gauss elimination/dense	D	n^3	n^2

- If the matrix is symmetric and positive-definite then preconditioned conjugate gradient may be the best candidate. The question then becomes which preconditioner is the best, and this depends on the problem and on the computer.
- If **A** is not positive-definite use CGNR assuming the condition number is reasonable.
- If **A** is not symmetric then the first choice should be GMRES or GMRES(k) if memory is at a premium.
- However, if $\mathbf{A}^T$ is not available then the QMR algorithm, which is quite robust and as fast as GMRES, would be a good candidate because it works effectively even for ill-conditioned matrices.

Figure 9.17: Decision tree for which algorithm to use based upon the properties of A.

This is just one of the many possible scenarios. What makes this field interesting is that the choices are not unique!

9.7 AVAILABLE SOFTWARE FOR FAST SOLVERS

The basic algorithms we have presented in this chapter are relatively easy to program but more sophisticated versions with respect to preconditioning, restarts, orthogonalization, and parallel implementation are available in free software at **www.netlib.org.**

The direct solvers are part of ScaLAPACK and LAPACK++ whereas the iterative solvers are part of the Templates package [5].

Specifically, in ScaLAPACK/LAPACK++, for LU type operations the routine **SGETRF** performs LU factorization with pivoting based on the BLAS3 routines and therefore it is very efficient. A similar routine **SGETF2** is based on BLAS2 routines and it is also efficient. For the specific implementations involved see [26]. For symmetric positive-definite matrices the routines **SPOTRF** and **SPOTRS** perform Cholesky factorization of a matrix and solve a linear system, respectively. Finally, the routine **SPTTRF** performs an LDL^T factorization of a symmetric positive-definite matrix.

Also in ScaLAPACK/LAPACK++, for QR type operations the routine **SGEQRF** performs QR factorization and the routine **SGEQPF** performs QR factorization with column pivoting. The routine **SGERQF** performs RQ factorization and the routine **SGEHRD** reduces a general matrix to upper Hessenberg form.

The **cpptemplates** files available at **www.netlib.org** contains implementations of all the iterative solvers presented in this chapter for matrix–vector classes. In particular, the routines **cg.h** and **cheby.h** implement the conjugate gradient method and the preconditioned Chebyshev method, respectively, for symmetric positive-definite systems. The routines **cgs.h**, **gmres.h**, **qmr.h**, and **bicg.h** are suitable for nonsymmetric systems and their names indicate the corresponding algorithms.

9.8 HOMEWORK PROBLEMS

1. Find the condition number of the matrices

$$A = \begin{bmatrix} 0.001 & 1 \\ 1 & 1 \end{bmatrix} \text{ and } B = \begin{bmatrix} 7 & 6.990 \\ 4 & 4 \end{bmatrix}.$$

2. Let $\mathbf{A} = \mathbf{L}\,\mathbf{DL}^T$ be a symmetric positive-definite matrix and let $\mathbf{D} = \text{diag}\,(d_{ii})$. Then, show that

$$\kappa_2(\mathbf{A}) \geq \frac{\max(d_{ii})}{\min(d_{ii})},$$

where $\kappa_2(\mathbf{A})$ is the condition number of $\mathbf{A}$ in the L_2 norm.

3. For what values of ϵ is the matrix

$$\begin{bmatrix} 1 & \epsilon \\ \epsilon & 1 \end{bmatrix}$$

ill-conditioned? How will your results be affected if you are to compute in *single* or *double* precision?

4. Let us assume that the matrix **A** is *strictly* diagonally dominant, that is,

$$\sum_{i \neq j} |a_{ij}| < |a_{ii}|.$$

Show that if you apply the LU factorization procedure to **A** with partial pivoting, it has no effect on the rows; that is, no actual row exchange occurs. This proves what we discussed in Section 9.1.2 that no pivoting is required for a strictly diagonally dominant matrix.

5. **Almost triangular matrix – Hessenberg:** This matrix is defined by

$$a_{ij} = 0, \quad i > j + 1,$$

$$a_{ij} \neq 0, \quad i \leq j + 1.$$

Estimate the operation count for the LU factorization and the backward solve for this matrix.

6. Consider the matrix **A** written in a block 2×2 form with submatrices $\mathbf{A}_{ij}$, $i, j = 1, 2$, of equal size $m \times m$. Show that the Schur complement defined as

$$\mathbf{S} \equiv \mathbf{A}_{22} - \mathbf{A}_{21}\mathbf{A}_{11}^{-1}\mathbf{A}_{12}$$

overwrites the matrix $\mathbf{A}_{22}$ after m steps of Gaussian elimination without pivoting.

7. Apply Hager's algorithm (by hand calculation) to a (3×3) matrix whose rows $(\mathbf{r}_i, i = 1, 2, 3)$ are $\mathbf{r}_i = i + j - 1$, $j = 1, 2, 3$. Compute also the exact condition number in the L_1 norm and compare the two values.

8. Apply Hager's algorithm to estimate the condition number of the Hilbert $(n \times n)$ matrix defined by

$$h_{ij} = \frac{1}{i + j - 2}$$

for $n = 4$, 16, and 32. (Use the LAPACK routines or any other available routines.) What do you observe?

9. In the parallel LU program, we did not implement row pivoting. Modify the code given in the text to accomplish row pivoting.

10. Using the parallel LU program as a guide, implement an MPI program to accomplish Cholesky factorization.

11. Apply the *incomplete* Cholesky factorization to the tridiagonal matrix $(-1, 4, -1)$. Compare the results with the results from the standard Cholesky factorization. Does your conclusion hold for any banded matrix?

12. In the cyclic reduction code presented in this chapter, the matrix **A** is allocated as if it were a full matrix. Modify both the serial and the parallel code so that only the necessary amount of memory is used to store the tridiagonal matrix **A**.

13. Consider the following system:

$$-2x_1 + x_2 = F_1,$$
$$x_1 - 2x_2 + 2x_3 = F_2,$$
$$x_2 - 2x_3 + 2x_4 = F_3,$$
$$x_3 - 2x_4 + 2x_5 = F_4,$$
$$x_4 - 2x_5 + 2x_6 = F_5,$$
$$x_5 - 2x_6 + 2x_7 = F_6,$$
$$x_6 - 2x_7 = F_7.$$

Solve this system by hand using cyclic reduction. At what level does this system terminate, and with what equation? Is there sufficient information at the point of termination to obtain the solution? If so, accomplish the back substitution to obtain the answer.

14. Use the Householder transformation to show that if $\mathbf{H}_e$ is a Hessenberg matrix and $\mathbf{H}_e = \mathbf{QR}$ then the matrix $\mathbf{H}_e^* = \mathbf{RQ}$ is also a Hessenberg matrix.

15. The flop count for solving the overdetermined system $\mathbf{Ax} = \mathbf{b}$, where $\mathbf{A}$ is of size $m \times n$, is (choose one)

(a) $mn^2/2 + n^3/6$ for normal equations and $mn^2/2 - n^3/6$ for the Householder QR method.

(b) the reverse of (a).

(c) none of the above.

16. The flop count for QR factorization of an $n \times n$ matrix with column pivoting using the Householder method is (choose one)

(a) $\dfrac{5}{3}n^3$.

(b) $\dfrac{5}{4}n^3$.

(c) $\dfrac{4}{5}n^2$.

17. The number of additions and multiplications in Cholesky factorization is roughly half that of LU factorization.

(a) True.

(b) False.

18. The QR method conserves the bandwidth of a matrix (choose one)

(a) always.

(b) in some cases.

(c) never.

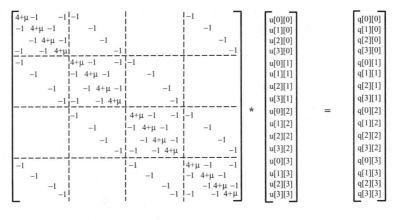

Figure 9.18: Matrix system Au = q for N = 4.

19. The QR factorization of a matrix **A** is (choose one)

    (a) always unique.

    (b) unique if **A** is nonsingular.

    (c) not unique.

20. The most efficient way of distributing a matrix on a parallel machine (choose one)

    (a) is by rows.

    (b) is by columns.

    (c) depends on the problem one is trying to solve.

21. Define $h = \frac{1}{N}$, $\mu = h^2$, and $q[i][j] = (8\pi^2 + 1)h^2 \sin(2\pi hi)\sin(2\pi hj)$, where $i, j = 0, \ldots, N-1$. Let **A** be of the form given in Figure 9.18.
    Solve the matrix system **Au** = **q** for **u** using the following methods:

    (a) Serial Jacobi.

    (b) Parallel Jacobi.

    (c) Serial conjugate gradient.

    (d) Serial preconditioned conjugate gradient, preconditioned using incomplete Cholesky.

    (e) Parallel conjugate gradient.

    (f) Parallel preconditioned conjugate gradient, preconditioned using incomplete Cholesky.

Solve for both $N = 4$ and $N = 20$. Here N denotes the number of points used in both the x- and y-directions (hence the total number of grid points is N^2, which corresponds to the rank of the matrix for which we are solving). For the serial algorithms, provide a graphical plot of the solution $u[i][j]$ at the points (hi, hj) (either a contour or surface plot). For the parallel algorithms, show the parallel speedup using different number of processors (this will require you to use the *MPI_Wtime* function to time your runs).

22. Solve the Poisson equation on a three-dimensional grid $N \times N \times N$ using a second-order finite difference discretization with Dirichlet boundary conditions. Employ the following (serial) algorithms:

    (a) Conjugate gradients.

    (b) Conjugate gradients with incomplete Cholesky as preconditioner.

    (c) SSOR with Chebyshev acceleration.

    (d) Jacobi.

    Estimate the computational work in terms of $\mathcal{O}(n^\alpha)$; that is, find α. Verify these estimates by solving for $n = N^3 = 64^3$ and timing your codes on the same computer.

23. In the text we presented a QR factorization example using the Hilbert matrix. At the conclusion of the example, we had constructed the matrix $\mathbf{R}$. From the values of $\mathbf{w}$ found in the example, compute the matrix $\mathbf{Q}$ and show that indeed $\mathbf{A} = \mathbf{QR}$.

    (*Hint*: Recall that the Householder matrix is given by

    $$\mathbf{H} = \mathbf{I} - 2\frac{\mathbf{w}\mathbf{w}^T}{\mathbf{w}^T\mathbf{w}}.$$

    Construct $\mathbf{H}_1$ and $\mathbf{H}_2$ and use them to construct $\mathbf{Q}$ by the expressions given in the text.)

24. Modify the QR routine in the text so that it computes the value of $\mathbf{Q}$. You will need to modify the input arguments of the function to accept an SCMatrix Q, which you should fill in with the appropriate values.

25. Write a serial function that accomplishes QR decomposition of a tri-diagonal matrix using Givens rotations. The function should have at least the following three arguments: the matrix $\mathbf{A}$ as input and the matrices $\mathbf{Q}$ and $\mathbf{R}$ as output.

26. Create a function that solves the system $\mathbf{Ax} = \mathbf{b}$ for tridiagonal matrices $\mathbf{A}$ and uses the QR code you wrote previously. What property of both $\mathbf{Q}$ and $\mathbf{R}$ can we use to accomplish this efficiently?

27. Write a parallel program that accomplishes QR decomposition of a tri-diagonal matrix using Givens rotations. Partition the matrix $\mathbf{A}$ by rows across the processors. Design your program so that each processor has the rows of $\mathbf{Q}$ and $\mathbf{R}$ that correspond to the rows of $\mathbf{A}$ that reside on the processor.

28. Consider five symmetric Toeplitz matrices $\mathbf{A}$ with entries given by $(k = 1, \ldots, n)$

    $$a_k^{(1)} = 1/k, \quad a_k^{(2)} = 1/\sqrt{k}, \quad a_k^{(3)} = 1/k^2, \quad a_k^{(4)} = k, \quad a_k^{(5)} = \cos k/k$$

    and an arbitrary nonzero vector $\mathbf{b}$. Use PCGM to solve the systems $\mathbf{Ax} = \mathbf{b}$ with circulant preconditioners and experiment with different types (i.e., number of Toeplitz diagonals employed). Compare your results without CG preconditioning in terms of the number of iterations for sizes up to $n = 100$ and tolerance levels just above single machine accuracy.

29. Estimate the operation count for GMRES(k) for fixed k and compare it with GMRES assuming a large value of the order n of matrix $\mathbf{A}$. Does GMRES(k) converge for any value of k?

30. For the GMRES example problem given in the text, use the function provided to attempt GMRES(2). Add *cout* statements to report the residual. Try a variety of different initial guesses $\mathbf{x}_0$ and plot the residual versus iteration for each case. Is the convergence rate the same?

31. Consider the linear advection–diffusion equation

$$\frac{\partial u}{\partial t} + \frac{\partial u}{\partial x} = \nu \frac{\partial^2 u}{\partial x^2},$$

where ν is the diffusion coefficient, in the domain

$$x \in [0, 10] \quad \text{and} \quad t \in [0, 5].$$

We also assume periodic boundary conditions and that the initial conditions are

$$u(0 \le x \le 1; 0) = x(1 - x) \quad \text{and} \quad u(1 \le x \le 10; 0) = 0.$$

Employ a second-order upwind scheme for the advection and a central finite difference scheme for the diffusion (with a Crank–Nicolson in time) to discretize this problem. Invert the resulting system using GMRES(k) and experiment with different values of k to minimize the solution time. Use $n = 128$ points for the discretization. Does the value of optimum k depend on the time step Δt? Is this method unconditionally stable?

10

Fast Eigensolvers

In this chapter we introduce methods for solutions of the standard eigenvalue problem

$$\mathbf{Ax} = \lambda \mathbf{x},$$

where $\mathbf{A}$ is a square $n \times n$ matrix, as well as for generalized eigenproblems. The main theory is based on the solvers of the previous chapter for linear systems. Unlike, however, the methods of the previous chapter where both direct and iterative approaches are effective, in eigenvalue problems only iterative solvers are efficient. We start with the simple power method and its variants, and we proceed with more sophisticated methods including a method for nonsymmetric eigenproblems using the Arnoldi iteration. We classify the different eigensolvers as *local* or *global* depending on whether they are typically used to compute one or two eigenvalues or the entire spectrum, respectively.

We introduce one new MPI function, *MPI_Alltoall*, and demonstrate its use through some of the algorithms presented in this chapter. In addition, we reiterate the use of *MPI_Allgather* and *MPI_Allreduce* through example implementations of algorithms.

10.1 LOCAL EIGENSOLVERS

We have already seen in Chapter 2 that computing the eigenvalues accurately from the determinant may not always be possible. The Newton–Raphson method of Chapter 4 is an accurate method of computing the roots of the characteristic polynomial, but it can be extremely inefficient for large systems. In the following, we present a simple method to compute iteratively the *maximum* and *minimum* eigenvalues and corresponding eigenvectors. We can also compute any other eigenvalue for which we have a good initial guess.

10.1.1 Basic Power Method

The basic power method is a very simple method to obtain the *maximum* eigenvalue. The main idea is to obtain iterates from

$$\mathbf{x}^{k+1} = c\mathbf{Ax}^k,$$

where c is a normalization constant that prevents $\mathbf{x}^{k+1}$ from becoming too large. After many iterations ($k \to \infty$), $\mathbf{x}^{k+1}$ will converge to the eigenvector $\mathbf{v}_1$ of $\mathbf{A}$ corresponding to the maximum eigenvalue λ_1. Here, we assume that there exists an eigenvalue λ_1 that dominates, that is,

$$|\lambda_1| > |\lambda_2| \geq |\lambda_3| \ldots \geq |\lambda_n|.$$

We can initialize this iteration by an arbitrary (nonzero) vector $\mathbf{x}^0$.

To see why this process converges and at what rate, we project the initial guess $\mathbf{x}^0$ to the space spanned by all the eigenvector $\mathbf{v}_i$ of $\mathbf{A}$, that is,

$$\mathbf{x}^0 = c_1 \mathbf{v}_1 + c_2 \mathbf{v}_2 + \cdots + c_n \mathbf{v}_n,$$

and thus

$$\mathbf{x}^k = \mathbf{A}\mathbf{x}^{k-1} = \ldots = A^k \mathbf{x}^0 = c_1 \lambda_1^k \mathbf{v}_1 + \cdots + c_n \lambda_n^k \mathbf{v}_n.$$

Now, we see that

$$\frac{\mathbf{x}^k}{c_1 \lambda_1^k} = \mathbf{v}_1 + \frac{c_2}{c_1}\left(\frac{\lambda_2}{\lambda_1}\right)^k \mathbf{v}_2 + \cdots + \frac{c_n}{c_1}\left(\frac{\lambda_n}{\lambda_1}\right)^k \mathbf{v}_n$$

converges to $\mathbf{v}_1$ because all factors

$$\left(\frac{\lambda_i}{\lambda_1}\right)^k, \ i \neq 1,$$

are less than one and tend to zero for $k \to \infty$.

The *convergence rate* is determined by the relative magnitude of the second largest to the largest term, that is, by the ratio

$$\frac{|\lambda_2|}{|\lambda_1|},$$

which represents the most resistive contribution to the error. The smaller this ratio is the faster the convergence is.

The following pseudo-code summarizes the algorithm:

Initialize: $\mathbf{x}^0$
Begin Loop: for $k = 1, 2, \ldots$

$$\hat{\mathbf{x}}^k = \mathbf{A}\mathbf{x}^{k-1}$$

$$\mathbf{x}_k = \frac{\hat{\mathbf{x}}^k}{\max(\hat{\mathbf{x}}^k)}$$
endfor

End Loop:

Here, the operator $\max(\mathbf{y})$ of a vector $\mathbf{y}$ returns the entry of $\mathbf{y}$ with the maximum modulus. Hence if $\mathbf{y} = (4.32, -9.88, 2.9)^T$, $\max(\mathbf{y}) = -9.88$ since $|-9.88| > |4.32| > |2.9|$. This operation is used merely for normalization of the eigenvector. Upon termination of the loop, $\max(\hat{\mathbf{x}}^k) \to \lambda_1$ and $\mathbf{x}^k \to \mathbf{v}_1$.

Table 10.1: Sequence converging to the largest eigenvalue of the 3 × 3 Hilbert matrix.

EXAMPLE. Let us consider the 3 × 3 Hilbert matrix

$$\mathbf{A} = \begin{bmatrix} 1 & \frac{1}{2} & \frac{1}{3} \\ \frac{1}{2} & \frac{1}{3} & \frac{1}{4} \\ \frac{1}{3} & \frac{1}{4} & \frac{1}{5} \end{bmatrix}$$

Iteration	Eigenvalue iterate
0	1.833333333
1	1.437878788
2	1.410835968
3	1.408537172
4	1.408337881
5	1.408320573
6	1.40831907
7	1.40831894
8	1.408318928

to which we will apply the power method to find its maximum eigenvalue. Starting with an initial guess of $(1, 1, 1)^T$, we obtain the sequence of eigenvalue iterates listed in Table 10.1. The iteration terminates when the absolute difference between successive iterates is less than 10^{-7}. In this algorithm the value of λ_1 is estimated from the maximum component of $\mathbf{x}^k$. However, any other norm can be used, for example, the L_2 norm

$$\lambda_1 = \frac{\parallel \mathbf{x}^{k+1} \parallel}{\parallel \mathbf{x}^k \parallel} = \frac{\parallel \mathbf{A}\mathbf{x}^k \parallel}{\parallel \mathbf{x}^k \parallel},$$

or alternatively the eigenvalue can be computed via the *Rayleigh quotient*. This is defined by

$$R(\mathbf{A}, \mathbf{x}^k) = \frac{(\mathbf{x}^k)^T \mathbf{A}\mathbf{x}^k}{\parallel \mathbf{x}^k \parallel^2}.$$

If $\mathbf{x} = \mathbf{v}_1$ (i.e., the first eigenvector), then obviously $R(\mathbf{A}, \mathbf{v}_1) = \lambda_1$. In general, if $\mathbf{A}$ is a *symmetric matrix* and $\mathbf{x}$ is a close approximation to the eigenvector $\mathbf{v}_1$, the Rayleigh quotient is close to the corresponding eigenvalue λ_1. This can be seen by projecting $\mathbf{x} = \sum_{i=1}^n c_i \mathbf{v}_i$, as before, where the $\mathbf{v}_i$ are orthonormal owing to the symmetry of $\mathbf{A}$, and $\mathbf{v}_i^T \mathbf{v}_i = 1$. Then

$$R(\mathbf{A}, \mathbf{x}) = \frac{\mathbf{x}^T \mathbf{A}\mathbf{x}}{\mathbf{x}^T \mathbf{x}} = \frac{(c_1\mathbf{v}_1 + \cdots + c_n\mathbf{v}_n)^T \mathbf{A}(c_1\mathbf{v}_1 + \cdots + c_n\mathbf{v}_n)}{c_1^2 + c_2^2 + \cdots + c_n^2}$$

$$= \frac{\lambda_1 c_1^2 + \lambda_2 c_2^2 + \cdots + \lambda_n c_n^2}{c_1^2 + c_2^2 + \cdots + c_n^2}$$

$$= \lambda_1 \left[\frac{1 + \left(\frac{\lambda_2}{\lambda_1}\right)\left(\frac{c_2}{c_1}\right)^2 + \cdots + \left(\frac{\lambda_n}{\lambda_1}\right)\left(\frac{c_n}{c_1}\right)^2}{1 + \left(\frac{c_2}{c_1}\right)^2 + \cdots + \left(\frac{c_n}{c_1}\right)^2} \right].$$

Because of our assumption that $\mathbf{x} \approx \mathbf{v}_1$ we have that $c_1 \gg c_i$, $\forall i \neq 1$, and thus, the quantity in brackets tends to 1, and correspondingly $R(\mathbf{A}, \mathbf{x})$ tends to λ_1.

The convergence of the power method can be enhanced by *shifting* the eigenvalues, so instead of multiplying the initial guess by powers of $\mathbf{A}$ we multiply by powers of $(\mathbf{A} - \sigma\mathbf{I})$, which has eigenvalues $(\lambda_i - \sigma)$ but the same eigenvectors. The corresponding convergence rate is then estimated by

$$\left| \frac{\lambda_2 - \sigma}{\lambda_1 - \sigma} \right|.$$

We can exploit this to enhance convergence by carefully choosing σ to significantly reduce this fraction. If all the eigenvalues are real, the best shift is either

$$\sigma = \frac{1}{2}(\lambda_2 + \lambda_n)$$

or

$$\sigma = \frac{1}{2}(\lambda_1 + \lambda_{n-1})$$

depending on whether $(\lambda_1 - \lambda_2)$ or $(\lambda_{n-1} - \lambda_n)$ is larger, respectively.

REMARK: If the eigenvalue λ_1 is complex the power method fails unless complex arithmetic is used with an initial complex vector $\mathbf{x}^0$.

10.1.2 Inverse Shifted Power Method

To selectively compute the *minimum* eigenvalue we can again apply the power method by multiplying by powers of the inverse (i.e., $\mathbf{A}^{-1}$). Thus, the iteration procedure here is

$$\mathbf{A}\mathbf{x}^{k+1} = c\,\mathbf{x}^k,$$

where again c is a normalization constant. This method is most effective with a proper shift, so the modified iteration is

$$(\mathbf{A} - \sigma\mathbf{I})\mathbf{x}^{k+1} = c\,\mathbf{x}^k,$$

and the solution will converge to the smallest shifted eigenvalue $|\lambda_n - \sigma|$ and the corresponding eigenvector, assuming that the shift σ is close to λ_n (the smallest eigenvalue). The rate of convergence is now

$$\frac{|\lambda_n - \sigma|}{|\lambda_{n-1} - \sigma|},$$

so if σ is close to λ_n, this ratio is very small and convergence is very fast. Clearly, if σ is close to any other eigenvalue λ_i the corresponding contribution dominates and then we obtain the eigenpair $(\lambda_i, \mathbf{v}_i)$. Hence, if we have a collection of approximations σ_i to the true eigenvalues λ_i, we can use the inverse shifted power method to obtain all the eigenpairs $(\lambda_i, \mathbf{v}_i)$.

The following pseudo-code summarizes the algorithm:

Initialize: Choose $\mathbf{x}^0$
             Choose σ
             Factorize $\mathbf{A} - \sigma\mathbf{I} = \mathbf{L}\,\mathbf{U}$

Begin Loop: for $k = 1, 2, \ldots$

$$\hat{\mathbf{x}}^k = \mathbf{U}^{-1}\mathbf{L}^{-1}\mathbf{x}^{k-1}$$

$$\mathbf{x}^k = \frac{\hat{\mathbf{x}}^k}{\max(\mathbf{x}^k)}$$

if $|R(\mathbf{A}, \mathbf{x}^k) - R(\mathbf{A}, \mathbf{x}^{k-1})| < \epsilon$

        return
    endfor

Upon termination (after the tolerance ϵ is reached), $\mathbf{x}^k$ converges to the desired eigenvector, and the corresponding eigenvalue can be computed from the Rayleigh quotient.

REMARK 1: Note that we do not actually compute explicitly the inverse $\mathbf{A}^{-1}$ or $(\mathbf{A} - \sigma\mathbf{I})^{-1}$; we simply perform an LU factorization only once outside the loop. The computational complexity of this algorithm is $\mathcal{O}(n^2)$ times the number of iterations plus the initial $\mathcal{O}(2n^3/3)$ cost for the LU factorization.

REMARK 2: If an iterative solver is used instead of the LU factorization for the linear solver, then a slightly more stringent tolerance can be used for the linear solver compared to the desired accuracy in eigenvalue. This idea can be used when $\mathbf{A}$ is sparse and may result in substantial savings.

REMARK 3: To accelerate convergence, we can start with a few iterations using the standard power method, obtain a first good guess and corresponding shift σ via the Rayleigh quotient, and then switch to the inverse iteration method.

REMARK 4: The matrix $(\mathbf{A} - \sigma\mathbf{I})$ is ill-conditioned; however, in practice the error associated with this seems to favor the inverse iteration as it grows toward the direction of the desired eigenvector. Therefore, the inverse shifted power method is a *stable* method.

We can modify the inverse shifted power method and enhance convergence even more (to third order) if we update the value of the shift adaptively using the **Rayleigh quotient**.

The following algorithm presents this modification:

Initialize: Choose $\mathbf{x}^0$

Compute $\sigma_0 = \dfrac{(\mathbf{x}^0)^T \mathbf{A} \mathbf{x}^0}{(\mathbf{x}^0)^T \mathbf{x}^0}$

Begin Loop: for $k = 0, 1, \ldots$

$$\mathbf{L}^k \mathbf{U}^k = \mathbf{A} - \sigma_k \mathbf{I}$$

$$\hat{\mathbf{x}}^{k+1} = (\mathbf{U}^k)^{-1}(\mathbf{L}^k)^{-1}\mathbf{x}^k$$

$$\mathbf{x}^{k+1} = \frac{\hat{\mathbf{x}}^{k+1}}{\max(\hat{\mathbf{x}}^{k+1})}$$

$$\sigma_{k+1} = \frac{(\mathbf{x}^{k+1})^T \mathbf{A} \mathbf{x}^{k+1}}{(\mathbf{x}^{k+1})^T \mathbf{x}^{k+1}}$$

if $|\sigma_{k+1} - \sigma_k| < \epsilon$

return

endfor

End Loop

REMARK 5: Although this algorithm triples the number of correct digits in each iteration it requires $\mathcal{O}(n^3)$ work at each iteration because the matrix $(\mathbf{A} - \sigma_k \mathbf{I})$ changes in each iteration. A more economical approach is to "freeze" σ_k for a few iterations so that the LU decomposition is not employed in each iteration. The resulting convergence rate is then *less than cubic,* but overall this is a more efficient approach.

PUTTING IT INTO PRACTICE

We now present an implementation of the inverse shifted power method with Rayleigh quotient adaptation. This function takes two inputs: the matrix $\mathbf{A}$, for which we are interested in finding an eigenvalue and eigenvector, and a vector $\mathbf{x}$ containing the initial guess $\mathbf{x}^0$. This function has as its return value an eigenvalue of $\mathbf{A}$, and it places the corresponding eigenvector associated with the eigenvalue in the vector $\mathbf{x}$.

Software

Suite

```
double ISPowerMethod(SCMatrix &A, SCVector &x){
   const int maxit = 100;
   const double tol = 1.0e-7;
   double tmp,sigma1,sigma2;
   SCMatrix Amod(A.Rows());
```

```
SCVector y(A.Rows());

// Calculation of the Rayleigh quotient
y = A*x;
sigma1 = dot(y,x)/dot(x,x);

for(int k=0;k<maxit;k++){
  Amod = A;

  for(int i=0;i<Amod.Rows();i++)
    Amod(i,i) = Amod(i,i) - sigma1;

  // Use LU solver from Chapter 9 to obtain solution x
  GaussElimination(Amod, x, 1);

  // Normalize with the element of maximum modulus
  tmp = x.ElementofMaxMod();
  x = x/tmp;

  y = A*x;
  sigma2 = dot(y,x)/dot(x,x);

  if(fabs(sigma1-sigma2) < tol)
    return sigma2;

  sigma1 = sigma2;
}

cout << "ISPowerMethod - Max number of iterations reached\n";
return sigma2;
}
```

REMARK 6: A downside of this implementation is that we require storage of an additional matrix MatAmod having the same size as **A**. We have chosen to do this because we want to be able to reuse the LU solver we implemented in Chapter 9. If memory were at a premium, we could rewrite the LU solver to take into account the modification to the diagonal entry, and hence we would not need to store an additional matrix.

EXAMPLE. Let us consider the 3×3 Hilbert matrix

$$\mathbf{A} = \begin{bmatrix} 1 & \dfrac{1}{2} & \dfrac{1}{3} \\ \dfrac{1}{2} & \dfrac{1}{3} & \dfrac{1}{4} \\ \dfrac{1}{3} & \dfrac{1}{4} & \dfrac{1}{5} \end{bmatrix}$$

and use the inverse shifted power method to solve for the maximum eigenvalue. Using the preceding program, if we take the initial eigenvector guess to be

$$\begin{bmatrix} 1.0 \\ 1.0 \\ 1.0 \end{bmatrix},$$

we obtain the eigenvalue 1.40832 and corresponding eigenvector

$$\begin{bmatrix} 1.0 \\ 0.556033 \\ 0.390908 \end{bmatrix}.$$

Observe that this is the same maximum eigenvalue we found before using the power method (as it should be!). If, however, we take the initial eigenvector guess to be

$$\begin{bmatrix} 0.4 \\ -0.4 \\ -0.4 \end{bmatrix}$$

we obtain the eigenvalue 0.122327 and corresponding eigenvector

$$\begin{bmatrix} -0.843517 \\ 0.813998 \\ 1.0 \end{bmatrix}.$$

As was pointed out earlier, the inverse shifted power method allows us to pick up different eigenvalues (other than just the minimum) based upon the initial eigenvector guess. In this case, our initial guess provided us with the second largest eigenvalue of the Hilbert matrix.

10.2 HOUSEHOLDER DEFLATION

The Householder transformation is very useful in "deflating" a matrix [i.e., reducing its size from $n \times n$ to $(n-1) \times (n-1)$]. This is often needed in eigensolvers, especially in conjunction with local and semidirect methods. The objective is to compute the subdominant eigenvalues after we compute the maximum or minimum eigenvalue with the power method or inverse power method, respectively.

Let us assume that we have computed the maximum eigenvalue λ_1 and the corresponding eigenvector $\mathbf{v}_1$. Recall from Section 9.3 that we can then obtain a Householder matrix $\mathbf{H}$ by

$$\mathbf{H}\mathbf{v}_1 = \begin{bmatrix} \alpha \\ 0 \\ \vdots \\ 0 \end{bmatrix} = \alpha \mathbf{e}_1.$$

We now construct the matrix $\mathbf{G} \equiv \mathbf{HAH}^T$ and investigate its structure. Since $(\lambda_1, \mathbf{v}_1)$ is an eigenpair it satisfies

$$\mathbf{Av}_1 = \lambda_1 \mathbf{v}_1 \Rightarrow \mathbf{HAv}_1 = \lambda_1 \mathbf{Hv}_1$$

$$\Rightarrow \mathbf{HA} \cdot \mathbf{I} \cdot \mathbf{v}_1 = \lambda_1 \mathbf{Hv}_1 \Rightarrow \mathbf{HA} \cdot (\mathbf{H}^T\mathbf{H}) \cdot \mathbf{v}_1 = \lambda_1 \mathbf{Hv}_1$$

$$\Rightarrow \mathbf{H} \cdot \mathbf{A} \cdot \mathbf{H}^T(\mathbf{Hv}_1) = \lambda_1(\mathbf{Hv}_1),$$

where we recall that $\mathbf{H}$ is orthonormal and thus $\mathbf{I} = \mathbf{H}^T \cdot \mathbf{H}$. We also have by definition that

$$\mathbf{Hv}_1 = \alpha \mathbf{e}_1$$

so by substituting into the previous equations, we obtain

$$\mathbf{H} \cdot \mathbf{A} \cdot \mathbf{H}^T(\alpha \mathbf{e}_1) = \lambda_1 \alpha \mathbf{e}_1 \Rightarrow \mathbf{Ge}_1 = \lambda_1 \mathbf{e}_1 = \begin{bmatrix} \lambda_1 \\ 0 \\ \vdots \\ 0 \end{bmatrix}.$$

Therefore, the matrix $\mathbf{G}$ has the form

$$\mathbf{G} = \begin{bmatrix} \lambda_1 \ast \ast & \ast & \ast \ast \\ \vdots & \mathbf{A}_{n-1} \\ 0 \end{bmatrix},$$

where $\mathbf{A}_{n-1}$ is a submatrix $(n-1) \times (n-1)$ that has the same $(n-1)$ remaining eigenvalues of $\mathbf{A}$. Stars denote values changed by the procedure. This can be seen by computing

$$\det(\mathbf{G} - \lambda \mathbf{I}) = (\lambda_1 - \lambda) \cdot \det(\mathbf{A}_{n-1} - \lambda \mathbf{I}) = 0.$$

To compute the first subdominant eigenvalue of $\mathbf{A}$ we then need to apply the power method to $\mathbf{A}_{n-1}$, repeat the process once more, and so on.

We now recapitulate the basic algorithm:

1. Compute the maximum eigenvalue λ_1 and the corresponding eigenvector $\mathbf{v}_1$ using the power method or shifted inverse power method.
2. Obtain the Householder matrix $\mathbf{H}$ using the eigenvector $\mathbf{v}_1$.
3. Form the matrix $\mathbf{G} = \mathbf{HAH}^T$.
4. Extract the eigenvalue at G_{11}.
5. Define $\mathbf{A}_{n-1} \equiv G_{2:n,2:n}$.
6. Repeat the process on the newly defined matrix $\mathbf{A}_{n-1}$.

The deflation procedure can be applied efficiently if we want to compute *two* to *three* eigenvalues. For a larger number of eigenvalues we need to switch to global eigensolvers (see Section 10.3).

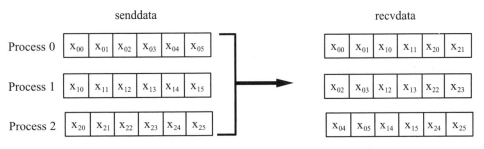

senddata · recvdata

Figure 10.1:
MPI_Alltoall schematic demonstrating data distribution to all processes of two data objects from each process.

REMARK: Another deflation procedure is to subtract the contribution $\lambda_1 \mathbf{v}_1 \mathbf{v}_1^T$, from the matrix $\mathbf{A}$, so the new matrix

$$\mathbf{A}_1 \equiv \mathbf{A} - \lambda_1 \mathbf{v}_1 \mathbf{v}_1^T$$

has eigenvalues $0, \lambda_2, \lambda_3, \dots, \lambda_n$. However, this procedure could sometimes be unstable, unlike the Householder deflation, which is always stable.

PUTTING IT INTO PRACTICE

We will now present a program for accomplishing one iteration of the algorithm just recapitulated. To accomplish this algorithm, we must introduce a new MPI function, *MPI_Alltoall*. This function allows a "scatter" from each process simultaneously (see Figure 10.1). We will now present the function call syntax, argument list explanation, usage example, and some remarks.

Software Suite

MPI_Alltoall

FUNCTION CALL SYNTAX

```
int MPI_Alltoall(
        void*          sendbuf     /*  in   */,
        int            sendcount   /*  in   */,
        MPI_Datatype   sendtype    /*  in   */,
        void*          recvbuf     /*  out  */,
        int            recvcount   /*  in   */,
        MPI_Datatype   recvtype    /*  in   */,
        MPI_Comm       comm        /*  in   */)
```

MPI

UNDERSTANDING THE ARGUMENT LIST

MPI

- *sendbuf* – starting address of the send buffer.
- *sendcount* – number of elements in the send buffer.
- *sendtype* – data type of the elements in the send buffer.
- *recvbuf* – starting address of the receive buffer.
- *recvcount* – number of elements for any *single* receive.

- *recvtype* – data type of the elements in the receive buffer.
- *comm* – communicator.

EXAMPLE OF USAGE

```
int mynode, totalnodes;
int datasize; // number of data units to be sent/recv
               // from each process

MPI_Init(&argc,&argv);
MPI_Comm_size(MPI_COMM_WORLD, &totalnodes);
MPI_Comm_rank(MPI_COMM_WORLD, &mynode);

// Determine datasize

double * senddata = new double[datasize*totalnodes];
double * recvdata = new double[datasize*totalnodes];

// Fill in senddata array for each process

MPI_Alltoall(senddata,datasize,MPI_DOUBLE,recvdata,datasize,
             MPI_DOUBLE,MPI_COMM_WORLD);

// At this point, each process has received from each
// process the contents of senddata and stored them
// in recvdata according to the process ordering
```

REMARKS

- *MPI_Alltoall* is a collective operation (i.e., it should be called by all processes within the communicator).
- Both the *sendbuf* and *recvbuf* arrays are relevant on all processes in the communicator.
- In most cases the *sendtype* and *recvtype* are identical and the value of *sendcount* and the value of *recvcount* are identical. MPI requires that the amount of data sent (sendcount times the size in bytes of the datatype sendtype) equals the amount of data received (recvcount times the size in bytes of the datatype recvtype) per process/root pair.
- The allocated size of both the *sendbuf* and *recvbuf* arrays should be at least equal to the value of *recvtype* times the number of processes (*totalnodes*).

We now present an MPI program to accomplish one iteration of the previously presented Householder deflation algorithm. In this program, we assume that the size of the matrix is divisible by the number of processes used. For the purpose of this example, we will once again use the Vandermonde matrix formed at the Chebyshev points. It will be distributed by rows across the processes (each process forming only those rows it needs). Observe that we will once again use *MPI_Allreduce* and *MPI_Allgather* (as part of the power method algorithm), and that we introduce the use of *MPI_Alltoall*.

We now present the source code for this program and will provide some remarks following it.

```cpp
#include <iostream.h>
#include <iomanip.h>
#include "SCmathlib.h"
#include "SCchapter3.h"
#include<mpi.h>

void ChebyVandermonde(int npts, double *A, int row);

// Global variable to set size of the system
const int size = 10;

int main(int argc, char *argv[]){
  int i,j,k,index,cnt;
  int mynode, totalnodes;
  double tmps1,tmps2,sum,total;
  const int maxit = 1000; //maximum number of iterations
                          //for the power method

  MPI_Init(&argc,&argv);
  MPI_Comm_size(MPI_COMM_WORLD, &totalnodes);
  MPI_Comm_rank(MPI_COMM_WORLD, &mynode);

  int numrows = size/totalnodes;
  double **A_local   = new double*[numrows];
  double **A_local_t = new double*[numrows];
  double * xold = new double[size];
  double * xnew = new double[numrows];
  double * tmparray = new double[size];

  for(i=0;i<numrows;i++){
    A_local[i] = new double[size];
    A_local_t[i] = new double[size];
    index = mynode*numrows + i;
    ChebyVandermonde(size,A_local[i],index);
  }

  /****************************************************/
  /* Use the power method to obtain the first eigenvector */
  /****************************************************/

  // Initialize starting vector to 1.0
  for(i=0;i<size;i++)
    xold[i] = 1.0;

  for(int it=0;it<maxit;it++){
    // Matrix-vector multiplication
    for(i=0;i<numrows;i++)
      xnew[i] = dot(size,A_local[i],xold);
```

```
    // Compute Euclidian norm of new vector
    sum = 0.0;
    for(i=0;i<numrows;i++)
      sum += xnew[i]*xnew[i];
    MPI_Allreduce(&sum,&total,1,MPI_DOUBLE,
                  MPI_SUM,MPI_COMM_WORLD);
    total = sqrt(total);

    // Scale vector by its norm
    for(i=0;i<numrows;i++)
      xnew[i] = xnew[i]/total;

    // Gather (Allgather) new vector to all processors
    MPI_Allgather(xnew,numrows,MPI_DOUBLE,tmparray,numrows,
  MPI_DOUBLE,MPI_COMM_WORLD);

    // Compute difference between old and new vector
    sum = 0.0;
    for(i=0;i<size;i++){
      sum += (xold[i]-tmparray[i])*(xold[i]-tmparray[i]);
      xold[i] = tmparray[i]; //replace old with new
    }

    if(sqrt(sum) < 1.0e-7) //termination condition
      break;
  }

  // Modify eigenvector per Householder transformation
  xold[0] = xold[0] + Sign(xold[0]);

  /**********************************************/
  /* Compute S = A*H (S is a temporary state    */
  /* stored in A_local)                         */
  /**********************************************/

  tmps1 = dot(size,xold,xold);
  for(i=0;i<numrows;i++){
    tmps2 = dot(size,A_local[i],xold);
    for(j=0;j<size;j++)
      A_local[i][j] = A_local[i][j] - 2.0*tmps2*xold[j]/tmps1;
  }

  /****************************/
  /* Transpose temporary state S */
  /****************************/

  for(i=0;i<numrows;i++){
    MPI_Alltoall(A_local[i],numrows,MPI_DOUBLE,tmparray,
                 numrows, MPI_DOUBLE,MPI_COMM_WORLD);
```

```
      cnt = 0;
      for(k=0;k<totalnodes;k++)
        for(j=0;j<numrows;j++)
  A_local_t[j][i+k*numrows] = tmparray[cnt++];
    }

    /**************************/
    /* Compute G = H*S = H*A*H */
    /**************************/

    tmps1 = dot(size,xold,xold);
    for(i=0;i<numrows;i++){
      tmps2 = dot(size,A_local_t[i],xold);
      for(j=0;j<size;j++)
        A_local_t[i][j] = A_local_t[i][j] -
                          2.0*tmps2*xold[j]/tmps1;
    }

    /*****************************************************/
    /* Transpose G so that it is stored by rows across the   */
    /* processors, just as the original A was stored        */
    /*****************************************************/

    for(i=0;i<numrows;i++){
      MPI_Alltoall(A_local_t[i],numrows,MPI_DOUBLE,tmparray,
                   numrows, MPI_DOUBLE,MPI_COMM_WORLD);
      cnt = 0;
      for(k=0;k<totalnodes;k++)
        for(j=0;j<numrows;j++)
  A_local[j][i+k*numrows] = tmparray[cnt++];
    }

    for(i=0;i<numrows;i++){
      delete[] A_local[i];
      delete[] A_local_t[i];
    }
    delete[] A_local;
    delete[] A_local_t;
    delete[] tmparray;
    delete[] xold;
    delete[] xnew;

    MPI_Finalize();
}

void ChebyVandermonde(int npts, double *A, int row){
  int i,j;
  double * x = new double[npts];
```

```
    ChebyshevPoints(npts,x);

    for(j=0;j<npts;j++)
      A[j] = pow(x[row],j);

    delete[] x;
}
```

REMARK 1: Because of the particular form of the Householder matrix, we do not have to form it explicitly. By taking advantage of this form, we can accomplish the matrix multiplication of $\mathbf{A} * \mathbf{H}$ in $\mathcal{O}(n^2)$ operations instead of the normal $\mathcal{O}(n^3)$ operations necessary for an arbitrary matrix–matrix multiplication.

REMARK 2: Observe that we use the *MPI_Alltoall* function to transpose the intermediary stage $\mathbf{A} * \mathbf{H}$ so that we can accomplish premultiplication by $\mathbf{H}$ again. Examine the indexing carefully following the MPI call. After receiving the array *tmparray*, we must now partition it properly across the rows that a processor holds.

REMARK 3: In general, the *MPI_Alltoall* function call is one of the most taxing communication calls because it requires the exchange of information from each process to all other processes. Because of this fact, the *MPI_Alltoall* function is often used in benchmarking the communication capability of parallel machines.

10.3 GLOBAL EIGENSOLVERS

Unlike local eigensolvers global methods for eigenproblems do not require a good initial guess for an eigenvalue. In addition, they provide the entire eigenspectrum. We will discuss two such approaches that are based on two different concepts: the *QR method* and the *Lanczos method*. The first one is *semidirect* and general whereas the second one is *iterative* and suitable for symmetric sparse eigensystems.

10.3.1 The QR Eigensolver

The main idea of this method is to construct a sequence of *similar* matrices $\mathbf{A}_1, \mathbf{A}_2, \ldots, \mathbf{A}_k$, where $\mathbf{A}_1 = \mathbf{A}$, and $\mathbf{A}_k$ approaches an upper triangular matrix, as $k \to \infty$, of the form

$$
\mathbf{A}_k \to \begin{bmatrix} \lambda_1 & * & * & \ldots & * \\ & \lambda_2 & * & \ldots & * \\ & & \lambda_3 & \ldots & \vdots \\ & & & \ddots & \\ \mathbf{O} & & & & \lambda_n \end{bmatrix}.
$$

The *Schur triangulization theorem* [46] guarantees that this triangular matrix exists if an orthonormal matrix $\mathbf{Q}$ is involved in the similarity transformation. If the matrix $\mathbf{A}$ is symmetric, we know that all the eigenvalues are real; the scalar entries on the diagonal correspond to those real eigenvalues. If the matrix is nonsymmetric, however, we may encounter complex eigenvalues, which manifest themselves as 2×2 submatrices on the diagonal in the form

$$\mathbf{A}_k \rightarrow \begin{bmatrix} \lambda_1 & * & * & * & \ldots & \ldots & * \\ 0 & a_{22} & a_{23} & * & \ldots & \ldots & * \\ 0 & a_{32} & a_{33} & * & \ldots & \ldots & * \\ 0 & 0 & 0 & \lambda_4 & & & \vdots \\ \vdots & & & & \lambda_5 & & \\ & & & & & \ddots & \\ 0 & & & & & & \lambda_n \end{bmatrix}.$$

These 2×2 submatrices appear also for double eigenvalues and they are sometimes referred to as *bumps*. The eigenvalues λ_2 and λ_3 can then be obtained by simply solving the second-order characteristic polynomial of the 2×2 submatrix.

We now present the basic QR iteration:

Initialize: $\mathbf{A}_0 = \mathbf{A}$ and $\mathbf{A}_0 = \mathbf{Q}_0 \mathbf{R}_0$

Begin Loop: $\mathbf{A}_1 = \mathbf{R}_0 \mathbf{Q}_0$ and $\mathbf{A}_1 = \mathbf{Q}_1 \mathbf{R}_1$

$\mathbf{A}_2 = \mathbf{R}_1 \mathbf{Q}_1$ and $\mathbf{A}_2 = \mathbf{Q}_2 \mathbf{R}_2$

$\vdots$

REMARK: The key observation to make in this algorithm is that we alternate between $\mathbf{Q}_i \mathbf{R}_i$ decompositions and $\mathbf{R}_i \mathbf{Q}_i$ products.

To prove that all matrices in the sequence are *similar*, we first examine

$$\mathbf{A}_1 = \mathbf{R}_0 \mathbf{Q}_0 = (\mathbf{Q}_0^T \mathbf{A}_0) \mathbf{Q}_0 \,;$$

since $\mathbf{Q}_0^T \mathbf{Q}_0 = \mathbf{I}$ we conclude that $\mathbf{A}_1$ is similar to $\mathbf{A}_0 = \mathbf{A}$.

This applies to iteration k as well, that is,

$$\mathbf{A}_k = \mathbf{R}_{k-1} \mathbf{Q}_{k-1} = (\mathbf{Q}_{k-1}^T \mathbf{A}_{k-1}) \mathbf{Q}_{k-1}.$$

The method *converges* if all eigenvalues have *different magnitude*, and the sequence of the diagonal will be

$$|\lambda_1| > |\lambda_2| > \ldots > |\lambda_n|$$

(see [94]); the rate of convergence is

$$\frac{|\lambda_{i+1}|}{|\lambda_i|}.$$

We note here that a similar sequence can be generated with about the same or even less computational cost by using the LU decomposition, instead of the QR factorization, this is the *LR method*. However, no pivoting can be employed as this will destroy the upper triangular structure and may change the eigenvalues (e.g., sign); thus the LU procedure will be unstable. We also note that, unlike the LU factorization, the QR decomposition can be applied to a *singular* matrix. So overall, the QR eigensolver is the preferred solution. However, a case for which the LU factorization may be used over the QR is when we have a *banded* and diagonally dominant matrix **A**. The reason is that LU preserves the bandwidth, unlike the QR approach, which fills in the (initially) zero off-diagonal elements at the rate of one additional diagonal on each side per iteration. The diagonal dominance of **A** guarantees that no pivoting is needed for stability, so overall the LR eigensolver will be a faster method in this case.

10.3.2 The Hessenberg QR Eigensolver

The basic QR method has two main disadvantages:

1. It requires QR factorization in each step, which costs

$$ \mathcal{O}\left(\frac{4n^3}{3}\right), $$

   that is, twice as much as an LU decomposition.
2. It also diverges if two eigenvalues have the same magnitude.

Fortunately, both problems have been solved!

With regards to the cost, the main idea is to *first transform* the matrix **A** to an upper Hessenberg matrix, that is,

$$ \mathbf{A} \longrightarrow \mathbf{H} $$

(see Section 9.3.1), and subsequently perform QR factorization on **H**. The method works because all subsequent matrices maintain the *Hessenberg* form, as can be verified with an example The initial cost to perform the Hessenberg reduction is

$$ \mathcal{O}\left(\frac{5}{3}n^3\right); $$

however, the QR factorization of a Hessenberg matrix is $\mathcal{O}(n^2)$, and this is the cost we incur in every iteration. Therefore, the Hessenberg QR eigensolver is an $\mathcal{O}(n)$ more efficient than the basic QR eigensolver.

10.3.3 Shifted QR Eigensolver

The convergence rate is at most *linear* for the QR eigensolver, that is, the error in every iteration is

$$ \epsilon_{k+1} \sim C\epsilon_k, $$

where $\epsilon_k \equiv \lambda_n - (a_{nn})_k$.

This is dictated by the ratio

$$\frac{|\lambda_{i+1}|}{|\lambda_i|},$$

which we want to make as small as possible. We can employ the idea of a *shift* similar to what we did in the power method (see Section 10.1.1).

Let us first assume that we have only *real* and *simple* eigenvalues. Instead of applying the QR factorization to $\mathbf{H}$ we will apply it to $(\mathbf{H} - \sigma\mathbf{I})$, thereby shifting the entire eigenspectrum by σ to $(\lambda_i - \sigma)$.

Specifically, we choose σ such that the element in the position $(n, n-1)$ converges to zero (i.e. $h_{n,n-1} \to 0$) as rapidly as possible.[1] Upon convergence, the entry in the position (n, n) (after we subtract the shift σ) will be the desired eigenvalue. Clearly, the closest estimate to λ_n we have is $h_{nn}^{(k)}$ of the matrix $\mathbf{H}_k$.

The modified algorithm to generate the sequence is then as follows:

Perform QR factorization: $\mathbf{H}_k - h_{nn}^{(k)}\mathbf{I} = \mathbf{Q}_k\mathbf{R}_k$
Obtain new iterate: $\mathbf{H}_{k+1} = \mathbf{R}_k\mathbf{Q}_k + h_{nn}^{(k)}\mathbf{I}$

and so on.

Then $\mathbf{H}_{k+1}$ is similar to $\mathbf{H}_k$ because

$$\mathbf{H}_{k+1} = \mathbf{Q}_k^T\mathbf{Q}_k\mathbf{R}_k\mathbf{Q}_k + \sigma\mathbf{I}$$
$$= \mathbf{Q}_k^T(\mathbf{Q}_k\mathbf{R}_k)\mathbf{Q}_k + \sigma\mathbf{I}$$
$$= \mathbf{Q}_k^T[\mathbf{Q}_k\mathbf{R}_k + \sigma I]\mathbf{Q}_k$$
$$= \mathbf{Q}_k^T\mathbf{H}_k\mathbf{Q}_k.$$

- The convergence of the shifted method is *quadratic* in general but increases to *cubic* if the original matrix $\mathbf{A}$ is symmetric.

For *double* or *complex* eigenvalues the shift strategy has to change to deal effectively with the "bumps" in the diagonal of the $\mathbf{A}_k$ matrix, as discussed earlier. Specifically, we modify the algorithm so that each iteration has two substeps. We can use the eigenvalues λ_2 and λ_3 of the submatrix to obtain the iterates as follows:

$$\mathbf{H}_1 - \lambda_2\mathbf{I} = \mathbf{Q}_1\mathbf{R}_1,$$
$$\mathbf{H}_2 = \mathbf{R}_1\mathbf{Q}_1 + \lambda_2\mathbf{I},$$
$$\mathbf{H}_2 - \lambda_3\mathbf{I} = \mathbf{Q}_2\mathbf{R}_2,$$
$$\mathbf{H}_3 = \mathbf{R}_2\mathbf{Q}_2 + \lambda_3\mathbf{I},$$

and so on, for subsequent iterations.

This method requires complex arithmetic because λ_2 and λ_3 may be a complex pair, which is certainly a disadvantage. However, Wilkinson [94] has come up with

---

[1] A convergence criterion used in practice is to take $|h_{i,i-1}^{(k)}| < C[|h_{ii}^{(k)}| + |h_{i-1,i-1}^k|]$.

another method that avoids complex arithmetic and is based on the sum $(\lambda_2 + \lambda_3)$ and the product $\lambda_2 \cdot \lambda_3$ of the complex pair.

REMARK: After the last eigenvalue λ_n has been obtained, deflation of the Hessenberg matrix can be applied to find the next one at reduced computational cost. In general, it takes about two to three QR iterations to compute one eigenvalue. The *total cost* is about $\mathcal{O}(10n^3)$, but such an operation count is approximate and problem dependent.

10.3.4 The Symmetric QR Eigensolver: Wilkinson Shift

Symmetric matrices are special, first because they have only *real* eigenvalues but also because the Hessenberg transformation reduces the matrix to a symmetric *tridiagonal* matrix. The QR iteration maintains this property for the entire sequence. The other good news is that the QR factorization of a symmetric tridiagonal matrix costs only $\mathcal{O}(n)$, instead of $\mathcal{O}(n^2)$ for the Hessenberg matrix. Therefore, the computational cost in this case is $\mathcal{O}(n)$ times the number of iterations to converge to all eigenvalues.

Wilkinson [94] has suggested that instead of using the $h_{nn}^{(k)}$ as the shift σ to accelerate convergence, a more effective way is to use the eigenvalue of the 2×2 matrix

$$\begin{bmatrix} h_{n-1,n-1} & h_{n,n-1} \\ h_{n,n-1} & h_{nn} \end{bmatrix},$$

which is closer to the entry h_{nn}. Convergence of the symmetric QR eigensolver is *cubic* and the operation count is $\mathcal{O}(n^2)$, but there is an $\mathcal{O}(\frac{2}{3}n^3)$ cost associated with the reduction of **A** to a tridiagonal matrix.

10.3.5 Parallel QR Eigensolver: Divide and Conquer

A fully parallel algorithm for the symmetric eigenvalue problem was developed by Dongarra and Sorensen [32]. It is based on the QR iteration and the divide-and-conquer approach we have encountered many times in this book; that is, we split the problem into two subproblems, each of which is further split into two subproblems, and so on.

First, by reducing **A** to its Hessenberg form (recall Section 9.3.1), we tridiagonalize the full symmetric matrix $\mathbf{A} \to \mathbf{T}$, where the latter has the form

$$\mathbf{T} = \begin{bmatrix} a_1 & b_1 & & & \\ b_1 & a_2 & b_2 & & \mathbf{O} \\ & \ddots & \ddots & \ddots & \\ & & b_{n-2} & a_{n-1} & b_{n-1} \\ \mathbf{O} & & & b_{n-1} & a_n \end{bmatrix}.$$

We then divide $\mathbf{T}$ into two symmetric tridiagonal matrices of half size as follows:

$$
\mathbf{T}_1 =
\begin{bmatrix}
a_1 & b_1 & & & & \\
b_1 & a_2 & b_2 & & & \mathbf{O} \\
& \ddots & \ddots & \ddots & & \\
& & b_{k-2} & a_{k-1} & b_{k-1} & \\
\mathbf{O} & & & b_{k-1} & a_k & -b_k
\end{bmatrix}
$$

and

$$
\mathbf{T}_2 =
\begin{bmatrix}
(a_{k+1} - b_k) & & b_{k+1} & & & \\
b_{k+1} & a_{k+2} & & b_{k+2} & & \mathbf{O} \\
\ddots & & \ddots & & & \ddots \\
& & & & & b_{n-1} \\
\mathbf{O} & b_{n-1} & & & a_n &
\end{bmatrix},
$$

so that

$$
\mathbf{T} =
\begin{bmatrix}
\mathbf{T}_1 & 0 \\
0 & \mathbf{T}_2
\end{bmatrix}
+ b_k \mathbf{z}\mathbf{z}^T,
$$

where

$$
\mathbf{z} =
\begin{bmatrix}
0 \\
\vdots \\
0 \\
1 \\
1 \\
\vdots \\
0
\end{bmatrix},
$$

with the two 1s being the kth and $(k+1)$th entries. Next, we can diagonalize both $\mathbf{T}_1$ and $\mathbf{T}_2$ using appropriate orthogonal matrices $\mathbf{Q}_1$ and $\mathbf{Q}_2$ as follows:

$$
\mathbf{T}_1 = \mathbf{Q}_1 \mathbf{D}_1 \mathbf{Q}_1^T \text{ and } \mathbf{T}_2 = \mathbf{Q}_2 \mathbf{D}_2 \mathbf{Q}_2^T,
$$

where

$$
\mathbf{D}_1 \equiv
\begin{bmatrix}
d_1 & & & \\
& d_2 & & \mathbf{O} \\
& & \ddots & \\
\mathbf{O} & & & d_k
\end{bmatrix}
\text{ and } \mathbf{D}_2 \equiv
\begin{bmatrix}
d_{k+1} & & & \\
& d_{k+2} & & \mathbf{O} \\
& & \ddots & \\
\mathbf{O} & & & d_n
\end{bmatrix}
$$

and

$$
\mathbf{D} \equiv
\begin{bmatrix}
\mathbf{D}_1 & 0 \\
0 & \mathbf{D}_2
\end{bmatrix}.
$$

Based on this definition and by introducing

$$\xi = \begin{bmatrix} \mathbf{Q}_1 & 0 \\ 0 & \mathbf{Q}_2 \end{bmatrix}^T \mathbf{z}$$

we can rewrite the matrix $\mathbf{T}$ as

$$\mathbf{T} = \begin{bmatrix} \mathbf{Q}_1 & 0 \\ 0 & \mathbf{Q}_2 \end{bmatrix} \left\{ \begin{bmatrix} \mathbf{D}_1 & 0 \\ 0 & \mathbf{D}_2 \end{bmatrix} + b_k \xi \xi^T \right\} \begin{bmatrix} \mathbf{Q}_1 & 0 \\ 0 & \mathbf{Q}_2 \end{bmatrix}^T,$$

which shows that the matrix $\mathbf{T}$ is *similar* to the matrix

$$\mathbf{G} \equiv \mathbf{D} + b_k \xi \xi^T.$$

The eigenvalues λ_i of $\mathbf{G}$ are given by the following equation:

$$1 + b_k \sum_{i=1}^{n} \frac{\xi_i^2}{d_i - \lambda} = 0, \tag{10.1}$$

where ξ_i are the elements of the vector ξ. Observe that the problem has been reduced to the root-finding problem:

- *Find λ such that $f(\lambda) = 0$, where $f(\lambda) = 1 + b_k \sum_{i=1}^{n} \frac{\xi_i^2}{d_i - \lambda}$.*

The equation for $f(\lambda)$ is known as the **secular equation**. In [26] several approaches to solving Equation (10.1) are presented. Having computed the eigenvalues λ_i of $\mathbf{G}$, which are also eigenvalues of $\mathbf{A}$, we can now compute the eigenvectors. First, the corresponding eigenvectors of $\mathbf{G}$ are (see [26, 32])

$$\mathbf{y}_i = (\mathbf{D} - \lambda_i \mathbf{I})^{-1} \xi.$$

Finally, the eigenvectors of the original matrix $\mathbf{A}$ are given by

$$\mathbf{v}_i = \begin{bmatrix} \mathbf{Q}_1 & 0 \\ 0 & \mathbf{Q}_2 \end{bmatrix} \mathbf{y}_i.$$

Clearly, this is the first level of dividing the problem. We can now repeat *recursively* this process for $\mathbf{T}_1$ and $\mathbf{T}_2$, which are also tridiagonal and half the size of the original matrix. These, in turn, can be further divided into two, and so on.

Software

Suite

PUTTING IT INTO PRACTICE

We now present a parallel implementation of the parallel QR eigensolver just discussed. This program solves for a very simple symmetric tridiagonal matrix consisting of the values $0.5, 1.5, \ldots$ on the diagonal and the value 0.3 on the off diagonals. This matrix was chosen for two reasons: First, it is diagonally dominant, similar to most matrices we encountered when using finite difference discretizations; second, all the eigenvalues of this matrix are simple (i.e., the multiplicity of each eigenvalue is exactly one). The rationale behind the second point will be presented in the remarks following the program.

For simplicity, we assume that the number of MPI processes used is a power of 2. This being the case, an example partitioning of a matrix of size 50 is presented in Figure 10.2.

Figure 10.2 is to be understood as follows. Suppose that we have eight processes $P_0, \ldots, P_7$ on which to solve for a matrix **A** of size 50. First, traversing down the tree, we see that using the algorithm described, we continuously subdivide the problem until each processor has assigned to it some subproblem to solve. In this case, P_0 solves a subproblem of size 6, P_1 solves a subproblem of size 6, etc. Each of these subproblems is solved in parallel by each individual process. When all the

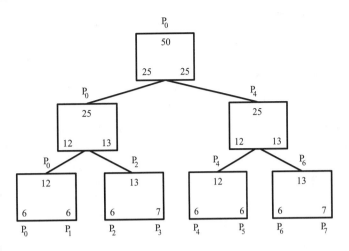

subproblems have been solved, a fan-in style algorithm is employed to complete the computation. Traversing back up the partitioning tree, we see that processes P_0 and P_1 combine their subproblems, each of size 6, into one subproblem of size 12, which is now solved on process P_0. In this implementation, P_1 remains idle throughout the remainder of the computation. Similarly, other processes combine their subproblems pairwise until finally the original problem of size 50 is solved.

Figure 10.2: Computational partitioning of a matrix of size 50. This partitioning is explained in the text.

We now present a C++/MPI code to accomplish the parallel QR eigensolver procedure just described. We first present the commented code and then conclude with some remarks about the code.

```cpp
#include <iostream.h>
#include <iomanip.h>
#include "SCmathlib.h"
#include "SCchapter10.h"
#include<mpi.h>

// Global variable to set size of the system
const int size = 50;

int main(int argc, char *argv[]){
  int i,j,k,ll,m,isum,ioffset,cnt,N1,N2;
  int mynode, totalnodes;
  MPI_Status status;
  double bn,*tmpd,**tmpdd;

  MPI_Init(&argc,&argv);
  MPI_Comm_size(MPI_COMM_WORLD, &totalnodes);
  MPI_Comm_rank(MPI_COMM_WORLD, &mynode);

  // Set up storage on each process
  double * a = new double[size];
  double * b = new double[size];
```

```
double * lambda = new double[size];
double ** Q  = CreateMatrix(size,size);
double ** Q1 = CreateMatrix(size,size);
double ** Q2 = CreateMatrix(size,size);
double * xi = new double[size];
double * d  = new double[size];

int ** index = ICreateMatrix(totalnodes,totalnodes);
double ** adjust = CreateMatrix(totalnodes,totalnodes);

//Form the Matrix A
for(i=0;i<size;i++){
  a[i] = i+1.5;
  b[i] = 0.3;
}

//Set up recursive partitioning of the matrix.
//Each process will solve for some subset of the problem

index[0][0] = size;
for(i=0;i<log2(totalnodes);i++){
  isum = 0;
  for(j=0;j<pow(2,i);j++){
    index[i+1][2*j] = index[i][j]/2;
    index[i+1][2*j+1] = index[i][j] - index[i+1][2*j];
    isum += index[i+1][2*j];
    adjust[i][j] = b[isum-1];
    a[isum-1] = a[isum-1] - b[isum-1];
    a[isum]   = a[isum]   - b[isum-1];
    isum += index[i+1][2*j+1];
  }
}

// Each process solves recursively for its subpart of
// the problem.

ioffset = (int) log2(totalnodes);
isum = 0;
for(k=0;k<mynode;k++)
  isum += index[ioffset][k];

TDQREigensolver(index[ioffset][mynode],&a[isum],
                &b[isum],d,Q1);

// Fan-in algorithm to finish solving system

for(i=0;i<log2(totalnodes);i++){
  isum = 0; cnt = 0;
  for(j=0;j<totalnodes;j+=(int)pow(2.0,i)){
```

```
        if(mynode == j){
          if(isum%2==0){
            MPI_Recv(d+index[ioffset][isum],index[ioffset]
                       [isum+1],MPI_DOUBLE, j+(int)pow(2.0,i),1,
                       MPI_COMM_WORLD,&status);
            for(k=0;k<index[ioffset][isum+1];k++)
              MPI_Recv(Q2[k],index[ioffset][isum+1],MPI_DOUBLE,
                         j+(int)pow(2.0,i),1,MPI_COMM_WORLD,
                         &status);
            N1 = index[ioffset][isum];
            N2 = index[ioffset][isum+1];
            bn = adjust[ioffset-1][cnt++];
          }
          else{
            MPI_Send(d,index[ioffset][isum],MPI_DOUBLE,
                       j-(int)pow(2.0,i),1,MPI_COMM_WORLD);
            for(k=0;k<index[ioffset][isum];k++)
              MPI_Send(Q1[k],index[ioffset][isum],MPI_DOUBLE,
                         j-(int)pow(2.0,i),1,MPI_COMM_WORLD);
          }
        }
        isum++;
      }

      for(j=0;j<totalnodes;j+=(int)pow(2.0,i+1)){
        if(mynode == j){
          cnt = 0;
          for(k=0;k<N1;k++)
            xi[cnt++] = Q1[N1-1][k];
          for(k=0;k<N2;k++)
            xi[cnt++] = Q2[0][k];

          // Solve for the secular equation to
          // obtain eigenvalues
          SolveSecularEq(bn,N1+N2,d,xi,lambda);

          // Form the Q matrix from Q1 and Q2
          for(k=0;k<N1;k++){
            for(ll=0;ll<N1+N2;ll++){
              Q[k][ll] = 0.0;
              for(m=0;m<N1;m++)
                Q[k][ll] += Q1[k][m]*xi[m]/(d[m]-lambda[ll]);
            }
          }
          for(k=0;k<N2;k++){
            for(ll=0;ll<N1+N2;ll++){
```

```
                    Q[N1+k][11] = 0.0;
                    for(m=0;m<N2;m++)
                       Q[k+N1][11]  += Q2[k][m]*xi[N1+m]/
                                       (d[N1+m]-lambda[11]);
                }
            }

            // Normalize the Q matrix so that each eigenvector
            // has length one
            double sum;
            for(k=0;k<N1+N2;k++){
              sum = 0.0;
              for(11=0;11<N1+N2;11++)
                sum+= Q[11][k]*Q[11][k];
              sum = sqrt(sum);
              for(11=0;11<N1+N2;11++)
                Q[11][k] = Q[11][k]/sum;
            }

            // Swap d and lambda arrays for use in the
            // next part of the fan-in algorithm
            tmpd = d;
            d = lambda;
            lambda = tmpd;

            // Swap Q and Q1 for use in the
            // next part of the fan-in algorithm
            tmpdd = Q1;
            Q1 = Q;
            Q = tmpdd;
          }
       }
    ioffset = ioffset - 1;
  }

  if(mynode==0){
    cout << "The eigenvalues are: " << endl;
    for(k=0;k<size;k++)
      cout << d[k] << endl;
  }

  MPI_Barrier(MPI_COMM_WORLD);

  delete[] a;
  delete[] b;
  delete[] lambda;
  delete[] xi;
  delete[] d;
```

```
        DestroyMatrix(Q,size,size);
        DestroyMatrix(Q1,size,size);
        DestroyMatrix(Q2,size,size);
        DestroyMatrix(adjust,totalnodes,totalnodes);
        IDestroyMatrix(index,totalnodes,totalnodes);

        MPI_Finalize();
    }
```

REMARK 1: Each process initially solves its assigned subproblem using the recursive routine *TDQREigensolver*, which can be found in the *software suite*. Observe that the parallel code resembles the serial *TDQREigensolver* solver – understanding the serial code will greatly help in interpreting the parallel code.

REMARK 2: To solve the secular equation we use a routine *SolveSecularEq*, which can be found in the *software suite*. This routine implements a very simple bisection algorithm for finding the roots of the secular equation. One assumption of this routine is that all the roots are distinct. More complicated methodologies that handle a wider variety of cases can be found in [26]. Commonly, a modified Newton–Raphson method is used for solving such problems.

REMARK 3: It should be pointed out that solving for the eigenvectors using the equation

$$\mathbf{y}_i = (\mathbf{D} - \lambda_i \mathbf{I})^{-1} \boldsymbol{\xi}$$

is not always numerically stable because two values of λ_i very close to each other will produce nearly parallel eigenvectors. In [26], several alternative methods that are more numerically stable are presented.

REMARK 4: In [32], a discussion is provided as to how one might keep all processors busy during the fan-in procedure. In the example code given here, when a process has completed its subproblem and if it is not involved in the fan-in process, it will remain idle. However, as pointed out in [32], the idle processes could be called back into service to work on solving the secular equation or for accomplishing parts of the matrix multiplications that are required. This will enhance the parallel efficiency.

10.3.6 The Lanczos Eigensolver

This algorithm, developed by Lanczos in the 1950s, is particularly useful for large *symmetric* matrices that are *sparse*. The QR method can also be used for such systems, but it does not maintain the sparsity of the new matrices in each iteration and thus becomes inefficient.

The key idea in Lanczos's approach is to make use of all the previous iterates

$$\mathbf{v}, \mathbf{A}\mathbf{v}, \mathbf{A}^2\mathbf{v}, \dots, \mathbf{A}^{k-1}\mathbf{v}$$

produced in a power method iteration. These k vectors form the so-called Krylov space:

$$\mathcal{K}_k(\mathbf{A}, \mathbf{v}) = \text{span } \{\mathbf{v}, \mathbf{A}\mathbf{v}, \mathbf{A}^2\mathbf{v}, \dots, \mathbf{A}^{k-1}\}$$

of dimension k. In principle, after n iterations assuming that all

$$\mathbf{v}, \mathbf{Av}, \ldots, \mathbf{A}^{n-1}\mathbf{v}$$

are linearly independent, we can express any vector $\mathbf{x}$ in terms of the basis formed by the vectors generated by that sequence. However, this sequence is not computationally friendly, and there is a *bias* toward the maximum eigenvalues of $\mathbf{A}$. The idea is then to orthogonalize these vectors but to do it fast, that is, to not use Gram–Schmidt or Householder but to use something new! The new orthonormalization will be based on the magic *three-term recurrence* formula. We have already seen how to use recurrence relations in the context of orthogonal polynomials (see Section 3.1) and also in the conjugate gradient method (see Section 4.1.7).

Assuming that we have produced the orthonormal vectors from the preceding sequence

$$\mathbf{q}_1, \mathbf{q}_2, \ldots, \mathbf{q}_k$$

then we can construct the orthornormal matrix $\mathbf{Q}$ by employing $\mathbf{q}_i$ as its columns. We also recall that

$$\mathbf{Q}^T\mathbf{Q} = \mathbf{I},$$

which is the condition of orthonormality.

We can then transform $\mathbf{A}$ to its *similar* matrix $\mathbf{T}$ using the similarity transformation, that is,

$$\mathbf{Q}^T\mathbf{AQ} = \mathbf{T} \text{ or } \mathbf{AQ} = \mathbf{QT}.$$

Clearly, the eigenvalues of $\mathbf{A}$ are the same as the eigenvalues of the matrix $\mathbf{T}$. The latter is a tridiagonal matrix of the form

$$T_k = \begin{bmatrix} \alpha_1 & \beta_1 & & & \\ \beta_1 & \alpha_2 & \beta_2 & & \mathbf{O} \\ & \ddots & \ddots & \ddots & \\ & & & & \beta_{k-1} \\ \mathbf{O} & & \beta_{k-1} & \alpha_k \end{bmatrix}.$$

The tridiagonal structure of $\mathbf{T}$ is a consequence of the three-term magic formula, so the columns of $\mathbf{Q}$ satisfy

$$\mathbf{Aq}_i = \beta_{i-1}\mathbf{q}_{i-1} + \alpha_i\mathbf{q}_i + \beta_i\mathbf{q}_{i+1}, \quad i = 1, 2, \ldots.$$

We can now compute the coefficients α_i and β_i from the orthonormality conditions. First, multiplying the previous equation by $\mathbf{q}_i^T$ we obtain

$$\mathbf{q}_i^T\mathbf{Aq}_i = \beta_{i-1}\mathbf{q}_i^T\mathbf{q}_{i-1} + \alpha_i\mathbf{q}_i^T\mathbf{q}_i + \beta_i\mathbf{q}_i^T\mathbf{q}_{i+1},$$

where $\mathbf{q}_i^T\mathbf{q}_i = 1$; also $\mathbf{q}_i^T\mathbf{q}_{i-1} = 0$ and $\mathbf{q}_i^T\mathbf{q}_{i+1} = 0$, owing to the orthonormality condition. Therefore, from this equation we obtain

$$\alpha_i = \mathbf{q}_i^T\mathbf{Aq}_i.$$

Conversely, assuming that α_i is obtained from this formula we can prove that $\mathbf{q}_{i+1} \perp \mathbf{q}_i$ by induction.

The coefficient β_i is also obtained from the recurrence formula

$$\mathbf{r}_i \equiv \beta_i \mathbf{q}_{i+1} = \mathbf{A}\mathbf{q}_i - \alpha_i \mathbf{q}_i - \beta_{i-1} \mathbf{q}_{i-1}$$

if we further assume that

$$\beta_i \neq 0 \Rightarrow \beta_i = \| \mathbf{r}_i \|_2$$

and

$$\mathbf{q}_{i+1} = \frac{\mathbf{r}_i}{\beta_i}.$$

All vectors $\mathbf{q}_{i+1}$ generated by the three-term sequence are orthogonal to all $\mathbf{q}_k$, $k < i$, given the symmetry of the matrix $\mathbf{A}$. This can be proved by induction as follows. First, we assume that

$$\mathbf{q}_{i+1} \perp \mathbf{q}_i \text{ and } \mathbf{q}_{i+1} \perp \mathbf{q}_{i-1}.$$

From the previous step (of the induction process) we have already that the condition

$$\mathbf{q}_i \perp \mathbf{q}_k, \quad k < i,$$

is valid. We will then prove that $\mathbf{q}_{i+1} \perp \mathbf{q}_k$ but first we prove that the vectors $\mathbf{q}_k$ and $\mathbf{q}_i$ are A-orthogonal. For this, we multiply the three-term recurrence formula by $\mathbf{q}_k$ ($k \leq i - 2$) to get

$$\mathbf{q}_k^T \mathbf{A}\mathbf{q}_i = (\mathbf{q}_k^T \mathbf{A}^T)\mathbf{q}_i = (\mathbf{A}\mathbf{q}_k)^T \mathbf{q}_i \text{ (owing to symmetry)}$$

$$= [\beta_{k-1}\mathbf{q}_{k-1} + \alpha_k\mathbf{q}_k + \beta_k\mathbf{q}_{k+1}]^T \mathbf{q}_i$$

$$= \beta_{k-1}\mathbf{q}_{k-1}^T\mathbf{q}_i + \alpha_k\mathbf{q}_k^T\mathbf{q}_i + \beta_k\mathbf{q}_{k+1}^T\mathbf{q}_i$$

$$= 0 + 0 + 0$$

$$\Rightarrow \mathbf{q}_k^T(\mathbf{A}\mathbf{q}_i) = 0.$$

Now, multiplying the three-term formula again we have

$$\beta_i\mathbf{q}_k^T\mathbf{q}_{i+1} = \mathbf{q}_k^T\mathbf{A}\mathbf{q}_i - \alpha_i\mathbf{q}_k^T\mathbf{q}_i - \beta_{i-j}\mathbf{q}_k^T\mathbf{q}_{i-1} = 0 + 0 + 0,$$

so we have proved by induction that $\mathbf{q}_{i+1}$ is orthogonal to all previous $\mathbf{q}_i$. We note here that each induction step has two substeps: the first shows the A-orthogonality and the second gives the final result.

In practice, the problem is that the orthogonality is *not* preserved. In fact, as soon as one eigenvalue converges all the basis vectors $\mathbf{q}_i$ pick up perturbations biased toward the direction of the corresponding eigenvector and orthogonality is lost. This has been analyzed in detail by Paige [74], who found that a "ghost" copy of the eigenvalue will appear again in the tridiagonal matrix $\mathbf{T}$. The straightforward remedy is to fully reorhonormalize the sequence by using Gram–Schmidt or even QR. However, either approach would be expensive if the dimension of the Krylov space is large, so instead a *selective reorthonormalization* is pursued. More specifically, the practical approach is to orthonormalize *halfway*, that is, within half machine precision $\sqrt{\epsilon_M}$ (see [4]).

The following algorithm presents an orthogonalized version of the basic Lanczos algorithm for symmetric matrices.

LANCZOS ALGORITHM

Initialize: Choose $\mathbf{q}_0 = 0$; arbitrary $\mathbf{r} \neq 0$; and $\beta_0 = \| \mathbf{r} \|_2$

Begin Loop: for $j = 1, \ldots$

$$\mathbf{q}_j = \frac{\mathbf{r}}{\beta_{j-1}}$$

$$\mathbf{r} = \mathbf{A}\mathbf{q}_j$$

$$\alpha_j = \mathbf{q}_j^T \mathbf{r}$$

$$\mathbf{r} = \mathbf{r} - \mathbf{q}_{j-1}\beta_{j-1}$$

$$\mathbf{r} = \mathbf{r} - \mathbf{q}_j\alpha_j$$

Orthogonalize if necessary

$$\beta_j = \| \mathbf{r} \|_2$$

Compute approximate eigenvalues of $\mathbf{T}_j$

Test for convergence

endfor

End Loop

REMARK 1: The algorithm can be implemented using a single matrix–vector product per iteration and BLAS1 routines (i.e., *ddot* and *daxpy*). Only three vectors need to be stored at any given time, that is, $\mathbf{r}$, $\mathbf{q}_j$, and $\mathbf{q}_{j-1}$, although there are also algorithms that require only two stores but these are more difficult to implement.

REMARK 2: We note that if we have n iterations in the loop for the Lanczos algorithm we will obtain the entire eigenspectrum of $\mathbf{T}$ and therefore of $\mathbf{A}$. This can be done with a standard QR method operating on a tridiagonal matrix, which requires only *linear* work. However, we can stop at any iteration $j < n$ and the resulting matrix $\mathbf{T}_j$ will have approximate values for the first j eigenvalues of the matrix $\mathbf{A}$. Hence, this method is both *local* in that we can obtain a subset of the eigenvalues but also *global* since we can obtain the entire eigenspectrum.

REMARK 3: If the eigenvalues of $\mathbf{A}$ are not well separated, then we can use a *shift* and employ the matrix

$$(\mathbf{A} - \sigma\mathbf{I})^{-1},$$

following the shifted inverted power method to generate the appropriate Krylov subspaces.

REMARK 4: The Lanczos algorithm can be extended to nonsymmetric systems (see modified algorithms in [4, 79]).

10.4 GENERALIZED EIGENPROBLEMS

So far we have dealt with linear eigenvalue problems, but in applications we often encounter problems of the form

$$\mathbf{A}(\lambda)\mathbf{v} = 0,$$

where $\mathbf{A}(\lambda)$ is a matrix function of λ. The general problem can be, in theory, solved using the Newton–Raphson method for systems. However, we have $(n + 1)$ unknowns $\lambda, \mathbf{x}_i, \ldots, \mathbf{x}_n$ and only n equations. To close the system we introduce the condition of normalization, which provides the $(n + 1)$th equation.

Other special forms of the generalized eigenproblem can be handled with more efficient approaches. We demonstrate a few examples next.

In its simplest form the generalized eigenproblem may be written as

$$\mathbf{A}\mathbf{v} = \lambda\mathbf{B}\mathbf{v}.$$

Assuming that $\mathbf{B}$ is not singular, we can turn this into

$$(\mathbf{B}^{-1}\mathbf{A})\mathbf{v} = \lambda\mathbf{v},$$

which is similar to the standard eigenproblem presented earlier. However, there is still concern if $\mathbf{B}$ is not singular but *nearly singular*. The algorithm in the next section deals with this case.

10.4.1 The QZ Eigensolver

When the matrix $\mathbf{B}$ is almost singular, it is not accurate to construct $\mathbf{B}^{-1}\mathbf{A}$ explicitly to find its eigenvalues. Instead, we transform $\mathbf{A}$ and $\mathbf{B}$ simultaneously to simpler forms and then compute the eigenvalues. This is accomplished in two steps.

In the *first step*, we pre- and postmultiply $\mathbf{A}$ and $\mathbf{B}$ by two orthonormal matrices $\mathbf{Q}$ and $\mathbf{Z}$ to achieve

$$\mathbf{A}^* = \mathbf{Q}^T\mathbf{A}\mathbf{Z} \quad (\textit{upper Hessenberg matrix}),$$

$$\mathbf{B}^* = \mathbf{Q}^T\mathbf{B}\mathbf{Z} \quad (\textit{upper triangular matrix}).$$

In the *second step*, we apply QR to the matrix pair $\mathbf{A}^*$ and $\mathbf{B}^*$ to reduce them further to an upper triangular form.

The eigenvalues of the generalized problem $\mathbf{A}\mathbf{v} = \lambda\mathbf{B}\mathbf{v}$ after triangulization of $\mathbf{A}$ are given by

$$\lambda_i = \begin{cases} a_{ii}^*/b_{ii}^* & \text{if } b_{ii}^* \neq 0, \\ \infty & \text{if } b_{ii}^* = 0 \text{ and } a_{ii}^* \neq 0. \end{cases}$$

For details on the algorithm we refer the reader to [70] and [21, 79].

10.4.2 Singular Eigenproblems

Many interesting applications involve a *singular* matrix $\mathbf{B}$, for example, the Orr–Sommerfeld equation in fluid dynamics [80]. In this case we can employ a local iteration procedure similar to the inverse power method. To this end, we solve the original system along with its adjoint, that is,

$$[\mathbf{A} - (\lambda_k - \sigma)\mathbf{B}]\,\mathbf{u}^{k+1} = \sigma\mathbf{B}\mathbf{u}^k,$$

$$[\mathbf{A} - (\lambda_k - \sigma^*)\mathbf{B}]^T\,\mathbf{v}^{k+1} = \sigma\mathbf{B}^T\mathbf{v}^k,$$

where σ and σ^* are normalization constants. We assume that we have some good initial guesses λ_1, $\mathbf{u}^0$, and $\mathbf{v}^0$. If $\mathbf{A}$ and $\mathbf{B}$ are symmetric these two equations are identical. For nonsymmetric systems this formulation with the *adjoint* accelerates convergence.

The eigenvalue is obtained through a generalized Rayleigh quotient of the form

$$\lambda_{k+1} = \frac{\mathbf{v}_k^T\mathbf{A}\mathbf{u}^k}{\mathbf{v}_k^T\mathbf{B}\mathbf{u}^k},$$

which will also be used in the next iteration. The convergence rate of this local method is *third order*.

10.4.3 Polynomial Eigenproblems

We now consider the *second-order* polynomial eigenproblem of the form

$$[\mathbf{A}\lambda^2 + \mathbf{B}\lambda + \mathbf{C}]\mathbf{v} = 0,$$

where $\mathbf{A}$ is nonsingular. By setting $\mathbf{x} = \mathbf{v}$ and $\mathbf{y} = \lambda\mathbf{v}$, this equation can be rewritten as

$$\mathbf{A}\lambda\mathbf{y} + \mathbf{B}\mathbf{y} + \mathbf{C}\mathbf{x} = 0,$$

which can be recast as

$$\mathbf{G}_2\mathbf{y} + \mathbf{G}_1\mathbf{x} = \lambda\mathbf{y},$$

with $\mathbf{G}_2 = -\mathbf{A}^{-1}\mathbf{B}$ and $\mathbf{G}_1 = -\mathbf{A}^{-1}\mathbf{C}$. Finally, we put it in block matrix form as

$$\begin{bmatrix} 0 & \mathbf{I} \\ \mathbf{G}_1 & \mathbf{G}_2 \end{bmatrix} \begin{bmatrix} \mathbf{x} \\ \mathbf{y} \end{bmatrix} = \lambda \begin{bmatrix} \mathbf{x} \\ \mathbf{y} \end{bmatrix}.$$

The solution of this eigenproblem is a *linear* $2n \times 2n$ system and can be solved using any of the local or global eigensolvers from the previous section.

10.5 ARNOLDI METHOD: NONSYMMETRIC EIGENPROBLEMS

In the previous chapter we presented the Arnoldi iteration, which transforms a nonsymmetric matrix $\mathbf{A}$ to a Hessenberg matrix $\mathbf{H}$. In fact, the Arnoldi iteration can go part way; if the matrix $\mathbf{A}$ has order n then the matrix $\mathbf{H}$ can have order m with $m < n$, and we denote it by $\mathbf{H}_m$.

We now address the question of how exactly we locate the eigenvalues of $\mathbf{A}$. We need to first find the eigenvalues of $\mathbf{H}_m$ (which is why we bothered with this Hessenberg reduction). To this end, we can employ a QR iteration for $\mathbf{H}_m$ to find the eigenpairs $(\lambda_i^{(m)}, \mathbf{y}_i^{(m)})$. However, these eigenvalues are only approximations to eigenvalues of $\mathbf{A}$. The accuracy increases as m increases, and the convergence rate is (approximately) linear for this method, although this is not always the case; rigorous analysis is difficult to perform (see [79]).

To assess the convergence of the method we need the residual. A good and cheap way to compute the residual is to consider the magnitude of the last component of the eigenvector $\mathbf{y}_i^{(m)}$, or more specifically the quantity

$$h_{m+1,m}|\mathbf{e}_m^T\mathbf{y}_i^{(m)}| = \| (\mathbf{A} - \lambda_i^{(m)}\mathbf{I})\mathbf{r}_i^{(m)} \|_2, \tag{10.2}$$

where $\mathbf{r}_i^{(m)}$ is the so-called Ritz approximate eigenvector defined by

$$\mathbf{r}_i^{(m)} = \mathbf{V}_m\mathbf{y}_i^{(m)}.$$

This equality is based on the equation

$$(\mathbf{A} - \lambda_i^{(m)}\mathbf{I})\mathbf{r}_i^{(m)} = h_{m+1,m}\mathbf{e}_m^T\mathbf{y}_i^{(m)}\mathbf{v}_{m+1},$$

which is derived from the fundamental Arnoldi relationship, namely,

$$\mathbf{A}\mathbf{V}_m = \mathbf{V}_m\mathbf{H}_m + h_{m+1,m}\mathbf{v}_{m+1}\mathbf{e}_m^T.$$

Multiplying this equation by $\mathbf{y}_i^{(m)}$ and utilizing the fact that $\mathbf{H}_m\mathbf{y}_i^{(m)} = \lambda_i^{(m)}\mathbf{y}_i^m$, we have that

$$\mathbf{A}\underbrace{\mathbf{V}_m y_i^{(m)}}_{\mathbf{r}_i^{(m)}} - \lambda_i^{(m)}\underbrace{\mathbf{V}_m\mathbf{y}_i^{(m)}}_{\mathbf{r}_i^{(m)}} = h_{m+1,m}\mathbf{v}_{m+1}\mathbf{e}_m^T\mathbf{y}_i^{(m)}.$$

Taking the L_2 norm of both sides and using the fact that $\| \mathbf{v}_{m+1} \|_2 = 1$ we obtain Equation (10.2).

10.6 AVAILABLE SOFTWARE FOR EIGENSOLVERS

The basic algorithms we have presented in this chapter are relatively easy to program, but more sophisticated versions with respect to preconditioning, restarts, orthogonalization, and parallel implementation are available in free software at **www.netlib. org.**

Here we briefly mention some of the most popular packages.

- For reduction of a dense matrix to a tridiagonal form using Householder transformations, the routines **xSYTRD** and **HETRD** for real and complex matrices are available in LAPACK. The corresponding routines in ScaLAPACK are **PxSYTRD** and **PxHETRD**.

- For various QR eigensolvers the routines **xSTEQR** and **xSTERF** are available in LAPACK.
- The parallel divide-and-conquer eigensolver we presented in this chapter is implemented in the routine **xSTEVD** of LAPACK. It is much faster than xSTEQR but requires more memory.
- The Lanczos algorithm is available in packages implemented by various authors. For example, the code **LANCZOS** presented in [19] implements the version without orthogonalization; the code **LANZ** in [61] involves partial orthogonalization; and the codes **LANSO** and **PLANSO** for the serial and parallel version, respectively, produced by researchers at UC Berkeley involve periodic orthogonalization.
- For Arnoldi eigensolvers the package **ARPACK**, which stands for ARnoldi PACKage, is available in both FORTRAN as well as in C++; the latter is called ARPACK++. Specifically, **ARPACK++** has a good C++ interface to the original ARPACK codes so that the C++ users do not have to deal with the reverse communication interface problems that characterize the FORTRAN routines of ARPACK.
- For generalized eigenproblems, a simple driver routine **xSYGV** exists in LAPACK that is based on the QR method. A more sophisticated version **xSYGVX** chooses from a number of eigensolvers based on efficiency for a particular problem. For the parallel divide-and-conquer method, there is the routine **xSYGVD**, which is based on the simple driver of LAPACK.

10.7 HOMEWORK PROBLEMS

1. Show that the matrix $\mathbf{A} = \mathbf{LU}$, where $\mathbf{L}$ is a unit lower triangular and $\mathbf{U}$ is upper triangular, has the same eigenvalues with the matrix $\mathbf{B} = \mathbf{UL}$.

2. The power method to finding eigenvalues is applicable to (choose one)

   (a) symmetric matrices.

   (b) symmetric, positive-definite matrices.

   (c) general matrices.

3. Write a C++ code to test the convergence rate of the inverted shifted power method applied to the matrix resulting from the two-dimensional discretization of

   (a) $\nabla^2 u = \lambda u$ (symmetric),

   (b) $\nabla^2 u - u_x - u_y = \lambda u$ (nonsymmetric)

   on a square domain $[0, 1] \times [0, 1]$ with second-order finite differences. We assume that the boundary conditions are all homogeneous. Plot the error in predicting the minimum eigenvalue versus the iteration number to estimate the convergence rate.

4. Prove that the QR iteration maintains the Hessenberg structure, which is a key step in applying efficiently the QR algorithm.

5. Show that the eigenvalues of the tridiagonal matrix defined by

$$d_{ii} = 2, \quad i = 1, \ldots, n,$$

$$d_{i,i-1} = -1, \quad i = 2, \ldots, n,$$

$$d_{i-1,i} = -1, \quad i = 2, \ldots, n,$$

are given by

$$\lambda_j = 2 - 2\cos(j\pi/(n+1))$$

with corresponding eigenvectors

$$\mathbf{v}_j = [\sin(j\pi/(n+1)), \ \sin(2j\pi/(n+1)), \ldots, \sin(nj\pi/(n+1))]^T.$$

Then, use the power method and the inverse power method to compute the maximum and minimum eigenvalues for $n = 50$. What is the convergence rate of the two methods for this problem?

6. Construct a QR eigensolver for a symmetric positive-definite matrix $\mathbf{A}$ using the Cholesky decomposition. Estimate the operation count and write a C++ code for the matrix resulting from the discretization of

$$\nabla^2 u - u = \lambda u \quad \text{in} \quad [0, 1] \times [0, 1].$$

Is your theoretical estimate consistent with what you find experimentally by timing your solver. (Use a sufficiently large number of grid points, e.g., a grid of 100×100.)

7. Consider a symmetric Topeliz matrix with entries $a_k = 1/k$, $k = 1, \ldots, n$. We want to apply Rayleigh quotient iteration to it. First, show that the shifted matrix $(\mathbf{A} - \sigma_k\mathbf{I})$, where σ_k is the Rayleigh quotient, remains a Topeliz matrix. Then compute the largest three and the smallest three eigenvalues of $\mathbf{A}$ for $n = 25$, 50, and 100. What is the convergence rate you observe?

8. Consider five symmetric Toeplitz matrices $\mathbf{A}$ with entries given by ($k = 1, \ldots, n$)

$$a_k^{(1)} = 1/k, \quad a_k^{(2)} = 1/\sqrt{k}, \quad a_k^{(3)} = 1/k^2, \quad a_k^{(4)} = k, \quad a_k^{(5)} = \cos k/k,$$

and construct corresponding circulant matrices $\mathbf{C}$ employing different number of Toeplitz diagonals. Compute the three largest and three smallest eigenvalues of the matrix $\mathbf{C}^{-1}\mathbf{A}$ and compare with the corresponding eigenvalues of $\mathbf{A}$. Use $n = 20, 30, \ldots, 100$. What do you observe?

9. Consider the finite difference discretization of the Helmholtz eigenvalue problem

$$\nabla^2 u - 4u = \lambda u$$

in the domain $[0, 1] \times [0, 1]$. Apply the QR and LR (based on LU) eigensolvers and compute the CPU time required to obtain the entire eigenspectrum. Consider a grid with $N \times N$ and $N = 128$, 256, and 512.

10. Let $\mathbf{T}$ be a block tridiagonal matrix of order $n^2 \times n^2$ with $\mathbf{A}$ of order $n \times n$ in the diagonal and $\mathbf{B}$ also of order $n \times n$ in the two off diagonals. Assuming that we

decompose $\mathbf{A}$ and $\mathbf{B}$ as follows:

$$\mathbf{Q}\mathbf{A}\mathbf{Q}^T = \text{diag}(a_1, a_2, \ldots, a_n),$$

$$\mathbf{Q}\mathbf{B}\mathbf{Q}^T = \text{diag}(b_1, b_2, \ldots, b_n),$$

find analytical expressions for the n^2 eigenpairs of $\mathbf{T}$ in terms of a_i, b_i, and $\mathbf{Q}$.

11. Consider the $n \times n$ matrix $\mathbf{A}$, the entries of which are computed from

$$a_{ij} = \frac{ij}{(i+j)^2}.$$

Compute the eigenvalues and eigenvectors of this matrix using the Lanczos algorithm for $n = 5$, 10, and 20 at different levels of accuracy.

12. Prove that the Householder matrix is symmetric.

13. Show how a Householder matrix $\mathbf{H}$ of size $n \times n$ times a vector $\mathbf{x}$ of size n can be accomplished in $\mathcal{O}(n)$ operations. Explain how this implies that an $n \times n$ matrix $\mathbf{A}$ can be premultiplied by $\mathbf{H}$ in $\mathcal{O}(n^2)$ operations.

14. Using the MPI program presented in this chapter, write an MPI program that accomplishes the full Householder deflation to obtain all the eigenvalues.

    (a) First explain how the rows of the matrix $\mathbf{A}$ should be partitioned to maximize parallel performance (block partitioning, cyclic partitioning, etc). Show diagrammatically why one partitioning is preferable over another.

    (b) For a 6×6 system and two processes, show by diagram the communication pattern that you would use for the full deflation.

    (*Hint*: You will need to use the variable length versions of *MPI_Allgather* and *MPI_AlltoAll* (*MPI_Allgatherv* and *MPI_Alltoallv*).)

15. Write a simple MPI program using *MPI_Alltoall* to transpose a matrix $\mathbf{A}$ of size N. Using the *MPI_Wtime* function, perform the following timings:

    (a) For a fixed number of processes, $P = 2$ and $P = 4$, plot the time to transpose matrices of size $n = 10, 20, 30, 40$, and 100. What scaling do you see? Document the machine on which you were running, the number of processors the machine has, etc.

    (b) For a fixed matrix size $n = 100$, plot the time to transpose a matrix on $P = 2, 4$, and 8 processors. What scaling do you encounter?

16. In the parallel QR eigensolver presented in the text, each process requires storage for full Q, Q1, and Q2 arrays. Modify the program so that only the minimal amount of memory is used.

17. Write a C++/MPI program that solves the secular equation in parallel.

18. In the parallel QR eigensolver presented in the text, a fan-in algorithm was used to combine the solved subproblems. Suppose, however, that instead of using a

fan-in algorithm, we solve the problem as follows: Let a master node partition the problem into P subproblems, having each process solve its subproblem (just as in the program we presented). Instead of fanning in, have the master node be in charge of the combination effort, using the other processes to solve in parallel the secular equation and the matrix multiplications.

(a) Implement the algorithm just described.

(b) Which algorithm is faster, the fan-in or the newly proposed algorithm? For matrices of size 50 and 100, perform timing tests on 2, 4, and 8 processors. What can you conclude?

Appendix A

C++ Basics

A.1 COMPILATION GUIDE

For the purposes of this compilation example, we will assume that we are using the GNU g++ compiler to compile a C++ program we have written contained within the file *myprog.cpp*. In the following examples, the argument following the "-o" flag designates the file name to be used for the output. If no "-o" option is specified, most compilers default to using the name "a.out." We now present several different programming scenarios:

- No user-defined libraries or user-defined header files are needed, and no special system libraries (such as those associated with *math.h*) are needed):

    ```
    g++ -o myprog myprog.cpp
    ```

- No user-defined libraries or user-defined header files are needed, but the special system library corresponding to *math.h* is needed:

    ```
    g++ -o myprog myprog.cpp -lmath
    ```

- User-defined libraries, user-defined header files, and the special system library corresponding to *math.h* are needed:

    ```
    g++ -o myprog myprog.cpp -I/users/kirby/includes -L/users/
        kirby/libs -lSCmathlib -lmath
    ```

    The string following the "-I" flag designates the location of the user-defined header files to be included. The string following the "-L" flag designates the location of the user-defined libraries to be included. The string "-lSCmathlib" links the program with the user-defined library we created, and the string "-lmath" links the program with the system math library corresponding to *math.h*.

A.2 C++ BASIC DATA TYPES

C++ has a set of standard data types representing the most common basic storage units of the language. They can be partitioned as follows:

1. a Boolean type (*bool*);

2. integer types (such as *int*):
   (a) *int*,
   (b) *unsigned int*,
   (c) *signed int*,
   (d) *short int* (short-handed declaration is *short*),
   (e) *long int* (short-handed declaration is *long*);
3. floating-point types (such as *float*):
   (a) *float* (single precision),
   (b) *double* (double precision),
   (c) *long double* (extended double precision);
4. character types (such as *char*):
   (a) *char*,
   (b) *unsigned char*,
   (c) *signed char*;
5. a type *void* that represents the absence of information; and
6. types constructed from the preceding types:
   (a) pointer types (such as *int **),
   (b) reference types (such as *int&*),
   (c) array types (such as *int*[]).

We refer the reader to [86] for a complete description and usage explanation of the data types listed here.

A.3 C++ LIBRARIES

A.3.1 Input/Output Library – iostream.h

Here we present three additional operations found within the C++ *iostream* system library that were not discussed previously. For more information about the contents of *iostream.h*, we refer the reader to [86].

- **cin.get(ch)** allows the user to obtain from standard input the next character (including white space and the end-of-line character). This function takes in its argument list a variable of type *char*, into which it places the character obtained from standard input (i.e., this variable is passed by reference).
- **cin.eof()** returns nonzero (true) if end-of-file has been encountered in the standard input stream.
- **cout.put(ch)** allows the user to print to standard output a single character. This function takes in its argument list a variable of type *char*, the contents of which are printed to standard output.

A.3.2 Input/Output Manipulation Library – iomanip.h

Next we present a list of a few of the input/output manipulation operations that can be found in the C++ *iomanip* system library. For more information about the contents of *iomanip.h*, we refer the reader to [86].

- **cout** << **setiosflags(ios::flag)** – sets/resets the I/O flag. The designator *flag* may be one of the following:
  1. *fixed* – floating point output will be printed in fixed format (not using scientific notation),
  2. *scientific* – floating point output will be printed in scientific notation, or
  3. *showpoint* – decimal points and trailing zeroes are displayed.
- **cout** << **setprecision(i)** – sets the number of decimal places of accuracy to be used when printing floating point (*float/double*) values. This function takes as input an integer variable representing the number of digits to be used.
- **cout** << **setw(i)** – sets the field width to be used for the next item printed. This function takes as input an integer variable that designates the number of characters used to determine the field width.
- **cout** << **endl** – indicates the ending of one line of output and the initiation of a new line of output.

A.3.3 Mathematics Library – math.h

The following is a list of some of the mathematical operations that can be found in the C++ math library. For more information about the contents of *math.h*, we refer the reader to [86].

$\sin(x)$	Sine of x.
$\cos(x)$	Cosine of x.
$\tan(x)$	Tangent of x.
$\text{asin}(x)$	$\text{Sin}^{-1}(x)$ in range $[-\pi/2, \pi/2]$, $x \in [-1, 1]$.
$\text{acos}(x)$	$\text{Cos}^{-1}(x)$ in range $[0, \pi]$, $x \in [-1, 1]$.
$\text{atan}(x)$	$\text{Tan}^{-1}(x)$ in range $[-\pi/2, \pi/2]$.
$\text{atan2}(y, x)$	$\text{Tan}^{-1}(y/x)$ in range $[-\pi, \pi]$.
$\sinh(x)$	Hyperbolic sine of x.
$\cosh(x)$	Hyperbolic cosine of x.
$\tanh(x)$	Hyperbolic tangent of x.
$\exp(x)$	Exponential function e^x.
$\log(x)$	Natural logarithm $\ln(x)$, $x > 0$.
$\log 10(x)$	Base-10 logarithm $\log_{10}(x)$, $x > 0$.
$\text{pow}(x, y)$	x^y. A domain error occurs if $x = 0$ and $y \leq 0$, or if $x < 0$ and y is not an integer.
$\text{sqrt}(x)$	$\sqrt{x}$, $x \geq 0$.
$\text{cdil}(x)$	Smallest integer not less than x, as a double.
$\text{floor}(x)$	Largest integer not greater than x, as a double.
$\text{fabs}(x)$	Absolute value $|x|$.
$\text{ldexp}(x, n)$	$x \cdot 2^n$.
$\text{frexp}(x, \text{int *exp})$	Splits x into a normalized fraction in the interval $[1/2, 1]$, which is returned, and a power of 2, which is stores in *exp. If x is zero, both parts of the result are zero.

modf(x, double *ip)   Splits x into integral and fractional parts, each with the same sign as x. It stores the integral part in *ip and returns the fractional part.

fmod(x, y)   Floating point remainder of x/y, with the same sign as x. If y is zero, the result is implementation-defined.

A.4 OPERATOR PRECEDENCE

Table A.1 provides the C++ convention used for operator precedence. This list is ordered from highest to lowest precedence.

A.5 C++ AND BLAS

Many of the C++ programs presented in this book can be reprogrammed to use BLAS for almost all of the mathematics operations. We did not originally program things using BLAS for pedagogical reasons; we attempted to use every programming example to expand the reader's familiarity with C++ constructs.

Table A.1: C++ convention used for operator precedence. Unary +, −, and * have higher precedence than the binary forms.

Operations	Associativity
( ) [ ] → .	Left to right
! ~ ++ -- + − * & (type) sizeof	Right to left
* / %	Left to right
+ −	Left to right
<< >>	Left to right
< <= > >=	Left to right
== !=	Left to right
&	Left to right
^	Left to right
|	Left to right
& &	Left to right
| |	Left to right
?:	Right to left
= += −= *= /= %= &= ^= |= <<= >>=	Right to left
,	Left to right

When combining C++ and BLAS, the reader should consult the Web site
`http://www.netlib.org/blas/,` which contains explicit documentation for linking C programs to BLAS. One modification that C++ requires is that BLAS function declarations should be done as follows:

```
extern "C" {
   void   daxpy_(int*, double*, double *, int*, double *, int*);
}
```

This notifies the compiler to use the C programming language function name convention.

Appendix B

MPI Basics

B.1 COMPILATION GUIDE

For the purposes of this compilation example, we will assume that we are using the GNU g++ compiler to compile a C++ program we have written contained within the file *myprog.cpp*. We will also assume that the machine on which you are trying to compile is a parallel machine with some version of MPI installed. You will need to contact your system administrator to find out the exact version of MPI that is available and the paths on your local architecture. In the following examples, the argument following the "-o" flag designates the file name to be used for the output. If no "-o" option is specified, most compilers default to using the name "a.out." We now present several different programming scenarios:

- No user-defined libraries or user-defined header files are needed, and no special system libraries (such as those associated with *math.h*) are needed other than the MPI libraries:

      g++ -o myprog myprog.cpp -lmpi

- No user-defined libraries or user-defined header files are needed, but the special system library corresponding to *math.h* is needed along with the MPI libraries:

      g++ -o myprog myprog.cpp -lmath -lmpi

- User-defined libraries, user-defined header files, and the special system library corresponding to *math.h* are needed along with the MPI libraries:

      g++ -o myprog myprog.cpp -I/users/kirby/includes -L/users/
          kirby/libs -lSCmathlib -lmath -lmpi

The string following the "-I" flag designates the location of the user-defined header files to be included. The string following the "-L" flag designates the location of the user-defined libraries to be included. The string "-lSCmathlib" links the program with the user-defined library we created, and the string "-lmath" links the program with the system math library corresponding to *math.h*. The string "-lmpi" links the MPI libraries.

You will need to contact your system administrator to verify the exact command used on your computing architecture to run an MPI program. In general, most architectures execute MPI programs in a fashion similar to the following:

```
mpirun -np 4 myprog
```

where "mpirun" is a special program used for starting execution on the parallel machine, "-np 4" indicates the number of processes requested, and "myprog" denotes the program executable that is compiled.

B.2 MPI COMMANDS

In this section we present an extended list of the MPI datatypes, MPI reduction operations, and MPI function declarations.

B.2.1 Predefined Variable Types in MPI

MPI DATATYPE	C DATATYPE
MPI_CHAR	Signed char
MPI_SHORT	Signed short int
MPI_INT	Signed int
MPI_LONG	Signed long int
MPI_UNSIGNED_CHAR	Unsigned char
MPI_UNSIGNED_SHORT	Unsigned short int
MPI_UNSIGNED	Unsigned int
MPI_UNSIGNED_LONG	Unsigned long int
MPI_FLOAT	Float
MPI_DOUBLE	Double
MPI_LONG_DOUBLE	Long double
MPI_BYTE	
MPI_PACKED	

B.2.2 Predefined Reduction Operators in MPI

OPERATION NAME	MEANING
MPI_MAX	Maximum
MPI_MIN	Minimum
MPI_SUM	Sum
MPI_PROD	Product
MPI_LAND	Logical and
MPI_BAND	Bitwise and
MPI_LOR	Logical or
MPI_BOR	Bitwise or

MPI_LXOR	Logical exclusive or
MPI_BXOR	Bitwise exclusive or
MPI_MAXLOC	Maximum and location of maximum
MPI_MINLOC	Minimum and location of minimum

B.2.3 MPI Function Declarations

- **MPI_Get_count**

```
int MPI_Get_count(
        MPI-Status*    status     /*  in   */,
        MPI_Datatype   datatype   /*  in   */,
        int*           count      /*  out  */)
```

- **MPI_Recv**

```
int MPI_Recv(
        void*          message    /*  out  */,
        int            count      /*  in   */,
        MPI_Datatype   datatype   /*  in   */,
        int            source     /*  in   */,
        int            tag        /*  in   */,
        MPI_Comm       comm       /*  in   */,
        MPI_Status*    status     /*  out  */)
```

- **MPI_Send**

```
int MPI_Send(
        void*          message    /*  in   */,
        int            count      /*  in   */,
        MPI_Datatype   datatype   /*  in   */,
        int            dest       /*  in   */,
        int            tag        /*  in   */,
        MPI_Comm       comm       /*  in   */)
```

- **MPI_Bsend**

```
int MPI_Bsend(
        void*          message    /*  in   */,
        int            count      /*  in   */,
        MPI_Datatype   datatype   /*  in   */,
        int            dest       /*  in   */,
        int            tag        /*  in   */,
        MPI_Comm       comm       /*  in   */)
```

- **MPI_Rsend**

```
int MPI_Rsend(
        void*        message    /*  in  */,
        int          count      /*  in  */,
        MPI_Datatype datatype   /*  in  */,
        int          dest       /*  in  */,
        int          tag        /*  in  */,
        MPI_Comm     comm       /*  in  */)
```

- **MPI_Ssend**

```
int MPI_Ssend(
        void*        message    /*  in  */,
        int          count      /*  in  */,
        MPI_Datatype datatype   /*  in  */,
        int          dest       /*  in  */,
        int          tag        /*  in  */,
        MPI_Comm     comm       /*  in  */)
```

- **MPI_Buffer_attach**

```
int MPI_Buffer_attach(
        void*        buffer     /*  in  */,
        int          size       /*  in  */)
```

- **MPI_Buffer_detach**

```
int MPI_Buffer_detach(
        void*        buffer_address  /*  out  */,
        int          size_ptr        /*  out  */)
```

- **MPI_Ibsend**

```
int MPI_Ibsend(
        void*        message    /*  in  */,
        int          count      /*  in  */,
        MPI_Datatype datatype   /*  in  */,
        int          dest       /*  in  */,
        int          tag        /*  in  */,
        MPI_Comm     comm       /*  in  */,
        MPI_Request* request    /*  out  */)
```

- **MPI_Irecv**

```
int MPI_Irecv(
        void*        message    /*  out  */,
        int          count      /*  in  */,
        MPI_Datatype datatype   /*  in  */,
```

```
        int         dest        /*   in    */,
        int         tag         /*   in    */,
        MPI_Comm    comm        /*   in    */,
        MPI_Request* request    /*   out   */)
```

- **MPI_Irsend**

```
int MPI_Irsend(
        void*       message     /*   in    */,
        int         count       /*   in    */,
        MPI_Datatype datatype   /*   in    */,
        int         dest        /*   in    */,
        int         tag         /*   in    */,
        MPI_Comm    comm        /*   in    */,
        MPI_Request* request    /*   out   */)
```

- **MPI_Isend**

```
int MPI_Isend(
        void*       message     /*   in    */,
        int         count       /*   in    */,
        MPI_Datatype datatype   /*   in    */,
        int         dest        /*   in    */,
        int         tag         /*   in    */,
        MPI_Comm    comm        /*   in    */,
        MPI_Request* request    /*   out   */)
```

- **MPI_Issend**

```
int MPI_Isend(
        void*       message     /*   in    */,
        int         count       /*   in    */,
        MPI_Datatype datatype   /*   in    */,
        int         dest        /*   in    */,
        int         tag         /*   in    */,
        MPI_Comm    comm        /*   in    */,
        MPI_Request* request    /*   out   */)
```

- **MPI_Request_free**

```
int MP_Request_free(
        MPI_Request* request    /*   in/out */)
```

- **MPI_Test**

```
int MP_Test(
        MPI_Request* request    /*   in/out */,
        int*        flag        /*   out    */,
        MPI_Status* status      /*   out    */)
```

- **MPI_Testall**

```
int MP_Testall(
        int           array_size   /*  in     */,
        MPI_Request*  requests[ ]  /*  in/out */,
        int*          flag         /*  out    */,
        MPI_Status    statuses[ ]  /*  out    */)
```

- **MPI_Testany**

```
int MP_Testany(
        int           array_size      /*  in     */,
        MPI_Request   requests[ ]     /*  in/out */,
        int*          completed_index /*  out    */,
        int*          flag            /*  out    */,
        MPI_Status*   status          /*  out    */)
```

- **MPI_Testsome**

```
int MP_Testsome (
        int           array_size      /*  in     */,
        MPI_Request   requests[ ]     /*  in/out */,
        int*          completed_count /*  out    */,
        int           indices[ ]      /*  out    */,
        MPI_Status    statuses[ ]     /*  out    */)
```

- **MPI_Wait**

```
int MPI_Wait(
        MPI_Request*  request  /*  in/out */,
        MPI_Status*   status   /*  out    */)
```

- **MPI_Waitall**

```
int MP_Waitall(
        int           array_size   /*  in     */,
        MPI_Request   requests[ ]  /*  in/out */,
        MPI_Status    statuses[ ]  /*  out    */)
```

- **MPI_Waitany**

```
int MP_Waitany(
        int           array_size      /*  in     */,
        MPI_Request   requests[ ]     /*  in/out */,
        int*          completed_index /*  out    */,
        MPI_Status*   status          /*  out    */)
```

- **MPI_Waitsome**

```
int MP_Waitsome(
        int         array_size      /*  in      */,
        MPI_Request requests[ ]      /*  in/out  */,
        int*        completed_count  /*  out     */,
        int         indices[ ]       /*  out     */,
        MPI_Status  statuses[ ]      /*  out     */)
```

- **MPI_Cancel**

```
int MP_Cancel(
        MPI_Request* request  /*  in  */)
```

- **MPI_Iprobe**

```
int MP_Iprobe(
        int         source /*  in   */,
        int         tag    /*  in   */,
        MPI_Comm    comm   /*  in   */,
        int*        flag   /*  out  */,
        MPI_Status* status /*  out  */)
```

- **MPI_Probe**

```
int MPI_Pobe(
        int         source /*  in   */,
        int         tag    /*  in   */,
        MPI_Comm    comm   /*  in   */,
        MPI_Status* status /*  out  */)
```

- **MPI_Test_cancelled**

```
int MPI_Test_cancelled(
        MPI_Status*  status /*  in   */,
        int*         flag   /*  out  */)
```

- **MPI_Bsend_init**

```
int MPI_Bsend_init(
        void*        message  /*  in   */,
        int          count    /*  in   */,
        MPI_Datatype datatype /*  in   */,
        int          dest     /*  in   */,
        int          tag      /*  in   */,
        MPI_Comm     comm     /*  in   */,
        MPI_Request* request  /*  out  */)
```

- **MPI_Recv_init**

```
int MPI_Recv_init(
        void*        message    /*  out  */,
        int          count      /*  in   */,
        MPI_Datatype datatype   /*  in   */,
        int          source     /*  in   */,
        int          tag        /*  in   */,
        MPI_Comm     comm       /*  in   */,
        MPI_Request* request    /*  out  */)
```

- **MPI_Rsend_inti**

```
int MPI_Rsend_init(
        void*        message    /*  in   */,
        int          count      /*  in   */,
        MPI_Datatype datatype   /*  in   */,
        int          dest       /*  in   */,
        int          tag        /*  in   */,
        MPI_Comm     comm       /*  in   */,
        MPI_Request* request    /*  out  */)
```

- **MPI_Send_int**

```
int MPI_Send_init(
        void*        message    /*  in   */,
        int          count      /*  in   */,
        MPI_Datatype datatype   /*  in   */,
        int          dest       /*  in   */,
        int          tag        /*  in   */,
        MPI_Comm     comm       /*  in   */,
        MPI_Request* request    /*  out  */)
```

- **MPI_Ssend_init**

```
int MPI_Ssend_init(
        void*        message    /*  in   */,
        int          count      /*  in   */,
        MPI_Datatype datatype   /*  in   */,
        int          dest       /*  in   */,
        int          tag        /*  in   */,
        MPI_Comm     comm       /*  in   */,
        MPI_Request* request    /*  out  */)
```

- **MPI_Start**

```
int MPI_Start(
        MPI_Request *request   /*  in/out  */)
```

- **MPI_Startall**

```
int MPI_Startall(
        int         array_size  /*  in      */,
        MPI_Request requests[ ]  /*  in/out  */)
```

- **MPI_Sendrecv**

```
int MPI_Sendrecv(
        void*         sendbuf    /*  in   */,
        int           sendcount  /*  in   */,
        MPI_Datatype  sendtype   /*  in   */,
        int           dest       /*  in   */,
        int           sendtag    /*  in   */,
        void*         recvbuf    /*  out  */,
        int           recvcount  /*  in   */,
        MPI_Datatype  recvtype   /*  in   */,
        int           source     /*  in   */,
        MPI_Datatype  recvtag    /*  in   */,
        MPI_Comm      comm       /*  in   */,
        MPI_Status*   status     /*  out  */)
```

- **MPI_Address**

```
int MPI_Address(
        void*       location  /*  in   */,
        MPI_Aint*   address   /*  out  */)
```

- **MPI_Get_elements**

```
int MPI_Get_elements(
        MPI_Status*   status    /*  in   */,
        MPI_Datatype  datatype  /*  in   */,
        int*          count     /*  out  */)
```

- **MPI_Type_commit**

```
int MPI_Type_commit(
        MPI_Datatype datatype  /*  in/out  */)
```

- **MPI_Type_contiguous**

```
int MPI_Type_contiguous(
        int            count    /*  in   */,
        MPI_Datatype   oldtype  /*  in   */,
        MPI_Datatype*  newtype  /*  out  */)
```

- **MPI_Type_extent**

```
int MPI_Type_extent(
        MPI_Datatype datatype  /*  in   */,
        MPI_Aint*    extent    /*  out  */)
```

- **MPI.Type.free**

```
int MPI_Type_free(
        MPI_Datatype  datatype  /*  in/out  */)
```

- **MPI.Type.hindexed**

```
int MPI_Type_hindexed(
        int           count                /*  in   */,
        int           blocklengths[ ]      /*  in   */,
        MPI_Aint      displacements[ ]     /*  in   */,
        MPI_Datatype  oldtype              /*  in   */,
        MPI_Datatype* newtype              /*  out  */)
```

- **MPI.Type.hvector**

```
int MPI_Type_hvector(
        int           count         /*  in   */,
        int           blocklength   /*  in   */,
        MPI_Aint      stride        /*  in   */,
        MPI_Datatype  oldtype       /*  in   */,
        MPI_Datatype* newtype       /*  out  */)
```

- **MPI.Type.indexed**

```
int MPI_Type_indexed(
        int           count              /*  in   */,
        int           blocklength[ ]     /*  in   */,
        int           displacements[ ]   /*  in   */,
        MPI_Datatype  oldtype            /*  in   */,
        MPI_Datatype* newtype            /*  out  */)
```

- **MPI.Type.1b**

```
int MPI_Type_1b(
        MPI_Datatype  datatype      /*  in   */,
        MPI_Aint*     displacement  /*  out  */)
```

- **MPI.Type.size**

```
int MPI_Type_size(
        MPI_Datatype  datatype  /*  in   */,
        int*          size      /*  out  */)
```

- **MPI.Type.struct**

```
int MPI_Type_stuct(
        int           count              /*  in   */,
        int           blocklengths[ ]    /*  in   */,
        MPI_Aint      displacements[ ]   /*  in   */,
        MPI_Datatype  types[ ]           /*  in   */,
        MPI_Datatype* newtype            /*  out  */)
```

- **MPI_Type_ub**

```
int MPI_Type_ub(
        MPI_Datatype    datatype        /* in   */,
        MPI_Aint*       displacement    /* out  */)
```

- **MPI_Type_vector**

```
int MPI_Type_vector(
        int             count           /* in   */,
        int             blocklength     /* in   */,
        int             stride          /* in   */,
        MPI_Datatype    oldtype         /* in   */,
        MPI_Datatype*   newtype         /* out  */)
```

- **MPI_Pack**

```
int MPI_Pack(
        void*           inbuf           /* in     */,
        int             incount         /* in     */,
        MPI_Datatype    datatype        /* in     */,
        void*           pack_buf        /* out    */,
        int             pack_buf_size   /* in     */,
        int*            position        /* in/out */,
        MPI_Comm        comm            /* in     */)
```

- **MPI_Pack_size**

```
int MPI_Pack_size(
        int             incount   /* in   */,
        MPI_Datatype    datatype  /* in   */,
        MPI_Comm        comm      /* in   */,
        int*            size      /* out  */)
```

- **MPI_Unpack**

```
int MPI_Unpack(
        void*           pack_buf        /* in     */,
        int             pack_buf_size   /* in     */,
        int*            position        /* in/out */,
        void*           outbuf          /* out    */,
        int             outcount        /* in     */,
        MPI_Datatype    datatype        /* in     */,
        MPI_Comm        comm            /* in     */)
```

- **MPI_Barrier**

```
int MPI_Barrier(
        MPI_Comm   comm  /* in */)
```

- **MPI_Bcast**

```
int MPI_Bcast(
        void*           buffer      /* in/out  */,
        int             count       /* in      */,
        MPI_Datatype    datatype    /* in      */,
        int             root        /* in      */,
        MPI_Comm        comm        /* in      */)
```

- **MPI_Allgather**

```
int MPI_Allgather(
        void*           sendbuf     /* in  */,
        int             sendcount   /* in  */,
        MPI_Datatype    sendtype    /* in  */,
        void*           recvbuf     /* out */,
        int             recvcount   /* in  */,
        MPI_Datatype    recvtype    /* in  */,
        MPI_Comm        comm        /* in  */)
```

- **MPI_Allgatherv**

```
int MPI_Allgatherv(
        void*           sendbuf          /* in  */,
        int             sendcount        /* in  */,
        MPI_Datatype    sendtype         /* in  */,
        void*           recvbuf          /* out */,
        int             recvcounts[ ]     /* in  */,
        int             displacements[ ]  /* in  */,
        MPI_Datatype    recvtype         /* in  */,
        MPI_Comm        comm             /* in  */)
```

- **MPI_Alltoall**

```
int MPI_Alltoall(
        void*           sendbuf     /* in  */,
        int             sendcount   /* in  */,
        MPI_Datatype    sendtype    /* in  */,
        void*           recvbuf     /* out */,
        int             recvcount   /* in  */,
        MPI_Datatype    recvtype    /* in  */,
        MPI_Comm        comm        /* in  */)
```

- **MPI_Alltoallv**

```
int MPI_Allgatherv(
        void*           sendbuf                    /*  in   */,
        int             sendcounts[ ]              /*  in   */,
        int             send_displacements[ ]      /*  in   */,
        MPI_Datatype    sendtype                   /*  in   */,
        void*           recvbuf                    /*  out  */,
        int             recvcounts[ ]              /*  in   */,
        int             recv_displacements[ ]      /*  in   */,
        MPI_Datatype    recvtype                   /*  in   */,
        MPI_Comm        comm                       /*  in   */)
```

- **MPI_Gather**

```
int MPI_Gather(
        void*           sendbuf      /*  in   */,
        int             sendcount    /*  in   */,
        MPI_Datatype    sendtype     /*  in   */,
        void*           recvbuf      /*  out  */,
        int             recvcounts   /*  in   */,
        MPI_Datatype    recvtype     /*  in   */,
        MPI_Comm        comm         /*  in   */)
```

- **MPI_Gatherv**

```
int MPI_Gatherv(
        void*           sendbuf                /*  in   */,
        int             sendcount              /*  in   */,
        MPI_Datatype    sendtype               /*  in   */,
        void*           recvbuf                /*  out  */,
        int             recvcounts[ ]          /*  in   */,
        int             displacements[ ]       /*  in   */,
        MPI_Datatype    recvtype               /*  in   */,
        int             root                   /*  in   */,
        MPI_Comm        comm                   /*  in   */)
```

- **MPI_Scatter**

```
int MPI_Scatter(
        void*           sendbuf      /*  in   */,
        int             sendcount    /*  in   */,
        MPI_Datatype    sendtype     /*  in   */,
        void*           recvbuf      /*  out  */,
        int             recvcount    /*  in   */,
        MPI_Datatype    recvtype     /*  in   */,
        int             root         /*  in   */,
        MPI_Comm        comm         /*  in   */)
```

- **MPI_Scatterv**

```
int MPI_Scatterv(
        void*          sendbuf             /* in  */,
        int            sendcounts[ ]       /* in  */,
        int            displacements[ ]    /* in  */,
        MPI_Datatype   sendtype            /* in  */,
        void*          recvbuf             /* out */,
        int            recvcount           /* in  */,
        MPI_Datatype   recvtype            /* in  */,
        int            root                /* in  */,
        MPI_Comm       comm                /* in  */)
```

- **MPI_Allreduce**

```
int MPI_Allreduce(
        void*          operand    /* in  */,
        void*          result     /* out */,
        int            count      /* in  */,
        MPI_Datatype   datatype   /* in  */,
        MPI_Op         operator   /* in  */,
        MPI_Comm       comm       /* in  */)
```

- **MPI_Op_create**

```
int MPI_Op_create(
        MPI_User_function*   function   /* in  */,
        int                  commute    /* in  */,
        MPI_Op               operator   /* out */)
```

- **MPI_Op_free**

```
int MPI_Op_free(
        MPI_Op*   operator   /* in/out */)
```

- **MPI_Reduce**

```
int MPI_Reduce(
        void*          operand    /* in  */,
        void*          result     /* out */,
        int            count      /* in  */,
        MPI_Op         operator   /* in  */,
        int            root       /* in  */,
        MPI_Comm       comm       /* in  */)
```

- **MPI_Reduce_Scatter**

```
int MPI_Reduce_scatter(
        void*           operand         /*  in    */,
        void*           recvbuf         /*  out   */,
        int             recvcounts[ ]   /*  in    */,
        MPI_Datatype    datatype        /*  in    */,
        MPI_Op          operator        /*  in    */,
        MPI_Comm        comm            /*  in    */)
```

- **MPI_Scan**

```
int MPI_Scan(
        void*           operand    /*  in    */,
        void*           result     /*  out   */,
        int             count      /*  in    */,
        MPI_Datatype    datatype   /*  in    */,
        MPI_Op          operator   /*  in    */,
        MPI_Comm        comm       /*  in    */)
```

- **MPI_Comm_group**

```
int MPI_comm_group(
        MPI_Comm      comm    /*  in    */,
        MPI_Group*    group   /*  out   */)
```

- **MPI_Group_compare**

```
int MPI_Group_compare(
        MPI_Group     group1   /*  in    */,
        MPI_Group     group2   /*  in    */,
        int*          result   /*  out   */)
```

- **MPI_Group_difference**

```
int MPI_Group_difference(
        MPI_Group     group1     /*  in    */,
        MPI_Group     group2     /*  in    */,
        MPI_Group*    newgroup   /*  out   */)
```

- **MPI_Group_excl**

```
int MPI_Group_excl(
        MPI_Group     group      /*  in    */,
        int           n          /*  in    */,
        int           ranks[ ]   /*  in    */,
        MPI_Group*    newgroup   /*  out   */)
```

- **MPI_Group_free**

```
int MPI_Group_free(
        MPI_Group*    group   /*  in/out   */)
```

- **MPI_Group_incl**

```
int MPI_Group_incl(
        MPI_Group    group     /* in  */,
        int          n         /* in  */,
        int          ranks[ ]  /* in  */,
        MPI_Group*   newgroup  /* out */)
```

- **MPI_Group_intersection**

```
int MPI_Group_intersection(
        MPI_Group         group1    /* in  */,
        MPI_Group         group2    /* in  */,
        MPI_Group*        newgroup  /* out */)
```

- **MPI_Group_range_excl**

```
int MPI_Group_range_excl(
        MPI_Group         group        /* in  */,
        int               n            /* in  */,
        int               ranges[ ][3] /* in  */,
        MPI_Group*        newgroup     /* out */)
```

- **MPI_Group_range_incl**

```
int MPI_Group_range_incl(
        MPI_Group         group        /* in  */,
        int               n            /* in  */,
        int               ranges[ ][3] /* in  */,
        MPI_Group*        newgroup     /* out */)
```

- **MPI_Group_rank**

```
int MPI_Group_rank(
        MPI_Group    group  /* in  */,
        int*         rank   /* out */)
```

- **MPI_Group_size**

```
int MPI_Group_size(
        MPI_Group    group  /* in  */,
        int*         size   /* out */)
```

- **MPI_Group_translate_ranks**

```
int MPI_Group_translate_ranks(
        MPI_Group         group1    /* in  */,
        int               n         /* in  */,
        int               ranks[ ]  /* in  */,
        MPI_Group*        group2    /* in  */,
        int               ranks2[ ] /* out */)
```

- **MPI_Group_union**

```
int MPI_Group_union(
        MPI_Group    group1    /*  in   */,
        MPI_Group*   group2    /*  in   */,
        MPI_Group*   newgroup  /*  out  */)
```

- **MPI_Comm_compare**

```
int MPI_Comm_compare(
        MPI_Comm     comm1    /*  in   */,
        MPI_Comm     comm2    /*  in   */,
        int*         result   /*  out  */)
```

- **MPI_Comm_create**

```
int MPI_Comm_create(
        MPI_Comm     comm1      /*  in   */,
        MPI_Group    new_group  /*  in   */,
        MPI_Comm*    new_comm   /*  out  */)
```

- **MPI_Comm_dup**

```
int MPI_Comm_dup(
        MPI_Comm     comm      /*  in   */,
        MPI_Comm*    new_comm  /*  out  */)
```

- **MPI_Comm_free**

```
int MPI_Comm_free(
        MPI_Comm*    comm  /*  in/out  */)
```

- **MPI_Comm_rank**

```
int MPI_Comm_rank(
        MPI_Comm     comm    /*  in   */,
        int*         result  /*  out  */)
```

- **MPI_Comm_size**

```
int MPI_Comm_size(
        MPI_Comm     comm  /*  in   */,
        int*         size  /*  out  */)
```

- **MPI_Comm_split**

```
int MPI_Comm_split(
        MPI_Comm     old_comm    /*  in   */,
        int          split_key   /*  in   */,
        int          rank_key    /*  in   */,
        MPI_Comm*    new_comm    /*  out  */)
```

- **MPI.Comm.remote.group**

```
int MPI_Comm_remote_group(
        MPI_Comm               comm    /*  in   */,
        MPI_Group*             group   /*  out  */)
```

- **MPI.Comm.remote.size**

```
int MPI_Comm_remote_size(
        MPI_Comm               comm    /*  in   */,
        int*                   size    /*  out  */)
```

- **MPI.Comm.test.inter**

```
int MPI_Comm_test_inter(
        MPI_Comm               comm    /*  in   */,
        int*                   flag    /*  out  */)
```

- **MPI.Intercomm.create**

```
int MPI_Intercomm_create(
        MPI_Comm               loca_comm      /*  in   */,
        int                    local_leader   /*  in   */,
        MPI_Comm               peer_comm      /*  in   */,
        int                    remote_leader  /*  in   */,
        int                    tag            /*  in   */,
        MPI_Comm*              intercomm      /*  out  */)
```

- **MPI.Intercomm.merge**

```
int MPI_Intercomm_merge(
        MPI_Comm               intercomm /*  in   */,
        int                    high      /*  in   */,
        MPI_Comm*              intracomm /*  out  */)
```

- **MPI.Attr.delete**

```
int MPI_Attr_delete(
        MPI_Comm         comm    /*  in   */,
        int              keyval  /*  in   */)
```

- **MPI.Attr.get**

```
int MPI_Attr_get(
        MPI_Comm         comm           /*  in   */,
        int              keyval         /*  in   */,
        void*            attribte_ptr   /*  out  */,
        int*             flag           /*  out  */)
```

- **MPI_Attr_put**

```
int MPI_Attr_put(
        MPI_Comm    comm        /*  in  */,
        int         keyval      /*  in  */,
        void*       attribute   /*  in  */)
```

- **MPI_Keyval_create**

```
int MPI_Keyval_create(
        MPI_Copy_function*      copy_fn     /*  in   */,
        MPI_Delete_function*    delete_fn   /*  in   */,
        int*                    keyval      /*  out  */,
        void*                   extra_arg   /*  in   */)
```

- **MPI_Keyval_free**

```
int MPI_Keyval_free(
        int*        keyval  /*  in/out  */,
```

- **MPI_Topo_test**

```
int MPI_Topo_test(
        MPI_Comm    comm        /*  in   */,
        int*        top_type    /*  out  */)
```

- **MPI_Cart_coords**

```
int MPI_Cart_coords(
        MPI_Comm    comm        /*  in   */,
        int         rank        /*  in   */,
        int         max_dims    /*  in   */,
        int         coords[ ]   /*  out  */)
```

- **MPI_Cart_create**

```
int MPI_Cart_create(
        MPI_Comm    old_comm    /*  in   */,
        int         ndims       /*  in   */,
        int         dims[ ]     /*  in   */,
        int         periods[ ]  /*  in   */,
        int         reorder     /*  in   */,
        MPI_Comm*   cart_comm   /*  out  */)
```

- **MPI_Cartdim_get**

```
int MPI_Cartdim_get(
        MPI_Comm    comm    /*  in   */,
        int*        ndims   /*  out  */)
```

- **MPI_Cart_get**

```
int MPI_Cart_get(
        MPI_Comm    comm        /*  in   */,
        int         max_dims    /*  in   */,
        int         dims[ ]      /*  out  */,
        int         periods[ ]   /*  out  */,
        int         coords[ ]    /*  out  */)
```

- **MPI_Cart_map**

```
int MPI_Cart_map(
        MPI_Comm    comm        /*  in   */,
        int         ndims       /*  in   */,
        int         dims[ ]      /*  in   */,
        int         periods[ ]   /*  in   */,
        int*        newrank     /*  out  */)
```

- **MPI_Cart_rank**

```
int MPI_Cart_rank(
        MPI_Comm    comm        /*  in   */,
        int         coords[ ]    /*  in   */,
        int*        rank        /*  out  */)
```

- **MPI_Cart_shift**

```
int MPI_Cart_shift(
        MPI_Comm    comm            /*  in   */,
        int         direction       /*  in   */,
        int         displacement    /*  in   */,
        int*        rank_source     /*  out  */,
        int*        rank_dest       /*  out  */)
```

- **MPI_Cart_sub**

```
int MPI_Cart_sub(
        MPI_Comm    comm            /*  in   */,
        int         free_coords[ ]   /*  in   */,
        MPI_Comm*   newcomm         /*  out  */)
```

- **MPI_Dims_create**

```
int MPI_Dims_create(
        int         nnodes      /*  in     */,
        int         ndims       /*  in     */,
        int         dims[ ]      /*  in/out */)
```

- **MPI_Graph_create**

```
int MPI_Graph_create(
        MPI_Comm      old_comm     /*  in   */,
        int           nnodes       /*  in   */,
        int           index[ ]     /*  in   */,
        int           edges[ ]     /*  in   */,
        int           reoder       /*  in   */,
        MPI_Comm      graph_comm   /*  out  */)
```

- **MPI_Graphdims_get**

```
int MPI_Graphdims_get(
        MPI_Comm      comm     /*  in   */,
        int*          nnodes   /*  out  */,
        int*          edges    /*  out  */)
```

- **MPI_Graph_get**

```
int MPI_Graph_get(
        MPI_Comm    comm        /*  in   */,
        int         max_index   /*  in   */,
        int         max_edges   /*  in   */,
        int         index[ ]    /*  out  */,
        int         edges[ ]    /*  out  */)
```

- **MPI_Graph_map**

```
int MPI_Graph_map(
        MPI_Comm    comm       /*  in   */,
        int         nnodes     /*  in   */,
        int         index[ ]   /*  in   */,
        int         edges[ ]   /*  in   */,
        int*        newrank    /*  out  */)
```

- **MPI_Graph_neighbors**

```
int MPI_Graph_neighbors(
        MPI_Comm    comm            /*  in   */,
        int         rank            /*  in   */,
        int         max_neighbors   /*  in   */,
        int         neighbors[ ]    /*  out  */)
```

- **MPI_Graph_neighbors_count**

```
int MPI_Graph_neighbors_count(
        MPI_Comm      comm         /*  in   */,
        int           rank         /*  in   */,
        int*          nneighbors   /*  out  */)
```

- **MPI_Get_processor_name**

```
int MPI_Get_processor_name(
        char*                   name        /* out */,
        int*                    resultlen   /* out */)
```

- **MPI_Errhandler_create**

```
int MPI_Errhandler_create(
        MPI_Handler_function*   function    /* in  */,
        MPI_Errhandler*         errhandler  /* out */)
```

- **MPI_Errhandler_free**

```
int MPI_Errhandler_free(
        MPI_Errhandler*    errhandler /* in/out */)
```

- **MPI_Errhandler_get**

```
int MPI_Errhandler_get(
        MPI_Comm           comm        /* in  */,
        MPI_Errhandler*    errhandler  /* out */)
```

- **MPI_Errhandler_set**

```
int MPI_Errhandler_set(
        MPI_Comm           comm        /* in  */,
        MPI_Errhandler*    errhandler  /* in  */)
```

- **MPI_error_class**

```
int MPI_Error_class(
        int                errorcode   /* in  */,
        int*               errorclass  /* out */)
```

- **MPI_Error_string**

```
int MPI_Error_string(
        int                errorcode   /* in  */,
        char*              string      /* out */,
        int*               resultlen   /* out */)
```

- **MPI_Wtick**

```
doube MPI_Wtick(void)
```

- **MPI_Wtime**

```
doube MPI_Wtime(void)
```

- **MPI_Abort**

```
doube MPI_Abort(
        MPI_comm  comm        /* in */,
        int       error_code  /* in */)
```

- **MPI_Finalize**

```
int MPI_Finalize(void)
```

- **MPI_Init**

```
int MPI_Init(
        int*    argc_ptr     /*  in/out  */,
        char**  argv_ptr[ ]  /*  in/out  */)
```

- **MPI_Initialized**

```
int MPI_Initialized(
        int*            flag  /*  out  */)
```

B.2.4 MPI Constants and Definitions

- **Error Classes**

```
MPI_SUCCESS
MPI_ERR_BUFFER
MPI_ERR_COUNT
MPI_ERR_TYPE
MPI_ERR_TAG
MPI_ERR_COMM
MPI_ERR_RANK
MPI_ERR_REQUEST
MPI_ERR_ROOT
MPI_ERR_GROUP
MPI_ERR_OP
MPI_ERR_TOPOLOGY
MPI_ERR_DIMS
MPI_ERR_ARG
MPI_ERR_UNKNOWN
MPI_ERR_TRUNCATE
MPI_ERR_OTHER
MPI_ERR_INTERN
MPI_PENDING
MPI_ERR_IN_STATUS
MPI_ERR_LASTCODE
```

- **Assorted Constants**

```
MPI_BOTTOM
MPI_PROC_NULL
MPI_ANY_SOURCE
MPI_ANY_TAG
```

```
MPI_UNDEFINED
MPI_BSEND_OVERHEAD
MPI_KEYVAL_INVALID
```

- **Error Handling Specifiers**

```
MPI_ERRORS_ARE_FATAL
MPI_ERRORS_RETURN
```

- **Maximum Sizes for Strings**

```
MPI_MAX_PROCESSOR_NAME
MPI_MAX_ERROR_STRING
```

- **Basic Datatypes**

```
MPI_CHAR
MPI_SHORT
MPI_INT
MPI_LONG
MPI_UNSIGNED_CHAR
MPI_UNSIGNED_SHORT
MPI_UNSIGNED
MPI_UNSIGNED_LONG
MPI_FLOAT
MPI_DOUBLE
MPI_LONG_DOUBLE
MPI_BYTE
MPI_PACKED
MPI_LONG_LONG_INT    /*  optional  */
```

- **Datatypes for Reduction Functions**

```
MPI_FLOAT_INT
MPI_DOUBLE_INT
MPI_LONG_INT
MPI_2INT
MPI_SHORT_INT
MPI_LONG_DOUBLE_INT
```

- **Datatypes for Building Derived Types**

```
MPI_UB
MPI_LB
```

- **Predefined Communicators**

```
MPI_COMM_WORLD
MPI_COMM_SELF
```

- **Results of Communicator and Group Comparisons**

    ```
    MPI_IDENT
    MPI_CONGRUENT
    MPI_SIMILAR
    MPI_UNEQUAL
    ```

- **Attrbute Keys for Implementation Information**

    ```
    MPI_TAG_UB
    MPI_IO
    MPI_HOST
    MPI_WTIME_IS_GLOBAL
    ```

- **Collective Reduction Operations**

    ```
    MPI_MAX
    MPI_MIN
    MPI_SUM
    MPI_PROD
    MPI_MAXLOC
    MPI_MINLOC
    MPI_BAND
    MPI_BOR
    MPI_BXOR
    MPI_LAND
    MPI_LOR
    MPI_LXOR
    ```

- **Null Handles**

    ```
    MPI_GROUP_NULL
    MPI_COMM_NULL
    MPI_DATATYPE_NULL
    MPI_REQUEST_NULL
    MPI_OP_NULL
    MPI_ERHANDLER_NULL
    ```

- **Empty Group**

    ```
    MPI_GROUP_EMPTY
    ```

- **Topologies**

    ```
    MPI_GRAPH
    MPI_CART
    ```

B.2.5 Type Definitions

The following type definitions are in the file mpi.h.

- **Opaque Types**

  ```
  MPI_Aint
  MPI_Status
  ```

- **Handles to Assorted Structures**

  ```
  MPI_Group
  MPI_Comm
  MPI_Datatype
  MPI_Request
  MPI_Op
  ```

- **Prototypes for User-Defined Functions**

  ```
  typedef int MPI_Copy_function(
          MPI_Comm                    oldcomm,
          int                         keyval,
          void*                       extra_arg,
          void*                       attribute_val_in,
          void*                       attribute_val_out,
          int                         flag)

  typedef int MPI_Delete_function(
          MPI_Comm                    comm,
          int                         keyval,
          void*                       attribute_val
          void*                       extra_arg)

  typedef void MPI_Handler_function(
          MPI_Comm*                   comm,
          int*                        error_code,
                                      ...)

  typedef void MPI_User_function(
          void*                       invec,
          void*                       inoutvec,
          int*                        len,
          MPI_Datatype*               datatype)
  ```

Bibliography

[1] M. Abramowitz and I. A. Stegun. *Handbook of Mathematical Functions*. Dover, New York, 1972.

[2] G. Amdahl. The validity of the single processor approach to achieving large scale computing capabilities. In *AFIPS Conf. Proc.*, vol. 30, pp. 483–485, 1967.

[3] W. Arnoldi. The principle of minimized iteration in the solution of the matrix eigenvalue problem. *Quart. Appl. Math.*, 9:17–29, 1951.

[4] Z. Bai, J. Demmel, J. Dongarra, A. Ruhe, and H. van der Vorst. *Templates for the Solution of Alebraic Eigenvalue Problems: A Practical Guide*. SIAM, Philadelphia, 2000.

[5] R. Barrett, M. Berry, T. F. Chan, J. Demmel, J. Donato, J. Dongarra, V. Eijkhout, R. Pozo, C. Comine, and H. Van der Vorst. *Templates for the Solution of Linear Systems: Building Blocks for Iterative Methods*. SIAM, Philadelphia, 1994.

[6] A. Bayliss and E. Turkel. Mappings and accuracy of Chebyshev pseudo-spectral approximation. *J. Comput. Phys.*, 101:349–359, 1992.

[7] D. J. Becker, T. Sterling, D. Savarese, J. E. Dorband, U. A. Ranawake, and C. V. Packer. BEOWULF: A parallel workstation for scientific computation. In *Proceedings of International Conference on Parallel Processing*, pp. 11–14, 1995.

[8] A. Bjorck. Numerics of Gram–Schmidt orthogonalization. *Linear Algebra and its Applications*, 197:297–316, 1994.

[9] E. K. Blum. A modification of the Runge–Kutta fourth-order method. *Math. Comput.*, 16:176–187, 1962.

[10] A. Brandt. *Multigrid Techniqus: Guide with Applications to Fluid Dynamics*. GMD-Studien, No. 85, Gesellschaft fur Mathematik and Datenver-arbeitung, St. Augustin, Bonn, 1984.

[11] W. L. Briggs, V. E. Henson, and S. F. McCormick. *A Multigrid Tutorial*, 2nd ed. SIAM, Philadelphia, 2000.

[12] J. M. Burgers. A mathematical model illustrating the theory of turbulence. *Adv. Appl. Mech.*, 1:171–199, 1948.

[13] B. Buzbee, G. Golub, and C. Nielsen. On direct methods for solving Poisson's equation. *SIAM J. Numer. Anal.*, 7:627–656, 1970.

[14] H. Casanova and J. J. Dongarra. Applying NetSolve's network enabled server. *IEEE, Comput. Sci. Eng.*, 5(3):57–66, 1998.

[15] M.-H. Chen, Q.-M. Shao, and J. G. Ibrahim. *Monte Carlo Methods in Bayesian Computation*. Springer-Verlag, Berlin, 2000.

[16] C. K. Chui. *Wavelets: A Mathematical Tool for Signal Analysis*. SIAM, Philadelphia, 1997.

[17] J. W. Cooley and J. W. Tukey. An algorithm for the machine computation of Fourier series. *Math. Comput.*, 19:297–301, 1965.

[18] R. Courant, K. O. Friedrichs, and H. Lewy. Uber die partiellen differenzengleichungen der mathematischen. *Math. Ann.*, 100:32–74, 1928.

[19] J. K. Cullum and R. A. Willoughby. *Lanczos Algorithms for Large Symmetric Eigenvalue Computations, Volume 1, Theory*. Birkhauser, Boston, 1985.

[20] G. Dahlquist. Convergence and stability in the numerical integration of ordinary differential equations. *Math. Scand.*, 4:33–53, 1956.

[21] B. N. Datta. *Numerical Linear Algebra*. Brooks/Cole, Pacific Grove, CA, 1995.

[22] I. Daubechies. *Ten Lectures on Wavelets*. SIAM, Philadelphia, 1992.

[23] P. J. Davis and P. Rabinowitz. *Methods of Numerical Integration*, 2nd ed. Academic Press, San Diego, 1984.

[24] E. F. Van de Velde. *Concurrent Scientific Computing*. Texts in Applied Mathematical Sciences Series, Springer-Verlag, Berlin, 1994.

[25] J. W. Demmel. On floating point errors in Cholesky. Technical report, LAPACK Working Notes, Department of Computer Science, University of Tennessee at Knoxville, 1989.

[26] J. W. Demmel. *Applied Numerical Linear Algebra*. SIAM, Philadelphia, 1997.

[27] D. Dodson and J. Lewis. Issues relating to extension of the Basic Linear Algrebra Subprograms. *ACM SIGNUM Newslett.*, 20(1):2–18, 1985.

[28] J. J. Dongarra. Performance of various computers using standard linear equations software in a fortran environment. Computer Science Technical Report CS-89-85, University of Tennessee, March, 1990.

[29] J. J. Dongarra, J. DuCroz, I. Duff, and S. Hammarling. A set of Level 3 Basic Linear Algebra Subprograms. *ACM Trans. Math. Software*, 16:1–17, 1990.

[30] J. J. Dongarra, I. S. Duff, D. C. Sorensen, and H. A. van der Vorst. *Numerical Linear Algebra for High-Performance Computers*. SIAM, Philadelphia, 1998.

[31] J. J. Dongarra, F. Gustavson, and A. Karp. Implementing linear algebra algorithms for dense matrices on a vector pipeline machine. *SIAM Rev.*, 26:91–112, 1984.

[32] J. J. Dongarra and D. C. Sorensen. A fully parallel algorithm for the symmetric eigenvalue problem. *SIAM J. Sci. Stat. Comput.*, 8:S139–S154, 1987.

[33] J. J. Dongarra and F. Sullivan. Top ten algorithms of the century. *IEEE, Comput. Sci. Eng.*, vol. 2 Issue 1 pp: 22–23, January/February, 2000.

[34] C. G. Douglas, J. Hu, U. Rude, and M. Bittencourt. Cache based multigrid on unstructured two dimensional grids. In *Proceedings of Tenth GAMM Workshop on Parallel Multigrid Methods, Bonn, Germany*, 1998.

[35] B. Engquist and A. Majda. Absorbing boundary conditions for the numerical solution of waves. *Math. Comput.*, 31:629–651, 1977.

[36] M. Flynn. Very high speed computing systems. *Proc. IEEE*, 54:1901–1909, 1966.

[37] B. Fornberg. Generation of finite difference formulas on arbitrary spaced gris. *Math. Comput.*, 51:699–706, 1988.

[38] I. Foster and C. Kesselman. *The Grid: Blueprint for a New Computing Infrastructure*. Kaufman, Los Altos, CA, 1998.

[39] R. Freund and N. Nachtigal. QMR: A quasi-minimal residual method for non-Hermitian linear systems. *Numer. Math.*, 60:315–339, 1991.

[40] M. Frigo and S. G. Johnson. FFTW: An adaptive software architecture for the FFT. In *Proceeding ICASSP Conference*, vol. 3, pp. 1381–1384, 1998.

[41] P. R. Garabedian. Estimation of the relaxation factor for small mesh size. *Math. Tables Aids Comput.*, 10:183–185, 1956.

[42] C. W. Gear. *Numerical Initial Value Problems in Ordinary Differential Equations*. Prentice Hall, New York, 1971.

[43] A. Ghizzetti and A. Ossicini. *Quadrature Formulae*. Academic Press, San Diego, 1970.

[44] S. K. Godunov and V. S. Ryabenkii. *The Theory of Difference Schemes*. North-Holland, Amsterdam, 1964.

[45] G. Golub and J. M. Ortega. *Scientific Computing: An Introduction with Parallel Computing*. Academic Press, San Diego, 1993.

[46] G. Golub and C. F. van Loan. *Matrix Computations*, 2nd ed. Johns Hopkins University Press, Baltimore, 1989.

[47] G. Golub and J. H. Wilkinson. Note on the iterative refinement of least squares solution. *Numer. Math.*, 9:139–148, 1966.

[48] W. J. Gordon and C. A. Hall. Transfinite element methods: Blending function interpolation over arbitrary curved element domains. *Numer. Math.*, 21:109–129, 1973.

[49] D. Gottlieb and S. A. Orszag. *Numerical Analysis of Spectral Methods: Theory and Applications.* SIAM-CMBS, Philadelphia, 1977.

[50] S. Gottlieb, C.-W. Shu, and E. Tadmor. Strong stability preserving high order time discretizations. *SIAM Rev.*, 43:89–112, 2001.

[51] W. Gropp, E. Lusk, and A. Skjellum. *Using MPI: Portable Parallel Programming with the Message-Passing Interface* 2nd ed. MIT Press, Cambridge, MA, 1999.

[52] W. W. Hager. Condition estimators. *SIAM J. Sci. Stat. Comput.*, 5:311–316, 1984.

[53] E. Hairer and G. Wanner. On the instability of the BDF formulas. *SIAM J. Numer. Anal.*, 20(6):1206–1209, 1983.

[54] W. W. Hargrove, F. M. Hoffman, and T. Sterling. The do-it-yourself supercomputer. *Sci. Am.*, August:72–79, 2001.

[55] M. Hestenes and E. Stiefel. Methods of conjugate gradients for solving linear systems. *J. Res. Natl. Bur. Stand.*, 49:409–436, 1952.

[56] C. Hirsch. *Numerical Computation of Internal and External Flows.* Wiley, New York, 1988.

[57] R. W. Hockney. *The Science of Computer Benchmarking.* SIAM, Software, Environments, Tools, Philadelphia, 1996.

[58] J. D. Hoffman. Relationship between the truncation errors of centered finite difference approximation on uniform and non-uniform meshes. *J. Comput. Phys.*, 46:469–474, 1982.

[59] T. J. Hughes. *The Finite Element Method: Linear Static and Dynamic Finite Element Analysis.* Prentice Hall, New York, 1987.

[60] A. Jameson, H. Schmidt, and E. Turkel. Numerical solutions of the Euler equations by finite volume methods using Runge–Kutta time stepping schemes. *AIAA Paper 81-1259*, 1981.

[61] M. T. Jones and M. L. Patrick. The Lanczos algorithm for the generalized symmetric eigenproblem on shared-memory architectures. *Appl. Numer. Math.*, 12:377–389, 1993.

[62] D. W. Kammler. *A First Course in Fourier Analysis.* Prentice Hall, New York, 2000.

[63] G. E. Karniadakis and S. J. Sherwin. *Spectral/hp Element Methods for CFD.* Oxford University Press, New York, 1999.

[64] S. K. Kim and A. T. Chronopoulos. A class of Lanczos-like algorithms implemented on parallel computers. *Parallel Comput.*, 17:763–778, 1991.

[65] H. O. Kreiss and J. Oliger. *Methods for the Approximate Solution of Time Dependent Problems.* World Meteorological Organization, International Council of Scientific Unions, Geneva, 1973.

[66] C. Lanczos. *Applied Analysis.* Dover, New York, 1988.

[67] C. Lawson, R. Hanson, D. Kincaid, and F. Krogh. Basic linear algebra subprograms for Fortran usage. *ACM Trans. Math. Software*, 5:308–329, 1979.

[68] S. K. Lele. Compact finite difference schemes with spectral-like resolutions. *J. Comput. Phys.*, 103:16–42, 1992.

[69] S. Mallat. Multiresolution approximation and wavelet orthonormal bases of $L^2(\mathbf{R})$. *Trans. Am. Math. Soc.*, 315:69–87, 1989.

[70] C. B. Moler and G. W. Stewart. An algorithm for generalized matrix eigenvalue problems. *SIAM J. Num. Anal.*, 10:241–256, 1973.

[71] H. Nessyahu and E. Tadmor. Non-oscillatory central differencing for hyperbolic conservation laws. *J. Comput. Phys.*, 87:408–463, 1990.

[72] A. M. Ostrowski. *Solutions of Equations and Systems of Equations.* Academic Press, San Diego, 1966.

[73] P. S. Pacheco. *Parallel Programming with MPI.* Kaufmann, Los Altos, CA, 1997.

[74] C. C. Paige. *The computation of eigenvalues and eigenvectors of very large sparse matrices.* PhD thesis, London University, 1971.

[75] W. H. Press, S. A. Teukolsky, W. T. Vetterling, and B. F. Flannery. *Numerical Recipes in C++.* Cambridge University Press, Cambridge, UK, 2002.

[76] J. K. Reid. *Large Sparse Sets of Linear Equations.* Academic Press, New York, 1971.

[77] P. D. Richtmyer and K. W. Morton. *Difference Methods for Initial Value Problems*, 2nd ed. Wiley-Interscience, London, 1967.

[78] P. J. Roache. *Fundamentals of Computational Fluid Dynamics.* Hermosa Publications, Albuquerque, 1998.

[79] Y. Saad. *Numerical Methods for Large Eigenvalue Problems.* Halsted Press, New York, 1992.

[80] H. Schlichting and K. Gersten. *Boundary Layer Theory*, 8th ed. Springer-Verlag, Berlin, 2000.

[81] T. Sterling, J. Salmon, and D. J. Becker, and D. Savarese. *How to Build a Beowulf: A Guide to the Implementation and Application of PC Clusters.* MIT Press, Cambridge, MA, 1999.

[82] H. Stone. An efficient parallel algorithm for the solution of a tridiagonal linear system of equations. *J. Assoc. comput. Mach.*, 20:27–38, 1973.

[83] G. Strang. A proposal for Toepliz matrix calculations. *Stud. Appl. Math.*, 74(2):171–174, 1986.

[84] G. Strang. *Linear Algebra and Its Applications*, 3rd ed. Harcourt Brace Jovanvich, San Diego, 1986.

[85] G. Strang. Wavelets and dilation equations: A brief introduction. *SIAM Rev.*, 31(4):614–627, 1989.

[86] B. Stroustrup. *The C++ Programming Language.* Wiley, New York, 1991.

[87] C. Temperton. Self-sorting mixed-radix fast Fourier transfroms. *J. Comput. Phys.*, 52:1–23, 1983.

[88] L. N. Trefethen and D. Bau III. *Numerical Linear Algebra.* SIAM, Philadelphia, 1997.

[89] R. S. Varga. *Matrix Iterative Analysis*, 2nd ed. Springer Series in Computational Mathematics, Springer-Verlag, Berlin, 2000.

[90] H. Wang. A parallel method for tridiagonal systems. *ACM Trans. Math. Software*, 7:170–183, 1981.

[91] R. F. Warming and R. W. Beam. Upwind second order difference schemes. *AIAA J.*, 24:1241–1249, 1976.

[92] P. Wesseling. *An Introduction to Multigrid Methods.* Wiley, New York, 1992.

[93] R. C. Whaley and J. J. Dongarra. Automatically tuned linear algebra software. In *Proceedings of Supercomputing'98*, 1998.

[94] J. Wilkinson. *The Algebraic Eigenvalue Problem.* Oxford University Press, New York, 1965.

[95] D. M. Young. *Iterative Solution of Large Linear Systems.* Academic Press, New York, 1971.

Index